A Collection of Treaties Between Great Britain and Other Powers;

A

COLLECTION

OF

TREATIES

BETWEEN

GREAT BRITAIN

AND

OTHER POWERS.

———

BY *GEORGE CHALMERS*, Esq.

———

VOL. I.

———

LONDON:
PRINTED FOR JOHN STOCKDALE, PICCADILLY.
M DCC XC.

PREFACE.

IT is always happy when private amufement can be made fubfervient to general convenience. Having enjoyed a pleafure in collecting the Treaties between Great Britain and other nations, in adjufting their dates, and in comparing their provifions, I prefumed to think that, were I to publifh the refult of my enquiries, ftatefmen, whofe duty leads them to confult national conventions, might find an utility where I had difcovered the gratifications of refearch and acquifition.

Without the correfpondence of Du Mont, the learning of Barbeyrac, or the zeal of Rouffet, it had been eafy to print a voluminous collection of treaties. My object, however, was not to make a big book, but an ufeful book; a commodious felection, which might lie handily on the table, and be readily infpected. With this defign, I have printed, in the following fheets, thofe treaties which are moft frequently perufed: I have referred to thofe treaties which are often confulted.

The collections of national conventions, which were publifhed at fucceffive periods, and in different countries, have not been always conveniently arranged, or accurately printed, at the fame time that they were univerfally allowed to be ufeful. They generally followed, indeed, a chronological order. But, from the

vaft

vaſt maſs of diſcordant matter, it was often a difficult
taſk to collect the treaties which belonged to any particular nation, or to adjuſt the ſtipulations which related to any ſpecified ſubject.

In the following collection, I have preſerved a chronological order, while I have brought together the
treaties which at various times have been formed with
each different nation. Without any ſtrong motive of
choice, I began with Ruſſia, in the north; I regularly
proceeded to the ſouth of Europe; I diverged afterwards to Africa and Aſia; and ended finally in America. I flatter myſelf this arrangement will be found
commodious. To the treaties, which belong to
each particular country, and which form a diſtinct
head, I have prefixed a chronological index of prior
treaties, for the purpoſe of tracing a principle of con-
nexion, and ſhewing where thoſe preceding conventions may be found. The uſefulneſs of this prefatory
index will be acknowledged by thoſe, who having been
engaged in much ſtudy, or in much buſineſs, have felt
the happineſs of knowing where to lay one's hand on
the thing that the preſſure of the moment required.
But, the brevity which I preſcribed to myſelf, did not
allow me to ſwell this prefatory index with the mention
of every agreement, either for the hire of troops, or the
performance of temporary ſtipulations. I was directed
by my notions of utility, either in publiſhing ſome
treaties, or in not mentioning others. The public,
whoſe convenience I have endeavoured to promote,
and to whoſe opinion I reſpectfully ſubmit, will ulti-
mately determine whether, in making this ſelection,
I have been directed by judgment, or by caprice.

The firſt treaty which was ever publiſhed in this nation, by *authority*, was the treaty with Spain, in 1604,
which was conducted by Sir Robert Cecil, the firſt Lord
Saliſbury, with ſuch wonderful talents and addreſs. No
treaty was printed, *without authority*, during any preceding period. It had been extremely dangerous for private

vate perfons, in the reign of King James, in the former, or in the fubfequent reign, to have publifhed
treaties with foreign Powers; becaufe to have done
this had been confidered as meddling with matters of
ftate, and punifhed as an infringement of prerogative.
The treaties of Charles I. were publifhed by authority.
Cromwell made many treaties, becaufe he was anxious,
like John IV. of Portugal, to procure the recognition
of other Powers: but, I doubt, whether he lived to
publifh them. The reign of Charles II. was fruitful
in treaties, which were printed by authority, often
fingly, and fometimes collectively. The four treaties
of Breda were publifhed by the King's fpecial command *, in 1667. A collection, comprehending feventeen treaties, beginning with the Commercial Treaty
with Spain, in 1667, and ending with the Algerine
treaty in 1682, was printed by direction of Lord Sunderland, the fecretary of ftate, in March 168⅘ †. Such
had been the fmallnefs of this impreffion, or fuch the
demand for it, that this ufeful code was reprinted in
1686. The falutary practice of publifhing by authority what was fo neceffary to be known, which had
been begun by King James, was continued by King
William, and by his royal fucceffors.

It was however in King William's councils, that it
was firft determined to print authoritatively the PUBLIC
CONVENTIONS of Great Britain with other Powers ‡.
It was owing to that determination, that the reign of
Queen Anne faw the publication of RYMER'S FOEDERA.

---

* By the affigns of J. Bill and C. Barker, the King's printers,
4to, 80 pages.

† By the affigns of J. Bill, and H. Hills, and T. Newcomb, the
King's printers. London, 1685, 4to, 269 pages.

‡ The warrant, empowering Thomas Rymer to fearch the public
repofitories for this great defign, was dated on the 26th of Auguft
1693. This warrant was renewed on the 3d of May 1707, when
Robert Sanderfon was appointed his affiftant. And, on the 15th of
February 1717, Sanderfon was continued the fingle conductor of
this laborious undertaking.

The

The first volume, commencing with the documents of the year 1201, was published in 1704; the twentieth volume, ending with the papers of 1654, was given to the world in 1735.

As historiographer these were not the only labours of Rymer: he left an unpublished collection, relating to the government and history of England, from the year 1115 to 1698, in fifty-eight volumes *, which the prudence of the house of peers directed to be placed in *The British Museum*, with the Cottonian manuscripts. Of men who have done great public services, we naturally wish to know something of the origin and the end. Thomas Rymer was born in the north of England; was educated at Cambridge; and, intending to make the law his profession, he entered himself a student of Gray's Inn. He first appeared as a poet and a critic in 1678; when he published *Edgar*, an heroic tragedy, which had scarcely preserved his name; and *Reflections on Shakespeare*, in 1693, which have drawn on him Warburton's indignation. On the decease of Shadwell, the great *Mac Flecnoe* of Dryden, in 1692, who, at once, celebrated King William's birth, as *Laureat*, and recorded King William's actions, as historiographer, the laurel was placed on the brow of Tate, and the pen of historian was delivered into the hand of Rymer. While collecting T<small>HE</small> F<small>OEDERA</small>, he also employed himself, like a royal historiographer, in detecting the *falshood* and ascertaining the *truth* of history †. He lived to publish

fifteen

---

* There is a list of this great collection in the seventeenth volume of the *Foedera*: and see Ayscough's Catalogue of the Museum MSS. vol. i. N° 4573—4630.

† He published, in 1702, his first letter to Bishop Nicholson: "Wherein, as he says, King Robert III. of Scotland is, beyond all dispute, freed from the imputation of bastardy." He soon after published his second letter to Bishop Nicholson; "containing an historical deduction of the alliances between France and Scotland: whereby the pretended old league with Charlemagne is disproved, and the true old league is ascertained." After his decease, there was published, in 1714, a small treatise "Of the Antiquity, Power,

and

fifteen folio volumes of the *public conventions;* and from his collections Sanderfon publifhed the fixteenth volume in 1715. Rymer finifhed his ufeful career in December, 1713, and was buried in the church of St. Clement's Danes. Yet, after all his labours, he is ofteneft remembered for his critical ftrictures on Shakefpeare: for, fuch has been the fingular fortune of this illuftrious poet, that whoever has connected himfelf with his name, either as commentator, pane-gyrift, or detractor, has been raifed up by the ftrength of his pinions, and will be carried through the ex-panfe of time by the continuance of his flight.

Robert Sanderfon, who had thus been Rymer's co-adjutor, continued *the Fœdera* after his death. The feventeenth volume, which is the moft ufeful of the whole, becaufe it contains an INDEX of the *perfons,* of the *things,* and of the *places,* that this and the fixteen preceding volumes comprehend, he publifhed in the year 1717. The eighteenth volume, which was re-publifhed with *the Caftrations,* he publifhed in 1726; the nineteenth in 1732, and the twentieth in 1735. Sanderfon, who was ufher of the court of Chancery, clerk of the chapel of the Rolls, and fellow of the Antiquary Society, died on the 25th of December, 1741.

A new edition of the firft feventeen volumes was publifhed in 1727, by George Holmes, with colla-tions and amendments. Holmes was born at Skip-ton, in Yorkfhire; he became clerk to Petyt, the keeper of the records in *the Tower,* about the year 1695; he continued almoft fixty years the deputy-

and Decay of Parliaments." And in the fame year,—" Some Tranflations from Greek, Latin, and Itaҳian Poets, with other Verfes and Songs, never before printed. By Thomas Rymer, late Hiftoriographer-royal." Thefe tranflations, verfes, and fongs, not being fufficient to make a volume in 12mo. were publifhed with *Curious Amufements;* by a Gentleman of Pembroke-hall in Cambridge.

keeper;

keeper; and, on account of his knowledge and his induftry, he was, by the recommendation of lord Hallifax, who was then chairman of a committee of the Houfe of Lords, appointed to methodize the records, on the death of Petyt, with a falary of £. 200 a year. This he enjoyed till his deceafe, in 1748, at the age of eighty-feven.—Such were the able and induftrious men to whom we owe *the Fœdera*, a work which is at once infinitely ufeful, and highly honourable to the Britifh nation.

The bookfellers at *the Hague* publifhed a third edition of *the Fœdera* in 1739, having contracted the twenty volumes into ten. In this edition the documents are tranflated into French, and printed in the oppofite column; and fome other papers of lefs ufefulnefs are added. With De Bure, I am inclined to confider this edition as the beft; becaufe, with equal accuracy, it contains more matter in lefs fpace.—Thus much with regard to thofe collections of treaties, which were publifhed by authority.

The reign of Queen Anne firft faw a collection of treaties, which was publifhed by private individuals, without authority. Two volumes appeared in 1710, which began with treaties of very early date, but of no validity, and comprehended documents rather hiftorical than diplomatic. A third volume was added, in 1713, without greater regard to felection, arrangement, or precifion. And when thefe treaties were republifhed by the London bookfellers, in 1732, a fourth volume was added, containing fuch additional documents as recent events had produced. In 1772, two fmall volumes of treaties were publifhed, beginning with the *grand alliance*, of 1689, and ending with the declarations of 1771, which concluded our difpute with regard to Falkland Iflands. A fupplemental volume was added in 1781, comprehending public papers, from 1495 to 1734, fome of greater and fome of lefs value. Thefe treaties were republifhed in 1785,

1785, arranged in chronological order, and expanded with additional matter; yet, comprehending something that is ufelefs amongft much that is good. During that active period, from the Revolution, in 1688, to recent times, our several treaties were fingly publifhed, as they were made, with commentaries, which fometimes explained, but oftener obfcured them, though the pens of our profoundeft fcholars were employed, with bifhop Hare at their head.

How early foreign nations began to publifh their treaties, I am unable to tell. *The articles of the twelve years truce*, between Spain and the United Netherlands*, which were concluded in April, 1609, were immediately printed by authority. The momentous treaties of the fubfequent age were fucceffively publifhed, as they were produced by various events. But the firft collection of public conventions, which comprehended the interefts of the European nations, was publifhed at Hanover, in 1693, by the illuftrious Leibnitz, in two folio volumes, under the title of *Codex juris gentium diplomaticus*. Leibnitz, who was born at Leipfic, in 1646, raifed himfelf by his genius and his labours to eminence among the high, and died in 1716, at the age of feventy.

During a bufy age of frequent negotiation, the public curiofity demanded frefh gratification. In 1700, four folio volumes of *National Agreements* were publifhed, under the infpection of James Bernard, who was born in Dauphiné; and, retiring into Switzerland and Holland, after the revocation of the edict of Nantz, became profeffor of philofophy at Leyden, and died in 1718. Thus, in the ardour of the public, and the interefts of the bookfellers, was laid the foundation of the CORPS UNIVERSEL DIPLOMATIQUE DU DROIT

---

* That famous truce was printed at Bruffels, by Rutger Velpius, the printer to the court, in 1609, quarto. I have this tract in my collection,

DES GENS. The labours of Bernard were expanded
and improved by the cares of Du Mont. This vaft
collection appeared in 1726. Du Mont was alfo a
French refugee, who, after ferving in the armies of
France, retired to Holland, and became hiftoriographer to the Emperor: after various publications, he
died in 1726, having acquired the rank of *Baron*. The
bookfellers at Amfterdam, willing to gratify the public tafte, and to promote their own gains, found other
workmen, when they determined to furnifh a SUPPLE-
MENT to the CORPS DIPLOMATIQUE. The celebrated
Barbeyrac gave them, in 1739, a large volume, comprehending *the ancient Treaties*, from the Amphictyonic
times to the age of Charlemagne, which he had ex-
tracted from the authors of Greece and Rome, and from
the monuments of antiquity. This is a work of vaft
and curious erudition. The performances of Bernard and Du Mont were only the labours of the hand:
the volume of Barbeyrac was the elaborate production of the head. John Barbeyrac, who muft not be
confounded with his uncle Charles Barbeyrac, was
born at Beziers, became profeffor of law firft at Lau-
fanne, and afterwards at Groningen, and finifhed his
ufeful courfe, in 1747. The bookfellers had fkilfully
refolved to divide their intended publication into three
parts: the firft was the hiftorical and chronological
collection of Barbeyrac, which has been already mentioned, and which was defigned as an introduction to
the diplomatic code, the fecond was properly *the Supplement*, being an extenfion and continuance of the voluminous works of Bernard and Du Mont; and the
third part was to confift of *the ceremonial of the courts
of Europe*. The performance of the two laft parts was
given to ROUSSET, the hiftoriographer of the Prince of
Orange, whofe diligence and whofe knowledge qualified him eminently for a tafk thus arduous and delicate.

A complete collection of General Treaties muft
confift of the following books: 1ft. Leibnitz's Codex,
in

in 1693; 2dly, The Corps Diplomatique, with its Supplement, in 1739, confisting of twenty volumes in folio, to which is annexed a copious index of matters; 3dly, St. Prieft's *Histoire de Traités de Paix du xvii Siecle, depuis la Paix de Vervins jufqu'à celle de Nimégue,* 1725, 2 *vol. in folio;* and 4thly, of the *Negotiations Sécretes, touching la Paix de Munfter et d'Ofnabrug,* 1725, 4 vol. in folio. Thefe ample collections begin with the eftablifhment of the AMPHICTYONS, 1496 years before the birth of Chrift, being the moft ancient treaty which is to be met with in the records of time; and end with the pacification of the troubles of Geneva, in May 1738.—Such, then, is the vaft mafs of papers which have originated from the reftlefnefs, or the wifdom, of Europe; and which every one muft poffefs, who is ambitious of extenfive knowledge, with regard to the difcordant interefts of the European Powers.

To all thefe muft be added, by thofe who are defirous to form a complete library, the collections, which have been publifhed with regard to particular negotiations: as the peace of Nimeguen; the peace of Ryfwick; the peace of Utrecht *: and to thefe may be added the ufeful collection of *acts, negotiations,* and *treaties,* from 1713 till 1748, in five-and-twenty 8vo. volumes †. The conventions of nations have not only been publifhed at large, but alfo in the abftract. Rouffet favoured the world, in 1736, with Les Intérêts des Puiffances de l'Europe, avec le Supplément, 4 vols. 4to.—Rouffet ceafed from his ufeful labours in Auguft 1762. Mably's *Droit Public de*

---

* Actes et Mémoires concernant la Paix de Nimégue, 1697, 4 tom. en 7 vol. in 12mo.—Actes et Mémoires concernant la Paix de Ryfwick, 1705, 4 vol. in 12mo.—Mémoires Politiques pour fervir à l'Hiftoire de la Paix de Ryfwick, par Jean Du Mont, 1699, 4 vol. in 12mo.—Actes, Mémoires, et autres Piéces authentiques, concernant la Paix d'Utrecht, 1714, 7 vol. in 8vo.

† Recueil des Actes, Negociations, et Traités, depuis la paix d'Utrecht, jufqu'a prefent, par Jean Rouffet.

l'Europe,

l'Europe, will be found a commodious manual, which is written with great knowledge, and arranged with uncommon skill. It has been continued to the peace of 1763, and enriched with the annotations of Rouffet, who was no favourable commentator. Mably and Rouffet parted with unkind sentiments of each other, though the bookfellers had endeavoured to make them agree.

But, of diplomatic researches, there must be an end. I have already exposed my ignorance to the eyes of those who have made the knowledge of the interests of Powers a profession, whilst I have only looked for entertainment amid other labours and other studies. If the following sheets shall be found an accommodation either to the public or to individuals, my design will be accomplished. I have one comfort, during the moment of publication, when I reflect, that if this collection do no great good, it can be attended with no other mischief than the addition of one more book to a class, which is already too numerous, or than the retardment of other works, on the same subject, which might be executed with better arrangement and greater accuracy.

Green Street,
Grosvenor Square,
23 October, 1790.

G. C.

THE

CONTENTS

OF VOL. I.

The

Page

The

The

A COLLECTION

A
COLLECTION
OF
TREATIES, &c.

RUSSIA.

1555.   THERE are copies of the moſt early privileges granted by the ſovereigns of Ruſſia to the Engliſh merchants, in *Hackluyt's Voyages*, ed. 1593. vol. i. p. 265–372-378-470-507; and in *Purchas's Pilgrims*, vol. iii. p. 754-59-61.

1556.   There are in the books of the Board of
1628.   Trade ten ſeveral grants of privileges by the ſovereigns of Ruſſia, to the Engliſh merchants, from December 1556 to June 1628.
                                              Trade, L. Nº 100.

1623.   Articles of perpetual league and alliance,
16 June. intercourſe, and commerce, between James, King of Great Britain, and Michael Pheodorowich, Emperor of Ruſſia.
                                Rym. Fœd. vol. xvii. p. 504.

1654.   There are copies of the terms on which
$\frac{31}{33}$ Aug. the Engliſh merchants were allowed to re-commence trade in Ruſſia.
                          Thurl. St. Pap. vol. ii. p. 558-62.

1734.
2d Dec'. A treaty of friendship, commerce, and navigation, between George II. King of Great Britain, &c. and the Empress Anne, of Russia, &c.

Pap. Off. L. 2.—*Board of Trade,* B. b. 16.—*Rousset's Sup. to the Corps Diplom.* tom. ii. p. 495.

1741.
3d April. The treaty concluded between Great Britain and Russia, at Petersburgh, with the separate and secret articles. *Pap. Off.* L. 3.

1742.
11 Dec'. The treaty concluded between Great Britain and Russia, at Moscow, with the separate and secret articles. *Pap. Off.* L. 4.

1755.
$\frac{12}{14}$ Sept. The treaty concluded between Great Britain and Russia, at Petersburgh, with the separate and secret articles.

Pap. Off. L. 16.—*Treat.* 1772. vol. ii. p. 137.—*Treat.* 1785. vol. iii. p. 30.

1766.
20 June. A treaty of commerce and navigation between Great Britain and Russia, concluded at Petersburgh.

Treat. 1772, vol. ii. p. 309-318.— *Treat.* 1785, vol. iii. p. 215-24.

[The following Treaty of Commerce and Navigation between Great Britain and Russia, 1766, is printed from the Treaties 1785, collated with an authentic copy, and corrected.]

Article I.

THE peace, friendship, and good understanding, which have hitherto happily subsisted between their Majesties of Great Britain and of all the Russias shall be ratified and confirmed by this treaty; so that from this time forward, and in all time coming, there shall be,

be, between the Crown of Great Britain on the one
hand, and the Crown of all the Ruffias on the other;
as alfo between the ftates, countries, kingdoms, dominions, and territories, that are fubject to them, a true,
fincere, firm, and perfect peace, friendfhip, and good
underftanding, which fhall laft for ever, and fhall be
inviolably obferved, as well by fea as by land, and on
the frefh waters; and the fubjects, people, and inhabitants on the one part and on the other, of what ftate or
condition foever they be, fhall perform to each other
all acts of kindnefs and affiftance poffible, and fhall
not do one another any hurt or injury whatever.

II. The fubjects of the two high contracting powers
fhall have full liberty of navigation and commerce in
all the ftates fituated in Europe, where navigation and
commerce are permitted at prefent, or fhall be permitted hereafter by the high contracting parties, to any
other nation.

III. It is agreed, that the fubjects of the two high
contracting parties fhall have leave to enter, trade, and
remain with their fhips, boats, and carriages, loaded or
unloaded, in all the ports, places, and towns, where
fuch leave is granted to the fubjects of any other nation; and the failors, paffengers, and fhips, as well
Britifh as Ruffian (though there fhould be among their
crews fubjects of fome other foreign nation) fhall be
received and treated as the moft favoured nation; and
neither the failors nor paffengers fhall be forced to enter,
againft their will, into the fervice of either of the two
contracting powers, excepting, however, fuch of their
fubjects as they may want for their own proper fervice; and if a domeftic or failor defert his fervice or
his fhip, he fhall be reftored. It is likewife agreed,
that the fubjects of the high contracting parties fhall
have leave to purchafe, at the current price, all forts
of commodities of which they may ftand in need; to
repair and refit their fhips, boats, and carriages; to
purchafe all kinds of provifions for their prefent fub-

fiftance

fiſtance of their voyage; and to remain or depart at
their pleaſure, without lett or impediment, provided
they conform to the laws and ordinances of the reſpective ſtates of the high contracting parties where they
may happen to be. In like manner the Ruſſian ſhips
that are navigating the ſea, and are met by Engliſh
ſhips, ſhall not be impeded in the courſe of their voyage, provided, in the Britiſh ſea, they conform to the
eſtabliſhed practice; but, on the contrary, ſhall receive
from them all kind of aſſiſtance, as well in the ports
of the dominion of Great Britain as in the open ſea.

IV. It is agreed, that the ſubjects of Great Britain
ſhall be at liberty to bring, by water or by land, into all
or into ſuch provinces of Ruſſia, where freedom of
trade is permitted to the ſubjects of any other nation, all ſorts of merchandiſe or effects, the traffic or
entry of which is not prohibited: and in like manner
the ſubjects of Ruſſia ſhall be at liberty to bring, buy
and ſell freely, in all, or in ſuch ſtates of Great Britain
where freedom of trade is permitted to the ſubjects of
any other nation, all ſorts of merchandiſe and effects,
the traffic and entry of which is not prohibited; which
is alſo to be equally underſtood of the manufactures
and products of the Aſiatic provinces, provided this
is not actually forbid by ſome law at preſent in force
in Great Britain; comprehending all ſorts of merchandiſe effects, which the ſubjects of any other
nation may buy there, and tranſport into other countries, particularly wrought and unwrought gold and
ſilver, excepting the current coin of Great Britain; and,
in order to preſerve a juſt equality between the Ruſſian
and Britiſh merchants, with regard to the exportation
of proviſions and other commodities, it is farther ſtipulated, that the ſubjects of Ruſſia ſhall pay the ſame
duties on exportation, that are paid by the Britiſh merchants on exporting the ſame effects from the ports
of Ruſſia; but then each of the high contracting parties ſhall reſerve to itſelf the liberty of making, in the
interior parts of its dominions, ſuch particular arrangements

ments as it shall find expedient for encouraging and extending its own navigation. The Ruffian merchants shall enjoy the same liberties and privileges as the British merchants of the Ruffian company enjoy; and, as the design of the two high contracting parties, and the intention of this treaty, is to facilitate the reciprocal commerce of their subjects, and to extend its limits and mutual advantages, it is agreed, that the British merchants trading in the dominions of Ruffia, shall have liberty, in case of death, a preffing exigency, or abfolute neceffity, when there are no other means of procuring money, or in case of bankruptcy, to difpofe of their effects, whether of Ruffian or foreign merchandife, in such manner as the perfons concerned shall find moft advantageous. The fame thing shall be obferved with regard to the Ruffian merchants in the dominions of Great Britain. All which, however, is to be underftood with this reftriction, that every fort of permiffion, on the one fide and on the other, fpecified in this article, shall not be in any thing contrary to the laws of the country; and the British, as well as the Ruffian merchants and their factors shall punctually conform to the rights, ftatutes, and ordinances of the country where they trade, in order to prevent all kind of fraud and impofition. 'Tis for this reafon, that the decifion of fuch events happening to the British compting-houfes in Ruffia, shall be fubmitted, at Peterfburgh, to the college of commerce, and in other towns where there is no college of commerce, to the tribunals that have the cognizance of commercial affairs.

V. It is agreed, that the subjects of Great Britain, if they have no rixdollars to pay the customs or other duties for the merchandize which they import or export, shall be allowed to pay them in other foreign coin of a known name and eftablished value, equal to that of the rixdollar, or in the current coin of Ruffia, the rixdollar valued at a hundred and twenty-five copecs (or pennies).

VI. All

VI. All poſſible aſſiſtance and diſpatch ſhall be given to the loading and unloading of ſhips, as well for the importation as the exportation of commodities, according to the regulations on that head eſtabliſhed; and they ſhall not be in any manner detained, under the penalties denounced in the ſaid regulations. In like manner, if the ſubjects of Great Britain make contracts with any chancery or college whatever, to deliver certain commodities or effects, upon notifying that ſuch commodities are ready to be delivered, and after they ſhall have been actually delivered at the time ſpecified in theſe contracts, they ſhall be received, and immediately thereupon the accounts ſhall be ſettled and cleared between the ſaid college or chancery and the Britiſh merchants, at the time fixed in the ſaid contracts. The ſame conduct ſhall be obſerved towards Ruſſian merchants in the dominions of Great Britain.

VII. It is agreed, that the ſubjects of Great Britain may, in all the towns and places of Ruſſia, where freedom of trade is permitted to any other nation, pay for the commodities they purchaſe in the ſame current coin of Ruſſia, which they take for the commodities they ſell, unleſs in their contracts they have ſtipulated the contrary; and this ought to be equally underſtood of Ruſſian merchants in the dominions of Great Britain.

VIII. In the places where embarkations are ordinarily made, permiſſion ſhall be granted to the ſubjects of the high contracting parties, to load their ſhips and carriages with, and tranſport by water or by land, all ſuch ſorts of commodities as they ſhall have purchaſed (with an exception, however, of thoſe whoſe exportation is prohibited) upon paying the cuſtoms, provided theſe ſhips and carriages conform to the laws.

IX. The ſubjects of the high contracting parties ſhall pay no greater duty for the importation or exportation of their commodities, than is paid by the ſubjects

jeéts of other nations. Neverthelefs, to prevent on both fides the defrauding of the cuftoms, if it fhould be difcovered that commodities have been entered clandeftinely, and without paying the cuftoms, they fhall be confifcated; but, befides that, no other punifhment fhall be inflicted upon the merchants on either fide.

X. Permiffion fhall be granted to the fubjeéts of the two contracting parties to go, come, and trade freely with thofe ftates, with which one or other of the parties fhall at that time, or at any future period, be engaged in war, provided they do not carry military ftores to the enemy. From this permiffion, however, are excepted places actually blocked up, or befieged, as well by fea as by land; but, at all other times, and with the fingle exception of military ftores, the abovefaid fubjeéts may tranfport to thefe places all forts of commodities, as well as paffengers, without the leaft impediment. With regard to the fearching of merchant fhips, men of war and privateers fhall behave as favourably as the reafon of the war, at that time exifting, can poffibly permit towards the moft friendly powers that fhall remain neuter; obferving, as far as may be, the principles and maxims of the law of nations, that are generally acknowledged.

XI. All cannon, mortars, mufkets, piftols, bombs, grenades, bullets, balls, fufees, flint-ftones, matches, powder, falt-petre, fulphur, breaft-plates, pikes, fwords, belts, cartouch-bags, faddles, and bridles, beyond the quantity that may be neceffary for the ufe of the fhip; or beyond what every man ferving on board the fhip, and every paffenger, ought to have, fhall be accounted ammunition or military ftores; and, if found, fhall be confifcated, according to law, as contraband goods or prohibited commodities; but neither the fhips nor paffengers, nor the other commodities found at the fame time, fhall be detained or hindered to profecute their voyage.

B 4   XII. If,

XII. If, what God forbid ! the peace fhould come to be broke between the two high contracting parties, the perfons, fhips, and commodities, fhall not be detained or confifcated; but they fhall be allowed, at leaft, the fpace of one year, to fell, difpofe, or carry off, their effects, and to retire wherever they pleafe; a ftipulation that is to be equally underftood of all thofe who fhall be in the fea or land fervice; and they fhall farther be permitted, either at or before their departure, to confign the effects which they fhall not as yet have difpofed of, as well as the debts that fhall be due to them, to fuch perfons as they fhall think proper, in order to difpofe of them according to their defire, and for their benefit; which debts, the debtors fhall be obliged to pay in the fame manner as if no fuch rupture had happened.

XIII. In cafe of a fhipwreck happening in any place belonging to one or other of the high contracting parties, not only fhall all kind of affiftance be given to the unhappy fufferers, and no fort of violence fhall be offered to them, but even the effects which they fhall have faved themfelves, or which they fhall have thrown overboard into the fea, fhall not be concealed, withheld, or damaged, under any pretext whatfoever; on the contrary, the above-faid effects and commodities fhall be preferved and reftored to them, upon their giving a moderate recompenfe to thofe who fhall have affifted them in faving their lives, their fhips, and their commodities.

XIV. Permiffion fhall be granted to Britifh merchants to build, buy, fell, and hire houfes in all the territories and towns of Ruffia, excepting, however, with regard to the permiffion of building and buying houfes in thofe towns of Ruffia which have particular rights of burgherfhip, and privileges inconfiftent with fuch indulgence; and it is exprefsly fpecified, that at St. Peterfburgh, Mofcow, and Archangel, the houfes which the Britifh merchants fhall buy, or caufe to
be

be built, fhall be exempt from all quartering of foldiers, as long as they fhall belong to them, and fhall
be inhabited by them , but with regard to the houfes
which they fhall hire or let, thefe fhall be fubject to
all the ufual charges of the town; the tenant and
landlord fettling that matter between them.   As to
every other town of Ruffia, the houfes which they
fhall purchafe or caufe to be built, in the fame
manner as thofe which they fhall hire or let, fhall
not be exempted from the quartering of foldiers.
Permiffion fhall likewife be granted the Ruffian merchants to build, buy, fell, and let houfes in Great
Britain and Ireland, in the fame manner as is done
by the fubjects of the moft favoured nations.   They
fhall enjoy the free exercife of the Greek religion in
their houfes, or in fuch places as are deftined for that
purpofe; and in like manner the Britifh merchants
fhall enjoy the free exercife of the Proteftant religion.   The fubjects of either power, eftablifhed in
Ruffia or in Great Britain, fhall have power to difpofe
of their eftates, and to leave them by will to whomfoever they think proper, following the cuftoms and
laws of their own proper country.

XV. Paffports fhall be granted to all Britifh fubjects who defire to quit the dominions of Ruffia, two
months after they fhall have fignified their defign of
departing, without obliging them to give fecurity; and
if, in that time, there appear no juft caufe for detaining them, they fhall be allowed to go; nor fhall
they be obliged to apply for that purpofe to any other
quarter than to the college of commerce, or to that
which may hereafter be eftablifhed in its place.   The
fame eafy methods of departing fhall, upon like occafions, and agreeable to the cuftom of the country, be
granted to Ruffian merchants, who want to quit the
dominions of Great Britain.

XVI. Britifh merchants, who fhall hire or employ domeftics, fhall, in this particular, be obliged

to conform themselves to the laws of this empire.
And Ruffian merchants fhall be equally obliged to do
the fame in Great Britain.

XVII. In all law-fuits and other proceedings, the
Britifh merchants fhall be amenable only to the college of commerce, or to that which fhall hereafter be
eftablifhed for the adminiftration of juftice between
merchants. But, if it fhould happen that the Britifh
merchants fhould have law-fuits in any place at a
diftance from the above-mentioned college of commerce, both they and the adverfe party fhall prefer
their complaints to the magiftrate of the faid towns;
with this provifo, however, that the Britifh merchants
fhall have the right to appeal from the fentence of
the magiftrate, and to demand that of the college of
commerce, if they find themfelves aggrieved. The
Ruffian merchants in the dominions of Great Britain
fhall, in their turn, have the fame protection and
juftice, which, according to the laws of that kingdom,
are granted to other foreign merchants, and fhall be
treated as the fubjects of the moft favoured nation.

XVIII. The Britifh merchants in Ruffia, and the
Ruffian merchants in Great Britain, fhall not be
obliged to fhew their books or papers to any perfon
whatever, unlefs it be to make proof in the courfe of
juftice; ftill lefs fhall the faid books or papers be
taken or detained from them. If, however, the cafe
fhould happen, that any Britifh merchant becomes
bankrupt, he fhall be amenable at St. Peterfburgh to
the college of commerce, or to that which fhall hereafter be eftablifhed for the adminiftration of juftice in
mercantile affairs, and in other remote towns, to the
magiftrate of the place; and he fhall be proceeded
againft according to the laws that are or fhall be
made for this purpofe. Neverthelefs, if the Britifh
merchants, without becoming bankrupt, refufe to pay
their debts, whether to the treafury of her Imperial
Majefty, or to individuals, it fhall be lawful to lay an

§   arreft

arreft upon part of their effects equivalent to their debts; and, in case thefe effects fhould not be fufficient for difcharging fuch debts, they may themfelves be arrefted and detained in cuftody, until fuch time as the greater part of their creditors, as well with refpect to number, as to the value of their refpective demands, have confented to their enlargement. With regard to their effects laid under arreft, they fhall remain as a depofit in the hands of thofe who fhall be named and duly authorifed for that purpofe, by the greater part of their creditors, as is above fpecified; which delegates fhall be obliged to appraife the effects as foon as poffible, and to make a juft and fair diftribution of them to all the creditors, in proportion to their refpective demands. The fame procedure fhall, in like cafes, be obferved towards the Ruffian merchants in the dominions of Great Britain, and they fhall. be there protected agreeably to the regulations made in the preceding article.

XIX. In cafe of complaints and law-fuits, three perfons of fair and unblemifhed character among the foreign merchants fhall, with a proper regard to circumftances, be named by the college of commerce, and where there is no fuch college, by the magiftrate, to examine the books and papers of the parties, and the report they fhall make to the college of commerce, or to the magiftrate, of what they fhall find in the faid books or papers, fhall be held a good proof.

XX. The commiffioners of the cuftoms fhall have the charge of examining the fervants or clerks of the Ruffian merchants, when they caufe their goods to be entered, whether they have, for that effect, the orders or full powers of the mafters; and if they have not fuch, they fhall not be credited. The fame conduct fhall be obferved towards the fervants of the Britifh merchants; and, when the faid fervants, having the orders or full powers of their mafters, fhall caufe their goods to be entered on account of their mafters, thefe

laft

last shall be as responsible as if they themselves had caused them to be entered. All the Russian servants employed in the shops shall likewise be registered, and their masters shall answer for them in the affairs of trade, and in the bargains which they make in their name.

XXI. In case the Russian merchants who are indebted to the British merchants withdraw from the places of their abode to other parts or districts, the college of commerce, after complaints shall have been made to them on the subject, and proofs of the debts have been adduced, shall cite them three times, allowing them a sufficient space to appear in person; and if they do not appear within the term prescribed, the said college shall condemn them, and shall send, at the expence of the plaintiff, an express to the Governors and Waywodes, with orders to put the sentence in execution, and thus shall oblige the debtors to pay the sums specified.

XXII. The brokerage shall be settled with justice, and the brokers shall be responsible for the quality of the goods and fraudulent package, and shall be obliged, after sufficient proofs produced against them, to make up the losses to which they have given occasion.

XXIII. A regulation shall be made to prevent the abuses that may be committed in the package of leather, hemp, and flax; and, if any dispute happen between the buyer and the seller concerning the weight or the tare, the commissioners of the customs shall determine it according to equity.

XXIV. In order the more effectually to encourage and promote the trade of Great Britain, it is agreed, that for the future the English woollen cloths, hereafter specified, shall not pay any greater duties on entry than are settled in this article, viz. English cloth for the use of the soldiery, shall pay (in rixdollars) only two copecs (or pennies) for every arsheen (or 71¼ yards)

yards) as a duty on entry; coarfe cloth of the county of York, known in the Ruffian Tariff by the name of Coftrogy, fhall only pay two copecs for every arfheen: broad flannel fhall only pay one copec per arfheen; narrow flannel fhall only pay three-fourths of a copec per arfheen, all as duty on entry. And in every thing that regards the impofts and duties payable on the importation or exportation of commodities in general, the fubjects of Great Britain fhall be always confidered and treated as the moft favoured nation.

XXV. The peace, friendfhip, and good under-ftanding fhall continue for ever between the high con-tracting parties; and, as it is cuftomary to fix a cer-tain term to the duration of treaties of commerce, the above-mentioned high contracting parties have agreed, that this treaty fhall continue for twenty years, counting from the day of figning; and, after the expiration of that term, they may agree upon the means to renew and prolong it.

XXVI. The prefent treaty of navigation and com-merce fhall be approved and ratified by his Britannic Majefty and by her Imperial Majefty; and the ratifi-cations, in due and lawful form, fhall be exchanged at St. Peterfburgh, in the fpace of three months, or fooner if poffible, counting from the day of figning.

In witnefs whereof, we the under-figned, in virtue of the full powers granted to us by his Majefty the King of Great Britain, and by her Imperial Majefty of all the Ruffias, have figned the prefent treaty, and thereto fet our feals. Done at St. Peterfburgh, this 20th day of June 1766.

(L. S.) *George Macartney.* (L. S.) *Nikita Panin.*
                         (L. S.) *Erneft, Count Munich.*
                         (L. S.) *Pr. A. Galitzin.*
                         (L. S.) *Gr. Teploff.*

The Edict of the Emprefs of Ruffia; *giving leave to all foreigners, of what nation or country foever, to carry on a free and unlimited trade, both by fea and land, with the feveral countries bordering upon the* Euxine, *which have lately been annexed to the* Ruffian *dominion; and allotting fpecially to fuch foreign nations the ports of* Cherfon *in the government of* Catherineflaw, Sebaftopolis *(formerly called* Acht-air*) and* Theodofia *(formerly called* Caffa*) both in the province of* Taurica, *where they may refide and carry on their traffic with the fame immunities and privileges, religious and civil, as are allowed at* Peterfburgh *and* Archangel.

W E Catherine the fecond, by the grace of God, Emprefs and Autocratice of all the Ruffias, of Mufcovy, Kiovia Wolodomiria, Novogorod, Czarina of Cazan, Czarina of Aftrachan, Czarina of Siberia, Czarina of the Cherfonefus Taurica, Lady of Pickof, and Great Duchefs of Smolenfko, Duchefs of Eftonia, Livonia, Carelia, Twer, Ingorie, Permio, Vitatkia, Bulgaria, and other places; Lady and Great Duchefs of the country of Lower Novogorod, Chernigof, Razan, Polofzk, Roftof, Jaroflof, Beloferfk, Uderfk, Obdorfk, Coudinfk, Wityrpfk, Mftiflawfk, and Sovereign of all the northern coafts, Lady of the Twerfky country, of the Carthalinian and Grauzinian Czars, of the country of Carbadinia; of the Princes of Circaffia, and thofe of the mountains, and of the other countries, Heirefs Lady, and Sovereign Ruler.

Our endeavours to increafe the trade of our own fubjects, and of the other nations throughout the Black Sea, and the Mediterranean, have met with the wifhed-for fuccefs; the treaty of commerce which we concluded with the Ottoman Porte on the 10th of June 1783, having finally removed thofe impediments and difficulties which, from the particular conftitution of the Turkifh government, had obftructed the faid trade

in

in every ftep of its progrefs; which can only be guard-
ed againft by the inftitution of proper laws for the protection of commerce, and by granting it that entire
freedom which its various fpeculations and turns fo indifpenfably require.   The principles of this unlimited
freedom we have adopted, and followed from the
earlieft period of our government, as is manifeft from
the feveral edicts and regulations which have been
iffued from our throne; and we now extend thefe
edicts and regulations in their utmoft latitude to the
trade. of the Black Sea.   The fecurity and convenience
of that commerce are now fully provided for by the
annexation of the province of Taurica, and the neigh-
bouring territories, to our other dominions; we have
opened therein divers fea ports for the ufe of all perfons who will carry away from thence the produce of
Ruffia, and bring thither the produce and manufactures of other countries.

It is well known, that the laft Turkifh war (a war
which, during the fix years that it lafted, was figna-
lized by fo many victories of our arms) was no fooner
concluded than we erected within the government of
Catherineflaw, upon the river Dniper, and at a fhort
diftance, the city of Cherfon: it having appeared to
us that that fituation was particularly commodious, as
well for exporting the produce of Ruffia as for importing, from other countries, fuch things as might be
ufeful to us; and we fecured the trade thereof by the
moft effectual means of defence, encouraging it moreover by fuch helps as were beft fuited to it, and were
not inconfiftent with the general principles of commerce.

This town, as alfo Sebaftopolis (formerly called
Acht-air) and Theodofia (formerly called Caffa) both
which latter are fituated in the province of Taurica,
and are provided with excellent fea-ports, we have,
on account of the commodioufnefs of their fituation,
ordered to be opened to all nations, living in amity
with

with our empire, for the purpofes of their commercial intercourfe with our faithful fubjects. Accordingly, we moft folemnly declare, by thefe prefents,
that all fuch nations are at liberty to come to the faid
ports, either in their own or hired veffels, and under
their own colours, as alfo to repair thither by land;
and they are likewife free to depart from thence at
their pleafure, paying the duties of importation and
exportation agreeable to the tariffs eftablifhed in the
refpective cuftom-houfes.—Moreover, all perfons, of
what nations and countries foever, may remain in
thefe towns as long as their bufinefs or inclinations
may lead them, and enjoy the free exercife of their
religion, agreeably to thofe laudable inftitutions which
have been handed down to us from our anceftors,
fovereigns of Ruffia, and which we ourfelves have confirmed and augmented, permitting all ftrangers refiding in Ruffia to worfhip the Almighty agreeably to
the religion of their forefathers, offering prayers to
him, together with our own fubjects, that he will increafe the welfare and ftrengthen the power of our
empire. We give leave to all and every one to carry
on their trade with abfolute freedom, either fingly or
in companies, promifing by our Imperial word, that
all foreigners fhall enjoy the fame privileges in thofe
three towns as they enjoy in our Imperial city of St.
Peterfburgh, and in our provincial town of Archangel; and in cafe of a war, every one fhall be fecured by the principles of that neutral fyftem which
we have erected, and which, on our part, fhall be
kept facred and inviolable. Finally, if any foreigners
fhall wifh to fettle in thefe or any other towns or places
of our empire, and to become our fubjects, we will
receive them moft gracioufly under our dominion, promifing that they fhall not only be allowed the free exercife of their religion (as mentioned above) but the
full enjoyment of all fuch privileges and exemptions
with regard to trade and navigation as have been
granted to our other fubjects; as alfo to erect fabrics
and

and manufactories, paying only such taxes as shall be paid by our other subjects of the same condition with themselves. All persons, who shall thus become our subjects, shall be at liberty, they and their descendants, to remain under our government as long as may be agreeable to them, or as their interest may require; and in case they should afterwards chuse to withdraw from the same, they shall be freely permitted so to do, on paying the taxes that had been laid upon them for three years to come. The particular privileges which will be granted to the above-mentioned towns will be set forth in their respective charters, which are speedily to be published.

Given at St. Petersburgh, the 22d of February 1784, and in the 22d year of our reign.

The original was signed with her Imperial majesty's own hand.

S W E D E N.

1654.
11 April.   THE treaty of peace between Oliver
              Cromwell and Chriſtina Queen of
Sweden, concluded at Upſal.
                      Treat. 1732, vol. iii. p. 89.
                      Treat. 1785, vol. i. p. 69.

1656.   . The treaty between Oliver Cromwell and
17 July.   Charles Guſtavus King of Sweden, concluded at Weſtminſter, confirming and ex-
plaining the treaty of Upſal.
                      Treat. 1732, vol. iii. p. 162.

1661.   The treaty of alliance and commerce be-
21 Oct.   tween Charles II. King of Great Britain,
&c. and Charles King of Sweden, concluded
at Whitehall.
                      Pap. Off. H. 2.
                      Treat. 1732, vol. iii. p. 240.
                      Treat. 1772, Suppl. p. 28.

1665.   The treaty of alliance and commerce be-
1 Mar.   tween Great Britain and Sweden, concluded
at Stockholm. *Pap. Off.* H. 3.

1666.   The treaty of commerce between Great
16 Feb.   Britain and Sweden, concluded at Stockholm.

1668.   The treaty between Great Britain, Swe-
25 Apr.   den, and the States General, with the ſeparate articles, concluded at the Hague.
                      . *Pap. Off.* H. 5.

1674.   The treaty of alliance and commerce
30 Sept.   concluded between Great Britain and Swe-
10 Oct.   den, concluded at Weſtminſter.
                      Pap. Off. H. 7.

                                        1699.

1699.   The treaty between Great Britain, Swe-
$\frac{2\cdot9}{3\cdot0}$ Dec.   den, and the States General, with the fepa-
1700.   rate and fecret articles, concluded at Lon-
$\frac{1\cdot1}{2\cdot7}$ Jan.   don and the Hague.

> *Pap. Off.* H. 9.
> *Treat.* 1785, vol. i. p. 313.

1703.   The defenfive alliance between Great
$\frac{5}{1\cdot6}$ Aug.   Britain, Sweden, and the States General,
with the feparate article, concluded at the
Hague. *Pap. Off.* H. 10.

1720.   The treaty of alliance and mutual affift-
21 Jan.   ance, with the feparate articles, concluded at
Stockholm.

> *Pap. Off.* H. 13.
> *Treat.* 1732, vol. iv. p. 106.
> *Rouffet, Recueil Hiftorique,* tom. ii.
> p. 476.

1727.   The acceffion of Sweden to the treaty of
14 Mar.   Hanover, 3d Sept. 1725, between Great
Britain, France, and Pruffia, with the feparate and fecret articles.

> *Pap. Off.* H. 16.
> *Treat.* 1732, vol. iv. p. 162.
> *Rouffet, Recueil Hiftorique,* tom. iii.
> p. 314.

1766.   The treaty of alliance and commerce be-
5 Feb.   tween Great Britain and Sweden.

The

The Treaty of Peace between Oliver Cromwell, *Protector of the Commonwealth of* England, *and* Christina, *Queen of* Sweden, *concluded at* Upsal *the 11th of* April, 1654.

WE the underwritten Axel Oxenstiern, Chancellor of the kingdom, and Provincial Judge of the Western Nordelles, Swedish Lapland, and Jempterland, Count of the Southern Morea, Free Baron in Kimith, Lord in Tyholm and Tidoen, Knight; and Eric Oxenstiern, Son of Axel, President of the General College of Commerce, Count of Southern Morea, Free Baron in Kimith, Lord in Tidoen, and of Vybium and Gorwats, Senators and Plenipotentiaries of the most Serene and most Potent Princess and Lady, the Lady Christina, by the Grace of God of the Swedes, Goths, and Vandals, Queen, Great Princess of Finland, Duchess of Esthonia, Carelia, Bremen, Verden, Stetin, Pomerania, Cassuben, and Vandalia, Princess of Rugen, also Lady of Ingria and Wismar, &c. and Senators and Plenipotentiaries also of the kingdom of Sweden, do hereby make known and testify, That as there has been a good and amicable correspondence, time out of mind, between the Swedish and English nations; and that as for renewing and increasing the same, it has been thought convenient that the most illustrious and most excellent Lord Bulstrode Whitlock, Constable of Windsor Castle, and one of the Commissioners of the Great Seal of England, should come to her Sacred Royal Majesty, by the command and in the name of Oliver, Lord Protector of the republic of England, Scotland, and Ireland, and the dominions thereof, sufficiently authorized and instructed to transact the affairs hereafter mentioned; so on the other hand, her said sacred Royal Majesty having furnished us with the like full powers, has graciously enjoined us, that after consultation held with the aforesaid Lord Ambassador, on such matters as shall be thought most agreeable to the present

circumstances

circumftances of affairs, for eftablifhing the freedom of commerce and navigation, and corroborating a mutual friendfhip, fomething certain might be determined, and comprehended under certain articles of a mutual treaty: For which reafon, after mature deliberation, we agreed to the points hereafter following, as they are clearly exprefled in the articles of this treaty.

I. There fhall be and remain hereafter between the Queen and kingdom of Sweden, and the Lord Protector and the republic aforefaid, and all and fingular their dominions, kingdoms, countries, provinces, iflands, lands, colonies, cities, towns, people, citizens, inhabitants, and all their fubjefts and inhabitants, a good, fincere, firm, and perpetual peace, amity, goodwill, and correfpondence, fo that both parties fhall love each other with the moft entire affeftion.

II. The aforefaid confederates, and the fubjefts, people, and inhabitants of both dominions, as occafion offers, fhall take care of and promote their mutual advantage; fhall alfo certify one another of any dangers which they fee threatened to either from the confpiracies and machinations of their enemies, and fhall oppofe and hinder the fame, as far as lies in their power. And it fhall not be lawful for either of the confederates, either for himfelf, or by any other perfons whatfoever, to aft, treat of, or endeavour any thing to the inconveniency or detriment of the other, in any part of their lands or dominions whatfoever, whether by land or fea; nor fhall either of the confederates favour the rebels or enemies of the other, nor receive, or admit into their dominions, any rebels or traitors, who fhall form any contrivance againft the ftate of the other, much lefs afford them any advice, afliftance, or favour, or fuffer or permit any fuch afliftance to be given them by the fubjefts, people, and inhabitants of either nation.

III. The faid Queen and kingdom, and the aforefaid Lord Proteftor and republic, fhall be very care-

ful

ful to remove all thofe impediments, as far as lies in
their power, which have hitherto interrupted the confederates freedom of navigation, and commerce between the two nations, through the dominions, lands,
feas, and rivers of both, with other people and nations;
and they fhall be juftified in afferting, eftablifhing,
defending, and promoting the abovementioned liberty
of navigation, and of all merchandize on both fides,
againft all difturbers whatfoever ; without fuffering any
thing to be done or committed, contrary to this article,
either by themfelves, or their fubjefts or people.

IV. It is granted, and it fhall be free for both of the
faid confederates, and their inhabitants and fubjefts, to
have free ingrefs and egrefs, refidence or paffage, in,
through, or from the kingdoms, countries, provinces,
lands, iflands, cities, and towns, walled or unwalled, fortified or not fortified, dominions and territories whatfoever, of the other confederate, freely and fecurely,
without any licenfe or fafe-conduft, general or fpecial ;
and in the mean time to buy and purchafe all necef-
ries for their fuftenance and ufe, where they think fit,
and that they be treated with all manner of benevolence. It fhall likewife be lawful for both of the confederates, and their fubjefts and inhabitants, to merchandife, traffic, and trade, in all places where commerce has been carried on at any time hitherto, in
whatfoever goods and wares they pleafe ; and every one
fhall have leave to import and export the fame at difcretion ; provided they pay the duties, and obferve the
laws and orders of the aforefaid kingdom and republic, relating to merchandize, or any other right.
Which things being prefuppofed, the people, fubjefts,
and inhabitants of either of the confederates, fhall have
and poffefs in the countries, lands, dominions, and
kingdoms of the other, as full and ample privileges,
and as many exemptions, immunities, and liberties, as
any foreigner doth or fhall poffefs in the dominions and
kingdoms of the faid confederates.

V. The

V. The merchants, captains, masters of ships, mariners, and all men whatsoever, their ships, and all merchandize and goods in general, of either of the confederates, their subjects and inhabitants, shall not be put or detained under arrest, on any public or private account, by virtue of any general or special edict, in any of the territories, harbours, stations, shores, or dominions whatsoever, of the other confederate, for public use, warlike expeditions, or any other cause, much less for the private use of any person; nor be compelled by any sort of violence, nor in any wise molested or injured. Provided nevertheless, that arrests which are agreeable to justice and equity be not prohibited, if made according to the ordinary forms of law, and not to gratify the passions of private persons, but as indispensably requisite for the administration of law and justice.

VI. That if one or more ships of either of the confederates, whether ships of war, or private ships of burthen belonging to their subjects, citizens, and inhabitants, be drove by stress of weather, or pursued by pirates and enemies, or compelled by other urgent necessity to any harbours, stations, or shores whatsoever, of the other confederate, they shall be there received with all kindness and humanity, and enjoy amicable protection, without being hindered in any measure from refitting themselves intirely, and from buying all necessaries for their sustenance, repair, and conveniency, at a fair price; nor shall they be hindered on any account from weighing anchor, and departing from any port and station, when they please, without paying the customs, or any imposts, so long as they do not contravene or transgress the statutes, orders, and customs of the place, to which the ships shall be retired, or where they stay.

VII. For the like reason, if one or more ships, whether public or private, of either of the confederates, their subjects or inhabitants, have run ashore, suffered

wreck,

wreck, or any lofs or damage whatfoever, or fhall
hereafter, upon the coafts or any territories whatfoever
of the other confederate, .the fufferers fhall be kindly
and friendly relieved, and affifted for a proper reward.
Provided that .whatfoever be recovered of the faid
wreck, or any lofs or damage, be fecured, preferved,
and reftored to the rightful owner, or his reprefen-
tative.

VIII. That if the fubjects and inhabitants of either
of the confederates, whether they are merchants and
their factors, fervants, captains, mafters of fhips, mariners, or others, travelling or fojourning, for any other
reafon, in the dominions of the other confederate, want
the affiftance of the magiftrates, either to plead any
caufe in the courts of juftice in their name for the recovery of their debts, or for other lawful reafons, it
fhall be courteoufly afforded to them readily, and according to the equity of the cafe; and juftice fhall be
adminiftered without tedious and unneceffary delays.
They fhall not in any manner, or for any pretence, be
hindered in tranfacting their affairs, contracting for
merchandize, receiving the price for them, and performing their journies, but fhall be treated every
where with the moft friendly offices; and it fhall be
fiee for them on both fides to wear arms for felf-de-
fence, on the fhores, or in the fhips, harbours, and
public places whatfoever of the other confederate.
Provided they do not give the governors and magiftrates of any place whatfoever, any juft fufpicion of
any machinations againft the public or private peace;
and whofoever behave modeftly and innocently, fhall
be protected from violence and trouble.

IX. It fhall be lawful for the faid confederates, and
each of them, their people and fubjects, to buy and
export from their refpective countries, dominions, and
kingdoms, arms and warlike ftores of all forts,
and fhips, into one another's harbours, ftations, and
fhores, to hale them afhore with fafety and freedom
to

to refide there, and to depart from thence, provided they behave modeftly, peaceably, and conformably to the laws and cuftoms of the feveral places, and do not in any refpeft hinder the freedom of commerce. In like manner, the Dutch fhips fhall have free accefs to the ports of the other confederate, and free anchorage there : but if their number be fuch as may give manifeft fufpicion, they fhall not enter without confent and leave firft obtained from that confederate, whofe harbours they are at; unlefs they are drove in by tempefts, or by violence, or by danger at fea : in which cafe they fhall fignify the reafon of their coming to the governor or chief magiftrate of the place, but fhall not ftay there longer than the time granted by the governor, or chief magiftrate of the place, as aforefaid, nor longer than they obferve this article, and thofe other conditions hereafter ftipulated.

X. It fhall be lawful for the fubjefts and inhabitants of the Queen and kingdom of Sweden, to travel fafely, and without moleftation, in England, Scotland, and Ireland, and all the dominions thereof, and to pafs through the fame whither they pleafe, by land or fea, to any nations whatfoever, and freely to trade and traffic with them in all forts of merchandize, to import them thither, and to export them from thence : and the people of the aforefaid republic fhall enjoy the fame liberties in the kingdoms, dominions, and territories of the Queen and kingdom of Sweden, on condition that the laws, ordinances, and prerogatives of each nation refpeftively, which relate to commerce and merchandize, be obferved on both fides.

XI. Although the preceding articles of this treaty, and the laws of friendfhip forbid, that either of the confederates fhall give aid and affiftance to the enemies of the other, yet it muft by no means be underftood, that that confederate, with the fubjefts and inhabitants, who are not involved in war, fhall carry on no manner of trade and navigation with the enemies of

that

that confederate who is engaged in the war. Only
it is hereby provided, in the mean time, till all the
rules appertaining to this matter are settled, that no
merchandize of that fort which shall be deemed contraband (which shall be specified by a particular catalogue, to be settled within four months) shall be carried to the enemies of the other, without danger of
being made prize, and without hopes of redemption,
if they are seized by the other confederate.

XII. Lest that such free navigation or passage of
one of the confederates, or his or her subjects and inhabitants, while the other confederate is at war, by
land or sea, with other nations, should be prejudicial
to the other confederate; and lest hostile goods and
wares should be concealed under the disguise of friendship; for removing all suspicion and fraud, it is thought
fit that all ships, carriages, wares, and men, belonging
to either of the confederates, shall be duly furnished
in their journies and voyages with safe-conducts, commonly called passports and certificates, which shall be
signed by the chief governor or magistrate of the chief
province, or city from whence they came, and be regulated in all things according to the forms that shall
be agreed on within the space of six months from the
date hereof: And when the merchandize, goods, ships,
men of either of the confederates, and their subjects
and inhabitants, shall meet or be met by the ships of
war, public or private, or the subjects and inhabitants
of the other confederate in the open sea or straits, harbours, stations, lands, or other places wheresoever
they shall come together, after producing their safe-
conducts and certificates, nothing farther shall be demanded of them, no inquiry whatsoever shall be made
into the ships, goods, or men, much less shall they be
injured, damaged, or molested, but shall be freely let
go to prosecute their journey, voyage, or business. And
if any thing be committed by either party contrary to
the genuine meaning of this article, both of the confederates shall inflict a severe punishment on their subjects

jects and inhabitants, the contraveners, and shall take care that plenary and immediate satisfaction be given to the other injured confederate, or his subjects and inhabitants; for all loss and expences.

XIII. If it also happen heieafter, during this friend-ship and treaty, that any of the people and subjects of either of the confederates attempt or endeavour any thing contrary to this league, or any article thereof, by land or sea, or elsewhere, this friendship, league, and contract shall not be interrupted or dissolved be-tween the said confederates on that account, but shall nevertheless remain and continue intire, and those par-ticular men only shall be punished, who shall violate this treaty, and right and justice shall be administered to those who receive the injury, and all manner of sa-tisfaction shall be made them for the loss and injury within the space of twelve months after the restitution demanded. And if the said delinquents, and those who are guilty of the violence committed, refuse to stand and submit to justice, or to make satisfaction within the day appointed, their estates, goods, and possessions whatsoever, shall be confiscated and sold for the just and full satisfaction of the injuries which they have committed; and the delinquents and guilty persons themselves, when they come into the power of the other state, shall moreover suffer due punish-ment, according to the nature of the offence. And restitution and satisfaction shall be made speedily, and without delay, to the party injured, and his or her sub-jects and inhabitants, for the losses and damages which either of the confederates suffered by the other, dur-ing the war betwixt England and the United Provin-ces of the Netherlands.

XIV. The present treaty and confederacy shall de-rogate nothing from any preheminence, right, and do-minion whatsoever, of either of the confederates, in their seas, straits, and waters whatsoever, but shall have and retain the same to themselves, in as ample

§   a manner

a manner as they have hitherto enjoyed them, and as by right to them belongs.'

XV. Whereas therefore it is the primary inftitution of this treaty, that fuch a freedom of navigation and commerce, as is defcribed in the foregoing articles, may be and remain on both fides, to both of the confederates, their fubjects and inhabitants, in the Baltic Sea, the Sound, the North Sea, the Britifh Ocean, the Mediterranean, and the Channel, and the other feas in Europe, both parties fhall endeavour heartily, with their joint advice, help, and affiftance, that the aforefaid mutual freedom of navigation and commerce may be eftablifhed and promoted, in all the feas and, ftraits aforefaid, and defended, if occafion fhall require, againft all difturbers, who fhall attempt to interrupt, prohibit, hinder, conftrain, or force it for their own pleafure, and for the fake of injuring the confederates. And both of the faid confederates fhall contribute friendly and readily to promote the advantages and remove the difadvantages of each other; faving the treaties heretofore entered into, and ftill fubfifting, between both nations, and other kingdoms, republics, and ftates. And hereafter neither of the confederates fhall by any means enter into any treaty, or make any contract with other foreign nations and ftates whatfoever, to the leaft prejudice of this prefent treaty, without the previous knowledge and confent of the other confederate; or if any thing fhall hereafter be ftipulated with others, it fhall be accounted of no effect, and fhall yield in all refpects to this mutual convention. As to the mutual aid or affiftance to be given one another for the defence of this treaty, and the freedom of commerce and navigation, when it fhall be neceffary, and reafon requires, a more particular agreement fhall be made,' according to the circumftances of time, &c.

XVI. As to the other advantages to be enjoyed, and laws to be conformed to by the men of war,.

which

which arrive at the harbours or ftations of either of the confederates, the trade to be carried on in America, alfo as to the catching of herrings, and other fifh what-foever, the appointing of ftaples and emporiums of commerce, and the regulating of other matters and conditions, which may be required for the greater il-luftration of the foregoing articles, the fame fhall be fettled, as hereafter fhall be mutually agreed, by a fpe-cial treaty or covenant.

XVII. But thofe things to which we have confent-ed in the former articles fhall immediately from this inftant be in full force, and duly obferved by both parties, and by all who are united on both fides by allegiance, faith, and obedience. And to the intent that hereafter they may be rendered the more ftable and firm, as well by her moft gracious Royal Majef-ty, as by the Lord Protector of the republic of Eng-land, Scotland, and Ireland, and their dominions, in the name of his Highnefs, and the faid republic, they fhall be fubfcribed, figned, and ratified within the term of four months, with the very hands and feals of her Majefty and his Highnefs.

In confirmation of all that is above written, and in witnefs that they fhall be facredly obferved, and rati-fied within the day aforefaid, on the part of her Royal Majefty, our moft gracious Lady, we have fubfcribed thefe prefents with our hands, and fealed them with our feals. Done at Upfal the 11th of April, 1654.

The Treaty between Charles Guftavus *King of* Swe-den, *and* Oliver Cromwell *Protector of* England; *whereby the Treaty of Alliance made between thofe two States the* 11th *of* April 1654, *is confirmed and explained.* Done at London, Anno 1656.

I Chriftiern Bonde, Free Baron of Layhela, Lòrd of Ymfifholm, Bordfoo, and Springeftadt, &c. Se-nator of the kingdom of Sweden, and of the moft Se-

rene

rene and Potent Prince and Lord, the Lord Charles
Guftavus, by the grace of God King of the Swedes,
Goths, and Vandals, Great Prince of Finland, Duke
of Efthonia, Carelia, Bremen, Verden, Stetin, Pomerania, Caffuben, and Vandalia, Prince of Rugen, Lord
of Ingria and Wifmar, alfo Count Palatine of the
Rhine, and Duke of Bavaria, Juliers, Cleves, and
Mons, and Ambaffador Extraordinary from that Prince
to the moft Serene and moft High Oliver Lord Protector of England, Scotland, and Ireland, and the dominions thereof, and to the republic of England; do
hereby make known and teftify to all and every one
whom it concerns, or whom it may in any meafure
concern, That whereas in the treaty made at Upfal,
the 11th of April 1654, between the moft Serene and
Potent Princefs Chriftina, by the grace of God Queen
of the Swedes, Goths, and Vandals, Great Princefs of
Finland, Duchefs of Efthonia, Carelia, Bremen, Verden, Stetin, Pomerania, Caffuben, and Vandalia, Princefs of Rugen, Lady of Ingria and Wifmar, and the
kingdom of Sweden, and the faid Lord Protector of
the republic of England, &c. certain affairs, relating
as well to the eftablifhment of mutual friendfhip, as to
the advantages of commerce and navigation, were deferred to a more convenient time. And whereas it
hath feemed good to his faid moft Serene Royal Majefty of Sweden, to fend me over to England, vefted
with fufficient powers to tranfact the fame, and the
other affairs which follow; therefore, after a conference
with the Lords Commiffioners of the faid moft Serene
Lord Protector, viz. the moft noble Lord Nathaniel
Fiennes, one of the Keepers of the Great Seal, and of
his Highnefs's Privy Counfellors, Sir Bulftrode Whitlock, Knight, one of the Commiffioners of his Highnefs's Treafury, and Conftable of Windfor Caftle,
and Walter Strickland, Efq; both Members alfo of his
Highnefs's faid Privy Council, furnifhed with fufficient
powers and commands for this purpofe; and after
we had mutually imparted our opinions, and maturely

confidered

confidered the following points, we agreed as is clearly and perfpicuoufly expreffed in the words of the under-written articles.

I. It fhall be lawful for either of the confederates to raife any foldiers and feamen by beat of drum with-in the kingdoms, countries, and cities of either; and alfo to hire men of war and fhips of burden, obferv-ing only the following conditions.

1. Whichfoever of the confederates defires to have a mufter, he fhall notify his intention to his ally, and fpecify the places in which he thinks fuch levies may moft conveniently be made; and if the condition of the other ally will not permit that the levy fhould be made in that place, then the other, being fo required, fhall appoint another place more convenient for his purpofe, and as little as poffible to the detriment of both parties.

2. As to the number of foldiers to be raifed, or of fhips to be hired, regard fhall be had to the affairs and circumftances of that confederate in whofe king-doms and dominions the mufters are to be made; left if a greater number of forces be required than is fit-ting, the other fhould find the want of them, or be dif-appointed of them for his own occafions.

3. When foldiers are raifed in that country, they fhall not take arms, nor fo much as on board the fhips, till they come within twenty leagues of the place where they are to be fet afhore.

4. The colonels or captains fhall raife no foldiers who are already entered into the pay of another king or ftate, nor fhall they entice any from their co-lours.

5. The foldiers, failors, and fhips, raifed or hired, as above, in the kingdoms and countries of either of the confederates, fhall not be raifed againft the friends or allies of the other, to the violation of the treaties concluded and now fubfifting between one another and their allies.

II. Whereas

. II: Whereas in the XIth article of the treaty lately made at Upſal in 1654, betwixt England and Sweden, it was agreed and ſpecified what goods and merchandize ſhould hereafter be declared contraband and prohibited; it is now by virtue of the ſaid article eſtabliſhed, that only thoſe hereafter mentioned ſhall be reckoned prohibited, and conſequently not to be diſpoſed of to the enemies of either, viz. bombs with their fuſees and other appurtenances, fire-balls, gun-powder, matches, cannon-ball, ſpears, ſwords, lances, pikes, halberts, guns, mortars, petards, granadoes, muſket-reſts, bandaliers, ſaltpetre, muſkets, muſket-balls, helmets, head-pieces, breaſt-plates, coats of mail, cuiraſſes, and the like kind of arms; ſoldiers, horſes, with all their furniture, piſtols, holſters, belts, and all other warlike inſtruments; and alſo ſhips of war. Money ſhall alſo be reckoned among the goods with which the enemies are not to be ſupplied, and which it ſhall not be lawful to carry to the enemies of either, any more than the things above mentioned, on the penalty of being made prize without hopes of redemption, if they are ſeized by either of the confederates. Nor ſhall either of the confederates permit that the enemies or rebels of the other be aſſiſted by any of their ſubjects, or that their ſhips be ſold, lent, or in any manner made uſe of by the enemies or rebels of the other, to his diſadvantage or detriment.

III. But it ſhall be lawful for either of the confederates, and his people or ſubjects, to trade with the enemies of the other, and to carry them any goods whatſoever, which are not excepted as above, without any impediment: Provided they are not carried to thoſe ports or places which are beſieged by the other; in which caſe they ſhall have leave either to ſell their goods to the beſiegers, or to repair with them to any other port which is not beſieged.

IV. Whereas in the XIth article of the treaty concluded at Upſal the 11th of April, 1654, between

Sweden

Sweden and England, it was agreed, that although it
was precautioned and prohibited by the preceding articles, that either of the confederates should give aid
and assistance to the enemies of the other, yet it ought
not to be understood, that that confederate who is not
involved in war with the enemy of the other, shall not
be allowed to carry on trade with the said enemy of
that confederate: but it was only provided thereby,
till there should be a farther agreement concerning this
matter, that no goods or merchandize which we commonly call contraband shall be carried to the enemy
of the other, without danger of being made prize, and
without hopes of redemption, if they are seized by the
other confederate. In like manner, whereas by the
XIIth article of the said treaty, for the evading of all
suspicions, left the navigation or commerce of one of
the confederates, whether by land or sea, should be
carried on during war to the prejudice of the other
confederate, or left the goods of enemies should be
carried under the disguise of the goods of friends, it
was stipulated and concluded, that all ships, carriages,
wares, and men, belonging to the other of the confederates, should be furnished in their journey and passage
with safe-conducts, commonly called passports, and
certificates, signed by the chief governor or magistrate
of that province and city from whence they came ; and
that those forms of the passports and certificates were
to be observed on which the confederates should mutually agree on both sides; and when the merchandize, goods, ships, men of either of the confederates,
and his subjects and inhabitants, shall meet or be met
by the ships of war, public or private, or the subjects
and inhabitants of the other confederate, in the open
sea, straits, harbours, havens, lands, and other places,
wheresoever or howsoever they shall come together,
after producing only their safe-conducts and certificates
nothing farther should be demanded of them, no inquiry whatsoever should be made into the ships, goods,
or men, much less should they be injured, damaged,

or molested; but should be freely let go to prosecute their journey and purpose, as is above signified.

And whereas by the XIVth article it was stipulated, that the said treaty and confederacy should derogate nothing from any preheminence of right and dominion whatsoever of either of the confederates, in any of their seas, straits, and waters whatsoever, but that they should have and retain the same to themselves in as ample a manner as they had all along enjoyed them, and as by right to them belonged; Now therefore that a fitting draught of such certificates and passports may be formed and observed, which may be answerable to the meaning of the aforesaid articles, it is agreed and concluded on both sides, That for avoiding all frauds and concealments whatsoever of the enemies goods, and all occasions of quarrels as to any certificates and passports, such forms as are underwritten verbatim shall be observed, and subscribed and signed by the chief magistrate of that province and city from whence they come; that then the true names of the ships, carriages, merchandize, and masters of the ships be specified; as also the punctual days and times, without any fraud, together with other descriptions of that sort, which are expressed in the following form of a safe-conduct or certificate. Wherefore, if any person who shall declare upon the oath by which he is bound to his king, state, or city, that he has given in a true account, be convicted by sufficient proof of having concealed any fraud by his permission under his said declaration, he shall be severely punished as a transgressor of the said oath.

We N. N. governor or chief magistrate of the province or city of N. [the title or office of the respective government of that place being added] do make known and certify, that on the   day of the month of   A°   N. N. N. citizens and inhabitants of N. and who are engaged and bound as subjects of his most Serene Royal Majesty of Sweden, and

and to our city, or of the most Serene Lord Protector our most gracious Lord, and to our city, personally appeared before us in the city or town of *N.* in the dominion [of his most Serene Royal Majesty of Sweden, or of the most Serene Lord Protector of England, just as it shall happen] and declared to us, that the ship or vessel called *N.* of   about
lasts or tons, belongs to the port, city, or town of *N.* in the dominion of *N.* and that the said ship does rightfully belong to him or other subjects of his most Serene Royal Majesty of Sweden, or of the most Serene Lord Protector, that she is now bound directly from the port *N.* to the port *N.* laden with the following merchandize, viz. [here shall be specified the goods, with their quantity and quality; for example, about so many chests or bales, hogsheads, &c. according to the quantity and condition of the goods] and affirmed upon oath to the aforesaid *N.* that the said goods or merchandize belong only to the subjects of his most Serene Royal Majesty of Sweden, the most Serene Lord Protector of England; or expressing to whatever other nation they belong, and that *N. N. N.* have declared upon their said oath that the said goods above specified, and no others, are already put on board or are to be put on board the abovenamed ship for the said voyage, and that no part of those goods belongs to any one whatsoever, but the persons abovementioned; and that no goods are disguised or concealed therein by any fictitious name whatsoever, but that the merchandize abovementioned is truly and really put on board, for the use of the said owners and no others; and that the captain of the said ship named *N. N.* is a citizen of the city of *N.* Therefore whereas after strict examination by us the abovementioned [governor or chief magistrate of the city aforesaid] it fully appears that the goods on board the said ship or vessel are free, and do truly and really belong to the subjects of his most Serene Royal Majesty of Sweden, or of the most Serene Protector, or to the inhabitants of

other

other nations abovementioned; We do moſt humbly and earneſtly require it of all and ſingular the powers by land and ſea, kings, princes, republics, and free cities; alſo of the generals of armies, admirals, commanders, officers and governors of ports, and all others to whom the cuſtody of any harbour or ſea is committed, which meet this ſhip in her voyage; or if ſhe happen to fall in, among, or paſs through their ſquadrons, or to ſtay in their harbours, that for the ſake of the treaties and friendſhip which ſubſiſt reſpectively between them, or whoever are his ſuperiors, and the moſt Serene King of Sweden, or the moſt Serene Lord Protector our moſt gracious Lord, they will not only permit the ſaid captain with the ſhip *N*. and the men, goods, and merchandize to her belonging, to proſecute her voyage freely without lett and moleſtation; but alſo, if he think fit to depart elſewhere from ſuch harbour, that they will ſhew all kind offices to him and his ſhips as a ſubject of his, moſt Serene Royal Majeſty of Sweden, or of the moſt Serene Lord Protector, as they ſhall in like manner experience the ſame from our moſt Serene King, or our moſt Serene Lord Protector, and all his miniſters and ſubjects in the like or any other caſe. In witneſs whereof we have taken care that theſe preſents ſigned by our hands be ſealed with the ſeal of our city. Given at our court.

.V. Neither of thoſe confederates ſhall ſuffer the ſhips, veſſels, goods, or merchandize of the other, or of his people or ſubjects, which are taken at ſea or elſewhere by enemies or rebels, to be brought into their ports or dominions, but ſhall publicly forbid any thing of that kind to be done; and if any ſhips, veſſels, goods, or merchandize of either, or his people or ſubjects, taken at ſea or elſewhere, ſhall be carried into the ports or countries of the other by any enemy or rebel of the confederates, or either of them, that confederate into whoſe harbours they ſhall be carried, ſhall not ſuffer the ſame or any part thereof to be ſold in that port, or any other place in their dominion; but

ſhall

shall take care that the master of the ship or vessel so taken, as also the mariners and passengers, shall as soon as they arrive, be immediately set at liberty, together with all the prisoners, subjects of either kingdom or republic, as many as shall be brought thither; nor shall he permit the said ship and vessel to stay in that harbour, but shall command the said ship, with her goods, merchandize, and lading, immediately to leave the harbour. Provided nevertheless, that nothing in this article be turned to the prejudice of the treaties formerly entered into by either of the confederates with other nations; and where these things do not interfere, the above article shall remain in full force.

VI. It shall be free for the men of war and guard-ships of either of the confederates to enter into the ports, havens, or rivers of the other, where such ships use to repair, and there to cast anchor, stay, and to depart from thence without any injury or molestation; provided these conditions are observed.

1. That it shall not be free to carry into the harbours of the confederate any squadron, exceeding five or six ships, without giving some notice thereof beforehand.

2. That the commander of the squadron and ships shall without delay exhibit his letters of safe-conduct to the governor of the castle, fort, city, or province, or acquaint the magistrate of the place where he arrives with the reasons of his coming, and for what end, and how long he designs to stay in that port or haven.

3. That such ships shall not come or stay nearer to those castles or forts than is convenient.

4. That the mariners, ships companies, and soldiers, shall not go ashore in bodies above 40 at a time, nor in any number that may give suspicion.

5. That while they are there they shall not do any damage to any person, not so much as their enemies; and above all shall not stop or obstruct the passage of any merchant ships whatsoever, into or out of the harbour.

·6. That they shall not leave their station for the sake, of infesting the navigation of any nation whatever.

·7. That they shall in all respects live and behave modestly, quietly, and conformably to the laws and customs of every place, and have special regard to the reciprocal friendship between the confederates.. Where the terms aforesaid are rightly observed according to the true meaning of the words, it shall be lawful for the men of war of either confederate to keep upon the coasts, and continue in the harbours of the other confederate, whether for avoiding tempests and enemies, or for rendezvousing and assembling merchant ships, or any other just causes. But if either of the confederates shall think it advantageous or necessary to enter the ports of the other confederate with a greater number of ships, and to enjoy the conveniences thereof, he shall signify the same to his confederate two months beforehand, during which time the ways and means of admitting the same shall be settled.

VII. Whereas it is provided by the aforesaid treaty at Upsal, that satisfaction should be given for the losses which either of the confederates or his people or subjects sustained from the other, or his people or subjects, during the war between the Republic and the States of the United Netherlands, it is now agreed, that three commissioners shall be delegated and deputed on each side, who shall take cognizance of, and decide all those disputes; which commissioners shall meet at London, the first day of January next. And the three commissioners abovementioned, so chosen and deputed on both sides, shall have power to take all those things into their consideration which shall be exhibited or proposed on both sides, and which happened in the said period, as well concerning the restitution of the ships or goods hitherto detained, as the satisfaction for losses sustained by the detaining of the ships of either of the confederates, which are already or shall hereafter be released; or if it can be conveniently done in any other manner, they shall judge of them summarily, according to right and reason, without any appeal

peal or forms of law; and both parties shall make it
their chief business and endeavour that what is just
and right be transacted in the controversies aforesaid
without any delay, and that what is taken-away be restored, and satisfaction performed and made fully and
really for the losses and expences, according to the tenor of the XIIIth article of the aforesaid treaty at Upsal.   But if the said commissioners cannot agree in any
reasons or foundations whatsoever of the proofs relating
to such restitution or satisfaction, then those differences
shall be left to another convention of the confederates.
And that this may be done with the least loss of time,
they shall use their endeavour to finish the cognizance
of all these matters in question within six months after
the first meeting; and the restitution and satisfaction
for those losses shall be made and performed fully and
without delay, within the space of a month after sentence is passed, by that king or state whose subjects
shall be doomed to perform the satisfaction.

VIII. The subjects of the said most Serene Lord
Protector and the said republic shall also hereafter enjoy all the prerogatives in the several branches of trade,
which they used to carry on in Prussia and Poland, or
elsewhere in the dominions of the said most Serene
King of Sweden, which they enjoyed heretofore, in
preference to other nations; and if at any time they
desire farther privileges, their desires shall be gratified
by all the means possible: And if the said most Serene
King of Sweden shall grant greater and more ample
privileges than the abovementioned, in Poland and
Prussia, to any nation besides, or people not subject to
him, or shall suffer any nation or people to enjoy such
larger privileges there, then the people and citizens of
this republic shall enjoy the same privileges in all respects, after they have desired it of his most Serene
Royal Majesty.   And moreover, if any edicts that
have been published since 1650, happen to be burden-
some to the English and Scots, dwelling or trading in
Poland and Prussia, the same shall after this time be

of no force, as far as it can be rendered fo in the dominions of the moſt Serene King of Sweden; but the ſubjects of the ſaid Lord Protector ſhall hereafter be entirely free from thoſe burdens.

IX. As to the commerce to be carried on in America, it is expreſsly provided by law, that the ſubjects of no republic beſides ſhall be impowered to trade there in common without a ſpecial licence: but if any of the ſubjects of the moſt Serene King of Sweden, furniſhed with his recommendations, ſhall privately ſolicit ſuch licence of the Lord Protector to trade to any of thoſe colonies whatſoever, he will in this reſpect comply with the deſire of his moſt Serene Royal Majeſty of Sweden, as far as the ſtate of his affairs and of the republic will for that time permit.

X. It ſhall be free for the ſubjects of the moſt Serene King of Sweden, to fiſh and catch herrings and other fiſh in the ſeas and on the coaſts which are in the dominion of this republic, provided the ſhips employed in the fiſhery do not exceed a thouſand in number: nor while they are fiſhing ſhall they be any ways hindered or moleſted; nor ſhall any charges be demanded on the account of the fiſhing by the men of war of this republic, nor by thoſe who are commiſſioned privately to trade at their own expence, nor by the fiſhing veſſels on the northern coaſts of Britain, but all perſons ſhall be treated courteouſly and amicably, and ſhall be allowed even to dry their nets on the ſhore, and to purchaſe all neceſſary proviſions from the inhabitants of thoſe places at a fair price.

XI. It is alſo agreed and concluded, that the preſent treaty, and all and ſingular the things therein contained and included by the aforeſaid ambaſſador of his ſaid moſt Serene Royal Majeſty of Sweden, and the commiſſioners of the moſt Serene Lord Protector, ſhall be confirmed and ratified within four months next enſuing (or ſooner if poſſible) by the letters patent of the ſaid King and Protector, ſealed in due and authentic

tic form with their great feal; and that the mutual
inftruments fhall be exchanged on both fides within
the term aforefaid.

The Commiffion from the moft Serene Lord Protector.

OLIVER, Protector of the republic of England,
Scotland, and Ireland, &c.   To all and fingular to
whom thefe prefents fhall come, greeting.   Know ye,
That whereas in the treaty made at Upfal between us
and the moft Serene and Potent Princefs Chriftina,
&c. fome points relating to the eftablifhment of a mutual amity, and to the advantages of trade and navigation, were adjourned to a more convenient oppor-
tunity; and whereas the moft Serene and Potent
Prince and Lord Charles Guftavus, &c. hath fent to
us as his ambaffador the moft noble Lord Chriftiern
Bonde, &c. vefted with full powers to tranfact thofe
and other affairs; we being entirely fatisfied of the
probity, fidelity, care, and prudence of our well-beloved
Nathaniel Fiennes, &c. Bulftrode Whitlock, &c. and
Walter Strickland, &c. have, by the advice of our
council, made, conftituted, and appointed, and by
thefe prefents do make, conftitute, and appoint them
our true and undoubted commiffioners, plenipotentiaries, and deputies, giving and granting to them,
or any two of them, full authority and power, and a
general and fpecial command, to treat, conclude, and
determine with the faid lord ambaffador of the faid
moft Serene King, of and concerning all the premifes,
under fuch regulations, heads, forms, promifes, reftrictions, and fecurities, which they fhall think requifite for the due obfervation of the conventions.   And
whatfoever our faid commiffioners fhall agree and
conclude with the faid lord ambaffador, we promife
bonâ fide (obliging ourfelves and our fucceffors by
thefe prefents) to obferve, perform, and ratify in every
point, in the beft manner poffible, as if we ourfelves
were prefent.   In witnefs whereof we have figned thefe
prefents with our own hand, and caufed our great feal
of

of England to be affixed to them. Given at our palace of Weftminfter the 15th day of July, O. S. Anno 1656.   **OLIVER, P.**

The Commiffion of his moft Serene Royal Majefty of
Sweden.

WE Charles Guftavus, &c. &c. do certify and make known, that whereas it is natural to thofe who are in the moft fincere friendfhip, to defire that the fame may be improved and increafed every day; and whereas it is for the common intereft of our kingdom, and of the republic of England, Scotland, and Ireland, and of our good friend the moft Serene and moft High Oliver Lord Protector of that republic, and the dominions thereof, that we fhould concert a clofer league than what has been hitherto, efpecially at this time, when it is very manifeft that many perfons are confpiring our deftruction:

We have therefore given it in command, as we do by thefe prefents in the beft form command and commiffion our well-beloved Lord Chriftiern Bonde, &c. our ambaffador extraordinary, a man of known prudence, circumfpection, and probity, to treat, ftipulate, and conclude a ftricter league between us, and all things thereunto appertaining, with thofe perfons who fhall be deputed with full powers for that purpofe, on the part of the Lord Protector, and of the faid republic. And whatfoever our abovenamed ambaffador extraordinary fhall tranfact, conclude, and eftablifh with the plenipotentiaries of the Lord Protector and of the faid republic, fhall by us be ratified and performed to all intents and purpofes. In witnefs and confirmation whereof, we have commanded thefe prefents, figned by our own hand, to be fealed with our great feal. Given at our palace of Stockholm the 15th day of June, 1656.

         CHARLES GUSTAVUS.
                 Cantberfteen.

                                     In

In witness of all and fingular the premifes, we the commiffioners of the moft Serene and the moft High Protector of the republic of England, Scotland, Ireland, &c. by virtue of our aforefaid commiffion, or full powers, have figned the prefent treaty, confifting of eleven articles, with our hands, and fealed it with our feals.   Done at Weftminfter July 17, Anno 1656.

A Convention relating to the fecond Article in the Treaty betwixt Sweden and England.   Done at Weftminfter July 17, Anno 1656.

WHEREAS in the fecond article of the treaty concluded at Weftminfter, anno 1656, betwixt England and Sweden, it is declared as a point agreed and ratified by the commiffioners of the moft Serene Protector, and by the lord ambaffador of the moft Serene King of Sweden, that only the goods, merchandize, and other things mentioned in that article, fhould hereafter be deemed as contraband, and publicly prohibited.   And whereas the moft Serene Lord Protector has propofed by his commiffioners, and has ftipulated with the aforefaid ambaffador extraordinary, that as long as the war continues betwixt the Englifh and the Spaniards, none of the goods and merchandize following fhall, under a penalty to be hereafter expreffed, be carried from the dominions of the moft Serene King of Sweden, to any part of the Spanifh dominions; and whereas to the intent that this might be granted with the more eafe, it has been alfo propofed that a conference fhould be held for afcertaining the price to be given by the Englifh merchants, for all thofe goods which fhall come from the Swedifh dominions; and whereas the aforefaid ambaffador faid he could not give his confent to the faid demand, becaufe he had it not in his inftructions from his moft Serene King, and therefore left it entirely to the difcretion of his moft Serene Majefty; it is declared by this writing, that the faid fecond article, if the moft Serene King will agree to and ratify it, fhall be only ratified upon this condition, That as long as the war

continues

continues betwixt the republic of England and the Spaniards, neither his Swedish Majesty, nor any of his people, shall carry pitch, tar, hemp, cables, sail-cloth, or masts, to any places in the dominions of Spain, but on the contrary, the said King shall most expressly forbid it; and if any such merchandize shall be carried thither contrary to this agreement, the same shall be liable to be seized by, and forfeited to the English. Wherefore it is most expressly provided, that if the said King shall not consent to it, then all the said second article relating to contraband goods (as also the third article which depends thereupon) shall imme-diately become of no force, and the question relating to the specification of contraband goods, shall remain in the state that it was before the time there was any treaty about it at London; nevertheless the rest of the articles shall remain in full force. And moreover, it is agreed and concluded on both sides, by virtue of the several powers granted to them, that although the pre-sent article be not inserted in the said treaty, it shall be of the same force and virtue as the treaty itself. Done at Westminster, July 17, 1656.

Nathaniel Fiennes, (L. S.)
Bulstrode Whitlock, (L. S.)
Walter Strickland, (L. S.)

[The following Treaty of 1661 is printed from the Supplement to the Treaties 1772, collated with the original, and freed from several errors.]

The Treaty of Alliance concluded between Charles II. *his Royal Majesty of* Great Britain, *and* Charles XI. *his Royal Majesty of* Sweden, *for the confirma-tion of their friendship, and for the mutual security of their dominions and trade. Done at* Whitehall, *October* 21, 1661.

WE, Charles, by the grace of God, King and Hereditary Prince of the Swedes, Goths, and Vandals,

dals, Great Prince of Finland, Duke of Schonen, Efthonia, Livonia, Carelia, Bremen, Verden, Stetin, Pomerania, Caffuben, and Vandalia, Prince of Rugen, Lord of Ingria and Wifmar, alfo Count Palatine of the Rhine, Bavaria, Juliers, Cleves, and Bergen, &c. defire to make known to all and fingular the perfons whom it doth, or whom it may, in any manner whatfoever concern. Whereas we lately fent to England our ambaffador extraordinary, as we did before him our envoy extraordinary, plenipotentiaries, in order to renew the antient friendfhip, and to make a mutual league with the moft ferene and moft potent Prince, our deareft brother, coufin, friend, and ally, the Lord Charles the Second, by the grace of God, King of Great Britain, France, and Ireland, Defender of the Faith, &c. And they having in like manner found a fingular inclination in the faid King to the common union and ftrict amity of the two kingdoms, it came to pafs that when commiffioners were appointed alfo on his part, and vefted with full powers to confolidate a friendfhip, and conclude a league, feveral congreffes and debates were held at London; in which the negociation was fo far promoted, that the following treaty, and the articles therein contained, were agreed upon in due form.

After it had feemed good to the moft ferene and potent Prince and Lord, Charles, by the grace of God, King and Hereditary Prince of the Swedes, Goths, and Vandals, Great Prince of Finland, Duke of Schonen, Efthonia, Livonia, Carelia, Bremen, Verden, Stetin, Pomerania, Caffuben, and Vandalia, Prince of Rugen; Lord of Ingria and Wifmar, alfo Count Palatine of the Rhine, Duke of Bavaria, Juliers, Cleves, and Bergen, &c. to confirm and eftablifh the exercife of that moft ftrict amity and mutual commerce which has continually exifted for fo many ages between the famous kingdoms of Sweden and England, with new laws, efpecially at this time when the moft ferene and moft potent Prince and Lord, the

Lord

Lord Charles the Second, by the grace of God, King of Great Britain, France, and Ireland, Defender of the Faith, &c. was most happily restored to his antient kingdoms; and for that end, his aforesaid Royal Majesty of Sweden sent his Excellency Nicholas Brahe, Senator of the Kingdom, Admiral and Counsellor of the College of Admiralty, Count in Visingburg, Lord Baron de Cajarta, Lord de Ridobbholm and Scaffnegen, &c. as Ambassador Extraordinary to his Royal Majesty of Great Britain, to the end that when he had performed the solemn office of congratulation, he might put the last hand to the treaty of mutual friendship and commerce, the form and tenor of which had been already settled between the most noble John Frederick de Frisendorf, Lord in Herdick and Kirup, &c. Privy Counsellor of his Swedish Majesty, and formerly commissioned to treat of this affair in quality of ambassador extraordinary to his Sacred Royal Majesty of Great Britain, and the lords commissioners particularly deputed to this purpose by his Sacred Royal Majesty of Great Britain. And whereas his Sacred Royal Majesty of Great Britain, favouring the same propension and inclination, solemnly appointed the most noble Lords of his Royal Majesty's Privy Council, viz. Thomas Earl of Southampton, Lord High Treasurer of England, John Lord Roberts, Lord Privy Seal, Edward Earl of Manchester, Lord Chamberlain of the King's Houshold, George Earl of Norwich, Captain of the Royal Band of Pensioners, Arthur Earl of Anglesey, Frederick Lord Cornwallis, Treasurer of the King's Houshold, Anthony Lord Ashley, Chancellor of the Exchequer, Sir George Carteret, Baronet, Vice-Chamberlain of the King's Houshold, Sir Edward Nicholas, Knight, and Sir William Morrice, Knight, two of his Majesty's principal Secretaries of State, to treat of this affair; the ambassador and envoy aforesaid met them, and after divers consultations on both sides, the following articles were at length, by God's blessing, clearly,

clearly, perfpicuoufly, and irrevocably agreed to on both fides.

I. In the firft place, it is concluded and agreed, that hereafter there be and remain a good, fincere, firm, and perpetual peace, friendfhip, good-will, and correfpondence, fo that both parties may carry it to each other with the fincereft love and affeftion.

II. The faid confederates and their dominions, fubjefts, people, and inhabitants, fhall, on all occafions, take care of and promote each other's advantage; and fhall alfo certify one another of any dangers threatened, and confpiracies and machinations formed by the enemies of either, and fhall oppofe and hinder them as far as lies in their power. Nor fhall it be lawful for either of the confederates, by himfelf, or by any other perfons whomfoever, to negociate or attempt any thing to the hurt or difadvantage of the other's lands or dominions whatfoever, any where, either by land or fea; nor fhall he by any means protect the enemies or rebels to the prejudice of the other confederate, nor receive or admit into his dominions any rebel or traitor, who fhall make any attempt againft the eftate of the other; much lefs fhall he afford them any advice, aid, or countenance, or fuffer any advice, affiftance, or favour to be given them by his fubjefts, people, and inhabitants.

III. The faid kings and kingdoms fhall with all candour and diligence take all the care poffible, that the impediments which have hitherto interrupted the freedom of navigation and commerce, not only between both nations, but alfo throughout the dominions, countries, feas, and rivers of both, with other people and nations, be removed, And they fhall fincerely endeavour to affert, eftablifh, defend, and promote the aforefaid freedom of navigation and commerce on both fides, againft all difturbers of it whomfoever, by the methods agreed on in this treaty, or by fuch as may hereafter be agreed on; and fhall not

4   fuffer

suffer any thing to be done or committed contrary to this treaty, either by themselves or by their subjects and people, either by their own, or any one else's fault.

IV. It shall be free for both of the said confederates, and their inhabitants and subjects, to enter by land or sea, or by any other manner of way, into the kingdoms, countries, provinces, territories, islands, cities, villages, towns walled or unwalled, fortified or unfortified, harbours, dominions, or jurisdictions whatsoever, freely and securely, without any license or safeconduct, general or special; and there to pass and repass, to reside therein, or to travel through the same, and in the mean time to buy provisions and all necessaries, and for hire acquire every convenience; and they shall be treated with all manner of civility. It shall be lawful also for both of the confederates and their subjects, citizens, and inhabitants, to trade, traffic, and exercise commerce in all places wheresoever commerce has been at any time hitherto used, and in whatsoever goods and merchandize they please, provided they are not contraband; and they shall have leave to import and export them at discretion, the due customs being always paid, and the laws and ordinances of both kingdoms, whether relating to merchandize or any other right, always observed. Which things being presupposed, the people, subjects, and inhabitants of one of the confederates shall have and hold in the countries, lands, dominions, and kingdoms of the other, such full and ample privileges, and as many exemptions, liberties, and immunities, as any foreigner whatsoever doth or shall enjoy in the said dominions and kingdoms on both sides.

V. Neither the merchants, captains of ships, masters, mariners, or other persons whatsoever, nor the ships or any goods and merchandize of either of the confederates, or his subjects or inhabitants, shall in in any public or private name, by virtue of any general or special edict, be seized or laid under embargo in

any

any of the countries, harbours, roads, shores, or do-minions whatsoever, of the other confederate, for the public use, military expeditions, or for any other cause, much less for any one's private use; nor be compelled by any manner of violence, nor in any wise molested or injured. Provided only, that such embargoes as are agreeable to law and equity be not prohibited, if they are made according to the ordinary forms of law, not for the sake of indulging any one's private resentment, and are indispensably necessary for the administration of right and justice.

VI. But if one or more ships of either of the con-federates, their subjects, citizens, or inhabitants, whe-ther ships of war or private merchantmen, are drove by storms, pirates, enemies, either public or private, or other urgent necessity, into the harbours, havens, or upon any of the coasts whatsoever of the other con-federate, they shall be received courteously, and with all civility, and enjoy friendly protection without being in any respect hindered from the means of refitting entirely, and from purchasing whatever they want for their provision, repair, and conveniency, at the mar-ket price. Nor shall they on any account be prohi-bited to depart in like manner from such port and haven when they please, without paying the duties and customs; so long as nothing be done or com-mitted contrary to the statutes and ordonnances of the place to which the said ships shall be carried, or where they shall stay.

VII. For the like reason, if any one or more ships, public or private, of either of the confederates, or his subjects and inhabitants, have run ashore, been cast away, or (which God forbid) suffered any wreck, or loss whatsoever, or shall suffer any hereafter, the suf-ferers shall be kindly and friendly relieved, and have such assistance for a reasonable hire, that whatsoever remains of the loss, wreck, or other damage, may be preserved and restored to the owners and proprietors;

provided they or their attornies or proctors lay claim to the said ships and goods within twelve months after the wreck happened; saving always the laws and customs of both nations.

VIII. That if the subjects and inhabitants of either of the confederates, whether they be merchants with their factors, servants, captains, and masters of ships, mariners, or whether they are travellers or residents in the dominions of the other confederates, or agents in their name in any court of justice, either for the recovery of their debts, or other lawful reasons, if they want the assistance of the magistrates they shall have it with speed, and according to the equity of the cause, and justice shall be administered without tedious and unneceffary delays. They shall in no sort, nor under any pretence, be hindered, but find all the moft friendly offices in the dispatch of their affairs, in the purchase and sale of goods, in the payments to be made for them, and hire to be given, and in performing their journies. It shall also be free for them on both fides, as they pass, repass, or walk on the shores, or to and from the ships, harbours, and public places of either confederate, to carry arms in their own defence; provided they do not give the governors and magistrates of any place whatsoever, any just suspicion that they are in a plot against the peace of the public, or of private persons. And whosoever behaves modeftly, shall in a special manner be protected from all injury, violence, and trouble.

IX. It shall be lawful for the said confederates, and the people and subjects of both, to buy and export out of the respective countries, dominions, and kingdoms of either, all manner of arms and military equipage, and safely and freely to navigate or carry their ships to any ports, havens, and shores of either, there to stay, and thence to depart: provided they behave modeftly, peaceably, and agreeably to the laws and customs of each place, and do not in any respect hinder the free-

dom

dom of commerce. In like manner, men of war and guardſhips ſhall have free acceſs to the ports, havens, or rivers, of the other confederate; and it ſhall be free for them to caſt anchor, ſtay, and depart from thence without any injury or moleſtation, provided theſe conditions are obſerved:

1. That the ſquadron to be carried into the harbour of the confederate, ſhall not exceed the number of five or ſix ſhips, without giving notice thereof beforehand.

2. That the commander of the ſquadron, and ſhips, ſhall without delay exhibit his letters of ſafe-conduct to the governor or magiſtrate of the caſtle, fort, city, or province, whereſoever they arrive, and give notice of the reaſon of his coming, and for what end, and how long he deſigns to ſtay in that port or haven.

3. That ſuch ſhips ſhall not come or ſtay nearer to thoſe forts than is convenient.

4. That the mariners, ſhips' companies, and ſoldiers, ſhall not go aſhore in bodies above forty at a time, nor in any number that may give ſuſpicion.

5. That while they are there, they ſhall not do any damage to any perſon, not even to their enemies; and above all, ſhall not ſtop or obſtruct the paſſage of any merchant-ſhips whatſoever, into or out of the harbour.

6. That they ſhall not go out of the haven for the ſake of infeſting the navigation of any nation whatſoever.

7. That they ſhall in all reſpects live and behave modeſtly, and conformably to the laws and cuſtoms of every place, and ſpecial regard to the reciprocal friendſhip between the confederates. If either of the confederates ſhall think it advantageous, or neceſſary, to enter the ports of the other confederate with a greater number of ſhips, and to enjoy the conveniences thereof, he ſhall ſignify the ſame to his confederate two months beforehand, during which time, the ways and means of admitting the ſame ſhall be ſettled; but if the ſhips of either are drove into the ports of the

other,

other, for avoiding tempefts or enemies, in fuch cafe the reafon of their coming fhall be notified to the governor or chief magiftrate of the place, nor fhall. they ftay there longer than the time granted by the governor or chief magiftrate; a regard being always had to the laws and conditions aforefaid in this article.

X. It fhall be lawful for any of the fubjects and inhabitants of Sweden whatfoever, to travel in England and all the dominions thereof, and to pafs through the fame by land or fea at pleafure, to any other nations whatfoever, and to inftitute commerce with them, and freely to traffic in all kinds of merchandize, and the fame to carry thither and export from thence; and the fubjects of the King of Great Britain fhall enjoy the fame liberties in the kingdoms, dominions, and territories of the King of Sweden, on condition that the laws, ordonnances, and peculiar prerogatives of every nation, relating to commerce and merchandize, be obferved on both fides.

XI. Although the foregoing articles of this treaty, and the laws of friendfhip do forbid, that either of the confederates fhall give aid and fupplies to the enemies of the other, yet it is by no means to be underftood that that confederate, with his fubjects and inhabitants, who is not a party in war, fhall be denied the liberty of trade and navigation with the enemies of that confederate who is involved in fuch war; provided only that no goods called contraband, and efpecially money, no provifions, nor arms, nor bombs with their fufees and other appurtenances; no fire-balls, gunpowder, matches, cannon-ball, fpears, fwords, lances, pikes, halberts, guns, mortars, petards, grenadoes, mufket-refts, bandaliers, falt-petre, mufkets, mufket-bullets, helmets, head-pieces, breaft-plates, coats of mail, commonly called cuiraffes, and the like kind of arms, nor troops, horfes, or any thing neceffary for the equipment of cavalry, nor piftols, belts, or any other inftruments of war, nor fhips of war, and guard-fhips, be be carried to the enemies of the other confederate, under the penalty, that if either of the confederates fhall feize the fame as a booty, the fame fhall be abfolutely retained. Nor fhall either of the confederates permit that the rebels or enemies of the other be affifted by the endeavours of any of his fubjects, or that their fhips be fold, lent, or in any manner made ufe of by the enemies or rebels of either, to his difadvantage or detriment. But it fhall be lawful for either of the confederates, and his people or fubjects, to trade with the enemies of the other, and to carry them any merchandize whatfoever (excepting what is above excepted) without any impediment; provided they are not carried to thofe ports or places which are befieged by the other, in which cafe they fhall have free leave either to fell their goods to the befiegers, or to repair with them to any other port which is not befieged.

XII. For the evading of all fufpicion and collufion, left the free navigation or intercourfe of one of the confederates and his fubjects, and inhabitants by land or fea, with other nations, while the other confederate is at war, fhould be carried on to the prejudice of the other confederate, and left the enemies goods and merchandize fhould be concealed under the difguife of the goods of friends, it is ftipulated that all fhips, carriages, wares, and men, belonging to the other of the confederation, fhall be furnifhed in their journies and voyages with fafe-conducts, commonly called paffports and certificates, fuch as are underwritten, verbatim, figned and fubfcribed by the chief magiftrate of that province and city, or by the chief commiffioners of the cuftoms and tolls, and fpecifying the true names of the fhips, carriages, goods, and mafters of the veffels, as alfo the exact dates, together with other defcriptions of that fort, as are expreffed in the following form of a fafe-conduct and certificate. Wherefore if any perfon fhall affirm, upon the oath by which he is bound to the King, ftate,

or

or city, that he has given in true accounts, and be convicted on sufficient proof, that any fraud has been concealed under his affirmation, by his consent, he shall be severely punished as a transgressor of the said oath.

We *N. N.* governor or chief magistrate, or the commissioners of the duties and customs of the city or province of *N.* [the title or office of the respective government of that place being added] do make known and certify, that on the   * day of the month of
in the year of   *N. N. N.* citizens and inhabitants of *N.* and subjects of his Sacred Royal Majesty of Sweden, or of his Sacred Royal Majesty of Great Britain, personally appeared before us in the city or town of *N.* in the dominions of his Sacred Royal Majesty of Sweden, or of his Sacred Royal Majesty of Great Britain, [as the case shall happen] and declared to us upon the oath by which they are related and bound to our Most Gracious Sovereign, his Sacred Royal Majesty of Sweden, and to our city, or to his Sacred Royal Majesty of Great Britain, and to our city, that the ship or vessel called *N.* of about   lasts or tons, belongs to the port, city, or town of *N.* in the dominions of *N.* and that the said ship does rightfully belong to him or other subjects of his Sacred Royal Majesty of Sweden, or his Sacred Royal Majesty of Great Britain, that she is bound directly from the port of *N.* to the port of *N.* laden with the following merchandize, viz. [here shall be specified the goods, with their quantity and quality; for example, about so many chests or bales, about so many hogsheads, &c. according to the quantity and condition of the goods] and affirmed on the oath aforesaid, that the said goods and merchandize belong only to *N.* one of the subjects of his Sacred Royal Majesty of Great Britain; or to *N.* of *N. N. N.* [or expressing whatever other nation they are subjects of] and that *N. N. N.* declared upon their said oath, that the said goods above specified, and no others, are already put on board, or are to be put on board the abovenamed ship for the said voyage. and that no part

5   of

of thofe goods belongs to any other perfon whatfoever but thofe abovementioned; and that no goods
are difguifed or concealed therein by any fictitious name
whatfoever, but that the wares abovementioned are
truly and really put on board for the ufe of the faid
owners, and no others, and that the captain of the faid
fhip named N. is a citizen of the city of N. Therefore,
whereas after ftrict examination by us [the governor
or chief magiftrate or commiffioners of the duties and
cuftoms of the city aforefaid] it fully appears that the
faid fhip or veffel, and the goods on board the fame,
are free, and do truly and really belong to the fubjects
of his Sacred Royal Majefty of Sweden, or of his
Sacred Royal Majefty of Great Britain, or to the inhabitants of other nations as aforefaid, we do moft
humbly and earneftly require it of all and fingular
the powers by land and fea, kings, princes, republics,
and free cities, alfo of the generals of armies, admirals, commanders, officers, and governors of ports,
and all others to whom the cuftody of any harbour or
fea is committed, which happen to meet this fhip in her
voyage, or if fhe chance to fall in, among, or pafs
through their fquadrons, or to ftay in their harbours,
that for the fake of the treaties and friendfhip which
fubfift refpectively between them, or whoever are his
fuperiors, and his Sacred Royal Majefty our Moft
Gracious Sovereign the King of Sweden, or his Sacred
Royal Majefty our Moft Gracious Sovereign the King
of Great Britain, that they will not only permit the faid
captain with the fhip N. and the men, goods, and merchandize to her belonging, to profecute her voyage
freely, without lett or moleftation, but alfo, if he think
fit to depart out of the faid harbour elfewhere, that
they will fhew all kind offices to him, and his fhip,
as a fubject of his Sacred Royal Majefty of Sweden,
or of his Sacred Royal Majefty of Great Britain, as
they fhall in like manner experience the fame from his
Sacred Royal Majefty of Sweden, or from his Sacred
Royal Majefty of Great Britain, and from all his minif-

E 4   ters

fers and subjects, in the like, or any other case. In witness whereof we have taken care that these presents, signed by our own hands, be sealed with the seal of our city. Given, &c.

. Therefore, when the merchandize, goods, ships, or men, of either of the confederates, and his subjects and inhabitants, shall meet, or be met in the open sea, streights, in harbours, havens, countries, or other places whatsoever, by men of war or privateers, or by the subjects and inhabitants of the other confederate, after producing only their safe-conducts and certificates aforesaid, nothing farther shall be demanded of them, no enquiry whatsoever shall be made into the goods, ships, or men, much less shall they be injured, damaged, or molested, but shall be freely let go to prosecute their voyage and purpose. But if this solemn and stated form of the certificate be not produced, or there be any other just and urgent cause of suspicion, then this ship ought to be searched, which shall only be deemed justifiable in this case, and not otherwise. If any thing be done by either party contrary to the genuine meaning of this article, both of the confederates shall take care that the severest punishment, due to the most heinous crimes, be inflicted on such of his subjects and inhabitants as are the offenders, for their contempt and transgression of the Royal commands; and that plenary and immediate satisfaction be made to the injured confederate, his subjects and inhabitants, for all loss and expences.

XIII. Neither of these confederates shall suffer the ships, vessels, goods, or merchandize of the other, or of his people or subjects, which are taken at sea, or elsewhere, by enemies or rebels, to be brought into his ports and dominions, but shall publicly forbid any thing of that kind to be done. And if any ships, vessels, goods, and merchandize of either, or his people or subjects taken at sea, or elsewhere, shall be carried into the ports or countries of the other, by any enemy

OF

or rebel of the confederates, or either of them, such confederate shall not suffer the same, or any part thereof, to be sold in that port, or any other place in their dominion; but shall take care that the master of the ship, or vessel, so taken, as also the mariners and passengers, shall, as soon as they arrive, be immediately set at liberty, together with as many prisoners, subjects of either kingdom, as shall be brought thither; nor shall he permit the said ship and vessel to stay in that harbour, but shall command the said ship, with her goods, merchandize, and lading, immediately to leave the port. Provided nevertheless, that nothing in this article be turned to the prejudice of the alliances formerly entered into by either of the confederates with other nations; and where these things do not interfere, the above article shall remain in full force.

XIV. If it shall also happen hereafter, while this friendship and alliance subsists, that any of the people and subjects of either of the confederates does or endeavours any thing contrary to this treaty, or any part thereof, by land, sea, or in any waters, this friendship, treaty, and covenant, between the said confederates, shall not on that account be interrupted or dissolved, but shall nevertheless continue and remain entire. And those private persons only shall suffer punishment who shall violate this treaty; and they who receive injury, shall have right and justice administered, and satisfaction made to them for all their loss and injury, within twelve months after the demand of such restitution. But if such delinquents and persons, guilty of the violence committed, shall refuse to appear and submit to justice, or to make satisfaction within the term aforesaid, whoever they are, they shall be renounced as enemies of both states, and their substance, goods, and possessions, what and how great soever they are, shall be forfeited and exposed to sale, towards making full and just satisfaction for the injuries which they have committed; and the offenders themselves, when they come

come into the jurisdiction of either state, shall, moreover, suffer condign punishment according to the nature of the crime.

XV. The present treaty and confederacy shall derogate nothing from any pre-eminence, law, and dominion whatsoever of either of the confederates, in any of their seas, firths, and waters whatsoever, but they shall have and hold the same in as ample a manner as they have hitherto enjoyed them, and as to them of right appertains.

XVI. Whereas, therefore, it is the principal end of this treaty, that such a freedom of navigation and commerce as is described in the foregoing articles may be and remain on both sides, to both the confederates, their subjects and inhabitants, in the Baltic, the Sound, the Northern, Western, British, and Mediterranean seas, and the Channel, and all the other seas of Europe, both sides shall sincerely contribute their joint advice, aid, and assistance, that the said mutual freedom of navigation and commerce may be established in all the said seas and firths, and (if there be occasion) that it be defended against all disturbers who shall offer to interrupt, prohibit, hinder, or constrain it for their own pleasure, and for the sake of injuring the confederates: and both of the said confederates shall, in the most courteous manner, shew their good-will and readiness for promoting the advantages, and lessening the inconveniences of the other confederate; saving nevertheless, those treaties heretofore entered into by both nations with other kingdoms, republics, and states, which shall subsist in full force. But hereafter neither of the confederates shall by any means enter into a treaty, or make any contract with other foreign nations and people whatsoever, to the prejudice of the present treaty in any respect, without the previous knowledge and consent of the other confederate: and if any thing be otherwise stipulated hereafter with others, it shall be
reckoned

reckoned null and void, and altogether give place to this mutual convention.

XVII. And thefe things which we have agreed to in the foregoing articles, fhall immediately from this inftant be in full force, and fincerely and duly obferved by both parties, and by all perfons who are engaged to either by obedience, duty, and allegiance. And to the end that the faid articles may be and remain the more ftable and firm hereafter, they fhall within the fpace of fix months be figned, fealed, and ratified, by the hands and feals of our Moft Gracious Sovereign his Sacred Royal Majefty of Sweden, and his Sacred Royal Majefty of Great Britain.

In witnefs and confirmation of all and fingular the premifes, the prefent treaty has been figned and fealed with the hands and feals of the Ambaffador Extraordinary of his Sacred Royal Majefty of Sweden, and alfo of his Envoy. Done at Whitehall, the 21ft day of October, 1661.

> *Nicholas Brahe*,   (L. S.)
> *J. F. a Frifendorff*, (L. S.)

We, therefore, Charles, by the grace of God King and Hereditary Prince of the Swedes, Goths, and Vandals, Great Prince of Finland, &c. have commended, approved, and ratified, as we do by thefe prefents commend, approve, and ratify, in the beft manner, the articles above expreffed and inferted in the inftrument of the treaty, as made in purfuance of our commands; promifing on our Royal word, and in the name of ourfelves and the Kings our fucceffors, that we will inviolably, and *boná fide* obferve and perform them, and that we will not fuffer them to be violated in any meafure, by our own fubjeéts or others whomfoever. In witnefs whereof we have commanded thefe prefents, figned by our moft honoured and dear Mother, and by our other Adminiftrators refpeétively, to
be

be fealed with our great feal. Done at Stockholm, anno 1661.

    Hedwig Eleonora, (L. S.)

 Peter Brahe, Count in Vifingburg, Droffart of the kingdom of Sweden.

 Magnus Gabriel de la Gardie, Chancellor of the kingdom.

 Guftavus Bancrius, Deputy Marfhal of the kingdom.

 Claudius Bielkenftierna, Vice Admiral of the kingdom.

 Guftavus Bondt, Treafurer of the kingdom.

[The following Treaty of 1766 is printed from an authentic copy.]

AU nom de la très Sainte Trinité. Leurs Majeftés le Roi de la Grande Bretagne et le Roi de Suede n'ayant rien de plus à cœur que de cimenter et d'affermir de plus en plus entr'elles leurs Royaumes et Sujets, cette ancienne amitié et confiance fincere qui depuis les tems les plus reculés a toujours fubfifté entre leurs Couronnes et leurs Sujets, et de contribuer en tout ce qui depend d'elles à des vues auffi falutaires que celles qui ont toujours fait la bafe de leurs liaifons, leurs Majeftés ont jugé à-propos de nommer et d'autorifer leurs Commiffaires refpectifs : Savoir, de la part de Sa Majefté le Roi de la Grande Bretagne, fon Envoyé Extraordinaire à la Cour de Suede M. le Chevalier Jean Goodricke, Baronet d'Angleterre ; et de la part de Sa Majefté le Roi de Suede, Son Excellence M. le Comte Charles Guftave de Lowenhielm, Senateur du Roi et du Royaume, Préfident du Confeil Royal de la Chancellerie, Chancelier de l'Univerfité de Lund, Chancelier, Chevalier et Commandeur des Ordres du Roi ; Son Excellence M. le Baron Charles de Lagenberg, Senateur du Roi et du Royaume, Préfident de la Commiffion Nomothetique, Chevalier et Commandeur des Ordres du Roi ; Son Excellence M. le Baron

Frederic Friefendorff, Senateur du Roi et du Royaume, Confeiller du Confeil Royal de la Chancellerie,
Chevalier et Commandeur des Ordres du Roi; Son
Excellence M. le Comte Adam de Horn, Senateur
du Roi et du Royaume, Grand Maréchal de la Cour,
Chevalier et Commandeur des Ordres du roi; Son
Excellence M. Axel de Lagerbielcke, Senateur du Roi
et du Royaume, et Commandeur de l'Ordre de l'Epée;
comme auffi M. le Baron Joachim de Dieben, Secretaire d'Etât, Chevalier de l'Ordre de l'Etoile du
Nord, et Secretaire des Ordres du Roi, et M. Charles
de Lagerflycht Confeillier du Confeil Royal de la Chancellerie; lefquels, après avoir réciproquement commu-
niqué et échangé leurs pleins pouvoirs, font convenus,
au nom et de la part de leurs fufdites Majeftés, des
articles fuivans d'un traité d'alliance et d'amitié.

I. Les deux hauts Alliés s'engagent, pour eux, leurs
héritiers et fucceffeurs, et leurs Sujets refpectifs, de
vouloir, comme de bons et fidéles amis et alliés, fe
procurer mutuellement tout le bien, avantage et con-
fidération poffible, et de contribuer de l'un côté et de
l'autre à tout ce qui pourra fervir à refferrer de plus
en plùs les noeuds d'une amitie fincére et permanente.

II. Les Sujets des deux Puiffances jouiront réci-
proquement, dans les royaumes, ports, rades, riviéres,
&c. de l'une et de l'autre, de tous les droits, avantages et immunités dont jouiffent ou pourront jouir ci-
après les nations les plus favorifées, excepté dans le
cas contenu dans le 3me article du traité prelimi-
naire de commerce conclu entre les couronnes de
Suede et de France, le $\frac{14}{25}$ d'Avril 1741, concernant
les droits à payer dans le port de Wifmar.

III. Ce traité d'amitié ne tendra à l'offenfe de
qui que ce foit, et encore moins à celle des amis et
alliés des hauts contractans, mais fervira uniquement
à fortifier et à confolider l'amitié et la confiance ré-
ciproque entre les deux Rois, de même que la tran-
quillité et le bien-être de leurs Royaumes et Sujets
refpectifs.   IV. Et

IV. Et afin que cette alliance d'amitié puiffe contribuer de plus en plus au bien, à l'avantage et à la fûreté des deux Couronnes, leurs Majeftés fe concerteront entre elles, lorfque le tems et les conjonctures le permettront, fur des engagements ultérieurs relativement à leurs intérêts refpectifs.

V. En attendant, leurs Majeftés, les Rois de la Grande Bretagne et de Suede, s'engagent également, comme de fidéles amis et alliés, de fe prêter réciproquement tous les bons offices que les circonftances pourroient exiger pour la fureté de leurs Royaumes, Pays, Poffeffions et Sujets en Europe.

VI. Ce traité fera ratifié par leurs Majeftés, le Roi de la Grande Bretagne et le Roi de Suede, et les ratifications feront échangées dans deux mois, ou plutôt, fi faire fe peut.

En foi de quoi nous avons, en vertu de nos pleins pouvoirs, figné les articles ci-deffus, et y avons appofé les cachets de nos armes. Fait à Stockholm le 5me de Fevr. 1766.

J. Goodricke, (L. S.)	*Carl. Guftaf Lewenhielm,* (L. S.)
	Carl. Lagerberg, (L. S.)
	Fred. Friefendorff, (L. S.)
	Ad. Horne, (L. S.)
	A. Lagerbielcke, (L. S.)
	J. Von Dieben, (L. S.)
	C. Lagerflycht, (L. S.)

DENMARK.

DENMARK.

1640.
22 Apr.
THE treaty of commerce, and concerning the duties in the Sound, between Charles I. King of Great Britain, and Christian IV. King of Denmark, concluded at Flensburgh.
Pap. Off. F. 5.
Board of Trade. Treaties.

1654.
15 Sept.
The treaty of peace and alliance between Oliver Cromwell, and Frederick III. King of Denmark, concluded at Westminster.
Treat. 1732, vol. iii. p. 136.
Treat. 1785, vol. i. p. 75.
Trait. de Paix, tom. iii. p. 664.

1665.
29 Apr.
The treaty of commerce between Charles II. King of Great Britain, and Frederick III. King of Denmark, with the secret article.   *Pap. Off. F. 6.*

1665.
18 Oct.
The treaty of offensive and defensive alliance between Great Britain and Denmark, concluded at Copenhagen.
Pap. Off. F. 7.

1670.
11 July.
The treaty of alliance and commerce between Charles II. King of Great Britain, and Christian V. King of Denmark.
Pap. Off. F. 8.

1690.
3 Nov.
The treaty of defensive alliance between Great Britain, Denmark, and the States General, with the secret articles, concluded at Copenhagen.
Pap. Off. F. 10.

1691

1691.
10 June. A provisional treaty of navigation and commerce between Great Britain and Denmark. *Pap. Off.* F. 11.
Board of Trade, F. 60.

1696.
3 Dec. The treaty between Great Britain, Denmark, and the States General, with the secret articles, concluded at the Hague.
Pap. Off. F. 15.

1701.
15 June. The treaty between Great Britain and the States General on the one part, and Denmark on the other, with the secret article, concluded at Copenhagen.
Pap. Off. F. 16.
Rouffet's Suppl. Corps Diplomatique, tom. ii. part 2, p. 6.

1720.
24 June. The King of Denmark's order about the diftribution of wreck in the territories of Denmark.
Pap. Off. F. 22.

1727.
16 Apr. The treaty of mutual defence between Great Britain, Denmark, and France, concluded at Copenhagen, with the feparate and fecret articles.
Pap. Off. F. 24.
Rouffet's Recueil Hiftorique, tom. iv. p. 244.
Treat. 1732, vol. iv. p. 167.
Treat. 1785, vol. ii. p. 295.

1734.
30 Sept. The treaty between Great Britain and Denmark, with the fecret articles, concluded at Weftminfter.
Pap. Off. F. 26.

1739.
14 Mar, The treaty between Great Britain and Denmark, with the fecret articles, concluded at Copenhagen.
Pap. Off. F. 27.

The

The Treaty of Peace and Alliance between Frederick III. *King of* Denmark, *and* Oliver Cromwell, *Protector of the Republic of* England. *Done at* Weftminfter, *Sept.* 15, 1654.

WHEREAS the moft Serene and Potent Prince and Lord, the Lord Frederick III. by the grace of God, King of Denmark, Norway, the Vandals and the Goths, Duke, of Slefwic, Holftein, Stormar, and Ditmarfh, Earl of Oldenburg and Delmenhorft, confidering the many great ties of friendfhip and alliances, by which the Danifh and Englifh nations have been engaged to each other for fo many ages paft, and how convenient and neceffary it is in every refpect, that this friendfhip and confederacy fhould be corroborated and increafed by farther reciprocal offices of friendfhip, did, for that end, fend the noble Lord Henry Williamfon Rofenwinge, governor of the monaftery of Draxe Marchienfis, and his extraordinary deputy, to the moft Serene Lord Oliver the Protector, and to the republic of England, Scotland, and Ireland; who, out of a defire and affection to concur to the fame purpofe, and to remove every impediment which might obftruct the prefervation of a fincere and mutual friendfhip, and in any wife hinder the promoting of commerce on both fides, has been pleafed to give it in charge to us the underwritten privy counfellors of his Highnefs, to treat with the faid lord deputy; and by virtue of our commiffions exhibited on both fides, and feveral conferences held from one time to another, we have at length agreed and concluded the following articles.

I. That from this day, there fhall be a firm, entire, and fincere friendfhip, peace, and confederacy, as well by land as by fea, and on the rivers, between the King and kingdom of Denmark and Norway, and the Protector and republic of England, Scotland, and Ireland, and the dominions, countries, and cities under both their dominions, and the people, inhabitants, and fubjects

jects of each, of what rank and dignity foever they be; fo that neither party fhall by themfelves or others, do any thing directly or indirectly, or, as far as lies in their power, fuffer any thing to be done, to the lofs or detriment of the other, but the one fhall affift the other with all good offices, and promote the advantage and benefit of the other to their utmoft.

II. That there fhall be a trade, navigation, and free commerce between the fubjects of the King of Denmark and Norway, and the people of the republic of England, in the kingdoms, dominions, countries, provinces, emporiums, and harbours of either, according to the regulation which is hereafter more clearly explained. And the magiftrates, and other governors and officers of places, fhall ufe their greateft diligence that the fame may be ufed and enjoyed on both fides, freely and fecurely, without any let or moleftation.

III. The people, fubjects, and inhabitants of both the confederates, of whatfoever degree or condition, fhall treat one another in all things courteoufly and amicably, fo that whenever they pleafe, they may have free accefs by land or water to each other's countries, territories, towns walled or unwalled, fortified or not fortified, harbours, and dominions; and there, without any impediment, buy what provifions they want for their ufe, excepting thofe colonies, iflands, harbours, and places under the jurifdiction of either, to which navigation or trade is prohibited, without fpecial leave or licenfe firft obtained from the other party to which fuch colonies, iflands, harbours, and places belong. But in all other places, it fhall be entirely free for both nations to trade and traffic in whatfoever merchandize they fhall think fit, and the fame to carry, fell, or export when and whither they pleafe; provided they pay the cuftoms, and faving all the laws and ftatutes of either's dominions.

IV. That all offences, difputes, and controverfies, arifen between the King of Denmark and the republic
of

of England, or done and committed by either party, or the people and subjects of either, by reason or on account of the detaining of any English ships, together with their lading, in the Sound, since the 18th of September, 1652, shall, by virtue of this treaty, cease, and be condemned to perpetual oblivion, in such manner, that neither of the said parties shall prosecute or in any wise molest the other on account of such detainer, or for any injuries and damages thereby occasioned. Provided nevertheless, and be it understood, that this article shall not extend, nor be construed to extend, to the rescinding or weakening of that contract in the 28th and 29th articles of the late treaty of peace, between his Highness the Lord Protector, and the Lords the States General of the United Provinces, for restoring the ships therein mentioned, together with their lading, and making good the damages as therein expressed; but the said contract shall remain firm and intire, and shall be duly and truly performed and fulfilled, according to the proper and genuine sense and meaning of the said articles.

V. That neither of the said parties, nor the subjects or people of either, shall by land or sea, or elsewhere, act, do, endeavour, negotiate, or attempt any thing against the other, or the subjects and people of the other, nor give, lend, administer, or consent to the giving, lending, or administering of any assistance or favour to the fugitives or rebels of the other; but both parties shall expressly and effectually oppose, resist, and really hinder all and every person and persons living or residing in the dominions of either, or happening to be in the dominions of either the one or the other, who shall act, do, negotiate, or attempt any thing against the other. Nor shall either of the parties receive or suffer any of the rebels or fugitives of the other to be received in their dominions, territories, and countries, harbours, bays, or districts; nor shall give, lend, or grant to any such fugitives or rebels, either within or without their territories, lord-

ships,

ſhips, lands, harbours, bays, or diſtricts, any aid, counſel, lodging, money, ſoldiers, ſhips, proviſions, arms,
&c. or permit or tolerate ſuch things to be given, lent,
or granted, by any perſons whatſoever, living out of
their dominions.

VI. That the people or inhabitants of the republic
of England, ſailing to any of the kingdoms, territories, or dominions whatſoever, of the King of Denmark and Norway, or trading to the ſame, ſhall not
pay more or greater cuſtoms, tribute, toll, or other
duties, or in any other manner, than the people of the
United Provinces of the Netherlands, or other foreigners (the Swedes only excepted) trading thither,
and paying the leſſer cuſtoms, do or ſhall pay; and
they ſhall enjoy all the other liberties, immunities, and
privileges, in going, returning, and ſtaying, as alſo in
fiſhing or trading, as the people of any foreign nation
whatſoever, trading in the ſaid kingdoms and dominions of the King of Denmark and Norway, do or
ſhall enjoy; and the ſubjects of the King of Denmark
and Norway ſhall uſe or enjoy the ſame privileges, in
all the dominions and countries of the republic of
England.

VII. If the ſubjects and inhabitants of either of the
confederates, with their ſhips, are compelled, either by
pirates, or by ſtreſs of weather, or by any other inconveniency, to ſeek ſhelter in the rivers, friths, bays, or
harbours of the other confederate, it is agreed that they
ſhall be courteouſly and kindly treated by the magi-
ſtracy and inhabitants of the place; and it ſhall be lawful for them to furniſh themſelves with what neceſſaries they want for rigging their ſhips, at the market-
price, and from thence freely to put to ſea again, without any hindrance and ſearch, and without paying any
toll or cuſtom. Provided they put none of their goods
or bales aſhore, or expoſe them to ſale; nor receive on
board any perſons guilty or ſuſpected of crimes, or
any contraband goods; nor, in fine, do any thing that

3   may

may be repugnant to the laws, ſtatutes, or cuſtoms of ſuch place and harbour to which they arrive.

VIII. If the ſhips of either of the confederates, his ſubjects and inhabitants, whether they are men of war or merchant ſhips, happen to run aſhore, or in any caſe whatſoever (which God forbid) to ſuffer wreck on the coaſts of the other party, the ſaid ſhips, with all their rigging, goods, and merchandize, or whatſoever ſhall be left of them, ſhall be reſtored to the maſters and proprietors, provided they or their plenipotentiaries or attornies lay claim to the ſaid ſhips and goods within a year after ſuch ſhipwreck happens; and the ſubjects or inhabitants living on ſuch ſhores and coaſts ſhall be obliged to give preſent ſuccour and relief to thoſe that are in danger, to the utmoſt of their power, and ſhall uſe all their endeavour either to ſet the ſhip free, or to ſave her goods, merchandize, rigging, and every thing elſe in their power from being caſt away, and convey the ſame to a ſafe place, that they may be reſtored to the owners, on condition that they pay the charges, and ſuch rewards as they ſhall deſerve, by whoſe labour and diligence the things and goods were recovered and ſecured.

IX. Both parties ſhall cauſe juſtice and equity to be adminiſtered to one another's people and ſubjects, according to the laws and ſtatutes of each country, ſpeedily, and without tedious and unneceſſary formalities and expences, in all cauſes and controverſies now depending, or that may ariſe hereafter.

X. That if any thing ſhall happen to be done, or attempted, by any of the ſubjects and inhabitants of the King of Denmark, or of the people and inhabitants of the republic of England, contrary to this treaty, or any member thereof, by land, ſea, or the freſh waters, this alliance, friendſhip, and union between the parties aforeſaid ſhall not therefore be interrupted or infringed, but ſhall neverthelefs remain intire, and be in full force, and thoſe perſons only who ſhall act con-

trary

trary to the said treaty shall be punished, and none other; and justice shall be done, and satisfaction given to those whom it concerns, by all those, who, by land, sea, or other waters, act any thing contrary to this alliance, within the space of a year after justice shall be demanded. But if the breakers of the treaty do not appear, nor surrender themselves to trial, nor give satisfaction within the term mentioned, those very persons shall be deemed enemies to both the parties; and, as far as the laws and statutes of every country and place will permit and authorize, all their goods, estates, and revenues whatsoever, shall be confiscated and sold, to make full and just satisfaction for the injuries by them committed, and their persons shall be liable to those punishments which their respective crimes deserve.

XI. It is also agreed and concluded, that the ships of the inhabitants of the republic of England, together with their lading and merchandize, which sail beyond the fort of Gluckstadt, or any other places and towns under the dominion of the King of Denmark, situate on the bank of the river Elbe, shall, both going and returning, be free and exempt from all tribute, toll, search, stoppage, or molestation.

XII. That firs, masts, and the other sorts of timber, after they are put on board the ships of the inhabitants of the republic of England, shall be subject to no farther visitation, but all visitation or search shall be made beforehand; and if there be then found any prohibited timber, the same shall be stopped on the spot, before it is carried on board the ships. Nor shall the persons or goods of the people of the said republic be for this cause arrested, or in any wise molested by being in any manner detained; and only the subjects of the King of Denmark, who shall presume to sell and alienate such prohibited timber, shall be duly punished for the offence.

XIII. For

XIII. For the greater fecurity of commerce, and the liberty of navigation, it is agreed and concluded, that neither party fhall, if it be in their power, permit common pirates, or other robbers of this fort, to harbour in any parts of the other's kingdom or country, nor fhall fuffer any of the inhabitants or people of the other, to receive or affift them in reality, or by countenance, but on the contrary, fhall do their endeavour that the faid pirates or robbers, and their piratical partners and accomplices, be apprehended and brought to condign punifhment; and that the fhips and the merchandize, as much of it as can be found, be reftored to their lawful owners, or their attornies, provided their right appear from due proofs according to law in the proper courts.

XIV. It is agreed that there fhall be always free accefs for the fubjects and people of either of the parties to the harbours and coafts of the other confederate, and it fhall be lawful for them to ftay therein, and to return from thence, not only with merchant fhips, and fhips of burthen, but alfo with men of war, whether they are fhips of the ftate, or fuch as are privately commiffioned, whether they are drove in by ftrefs of weather, or for avoiding the danger of the fea, whether to repair their fhips, or to buy provifions, Provided they do not exceed the number of fix men of war, if they enter of their own accord, nor ftay longer in or about the harbours than fhall be needful for the repair of the fhips, buying provifions, or for other neceffary occafions. And if upon occafion they fhall offer to go to fuch ports with a greater number of men of war, it fhall not by any means be lawful for them fo to do, without notice given in time by letters of their arrival, and without leave firft obtained from thofe to whom the faid harbours fhall belong. But if by ftrefs of weather, or other urgent neceffity, they are compelled to feek harbour, in fuch cafe, without any token or notice preceding, the fhips fhall not be reftrained to any certain number;

on

on condition, neverthelefs, that their commander, immediately after their arrival, do certify the chief magiftrate or commander of the place, fort, or coaft to which they arrive, of the reafon of his coming, and that he ftay there no longer than he fhall be fuffered by the chief magiftrate or commander, and do neither commit nor attempt any hoftility in the harbours which he enters, nor do any thing in prejudice of that confederate to whom they belong.

XV. If either of the confederates fhall think it of fervice to himfelf or his fubjects to appoint deputies, refidents, commiffioners, or other minifters of whatfoever title or character, to manage their affairs in the courts or tribunals of the other, it is agreed and concluded, that the faid minifters fhall be favourably admitted, according to the credentials which they bring, and be received with fitting refpect and honour, and fhall be under the protection of the other confederate, and fafe from all manner of injury and violence. Provided they do not commit, or attempt any thing to the lofs and prejudice of the confederate to whom they are fent.

XVI. Whereas fince the 26th of April, 1654, and the firft of June, 1646, certain treaties and alliances were entered into concerning cuftoms in the Sound, and other things, between the moft Serene King of Denmark of glorious memory, and the States of England, at that time affembled in parliament, it is agreed and concluded, that the faid treaties and alliances fhall not in any wife by the prefent treaty be deemed to be fet afide or repealed, but remain in their former force and vigour, as well on the part of his moft Serene Royal Majefty now reigning, as on the part of the moft High Lord Protector of the republic of England; who both bind themfelves again by the vigor and virtue of this prefent treaty, to perform the faid treaties reciprocally and really, and that they will take care that the fame, and every one of their

articles

articles be performed, and effectually obferved, according to their true and proper meaning, by their fubjects and people.

XVII. Finally, it is agreed and concluded, that both parties fhall fincerely and *bonâ fide* obferve all and fingular the articles contained and eftablifhed in the prefent treaty and alliance, and caufe them to be obferved by all the fubjects, inhabitants, and people, of the Moft Serene King of Denmark and Norway, and of the republic of England, univerfally; and that they fhall not contravene, or caufe them to be contravened, directly or indirectly; and fhall confirm and ratify all and fingular the contents, in fufficient and valid form, fubfcribed with their hands, and fealed with their great feals; and fhall *bonâ fide* and really deliver, or caufe the fame to be delivered, reciprocally to deputies appointed for that purpofe, within the fpace of three months, or fooner, if poffible.

In witnefs of all and fingular the premifes, I the Deputy Extraordinary of the Moft Serene and Potent King of Denmark and Norway, and we the Counfellors and Commiffioners of his Moft Serene Highnefs the Lord Protector of the republic of England, Scotland, and Ireland, have with our hands and feals figned and fealed the prefent treaty, confifting of feventeen articles. Done at Weftminfter, Sept. 15, 1654.

[The following is printed from the treaty, which was publifhed by authority in 1636.]

Articles of Peace and Alliance between the Moft Serene and Mighty Prince, Charles *the Second, by the grace of God, King of* England, Scotland, France, *and* Ireland, *Defender of the Faith,* &c. *and the Moft Serene and Mighty Prince,* Frederick III. *King of* Denmark

Denmark *and* Norway.   *Concluded* $\frac{11}{11}$ *day of* July, 1667.

I. FIRST, It is covenanted, concluded, and agreed, that there be from this day a perpetual, firm, and inviolable peace between the Moſt Serene and Moſt Mighty Prince, Charles the Second, King of Great Britain, and the Moſt Serene and Moſt Mighty Prince, Frederick the Third, King of Denmark and Norway, between their heirs and ſucceſſors, and their kingdoms, principalities, earldoms, iſlands, cities, forts, lands, ſubjects, and inhabitants, of what ſtate and quality ſoever: and ſo as to maintain and promote each other's good no leſs than their own, and to avert and hinder, with all poſſible ſtudy, the damage and deſtruction of one another. And in this reſpect it ſhall be free for the ſubjects of either King to exerciſe a mutual navigation and commerce without moleſtation, and with their merchandizes to come to each other's kingdoms, provinces, marts, ports, and rivers, and there to abide and traffic.

II. At this preſent ſhall ceaſe between the aforeſaid Kings, and their kingdoms, principalities, earldoms, people, and ſubjects, both by land and ſea, all enmity, war, and hoſtility; that is to ſay, in the Northern ocean, and in the Baltic ſea, and the Channel, within twenty-one days; from the mouth of the ſaid ſtraight or channel to the Cape of St. Vincent, within ſix weeks; and then within the ſpace of ten weeks beyond the ſaid cape on this ſide the equinoctial line or equator, as well in the ocean as the Mediterranean ſea: finally, within the ſpace of eight months, beyond the bounds of the aforeſaid line all over the world, without any exception or further diſtinction of time or place; all days, weeks, and months, to be computed from the ſubſcription of the preſent agreement, and the publication of the ſame here made at Breda. And whatſoever ſhall be taken and ſeized after the aforeſaid days, by either King, or their ſubjects,

jects, to whom commiffions have been granted, it
fhall be wholly reftored back again to him or them
from whom the fame was taken; and furthermore,
full fatisfaction fhall be made for the damages to him
or them thereby arifing, or the charges they have been
at; and every perfon herein offending, fhall be punifhed as his offence deferves.

III. It is alfo agreed and concluded, that all differences on both fides, fufpicions, and ill-will, both on
the part of the Moft Serene King of Great Britain,
and on the part of the Moft Serene King of Denmark,
&c. and likewife for fingular the minifters, officers,
and fubjects of them, be buried and abolifhed by a
perpetual oblivion. And further, from this prefent
fhall expire, be annulled, and for ever cancelled, all
damages, offences, injuries by word or writing, that
either the one has done the other, or has been fuffered
by the one from the other, from the very firft beginning of the now ceafing war to this day, and the determined point of time wherein all diffenfions, difcords, differences, and enmities, fhall ceafe and be
laid afide: by name, the affault and defence made at
Bergen in Norway, and in whole, whatfoever either
followed from thence, or does thereon depend; in fuch
manner, as that neither of the faid parties, by reafon of
any damage of this kind, offence, or charges, do, under
any pretence whatfoever, caufe the other any trouble,
much lefs for this caufe endeavour or attempt any kind
of hoftility.

IV. All prifoners on both fides, of whatfoever fortune or rank, fhall be forthwith fet at liberty without
any ranfom.

V. All fhips, goods, or the like, that in this turbu-
lent feafon, in the heat of this very war between both
the above-mentioned Kings and their fubjects, have
been taken by the one from the other, or that either
party has confifcated and feized of the goods and pretenfions of perfons or fubjects of the other nation;
as

as also all the expences of war on both sides, shall be compensated by a like mutual abolition. In such manner, as are together comprehended in this compensation, those debts of the subjects of the King of Great Britain, which have been on the part of Denmark confiscated; but in this sense, that whatever debts of this kind unto the tenth day of May old stile, and twentieth new stile, by virtue of confiscation or reprisals, have been by subjects paid and received, do remain utterly abolished and satisfied; and that it be not lawful for the creditors of such debts for the future to pretend any thing upon this account, much less to urge payment of such for any reason, or under any pretence whatsoever. But of such debts as on the said day have not been paid and received, it shall be lawful for the creditors, subjects of the King of Great Britain, to demand and prosecute the payment, by the ordinary way of justice. Excepting nevertheless, 120,000 rix-dollars, more or less (namely, accruing from a certain controversy which arose between Christian the Fourth, of most glorious memory, King of Denmark and Norway, and the Parliament of England, by reason of sending aid to Charles the First of most glorious memory, King of Great Britain) for which the King of Denmark and Norway bound himself, and gave his bond to a company of certain English merchants trading at Hamburgh, and there either now living, or that have heretofore lived; which claim of 120,000 rix-dollars or thereabouts, being confiscate, shall be now by virtue of the present treaty accounted as null, dead, and utterly abolished; in such manner, that the creditors of that debt are not either now, or at any time hereafter, therefore to demand or pretend any thing. In like manner as is also covenanted and agreed in most significant words, that no pretension shall be at any time made, by reason of such ships and goods so seized, and debt or money lent, in such manner as aforesaid abolished and confiscated; but that all shall on both sides by a solemn compensation be for ever accounted

counted as null and void: yet fo that lands and immoveable goods be not comprehended in the aforefaid voidance and annullation, but that they be without any difficulty or impediment reftored back to thofe, who before the denouncing of the prefent war were the poffeffors and proprietors of them.

VI. It is covenanted and agreed on both fides, That under the laft-mentioned compenfation, neither countries, nor iflands, nor cities, nor forts, nor ports, nor other like places, are to be underftood. But if it fhall be found, that either party during this war hath either taken any fuch, in or out of Europe, or may yet take within the time-limited in the fecond article, whatfoever it be, it fhall be, without any compenfation and lofs, together with all, even the fmalleft things thereto appertaining, forthwith reftored to him whofe it was before, and in the fame condition wherein it was then when it was taken, without tergiverfation, delay, or any kind of pretence.

VII. Under this prefent treaty of peace fhall be comprehended thofe, who before the exchange of ratifications, or afterwards within fix months, fhall be by common confent nominated by both parties. And, as the covenanting parties do thankfully acknowledge the friendly offices and unwearied endeavours, whereby the Moft Serene King of Sweden interpofing his mediation, hath through the affiftance of God promoted and carried on this beneficial work of pacification unto the defired conclufion; fo to teftify their like affection, it is decreed and covenanted, by the common confent of all the parties, that his above-mentioned Majefty of Sweden, with all his kingdoms, dominions, provinces, and rights, be included in this treaty, and comprehended in the prefent pacification, after the beft and moft effectual manner that may be.

VIII. Laftly, It is concluded, covenanted, and agreed, that the forefaid Moft Serene and Moft Potent Kings fhall fincerely and *bonâ fide* obferve all and

fingular

singular the articles contained and established in this present treaty, and shall cause the same to be observed by their subjects and inhabitants, neither shall they directly or indirectly transgress them, or suffer them to be transgressed by their subjects or inhabitants directly or indirectly: and they shall ratify and confirm all and every thing as they are above covenanted, by letters patent, subscribed with their hands, and corroborated with their great seals, conceived and written in sufficient, valid, and effectual form, and shall reciprocally deliver, or cause the same to be delivered here at Breda, *bona fide*, really and effectually, within the space of four weeks next ensuing the date of these presents, or sooner if it may be done.

Breda, the $\frac{1}{11}$ day of July, 1667.

[The following is printed from the treaty which was published by authority in 1686.]

Articles of Alliance and Commerce between the Most Serene and Potent Prince, Charles *the Second, by the grace of God, King of* England, Scotland, France, *and* Ireland, *Defender of the Faith, &c. and the Most Serene and Potent Prince,* Christian *the Fifth, by the grace of God, King of* Denmark, Norway, *&c. Concluded at* Copenhagen, *the* 11*th day of* July, 1670.

I. THAT there be between the two Kings, their heirs and successors; as also their kingdoms, principalities, provinces, estates, counties, islands, cities, subjects, and vassals, of what condition, dignity, and degree soever, by land and sea, in rivers, fresh-waters, and all places whatsoever, as well in Europe as out of Europe, now and for the time to come, a sincere, true, and perfect friendship, peace, and confederation; so as that neither party do any wrong, injury, or prejudice to the kingdoms, principalities, provinces, and
eftates,

eftates, or to the inhabitants and fubjects of the other;
nor fuffer any to be done by others, as much as in him
is: but rather live as friends together, ufing each other
with good-will and refpect; and promoting upon all
occafions the interefts and advantages of each other,
and their fubjects, as if they were their own: and preventing and hindering with all their power, by their
affiftance and advice, any damage, wrong, and injury,
that may be offered them.

II. Neither of the forefaid Kings and their heirs
fhall confent to any thing that may be to the prejudice
or detriment of his ally; but if either of the Kings
fhall know that any thing is propofed, or is in agitation
or contrivance, or that will be propofed, agitated, or
contrived, which may tend to the detriment of the
other, he fhall be obliged to fignify the fame unto him
without delay, and in the mean time to hinder and
prevent it by all ways poffible.

III. The forefaid Kings for themfelves, their heirs
and fucceffors, mutually do undertake and promife,
That they will not aid or furnifh the enemies of either
party, that fhall be aggreffors, with any provifions of
war, as foldiers, arms, engines, guns, fhips, or other
neceffaries for the ufe of war, or fuffer any to be
furnifhed by their fubjects: but if the fubjects of either Prince fhall prefume to act contrary hereunto,
then that King, whofe fubjects fhall have fo done, fhall
be obliged to proceed againft them with the higheft
feverity, as againft feditious perfons, and breakers of
the league.

IV. It is further covenanted and agreed, That if at
any time hereafter, any prince or ftate fhall invade, or
by any hoftile way attempt upon the hereditary kingdoms, provinces, counties, towns, iflands, territories,
or dominions of the King of Denmark, which he
now poffeffeth, then the King of Great Britain fhall
affift the faid King of Denmark in time, with fuch
number of land forces and fhips of war, againft fuch
aggreffor,

aggreffor, as fhall fuffice to repel the force, and as the ftate of the faid King's affairs fhall require. And the faid King of Great Britain fhall therefore with all his power endeayour to hinder, that by fuch invafion or difturbance the King of Denmark be not prejudiced in any wife in his kingdoms, dominions, or rights. And if the faid King of Great Britain, or the faid King of Denmark, fhall contract or make any league, alliance, or union with any other king, prince, commonwealth, or ftate, they fhall refpectively endeavour to comprehend therein each other, and their dominions (as much as in them lies) if they fhall defire to be comprehended.

V. It fhall be lawful for the fubjects of both Kings, with their commodities and merchandize both by fea and land, in time of peace, without licence or fafe-conduct general or fpecial, to come to the kingdoms, provinces, mart towns, ports, and rivers of each other; and in any place therein to remain and trade, paying ufual cuftoms and duties ; referving neverthelefs to either Prince his fuperiority and regal jurifdiction in his kingdoms, provinces, principalities, and territories, refpectively.

VI. It is notwithftanding covenanted and concluded, that the fubjects of the King of Great Britain fhall in no wife come to the prohibited ports, of which mention is made in precedent treaties, nor colonies, without the fpecial licence of the King of Denmark firft defired and obtained; unlefs they fhall be compelled to make thither, and enter therein, by ftrefs of weather, or purfuit of pirates ; in which cafe, neither fhall it be lawful for them to buy or fell. As alfo in like manner the fubjects of the King of Denmark fhall not come to the Britifh colonies, unlefs by fpecial licence of the King of Great Britain firft defired and obtained.

VII. It fhall be lawful for the fubjects of the Moft Serene King of Denmark to bring into their own

ftores

ſtores and warehouſes in England, Scotland, and Ireland, and other the ports of the King of Great Britain in Europe, ſuch commodities as now, or hereafter ſhall be of the growth and production of the eſtates, countries, and dominions, ſubject to the King of Denmark, or of the manufacture thereof, and likewiſe ſuch as come from any part of the river of Elbe.

In like manner ſhall it be lawful for the ſubjects of the King of Great Britain to import and bring into Denmark, Norway, and all other ports and colonies not prohibited of the King of Denmark, all kinds of merchandize which now or hereafter ſhall be produced or made in the kingdoms, countries, and eſtates under the ſubjection of the King of Great Britain. But if at any time hereafter it be permitted to any foreign nations, to bring all kinds of commodities without exception, into England, Scotland, and Ireland, and other the ports belonging to the King of Great Britain, then the ſame alſo ſhall be lawful for the ſubjects of the King of Denmark: which in like manner ſhall be permitted to the ſubjects of the King of Great Britain, upon the like occaſion, in the prohibited ports and colonies of the King of Denmark.

VIII. It is alſo covenanted and agreed, that the people and ſubjects of the King of Great Britain, ſailing to any the hereditary kingdoms, countries, or dominions of the King of Denmark, or trading in the ſame, ſhall pay no more or greater cuſtoms, tribute, toll, or other duties, nor in any other manner than the people of the United Provinces of the Low Countries, and other ſtrangers (the Swede only excepted) trading thither, and paying leſſer cuſtoms, do or ſhall pay; and in going, returning, and ſtaying, as alſo in fiſhing and trading, and all other things, ſhall enjoy the ſame liberties, immunities, and privileges, which the people of any foreign country in the ſaid kingdoms and dominions of the King of Denmark, abiding and

trading,

trading, do or shall enjoy. And so on the other side, the people and subjects of the King of Denmark shall have and enjoy the same privileges in the countries and territories of the King of Great Britain; to wit, that the people and subjects of the King of Denmark, sailing to any the kingdoms, countries, or dominions of the King of Great Britain, or trading in the same, shall not pay any more or greater customs, tributes, toll, or other duties, nor in any other manner, than the people of the United Netherlands, or other strangers trading thither, and paying lesser customs, do or shall pay: and in going, returning, and staying, as also in fishing and trading, and all other things, shall enjoy the same liberties, immunities, and privileges, which the people of any other foreign country in the said kingdoms and dominions of the King of Great Britain, abiding and trading, do or shall enjoy: but so, as that the power of each King of making or altering customs, or other duties, as they shall see occasion, in their respective kingdoms, countries, dominions, and ports, remain full and entire; provided the foresaid equality be strictly observed on both sides in manner aforesaid.

IX. It is also covenanted, that when the subjects of either King have imported their commodities into the dominions of the other, have paid the usual customs for them, and undergone their search, it shall be free and lawful for them to bring their said commodities into their own proper storehouses and cellars, or into places which they shall think most fit and convenient, and there store them; nor shall any magistrate or officer of any the cities or ports of either, impose upon them any cellars or storehouses without their consent.

X. The subjects of either crown trading upon the seas, and sailing by the coasts of either kingdom, shall not be obliged to come into any port, if their course were not directed thither; but shall have liberty to pursue their voyage without hinderance or detention,

tion, whitherfoever they pleafe. Nor fhall they, being by tempeft forced into port, and there remaining, be obliged to unlade their cargo, or to barter or fell any part thereof; but it fhall be lawful for them to difpofe of it as they fhall think fit, and to do any other thing which they fhall judge moft for their advantage: provided nothing be done that may be to the defrauding of either Prince of his due rights and cuftoms.

XI. It is alfo agreed, that after any planks, mafts, and other forts of timber, have been once put on board the fhips of the fubjects or people of the King of Great Britain, they fhall not be liable to any further fearch; but all fearch or fcrutiny fhall be made before; and if then, either oaken, or other prohibited timber be found, it fhall be prefently ftopped and detained upon the place, before it be put on board the fhips; nor fhall the people of the faid King of Great Britain, or his fubjects, be therefore molefted in their perfons or eftates by arreft, or other detention whatfoever; but only the fubjects of the King of Denmark, who fhall have prefumed to fell or alienate any the like prohibited timber, fhall be punifhed in due manner. And the people and fubjects of the King of Great Britain fhall have, poffefs, and enjoy all and fingular the contents and conceffions of this article, without any moleftation or interruption, fo long, and for all fuch time as the fubjects, or any of the people of the United Netherlands, fhall hold, poffefs, and enjoy, or might or ought to hold, poffefs, and enjoy the fame, or like privileges, by any treaty already made, or to be made, or by any contract, agreement, or permiffion.

XII. It is alfo concluded and agreed, that all fhips belonging to the fubjects of the King of Great Britain, and merchants, in their paffage through the Sound, under the Moft Serene King of Denmark and Norway, &c. fhall enjoy, after the fame manner, the benefit and privilege of deferring the payment of their

G 2 cuftoms

cuftoms until their return, as they held and enjoyed in
former years laft preceding the late war; but fo, neverthelefs, that the faid fhips and merchants bring with
them certificates under the feal of the officers of the
faid King of Great Britain deputed thereunto, tefti-
fying the faid fhips to belong to fubjefts of the
King of Great Britain; and likewife that before
their paffage they give fufficient and good fecurity for
paying the fame in place convenient, to the collectors
of the cuftoms of the faid King of Denmark, at their
return, or if they fhall not return, within three months
time at the fartheft, if they do not pay the fame at their
faid firft paffage.

XIII. And furthermore it is agreed, that whatfoever merchandize the fubjefts of the King of Great
Britain fhall land at Elfignore, and there lay in their
ftorehoufes, to no other end than to put on board again
entire, and tranfport them to other parts, they fhall be
obliged to pay only the fame duties for fuch merchandize, and no more, than is wont to be paid in this cafe
by the Dutch nation, or any other ftrangers: which
fhall be reciprocally obferved to the fubjefts of the
King of Denmark, after the fame manner, in England.

XIV. Alfo it is agreed, that the fhips and fubjefts
of the King of Great Britain fhall have their difpatch
at Elfignore as foon as they arrive there, without delay,
no fhips, of what nation foever, having preference
before them in this behalf: except the inhabitants of
certain places, who have anciently held a privilege to
that purpofe, and ftill do.

' XV. If any fubject of either Prince fhall happen
to die in the dominions or territories of the other, it
fhall be lawful for him to difpofe of his eftate, both
money and goods, in any manner whatfoever: and if
any one die within the kingdoms or provinces of the
other Prince without making any fuch difpofitions,
then the goods by him left, moveable or immoveable,
of whatever nature or condition the fame fhall be;

            fhall

fhall be faithfully preferved for the ufe of the right heir, and for fatisfaction of fuch debts as the party deceafed was juftly bound to pay: and to that end, fo foon as any fubject of either Prince fhall die in the other Prince's dominions, the conful or public minifter then refiding there fhall have right to poffefs the faid monies and goods, and fhall make inventories of the fame before fome magiftrate of the place; which goods fhall afterwards remain in his hands, to be anfwered to the heirs and creditors as aforefaid; but if no fuch conful or public minifter fhall be there, then it fhall be lawful for two merchants of the fame country with the party deceafed, to poffefs the goods left by him, to preferve them, and in like manner to anfwer them to the heirs and creditors.   Which notwithftanding is to be fo underftood, that no papers or books of accounts are by this article to be expofed to the infpection of the faid magiftrate, but only the real goods and merchandize of the deceafed, and that the faid magiftrate, within the fpace of forty-eight hours after notice given, and requeft made, fhall be obliged to be prefent, otherwife the faid inventories fhall be made without him.

XVI. It fhall be lawful for either of the confederates, and their fubjects or people, to trade with the enemies of the other, and to carry to them, or furnifh them with any merchandizes (prohibited only, which they call contrabanda, excepted) without any impediment, unlefs in ports and places befieged by the other; which neverthelefs if they fhall fo do, it fhall be free for them either to fell their goods to the befiegers, or betake themfelves to any other port or place not befieged.

XVII. It is alfo agreed, that it fhall be free and lawful for the fubjects of either Prince, trading in the dominions or ports of the other, there to remain and refide for the buying and felling commodities, without any reftriction of time, or limitation to be impofed upon them by any officers or magiftrates of the faid dominions or ports, they paying the accuftomed duties for all goods and merchandize by them imported or exported; and further provided that they trade with none but fuch as are citizens, or burghers of fome city or town within the kingdoms of Denmark or Norway, and that only by wholefale, and not by parcels or retail.

XVIII. Furthermore, for the better encouragement of trade and commerce, and for the utter avoiding of all frauds and difputes that may arife between the officers of ports and merchants, it is agreed and concluded, that all and fingular duties fhall be demanded and paid, according to the printed Tariff (or book of rates) wherein fhall be comprized all cuftoms and duties to be paid, as well for goods in the refpective ports, as for paffage through the Sound: and to the end that this may be the more ftrictly obferved, both Kings fhall not only enjoin his officers and collectors of his cuftoms, under the higheft penalty, not to do any thing that may fruftrate or elude this agreement; but alfo that they do not, by moleftation or exaction, caufe any trouble, or offer any injury to the fubjects of either King.

XIX. Moreover, it is concluded and agreed, that the King of Denmark fhall conftitute the overfeers of his cuftoms, or others, commiffioners for re-meafuring all fhips belonging to the fubjects of the King of Great Britain trading in Norway, according to their burthen and content, fo as that what has been hitherto not rightly obferved, either in excefs or defect, may be hereafter reduced into better order.

XX. But left fuch freedom of navigation or paffage of the one ally, and his fubjects and people, during the war that the other may have by fea or land with any other country, may be to the prejudice of the other ally, and that goods and merchandize belonging to the enemy may be fraudulently concealed under

under colour of being in amity; for the preventing of fraud, and clearing all fufpicion, it is thought fit, that the fhips, goods, and men, belonging to the other confederate, in their paffage and voyages, be accompanied with letters of paffport and certificate; the forms whereof to be as follows:

CHARLES *the Second, by the Grace of God, King of*
Great Britain, *&c.*

CHRISTIAN *the Fifth, by the Grace of God, King of*
Denmark *and* Norway, *&c.*

BE it known unto all and fingular to whom thefe our letters of fafe-conduct fhall be fhewn, That
our fubject and citizen of our city of
hath humbly reprefented unto us, that the fhip called
of the burthen of tons, doth belong unto them and others our fubjects, and that they are fole owners and proprietors thereof, and is now laden with the goods which are contained in a fchedule which fhe hath with her from the officers of our cuftoms, and do folely, truly, and really belong to our fubjects, or others in neutrality, bound immediately from the port of to fuch other place or places where fhe may conveniently trade with the faid goods, being not prohibited, nor belonging to either of the parties in hoftility, or elfe find a freight: which the forefaid our fubject, having attefted by a writing under his hand, and affirmed to be true by oath, under penalty of confifcation of the faid goods, we have thought fit to grant him thefe our letters of fafe-conduct: and therefore we do hereby refpectively pray and defire all governors of countries and feas, kings, princes, commonwealths, and free cities, and more efpecially the parties now in war, and their commanders, admirals, generals, officers, governors of ports, commanders of fhips, captains, freighters, and all others whatfoever

G 4 having

having any jurifdiction by fea, or the cuftody of any
port, whom the fhip aforefaid fhall chance to meet, or
among' whofe fleet or fhips it fhall happen to fall, or.
make ftay in their ports, that by virtue of the league
and amity, which we have with any king or ftate, they.
fuffer the faid mafter with the fhip,   perfons,
things, and all merchandize on board her, not only
freely and without any moleftation, detention, or impediment, to any place whatfoever to purfue his voyage, but alfo to afford him all offices of civility, as to
our fubject, if there fhall be occafion; which upon the
like or other occafion we and ours fhall be ready to
return.

· Given the   day of   in the ˙
    year

· WE the prefident, confuls, and fenators of the
city of   do atteft and certify, That
on the   day of   in the year
            perfonally before us came and appeared
            citizen and inhabitant of the city or town
of   and under the oath wherein he ftands
bound to our fovereign Lord the King, did declare
unto us, that the fhip or veffel called   ·
of the burthen of   tons, doth belong to
the port, city, or town of   in the province of   And that the faid fhip doth
juftly belong only to him and others, fubjects of our
faid fovereign Lord, and now bound directly from the
port of   laden with goods mentioned
in a fchedule received from the officers of the cuftoms;
and that he hath affirmed under the oath aforefaid,
that the forementioned veffel, with her goods and merchandize, doth only belong to fubjects of his Majefty,
and doth carry no goods prohibited, which belong to
either of the parties now in war.

    In teftimony whereof we have caufed this certificate
        to be fubfcribed by the fyndic of our city, and
        fealed with our feal.
    Given, &c.
                                            When

. When therefore the merchandize, goods, ships, or men of either of the confederates, and their subjects, and people, shall meet in open sea, straights, ports, havens, lands, and places whatsoever, the ships of war, whether public or private, or the men, subjects, and people of the other confederate; upon exhibiting only the foresaid letters of safe-conduct and certificate, there shall be nothing more required of them, nor shall search be made after the goods, ships, or men, nor shall they be any other ways whatsoever molested or troubled, but suffered with all freedom to pursue their intended voyage; but if this solemn and set form of passport and certificate be not exhibited, or that there be any other just and urgent cause of suspicion, then shall the ship be searched, which is nevertheless in this case only understood to be permitted, and not otherwise. If by either party any thing shall be committed contrary to the true meaning of this article, against either of the confederates, each of the said confederates shall cause his subjects and people offending to be severely punished, and full and entire satisfaction to be forthwith given, and without delay, to the party injured, and his subjects and people, for their whole loss and expences.

XXI. It is also concluded and agreed, that all ships of subjects and people of the King of Great Britain, together with their lading and merchandize, passing by the port of Gluckstad, or other places and towns under the dominion of the King of Denmark, situate upon the Elbe stream, both going and returning, shall be free and exempt from all custom, impost, search, seizure, and molestation, except only the case of search in the time of war, when the King of Denmark hath war with any other king or state.

XXII. If the subjects of either Prince be hurt or injured in the territories of the other, then the King of that place where the injury is done, shall take care that speedy justice be administered according to the

laws

laws and cuſtoms of the country; and that the perſons guilty be duly puniſhed, with ſatisfaction to be made to the party wronged.

XXIII. It is alſo agreed, that no ſhips whatſoever, veſſels, or merchandize laden on ſhips of whatſoever nature, kind, or quality, howſoever taken, belonging to any the ſubjects of either of the aforeſaid Kings, under any colour or pretence whatſoever, be adjudged prize, unleſs by a judicial examination and proceſs in form of law, in a court of admiralty for prizes taken at ſea, in that behalf lawfully conſtituted.

XXIV. Both parties ſhall cauſe juſtice and equity to be adminiſtered to the ſubjects and people of each other, according to the laws and ſtatutes of either country, ſpeedily, and without long and unneceſſary formalities of law and expences, in all cauſes and controverſies, as well now depending, as which may hereafter ariſe.

XXV. If the ſhips of either of the confederates, and their ſubjects and people, whether they be merchant-men, or men of war, ſhall happen to run on ground, or fall upon rocks, or be forced to lighten themſelves, or ſhall otherwiſe ſuffer ſhipwreck (which God forbid) upon the coaſts of either King, the foreſaid ſhips, with their tackle, goods, and merchandize, or whatſoever ſhall be remaining of them, ſhall be reſtored to their owners and proprietors; provided they or their agents and proctors do claim the ſaid ſhips and goods within the ſpace of a year and a day after ſuch ſhipwreck ſuf-fered, ſaving always the rights and cuſtoms of both nations. The ſubjects alſo and inhabitants dwelling upon the ſaid coaſts and ſhores, ſhall be obliged to come in to their help in caſe of danger, and as much as in them lies to give their aſſiſtance; and ſhall do their utmoſt endeavour either for the freeing of the ſhip, or ſaving the goods, merchandize, and apparel of the ſaid ſhip, and what elſe of the ſame they ſhall be able, and for the conveying the ſame into ſome ſafe

place

place in order to be restored to the owners; they paying salvage, and giving such recompence to the persons by whose assistance and diligence the said merchandize and goods shall have been recovered and preserved, as they shall deserve. And finally, both parties, in case of such misfortune, shall see observed on their side, what they would desire to have observed and done on the other side.

XXVI. The commanders of ships, or governors, soldiers, mariners, and company belonging to the same; as also the ships themselves, and the goods and merchandize on board them, shall not be detained by any arrest or seizure, upon any warrant either general or special, or for any cause, unless for the defence and preservation of the kingdom; which yet shall not be understood to be meant of arrests laid by authority of law, for debt contracted upon any other lawful occasion whatsoever, in which case it shall be lawful to proceed according to the rules of justice and law.

XXVII. It shall be free for the merchants of both kingdoms, their factors and servants, and also the masters and mariners of ships upon the sea, and in other waters, as likewise in the ports, and upon the coasts and lands of either confederate, going, returning, and walking, for the defence of their persons and goods, to carry any kind of portable arms, as well offensive as defensive, so that they give no just cause of suspicion to the commanders and magistrates of any place, of any plots or contrivances against the public or private peace.

XXVIII. The convoys or ships of war of either party, meeting in their voyage, or overtaking any merchants ships, or others, belonging to the other confederate or his subjects, and making the same course at sea, in Europe or out of Europe, shall be obliged to guard and defend them as long as they shall hold the same course together.

XXIX. For

. XXIX. For the greater fecurity of commerce and freedom of navigation, it is concluded and agreed, that neither part, as much as may be, and fhall lie in their powers, fhall permit that public pirates or, other robbers upon the fea, in any the ports of the other kingdom or country, have their receptacles or retreats, or fhall fuffer that any of the inhabitants or people of either Prince do receive them into their houfes, or fupply them with provifions, or be otherwife affifting to them; but, on the contrary, fhall endeavour that the faid pirates or robbers, and their partizans and accomplices, be apprehended and punifhed according to their demerit, and the fhips and goods, as much as can be found of them, reftored to the lawful owners or their agents, provided their right be made appear by due proof of law in the court of admiralty.

. XXX. It is concluded and agreed, that there fhall be at all times free accefs for the fubjects and people of either party, to the ports and coafts of both Princes, and it fhall be lawful for them to remain therein, and from thence again to depart, and alfo to pafs through the feas and territories whatfoever of either King refpectively (not committing any wafte or injury) not only with merchant-fhips, and fhips of burthen, but alfo with fhips of war, whether the fame be upon the public account, or acting by private commiffions; whether they enter by reafon of tempeft, and for avoiding the danger of the fea, or to refit or buy provifions: fo that they exceed not the number of fix fhips of war, if they enter of their own accord, nor fhall they remain longer in or about the ports than fhall be neceffary for the refitting of their fhips, buying provifions or other neceffaries: and if they fhould upon occafion defire to come into the faid ports with a greater number of fhips of war, it fhall in no wife be lawful for them to enter thereinto without firft giving timely notice by letter of their coming, and obtaining leave of thofe to whom the forefaid ports belong. But if by force of tempeft, or other urgent neceffity,

they

they shall be compelled to put into harbour, in such case, without any precedent notice, the ships shall not be restrained to a certain number; but with this condition neverthelefs, that their admiral or commander in chief, prefently after his arrival, shall make acquainted the chief magistrate or commander of the place, haven, or coast, whither they are come, with the cause of his coming; nor shall he stay longer there than shall be permitted him by the chief magistrate or commander, and shall not act or attempt any hostility in the ports whereinto he hath betaken himself, or any thing prejudicial to him of the two confederates to whom they shall belong.

XXXI. It shall not be lawful for the subjects of either King, or the inhabitants of the kingdoms or lands under their obedience, to procure of any prince or state who is at difference, or in open war with either of the confederates, letters patents, called commissions or reprisals, much less by virtue of such letters to molest or damnify the subjects of either. Both the said Kings shall strictly prohibit their subjects respectively, that they do not procure or accept from other princes or states any such commissions; but shall, as much as in them lies, forbid and hinder the committing of any depredations by virtue of such commissions.

XXXII. If any ship or ships belonging to the subjects of either King be taken in the ports of either by a third party, they in whose port, or within whose jurisdiction whatsoever the foresaid ships shall be taken, shall be mutually obliged to use their endeavour, together with the other party, for the finding and retaking the said ship or ships, and restoring them to the owners; which neverthelefs shall be done at the charge of the said owners, or the parties interested.

XXXIII. But if also in the ships taken by the subjects of either confederate, and brought into any port belonging to the other, there be found any seamen or other persons who are subjects of that confederate

derate .into .whofe· pórts or rivers the prize˙ fhall be brought, they fhall be civilly ufed by thofe who have taken them, and reftored to their liberty forthwith, and without ranfom.

XXXIV. But if a fhip of war, or any other, laden with prohibited˙goods belonging to the other crown, happen to be taken ; it fhall not be lawful for the captains or commanders who have taken her, to open or break up any chefts, tons, or bales on board the faid fhip, nor likewife to tranfport or otherwife alienate any of her merchandize, until they have been firft put on fhore, and an inventory thereof made before the judges of the admiralty.

XXXV. And for the greater fecurity of the fubjeas of both Kings, and for preventing of all violence towards them from the faid fhips of war ; all commanders of any the fhips of war belonging to the King of Great Britain, and all other his fubjeas whatfoever, fhall be ftriatly charged and required, that they do not moleft or injure the fubjeas of the King of Denmark; if they fhall do otherwife, they fhall be liable to anfwer it in their perfons and eftates, and fhall therein ftand bound until juft fatisfaction and compenfation fhall be made for the wrongs by them done, and the damage thereby fuftained or to be fuftained: in like manner fhall all commanders of the fhips of war belonging to the King of Denmark, and all other his fubjeas whatfoever, be ftraitly, under the fame penalties, charged and required that they do not moleft or injure the faid fubjeas of the King of Great Britain: provided neverthelefs, that all the forefaid actions be examined and adjudged by due and legal proceeding in the court of admiralty of both Kings; or if it fhall rather feem meet to either of the parties, being a ftranger in the place where the controverfy is to be decided, they fhall be examined before certain commiffioners, which both Kings, fo foon as they fhall be defired, fhall appoint to˙that end, that fo proceedings by this means

may

may be not only carried on without great expences, but alfo ended within three months at fartheft.

XXXVI. Both Kings fhall take care, that judgment and fentence, in things taken at fea, be given according to the rules of juftice and equity, by perfons not fufpected or interefted; and being once given by fuch judges as aforefaid, they fhall ftraitly charge and require their officers, and whom it fhall concern, to fee the fame put in due execution according to the form and tenor thereof.

XXXVII. If the ambaffadors of either King, or any other public minifters refiding with the other King, fhall happen to make complaint of any fuch fentence, that King to whom complaint fhall be made, fhall caufe the faid judgment and fentence to be re-heard and examined in his council, that it may appear whether all things requifite and neceffary have been performed according to the rules of this treaty, and with due caution: if the contrary fhall happen, it fhall be redreffed, which is to be done at the fartheft within three months time.

Neither fhall it be lawful, either before the giving of the firft fentence, or afterwards during the time of re-hearing, to unlade or fell and make away the goods in controverfy, unlefs it happen to be done by confent of parties, and to prevent the perifhing of the faid goods and merchandize.

XXXVIII. The faid Kings fhall have in each other's court their minifters, and in certain ports their confuls, for the better and more eafy communicating and propofing fuch things as they fhall think advantageous to the public intereft, or private concerns of any particular perfon.

XXXIX. No private injury fhall in any wife letten this treaty, nor fhall raife any difcord or hatred between the forefaid nations, but every man fhall anfwer for his own doings, and fhall be refponfible

therefore;

therefore; nor shall one man suffer for that which another has offended in, by having recourse to reprisals, or such like rigorous proceedings; unless justice be denied or delayed longer than is fitting. In which case it shall be lawful for that King, whose subject has received the injury, to proceed according to the rules and prescriptions of the law of nations, until reparation be made to the party injured; provided notwithstanding, that he have first in due manner advertised the other King thereof.

XL. Also it is agreed, that if the Hollander, or any other nation whatsoever (the Swedish nation only excepted) hath already, or shall hereafter obtain any better articles, agreements, exemptions, or privileges, than what are contained in this treaty, from the King of Denmark, that the same and like privileges shall be likewise granted to the King of Great Britain and his subjects, effectually and fully, to all intents and purposes; and on the other side, if the Hollander, or any other nation whatsoever, hath or shall obtain from his Majesty of Great Britain, any better articles, agreements, exemptions, or privileges, than what are contained in this treaty, that the same and like privileges shall be granted to the King of Denmark and his subjects also, in most full and effectual manner.

XLI. It is also concluded, that former treaties and leagues, at any time heretofore made between the foresaid confederates or their predecessors, Kings, as well for the kingdoms of Great Britain, &c. as for the hereditary kingdoms of Denmark and Norway, &c. respectively, be not in the least reputed or taken to be broken and abolished by any agreement, covenants, or articles in the present treaty contained; but that the same remain in full force, effect, and virtue, so far as they are not contrary or repugnant to the present treaty, or any article therein contained.

XLII. Finally, it is covenanted, concluded, and agreed, that the foresaid Kings shall sincerely and

bind

bonâ fide obferve all and fingular the articles contained and fet down in this treaty, and fhall caufe them to be obferved by their fubjects and people; nor fhall tranf-grefs the fame directly or indirectly, or fuffer the fame to be tranfgreffed by their fubjects or people, and fhall ratify and confirm all and fingular the premifes as be-fore agreed, by letters patents fubfcribed with their hands, and fealed with their great feals, in good, fuf-ficient, and effectual form, and fhall deliver the fame reciprocally within three months after the date of thefe prefents, or caufe them to be delivered, in good faith and reality, and with effect.

Given at Copenhagen, the 12th day of July, 1670.

The following Explanation of the Third Article of the Treaty of Alliance and Commerce, which was concluded in 1670, between their late Majefties, Charles *the* Second, *and* Chriftian *the Fifth, was made by a Convention, dated the 4th of* July, 1780.

LES deux Souverains contractants s'engagent réci-proquement, pour eux et pour leurs fucceffeurs, de ne point fournir aux ennemis de l'un ou de l'autre, en tems de guerre, aucun fecours, ni foldats, ni vaiffeaux, ni au-cuns des effets et marchandifes dites de contrebande; de défendre également à leurs Sujets de le faire; et de punir féverement, et comme des infracteurs de la paix, ceux qui oferoient contrevenir à leurs défenfes à cet égard. Mais, pour ne laiffer aucun doute fur ce qui doit être entendu par le terme de contrebande, on eft convenu, qu'on n'entend fous cette dénomination que les armes, tant à feu que d'autres fortes, avec leurs affortimens, comme canons, moufquets, mortiers, pe-tards, bombes, grenades, cercles-poiffés, fauciffes, affuts, fourchettes, banderollieres, poudre, meches, falpêtre, balles, piques, épées, morions, cuiraffes, hallebardes,

lances, javelines, chevaux, felles de cheval, fourreaux
de piftolets, baudriers, et généralement tous autres affortimens fervant à l'ufage de la guerre, de même que
le bois de conftruction, le goudron, ou poix réfine,
le cuivre en feuille, les voiles, chanvres et cordages,
et généralement tout ce qui fert directement à l'équip-
pement des vaiffeaux ; le fer non ouvragé, et les planches
de fapin cependant exceptés.

Mais il eft expreffément déclaré, que, dans ce genre
de marchandifes de contrebande, l'on ne comprend
point le poiffon et la viande fraîche ou falée, les fro-
mens, farines, bleds ou autres grains, les légumes,
l'huile, le vin, et généralement tout ce qui fert à la
nourriture et fuftentation de la vie ; et ainfi toutes ces
chofes pourront toujours fe vendre et tranfporter,
comme les autres marchandifes, même aux lieux tenus
par un ennemi des deux Couronnes, pourvu qu'ils ne
foient affiégés ou bloqués.

The

The HANSE TOWNS.

1435.
————
1578.

THERE were various treaties between England and the Hanse Towns, from 1435 to 1578, when their peculiar privileges, within this kingdom, were entirely abrogated by Queen Elizabeth.

   Rym. Fœd. vol. x. p. 627-57-666.
    vol. xi. p. 217-645-729-739-780-793.

167$\frac{2}{7}$.
12 Jan.

The city of Hamburgh's instrument, obliging itself to pay 35,000l. as compensation for the loss of certain English ships in the river Elbe.

   Pap. Off. R. 1.

1706.
11 Oct.

The treaty of commerce with Dantzic.

   Pap. Off. R. 4.
   Board of Trade, Q. 14.

1711.
31 Jan.

The convention with Hamburgh, about the herring trade.

   Pap. Off. R. 5.
   Board of Trade, O. 128.

17$\frac{19}{20}$.
3 Feb.

The convention with Hamburgh, about the herring trade.

   Pap. Off. R. 6.
   Board of Trade, P. 165.

1731.
17 Oct.

The convention with the city of Bremen, touching the commerce of herrings.

   Pap. Off. R. 7.
   Board of Trade, V. 88.

[The

[The following treaty of commerce, between Great Britain and Dantzic, is printed from a copy in the book of treaties, belonging to the late Board of Trade.]

The Treaty of Commerce with Dantzic, *dated* $\frac{11}{22}$ *October,* 1706.

WHEREAS her Sacred Majesty Anne, by the grace of God, of Great Britain, France, and Ireland, Queen, Defender of the Faith, at the request of her subjects, merchants residing in the city of Dantzic, most graciously commanded the Excellent and Reverend Dr. John Robinson, Doctor in Divinity, and Canon of the cathedral and metropolitical church of Christ at Canterbury, her Ambassador Extraordinary and Plenipotentiary, that he should confer with the most Noble Magistracy of the said city, in order to the removing certain grievances in trade, whereby the British merchants at Dantzic are oppressed; and the Magistracy aforesaid, being disposed and inclined to all those things which may be grateful and acceptable to her Majesty, and very much desiring that the British merchants residing at Dantzic, and those of Dantzic in Great Britain, may enjoy mutual advantages, hath named their deputies, the Noble Lords M. Gabriel von Boemeln, Consul, and John Ernest von der Linde, Consul and Syndic, to confer and treat upon that affair with the aforesaid Minister and Plenipotentiary: Whereupon the said Minister and Deputies consented and agreed unto the following articles.

I. As formerly and hitherto, so also hereafter for the future, it shall be lawful for the subjects of the kingdoms of Great Britain, to wit, England, Scotland, and Ireland, as of a nation in amity, freely to dwell at Dantzic, as long as they will, without any molestation, and exercise trade there; that is to say, to import whatsoever merchandizes of other nations, which it is lawful by sea or land to bring from foreign

reign parts to Dantzic, and, having paid the due, and usual customs, to keep them in cellars, warehouses, and storehouses, and thence sell them to the citizens of Dantzic; or if, perhaps, they cannot sell them, to export them again by sea, in what ships they shall think fit, having paid the duties at their going out, which the citizens themselves do; as also buy all merchandizes whatsoever of the citizens of Dantzic, and transport them by sea to what foreign parts soever they please; nevertheless always observing the laws and statutes of the said city respecting either commerce, or any other right or privilege whatsoever.

II. But as to herrings in particular, and every kind of salt fish, it shall be lawful to keep these goods brought by British subjects, and to put them in cellars, warehouses, and storehouses, and have the same privileges as the Dutch merchants dwelling in Dantzic: yet so, that they must declare in the customhouse the said merchandizes, as well as all others, according to the true consignment of the same, as also commit them to the care and inspection of officers sworn to approve and examine the same; but they shall not deliver any of the said goods into the buyers hands, before they are exposed by the officers upon the public bridge, and subjected to their approbation and examination: In like manner also, the subjects of Great Britain shall be allowed to export herrings and salt by sea, paying custom for the same, provided they cannot sell them at Dantzic (suspending as heretofore, so now, and as far as may be, without prejudice to the public good, the execution of an edict published in the month of March, in the year 1687), but when it shall be necessary to enforce the said edict, and put it in execution, the same shall be previously notified to the British merchants for the six preceding summer months. Moreover, because the aforesaid merchants ought not to enjoy the proper rights and privileges of the citizens in buying

and

and felling, neither fhall the Britifh fubjects, who
lodge with any citizen of Dantzic, and have no family of their own, be obliged to execute perfonal offices and employments, as for example, to undertake
the guardianfhip of others, the government of churches
and hofpitals, or thofe of any other kind whatfoever;
nor to pay the fubfidy that is impofed on the citizens
and inhabitants, or any other burthens, befides the
juft· and ufual duties at coming in and going out, for
their fhips and merchandizes, as much, namely, as
fhall be paid by the citizens themfelves, either for
their perfons or goods, and commodities whatfoever;
but others who have hired houfes and fixed habita-
tions at Dantzic, and ufe and dwell in them, and have
families of their own, they fhall hereafter pay and be
fubject to all duties and impofitions, without mur-
muring or refufal, which fhall be required not only
from the citizens, but from all the inhabitants in
general, an equality being always obferved, that they
are not more burthened than the other inhabitants.

. III. Moreover, there fhall be entire liberty as well
for the Britifh merchants themfelves, or if they have
a family, as for the Britifh heirs of the deceafed to
change place, and remove from Dantzic all their
goods and effects, whenever and wherefoever they
fhall think fit; and thofe of Dantzic, or any Dantzic heirs of the deceafed, fhall alfo equally enjoy the
fame right in all things in the kingdom of Great
Britain.

IV. A Britifh fhip being driven by ftorm going
into port and the river Weiffell, fhall pay nothing
more than the money to the pilots, and for clearing
out the ballaft (commonly called Lotfs and Bagger
Gild); but with this difference, that a fhip of great
burthen fhall bear the faid expences according to the
proportion of lafts which, for eafier entrance, fhe
unloadeth into leffer veffels. And a little fhip that
unloadeth no goods, fhall pay at leaft half the money
for

for clearing out ballaft (for hereafter a rate fhall be settled of the payments to pilots, according to certain fleets of fhips); but if fuch fhip fhall be brought to the city, or place appointed for repairing fhips, then it fhall pay all and fingular the impofitions ufually demanded of fhips, the expences to be paid to officers being within moderation, according to the proportion of the fhip; though the goods, which in that cafe the fhip hath landed for its neceffary repair, and afterwards' received back, fhall be free from any duty or impofition, and not like the reft of the loading.

And if there fhall be occafion to fell any part of the goods for the faid reparations, or to buy provifions, the accuftomed duties for this proportion of goods only fhall be paid; and it fhall not be lawful to take out any part of the goods, without leave firft obtained of the magiftrate.

But as often as any fhip which fhall arrive from foreign parts into the ftation of the Dantzic fhips, and bound with her loading to another place, fhall unload any goods to be carried into the city; or if any goods are to be carried on board any fhip arriving from foreign parts, and bound to another place, but not unloading any goods; in this cafe the whole cuftom muft be paid for the fhip, that is to fay, as much as is required in that cafe for the Dantzic fhips themfelves; but the other impofitions fhall be levied, as well upon view of the fhip as by reafon of the merchandizes, according to the proportion of lafts unloaded or imported. But if fuch fhip unloading any merchandize, has a mind to import into the city other goods in lieu of thofe unloaden, in that cafe the duties fhall be proportionably paid, according to the rate of the lafts which fhall remain imported.

V. For as much as the Britifh merchants, defiring to provide for the payment of the cuftoms in a manner lefs troublefome, but not with lefs fafety, did obtain from the magiftrates of Dantzic, by the conclu-

fion

fion of the States of the city of the 22d July, 1705, that inftead of the ufual money to be paid in the chamber. (cuftom-houfe) perfonal fecurity fhould be admitted to be taken, whereby all and fingular the merchants of the Britifh nation, refiding in Dantzic for the time being, were bound, and the faid States were pleafed again to prolong the fame method of fecurity for another year; it is therefore agreed, that the faid ufe of perfonal fecurity fhall remain to the end of the faid year, nor is it hereafter to be doubted that any thing fhall be changed therein, except it fhall be found by experience that the Britifh merchants abufe that conceffion, and perform not their part, or that other weighty confiderations require it otherwife.

VI. Whereas commerce and the credit of traders, which are mutually neceffary, cannot flourifh or fubfift without a ready adminiftration of juftice, the magiftrate fhall therefore take care that regard be had to the Britifh merchants in all caufes, and to their juft defires in this particular. And a Dantzic merchant being creditor in fpecie, fhall not arreft the perfon or goods of any Britifh merchant his debtor, who fhall be willing to give fufficient fecurity; and by the like fufficient fecurity to be given, a citizen of Dantzic that is debtor, fhall be refponfible to a Britifh merchant that is creditor and fuitor. The citizens of Dantzic fhall reciprocally enjoy the fame right in the kingdoms of Great Britain, &c.

VII. In caufes relating to trade carried on with foreigners, againft the rights of the city, the procefs againft Britifh merchants fhall be made in the fame manner and form of law as is ufual to proceed againft the citizens themfelves in the fentence of punifhment, according to the prefcription of the ftatute law hitherto conftantly obferved, and in this cafe exact equity fhall be obferved; nor fhall the magiftrate omit to take care as well to prevent the lengthening of fuits, as alfo to correct the other abufes, which by the malice

. lice and obstinacy of the parties themselves at law in this behalf may have broke in.

VIII. If differences shall happen to arise in civil causes merely maritime, between the commanders of British ships and their seamen, that shall require a quick dispatch, the plaintiff, upon the request of the adverse party, shall be referred to the minister of Great Britain (if there be any upon the place), or to two British merchants deputed for that purpose, that the dispute may be well and justly made up. But if that cannot be, the magistrate shall plainly, and without any expence of time or charge, take care to determine the matter, that the said seamen shall not desert their master and ship to whom they belong, except for the most weighty reasons.

IX. The British merchants residing at Dantzic shall have a minister for the worship of God, who shall perform divine service in a private house, and in the British language, and shall perform the other offices of his function for those of the British nation. And the said minister, whether he hath a house and family of his own or not, shall enjoy the same freedom as the merchants. He shall moreover enjoy, by the kind indulgence of the magistrate, an exemption of excise of beer for the use of his house, and consumption of his own family. And the ministers of the reformed religion at Dantzic shall hereafter be indulged in any such respectful privilege.

X. For preventing all abuses whatsoever in the measure of salt or pit coals, all the tons by which they are measured shall be exactly adjusted, and a review of them, whether they are altered in any part, shall be yearly appointed; and the coal inspector shall be severely prohibited hereafter from taking to himself any thing that shall accidentally fall upon the ground in unloading the coals out of the ship or cart, or shall be designedly thrown out, but he shall leave it to the true owner; and the measurers of salt shall be enjoined

to

to make juft and equal meafure, and to accept reward
from no perfon whatfoever, under the penalty of being removed from their office.

XI. And it fhall be lawful for the Britifh merchants,
in carrying their merchandizes between the city and
the ftation of the fhips, and vice verfa, to bring fmall
boats (commonly called boardings and ballaft boats)
for that purpofe, according to an order thereupon
made; nor fhall greater fieight be exacted of them
for their goods than from the citizens themfelves:
and moreover it fhall be lawful for the Britifh fubjects who trade in Poland, to bring the goods bought
there to Dantzic, to be fold to the citizens, and carry
away thofe bought of the citizens, with the fame freedom as the Poles have hitherto, and may do hereafter.

XII. For as much as experience hath taught, that,
under the name of tobacco imported from England
and Holland, at the port of the city of Dantzic, an
herb of the like fpecies is brought hither, though of
very different goodnefs from it, and therefore of a
quite different and much cheaper price, that we are
perplexed with exquifite and admitted frauds, and by
this means the revenue of cuftoms is prejudiced, and
private buyers craftily deceived; care fhall therefore
be taken, that the remedies introduced for preventing
thefe frauds may have their due effect, and other proper means ufed to obviate them hereafter.

For what remains; if any greater privileges, which
any wife refpect the perfons, fhips, or goods of foreigners at Dantzic, fhall be hereafter granted to any
foreign nation, the Britifh fubjects fhall in the like
manner fully enjoy the fame for themfelves, their
fhips, and commerce.

But after the noble Magiftracy by their Deputies
have propofed certain requefts, whereof the citizens
and merchants of Dantzic moft humbly folicit her
moft Serene and Potent Majefty of Great Britain's
conceffion, the forementioned Minifter and Plenipotentiary

tentiary of her said Majesty using his good offices therein, and have earnestly moved that certain inconveniences, which have for some time affected the navigation and commerce of the people of Dantzic, in the kingdom of Great Britain, may be kindly removed and abolished; and therefore conferences having been likewise set on foot upon this affair between the said Plenipotentiary and the Deputies of the Magistrates, all things being considered, they thought fit to provide for the requests and grievances of the citizens and merchants of Dantzic by the following articles.

XIII. The citizens and inhabitants of Dantzic shall enjoy in the kingdoms of Great Britain, the same rights and liberties which they have hitherto obtained, and are now in use; and it shall be therefore free for them to come to, either by land or sea, all the dominions, towns, and places whatsoever of England, Scotland, and Ireland, and to enter into all ports with their ships, merchandizes, and cargoes, freely and with all manner of security, and to remain therein as long as they please, without any hindrance, and to trade and deal by themselves, or their factors and servants, and to import at pleasure any merchandize of the product or manufacture of the territories of the said city of Dantzic or Prussia, or such as shall be first commonly brought from other parts to the port of Dantzic, to be transported thence by sea to other places and territories, and in like manner to export merchandize of all sorts; on this condition, nevertheless, that they pay and bear the customs and all other impositions that are equally to be paid and discharged by all other foreigners residing or trading there; and that they observe the laws, statutes, and customs of this or that place where they shall come, and conform themselves thereto. But so often as the masters of Dantzic ships buy salt or pit coals in specie (neo castri) at Newcastle, or at any places of the kingdom of Scotland, they shall not be obliged to pay, or be loaden with greater

impositions

impositions and costs, than other foreign nations doing the same are obliged to pay.

XIV. The ships of Dantzic being duly furnished with authentic passports and certificates, by which the propriety of the ships and cargo may certainly appear, and that they neither carry contraband goods, nor those of the enemy; they shall not be stopped by British privateers in the British seas, or elsewhere in their voyage, much less detained, visited or taken, and carried into the ports of Great Britain: but if this stated and usual form of certificate be not produced, or there be some other just and urgent ground of suspicion, then the ship may be visited, nevertheless, this permission is to be understood in such case only, and not otherwise: and if any thing shall be done contrary to the true and genuine sense and meaning of this article, a severe penalty shall be inflicted on the offenders, and ample satisfaction shall immediately be made, without any delay, to the party injured, for his loss, damage, and expences.

XV. As often as a ship of Dantzic, laden with goods on the account of British merchants, shall arrive in any port of Great Britain, the British merchants shall take care that it be unladen as soon as may be, and pay the Dantzic masters of ships the price of transportation or freight in ready money (and not in bills, but they shall repay the charges, that is to say, the money paid to the pilots) according to contract and agreement, for undertaking the voyage between the owners and masters of the ships.

XVI. For as much also as complaints and differences do often arise between the British merchants and masters of ships, for pretended damage done to their goods, and compensation thereof; wherefore, to obviate such things for the future, lest any thing be allowed not agreeable to justice and equity, it shall not be lawful for British merchants, upon view of certain pretended damage, to with-hold from the Dant-

zic

zic mafters of fhips as much as they pleafe and defire, of the price of hire for freight due to them; but
a juft and exact account of the real damage fhall be
taken, and the Dantzic mafters be obliged only to pay
the true value thereof.

XVII. As often as any Britifh merchant fhall po-
fitively and effectually agree with a Dantzic mafter of
a fhip, being in the kingdom of Great Britain with
his fhip, for the carrying of goods, they fhall, *bonâ
fide*, mutually perform and comply with fuch contract
and agreement; nor fhall it be lawful for the merchant, by preferring other fhips, though Britifh, to
detain the Dantzic fhip beyond the appointed time.
In like manner alfo, the Britifh mafters of fhips, as
often as they cut the cable, fhall be obliged to make
good the lofs accruing thereby to the Dantzic mafters of fhips who were not in fault, not only by paying one Englifh fhilling, but the true and juft price
thereof.

And, as all and fingular the premifes contained in
the foregoing articles are agreed and confented unto;
fo, after the approbation and ratification thereof by
the moft Serene and Potent Queen of Great Britain
fhall come and be exchanged with the ratification in
like manner to be delivered by the Noble Magiftracy
of Dantzic, they fhall conftantly and inviolably be obferved in all and every the points and claufes thereof.

In teftimony and greater confirmation whereof, the
Minifter and Plenipotentiary of the moft Serene
and Potent Queen of Great Britain, as well as
the Deputies of the Noble Magiftracy of Dantzic, have fubfcribed and ratified thefe articles with
their hands and feals. Done at Dantzic the $\frac{11}{13}$
day of October, in the year 1706.

J. Robinfon, (L. S.)   *Gabriel von Boemeln,*   (L. S.)
                         Jo. Erneft von der Linde, (L. S.)

[The

[The following is printed from the copy which was
publiſhed by authority in 1717.]

H A M B O U R G.

IN the Convention which was made in the year
1609, between the States of the province of Holland and this city, it is laid down as a certain principle, that Herrings caught before Midſummer-day
cannot be at their maturity; and therefore thoſe
States and this city agreed, that no Herrings caught
before that day ſhould be brought in and ſold here.
But Mr. Wich, Reſident of the King of Great Britain, having inſiſted with the Senate that his Majeſty's ſubjects might be allowed to bring Herrings here
as ſoon as they can; the Senate came to a reſolution
thereupon, which was entered in their Protocol the
3d of April, 1716, and a copy of it, ſigned by their
Secretary, was delivered to the ſaid Britiſh Reſident,
being as follows.

Extract from the Protocol *of the Senate of* Hambourg,
the 3d of April, 1716.

Reſolved to depute the Syndic, M. Sillem, and
M. van Sam, to communicate to the Reſident of his
Britannic Majeſty, an authentic copy of the treaty
made with the States of Holland; and to repreſent
to him, that he will ſee by it, how it has always been
laid down for an unalterable principle, that no Herring can come to its maturity before Midſummer-
day; for which reaſon the Senate cannot take upon
them to change the eſtabliſhed rule. However, the
Senate does hereby give aſſurance to the Reſident,
that if the ſubjects of his Britannic Majeſty can give
proof that there is no true ground for this principle
which has obtained, and will bring hither before
Midſummer-day Herrings in maturity, then the Senate will not make any difficulty to let them be imported.   *Nich. Luke Schaffshauſen,* Secretary.

This permiſſion was confirmed by the Senate, under
the privy ſeal of the city, on the 3d of July, 1716.

6

[The following Convention is printed from the original.]

Convention renouvellée et amplifiée, entre Sa Majefté Britannique et la Ville d'Hambourg, touchant le Commerce des Harengs. Fevrier 8me, 1719.

A SAVOIR qu'entre le féréniffime et très-puiffant Prince et Seigneur, George, Roi de la Grande Bretagne, &c. par fon Miniftre Réfident, Monfieur Cyrille de Wich, d'un côté; et la Louable République d'Hambourg, par les Députés de fon Honorable Senat, les Sieurs Jean Anderfon, Syndic, Pierre Burmefter, et Henry Dieteric Wiefe, Senateurs, de l'autre côté; en vertu de leurs Pouvoirs et Commiffions, la Convention de l'année 1711 a été renouvellée, expliquée et amplifiée dans les fuivans Articles, pour fervir de Reglement conftant au libre Commerce du Hareng qui fe pêche par les Sujets de Sa Majefté Britannique fur les côtes de fes Royaumes.

I. La Ville d'Hambourg accorde la permiffion, que le Hareng qui fe pêche fur les côtes de la Grande Bretagne foit apporté librement à ladite Ville, en payant les mêmes droits d'entrée qui fe payent ordinairement pour le Hareng Flamand ou Hollandois.

II. Ce Hareng, dès fon arrivée, fera tout mis dans le magazin, ou les magazins qu'on jugera les plus convenables et propres pour y être gardé, moyennant que les propriétaires en payent un loyer raifonnable par tonneau, felon qu'ils en pourront convenir avec le maître du magazin.

III. Ce Hareng fera ouvert dans la cour du magazin, de la même maniere que celui de Hollande, à la vue de tous ceux qui voudront y être préfens; la faumure en fera tirée; et après que le vuide des tonneaux fera rempli de bons poiffons, la faumure y fera remife, le poiffon reftant toujours dans fon premier tonneau, fans être rempacqueté d'un tonneau à l'autre. De plus, il fera taxé, et on mettra, felon fa qualité, la marque et le cercle convenables fur le fonds et au

milieu

milieu de chaque tonneau; et pour faire voir que ce n'est pas du Hareng Flamand ou Hollandois, mais celui de la Grande Bretagne, on fera brûler au fond de chaque tonneau un B couronné.

IV. Pour cette fin le Senat s'oblige de choisir et constituer deux taxadeurs, ordinairement dits *Wraquers*, et deux empacqueteurs; et afin qu'on ne les puisse pas soupçonner de partialité, ils n'auront aucune dépendance ni communauté avec les *Schonenfahrers*: Et ces dits *Wraquers* et empacqueteurs feront un serment solemnel, conforme au sens de cet Article, devant l'Honorable Senat, lequel serment leur sera réitéré tous les ans, au commencement de Juin, par les Députés du Senat.

V. Si les propriétaires, ou leurs commissionnaires, viennent en personne avec leur Hareng, ils auront la liberté de le vendre indifféremment aux bourgeois ou habitans de la Ville, à qui ils voudront: mais si, dans l'espace de huit jours, ils ne le pourroient débiter à ceux-ci, il leur sera permis de le vendre à quiconque ils voudront, ou même de l'envoyer hors de la Ville, à tel endroit qu'ils jugeront convenable.

VI. Quand les propriétaires voudront envoyer leur Hareng à des commissionnaires, pour le débiter, ils seront tenus de choisir leur commissionnaire, ou d'entre la Louable Société Anglicane, résidante dans la Ville, ou d'entre les bourgeois, qui, alors, le pourront vendre à quiconque leur plaira, ou l'envoyer hors de la Ville, où bon leur semblera.

VII. Outre ce dont on est déjà convenu ci-dessus, les Sujets de Sa Majesté Britannique jouiront toujours des mêmes privilèges et avantages dans ce Commerce des Harengs, qui font déjà accordés, ou qui pourroient à l'avenir être accordés, aux Sujets de Leurs Hautes Puissances, Messieurs les Etats Généraux des Provinces-Unies.

VIII. De même, il est permis aux Sujets de Sa Majesté Britannique d'apporter à Hambourg des Saumons,

mons, Merlus, Morues, et toute autre forte de poiſſon,
foit ſéchés ou fumés, en barriques ou ſalés; bien entendu qu'ils payent, comme de coutume, le droit
d'entrée ou gabelle modique: de la même maniere
il eſt reſervé aux habitans et bourgeois d'Hambourg,
de négocier, ſelon leur ancienne coutume, aux Provinces des Royaumes Britanniques, d'y mener des
marchandiſes, et de les troquer ou changer contre ces
ſortes de Poiſſons et d'autres denrées.

> En foi de quoi, et en vertu des Ordres et Plein-pou-
> voirs, que nous ſuſdits, le Miniſtre de la Grande
> Bretagne, et les Députés d'Hambourg, avons
> reçu de Sa Majeſté le Roi de la Grande Bretagne,
> d'une part, et de l'Honorable Senat, de l'autre,
> nous avons ſigné la préſente Convention renou-
> vellée, et y avons fait appoſer les ſceaux de nos
> armes. Fait à Hambourg, ce 8 Fevrier 1719.

(L. S.) *Cyrill Wich.*
> (L. S.) *Johann. Anderſon*, Syndicus.
> (L. S.) *Petrus Burmeſter*, Roſſman.
> (L. S.) *Henricus Ditericus Wieſe*, Senateur.

[The following Convention with the city of Bremen is printed from a copy in the books of the Board
of Trade, V. 8.]

*Convention conclue entre Sa Majeſté Britannique et la
Ville de Bremen, touchant le Commerce des Harengs,
1731.*

SOIT notoire à tous ceux qui y ont interêt, qu'en-
tre le ſéréniſſime et très-puiſſant Prince et Seigneur
George II. Roi de la Grande Bretagne, &c. &c. par
ſon Envoyé Extraordinaire le Chevalier, Baronet Cyrill
Wich, d'un côté; et la Louable République de Bremen,
par les Députés de ſon Honorable Senat, les Sieurs
Chriſtian Schöne, et Gaſpar à Rheden, Docteurs en
Droit, de l'autre côté; en vertu de leurs Pouvoirs et
Commiſſions; il a été conclu et arrêté les Articles

ſuivans, pour ſervir de Reglement conſtant au libre Commerce du Hareng qui ſe pêche par les Sujets de Sa Majeſté Britannique ſur les côtes de ſes Royaumes.

I. La Ville de Bremen accorde la permiſſion que le Hareng qui ſe pêche ſur les côtes de la Grande Bretagne, avant ou après le 24ᵉ de Juin N. St. ſoit apporté librement à ladite Ville, en payant les mêmes droits d'entrée qui ſe payent ordinairement pour le Hareng Flamand ou Hollandois, ſans qu'ils ayent beſoin de produire aucun certificat fermenté touchant le tems que ce Hareng ait été pêché ou pris.

II. Ce Hareng, dès ſon arrivée, ſera tout mis dans le magazin ou les magazins qu'on jugera les plus convenables et propres pour y être gardé, moyennant que les propriétaires en payent un loyer raiſonnable par tonneau, ſelon qu'ils en pourront convenir avec le maître du magazin.

III. Ce Hareng ſera ouvert dans la cour du magazin, à la vue de tous ceux qui voudront y être préſens; la ſaumure en ſera tirée; et après que le vuide des tonneaux ſera rempli de bons poiſſons, la ſaumure y ſera remiſe, le poiſſon reſtant toujours dans ſon premier tonneau, ſans être rempacqueté d'un tonneau à l'autre. De plus, il ſera taxé; et on mettra, ſelon ſa qualité, la marque et le cercle convenables ſur le fonds et au milieu de chaque tonneau: et pour faire voir que c'eſt du Hareng de la Grande Bretagne, on fera brûler au fond de chaque tonneau un B. couronné, auſſi bien que l'an de la pêche de ce Hareng.

IV. Pour cette fin, le Senat s'oblige de choiſir et conſtituer deux taxadeurs, ordinairement dits Wraquers et deux empacqueteurs; et afin qu'on ne les puiſſe pas ſoupçonner de partialité, ils feront un ſerment ſolemnel devant l'Honorable Senat, de taxer les Harengs Britanniques ſelon leur bonté et exacte valeur, et de les empacqueter avec tout le ſoin imaginable; lequel ſerment, conforme au ſens de cet Article, leur

ſera

fera réitéré tous les ans, au commencement de Juin, par les Députés du Sénat.

V. Si les propriétaires, où leurs commissionnaires, viennent en personne à Bremen avec leur Hareng, ils auront la liberté de le vendre indifféremment aux bourgeois ou habitans de la Ville, à qui ils voudront : mais si, dans l'espace de huit jours, ils ne pourroient débiter leurs Harengs à ceux-ci, il leur sera permis de les vendré à quiconque ils voudront, ou même de l'envoyer hors de la Ville, à tel endroit qu'ils jugeront convénable.

VI. Quand les propriétaires voudront envoyer leurs Harengs à des commissionnaires, pour les débiter, ils feront tenus de choisir pour commissionnaire un Marchand Britannique, demeurant à Bremen, ou quelque bourgeois de la Ville, qui alors le pourront vendre ou l'envoyer hors de la Ville, où bon leur semblera, selon le sens de l'Article précédent.

VII. Outre ce dont on est déjà convenu ci-dessus, les Sujets de Sa Majesté Britannique jouiront toujours des mêmes privileges et avantages dans ce trafic des Harengs, et tous autres commerces sans exception, qui sont deja accordés, ou qui pourroient à l'avenir être accordés, aux Sujets d'aucune Puissance la plus favorisée.

VIII. De même, il est permis aux Sujets de Sa Majesté Britannique d'apporter à Bremen des Saumons, Merlus, Morues, et toute autre sorte de poissons, soit séchés ou fumés, en barriques ou salés; bien entendu qu'ils payent le droit d'entrée, ou la gabelle modique.

De la même maniere, il est réservé aux habitans et bourgeois de Bremen de négocier, selon leur ancienne coutume, aux Provinces des Royaumes Britanniques, d'y mener des marchandises, et de troquer ou changer contre ces sortes de poissons et d'autres denrées.

IX. Tout ce qui eſt contenu dans les précédens Articles, ſera confirmé et ratifié par Sa Majeſté Britannique et le Senat de Bremen, dans les formes authentiques et uſitées, dans l'eſpace de ſix ſemaines, ou plutôt, ſi faire ſe peut; et les inſtrumens ſeront échangés dans le terme ſuſmentionné.

En foi de quoi, et en vertu des Ordres et Plein-pouvoirs que nous ſuſdits, l'Envoyé Extraordinaire de la Grande Bretagne, et les Deputés de Bremen, avons reçus de Sa Majeſté le Roi de la Grande Bretagne, d'une part, et l'Honorable Senat, de l'autre, nous avons ſigné la préſente Convention, et y avons fait appoſer les ſceaux de nos armes. Fait a Bremen, ce 17ᵉ d'Octobre 1731.

      (L. S.)   *Cyrill Wich.*
      (L. S.)   *Chretien Schöne* D.
      (L. S.)   *Gaſp. à Rheden.*

PRUSSIA.

PRUSSIA.

1701.
30 Dec.
THE treaty of alliance between Great Britain, Pruffia, and the States General, concluded at the Hague.
Pap. Off. I. 14.
Rouffet's Suppl. Corps Diplom. tom. ii. part 2. p. 12.

1702.
$\frac{9}{20}$ Jan.
The treaty of alliance between Great Britain and Pruffia, with the feparate article, concluded at London.
Pap. Off. I. 15.

1702.
18 Feb.
The King of Pruffia's acceffion to the grand alliance between the Emperor, Great Britain, and the States General.
Pap. Off. I. 16.

1719.
4 Aug.
The treaty between Great Britain and Pruffia, with the feparate and fecret article, concluded at Berlin.
Pap. Off. I. 26.

1723.
10 Oct.
The treaty between Great Britain and Pruffia, with the feparate and fecret articles, concluded at Charlottenburg.
Pap. Off. I. 27.

1725.
3 Sept.
The treaty between Great Britain, Pruffia, and France, with the feparate and fecret articles, concluded at Hanover.
Pap. Off. I. 29.
Treat. 1732, vol. iv. p. 146.
Treat. 1785, vol. ii. p. 274.

1742.

1742.   The treaty of defensive alliance between
18 Nov.   Great Britain and Pruffia, with the feparate
            and fecret article, concluded at Weftmin-
            fter.   *Pap. Off.* I. 32.

1745.   The preliminary articles between Great
$\frac{14}{25}$ Aug.   Britain and Pruffia, to ferve as a bafis for a
            treaty of peace between the King of Pruf-
            fia, the Queen of Hungary, and the King
            of Poland.
                        Pap. Off. I. 37, 38.

1756,   The feveral conventions between Great
   to   Britain and Pruffia.
1760.   *Pap. Off.* I. 39, 40, 41, 42, 43, 44,
                        Treat. 1785, vol. iii. p. 54—70.

1788.   The treaty of defenfive alliance, between
13 Aug.   Great Britain and Pruffia, concluded at
            Berlin.

[The following is printed from the copy, which was
publifhed by authority.]

*The Treaty of Defenfive Alliance between his Majefty
the King of Great Britain, and his Majefty the King
of Pruffia.*

THEIR Majefties the King of Great Britain, and
the King of Pruffia, being animated with a fincere
and equal defire to improve and confolidate the ftrict
union and friendfhip, which having been tranfmitted to
them by their anceftors, fo happily fubfift between
them, and to concert the moft proper meafures for
fecuring their mutual interefts, and the general tranquillity of Europe, have refolved to renew and ftrength-
en thefe ties by a treaty of defenfive alliance; and
they have authorized, for this purpofe (to wit) his
Majefty the King of Great Britain, the Sieur Jofeph
Ewart,

Ewart, his Envoy Extraordinary at the Court of Berlin; and his Majefty the King of Pruffia, the Sieur Ewald Frederick, Count de Hertzberg; his Minifter of State, and of the Cabinet, Knight of the Order of the Black Eagle: who, after reciprocally communicating their full powers to each other, have agreed upon the following articles:

I. There fhall be a perpetual, firm, and unalterable friendfhip, defenfive alliance, and ftrict and inviolable union, together with an intimate and perfect harmony and correfpondence between the faid moft Serene Kings of Great Britain and Pruffia, their heirs and fucceffors, and their refpective kingdoms, dominions, provinces, countries, and fubjects, which fhall be carefully maintained and cultivated, fo that the contracting powers fhall conftantly employ, as well their utmoft attention, as all thofe means which Providence has put in their power, for preferving at the fame time the public tranquillity and fecurity, for maintaining their common interefts, and for their mutual defence and guaranty againft every hoftile attack; the whole in conformity to the treaties already fubfifting between the high·contracting parties, which fhall remain in full force and vigour, and fhall be deemed to be renewed by the prefent treaty, as far as the fame fhall not be derogated from, with their own confent, by pofterior treaties, or by the prefent treaty.

II. In confequence of the engagement contracted by the preceding article, the two high contracting parties fhall always act in concert for the maintenance of peace and tranquillity; and in cafe either of them fhould be threatened with a hoftile attack by any power whatever, the other fhall employ his moft efficacious good offices for preventing hoftilities, for procuring fatisfaction to the injured party, and for effecting an accommodation in a conciliatory manner.

III. But if thofe good offices fhould not have the defired effect, in the fpace of two months, and either

of

of the two high contracting parties should be hostilely
attacked, molested, or disturbed in any of his dominions, rights, possessions, or interests, or in any manner
whatever, by sea or land, by any European power, the
other contracting party engages to succour his ally
without delay, in order to maintain each other reciprocally in the possession of all the dominions, territories, towns, and places, which belonged to them
before the commencement of such hostilities: for
which end, if his Prussian Majesty should happen to
be attacked, his Majesty the King of Great Britain
shall furnish to his Majesty the King of Prussia a succour of sixteen thousand infantry, and four thousand
cavalry; and if his Britannic Majesty should happen
to be attacked, his Majesty the King of Prussia shall
likewise furnish to him a succour of sixteen thousand
infantry, and four thousand cavalry; which respective
succours shall be furnished in the space of two months
after requisition made by the party attacked, and shall
remain at his disposal during the whole continuance of
the war in which he shall be engaged. These succours
shall be paid and maintained by the required power,
wherever his ally shall employ them; but the requiring
party shall supply them, in his dominions, with such
bread and forage as may be necessary, upon the footing to which his own troops are accustomed.

It is nevertheless agreed between the high contracting parties, that if his Britannic Majesty should be
in the case of receiving the succour in troops from his
Prussian Majesty, his Britannic Majesty shall not employ them out of Europe, nor even in the garrison of
Gibraltar.

If the injured and requiring party should prefer
succours in money to land forces, he shall have his
choice: and in case of the two high contracting parties
furnishing to each other the stipulated succours in
money, such succours shall be computed at one hundred thousand florins, Dutch currency, per annum, for
one thousand infantry, and at one hundred and twenty
                                                    thousand

thoufand florins, of the like value, for one thoufand cavalry, per annum, or in the fame proportion by the month.

IV. In cafe the ftipulated fuccours fhould not be fufficient for the defence of the requiring power, the required power fhall augment them, according to the exigency of the cafe, and fhall affift the former with his whole force, if circumftances fhall render it neceffary.

V. The high contracting parties hereby renew, in the moft exprefs terms, the provifional treaty of defenfive alliance which they concluded at Loo, on the 13th of June in the prefent year, and they again engage and promife to act, at all times, in concert, and with mutual confidence, for maintaining the fecurity, independance, and government of the republic of the United Provinces, conformably to the engagements which they have lately contracted with the faid republic; that is to fay, his Britannic Majefty, by a treaty concluded at the Hague, on the 15th of April, 1788, and his Pruffian Majefty, by a treaty figned the fame day at Berlin, which the faid high contracting parties have communicated to each other.

And if it fhall happen that, by virtue of the ftipulations of the faid treaties, the high contracting parties fhould be obliged to augment the fuccours to be given to the States General, above the numbers fpecified in the faid treaties, or to affift them with their whole force, the faid high contracting parties will concert together upon all that may be neceffary relative to fuch augmentation of fuccours to be agreed on, and to the employment of their refpective forces for the fecurity and defence of the faid republic.

In cafe either of the faid high contracting parties fhould happen, at any time hereafter, to be attacked, molefted, or difturbed, in any of his dominions, rights, poffeffions, or interefts, in any manner whatever, by fea or by land, by any other power, in confequence

and

and in hatred of the articles or ftipulations contained in the faid treaties, or of the meafures to be taken by the faid contracting parties refpectively, in virtue of thofe treaties, the other contracting party engages to fuccour and affift him againft fuch attack, in the fame manner, and by the fame fuccours as are ftipulated in the third and fourth articles of the prefent treaty; and the faid contracting parties promife, in all fimilar cafes, to maintain and guaranty each other in the poffeffion of all the dominions, towns, and places, which be-longed to them refpectively before the commencement of fuch hoftilities.

VI. The prefent treaty of defenfive alliance fhall be ratified by each party, and the ratifications fhall be exchanged in the fpace of fix weeks, or fooner, if it can be done.

In witnefs whereof, we the underwritten, being au-thorized by the full powers of their Majefties the Kings of Great Britain and of Pruffia, have in their names figned the prefent treaty, and have thereto fet the feals of our arms.

Done at Berlin, the thirteenth of Auguft, in the year of our Lord one thoufand feven hundred and eighty-eight.

(L. S.) *Jofeph Ewart.*   (L. S.) *Ewald Frederic,*
                                  Comte de Hertzberg.

The STATES GENERAL.

1578.
7 Jan.
THE treaty of alliance between Queen Elizabeth and the States General
Trait de Paix, tom. ii. p. 391.
Treat. 1732, vol. ii. p. 81.

1585.
10 Aug.
The treaty between the fame parties, concluded at Nonfuch.
Trait de Paix, tom. ii. p. 512.
Treat. 1732, vol. ii. p. 83.

1598.
16 Aug.
The treaty and renewment of alliance between Queen Elizabeth and the States General, concluded at Weftminfter.
Rym. Fæd. vol. xvi. p. 340.
Treat. 1732, vol. ii. p. 120.
Trait de Paix, tom. ii. p. 631.

1608.
27 June.
The defenfive and commercial treaty between King James and the States General.
Pap. Off. D. 1.
Rym. Fæd. vol. xvi. p. 687.

1624.
5 June.
The treaty for continuing the defenfive league between King James and the States General, in 1608, concluded at London.
Pap. Off. D. 3.
Treat. 1732, vol. ii. p. 226.
Trait de Paix, tom. iii. p. 213.

1625.
17 Sept.
The treaty of alliance offenfive and defenfive, between Charles I. King of Great Britain and the States General, concluded at Southampton.
Pap. Off. D. 4.
Treat. 1732, vol. ii. p. 248.
Trait de Paix, tom. iii. p. 231.

6   1654.

1654.
5 April.
The treaty of peace and union between Oliver Cromwell and the States General, concluded at Weftminfter.
> *Pap. Off.* D. 8.
> *Treat.* 1732, vol. iii. p. 67.
> *Treat.* 1785, vol. i. p. 44.
> *Trait de Paix*, tom. iii. p. 647.

1661.
11 Apr.
The convention for the regulation of the
pofts between England and the United Provinces, concluded at London.
> *Treat.* 1732, vol. iii. p. 234.
> *Treat.* 1785, vol. i. p. 159.

1667.
$\frac{21}{31}$ July.
The articles of peace and alliance between
King Charles II. and the United Nether-
lands, concluded at Bredah.

1668.
23 Jan.
The triple league between Great Britain,
the States General, and Sweden, concluded
at the Hague.
> *Pap. Off.* D. 13.
> *Treat.* 1732, vol. i. p. 136.

166$\frac{7}{8}$.
17 Feb.
The treaty of commerce betwixt Great
Britain and Holland, concluded at the Hague.
> *Pap. Off.* D. 14.
> *Treat.* 1732, vol. i. p. 146.
> *Treat.* 1785, vol. i. p. 190.

1668.
15 Apr.
The treaty between Great Britain, France,
and Holland, for procuring a peace between
France and Spain, concluded at St. Germain
en leye.
> *Treat.* 1732, vol. i. p. 152.
> *Treat.* 1785, vol. i. p. 193.

167$\frac{3}{4}$.
$\frac{9}{19}$ Feb.
The treaty of peace between Great Britain
and Holland, concluded at Weftminfter.
> *Pap. Off.* D. 17.
> *Treat.* 1732, vol. iii. p. 275.

1674.

1674.   The marine treaty between Great Britain
1 Dec.   and Holland, concluded at London.
Pap. Off. D. 18.

1675.   The articles between King Charles II. and
8 Mar.   the States General, for preventing difputes
between the Englifh and Dutch Eaft India
Companies.
Pap. Off. D. 21.

1678.   The treaty of a defenfive alliance between
$\frac{16}{26}$ Jan.   Great Britain and the States General, with
the feparate articles, concluded at the Hague.
Pap. Off. D. 24.
Treat. 1732, vol. i. p. 177.
Treat. 1785, vol. i. p. 211.

1678.   The treaty of defenfive alliance between
3 Mar.   Great Britain and the States General, concluded at Weftminfter.
Pap. Off. D. 26.
Treat. 1732, vol. i. p. 183.

1678.   The treaty of alliance between Great Bri-
$\frac{15}{25}$ July.   tain and the States General, concluded at
the Hague.
Pap. Off. D. 28.
Treat. 1732, vol. i. p. 188.

1689.   The grand alliance between Great Bri-
12 May. tain, the Emperor, and the States General,
20 Dec. concluded at Vienna.
Pap. Off. D. 30.
Treat. 1732, vol. i. p. 275.

1689.   The treaty of alliance between England
24 Aug. and Holland, concluded at Whitehall.
Pap. Off. 32.
Treat. 1732, vol. i. p. 287.

1690

1690.   The treaty between Great Britain, Hol-
20 Oct.   land, and Savoy, with the secret article, con-
         cluded at the Hague.
              Treat. 1732, vol. iii. p. 334.
              Treat. 1785, vol. i. p. 286.

1698.   The convention between Great Britain,
$\frac{4}{14}$ May.   Sweden, and the States General, for a de-
         fensive league, concluded at the Hague.
              Pap. Off. D. 36.
              Treat. 1732, vol. iii. p. 344.

1698.   The first treaty of partition in favour of
11 Oct.   the Electoral Prince of Bavaria, made be-
         twixt Great Britain, France, and the States
         General, concluded at the Hague.
              Pap. Off. 38.
              Treat. 1732, vol. i. p. 386.
              Treat. 1785, vol. i. p. 305.

1700.   The treaty of alliance between Great Bri-
$\frac{11}{22}$ Jan.   tain, Sweden, and the States General, usu-
         ally called The Second Partition Treaty,
         with the secret and separate articles, con-
         cluded at the Hague.
              Pap. Off. 39.
              Treat. 1732, vol. iii. p. 347.
              Treat. 1785, vol. i. p. 313.

1701.   The treaty of alliance between Great Bri-
20 Jan.   tain, Denmark, and the States General,
         concluded at Odensee.
              Treat. 1785, vol. i. p. 331.

1709.   The treaty between Great Britain and the
29 Oct.   States General, for securing the succession
         to the crown of Great Britain, and for set-
         tling a barrier to the States General, with
         the separate articles, concluded at the
         Hague.
              Pap. Off. 50.
              Treat. 1785, vol. i. p. 354.

1713. 29 Jan. —————— 13 Feb.	The treaty of guaranty for the Proteſtant ſucceſſion to the crown of Great Britain, and for the barrier of the States General, concluded at Utrecht. *Pap. Off.* D. 55. *Treat.* 1785, vol. i. p. 364.
1716. 6 Feb.	The treaty between Great Britain and the States General, for renewal of former alliances and conventions. *Pap. Off.* D. 58.
1717. 4 Jan.	The treaty of alliance between Great Britain, France, and the States General, for the guaranty of the treaties of Utrecht. *Pap. Off.* D. 59. *Rouſſet's Recueil Hiſtorique,* tom. i. p. 89. *Treat.* 1785, vol. ii. p. 185.
1718. 22 July. —————— 2 Aug.	The treaty uſually called The Quadruple Alliance, between Great Britain, France, and the States General, concluded at London. *Rouſſet's Recueil Hiſtorique,* tom. i. p. 180. *Treat.* 1785, vol. ii. p. 199.
1718. 22 Dec.	The convention between the Emperor, Great Britain, and the States General, for executing certain articles of the barrier treaty, ſigned at the Hague. *Pap. Off.* D. 61. *Rouſſet's Recueil Hiſtorique,* tom. i. p. 400. *Treat.* 1785, vol. ii. p. 228.
1726. 9 Aug.	The acceſſion of the States General to the treaty of Hanover, 1725. *Pap. Off.* D. 64. *Rouſſet's Recueil Hiſtorique,* tom. iii. p. 166. *Treat.* 1785, vol. ii. p. 281.

1731.

1731.
16 Mar.
The treaty of peace and alliance between the Emperor, Great Britain, and the States-General, concluded at Vienna.
> *Pap. Off.* D. 72.
> *Rouffet's Recueil Hiftorique*, vol. vi. p. 13.
> *Rouffet's Suppl. au Corps Diplomatique*, tom. ii. part 2, p. 288.
> *Treat.* 1785, vol. ii. p. 318.

1748.
18 Oct.
The treaty of peace between Great Britain, France, and the States General, concluded at Aix-la-Chapelle.
> *Pap. Off.* D. 88.
> *Treat.* 1785, vol. ii. p. 370.
> *See this Treaty*, vol. i. Table of Contents, art. FRANCE.

1784.
20 May.
The treaty of peace between Great Britain and the States General, concluded at Paris. *Treat.* 1785, vol. iii. p. 427.

1788.
15 Apr.
The treaty of defenfive alliance between Great Britain and the States General, concluded at the Hague.

An Agreement and Convention, fcr the Regulation and fpeedy Difpatch of the Pofts, betwixt England *and the* United Provinces. *At* London, April 11, 1661.

Articles drawn up and agreed to between his Excellency Simon van Hoorn, Ambaffador of the High and Mighty Lords the States General of the United Provinces of the Netherlands, in the name and by order of the venerable Lords the Burgomafters and Counfellors of Amfterdam, and of Henry Jacob vander Heyden, Poft-mafter of certain towns in the United Provinces, on one part; and Henry Bifhop, Efq; Mafter of the General Pofts of all England,

England, and from thence to all other kingdoms and countries, on the other part, in the 10th year of the reign of Charles II. King of England, Scotland, &c. Defender of the Faith.

I T has been reciprocally promifed and agreed betwixt the faid Simon van Hoorn, in name and by order of the faid Lords the Burgomafters and the Magiftrates of Amfterdam, as alfo of the faid Henry Jacob vander Heyden, and the faid Henry Bifhop, that a way and a method fhould be concerted which might be more commodious and more expeditious than thofe hitherto made ufe of for the fending of letters every week precifely from England to the United Provinces, and from the United Provinces to England, in fuch manner that letters fhould be brought every week directly from England to fome harbour of the faid United Provinces, and in like manner from the faid United Provinces to England.

For this end the following articles have been confidered and agreed to between the parties, viz.

The faid Henry Bifhop has agreed with and promifed the faid Lord Simon van Hoorn, as the perfon vefted with the full powers of the faid Lords the Burgomafters and the Magiftracy of Amfterdam, and of Henry Jacob vander Heyden, that he will keep ready, and maintain at his own expence, a fufficient number of veffels, built in England, by which once a week upon a certain day fixed, viz. Saturday, packets of letters fhall be brought from England to Amfterdam, and other towns and offices of the United Provinces; and that care fhall be taken that the faid packets of letters fhall be carried beyond fea, with as much expedition as the wind and weather will permit, and that they fhall be fafely delivered at Helvoetfluys, Flufhing, or fome other harbour which the contracting parties fhall agree on, unlefs hindered by fome misfortune that happens at fea.

VOL. I.   K   Alfo

Alfo the said Henry Bishop shall so order it, that the packets of letters which shall be sent from Amsterdam, or any other place in the United Provinces, be taken in every Saturday at such ports, and that they be carried in like manner to the ports of England, with as much expedition as the wind and weather will permit, and from thence forwarded to the offices at London, for delivery to such persons as they shall be directed to.

Moreover, the said Henry Bishop has agreed and promised the said Lord Simon van Hoorn, in the name and character as above, and made the like agreement with the said vander Heyden, that he will keep an exact account of the weight of all packets of letters that shall be sent by the way of Amsterdam to Hamburgh and Dantzic, or to any part of Italy or the North; and that computing from the day when the said account shall commence, he will cause a payment to be made every three months to the Lords Burgomasters and Magistrates of Amsterdam, at the rate of an English shilling for every ounce weight of letters that shall be sent that way to Hamburgh, Italy, or the northern countries.

The said Henry Bishop likewise promises the said Lords the Burgomasters and Magistrates of Amsterdam, to pay them 12 *d*. English for every ounce weight of letters from Italy, that shall be sent through the said city of Amsterdam to England; and as to the letters from Hamburgh, Dantzic, and the North, which are directed for England, they shall pay the common postage at Amsterdam, as was formerly practised at Antwerp.

In consideration of which, the said Henry Jacob vander Heyden promises the said Henry Bishop (the said Lords Burgomasters and the Magistrates of Amsterdam engaging in like manner to perform this contract, as far as concerns them) to pay or order to be paid the sum of 500 *l*. sterling every year for the charge and maintenance of the said ships; which sum, to be

paid

paid quarterly, viz. 125 l. every three months, shall commence from the 25th of December next ensuing the date and subscription of this contract. And if it happen that the said sum of 500 l. or a part thereof, be not paid to the said Henry Bishop in the manner aforesaid, by the said vander Heyden, in that case the said Lords the Burgomasters engage themselves, and promise to pay it to the said Bishop, or his order.

And the said Lords Burgomasters and Magistrates of Amsterdam do further promise the said Henry Bishop, to establish and carry on a constant post every week for Hamburgh and Dantzic, and for all the trading towns of Germany, the North, and Italy; and also that the said post shall make as much dispatch both forward and backward as ever any post did or can do, in these provinces; and that it shall keep a regular time and method both in setting out from Amsterdam, in arriving there, and in setting out from thence for England, and the like to all the other towns of the United Provinces. Whereupon the said Jacob vander Heyden obliges himself, and promises to settle fit persons in the towns, and especially at the ports, (which places shall hereafter be named by the parties) there to wait for, and receive all packets of letters that shall be brought over by the vessels of the said Henry Bishop, and to send them from one town to another with all speed, and with the same expedition to bring packets of letters from those towns to the harbours; and to put them on board the vessels of the said Bishop, which shall lie ready to receive them: the Lords Burgomasters and the Magistrates of Amsterdam promising also to cause the same to be executed accordingly, as far as it relates to them.

Moreover, the said Henry Jacob vander Heyden obliges himself (the Lords Burgomasters of Amsterdam promising it also on their part) that he will take care that the salaries of the clerks appointed, or to be appointed for that end in the several places;

shall

fhall be paid punctually and without delay; and that there fhall be always at Amfterdam, and the other towns of the United Provinces, a fufficient number of clerks capable to receive, diftribute, and fend all the packets that fhall be received and fent, to maintain a continual correfpondence with the faid Henry Bifhop's poft-mafters, and to keep exact regifters of all the packets received or fent, and of their weight.

The Lords Burgomafters and the Magiftrates of Amfterdam do likewife promife the faid Henry Bifhop, to give orders that the poftage of letters from England to Amfterdam be fo regulated, as not to exceed the rate that was paid for them, when they were brought by the way of Antwerp.

By means hereof, a firm and true friendfhip will be eftablifhed between the parties, with a fincere correfpondence, for the reciprocal profit and advantage of both parties; and if any difference happen between them, relating to the performance and execution of the faid articles and conditions, they fhall be referred to the decifion of fome impartial arbitrators, who fhall be named on both fides, and in whofe award both fides fhall acquiefce.

The parties have alfo agreed, that if any packets of the merchants, or other parcels neceffary to be communicated, be put into their hands, they fhall be fent on an extraordinary day, without ftaying for Saturday, which is the day intended for the common letters; but if for this reafon the faid Henry Bifhop be obliged to keep a greater, or twice the number of veffels, in fuch cafe the faid vander Heyden fhall take care, with the affiftance of the Lords the Burgomafters and the Magiftrates of Amfterdam, to pay or caufe to be paid to the faid Bifhop, at the end of every quarter, the fum of fixty-two pounds fterling, towards defraying the extraordinary charge of the veffels. And to the end it may appear that the parties are agreed in all the articles above written, they

they have figned them with their own hands. Done at London the 11th of April, 1661.

(Signed)   *Simon Van Hoorn.*
Henry Bifhop.

And underneath,
We the underwritten are witneffes to this inftrument.

John Widman.
Van Hulft.

[The following is printed from the copy publifhed by authority in 1686.]

> *Articles of Peace and Alliance between the Moft Serene and Mighty Prince,* Charles *the Second, by the Grace of God, King of* England, Scotland, France, *and* Ireland, *Defender of the Faith,* &c. *and the High and Mighty Lords, the States General of the* United Netherlands, *concluded the* $\frac{21}{31}$ *Day of* July, 1667.

I. FIRST, that from this day there be a true, firm, and inviolable peace, fincere friendfhip, a nearer and ftraiter alliance and union between the Moft Serene King of Great Britain, and the High and Mighty States General of the United Provinces of the Netherlands, and the lands, countries, and cities under the obedience of both parties, wherefoever fituate, and their fubjects and inhabitants, of what degree foever they be.

II. Alfo, that for the time to come, all enmities, hoftilities, difcords, and wars, between the faid Lord the King, and the forefaid Lords the States General, and their fubjects and inhabitants, ceafe and be abolifhed; and that both parties do altogether forbear and abftain from all plundering, depredation, harm-doing, injuries, and infeftation whatfoever, as well by land

as

as by sea, and in fresh-waters, every where; and especially through all tracts, dominions, places, and governments (of what condition soever they be) within the jurisdiction of either party.

III. Also, that all offences, injuries, damages, losses, which his said Majesty and his subjects, or the foresaid States General and their subjects, have on either side sustained during this war, or at any time whatsoever heretofore, upon what cause or pretence soever, be buried in oblivion, and totally expunged out of remembrance, as if no such things had ever past.

Furthermore, that the foresaid peace, friendship, and alliance may stand upon firm and unshaken foundations, and that from this very day all occasions of new dissention and difference may may be cut off; it is further agreed, that both the parties, and either of them, shall keep and possess hereafter, with plenary right of sovereignty, propriety, and possession, all such lands, islands, cities, forts, places, and colonies (how many soever) as during this war, or in any former times before this war, they have by force of arms, or any other way whatsoever, gotten and detained from the other party, and that, altogether after the same manner as they had gotten and did possess them the $\frac{10}{20}$ day of May last past, none of the same places being excepted.

IV. Moreover, that all ships, with their furniture and merchandize, and all moveables, which during this war, or at any time heretofore, have come into the power of either of the forementioned parties, or their subjects, be and remain to the present possessors, without any compensation or restitution; so as each one become and remain proprietor and possessor for ever of that which was so gotten, without any controversy, or exception of place, time, or things.

V. Moreover, that all actions, suits, and pretensions, whatsoever they be, or in what manner soever they have been restrained, circumscribed, defined, or reserved, ferved, in any articles of peace or alliance already made (and efpecially in the fifteenth article of that treaty which was figned in the year 1662) which his faid Majefty and the faid States General, or their fubjects, may or would profecute or move againft one another about fuch matters or things as have happened during this war, or in any former times, as well before as after the forefaid treaty of 1662, until the day of this prefent alliance, be and remain void, obliterated, and difannulled; as his faid Majefty and the faid States General fhall declare, and they do hereby declare, that by virtue of thefe prefents they will for ever totally renounce, even as hereby they do renounce, all fuch actions, fuits, and pretenfions, for themfelves and their fucceffors, fo as in regard of them nothing more may or ought ever to be urged on either fide, and nothing to be moved thereupon hereafter.

VI. But if after the $\frac{10}{10}$ day of May, expreffed in the precedent third article, or after the peace is made, or this treaty figned, either party fhall intercept and get from the other any lands, iflands, cities, forts, colonies, or other places whatfoever, all and every of them, without any diftinction of place or time, fhall be reftored *boná fide* in the fame ftate and condition wherein they fhall be found to be at the time whenfoever it fhall be known in thofe places that the peace is made.

VII. But to avoid all matter of ftrife or contention hereafter, that ufeth fometimes to arife concerning the reftitution or liquidation of fuch fhips, merchandize, and other moveables, as both parties, or either of them, may pretend to have been taken or gotten in places and coafts far diftant, after the peace is concluded, and before it be notified unto thofe places; it is agreed, that all fuch fhips, merchandize, and other moveables, which may chance to fall into either party's hands after the conclufion and publication of the prefent inftrument, in the Channel or Britifh fea, within the fpace of twelve days, and the fame in the North fea; and within the fpace of fix weeks, from the mouth of the Channel unto the Cape of St. Vincent; as alfo within the fpace of ten weeks beyond the faid Cape, and on this fide the Equinoctial Line or Equator, as well the ocean and Mediterranean fea, as elfewhere; and from thence within the fpace of eight months, beyond the terms of the forefaid Line, throughout all the world, fhall be and remain unto the poffeffors, without any exception or further diftinction of time or place, or any regard had to the making of reftitution or compen-fation.

VIII. It is alfo agreed, that under the forefaid re-nunciation and ftipulation, all letters whatfoever of reprifal, marque, and counter-marque, both general and particular, and others of that kind, by virtue whereof any hoftility may be exercifed for the future, ought alfo to be reckoned and comprehended; and by the public authority of this alliance they are inhibited and revoked. And if any perfons of either nation, after fuch revocation, fhall neverthelefs, under pretence or authority of fuch letters or commiffions already revoked, defign any new mifchief, or act any hoftility, after the peace is made, and the times fpecified in the precedent feventh article are elapfed, they are to be looked upon as difturbers of the public peace, and punifhed according to the law of nations, befides an entire reftitution of the thing-taken, or full fatisfaction of damages, to which they fhall be liable; notwithftand-ing any claufe whatfoever to the contrary, which may be inferted in the faid letters revoked as aforefaid.

IX. And whereas in countries far remote, as in Africa and America, efpecially in Guinea, certain pro-teftations and declarations, and other writings of that kind, prejudicial to the liberty of trade and navigation, have been emitted and publifhed on either fide by the governors and officers in the name of their fuperiors; it is in like manner agreed, that all and every fuch protef-
tations,

tations, declarations, and writings aforefaid, be abolifhed, and held hereafter for null and void; and that both the above-mentioned parties, and their inhabitants and fubjects, ufe and enjoy the fame liberty of trade and navigation, as well in Africa as in America, which they ufed and enjoyed, or of right might ufe and enjoy, at that time when the treaty of the year 1662 was fubfcribed.

X. Alfo, that prifoners on both fides, one and all, of what degree, dignity, or condition foever they be, fhall be fet at liberty, without ranfom, or any other price of their freedom; provided fatisfaction be made by them for debts which they have contracted for diet or any other lawful caufe.

XI. That the faid King of Great Britain, and the faid States Géneral, remain friends, confederate, united, and allied, for the defence and prefervation of the rights, liberties, and immunities of either ally and their fubjects, againft all whomfoever, who fhall endeavour to difturb the peace of either's ftate by fea or land, or fuch as living within either's dominions, fhall be declared public enemies to either.

XII. That neither the faid King of Great Britain, nor the faid States General, fhall act, do, endeavour, treat, or attempt any thing againft the other, or the fubjects of either, any where, by land or fea, or in any ports, liberties, creeks, or frefh-waters, upon any occafion whatfoever; and that neither they, nor the fubjects of either of them, fhall give, afford, or fupply any aid, counfel, or favour, nor confent that any thing be done, treated, or attempted by any other whofoever, to the harm or prejudice of the other, or the fubjects of either; but fhall exprefsly and actually oppofe, contradict, and really hinder all whomfoever, refiding or dwelling in either the refpective dominions, who fhall act, do, treat, or attempt any thing againft either of them.

XIII. That

XIII. That neither the said King, nor the said Commonwealth, nor any of the subjects of either, inhabiting or residing within their jurisdiction, shall cherish and assist the rebels of either party with any succour, counsel, or favour whatsoever; but shall expressly oppose, and effectually hinder all persons abiding, residing, or dwelling in either of their dominions, from supplying or furnishing any of those foresaid rebels, by sea or land, with any succour or assistance, either in men, ships, arms, warlike furniture, or other prohibited goods, or with money, provisions, or victuals: and all ships, arms, warlike furniture, or other forbidden goods, also money and provisions belonging to any person or persons whatsoever, which shall be supplied or furnished contrary to the meaning of this article, shall be confiscate and forfeited to that party where the persons offending shall be: and those who shall wittingly and willingly act, commit, attempt, or advise any thing contrary to the sense of this article, shall be judged enemies of both parties, and shall be punished as traitors, there where the offence shall be committed. But as touching the specification of prohibited or contraband goods, it shall be provided for hereafter.

XIV. That the said King of Great Britain, and the said States General, shall mutually, sincerely, and faithfully (as there is occasion) assist each other against the rebels of either, by sea or land, with men and ships, at the cost and charges of the parties who desire the same, in such proportion and manner, and upon such conditions, as afterward shall be agreed, and the present occasion shall require.

XV. That neither the said King, nor the said Commonwealth, nor the subjects of either, shall in any of their jurisdictions, countries, lands, havens, sea-ports, creeks, receive any rebel or rebels, fugitive or fugitives, of the other pary, declared, or to be declared, nor shall give or yield unto such declared rebels and
fugitives,

fugitives, in the places aforesaid, or elsewhere, though without their lands, countries, havens, sea-ports, creeks, or jurisdictions, any help, counsel, lodging, soldiers, ships, money, arms, ammunition, or victuals: as also neither of the states shall permit that such rebels or fugitives be received by any person or persons within their jurisdictions, countries, lands, sea-ports, havens, creeks, nor suffer that any help, counsel, lodging, favour, arms, ammunition, soldiers, ships, monies, or provision be given or yielded to such rebels and fugitives; but shall expresly and effectually oppose and really hinder the same.

XVI. That in case either of them by their public and authentic letters shall make known and declare unto the other, that any person or persons are or have been a rebel or rebels, fugitive or fugitives, and that they or any of them have been received, or reside, lie hid, or seek shelter, in their jurisdictions, lands, countries, sea-ports, or in any of them; then that party who shall have received such letters, or to whom such notice shall be given, or declaration made, shall within the space of twenty-eight days, to be accounted from the day that such notice was given, be bound to charge and command such rebel or rebels, fugitive or fugitives, to withdraw and depart out of their jurisdictions, lands, dominions, countries, and every of them: and in case any of the said rebels or fugitives do not withdraw and depart within fifteen days after such charge or command so given, then that they be punished with death, and loss of lands and goods.

XVII. That no rebel of the said King of Great Britain shall be received into any of the castles, cities, havens, jurisdictions, or other places, privileged or not privileged, which any person, of what dignity or degree soever he be, or shall be, hath within the dominions or territories of the United Provinces, by what right or title soever he doth or shall hold or possess the same, nor be permitted to be received into, or remain

in

in them, by any perfon, of what quality or degree
foever he be.   Neither fhall the faid States General
permit or fuffer, that in any of the aforefaid places,
any affiftance, counfel, or favour, with fhips, foldiers,
money, or provifion, or in any other manner, be given
or afforded unto any fuch rebel, by any perfon of what
degree or quality foever he be, but fhall openly and
exprefsly forbid and effectually hinder the` fame.
And if any perfon or perfons, of what degree or quality foever they be, dwelling or remaining within the
dominions of the faid United Provinces, or under their
command, fhall act any thing contrary to this agreement, that then all and fingular fuch perfons fo doing
fhall, for term of their lives refpectively, lofe and forfeit all fuch caftles, towns, villages, lands, and other
places which they or any of them at that time have,
or pretend to have, by what right or title foever.   In
like manner, no rebel of the faid ftates of the United
Provinces fhall be received into any caftles, towns,
havens, or other places, or any of them, privileged
or not privileged, which any perfon or perfons, of
what degree or quality foever they be, and by what
right or title foever he or they do or fhall hold and
poffefs, within the kingdoms or dominions of his faid
Majefty of Great Britain: nor fhall fuch rebel be fuffered to be received by any perfon or perfons whatfoever, or there to remain; neither fhall the King of
Great Britain permit or fuffer, that any counfel, affiftance, or favour, in any of the faid places, with fhips,
men, money, victuals, or in any other manner, be
given or afforded unto any fuch rebel, by any fuch
perfon or perfons, of what degree or quality foever
they be, but fhall openly and exprefsly forbid and
effectually hinder the fame.   And in cafe any of the
fubjects of the faid King, or within his dominions,
fhall do or attempt any thing againft this agreement,
that all and every perfon fo offending fhall in like
manner, for their refpective lives, lofe and forfeit all
fuch caftles, cities, towns, lands, and other places,
                                                    which

which they or any of them at that time, hath, or fhall pretend to have, by any right or title whatfoever.

XVIII. That the faid King of Great Britain and his fubjects, and all the inhabitants of his Majefty's dominions, and alfo the faid United Provinces, and their fubjects and inhabitants, of what rank or condition foever they be, fhall be bound to ufe each other kindly and friendly in every thing; fo that they may freely and fafely pafs by land or by water into each other's countries, cities, towns walled or unwalled, fortified or not fortified, and their havens, and all other their dominions fituate in Europe, to continue and abide therein fo long as they fhall pleafe, and may there buy fo much provifions as are, neceffary for their ufe, without any hinderance: and that likewife they may trade and traffic in goods and commodities of all forts, as to them fhall feem fit, and them to export and import at their pleafure, paying the ufual duties, faving to each country their particular laws and cuftoms. Provided that the fubjects and inhabitants of either fide, exercifing their trade in each other's countries and dominions, fhall not be obliged hereafter to pay any more cuftoms, impoft, or other duties, than according to that proportion which other foreign nations trading in the faid places do ufually pay.

XIX. That the fhips and veffels of the faid United Provinces, as well men of war as others, meeting any men of war of the faid King of Great Britain's in the Britifh feas, fhall ftrike the flag, and lower the top-fail in fuch manner as the fame hath been formerly obferved in any times whatfoever.

XX. And, for the greater freedom of commerce and navigation, it is agreed and concluded, that the faid King of Great Britain, and the faid States General, fhall not receive into their havens, cities, and towns, nor fuffer that any of the fubjects of either party do receive, pirates or fea-rovers, or afford them any entertainment, affiftance, or provifion; but fhall

endeavour

endeavour that the said pirates and sea-rovers, or their
partners, sharers, and abettors, be found out, apprehended, and suffer condign punishment, for the terror
of others: and all the ships, goods, and commodities
piratically taken by them, and brought into the ports
of either party, which can be found, nay, although
they be sold, shall be restored to the right owners,
or satisfaction shall be given either to their owners,
or to those who by letters of attorney shall challenge
the same; provided the right of their propriety be
made to appear in the court of admiralty by due
proofs according to law.

XXI. It shall not be permitted to the subjects of
the said King of Great Britain, and the inhabitants of
the kingdoms and countries under his obedience, or to
the inhabitants and subjects of the said United Provinces, to do or offer any hostility or violence to each
other, either by land or by sea, upon any pretence or
colour whatsoever: and consequently it shall not be
lawful for the said subjects or inhabitants to get commissions or letters of reprisal from any prince or state,
with whom either of the confederates are at difference,
or in open war; and much less by virtue of those
letters to molest or damnify the subjects of either
party.   Neither shall it be lawful for any foreign private men of war, who are not subjects to one nor
the other party, having commissions from any other
prince or state, to equip their ships in the harbours
of either of the aforesaid parties, or to sell or ransom
their prizes, or any other way to truck, as well the
ships and goods as any other lading whatsoever.
And it shall not be lawful for them to buy any victual,
but what shall be necessary to bring them to the next
port of that prince from whom they obtained their
said commissions.   And if perchance any of the subjects of the said King of Great Britain, or of the said
States General, shall buy or get to themselves by truck,
or any other way, such ship or goods which have been
taken by the subjects of one or the other party; in
such

such case the said subject shall be bound to restore the said ship or goods to the proprietors without any delay, and without any compensation or reimbursement of money paid or promised for the same; provided that they make it appear before the council of the said King of Great Britain, or before the said States General, that they are the right owners or proprietors of them.

XXII. That in case the said King of Great Britain, or the said States General, do make any treaty of amity or alliance with any other kings, republics, princes, or states, they shall therein comprehend each other and their dominions, if they desire to be therein comprehended; and shall give to the other notice of all such treaties, or friendship and alliance.

XXIII. That in case it happen, during this friendship, confederacy, and alliance, any thing shall be done or attempted by any of the subjects or inhabitants of either party against this treaty, or any part thereof, by land, sea, or fresh-waters, that nevertheless this amity and alliance between the said nations shall not thereby be broken or interrupted, but shall remain and continue in its full force; and that only those particular persons shall be punished, who have committed any thing against this treaty, and none else; and that justice shall be rendered and satisfaction given to all persons concerned, by all such who have committed any thing contrary to this treaty, by land or sea, or other waters, in any part of Europe, or any places within the Straits, or in America, or upon the coasts of Africa, or in any lands, islands, seas, creeks, bays, rivers, or in any places on this side the Cape of Good Hope, within twelve months space after justice shall be demanded; and in all places whatsoever on the other side the Cape (as hath been abovesaid) within eighteen months next ensuing after demand of justice shall be made in manner aforesaid. But in case the offenders against this treaty do not appear, and submit

5   mit

mit themfelves to judgment, and give fatisfaction within
the refpective times above expreffed, proportionable
to the diftance of the places, they fhall be declared
enemies of both parties, and their eftates, goods, and
revenues whatfoever, fhall be confifcated for due and
full fatisfaction of the injuries and wrongs by them
offered; and their perfons alfo, when they come within
the dominions of either party, fhall be liable unto fuch
punifhments as every one fhall deferve for his refpective offences.

XXIV. That the fubjects of the faid King of Great
Britain, and thofe which are under his jurifdiction,
may freely and fecurely travel in all the provinces of
the Low Countries, and all their dominions in Europe,
and through them by fea or land pafs to other places
there or beyond them, and through all quarters of the
United Provinces, cities, forts, or garrifons whatfoever, which are in any parts of the United Provinces,
or elfewhere in their dominions in Europe, as well
they themfelves exercifing trade in all thofe places, as
their agents, factors, and fervants may go armed or
unarmed (but if armed, not above forty in a company)
as well without their goods and merchandizes as with
them, wherefoever they pleafe. The people alfo and
inhabitants of the United Provinces fhall enjoy the
fame liberty and freedom in all the dominions of the
faid King in Europe; provided that they, and every
of them, do in their trade and merchandizing yield
obedience to the laws and ftatutes of either nation
refpectively.

XXV. That in cafe the merchant-fhips of the fubjects of either nation fhall by ftorm, pirates, or any
other neceffity whatfoever, be driven into any haven
of either dominion, they may depart fecurely and at
their pleafure, with their fhips and goods, without
paying any cuftoms or other duties; provided they
break no bulk, nor fell any thing; nor fhall they be
fubject to any moleftation or fearch, provided they do

not

not receive on board any perfons or goods, nor do any thing elfe contrary to the laws, ordinances, or cuftoms of the places where they (as aforefaid) fhall happen to arrive.

XXVI. That the merchants, mafters, and feamen of either party, their fhips, goods, wares, or merchandizes, fhall not be arrefted or feized in the lands, havens, roads, or rivers of the other, to ferve at war, or any other ufe, by virtue of any general or fpecial command, unlefs upon an extraordinary neceffity, and that juft fatisfaction be given for the fame; but fo as the fame fhall not derogate from the feizures and arrefts duly made in the ordinary courts of juftice of either nation.

XXVII. That the merchants on both fides, their factors and fervants, and alfo the mafters and other feamen, as well going as returning by fea, and other waters, as alfo in the havens of either party, or going on fhore, may carry and ufe, for the defence of themfelves and goods, all forts of weapons, as well offenfive as defenfive; but being come into their lodgings or inns, they fhall there lay by and leave their arms, until they be going on board again.

XXVIII. That the men of war or convoys of either nation, meeting or overtaking at fea any merchants fhip or fhips belonging to the fubjects or inhabitants of the other, holding the fame courfe, or going the fame way, fhall be bound, as long as they keep one courfe together, to protect and defend them againft all and every one who would fet upon them.

XXIX. That if any fhip or fhips of the fubjects or inhabitants of either nation, or of a neuter, be taken by a third party in the harbours of either, not being of the fubjects or inhabitants of either nation, they in or out of whofe haven or jurifdiction the faid fhips fhall be taken, fhall be bound to endeavour with the other party, that the faid fhip or fhips be purfued, brought back, and reftored to the owners; but all this fhall be done at the charges of the owners, or whom it concerns.

XXX. That fearchers, and other like officers on both fides, fhall regulate themfelves according to the laws of either nation, and fhall not impofe or demand more than they are allowed by their commiffions and inftructions.

XXXI. That if any injury be done or practifed by either nation, or the fubjects or inhabitants of the fame, againft the fubjects or inhabitants of the other, or againft any of the articles of this prefent treaty, or againft common right; yet neverthelefs no letters of reprifal, marque, or countermarque, fhall be granted by either fide, till juftice hath been firft demanded according to the ordinary courfe of law; but in cafe juftice be there denied or delayed, then that the faid King of Great Britain, and the faid States General, or commiffioners of that nation whofe fubjects and inhabitants have fuffered the wrong, fhall publicly require juftice from that other party, where (as abovefaid) it was denied or delayed, or from that power appointed to hear and decide fuch differences, that there may be a friendly compofure, or due procefs of law. But if ftill there happen more delays, and neither juftice be adminiftered, nor fatisfaction given within three months after fuch demand, that then letters of reprifal, marque, or countermarque, may be granted.

XXXII. It is alfo agreed, if at any time it happen (which God of his mercy forbid) that the differences now compofed between his faid Majefty and the faid States General fhould fefter, and break out again into open war, that then thofe fhips, merchandize, or any kind of moveables of either party, which fhall be found to be and remain in the ports, and under the command of the adverfe party on either fide, fhall not for all that be confifcated, or made obnoxious to any inconvenience; but the fpace of fix months fhall entirely

tirely be allowed to the fubjects and inhabitants of either party, that they may have leifure to tranfport from thence the forementioned things, and any thing elfe that is theirs, whither they fhall think fit, without any kind of moleftation.

XXXIII. That they who have obtained private commiffions from either party, before they receive fuch commiffions, fhall give good and fufficient caution before the judge of the court where they receive fuch commiffions, by refponfible men, who have no part or fhare in fuch fhips, that they fhall do no damage or injury to the fubjects or inhabitants of either fide.

XXXIV. It is alfo agreed and concluded, that the fubjects and inhabitants of either party fhall always have free accefs to each other's fea-ports, there to remain, and from thence to depart with the fame freedom; and not only with their merchant-fhips and lading, but alfo with their men of war, whether they belong to the faid King or States General, or unto fuch as have obtained private commiffions, whether they arrive through violence of tempeft, or other cafualty of the feas, or to mend their fhips, or to buy provifion, fo they exceed not the number of eight men of war, when they come there voluntarily, nor fhall remain or abide longer in the havens or places adjacent, than they fhall have a juft caufe, to repair their faid fhips, or to buy victuals or other neceffaries: and if a greater number of men of war fhould upon occafion defire to come unto fuch ports, they fhall in no cafe enter thereinto, until they have firft obtained leave from thofe to whom the faid havens do appertain; unlefs they be forced fo to do by ftorm, or fome force or neceffity, whereby they may avoid the danger of the fea: in which cafe alfo they fhall prefently make known the caufe of their coming unto the governor or chief magiftrate of the place, and fhall ftay no longer than the faid governor or chief magif-

L 2   trate

trate shall permit them, and shall not do any acts of hostility or other prejudice in the aforesaid havens during their abode there.

XXXV. Furthermore it is agreed and concluded, that both parties shall truly and firmly observe and execute this present treaty, and all and every the matters contained therein, and effectually cause the same to be observed and performed by the subjects and inhabitants of either nation.

XXXVI. Also, for further caution and assurance that this treaty and confederacy shall be duly and *bonâ fide* observed on the part of the said States General of the United Provinces and their people, it is concluded and agreed, as also the said States General by these presents do agree, and firmly oblige and bind themselves, that all and every one whom they, or the States of the Provinces shall at any time choose, appoint, or make captain-general, governor, or chief president, or stad-holder, general of armies or military forces by land, or admiral or general of the fleets, ships, or forces at sea, shall be bound and obliged by oath to confirm this treaty, and all the articles thereof, and promise sacredly upon oath, that they shall, as far as it is possible, religiously observe and execute the same, and, as much as concerns them, cause the same to be observed and executed by others.

XXXVII. Under this present treaty of peace those shall be comprehended, who shall be named by either party with common consent before the exchange of ratifications, or within six months after. But in the mean time, as the covenanting parties do thankfully acknowledge the friendly offices, and unwearied endeavours, whereby the most Serene King of Sweden, interposing his mediation, hath, through the assistance of God, promoted and carried on this beneficial work of pacification unto the desired conclusion; so, to testify their like affection, it is decreed and covenanted by the common consent of all the parties, that his above-
mentioned

mentioned Majesty of Sweden, with all his kingdoms, dominions, provinces, and rights, be included in this treaty, and comprehended in the prefent pacification, after the beft and moft effectual manner that may be.

XXXVIII. It is alfo covenanted, concluded, and agreed, that the prefent treaty, and all and every thing and things therein contained and concluded, fhall be confirmed and ratified by the faid King of Great Britain, and the faid States General of the United Provinces, by letters patents on both fides, fealed with the great feal in due and authentic form, within four weeks next enfuing, or fooner, if it can be done; and that within the faid time the ratifications on both fides fhall be exchanged at Breda; and that prefently after the delivery and exchange of the fame, this treaty and alliance fhall be publifhed in fuch form and place as is ufual.

Done at Breda, the $\frac{21}{31}$ day of July, 1667.

The feparate Article.

IF it happen that any tapeftry, hangings, carpets, pictures, or houfhold furniture of what kind foever, or precious ftones, jewels, rich curiofities, or other moveable goods whatfoever, belonging to the King of Great Britain, either now are, or hereafter fhall be found to be in the hands or power of the faid States General, or of any of their fubjects; the faid States General do promife, that they will in no wife protect the poffeffors of any moveables appertaining unto the faid King; which goods may be taken from them in fuch manner, that they, who fhall make difficulty to reftore them freely, may not be dealt withal by any means contrary to equity and juftice. And the faid States do promife to ufe their moft effectual endeavours, that a plain and fummary way of proceeding may be taken in this affair, without the ordinary form and method of procefs ufually obferved in courts; and that juftice be adminiftered, whereby his faid

Majefty

Majefty may be fatisfied, as far as poffibly may be, without the wrong of any one.

Alfo, that if any of thofe who are guilty of that horrible treafon and parricide committed upon King Charles the Firft of moft bleffed memory, and lawfully attainted, condemned, or convicted of the fame, either now are in the dominions of the faid States General, or fhall hereafter come thither; as foon as ever it fhall be known or fignified to the faid States General, or any of their officers, they fhall be apprehended, put into cuftody, and fent prifoners into England, or delivered into the hands of thofe whom the faid King of Great Britain fhall appoint to take charge of them, and bring them home.

Done at Breda the $\frac{21}{31}$ day of July, 1667.

His Majefty's Declaration concerning the Reftoring of all Places, Forts, &c. which his Subjects fhall have taken or recovered from the Dutch *after the* $\frac{10}{20}$ *day of* May *laft paft.*

CHARLES II. by the grace of God, King of Great Britain, France, and Ireland, Defender of the Faith, &c. We do hereby make known and teftify unto all and every perfon and perfons whom it doth or may any way concern, that whereas in the treaty of peace concluded at Breda the $\frac{21}{31}$ day of July, 1667, between us and the High and Mighty Lords States General of the United Netherlands, it is agreed in the third article, that each party is to hold and poffefs, for the time to come, with plenary right of fovereignty, propriety, and poffeffion, all fuch lands, iflands, cities, forts, places, and colonies, as during this war, or in any former times before this war, they have by force of arms, or any way whatfoever, gotten or detained from the other party, after the very fame manner as they had feized and did poffefs them on the $\frac{10}{20}$ day of May laft paft, not excepting any of the faid places, And whereas furthermore, for the avoiding of all matter

ter

ter of ftrife and contention, which ufeth fometimes to arife by reafon of reftitutions, it is alfo agreed in the fixth article, that if either party fhall intercept and get from the other any lands, iflands, cities, forts, colonies, and other places, after the faid $\frac{19}{10}$ day of May laft paft, all and every of the premiffes (without any diftinction of time and place) are forthwith to be reftored in the very fame condition wherein they fhall be found to be at the time whenfoever certain notice fhall come to thofe places that the peace is renewed : We do hereby require and command all our governors, officers, commanders, and foldiers, both by fea and land, of what quality and condition foever they be, as well within Europe as without, that they do not only forbear and totally abftain from all hoftility, according to the tenor of the forefaid treaty; but alfo, if at any time it fhall happen or come to pafs, that any lands, iflands, cities, forts, colonies, and other places, wherefoever fituated, fhall be taken from the United Netherlanders, or recovered from them and brought under our power, after the expiration of the faid $\frac{19}{10}$ day of May, that they reftore them all, without any delay or excufe, unto thofe perfons who fhall exhibit thefe letters patents, in fuch condition as they fhall be found in at the time when the renewing of the peace fhall be notified there, without any diminution, detraction, wafte, or embezzlement whatfoever, upon pain of our higheft difpleafure. Given at Weftminfter the nine and twentieth day of July, old ftile, and eighth day of Auguft, new ftile, in the year of our Lord 1667, and of our reign the nineteenth.

[The following is printed from the copy publifhed by authority in 1686.]

Articles of Navigation and Commerce between the Moft Serene and Mighty Prince, Charles *the Second, by the Grace of God, King of* England, Scotland, France, *and* Ireland, *Defender of the Faith, &c. and the High and Mighty Lords the States General*

L 4 *of*

of the United Netherlands, *concluded the* $\frac{21}{31}$ *day of* July, 1667.

WHEREAS by thofe articles of peace, union, and alliance, which are this day concluded between his Majefty the King of Great Britain, and the States General of the United Provinces, it is fpecially and carefully provided, that all the difmal and calamitous effects of war may forthwith ceafe, and that the peace fo much defired by all, may be reftored in all kingdoms and dominions of both parties, and unto all their fubjects and inhabitants: and the meafure of time and affairs hath not permitted them to weigh in an equal balance, and thereby exactly to adjuft all and every thing and things which were to be obferved and confidered about the forefaid articles, efpecially about thofe which belong to the rules of free navigation and trade; and that it may be feared, the inhabitants and fubjects of both parties may fall back again into new quarrels and diffentions, and the differences now compofed may bleed afrefh, if they be not bound up by fome certain laws about thofe things which concern navigation and the ufe of trade: therefore, by the mediation and endeavours of the Swedifh ambaffadors, the forementioned parties have further agreed unto thefe feparate articles.

I. That all fuch proclamations and acts of ftate, which either party hath publifhed, by reafon of this war, to the prejudice of the other party, againft the liberty of navigation and trade, be abrogated on both fides.

II. That for the elucidation of that act which the King of Great Britain caufed to be publifhed in the year 1660, for the encouragement of navigation in his own fubjects, whereby ftrangers are prohibited to import any commodities into England, but fuch as are of their own growth or manufacture; it may be lawful for the States General, and their fubjects, to carry alfo into England in their fhips, all fuch com-
　　　　　　　　　　　　　　　　modities

modities as growing, being produced, or manufactured in Lower or Upper Germany, are not usually carried so frequently and commodiously unto seaports (thence to be transported to other countries) any other way but through the territories and dominions of the United Netherlands, either by land or by rivers.

III. Whereas the King of Great Britain hath heretofore pressed, that merchandize and commodities on both sides might be reduced to a certain and convenient rule; the States General also have always aim at the same mark, that merchandize should be bounded and circumscribed within some certain laws of perpetual observation; and yet that business seems to require longer attention and labour, than that it can be speedily dispatched to the satisfaction of both parties; they are both content to remit the same unto a fitter occasion, that commissioners on both sides may meet together as soon as may be after this peace is concluded, who may resolve and agree about specifying and circumscribing the species of commodities, and the laws of navigation, and may set the same down in new and mutual covenants. Yet left in the mean time the inhabitants and subjects of both parties should be in suspence and doubt, as not knowing what kinds of commodities it may be lawful or unlawful to carry or supply unto the enemy of either party, after the manner and form of warlike provisions or succours, or under the title or pretence of merchandize; it is likewise covenanted and agreed, that the treaty of navigation and commerce made between the Most Christian King and the said States General (beginning from the 26th unto the 42d article inclusively) in that manner and tenor wherein they follow here, inserted in the French language, may provisionally serve for a rule and law, and so make way for the perfecting of a larger and fuller treaty concerning maritime commerce between the above-mentioned parties.

The

The forefaid articles follow.

26. All the fubjects and inhabitants of France may with all fafety and freedom fail and traffic in all the kingdoms, countries, and eftates which are or fhall be in peace, amity, or neutrality with France, without being troubled or difquieted in that liberty by the fhips, gallies, frigates, barques, or other veffels belonging to the States General, or any of their fubjects, upon oc-cafion and account of the hoftilities which may here-after happen between the faid States General and the abovefaid kingdoms, countries, and eftates, or any of them, which are or fhall be in peace, amity, or neu-trality with France.

27. This tranfportation and traffic fhall extend to all forts of merchandize, except thofe of contraband.

28. This term of contraband goods is underftood to comprehend only all forts of fire-arms and their appurtenances; as cannon, mufquets, mortar-pieces, petards, bombs, granadoes, fauciffes, pitched hoops, carriages, refts, bandeliers, powder, match, falt-petre, bullets, pikes, fwords, morions, head-pieces, cuiraffes, halberts, javelins, horfes, great faddles, holfters, belts, and other utenfils of war.

29. In this quality of contraband goods thefe fol-lowing fhall not be comprehended; wheat, corn, and other grain, gums, oils, wines, falt, nor generally any thing that belongs to the nourifhment and fuftenance of life, but fhall remain free as other merchandize and commodities not comprehended in the precedent article; and the tranfportation of them fhall be per-mitted even unto places in enmity with the faid States General, except fuch cities and places as are befieged, blocked up, or invefted.

30. It hath been agreed, that the execution of what is abovefaid fhall be performed in the manner follow-ing; that the fhips and barques with the merchan-dize of his Majefty's fubjects, being entered into any port of the faid States General, and purpofing to pafs from thence unto the ports of the faid enemies, fhall
be

be only obliged to shew unto the officers of the port of the said States out of which they would go, their passports, containing the specification of the lading of their ships, attested and marked with the ordinary seal and signing, acknowledged by the officers of the admiralty of those places from whence they first came, with the place whither they are bound, all in the usual and accustomed form: after which shewing of their passports in the form aforesaid, they may not be disquieted nor searched, detained nor retarded in their voyages, upon any pretence whatsoever.

31. The same course shall be used in regard of the French ships and barques which shall come into any roads of the countries under the obedience of the said States, not intending to enter into the ports, or being entered thereinto, not to unlade and break bulk; which ships may not be obliged to give account of their lading, but in case of suspicion that they carry unto the enemies of the said States any contraband goods, as was abovesaid.

32. And in case of such apparent suspicion, the said subjects of his Majesty shall be obliged to shew in the ports their passports in the form above specified.

33. But if they were come within the roads, or were met in the open sea by any of the said States ships, or private men of war their subjects; for avoiding of all disorder, the said ships of the United Provinces shall come no nearer unto the French barques than within cannon-shot, and may send their long-boat or shallop on board the French ships or barques, and cause only two or three men to go on board, unto whom the passports and certificates shall be shewn by the master or pilot of the French ship, in the manner above specified, according to the form of the said certificates which shall be inserted at the end of this treaty; by which passports and certificates proof may be made not only of the lading, but also of the place of the abode and residence as well of the master and pilot, as of the ship itself; to the end that by these

2   two

two ways it may be known whether they carry contraband goods; and that the quality as well of the
said ship as of its master and pilot may sufficiently appear: unto which passports and certificates entire
faith and credit ought to be given.   And to the end
that their validity may be the better known, and that
they may not be in any wise falsified and counterfeit,
certain marks and countersigns of his Majesty and the
said States General shall be given unto them.

34. And in case any merchandize and commodities
of those kinds which are before declared to be contraband and forbidden, shall by the means aforesaid
be found in the French vessels and barques bound for
the ports of the said States enemies; they shall be
unladen, and declared confiscate before the judges of
the admiralty of the United Provinces, or other
competent officers: but so, that the ship and barque,
or other free and allowed goods, merchandize, and
commodities found in the same ship, may not for
that cause be in any manner seized or confiscate.

35. It was furthermore agreed and covenanted,
that whatsoever shall be found laden by his Majesty's subjects upon a ship of the enemies of the said
States, although the same were not contraband goods,
shall yet be confiscate, with all that shall be found in
the said ship, without exception or reservation; but on
the other side also, all that shall be and shall be found
in the ships belonging to the Most Christian King's
subjects, shall be free and discharged, although the
lading or part thereof belong to the said States enemies; except contraband goods, in regard whereof
such rule shall be observed as hath been ordered in the
precedent articles.

36. All the subjects and inhabitants of the said
United Provinces shall reciprocally enjoy the same
rights, liberties, and exemptions in their trade and
commerce, within the ports, roads, seas, and estates of
his said Majesty (as hath been newly said) which his
said Majesty's subjects shall enjoy in those of the said

States,

States, and in open fea; it being to be underftood, that the equality fhall be mutual every way on both fides : And even in cafe the faid States fhould hereafter be in peace, amity, and neutrality with any Kings, Princes, and States, who fhould become enemies to his faid Majefty, either of the parties are mutually to ufe the fame conditions and reftrictions expreffed in the articles of this prefent treaty, which regard trade and commerce.

37. And the more to affure the fubjects of the faid States, that no violence fhall be offered them by the faid fhips of war, all the captains of the King's fhips, and others his Majefty's fubjects, fhall be charged and enjoined not to moleft or endamage them in any thing whatfoever, upon pain of being punifhed and made anfwerable in their perfons and goods for the damages and interefts fuffered, and to be fuffered, until due reftitution and reparation be made.

38. And for this caufe the captains and capers fhall from henceforth every one of them be obliged, before they go out, to give good and fufficient fecurity before competent judges, in the fum of fifteen thoufand livres tournois, to anfwer every one by himfelf for the mifcarriages they may commit in their courfes at fea, and for their captains and officers violations of this prefent treaty, and of the orders and proclamations of his Majefty, which fhall be publifhed by virtue and in conformity of the regulation therein made; upon pain of being cafhiered, and forfeiting the faid commiffions and licences : which fhall in like manner be practifed by the fubjects of the faid States General.

39. If it fhould happen that any of the faid French captains fhould make prize of a veffel laden with contraband goods, as hath been faid, the faid captains may not open nor break up the chefts, mails, packs, bags, cafk, and other boxes, or tranfport, fell, or exchange, and otherwife alienate them, until they have landed in the prefence of the judges of the admiralty,

miralty, and after an inventory hath by them been
made of the said goods found in the said vessels; unless the contraband goods making but a part of the
lading, the master or pilot of the ship should be content to deliver the said contraband goods unto the
said captain, and to pursue his voyage: in which
case the said master or pilot shall by no means be hindered from continuing his course and the design of
his voyage.

40. His Majesty being desirous that the subjects of
the said States may be used in all countries under
his obedience as favourably as his own subjects, will
give all necessary orders, that judgments and decrees
upon prizes which shall happen to be taken at sea,
may be given with all justice and equity, by persons
not suspected nor concerned in the matter under debate: and his Majesty will give precise and effectual
orders, that all decrees, judgments, and orders of justice already given and to be given, may be readily
and duly executed according to their forms.

41. And when the ambassadors of the said States
General, or any other of their public ministers residing in his Majesty's court, shall make complaint of
the judgments which shall be given, his Majesty will
cause a review to be made of the said judgments in
his council, to examine whether the order and precautions contained in the present treaty have been followed and observed, and to provide for the same according to reason; which shall be done within the
space of three months at the farthest: nevertheless,
neither before the first judgment, nor after it, during the time of the review, the goods and effects
which are claimed, may not be sold or unladen, unless it be with consent of the parties interested, to avoid
the spoiling of the said commodities, if they be pe-
rishable.

42. When process shall be moved in the first or second instance between those that have taken the prizes
at sea, and the persons interested therein, and the said
interested

interefted perfons fhall come to obtain a favourable judgment or decree, the faid judgment or decree fhall have its execution upon fecurity given, notwithftanding the appeal of him that took the prize; but the fame fhall not hold on the contrary. And that which is faid in this prefent, and in the precedent articles, for the caufing of good and fpeedy juftice to be done unto the fubjects of the United Provinces in the matter of prizes taken at fea by his Majefty's fubjects, fhall be underftood and practifed by the States General, in regard of prizes taken by their fubjects from thofe of his Majefty.

IV. It is alfo covenanted, that thefe above-written feparate articles, and all and every thing therein contained and concluded, fhall be confirmed and ratified by the faid King of Great Britain, and the faid States General of the United Provinces, by letters patents of both parties, fealed with their great feal in due and authentic form, within four weeks next enfuing, or fooner, if it may be; and mutual inftruments fhall be exchanged at Breda within the forefaid time; and the fame fhall be publifhed, after the delivery and exchange thereof, in the ufual form and place.

Done at Breda the $\frac{21}{31}$ day of July, 1667.

A Form of the Paſſports and Certificates that ought to be given in the Admiralty of France, to the Ships and Barques that go out thence, according to the Article of the prefent Treaty.

CÆSAR, Duke of Vendome, Peer and Great Mafter, Chief and Superintendant General of the navigation and commerce of France: To all who fhall fee thefe prefents, greeting.

We do make known, that we have granted leave and permiffion to   mafter and conductor of a fhip called   of the city of
                of the burthen of
                                 tons or thereabouts, being
at

'at prefent in the port and haven of
to go to   laden with   .af-
ter fearch fhall have been made 'of his fhip, and he
before his departure fhall make oath before the officers
that exercife the jurifdiction of maritime caufes, that
the faid veffel doth belong to one or more of his Majefty's fubjects, an act whereof fhall be put at the bottom of the prefents, as alfo to keep and caufe to be
kept by thofe aboard him, the orders and rules of the
marine, and fhall put into the regiftry the roll figned
and certified, containing the names and furnames, the
nativity and habitation of the men that are aboard him,
and of all that fhall embark themfelves, whom he
may not take on board without the knowledge and
permiffion of the marine officers ; and in every port or
haven where he fhall enter with his fhip, fhall make
appear to the officers and marine judges concerning
the prefent licence, and fhall make them faithful relation of what hath been done and hath paffed during
his voyage, and fhall carry the flags, arms, and colours, both the King's and ours, throughout his whole
voyage. In witnefs whereof, we have figned thefe
prefents, and caufed the feal of our arms to be put
thereunto, and the fame to be counterfigned by our
fecretary of the marine, the   . day of
          One thoufand fix hundred

(Signed) ·
Cæfar of Vendome. And underneath, By my Lord
Matharel. And fealed with the feal of the
arms of the faid Lord Admiral.

A Form of the Act containing the Oath.

WE   of the Admiralty of   do certify, that
                    · mafter of the fhip named
in the paffport above, hath taken the oath therein
mentioned. Made at   the.   . day of
          One thoufand fix hundred, &c.

Another

Another Form of the Certificates that ought to be given by the Cities and Sea Ports of the United Provinces, to the Ships and Barques that go from thence, according to the Article abovesaid.

TO the most Serene, most Illustrious, Illustrious, most Mighty, most Noble, Honourable, and Prudent Lords, Emperors, Kings, Commonwealths, Princes, Dukes, Comties, Barons, Lords, Burgomasters, Sheriffs, Counsellors, Judges, Officers, Justices, and Regents of all good cities and places, as well ecclesiastical as secular, who shall see or read these presents. We burgomasters and governors of the city of do make known, that ship-master, appearing before us, hath declared by solemn oath, that the ship called containing about lasts, of which he is at present the master, belongeth to inhabitants of the United Provinces, So help him God: And, as we would willingly see the said ship-master assisted in his just affairs, we do request you all in general and particular, that where the abovesaid master shall arrive with his ship and goods, it may please them to receive him courteously, and use him in due manner, suffering him, upon the usual rights of tolls and other charges, in, through, and nigh your ports, rivers, and territories, permitting him to sail, pass, frequent, and trade there where he shall think fit. Which we shall willingly acknowledge. In witness whereof we have caused the seal of our city to be thereunto put.

[The following is printed from the copy published by authority in 1686.]

Articles touching Navigation and Commerce, between the most Serene and Mighty Prince, Charles *the Second, by the Grace of God, King of* England, Scotland, France, *and* Ireland, *Defender of the Faith, &c. and the High and Mighty Lords the States Ge-*

neral of the United Netherlands; *concluded at the* Hague *the* ₁⁷₁ February, 166⅞.

WHEREAS, by the bleffing of Almighty God, for the mutual fafety of the two parties, as well as the common good of Chriftendom, a perpetual defenfive treaty was concluded, and figned on the 23d day of January laft paft, between the moft Serene and moft Potent Prince Charles the Second, and the High and Mighty Lords the States General of the United Netherlands, with ftipulation of confiderable fuccours, to be mutually given by the parties, as well by fea as land: And whereas the faid King and States did on the fame day, and by another inftrument, readily enter into a folemn treaty and agreement, for compofing the affairs of their neighbours, and reftoring peace to Chriftendom ; fo as nothing feems now remaining that can at any time hereafter interrupt a friendfhip and alliance renewed with fo equal defires, unlefs fuch controverfies as may otherwife hereafter happen to arife about determining the different forts and natures of merchandize, which being left dubious and uncertain, would give occafion to the further growth of fuch differences: And therefore, that it may appear with what fincerity and good faith the faid King, and the faid States, defire to preferve and entertain, not only for the prefent, but to all pofterity, the amity they lately contracted between them, they have at laft, for the taking away all grounds, not only of differences and mifunderftandings, but even of queftions and difputes; and fo utterly to cut off the hope and expectation of thofe, whoever they are, that may think it their intereft, by new controverfies, to endeavour the difturbance or interruption of the faid peace, mutually agreed on thefe following articles, which are to be on both fides, and for ever, obferved as the meafure and rule of fuch maritime affairs, and mutual fettlement of trade, or at left fo long, till, by the joint confent of both parties, commiffioners be appointed, and do meet in order to the framing a more full and ample treaty concerning

cerning this matter, and the laws and rules of commerce and navigation; as by farther experience shall be found most advantageous to the common good of both parties.

I. All the subjects and inhabitants of Great Britain may, with all safety and freedom, sail and traffic in all the kingdoms, countries, and estates, which are or shall be in peace, amity, or neutrality with Great Britain, without being troubled or disquieted in that liberty by the ships of war, gallies, frigates, barques, or other vessels belonging to the States General, or any of their subjects, upon occasion and account of the hostilities which may hereafter happen between the said States General and the abovesaid kingdoms, countries, and estates, or any of them, which are or shall be in peace, amity, or neutrality with Great Britain.

II. This freedom of navigation and traffic shall extend to all sorts of merchandize, except those of contraband.

III. This term of Contraband goods is understood to comprehend only all sorts of fire-arms and their appurtenances; as cannon, musquets, mortar-pieces, petards, bombs, granadoes, fire-crancels, pitched hoops, carriages, rests, bandeliers, powder, match, salt-petre, bullets, pikes, swords, morions, head-pieces, coats of mail, halberts, javelins, horses, great saddles, holsters, belts, and other utensils of war, called in French, Assortissemens servans à l'usage de la guerre.

IV. In this quality of contraband goods, these following shall not be comprehended; corn, wheat, or, other grain, and pulse; oils, wines, salt, or generally any thing that belongs to the nourishment and sustenance of life, but shall remain free as other merchandize and commodities not comprehended in the precedent article; and the transportation of them shall be permitted even unto places in enmity with the said States General, except such cities and places as are besieged, blocked up, or invested.

M 2   V. It

V. It hath been agreed, for the due execution of what is abovesaid, that the ships and barques of the English, laden with merchandize, being entered into any port of the said States General, and purposing to pass from thence unto the ports of their enemies, shall be only obliged to shew unto the officers of the port of the said States, out of which they would go, their passports, containing the specification of the lading of their ships, attested and marked with the ordinary seal of the officers of the admiralty of those places from whence they first came, with the place whither they are bound, all in the usual and accustomed form: after which shewing of their passports in the form aforesaid, they may not be disquieted nor searched, detained nor retarded in their voyages, upon any pretence whatsoever.

VI. The same course shall be used in regard of the English ships and vessels which shall come into any roads of the countries under the obedience of the said States, not intending to enter into the ports, or being entered thereinto, not to unlade and break bulk; which ships may not be obliged to give account of their lading, but in case of suspicion that they carry unto the enemies of the said States any contraband goods, as was abovesaid.

VII. And in case of such apparent suspicion, the said subjects of his Majesty shall be obliged to shew in the ports their passports in the form above specified.

VIII. But if they were come within the roads, or were met in the open sea by any of the said States ships, or private men of war of their subjects; for avoiding of all disorder, the said ships of the United Provinces, or of their subjects, shall not come near within cannon-shot of the English, but shall send out their long-boat, and cause only two or three men to go on board the English ships or vessels, unto whom the passports and certificates of the propriety of the ships shall be shewn by the master or captain of the English
ship,

ſhip, in the manner above ſpecified, according to the form of the ſaid certificates which ſhall be inſerted at the end of this treaty; by which paſſports and certificates proof may be made not only of the lading, but alſo of the place of the abode and reſidence of the maſter or captain, and name of the ſhip itſelf; to the end that by theſe two ways it may be known whether they carry contraband goods, and that the quality as well of the ſaid ſhip, as of its maſter or captain, may ſufficiently appear: unto which paſſports and certificates entire faith and credit ſhall be given. And to the end that their validity may be the better known, and that they may not be in any wiſe falſified and counterfeit, certain marks and counterſigns of his Majeſty and the ſaid States General ſhall be given unto them.

IX. And in caſe any merchandize and commodities of thoſe kinds which are before declared to be contraband and forbidden, ſhall by the means aforeſaid be found in the Engliſh ſhips and veſſels, bound for the ports of the ſaid States enemies, they ſhall be unladen, judicially proceeded againſt, and declared confiſcate before the judges of the admiralty of the United Provinces, or other competent officers: but ſo that the ſhip and veſſel, or other free and allowed goods, merchandize, and commodities found in the ſame ſhip, may not for that cauſe be in any manner ſeized or confiſcate.

X. It is furthermore agreed and covenanted, that whatſoever ſhall be found laden by his Majeſty's ſubjects upon a ſhip of the enemies of the ſaid States, although the ſame were not contraband goods, ſhall yet be confiſcate, with all that ſhall be found in the ſaid ſhip, without exception or reſervation: but on the other ſide alſo, all that ſhall be found in the ſhips belonging to the King of Great Britain's ſubjects, ſhall be free and diſcharged, although the lading or part thereof belong to the ſaid States enemies; except con-

traband

traband goods, in regard whereof such rule shall be observed as hath been ordered in the precedent articles.

XI. All the subjects and inhabitants of the said United Provinces shall reciprocally enjoy the same rights, liberties, and exemptions, in their trade and commerce upon the coasts, and in the ports, roads, seas, and estates of his said Majesty (as was now said) which his said Majesty's subjects shall enjoy in those of the said States, and in open sea; it being to be understood, that the equality shall be mutual every way on both sides, even in case the said States should hereafter be in peace, amity, and neutrality with any Kings, Princes, and States, who should become enemies to his said Majesty; so that either of the parties are mutually to use the same conditions and restrictions expressed in the articles of this present treaty, which regard trade and commerce.

XII. And the more to assure the subjects of the said States, that no violence shall be offered them by the ships of war belonging to his Majesty of Great Britain, or his subjects, all the captains of the King's ships, and all his Majesty's subjects that set out private men of war, shall be charged and enjoined not to molest or endamage them in any thing whatsoever, upon pain of being punished and made answerable in their persons and goods for all costs and damages, until due restitution and reparation be made.

XIII. And for this cause the captains and capers shall from henceforth every one of them be obliged, before they go out, to give good and sufficient security, before competent judges, in the sum of fifteen hundred pounds sterling, or fifteen thousand livres tournois, that they will give full satisfaction for any injuries or wrongs they may commit in their courses at sea, and for their captains and officers that shall violate this present treaty, and the orders and proclamations of his Majesty, which shall be published by virtue

tue and in conformity to the regulation therein made; upon pain of forfeiting their said commissions and licences: which shall in like manner be practised by the subjects of the said States General.

'XIV. If it should happen that any of the said French captains should make prize of a vessel laden with contraband goods, as hath been said, the said captains may not open nor break up the chests, mails, packs, bags, cask, or sell, or exchange, or otherwise alienate them, until they have landed them in the presence of the judges or officers of the admiralty, and after an inventory by them made of the said goods found in the said vessels; unless the contraband goods making but a part of the lading, the master of the ship should be content to deliver the said contraband goods unto the said captain, and to pursue his voyage: in which case the said master shall by no means be hindered from continuing his course and the design of his voyage.

XV. His Majesty being desirous that the subjects of the said States may be used, in all countries under his obedience, as favourably as his own subjects, will give all necessary orders, that judgments and decrees upon prizes which shall happen to be taken at sea, may be given with all justice and equity, by judges not suspected nor concerned in the matter under debate: and his Majesty will give precise and effectual orders, that all decrees, judgments, and orders of justice, already given and to be given, may be readily and duly executed according to the tenor of them.

XVI. And when the ambassadors of the said States General, or any other of their public ministers residing in his Majesty's court, shall make complaint of the judgments which shall be given, his Majesty will cause a review to be made of the said judgments in his council, to examine whether the order and precautions contained in the present treaty have been followed and observed, and to provide for the same ac-

cording

cording to right and equity; which shall be done within the space of three months at the fartheft: nevertheless, neither before the firft judgment, nor after it, during the time of the review, the goods and effects which are reclaimed may not be fold or unladen, unlefs it be with the confent of the parties interefted, to avoid the fpoiling of the faid commodities, if they be perifhable.

XVII. When procefs fhall be moved in the firft or fecond inftance between thofe that have taken the prizes at fea, and the perfons interefted therein, and the faid interefted perfons fhall come to obtain a favourable judgment or decree, the faid judgment or decree fhall have its execution upon fecurity given, notwithftanding the appeal of him that took the prize; but the fame fhall not hold on the contrary, where the fentence goes againft the claimers. And that which is faid in this prefent and in the precedent articles, for the caufing of good and fpeedy juftice to be done unto the fubjects of the United Provinces in the matter of prizes taken at fea by his Majefty's fubjects, fhall be underftood and practifed by the States General; in regard of prizes taken by their fubjects from thofe of his Majefty.

XVIII. But fince the conveniences and inconveniences of things and agreements cannot be difcovered but in procedure of time, and by obfervations drawn from mutual experience, it is therefore agreed between the faid King of Great Britain and the faid Lords the States of the United Netherlands, that at any time hereafter, when both parties fhall fo think it fitting, certain commiffioners by each party refpectively chofen, fhall meet by the common confent of both; who fhall make it their care and bufinefs to fupply whatever fhall be found wanting in the aforementioned articles, to change or limit whatever fhall not be convenient and commodious for both, and fully compleat a further treaty, both concerning thefe things and all other the laws of navigation.

XIX. All

XIX. All thefe agreements, and all and every thing. therein contained, fhall be confirmed and ratified by the faid King of Great Britain and the States General of the 'United Provinces, by letters patents of both parties, fealed with their great feal in due and authentic form, within four weeks next enfuing, or fooner if it may be, and mutual inftruments fhall be exchanged by each party within the time aforefaid.

Here follow certain forms, whereof mention is made in the eighth article,

A Form of the Certificates that ought to be given by thofe that have the ordinary Power of the Admiralty of England, *to the Ships and Veffels that go out thence, according to the Eighth Article of the prefent Treaty.*

high admiral of England, to all who fhall fee thefe prefents, greeting.

Thefe are to certify, that we have granted leave and permiffion· to   mafter and captain of the fhip called   of the city of of the burthen of tons, or thereabouts, being at prefent in the port and haven of   to go to   laden with   after fearch fhall have been made of his fhip, and he before his departure fhall have made oath before the officers that exercife the jurifdiction of maritime caufes, that the faid veffel doth belong to one or more of his Majefty's fubjects, an act whereof fhall be put at the bottom of thefe prefents, as alfo to keep and caufe to be kept by thofe aboard him, the orders and rules of the marine, and fhall put into the regiftry a lift figned and certified, containing the names and furnames, the nativity and habitation of the men that are aboard him, and of all that fhall embark themfelves, whom he may not take on board without the knowledge and permiffion of the marine officers; and in every port or haven where he fhall shall enter with his ship, shall shew the officers and marine judges this his present licence, and, having finished his voyage, shall make faithful relation of what hath been done and hath passed during all the time of his said voyage, and shall carry the flags, arms, and colours of his Majesty throughout his whole voyage. In witness whereof, we have signed these presents, and caused the seal of our arms to be put thereunto, and the same to be countersigned by our secretary of the marine, the   day of one thousand six hundred

    Signed

               And underneath,
        By   and sealed with the seal of the arms of the said high admiral.

A Form of the Act containing the Oath to be taken by the Master or Captain of the Ship.

WE   of the admiralty of   do certify, that   master of the ship named in the passport above, hath taken the oath therein mentioned. Given at   the   day of one thousand six hundred, &c.

    In testimony whereof we have hereunto set our hands.

The Form of the Certificates that ought to be given by the Burgomasters of the Cities and Sea-ports of the United Provinces, to the Ships and Vessels that go from thence, according to the Eighth Article abovesaid.

TO the most Serene, most Illustrious, most Mighty, most Noble, Honourable, and Prudent Lords, Emperors, Kings, Commonwealths, Princes, Dukes, Comtes, Barons, Lords, Burgomasters, Sheriffs, Counsellors, Judges, Officers, Justices, and Regents of all cities and places,

places, as well ecclefiaftical as fecular, who fhall fee or read thefe prefents. We burgomafters and governors of the city of   do certify, that
fhip-mafter, appearing before us, hath declared by folemn oath, that the fhip called
containing about   lafts, of which he is at prefent the mafter, belongeth to inhabitants of the United Provinces, So help him God: and, as we would willingly fee the faid fhip-mafter affifted in his juft affairs, we do requeft you, and every of you, where the abovefaid mafter fhall arrive with his fhip and goods, that you will pleafe to receive him courteoufly, and ufe him kindly, admitting him, upon paying the ufual dues, tolls, and other cuftoms, to enter into, remain in, and pafs from your ports, rivers, and territories, and there to trade, deal, and nego-ciate in any part or place, in fuch fort and manner as he fhall defire. Which we fhall moft readily ac-knowledge in the like occafion. In witnefs whereof we have caufed the feal of our city to be thereunto put.

In witnefs and confirmation of all and every part whereof, we the commiffioners of his faid Ma-jefty the King of Great Britain, and of the faid Lords the States General, having fufficient power given us thereunto, have figned thefe tables, and fealed them with our feals. At the Hague in Holland, the 17th of February in the year one thoufand fix hundred fixty-eight.

De Gellicum,   G. Hoolck,
    B. d' Afperen,   V. Unckell,
    John de Witt,   Jan. Van Iffelmuden,
    Van Crommon,   L. T. Van Starckenborck.

[The

[The following is printed from the copy publiſhed by authority in 1686.]

Articles of Peace between the moſt Serene and Mighty Prince, Charles *the Second, by the Grace of God, King of* England, Scotland, France, *and* Ireland, *Defender of the Faith, &c. and the High and Mighty Lords the States General of the* United Nether-lands; *concluded at* Weſtminſter *the* 1/9 *Day of* February, 167¾.

I. IT is concluded and agreed, that from this day there ſhall be a firm and inviolable peace, union, and friendſhip betwixt his Majeſty the King of Great Britain, and the High and Mighty Lords, the States General of the United Provinces, and betwixt all their ſubjeçts, whether within Europe or without, in all regions and places whatſoever.

II. That this good union betwixt the aboveſaid King and the ſaid States General may the ſooner take its effeçt, it is by them agreed and concluded, that immediately upon the publication of this treaty of peace, all açtions of hoſtility ſhall on both ſides be immediately forbid, and no commiſſion, inſtruçtion, or order, privately or publicly, direçtly or indireçtly, be on either ſide given or countenanced, for the infeſting, attacking, fighting, or ſpoiling of each other, their dominions or ſubjeçts; but, on the contrary, all peaceable and amicable comportments enjoined to the ſubjeçts of both nations.

III. But in reſpeçt the diſtances of places are ſo different, that the orders and commands of the reſpective ſovereigns cannot at the ſame time reach all their ſubjeçts, it hath been thought fit to appoint theſe following limits for the committing any açts of hoſtility or force upon each other; *viz.* that after the expiration of twelve days next following the publication of this treaty, no hoſtility ſhall be açted from the Soundings to the Naz in Norway; nor after the term of ſix

weeks,

weeks, betwixt the Soundings and Tangier; nor after the term of ten weeks, betwixt the said Tangier and the Equator, neither in the Ocean, Mediterranean, or elsewhere; nor after the term of eight months, in any part of the world: and whatsoever actions of hostility and force shall be committed after the expiration of the aforesaid terms, upon colour of whatsoever former commission, letters of mart, or the like, shall be deemed as illegal, and the actors obliged to make reparation and satisfaction, and punished as violators of the public peace.

IV. That the aforesaid States General of the United Provinces, in due acknowledgment on their part of the King of Great Britain's right to have his flag respected in the seas hereafter mentioned, shall and do declare and agree, that whatever ships or vessels belonging to the said United Provinces, whether vessels of war or others, or whether single or in fleets, shall meet in any of the seas from Cape Finisterre to the middle point of the land Van Staten in Norway, with any ships or vessels belonging to his Majesty of Great Britain, whether those ships be single or in greater number, if they carry his Majesty of Great Britain's flag or jack, the aforesaid Dutch vessels or ships shall strike their flag and lower their top-sail, in the same manner and with as much respect as hath at any time, or in any place, been formerly practised towards any ships of his Majesty of Great Britain or his predecessors, by any ships of the States General or their predecessors.

V. Whereas the colony of Surinam, and the articles made upon the surrender thereof 1667, betwixt William Biam, then governor thereof for his Majesty of Great Britain, and Abraham Quirini, commander for the States General, have in the execution of them administered much occasion of dispute, and contributed much to the late misunderstanding betwixt his Majesty and the said States General; to remove all grounds of future mistakes, the said States General do by these pre-
lents

fents agree and covenant with the faid King of Great
Britain, that not only the fore-named articles fhall be
executed without any manner of tergiverfation or equi-
vocation; but that likewife it fhall be free for his Majefty to depute one or more perfons thither, to fee the
condition of his fubjefts there, and to adjuft with them
a time for their departure; and that it fhall be lawful
for his Majefty to fend one, two, or three fhips at one
time, and thereon to embark and carry away the faid
fubjefts, their goods, and flaves; and that the then
governor there for the States General fhall not make
or execute any law, whereby the buying or felling of
land, paying of debts, or commutation of goods,
fhall be otherwife qualified to the Englifh, than it hath
or fhall be to all other inhabitants of the colony; but
that during their ftay they fhall enjoy the fame laws
and privileges of fuing for debts, and paying their
debts, making bargains and contrafts, as hath been
ufually praftifed amongft the other inhabitants; and
that whenfoever his Majefty of Great Britain fhall
defire of the States General fufficient and authentic
letters to the governor of the faid colony, to fuffer
the faid Englifh to depart, and permit the coming of
the faid fhips, the faid **States** General fhall, within
the fpace of fifteen **days after** fuch demand, deliver
unto whomfoever **deputed** by his Majefty of Great
Britain for that purpofe, full and fufficient letters and
inftruftions to their governor there, for permitting the
arrival of the fhips, as well as the embarking of fuch
of his Majefty's fubjefts as fhall declare themfelves
willing to go away, with their goods and flaves, to be
tranfported where his Majefty fhall direft.

VI. It is agreed and concluded, that whatever
country, ifland, town, haven, caftle, or fortrefs, hath
been or fhall be taken by either party from the other,
fince the beginning of the late unhappy war, whether
in Europe or elfewhere, and before the expiration of
the times above limited for hoftility, fhall be reftored
to the former owner in the fame condition it fhall be
in

in at the time of the publishing this peace; after which time there shall be no plundering of the inhabitants, or demolishing of the fortifications, or carrying away the artillery and ammunition belonging to any fort or castle at the time of its having been taken.

VII. That the treaty of Breda, made in the year 1667, as all other former treaties confirmed by the said treaty, be renewed, and remain in their full force and vigour, so far forth as they contradict nothing in this present treaty.

VIII. That the marine treaty made at the Hague between the two parties in the year 1668, be continued for nine months after the publication of this present treaty, unless it shall be otherwise agreed on by a subsequent treaty; and that in the mean time the consideration of a new one be referred to the same commissioners to whom the trade in the East Indies is referred in the subsequent article.

But if such commissioners, within three months after their first meeting, shall not agree upon a new marine treaty, then that matter shall also be referred to the arbitration of the most Serene Queen Regent of Spain, in the same manner as the regulation of the East India trade is referred to her Majesty in the said article next following.

IX. In respect that upon the mutual, free, and undisturbed enjoyment of trade and navigation, not only the wealth, but the peace likewise of both nations is most highly concerned; there ought nothing to be so much the care of both parties as a just regulation of trade, and particularly in the East Indies; and yet, in respect that the weightiness of the matter requireth much time to make firm and durable articles to the content and security of the subject on both sides, and on the other side, the bleeding condition of most part of Europe, as well as of the two parties concerned, earnestly demand a speedy conclusion of this treaty, the King of Great Britain is pleased to condescend to the

desires

defires of the States General, to have the confideration
of the fame referred to an equal number of commiffioners to be nominated by each party, the faid States
General engaging themfelves to fend thofe of their no-
mination to treat at London with thofe to be nominated
by his Majefty; and this within the fpace of three months
after the publication of this treaty; the number to be
nominated by each to confift of fix perfons: and in
cafe that after three months from the time of their firft
affembling, they fhall not have the good fuccefs to
conclude a treaty, the points in difference betwixt
them fhall be referred to the arbitrement of the moft
Serene Queen Regent of Spain, who fhall nominate
eleven commiffioners; and whatfoever the major part
of them fhall determine, as to the remaining differences, fhall oblige both parties; provided ftill, that
they deliver their judgment within the fpace of fix
months from the day of their affembling; which fhall
likewife be within the fpace of three months after the
faid moft Serene Queen Regent of Spain hath accepted
of the being umpire.

X. That whereas the moft Serene Queen Regent of
Spain hath given affurance to his Majefty of Great
Britain, that the faid States General fhould, upon the
making of the peace, pay unto his faid Majefty the
King of Great Britain, the fum of 800,000 patacoons,
the faid States General do promife and covenant to
pay the faid 800,000 patacoons in this following manner, *viz.* a fourth part as foon as the ratification of
this treaty fhall be mutually exhibited, and the reft the
three enfuing years, by equal portions.

XI. The aforefaid moft Serene King of Great
Britain, and the faid High and Mighty States General
of the United Provinces, fhall obferve fincerely, and
bond fide, all and fingular the matters agreed and concluded in this prefent treaty, and caufe the fame to be
obferved by their fubjects and inhabitants; nor fhall
they directly or indirectly violate any of them, or fuffer
                                                them

them to be violated by their subjects or inhabitants: and they shall ratify and confirm all and every thing as before agreed, by letters patent subscribed with their hands, and sealed with their great seals, conceived and written in sufficient, valid, and effectual form; and shall deliver, or cause the same to be delivered reciprocally, within four weeks after the date of these presents (or sooner if it may be) *bonâ fide*, really, and with effect.

XII. Lastly, as soon as the said ratifications shall have been duly and mutually exhibited and exchanged, the peace shall be proclaimed at the Hague within four and twenty hours after the delivery and exchange there made of the said ratifications.

Done at Westminster the $\frac{9}{19}$ day of February, $167\frac{3}{4}$.

[The following is printed from the copy published by authority in 1686.]

A Treaty Marine, between the most Serene and Mighty Prince, Charles *the Second, by the Grace of God, King of* England, Scotland, France, *and* Ireland, *Defender of the Faith,* &c. *and the High and Mighty Lords, the States General of the* United Netherlands, *to be observed throughout all and every the Countries and Parts of the World, by Sea and Land. Concluded at* London *the First Day of* December, 1674, *S. V.*

I. THAT it shall and may be lawful for all and every the subjects of the most Serene and Mighty Prince, the King of Great Britain aforesaid, with all freedom and safety to sail, trade, and exercise any manner of traffic in all those kingdoms, countries, and estates, which are, or at any time hereafter shall be in peace, amity, or neutrality with his said Majesty;

fo that they fhall not be any ways hindered or molefted in their navigation or trade, by the military forces,
nor by the fhips of war, or any other kind of veffels
whatfoever, belonging either to the High and Mighty
States General of the United Netherlands, or to their
fubjects, upon occafion or pretence of any hoftility or
difference which now is, or fhall hereafter happen between the faid Lords the States General, and any
princes or people whatfoever in peace, amity, or neutrality with his faid Majefty: and likewife, that it fhall
and may be lawful for all and every the fubjects of the
faid High and Mighty Lords the States General of
the United Netherlands, with all freedom and fafety
to fail, trade, and exercife any manner of traffic in
all thofe kingdoms, countries, and eftates, which are,
or at any time hereafter fhall be in peace, amity, or
neutrality with the aforefaid Lords the States; fo that
they fhall not be any ways hindered or molefted in their
navigation or trade, by the military forces, nor by the
fhips of war, or any other kind of veffels whatfoever,
belonging either to the moft Serene and Mighty King
above mentioned, or to his fubjects, upon occafion or
pretence of any hoftility or difference, which now is,
or fhall hereafter happen between his faid Majefty and
any princes or people whatfoever, in peace, amity, or
neutrality with the faid Lords the States.

II. Nor fhall this freedom of navigation and commerce be infringed by occafion or caufe of any war,
in any kind of merchandizes, but fhall extend to all
commodities which fhall be carried in time of peace;
thofe only excepted which follow in the next article,
and are comprehended under the name of Contraband.

III. Under this name of Contraband or prohibited
merchandizes fhall be comprehended only arms, pieces
of ordnance, with all implements belonging to them,
fire-balls, powder, match, bullets, pikes, fwords, lances,
fpears, halberds, guns, mortar-pieces, petards, granadoes,

does, mufquet-refts, bandeliers, falt-petre, mufquets, mufquet-fhot, helmets, corflets, breaft-plates, coats of mail, and the like kind of armature, foldiers, horfes, and all things neceffary for the furniture of horfes, holfters, belts, and all other warlike inftruments whatfoever.

IV. Thefe merchandizes following fhall not be reckoned among prohibited goods, *viz.* all kind of cloth; and all other manufactures woven of any kind of wool, flax, filk, cotton, or any other material; all forts of clothing and veftments, together with the materials whereof they ufe to be made; gold and filver, as well coined as not coined; tin, iron, lead, copper, and coals; as alfo wheat, barley, and all other kind of corn or pulfe; tobacco, and all kind of fpices, falted and fmoked flefh, falted and dried fifh, butter and cheefe, beer, oils, wines, fugars, and all fort of falt; and in general, all provifion which ferves for the nourifhment and fuftenance of life; likewife all kind of cotton, hemp, flax, and pitch, and ropes, fails, and anchors; alfo mafts and planks, boards and beams of what fort of wood foever, and all other materials requifite for the building or repairing fhips, but they fhall be wholly reputed amongft free goods, even as all other wares and commodities which are not comprehended in the next precedent article, fo that the fame may be freely tranfported and carried by the fubjects of his faid Majefty, even unto places in enmity with the faid States, as alfo on the other fide, by the fubjects of the faid States, to places under the obedience of the enemies of his faid Majefty; except only towns or places befieged, environed, or invefted, in French, Blocquees ou invefties.

V. And that all manner of differences and contentions on both fides, by fea and land, may from henceforth ceafe and be utterly extinguifhed, it is agreed, that all kind of fhips and veffels whatfoever, belonging to the fubjects of his faid Majefty, entering or

N 2   being

being entered into any road or port under the obedience of the Lords the States, and purpofing to pafs from thence, fhall be only obliged to fhew unto the officers acting in the ports of the faid States, or to the captains of the States fhips, or of private men of war (if any happen there to be) their paffport, commonly called a fea-brief (the form whereof is added at the end of thefe articles) nor fhall any money, or any thing elfe be exacted from them under that pretence; but if any fhip belonging to the fubjects of his Majefty of Great Britain fhall, in the open fea, or elfewhere, out of the dominions of the faid States, meet the fhips of war of the faid Lords the States, or private men of war of their fubjects, the faid fhips of the Lords the States, or of their fubjects, fhall keep at a convenient diftance, and only fend out their boat, and it fhall be lawful for them only with two or three men, to go on board the fhips and veffels of the fubjects of his Majefty, that the paffport (or fea-brief) of the propriety thereof, according to the form hereafter fpecified, may be fhewn to them by the captain or mafter of fuch fhip or veffel belonging to the fubjects of his Majefty; and the fhip which fhall fhew the fame fhall freely pafs, and it fhall not be lawful to moleft, fearch, detain, or divert the fame from her intended voyage: and all the fubjects of the Lords the States fhall enjoy in all things the fame liberty and immunity, they in like manner fhewing their paffport (or fea-brief) made according to the form prefcribed at the latter end of this treaty.

VI. But if any fhip or veffel belonging to the Englifh, or other fubjects of his Majefty, fhall be met making into any port in enmity with the Lords the States; or on the other fide, if any fhip belonging to the United Provinces of the Netherlands, or other fubjects of the Lords the States, fhall be met in her way making into any port under the obedience of the enemies of his faid Majefty, fuch fhip fhall fhew, not only a paffport (or fea-brief) according to the form hereunder prefcribed, wherewith fhe is to be furnifhed, but alfo her cocquets, exprefling the contents of the goods on board, given in the ufual form, by the officers of the cuftoms in the port from whence fhe came, whereby it may be known whether fhe is laden with any merchandizes prohibited by the third article of this treaty.

VII. But if by the fhewing the abovefaid cocquets exprefling the contents of the goods on board, given in the ufual form by the officers of the cuftoms in the port from whence fhe came (concerning the fhewing whereof it is above agreed) either party fhall difcover any kind of, merchandizes which in the third article of this treaty are declared to be contraband or prohibited, configned to any port under the obedience of their enemies, it fhall not be lawful to open the hatches of fuch fhip in which the fame fhall happen to be found, whether fhe belongs to the fubjects of his Majefty, or of the Lords the States, nor to unlock or break open the chefts, mails, packs, or cafks in the fame, nor to convey away any the leaft part of the merchandizes, before the whole be firft landed in the prefence of the officers of the admiralty, and inventoried; neither fhall it be any ways lawful to fell, exchange, or otherwife to alienate the fame, until fuch prohibited goods are rightly and lawfully proceeded againft, and that the judges of the admiralty have by their refpective fentences confifcated the fame: provided always, that as well the fhip itfelf, as the reft of the commodities found in the fame, which by this treaty are to be reputed free, fhall not, upon pretence of their being infected by fuch prohibited goods, be detained, much lefs confifcated for lawful prize; but if not the whole, but a part only of the lading confifts of contraband or prohibited commodities, and that the mafter of the fhip fhall be willing and ready to deliver them to the captor who feized the fame, in that cafe the captor fhall not compel the fhip to go out of her courfe, to any port he thinks fit, but fhall forthwith difmifs her, and upon

no account hinder her from freely profecuting her defigned voyage.

VIII. It is further agreed, that whatfoever fhall be
found laden by his Majefty's fubjects, upon any fhip
whatfoever belonging to the enemies of the Lords the
States, although the fame be not of the quality of contraband goods, may be confifcated; but on the contrary, all that which fhall be found in the fhips belonging to the fubjects of his Majefty fhall be accounted
clear and free, although the whole lading, or any part
thereof, by juft title of propriety, fhall belong to the
enemies of the Lords the States; except always contraband goods, which being intercepted, all things
fhall be done according to the meaning and direction
of the precedent articles; and by the fame reafon,
whatfoever fhall be laden by the fubjects of the Lords
the States, in any fhip whatfoever belonging to the
enemies of his Majefty, although the fame be not of
the quality of contraband goods, may be confifcated;
but on the other fide, all that which fhall be found in
the fhips belonging to the fubjects of the Lords the
States, fhall be accounted clear and free, although the
whole lading, or any part thereof, by juft title of
propriety, fhall belong to the enemies of his Majefty;
except always contraband goods, which being intercepted, all things fhall be done according to the meaning and direction of the precedent articles. And left
any damage fhould by furprize be done to the one
party who is in peace, when the other party fhall happen to be engaged in war, it is provided and agreed,
that a fhip belonging to the enemies of the one party,
and laden with goods of the fubjects of the other party,
fhall not infect or render the faid goods liable to confifcation, in cafe they were laden before the expiration
of the terms and times hereafter mentioned, after the
declaration or publication of any fuch war; viz. if the
goods were laden in any port or place between the
places or limits called the Soundings, and the Naz in
Norway, within the fpace of fix weeks after fuch declaration;

claration; of two months, between the faid place the Soundings, and the city of Tangier; and of ten weeks, in the Mediterranean Sea; or within the fpace of eight months in any other country or place of the world; fo that it fhall not be lawful to confifcate the goods of the fubjects of his Majefty, taken or feized in any fhip or veffel whatfoever of any enemy of the Lords the States, upon that pretence, but the fame fhall be without delay reftored to the pioprietors, unlefs they were laden after the expiration of the faid terms of time refpectively; but fo that it may not be lawful for them afterwards to carry to enemies ports the faid merchandizes which are called contraband, and for the reafon aforefaid fhall not be liable to confifcation; neither, on the other fide, fhall it be lawful to confifcate the goods of the fubjects of the Lords the States, taken or feized in any fhip or veffel whatfoever of an enemy of his Majefty, upon that pretence; but the fame fhall be forthwith reftored to the proprietors thereof, unlefs they were laden after the expiration of the faid terms of time refpectively; but fo, that it may not be lawful for them afterwards to carry to enemies ports the faid merchandizes which are called contraband, and for the reafon aforefaid fhall not be liable to confifcation.

IX. And the more to affure the fubjects of his Majefty and of the faid States, that no injury fhall be offered to them by the fhips of war or private men of war of either fide, all the captains of the fhips, as well of his Majefty as of the faid States, and all their fubjects who fhall fet out private men of war, and likewife their privileged companies, fhall be enjoined not to do any injury or damage whatfoever to the other; which if they do, they fhall be punifhed, and moreover be liable to fatisfy all cofts and damages, by reftitution and reparation, upon pain and obligation of perfon and goods.

N 4　　　　　X. For

X. For this cause, all the commanders of private men of war shall from henceforth be obliged, before they receive their commissions, to enter, before a competent judge, good and sufficient security, by able and responsible men, who have no part or interest in such ship, in the sum of fifteen hundred pounds sterling, or sixteen thousand five hundred gilders; and when they have above one hundred and fifty men, then in the sum of three thousand pounds sterling, or three and thirty thousand gilders, that they will give full satisfaction for any damages or injuries whatsoever, which they or their officers, or others in their service, shall commit in their courses at sea, contrary to this present treaty, or any other whatsoever, between his Majesty and the said States, and upon pain of revocation and annulling their said commissions, in which it shall be always inserted, that they have given such security as abovesaid; and likewise it is agreed, that the ship itself shall be also liable to make satisfaction for injuries and damages done by her.

XI. His Majesty and the said States, being desirous that the subjects of each other may be mutually treated, in all countries under their obedience respectively, with the like kindness as their own subjects, will give all necessary and effectual orders, the judgments upon prizes taken be given according to the rule of justice and equity, by judges beyond all suspicion, and not any way concerned in the cause under debate; and his Majesty and the said States will likewise give strict orders that all sentences already given, and which shall be hereafter given, be (according to the tenor thereof) duly put in execution, and obtain their effect.

XII. And whensoever the ambassadors of the said Lords the States, or any other their public ministers resident at the court of his most Serene Majesty of Great Britain, shall complain of the unjustness of sentences which have been given, his Majesty will cause the same to be reviewed and examined in his council,

that

that it may appear whether the orders and precautions prescribed in this treaty have been observed, and have had their due effect, and will also take care that the same be fully provided for, and that right be done to the party complaining, within the space of three months; and likewise, when the ambassadors or other public ministers of his Majesty, resident with the States General, shall complain of the unjustness of sentences, the said States will cause a review and examination thereof to be made in the assembly of the States General, that it may appear whether the orders and precautions prescribed in this treaty have been observed, and have had their due effect, and they will likewise take care that the same be fully provided for, and that right be done to the party complaining within the space of three months: nevertheless, it shall not any ways be lawful to sell or unlade the goods in controversy, either before the sentence given, or after it, during the review thereof, on either side, unless it be with the consent of the parties interested.

XIII. A suit being commenced between the takers of prizes on the one part, and the claimers thereof on the other, and a sentence or decree being given for the party reclaiming, the said sentence or decree (upon security given) shall be put in execution, notwithstanding the appeal made by him that took the prize, which shall not be observed, in case the sentence shall be given against the claimers.

XIV. And whereas the masters of merchants ships, and likewise the mariners and passengers, do sometime suffer many cruelties and barbarous usages, when they are brought under the power of ships which take prizes in time of war, the takers in an inhuman manner tormenting them, thereby to extort from them such confessions as they would have to be made; it is agreed, that both his Majesty, and the Lords the States General, shall, by the severest proclamations or placarts, forbid all such heinous and inhuman offences, and as many as

they

they fhall by lawful proofs find guilty of fuch acts, they
fhall take care that they be punifhed with due and juft
punifhments, and which may be a terror to others;
and fhall command that all the captains and officers
of fhips, who fhall be proved to have committed fuch
heinous practices, either themfelves, or by inftigating
others to act the fame, or by conniving while they
were done, fhall (befides other punifhments to be
inflicted proportionably to their offences) be forthwith
deprived of their offices refpectively; and every fhip
brought up as prize, whofe mariners or paffengers fhall
have fuffered any torture, fhall forthwith be difmiffed
and freed, with all her lading, from all further examination and proceedings againft her, as well judicial as
otherwife.

XV. It is alfo agreed, that the like feverity of punifhments fhall be inflicted upon thofe who, contrary
to the meaning of the one and twentieth article of the
treaty of peace concluded at Breda, fhall take commiffions from enemies, to feize the fhips of either ally
(or party) contrary to what is provided in the faid
article.

XVI. Laftly, it is agreed and concluded, that this
prefent treaty, and all and fingular the things therein
contained, fhall be with all convenient fpeed on both
fides ratified and confirmed, and that the ratifications
thereof fhall be, within two months from the date
hereof, rightly and reciprocally exchanged between
both parties, and alfo that the faid treaty fhall, within
one month after fuch exchanging of the ratifications,
be delivered in due and authentic form to the governors of the Englifh Eaft India and Africa companies,
and to the directors of the Dutch Eaft and Weft India
companies, and fhall with the firft conveniency be alfo
fent by his faid Majefty, and by the faid Lords the
States, to their refpective governors and commanders
in chief of their colonies and plantations in every part
of the world out of Europe, to the end that it may

be

be by them, and all others within their dominions and under their power, punctually observed and fulfilled. ;

The Form of the Passport (or Sea-brief) to be asked of, and given by the Lord High Admiral, or by those to whom the Exercise of Admiralty Jurisdiction is ordinarily committed, or by the Mayor or other chief Magistrate, or by the Commissioners or other principal Officers of the Customs in their respective Ports and Places within his Majesty's Dominions, to the Ships and Vessels sailing out thence, according to the Purport of the Fifth Article.

TO all unto whom these presents shall come, greeting. We   Lord High Admiral of ·   We   Lords Commissioners executing the office of the Lord High Admiral of   or We   Judge of the High Court of the Admiralty of   or We   the Mayor, or other Magistrate of   or We   Commissioners, or principal Officers of the Customs in the city or port of   do testify and make known, that   master or commander of the ship called the   hath appeared before us, and hath declared by solemn oath, that the said ship or vessel, containing about   tons, of which he is at present master or commander, doth belong to the inhabitants of · within the dominions of the most Serene and Mighty Prince, the King of England, Scotland, France, and Ireland, Defender of the Faith, &c. So help him God. And in regard it would be most acceptable to us, that the said master or commander be assisted in his just and lawful affairs, we do request you, and every of you, wheresoever the said master or commander shall arrive with his ship, and the goods laden on board and carried in her, that you would please to receive him courteously, and use him kindly, and admit him, upon paying the lawful and usual customs

and

and other duties, to enter into, remain in, and pafs
from your ports, rivers, and dominions, and there to
enjoy all kind of right of navigation, traffic, and commerce, in all places where he fhall think fit; which
we fhall moft willingly and readily acknowledge upon
all occafions. In teftimony and confirmation whereof,
we have with our hand figned thefe prefents, and
caufed them to be fealed with our feal, Dated at
in   the   day of
in the year of our Lord

*The Form of the Paffport (or Sea-brief) to be afked of,
and given by the Burgermafters of the Cities and
Ports of the United Netherlands, to the Ships or
Veffels failing from thence, according to the Purport
of the Fifth Article.*

TO the moft Serene, moft Illuftrious, moft Mighty, moft Noble, moft Honourable, and moft Prudent
Emperors, Kings, Governors of Commonwealths,
Princes, Dukes, Earls, Barons, Lords, Burgermafters,
Schepens, Counfellors, Judges, Officers, Juftices, and
Rulers of all cities and places, as well ecclefiaftical
as fecular, to whom thefe prefents fhall be fhewn; We
the burgermafters and rulers of the city of
do certify, that   mafter or fkipper of the
fhip   appeared before us, and declared by
folemn oath, that the faid fhip, called the   :
containing about   lafts, of which he is at
prefent mafter or fkipper, belongeth to the inhabitants
of the United Netherlands. So help him God. And
in regard it would be moft acceptable to us, that the
faid mafter or fkipper be affifted in his juft and lawful affairs, we do requeft you and every of you, wherefoever the faid mafter or fkipper fhall arrive with his
fhip, and the goods laden on board and carried in
her, that you would pleafe to receive him courteoufly,
and ufe him kindly, and admit him, upon paying the
lawful and ufual cuftoms and other duties, to enter
into, remain in, and pafs from your ports, rivers, and
dominions,

dominions, and there to enjoy all kind of right of navigation, traffic, and commerce, in all places where he shall think fit; which we shall most willingly and readily acknowledge upon all occasions. In testimony and confirmation whereof, we have caused the seal of our city to be hereunto put. Dated at
in   the   day of
in the year of our Lord

In testimony and confirmation of all and singular the premises, we the commissioners of his Majesty and the Lords the States General aforesaid, being sufficiently impowered thereunto, have to these presents subscribed our names, and sealed them with our seals, at London, the first day of December, 1674.

Tho. Culpeper	*J. Corver*
G. Downing	*G. Sautyn*
Richard Ford	*Samuel Beyer*
Will. Thomson	*And. Van Vossen*
John Jollife	*P. Duvelaer*
John Buckworth	*M. Michielzen.*

[The following is printed from the copy published by authority in 1686.]

Explanatory Declaration upon certain Articles of the Marine Treaties, concluded between his Majesty and the States General of the United Provinces, February 17, 166⅞, and December 1, 1674.

WHEREAS some difficulty hath arisen concerning the interpretation of certain articles, as well in the treaty marine which was concluded the first day of December, 1674, as in that which was concluded the 17th of February, 166⅞, between his Majesty of Great Britain on the one part, and the States General of the United Provinces of the Low Countries on the

the other, relating to the liberty of their respective
subjects to trade unto the ports of each other's enemies; We Sir William Temple, Baronet, Ambassador
Extraordinary from his said Majesty of Great Britain, in the name and on the part of his said Majesty; and We William Van Heuckelom, Daniel Van
Wyngaerden, Lord of Werckendam, Gaspar Fagel,
Counsellor and Pensioner of Holland and West Friesland, John de Mauregnault, John Baron of Reede
and Renswoude, William de Haren, Gretman of the
Bilt, Henry Ter Borgh, and Luke Alting, Deputies
in the Assembly of the said States General for the
States of Guelderland, Holland, Zealand, Utrecht,
Friesland, Overissell, Groningen, and the Omlands, in
the name and on the part of the said States General, have declared, as we do by these presents declare,
that the true meaning and intention of the said articles is and ought to be, that ships and vessels belonging to the subjects of either of the parties, can
and might, from the time that the said articles were
concluded, not only pass, traffic, and trade from a
neutral port or place to a place in enmity with the
other party, or from a place in enmity to a neutral
place, but also from a port or place in enmity, to a
port or place in enmity with the other party, whether
the said places belong to one and the same Prince or
State, or to several Princes or States, with whom the
other party is in war. And we declare, that this is
the true and genuine sense and meaning of the said articles; pursuant whereunto we understand that the
said articles are to be observed and executed on all occasions, on the part of his said Majesty and the said
States General, and their respective subjects; yet so,
that this declaration shall not be alledged by either
party for matters which happened before the conclusion of the late peace in the month of February, 167¾.
And we do promise, that the said declaration shall be
ratified by his said Majesty, and by the said States General, and that within two months, or sooner if possible,

ble, reckoning from the day and date of this declaration, the ratifications of the same shall be brought hither to the Hague, to be here exchanged. In witness whereof we have signed these presents at the Hague, this 30th day of December, 1675.

(L. S.) *W. Temple.* (L. S.) *W. Van Heuckelom.*
　　　　　　　　　(L. S.) *D. Van Wyngaerden.*
　　　　　　　　　(L. S.) *Gasp. Fagel.*
　　　　　　　　　(L. S.) *Jo. Mauregnault.*
　　　　　　　　　(L. S.) *John Baron van Reede*
　　　　　　　　　　　　 vry Heer van Renswoude.
　　　　　　　　　(L. S.) *W. Haren.*
　　　　　　　　　(L. S.) *H Ter. Borgh.*
　　　　　　　　　(L. S.) *L. Alting.*

[The following is printed from the copy published by authority in 1784.]

The Definitive Treaty of Peace and Friendship between his Majesty the King of Great Britain, *and their High Mightinesses the States General of the* United Provinces *of the* Low Countries.

In the name of the most holy and undivided Trinity, Father, Son, and Holy Ghost. So be it.

BE it known to all those whom it shall or may in any manner concern. The most Serene and most Potent Prince and Lord George the Third, by the grace of God, King of Great Britain, France, and Ireland, Duke of Brunswic and Lunenbourg, Arch-Treasurer and Elector of the holy Roman Empire, &c. and the High and Mighty Lords the States General of the United Provinces of the Low Countries, having laid the foundation of peace by the preliminary articles signed at Paris the second of September last; and his said Majesty and the said States General being desirous to complete so great and salutary a work, have

‑named

named and authorised, to wit, on the part of his Britannic Majesty, Daniel Hailes, Esq; his said Majesty's Minister Plenipotentiary to his most Christian
Majesty; and on the part of their High Mightinesses
the said States General, the most Noble and most Excellent Lords Mathew Lestevenon, Lord of Berkenroode and Stryen, Deputy to the States General of
the United Provinces of the Low Countries from the
province of Holland, and their Ambassador in Ordinary to his Majesty the most Christian King, and
Gerard Brantsen, Burgomaster and Senator of the
city of Arnheim, Counsellor and Grand Master of
the Mint of the Republic, Deputy to the States General of the United Provinces, and their Ambassador
Extraordinary and Plenipotentiary to his most Christian Majesty: who, after having duly communicated
to each other their full powers in good form, have
agreed upon the following articles.

I. There shall be a christian, universal, and perpetual peace, as well by sea as by land, and a sincere
and constant friendship shall be re-established, between
his Britannic Majesty, his heirs and successors, kingdoms, dominions, and subjects, and their High Mightinesses the said States General, and their dominions
and subjects, of what quality or condition soever they
be, without exception either of places or persons; so that
the high contracting parties shall give the greatest attention to the maintaining between themselves, and their
said dominions and subjects, this reciprocal friendship
and intercourse, without permitting hereafter, on either
part, any kind of hostilities to be committed, either
by sea or by land, for any cause or under any pretence
whatsoever: and they shall carefully avoid, for the
future, every thing which might prejudice the union
happily re-established, endeavouring, on the contrary,
to procure reciprocally for each other, on every occasion, whatever may contribute to their mutual glory,
interests, and advantage, without giving any assistance
or protection, directly or indirectly, to those who would
do

do any injury to either of the high contracting parties. There shall be a general oblivion of every thing which may have been done or committed, before or since the commencement of the war which is just ended.

II. With respect to the honours of the flag, and the salute at sea, by the ships of the Republic towards those of his Britannic Majesty, the same custom shall be respectively followed, as was practised before the commencement of the war which is just concluded.

III. All the prisoners taken on either side, as well by land as by sea, and the hostages carried away or given during the war, and who have not yet been restored, conformably to the preliminary treaty, shall be restored as soon as possible, without ransom; each Power respectively discharging the advances which shall have been made, for the subsistence and maintenance of their prisoners, by the Sovereign of the country where they shall have been detained, according to the receipts, attested accounts, and other authentic vouchers, which shall be furnished on each side : and sureties shall be reciprocally given for the payment of the debts which the prisoners may have contracted in the countries where they may have been detained until their entire release. And all ships, as well men of war as merchant-ships, which may have been taken since the expiration of the terms agreed upon for the cessation of hostilities by sea, shall likewise be restored, *bonâ fide*, with all their crews and cargoes : and the execution of this article shall be proceeded upon immediately after the exchange of the ratifications of this treaty.

IV. The States General of the United Provinces cede and guaranty, in full right, to his Britannic Majesty, the town of Negapatnam, with the dependencies thereof; but in consideration of the importance which the States General of the United Provinces annex to the possession of the aforesaid town, the King of Great Britain, as a proof of his good-will towards the said States, promises, notwithstanding this cession, to receive and treat with them for the restitution of the said town, in case the Lords the States should hereafter have an equivalent to offer him.

V. The King of Great Britain shall restore to the States General of the United Provinces, Trinquemale, as also all the other towns, forts, harbours, and settlements, which, in the course of the war, have been conquered, in any part of the world whatever, by the arms of his Britannic Majesty, or by those of the English East India Company, and of which he should be in possession; the whole in the condition in which they shall be found.

VI. The States General of the United Provinces promise and engage not to obstruct the navigation of the British subjects in the Eastern seas.

VII. Whereas differences have arisen between the English African Company, and the Dutch West India Company, relative to the navigation on the coasts of Africa, as also on the subject of Cape Apollonia; for preventing all cause of complaint between the subjects of the two nations on those coasts, it is agreed that commissaries shall be named, on each side, to make suitable arrangements on these points.

VIII. All the countries and territories which may have been, or which may be conquered, in any part of the world whatsoever, by the arms of his Britannic Majesty, as well as by those of the States General, which are not included in the present treaty, neither under the head of Cessions, nor under the head of Restitutions, shall be restored without difficulty, and without requiring any compensation.

. IX. Whereas by the ninth article of the preliminary treaty, a period was stipulated and appointed, by the high contracting parties, for the restitutions and evacuations to be made, on each side, of the towns, for-

5   tresses,

treffes, and territories which might have been conquered by their refpective arms, and of which they fhould be in poffeffion, excepting fuch as had been ceded; and whereas the term fpecified in the aforefaid ninth article is already expired, the high contracting parties engage reciprocally and *bonâ fide*, to obferve the faid ftipulations, and in cafe, by any accident or otherwife, the ceffions and reftitutions therein comprifed fhould not have taken place, to expedite immediately the neceffary orders, to the end that there may be no further delay in the accomplifhment of the faid ftipulations.

X. His Britannic Majefty and their High Mightineffes the aforefaid States General, promife to obferve fincerely, and *bonâ fide*, all the articles contained and eftablifhed in this prefent treaty; and they will not fuffer the fame to be infringed, directly or indirectly, by their refpective fubjects: and the faid high contracting parties guaranty to each other, generally and reciprocally, all the ftipulations of the prefent articles.

XI. The folemn ratifications of the prefent treaty, prepared in good and due form, fhall be exchanged in this city of Paris, between the high contracting parties, in the fpace of one month, or fooner, if it can be done, to be computed from the day of the fignature of the prefent treaty.

In witnefs whereof, we the under-written, their ambaffadors and minifters plenipotentiary, have figned with our hands, in their names, and by virtue of our full powers, the prefent definitive treaty, and have caufed the feals of our arms to be affixed thereto.

Done at Paris the 20th of May, one thoufand feven hundred and eighty-four.

Daniel Hailes. (L. S.)

Leftevenon van Berkenrode. (L. S.)
Brantfen. (L. S.)

Separate

Separate Article.

I. IT has been agreed and determined, that the French language, made ufe of in all the copies of the prefent treaty, fhall not form an example which may be alledged, or quoted as a precedent, or, in any manner, prejudice either of the contracting Powers; and that they fhall conform, for the future, to what has been obferved, and ought to be obferved, with regard to, and on the part of Powers, who are in the practice and poffeffion of giving and receiving copies of like treaties in a different language from the French; the prefent treaty having, neverthelefs, the fame force and virtue as if the aforefaid practice had been therein obferved.

In witnefs whereof, we the under-written Ambaffadors and Minifters Plenipotentiary of his Britannic Majefty, and of the States General of the United Provinces, have figned the prefent feparate article, and have caufed the feals of our arms to be affixed thereto.

Done at Paris, the twentieth of May, one thoufand feven hundred and eighty-four.

Daniel Hailes. (L. S.)
      Leftevenon van Berkenroode. (L. S.)
      Brantfen. (L. S.)

His Britannic *Majefty's Full Power.*

GEORGE *R.*

GEORGE the Third, by the grace of God, King of Great Britain, France, and Ireland, Defender of the Faith, Duke of Brunfwic and Lunenburgh, Arch-Treafurer and Prince Elector of the holy Roman Empire, &c. To all and fingular to whom thefe prefents fhall come, greeting. Whereas, in order to perfect the peace between us and the High and Mighty Lords the States General of the United Netherlands, which was happily begun by the preliminary articles, figned at Paris the fecond day of September laft, and to

bring'

bring the, fame to the defired conclufion, we have
thought fit to inveft fome proper perfon with full
power on our part; Know ye, that we, confiding entirely in the fidelity, diligence, ability, penetration, and
experience in affairs of our trufty and well-beloved
Daniel Hailes, Efq; our Minifter Plenipotentiary to
our good brother the moft Chriftian King, have
named, made, and conftituted, and, by thefe prefents,
do name, make, and conftitute him our true, certain
and undoubted Commiffioner, Procurator, and Plenipotentiary; giving and granting to him all and all
manner of power, faculty, and authority, as alfo our
general and fpecial command (fo that the general fhall
not derogate from the fpecial, nor contrarywife) at the
court of our faid good brother the moft Chriftian King,
for us, and in our name, to meet and confer with the
Ambaffadors, Commiffioners, Deputies, and Plenipotentiaries of the aforefaid Lords the States General of
the United Netherlands, being furnifhed with fufficient authority, and with them to agree, treat, confult,
and conclude upon the re-eftablifhing, as foon as may
be, of a firm and lafting peace, and fincere friendfhip
and concord; and for us, and in our name, to fign
whatever may be fo agreed upon and concluded; and
alfo to make, and mutually deliver and receive, a
treaty or treaties, or fuch other and fo many inftruments as fhall be requifite, upon the bufinefs concluded, and to tranfact all other matters, which may relate to the happily accomplifhing of the aforefaid work,
in as ample manner and form, and with equal force
and effect, as we, if we were prefent, could do and
perform: engaging and promifing, on our Royal word,
that we will approve, ratify, and accept, in every more
perfect form, whatever may happen to be tranfacted
and concluded by our faid Plenipotentiary, and that
we will never fuffer the fame to be violated or infringed
by any one, either in the whole or in part. In witnefs, and for the greater validity of all which, we have
caufed our great feal of Great Britain to be affixed to

thefe

thefe préfents, figned with our Royal hand. Given at our court at St. James's, the twenty-feventh day of April, in the year of our Lord one thoufand feven hundred and eighty-four, and in the twenty-fourth year of our reign.

The *Full Power* of the States General.

THE States General of the United Netherlands: To all who fhall fee thefe prefents, greeting. Whereas there is nothing we have more earneftly at heart, than that the war, in which we, together with other Powers, are involved, againft Great Britain, may be terminated by a general, folid, and lafting peace, and that, in order to accomplifh fo defirable and falutary a purpofe, negotiations may be forthwith begun; wherefore, moved by a defire of contributing whatever lies in our power to promote the negotiation for a general peace, and trufting that we fhall find the moft Serene King of Great Britain animated with the like fentiments, we, knowing the prudence, experience in affairs, and fidelity of the Lords Leftevenon de Berkenroode, our Ambaffador to his moft Chriftian Majefty, and Gerard Brantfen, Conful of the city of Arnheim, Counfellor and Mafter General of the Mint of the Republic, Deputy in ordinary from the province of Gueldres to our Affembly, and our Plenipotentiary, have authorifed, appointed, commiffioned, and deputed, as, by thefe prefents, we do authorife, appoint, commiffion, and depute them, granting full power, as well as general and fpecial command, to both of them conjointly, or to either of them in the abfence of the other, whether on account of illnefs, or of any other impediment whatfoever, to treat with him or them who fhall have been likewife invefted by his Britannic Majefty with the neceffary authority for that purpofe, concerning all things which fhall be judged expedient and requifite for concluding a general, lafting, and advantageous peace, to endeavour to remove all obftacles which may

occur,

occur, to act, agree, and ftipulate thereupon, in fuch manner as they fhall think proper, and generally to do all things relative thereto, which we ourfelves being prefent might do; promifing fincerely and *bonâ fide*, that we will accept, perform, and ratify every thing which the faid Lords our Ambaffador and Plenipotentiary fhall have ftipulated, promifed, or granted, and that we will iffue our letters of ratification in due form. Given at the Hague under our great feal, figned by the Prefident of our affembly, and counterfigned by our Greffier, the nineteenth day of Auguft, in the year one thoufand feven hundred and eighty-two.　　　　　　　　　　　　　R. *Sloet*, Pt.

By order of the aforefaid Lords the States General,
H. Fagel.

[The following is printed from the copy publifhed by authority in 1788.]

The Treaty of defenfive Alliance between his Majefty the King of Great Britain, and their High Mightineffes the States General of the United Provinces, figned at the Hague the 15th of April, 1788.

THE mutual and fincere friendfhip, which has fo long fubfifted between his Majefty the King of Great Britain, and the Lords the States General of the United Provinces, having been increafed and ftrengthened by the intereft, which his Britannic Majefty has lately manifefted in the prefervation of the independence of the Republic, and of its legal conftitution, his faid Majefty, and the faid Lords the States General of the United Provinces, have refolved, in order to cement, in the moft folid and lafting manner, the good harmony, confidence, and correfpondence between them, to form permanent engagements, by a treaty of defenfive alliance, for the good of both parties, and for the maintenance of the general tranquillity, as well as of their own in particular. To accomplifh fo falutary

lutary a purpofe, his Majefty the King of Great Britain has named and authorized Sir James Harris, Privy Counfellor, Knight of the Bath, Member of the Parliament of Great Britain, and his Majefty's ambaffador extraordinary and plenipotentiary to their High Mightineffes; and their High Mightineffes the States General of the United Provinces have named and authorized their Deputies for foreign affairs; who, after communicating to each other their full powers in due form, and having conferred together, have agreed upon the following articles:

I. There fhall be a fincere, firm, and conftant friendfhip and union between his Britannic Majefty, his heirs and fucceffors, and the Lords the States General of the United Provinces, fo that the high contracting parties fhall direct their utmoft attention to maintain this mutual friendfhip and correfpondence between them, and their dominions and fubjects; and they engage to contribute, as far as fhall be in their power, mutually to preferve and defend each other in peace and tranquillity.

II. In cafe either of the high contracting parties fhould be hoftilely attacked by any European Power, in any part of the world whatfoever, the other contracting party engages to fuccour its ally, as well by fea as by land, in order to maintain and guaranty each other mutually in the poffeffion of all the dominions, territories, towns, places, franchifes, and liberties, which belonged to them refpectively before the commencement of hoftilities.

III. His Britannic Majefty guaranties, in the moft effectual manner, the hereditary ftadtholderate, as well as the office of hereditary governor of each province, in the Serene Houfe of Orange, with all the rights and prerogatives thereto belonging, as forming an effential part of the conftitution of the United Provinces, according to the refolutions and diplomas of the years 1747 and 1748, by virtue of which the prefent Stadt-

holder

holder entered into the poſſeſſion of thoſe offices in 1766, and was reinſtated therein in 1788; engaging to maintain that form of government againſt all attacks and enterprizes, direct or indirect, of whatſoever nature they may be.

IV. The ſuccours mentioned in the ſecond article of this treaty of defenſive alliance, ſhall conſiſt, on the part of his Britannic Majeſty, of eight thouſand infantry, two thouſand cavalry, twelve ſhips of the line, and eight frigates; and, on the part of the States General, of five thouſand infantry, one thouſand cavalry, eight ſhips of the line, and eight frigates; which reſpective ſuccours ſhall be furniſhed in the ſpace of two months after requiſition made by the party attacked, and ſhall remain at its diſpoſal during the whole continuance of the war in which it ſhall be engaged, whilſt thoſe ſuccours (whether ſhips and frigates, or troops) ſhall be paid and maintained by the Power of whom they ſhall be required, wherever its ally ſhall employ them.

V. In caſe the ſtipulated ſuccours ſhould not be ſufficient for the defence of the Power requiring them, the Power to whom requiſition ſhall be made ſhall ſucceſſively augment them, according to the wants of its ally, whom it ſhall aſſiſt, even with its whole force, if circumſtances ſhould render it neceſſary; but it is expreſsly agreed, in all caſes, that the contingent of the Lords the States General ſhall not exceed ten thouſand infantry, two thouſand cavalry, ſixteen ſhips of the line, and ſixteen frigates.

VI. But as it may happen (conſidering the diſtance of ſeveral of the poſſeſſions of the two high contracting parties) that the advantages which ought to reſult to them reciprocally from the concluſion of the preſent treaty, may become illuſory, unleſs meaſures can be taken for the mutual defence of thoſe poſſeſſions, before their reſpective governors could receive orders from Europe for that purpoſe; it is ſtipulated and
agreed,

agreed, that in cafe either of them fhould be hoftilely attacked, or even menaced with an hoftile attack, in its poffeffions, whether in Africa or in Afia, by an European power, the governors of their fettlements in thofe two parts of the world fhall be enjoined to concert together the fuccour to be furnifhed, and, in cafe of need, to furnifh fuch fuccour, in the moft fpeedy and effectual manner, to the party attacked; and that orders to that effect fhall be expedited to the faid governors immediately after the conclufion of the prefent treaty: and in cafe the two high contracting parties fhould be obliged to furnifh the aforefaid fuccours, they fhall not permit the fhips of war, of what nature they may be, of the Power attacking, to enter into any of their ports in the aforefaid fettlements, until peace fhall be reftored between the party attacking, and the ally of the contracting party, unlefs the faid veffels be forced to take refuge there, to avoid perifhing, or being fhipwrecked.

VII. If it fhould happen that the two high contracting parties fhall be equally involved in a war againft a common enemy, they reciprocally promife each other not to difarm but by common confent; and they fhall communicate to each other confidentially the propofals for a peace, or truce, which may be made.

VIII. If the high contracting parties prefer furnifhing their fuccours of troops in money, they fhall be at liberty on each fide fo to do; and then fuch fuccour fhall be computed at one hundred thoufand florins, Dutch currency, per annum, for one thoufand infantry, and at one hundred and twenty thoufand florins, of the like value, for one thoufand cavalry, per annum, and in the fame proportion by the month.

IX. The Power requiring fhall be obliged, whether the fhips, frigates, and troops, with which it fhall have been furnifhed, remain for a long or fhort time in its ports, to provide whatever they may want, at the fame price as if they belonged to fuch Power itfelf.

It

It has been agreed, that the faid troops or fhips fhall not in any cafe be at the expence of the party requiring, but that they fhall neverthelefs remain at its difpofal, during the whole continuance of the war in which it fhall be engaged.   The fuccours above-mentioned fhall, with refpect to difcipline be fubject to the orders of the chief officer who commands them; and they fhall not be employed feparately, or otherwife than in concert with the faid commanding officer: with regard to the operations, they fhall be wholly fubject to the orders of the commander in chief of the Power requiring.

X. It is agreed, that until the two Powers conclude a treaty of commerce with each other, the fubjects of the Republic fhall be treated, in the kingdoms of Great Britain and Ireland, as the moft favoured nation; and the fame fhall be obferved in the United Provinces towards the fubjects of his Britannic Majefty. It is however to be underftood, that this article is not to extend to a diminution of the import duties payable upon linens.

XI. Whereas by the fourth article of the treaty of peace, figned in the month of June, 1784, his Britannic Majefty engaged to treat with the Lords the States General for the reftitution of Negapatnam, with its dependencies, in cafe the faid Lords the States General fhould in future have any equivalent to give; and whereas their High Mightineffes have now renewed their requeft for obtaining that reftitution, as well as for fettling and determining precifely the fenfe of the fixth article of that treaty, concerning the navigation of Britifh fubjects in the Eaftern feas; his Britannic Majefty, in order to manifeft his good-will towards the Republic, is difpofed to concur in thefe defires of their High Mightineffes, and even to fecure to the Republic additional and real commercial advantages in that part of the world, as foon as an equivalent for thofe objects can be agreed upon; in return for which his Britannic
Majefty

Majesty will require nothing but what is favourable to the reciprocal interests and security of the contracting parties in the Indies: and, to prevent the negotiations for such arrangements from retarding the conclusion of the present treaty, it is agreed, that they shall be begun as soon as possible, and be concluded in the space of six months from the date of the present treaty; and that the convention to be made thereon shall have the same force as if it was inserted in the treaty itself.

XII. The present treaty shall be ratified on each side, and the exchange of the ratifications shall be made in the space of six weeks, or sooner, if it can be done.

Done at the Hague, the fifteenth of April, one thousand seven hundred and eighty-eight.

(L. S.) *James Harris.*

(L. S.) *J. W. Comte de Welderen.*
(L. S.) *W. F. H. van Wassenaer.*
(L. S.) *L. P. van de Spiegel.*
(L. S.) *Guillaume de Citters.*
(L. S.) *W. N. Pesters.*
(L. S.) *Charles Bigot.*
(L. S.) *M. B. C. van Voërst v. Bergel.*

The AUSTRIAN NETHERLANDS.

1496
to
1506.

THERE are various commercial treaties with the Netherlands, from the *Intercurſus magnus* to the *Intercurſus malus*.

Rym. Fœd. vol. xii. p. 578-654-711. vol. xiii. p. 6-132.
Treat. 1732, vol. ii. p. 1-28.

1604.
18 Aug.

The articles of peace, intercourſe, and commerce, between Great Britain, Spain, and the Netherlands, concluded at London.

Treat. 1732, vol. ii. p. 131.

1648.
30 Jan.

The treaty of Weſtphalia, between the Emperor, Spain, the States General, and Sweden. *Mably, Dr. Pub.* vol. i. ch. i.

Treat. 1732, vol. i. p. 1. vol. ii. p. 335.
Treat. 1785, vol. i. p. 1-44.

1667.
$\frac{13}{23}$ May.

The articles of peace, alliance, and commerce, between Great Britain and Spain, uſually called, The Treaty of Madrid, which is hereafter printed, vol. ii. p. 5.

1701.
7 Sept.

The treaty between Great Britain, the Emperor, and the States General, concluded at the Hague; uſually called, The Second Grand Alliance.

Treat. 1732, vol. i. p. 415.
Treat. 1785, vol. i. p. 326.

1713.
$\frac{15}{23}$ July.

A convention for a proviſional regulation of trade in the Netherlands, concluded at Utrecht.

1715.
26 July.

The convention, made at London, relating to the duties payable on the importation

tation of Britiſh woollen cloths into the Auſtrian Netherlands.

    Pap. Off. A. 17.
    Treat. 1732, vol. iv. p. 444.
    Treat. 1785, vol. ii. p. 144.

1715.
15 Nov.

The Barrier treaty between Great Britain, the Emperor, and the States General, with the tariff of duties payable in the Auſtrian Netherlands, according to the 26th article of this treaty, concluded at Antwerp.

    Pap. Off. A. 18.
    Board of Trade, O. 52.
    Rouſſet, Recueil Hiſtorique, tom. i. p. 37.
    Treat. 1785, vol. ii. p. 148.

1716.
25 May.

The defenſive alliance between Great Britain and the Emperor, with the ſeparate and ſecret articles, and Count Volkra's declaration, dated the $\frac{29}{11}$ Auguſt, 1716, about the trade in Flanders; concluded at Weſtminſter. *Pap. Off.* A. 19.

    Rouſſet, Recueil Hiſtorique, tom. i. p. 469.
    Treat. 1785, vol. ii. p. 175.

1718.
22 July,
2 Aug.

The quadruple alliance between Great Britain, the Emperor, and the States General, with the ſeparate and ſecret articles, concluded at London.

    Pap. Off. A. 23.
    Rouſſet, Recueil Hiſtorique, tom. 1. p. 180.
    Treat. 1785, vol. ii. p. 199.

1718.
22 Dec.

The convention between Great Britain, the Emperor, and the States General, relating to the execution of certain points of the Barrier treaty, concluded at the Hague.

    Pap. Off. A. 26.
    Board of Trade, R. 164.
    Rouſſet, Recueil Hiſtorique, tom. i. p. 400.
    Treat. 1785, vol. ii. p. 228.

1731.

1731. 16 March.	The treaty between Great Britain, the Emperor, and the States General, with the separate and secret articles; concluded at Vienna. *Pap. Off.* A. 35.

> *Rouffet, Recueil Hiftorique,* tom. vi. p. 16.
>
> *Rouffet, Sup. au Corps Diplom.* tom. ii. part. ii. p. 288.
>
> *Treat.* 1785, vol. ii. p. 318.

1731. 22 July.	The treaty between Great Britain, the Emperor, and Spain, with the separate and secret articles; concluded at Vienna. *Pap. Off.* A. 36.

> *Rouffet, Recueil Hiftorique,* tom. vi. p. 193.
>
> *Rouffet, Sup. Corps Diplom.* tom. ii. part. ii. p. 307.
>
> *Treat.* 1785, vol. ii. p. 333.

1743. $\frac{2}{13}$ Sept.	The treaty of Worms, between Great Britain, Hungary, and Sardinia.

> *See it,* vol. ii. under the art. SAR-
>
> DINIA.
>
> *Treat.* 1785, vol. ii. p. 355.

[The following is printed from the copy which was publifhed by authority in 1713.]

A Provifional Regulation of Trade, in the Spanifh Low Countries, *made at* Utrecht *the* $\frac{11}{26}$ *Day of* July, 1713.

IN order to make a provifional regulation of the commerce in and through the Low Countries, as well thofe that are called Spanifh, as thofe that have been re-conquered and yielded, it is agreed,

I. That in all the places of importation or exportation in the faid Spanifh Low Countries, re-conquered and yielded up, the duties upon merchandize fhall be exacted and paid upon the fame foot as they were exacted and paid in the year 1680.

II. All

II. All forts of merchandize imported by the fubjects of Great Britain, or the United Provinces, which have formerly enjoyed the right of tranfit or paffage, fhall enjoy the fame for the future; and the merchandize of Great Britain, and the United Provinces, which have enjoyed this right of tranfit, fhall ftill enjoy the fame, although thofe who import them are not fubjects either of the Queen of Great Britain, or their High Mightineffes; and this duty fhall not exceed two and a half per cent.

III. All duties of entrance upon merchandize, coming out of the other parts of the Spanifh Low Countries, and entering into thofe which are called re-conquered and yielded, fhall ceafe; and not only the merchandize of Great Britain, and the United Provinces, that may be brought into thofe parts by others, but the fubjects alfo of Great Britain, and the United Provinces, fhall from this time be free from all duties of entrance for their merchandize in the faid Low Countries, which are re-conquered and delivered up.

IV. That the duties of confumption in the towns and other places of the Low Countries, that are reconquered and yielded up, fhall be altogether the fame upon the goods and merchandize of each nation, and the fame liberty of felling, or expofing them to fale, be allowed to both; and that the faid duties fhall not exceed what was cuftomary in the faid towns and places before the conqueft.

V. That the duty of exportation, which has been exacted for merchandize going out of the Low Countries, in order to pafs into the new conquefts, or places that have been yielded, fhall ceafe from this time; and the merchandize, likewife, which fhall be carried out of the faid Low Countries, in order to go to France, or any other country, either through the places lately re-conquered and delivered up, or any other, fhall pay but one duty of exportation, which fhall be that which was paid in the Spanifh Low Countries, in the

the year one thousand six hundred and eighty, and it shall not be lawful to exact more or less for the importation, exportation, or passage of merchandize, than was paid in the said year one thousand six hundred and and eighty, so long as this provisional regulation shall remain in force.

VI. As to the right of convoy, it is referred to the consideration of the ministers of the Queen of Great Britain, and their High Mightinesses, at Brussels.

VII. The Queen of Great Britain, and their High Mightinesses, shall give orders to their ministers at Brussels, to take such effectual methods, that all and every one of the articles of this provisional regulation may be speedily put in execution, and duly observed.

In witness whereof we have signed this instrument, and caused it to be sealed with our arms. Done at Utrecht, this $\frac{fifteenth}{twenty-sixth}$ day of July, in the year one thousand seven hundred and thirteen.

(L. S.) *Joh. Bristol*, C. P. S.
     (L. S.) *J. B. V. Randuyck.*
     (L. S.) *William Buys.*
(L. S.) *Strafford.* (L. S.) *S. V. Dussen.*
     (L. S.) *V. Gheel van Spanbroeeck.*
     (L. S.) *F. Baron de Reede de Rensf- woude.*
     (L. S.) *Graef van Kniphuisen.*

[The following is printed from the copy which was published by authority.]

The Treaty for settling the Barrier, &c. in the Netherlands, *between the most Serene and most Potent
Prince* Charles VI. *Emperor of* Germany, *&c.
and the most Serene and Potent Prince* George, *by
the Grace of God, King of* Great Britain, France,
and Ireland, *Defender of the Faith, &c. and the
High and Mighty Lords the* States General *of the*

United Netherlands; *concluded at* Antwerp *on the 15th of* November, 1715.

GEORGE, by the Grace of God, King of Great Britain, France, and Ireland, Defender of the Faith, &c. To all and fingular to whom thefe prefent letters fhall come, greeting. Whereas the Minifters Plenipotentiaries, as well on our part, as on thofe of his Imperial and Catholic Majefty, and of the High and Mighty Lords the States General of the United Netherlands, having met at Antwerp, and being impowered with fufficient orders and authority, did, on the fifteenth day of the prefent month of November, conclude and fign a certain treaty, in the following form and words.

IT having pleafed the Almighty to grant peace for fome time paft to Europe, and nothing being more defirable and neceffary, than to re-eftablifh and fecure every where, as much as can be, the common and public fafety and tranquillity, and their High Mightineffes the Lords the States General of the United Provinces, having engaged to deliver up the Netherlands to his Imperial and Catholic Majefty Charles VI. purfuant to what is ftipulated and agreed by the treaty made at the Hague on the feventh of September, one thoufand feven hundred and one, between his Imperial Majefty Leopold, of glorious memory, his Britannic Majefty, William III. alfo of glorious memory, and the faid States General, that the faid Powers fhould agree together upon what might relate to their mutual interefts, particularly with refpect to the manner by which the fecurity of the Netherlands might be eftablifhed, to ferve for a barrier to Great Britain, and to the United Provinces, and with refpect to the commerce of the inhabitants of the faid Netherlands, and of Great Britain, and of thofe of the United Provinces, and his Imperial and Catholic Majefty Charles VI. to whom the faid Netherlands fhall be delivered by this treaty, his Britannic Majefty George, both

3   now

now reigning, and both lawful heirs and succeffors of the faid Emperor and King, and the Lords the States General of the United Provinces, acting herein by the fame principles of friendfhip, and with the fame intention to procure and eftablifh the faid mutual fafety, and to corroborate more and more a ftrict union, have to this end nominated, conftituted, and appointed, for their Minifters Plenipotentiaries, that is to fay, his Imperial and Catholic Majefty, Jofeph Lothaire, Count Kinigfegg, his Chamberlain, Counfellor of War, and Lieutenant General of his armies; his Britannic Majefty, William Cadogan, Efq; his Envoy Extraordinary to their High Mightineffes the Lords the States General of the United Provinces, a Member of the Parliament of Great Britain, Mafter of the Robes to his Majefty, Lieutenant General of his armies, and Colonel of his fecond regiment of guards; and the States General, M. Bruno vander Duffen, ancient Burgomafter, Senator and Counfellor Penfionary of the city of Gouda, Affeffor in the Council of the Heemrades of Schieland, Dykegrave of the Crimpenerwaard; Adolphus Henry Count Rechteren, Lord of Almelo and Vriefeeven, &c. Prefident of the Lords the States of the Province of Overyffel, Droffard of the diftrict of Zalland; Seato van Gockinga, Senator of the city of Groninghen; and Adrian van Borfelle, Lord of Gueldermalfen, &c. Senator of the town of Flufhing; the three former, Deputies in the Affembly of the Lords the States General on the part of the provinces of Holland and Weftfrifeland, Overyffel, and Groninghen and the Ommelands, and the fourth, Deputy in the Council of State of the United Provinces; who, having met in the city of Antwerp, which by common confent had been named for the place of congrefs, and having exchanged their full powers, copies of which are inferted at the end of this treaty, after feveral conferences have agreed for, and in the name of his Imperial and Catholic Majefty, his Britannic Majefty,

and

and the Lords the States General, in the manner following.

I. The States General of the United Provinces
shall deliver up to his Imperial and Catholic Majesty, by virtue of the grand alliance in the year one
thousand seven hundred and one, and of the engagements into which they have since entered, immediately after the exchange of the ratifications of the present treaty, all the provinces and towns of the Netherlands, with their dependencies, as well those which
were possessed by the late King of Spain Charles II.
of glorious memory, as those which have not long
since been yielded by his late most Christian Majesty
also of glorious memory; which provinces and towns
together, as well those which shall be delivered up by
this present treaty, as those which have been already
delivered, shall for the future make and compose, in
all or in part, but one sole and indivisible, inalienable,
and unexchangeable demesne, which shall be inseparable from the dominions of the House of Austria in
Germany, to be enjoyed by his Imperial and Catholic Majesty, his successors and heirs, in full irrevocable
sovereignty and propriety, that is to say, with respect
to the former provinces, as they were enjoyed or ought
to have been enjoyed by the late King Charles II. of
glorious memory, conformably to the treaty of Ryswick, and as to the other provinces, in the manner
and on the conditions upon which they were yielded
and delivered up to the said Lords the States General by the late most Christian King of glorious memory, in favour of the most august House of Austria,
and without other incumbrances or mortgages, charged
thereon by the States General, and for their benefit.

II. His Imperial and Catholic Majesty promises and
engages, that no province, city, place, fortress, or territory of the said Netherlands, shall be yielded, transferred, given, or fall to the crown of France, or to
any Prince or Princess of the house and lineage of
France,

France, or to any other who shall not be the successor, heir, and possessor of the dominions of the House of Austria in Germany, either by gift, sale, exchange, marriage-contract, inheritance, succession by will, or in default of a will, or upon any other title or pretext whatsoever; so that no province, city, place, fortress, or territory of the Netherlands, shall ever be subject to any other Prince, than only to the successors to the said dominions of the House of Austria, except what has already been yielded to the King of Prussia, and what shall be yielded by this present treaty to the said Lords the States General.

III. As the security of the Austrian Netherlands will depend principally on the number of troops which may be kept up in the said countries, and in the places which are to form the barrier that has been promised to the Lords the States General by the grand alliance, his Imperial and Catholic Majesty, and their High Mightinesses, have agreed to maintain therein always, each at their own charge, a body of between thirty and thirty-five thousand men, of which his Imperial and Catholic Majesty shall furnish three-fifths, and the States General two-fifths, provided that if his Imperial and Catholic Majesty lessen his contingent, it shall be in the power of the said States General to lessen theirs, in proportion; and when there shall be a likelihood of war, or of an attack, the said body shall be augmented to forty thousand men, according to the same proportion; and in case of actual war, a further agreement shall be made for such forces as shall be judged necessary.

The repartition of the said troops in time of peace, so far as it relates to the places committed to the keeping of their High Mightinesses troops, shall be made by themselves only, and the repartition of the rest by the governor general of the Netherlands, acquainting each other mutually with the dispositions they shall make.

P 3 IV. His

IV. His Imperial and Catholic Majesty grants that the States General shall have a garrison intirely of their own troops in the towns and castles of Namur and Tournay, and in the towns of Menin, Furnes, Warneton, Ypres, and Fort Knocque; and the States General engage not to employ in the said places, troops which though in their pay, may belong to a prince or nation that may be at war against, or suspected to be in engagements contrary to the interests of his Imperial and Catholic Majesty.

V. It is agreed, that in the town of Dendermonde there shall be a joint garrison, which for the present shall be composed of one battalion of Imperial troops, and of one of those of the States General, and if hereafter it may be necessary to augment the said garrison, that augmentation shall be made equally with troops of both parties, and by common concert. The governor shall be appointed by the Emperor; who, as well as the subalterns, shall take an oath to the States General, never to do, or permit any thing to be done in the said town, which may be prejudicial to their service, with respect to the preservation of the said town and garrison, and he shall be obliged by the same oath to give free passage to their troops, whenever and as often as they shall desire it, provided it be previously asked, and only for a moderate number at a time. The whole according to the form which has been agreed on, and which shall be inserted at the end of this treaty.

VI. His Imperial and Catholic Majesty consents likewise, that in the places above granted to the States General, for keeping garrisons intirely their own, they may put such governors, commandants, and other officers who compose the Etat Major as they shall think fit, on condition that they shall not be chargeable to his Imperial and Catholic Majesty, nor to the towns and provinces, otherwise than for convenient lodging, and the emoluments arising from the fortifications,

and

and that they be not perfons who may be difagree-
able to or fufpected by his faid Majefty, for reafons
to be particularly alledged.

VII. Which governors, commandants, and officers,
fhall be intirely and abfolutely dependent on, and fubject to the fole orders and fole judicature of the States
General, in all that relates to the defence, guard, fecurity, and all other military concern of their places;
but the faid governors, as well as their fubalterns, fhall
be obliged to take an oath to his Imperial and Catholic Majefty, to keep the faid places faithfully under
the fovereignty of the Houfe of Auftria, and not to in-
termeddle in any other affair, according to the form
which has been agreed upon, and is inferted at the end
of this treaty.

VIII. The generals fhall give reciprocally, as well
in the towns where there fhall be a garrifon of his
Imperial and Catholic Majefty, as in thofe which are
intrufted to the keeping of the troops of their High
Mightineffes, the ufual honours according to their character, and the cuftom of each fervice; and in cafe
the governor general of the Netherlands comes into
the places committed to the keeping of the troops of
the States General, the honours fhall be fhewn him
which he is ufed to receive in the places where are
garrifons of his Imperial and Catholic Majefty; he
fhall alfo give out the word there; the whole without
prejudice to the fixth article.

And the governors, and in their abfence the commandants, fhall communicate to the faid governor general the difpofitions made by them, for the fecurity
and guard of the places committed to their care, and
he fhall have fit regard to the alterations which the
faid governor general may judge ought to be made in
them.

IX. His Imperial and Catholic Majefty grants the
exercife of their religion to the troops of the States General, wherever they fhall be in garrifon; but this fhall

be

be done in particular places that are convenient and proportioned to the number of the garrison, which the magistrates shall appoint and keep in repair in every town and place where none are already settled, which places shall not be distinguished by any exterior marks of a church; and the civil and military officers, as also the ecclesiastics, and all others whom it concerns, shall be strictly enjoined, on both sides, to hinder all occasion of scandal and contest which may arise on the subject of religion; and when any dispute or difficulty shall arise, it shall be made up amicably on both sides. And as to religion with respect to the inhabitants of the Austrian Netherlands, all things shall rest and remain on the same foot they were during the reign of King Charles II. of glorious memory.

X. All stores of war, artillery, and arms, of the States General; as also materials for the fortifications, corn in time of scarcity, provisions to be put into magazines, when there shall be a likelihood of war; as also cloth and furniture for cloathing the soldiers, which shall be certified to be intended for that use, shall pass free, and without paying any duties or tolls, by virtue of passports which shall be asked and granted upon a specification signed; on condition, however, that at the first custom-office of his Imperial and Catholic Majesty where the said stores, materials, arms, and mounting shall enter, the boats and other carriages may be duly searched, at the place where they are to be unloaded, to hinder the mixing of other merchandize among them, and for preventing all fraud and abuse, against which it shall always be free to use such precautions as by course of time and experience shall be judged necessary; nor shall the governors and their subalterns be permitted to obstruct in any wise the execution of this article.

XI. The States General shall change their garrisons and the dispositions of the troops in the towns and places committed to their own keeping, as they
shall

'fhall think fit; nor fhall the paffage of the troops which they fhall fend thither, or which they fhall draw from time to time, be hindered or ftopt under any pretext whatever: the faid troops fhall likewife, when the cafe may require, pafs through all the towns of Brabant and Flanders, and through all the open country, make bridges as well over the canal between Bruges and Ghent, as over all the other canals, and over all the rivers which fhall be in their routes; on condition, however, that they fhall be troops of a prince or of a nation not in war with his Imperial and Catholic Majefty, nor fufpected of any engagement or obligation contrary to his interefts, as is faid above in the fourth article, and that previoufly notice fhall be given, and requifition made to the governor general of the Netherlands, with whom the route and other neceffary points fhall be regulated by fome perfon commiffioned by their High Mightineffes.

The regulation made by the States General concerning the paffage of their troops, fhall be obferved, as it is obferved in their own country.

And the States General fhall endeavour to make the faid changes of garrifons, as well as the neceffary difpofitions for the fame, in fuch manner as may be leaft expenfive and inconvenient to the inhabitants.

XII. The common fafety requiring in time of war, or in imminent danger of war, that the States General fhould fend their troops into the places which fhall appear to be moft expofed to the hazard of being attacked or furprized, it is agreed between his Imperial and Catholic Majefty, and the States General, that their troops fhall be received into the faid places fo far as fhall be neceffary for their defence, when the cafe fhall apparently happen, provided that this be done by agreement, and by concert with the governor general of the Netherlands.

XIII. The States General may at their coft and expence caufe the faid towns and places to be fortified,

fied, either by new works, or by repairing the old, keep them up, and in general provide whatever they shall think neceffary for the fecurity and defence of the faid towns and places, except that they shall not caufe new fortifications to be built, without giving previous notice to the governor general of the Netherlands, and hearing his opinion and confiderations thereupon, nor shall they be charged to the account of the Emperor or of the country, but by his Majefty's confent.

XIV. For the fecurity of the communication between the United Provinces, and the towns and places of the barrier, his Imperial and Catholic Majefty shall caufe fuch meafures to be taken, that letters and meffengers, as well ordinary as extraordinary, may pafs freely to and from the towns and places of the barrier, and through thofe of other countries, on condition that the faid meffengers shall not charge themfelves with letters or packets of merchants or other private perfons, which, as well for the places of the barrier as for any other place, ought to be put into the poft-offices of his Imperial and Catholic Majefty.

XV. As for the artillery, magazines, and ftores of war, which their High Mightineffes have in the towns and places which they deliver up to his Imperial and Catholic Majefty, they shall be allowed to caufe the fame to be removed without any hinderance, and without paying any duties or tolls, as well what they themfelves have caufed to be conveyed thither, as the artillery marked with their arms, loft in the laft war, and otherwife belonging to them, which they shall have found in the faid places; unlefs his Imperial and Catholic Majefty defires to take the faid artillery and ftores of war on his own account, and agrees upon price with their High Mightineffes before the delivery of the places committed to the keeping of the troops of the States General; and as to the artillery and ammunition which are now in the places committed

ted to the keeping of the troops of the States General, they fhall be left in their keeping and difpofal, according to the inventories of them which fhall be drawn up and figned on both fides, before the exchange of the ratifications of the prefent treaty, without being allowed to caufe them to be removed elfewhere, unlefs by common confent; and the property of what is found in the faid places at the time of their ceffion or delivery, fhall remain in his Imperial and Catholic Majefty.

XVI. In cafe the provinces of the Auftrian Netherlands fhould be attacked, and it fhould happen (which God forbid) that the enemies armies fhould enter Brabant, there to act, and lay fiege to fome places in the faid province, or to fome of thofe which make its barrier; it fhall be lawful for their High Mightineffes to caufe their troops to take poffeffion and poft themfelves in the towns and places on the Demer, from the Schelde to the Maefe, as alfo to throw up intrenchments and lines, and make inundations, to prevent the farther progrefs of the enemies, in fuch manner as the reafon of war may require.

XVII. It being manifeft by the experience of the laft war, that for fecuring the frontiers of the States General in Flanders, it was neceffary to have feveral bodies of troops fo confiderable that the army was very much weakened by it; for preventing that inconvenience, and for the better fecuring the faid frontiers for the future, his Imperial and Catholic Majefty yields to the States General fuch forts, and as much territory of the Auftrian Flanders lying contiguous to their faid frontiers, as fhall be wanted for making the neceffary inundations, and for covering them effectually from the Schelde to the fea, in thofe places where they are not yet fufficiently fecured, and where they cannot be fo by inundations on thofe lands only which do already belong to the States General. For this end his Imperial and Catholic Majefty confents and approves,

approves, that for the future the limits of the States General in Flanders shall begin at the sea between Blankerberg and Heyst, at the place where are no Downs, provided that they shall not build nor permit the building of villages or houses near the said post, nor suffer any settlement of fishermen, nor make any sluices to the sea.

And their High Mightinesses do farther promise, that if they think fit to cause any fortifications to be built at the head of their new limits, they will take care not to diminish the strength of the Digue, and will not only take upon themselves the extraordinary expence which may be occasioned by means of the said fortifications, but will make good to the inhabitants of the Austrian Flanders all the losses which they may suffer, in case the sea should happen to make inundations by reason of the foresaid fortifications.

From the forementioned post a line shall be drawn directly to the Goteweegie, whence the line shall be continued to Heyst, from Heyst it shall extend to Driehoek and Swarte-Sluas, thence to Fort St. Donas, which his Imperial and Catholic Majesty yields in propriety and sovereignty to their High Mightinesses (provided the gates of the sluices at the said fort shall be and remain taken off in time of peace;) and likewise yields the ground situate to the north of the line above-described.

From Fort St. Donas the new limits of the States General shall extend to Fort St. Job, whence they shall turn into the antient limits near the town of Middlebourg, which limits shall stretch along the Zydlingsdyke to the place where the Eeckeloosewatergang and the Waterloop meet at a sluice.

Thence the Graaf Jansdyke shall carry them on to the village of Bouchoute (the persons interested in the sluices there being permitted to replace them where they were formerly) and from the said Bouchoute the line shall be continued directly to the antient limits of the States General.

His

His Imperial and Catholic Majesty yields likewise in full and entire sovereignty to the States General, the territory situate northward of the said line.

And whereas, for their entire security, it is necessary the inundation should be continued from Bouchoute to the canal of the Sas van Ghent along the Graaf Jansdyke, it shall be lawful for their High Mightinesses, in time of war, to possess and cause to be fortified all the sluices in the Graaf Jansdyke and Zydlingsdyke.

As for the town of Sas van Ghent, the limits shall be extended to the distance of two thousand geometrical paces, provided there be no villages included in that compass of ground.

And for the preservation of the lower Schelde, and of the communication between Brabant and that part of Flanders belonging to the States General, his Imperial and Catholic Majesty yields in full and entire propriety and sovereignty to the States General, the village and Polder of Doel, as also the Polders of St. Anne and of Ketenisse.

And whereas in time of war it will be needful, for the greater security, to make inundations by the sluices between the forts Mary and Pearl, his Imperial and Catholic Majesty will, as soon as the barrier shall be attacked, or the war begun, commit the keeping of fort Pearl and the sluices to their High Mightinesses; on condition, that when the war ceases, they shall restore those sluices, and the said fort Pearl, to his Imperial and Catholic Majesty, as also those which they shall have taken into their possession in the Graaf Jansdyke and Zidlingsdyke. The States General shall not make any inundation in time of peace, and when they think themselves obliged to make any in time of war, they shall previously give notice of it to the governor general of the Netherlands, and concert the matter with the generals commanding the armies in the Netherlands. Promising besides, that if by reason of the cession of some sluices (the free use of which the inhabitants

habitants of the Auftrian Flanders fhall retain in time
of peace) the faid inhabitants fhould happen to fuffer
fome damage or prejudice, either by the commanding or other military officers, the States General will
not only immediately redrefs the fame, but will likewife make good the lofs of the perfons concerned.

And feeing by this new fituation of the limits, it
will be neceffary to remove the cuftom-offices, for
preventing frauds, in which his Imperial and Catholic
Majefty, and their High Mightineffes, are equally
concerned, it fhall be agreed at what places to eftablifh
thofe offices, and what farther precautions to take, as
fhall be judged neceffary.

It is farther ftipulated by this article, that before the
ratification of the prefent treaty, a computation fhall
be made of the revenues which the Sovereign receives
from the lands that fhall be yielded to their High
Mightineffes by this article; as alfo of the profit that
has arifen to the Sovereign by the renewal of grants,
upon the foot on which they have been beftowed for
thefe thirty years laft paft; to be deducted and abated
out of the annual fubfidy of five hundred thoufand
crowns.

And the Roman Catholic religion fhall be preferved
and maintained in the places yielded as above, in all
refpects on the foot it is now exercifed there, and as it
was in the time of King Charles II. of glorious memory, and the privileges of the inhabitants fhall in
like manner be preferved and maintained.

The fort of Roden Huyfen fhall be razed, the differences concerning the canal of Bruges fhall be referred to the decifion of neutral arbitrators to be chofen
on both fides; but it is underftood that by the ceffion
of fort St. Donas, thofe of the town of Sluys fhall not
have more right to the faid canal than before that
ceffion.

XVIII. His Imperial and Catholic Majefty yields
to their High Mightineffes the States General for ever,
in full fovereignty and propriety, in the upper quarter
of

of Gelderland, the town of Venlo with its Banlieue, and the fort of St. Michael, as alfo the fort of Steven-fwaert with its territory or Banlieue, together with as much ground as is neceffary for enlarging their fortifications on this fide of the Maefe; and his faid Majefty promifes never to caufe to be built, or to fuffer another to build, any fortification, by what name foever, within the diftance of half a league of the faid fortrefs.

His Imperial and Catholic Majefty yields alfo to the States General the Ammanie of Montfort, confifting, (the villages of Swalmt and Elmt excepted, which he referves to himfelf) of the fmall towns of Neu-ftadt and Echt, with the following villages; that is to fay, Ohe, and Laeck, Roaftren, Braght, Befel, Belfen, Vlodorp, Poftert, Berg, Lin, and Montfort, to be poffeffed by the faid States General in the manner they were poffeffed and enjoyed by his Majefty King Charles II. of glorious memory, with the prefeétures, bourgs, fiefs, lands, eftates, quit-rents, rents, revenues, tolls, of what nature foever, fubfidies, contributions, and colleétions, feudal, domanial, and other rights what-foever, belonging to the faid places yielded as above; the whole however without prejudice to, and with a refervation of all the rights which may belong to his Majefty the King of Pruffia; and this notwithftanding all exceptions, pretenfions, or oppofitions, made or to be made, to difturb the States General in the peaceable poffeffion of the places yielded by the pre-fent article, all agreements, conventions, or difpofi-tions contrary to the prefent article being deemed null and of no validity. But it is underftood, that this ceffion is made with this exprefs claufe, that the ftatutes, antient cuftoms, and generally all the pri-vileges, civil and ecclefiaftical, as well with refpeét to the magiftrates and private perfons, as to the churches, convents, monafteries, fchools, feminaries, hofpitals, and other public places, with all their appurtenances and dependencies; as alfo the diocefan right of the

Bifhop

Bishop of Ruremonde, and generally whatever concerns the rights, liberties, immunities, functions, usages, ceremonies, and exercise of the Catholic religion, shall be preserved, and shall subsist without any change or innovation to be made directly or indirectly, in all the places yielded as above, in the manner as at the time of King Charles II. of glorious memory, and as it shall be explained on both sides more amply in case any dispute happens on this subject; and the magistracy, and other offices of the civil administration, shall not be given to any other persons than such as are of the Catholic religion.

The right of collating to benefices, which has hitherto been in the Sovereign, shall henceforward belong to the Bishop of Ruremonde, on condition that the said benefices shall not be given to other persons than such as shall not be disagreeable to the States General, for reasons to be particularly alledged.

It is also stipulated, that the States General shall not pretend to have acquired by the cession of the town of Echt any right of judicature, or of appeal, with relation to the chapter of Thorn, or other territories of the empire, and his Imperial and Catholic Majesty shall be free to name such place as he shall think proper for the said judicature or appeal.

And seeing the inhabitants of that part of the upper quarter which is thus yielded, can no longer remove their suits, in case of appeal, to the court at Ruremonde, their High Mightinesses shall be at liberty to erect a court of appeal for their subjects in such place of the province as they shall think fit.

It is farther agreed, that the duties of importation and exportation, which are levied all along the Maese, shall not be raised or lowered, in all or in part, but by common consent, of which duties his Imperial and Catholic Majesty shall have the produce to himself of what is collected at Ruremonde and Navagne, and the Lords the States General those which are collected at Venlo; and as those duties on the Maese in general,

as

as also thofe on the Schelde additionally, are appropriated to the payment of two diftinct annuities;
that is to fay, one of fourfcore thoufand, and one of
twenty thoufand florins yearly, by virtue of the contract
made and concluded the twenty-fixth of December,
one thoufand fix hundred eighty-feven, with his late
Majefty of Great Britain William III. it is agreed,
that their High Mightineffes, on account of the forementioned ceffion, fhall affift his Imperial and Catholic Majefty in the yearly payment of the faid annuities,
and other debts for which they may be mortgaged,
proportionably to the produce of the duties out and
in which they fhall receive, the whole accoiding to
the fettlements of the faid annuities.

And as to the debts and incumbrances contracted and
charged upon the generality of the upper quarter, the
States General fhall concur in the payment thereof,
as to their quota, according to the proportion fpecified
in the regifter of the whole upper quarter aforefaid.

All the records and papers which concern the upper
quarter of Guelderland, fhall remain as formerly in
the archives of Ruremond; but it is agreed that an
inventory or regifter of them fhall be made under the
joint infpection of the commiffioners of his Imperial
and Catholic Majefty, of his Pruffian Majefty, and
of the Lords the States General, and an authentic
copy of the faid inventory fhall be given to each of
the three Powers, that they may have always free accefs to all the papers and records for which they have
occafion, with refpect to that part which they poffefs
in the faid upper quarter of Guelderland, and of which
an authentic copy fhall be delivered to them at the
firft demand.

XIX. In confideration of the great charge and
extraordinary expence which the States General are
indifpenfably obliged to be at, as well for maintaining
the great number of troops, which they have engaged
themfelves by this prefent treaty to keep in the towns

above-named, as for defraying the great expence abfolutely neceffary for keeping up and repairing the fortifications of the faid places, and for furnifhing them
with ammunition and provifion, his Imperial and Catholic Majefty engages and promifes to caufe to be
paid annually to the States General the fum of five
hundred thoufand crowns, or twelve hundred and
fifty thoufand florins, Dutch money, over and above
the revenue of that part of the upper quarter of
Guelderland, yielded in propriety by his Imperial and
Catholic Majefty to the States General, by the eighteenth article of the prefent treaty; as alfo over and
above the expence for lodging the troops, according
to the regulation made in the year one thoufand fix
hundred ninety-eight, in the manner which fhall be
particularly agreed upon; which fum of five hundred
thoufand crowns, or twelve hundred and fifty thoufand
florins, Dutch money, fhall be fecured and charged,
as by this article it is fecured and charged upon all the
revenues in general of the Auftrian Netherlands, including therein the countries yielded by France, and
particularly upon the cleareft and leaft incumbered
revenues of the provinces of Brabant and Flanders,
and upon thofe of the countries, towns, caftellanies, and
dependencies yielded by France, as is more particularly agreed by a feparate article, as well for the
mortgage as for the method and terms of receiving
the faid fum; and the faid payment of the fubfidy of
five hundred thoufand crowns, or twelve hundred and
fifty thoufand florins, Dutch money, fhall begin from
the day of figning this prefent treaty; out of which
fhall be deducted, in proportion to the time, the revenues of the towns, caftellanies, and dependencies,
yielded by France, which fhall become due from the
faid day till the day when the faid Netherlands fhall
be delivered to his Imperial and Catholic Majefty, for
fo much as the States General fhall have received.

XX. His Imperial and Catholic Majefty confirms
and ratifies by this article the capitulations granted to
the

the provinces and towns of the Netherlands formerly called Spanish, at the time they were reduced to the obedience of his said Majesty; as also the general administration of the said country exercised therein by Great Britain and the States General of the United Provinces, representing the lawful Sovereign by their ministers who resided at Bruffels, and by the council of state appointed for the general government of the said Netherlands, in confequence of the power and instructions which were given to the said council, and of the requisitions which were made to it on the part of the two Powers, as well in matter of royalty, of justice, and of civil magiftracy, as of finances; as also the particular administration of the ftates and provinces, of the colleges, of the towns, and of the communities in the open country; together with the fovereign courts of juftice, and other inferior courts and judges; which acts of civil magiftracy, royalty, juftice, and finances, shall subsift and have their full and entire effect, according to the tenor of the said acts, and of the fentences given; the whole in the same manner as if they had been done by the lawful Sovereign of the country, and under his government.

XXI. All that is contained in the preceding article, shall likewife be obferved, ratified, and maintained on the part of his Imperial and Catholic Majefty with refpect to the upper quarter of Guelderland, and to the countries conquered from France (of which King Charles the Second, of glorious memory, was not poffeffed at his deceafe) as to all the difpofitions made in the name and on the part of the States General of the United Provinces.

And as for ecclefiaftical benefices and dignities, thofe on whom they have been conferred, and who are poffeffed of them, fhall not be difpoffeffed; and thofe who are not yet in poffeffion, fhall be admitted, without being oppofed therein, unlefs by the methods, and in the courfe of juftice, according to the laws and cuftoms of the country.

Q 2   XXII. His

XXII. His Imperial and Catholic Majesty acknowledges and promises to satisfy the obligations which were entered into on the part of his Catholic Majesty Charles II. of glorious memory, for the loans of money which their High Mightinesses have caused to be negotiated for his said Majesty, the list of which is subjoined at the end of this article; and as the States General have not yet had delivered to them the obligations of the States of the Spanish Netherlands for the sum of two hundred thousand florins a year, to be furnished by them for paying the interest and reimbursing the principal of fourteen hundred thousand florins taken up at interest in the year one thousand six hundred ninety-eight, to be employed in the necessary service of the frontiers of the said Spanish Netherlands, and of four years interest, amounting to the sum of two hundred twenty-four thousand florins, with which the said principal of fourteen hundred thousand florins is increased, which obligations the said King Charles II. of glorious memory had promised to cause to be delivered, but it was not done; his Imperial and Catholic Majesty hereby promises to cause the obligations to be entered into by the States of the Provinces of the said Netherlands, and to be delivered immediately after to the said States General, conformably to the tenor of the said obligation of his Catholic Majesty of the thirtieth of May, one thousand six hundred ninety-eight, at the first meeting of the States, or at farthest within the term of two months after the exchange of the ratifications of this treaty.

A Memorial of the Loans negotiated at the Request of his Catholic Majesty Charles II. *of glorious Memory.*

THE first loan was of one million five hundred seventy-five thousand florins, on the duties in and out collected at the Mary, at five per cent. by a deed bearing date the thirteenth of December, one thousand six hundred and ninety. } f. 1,575,000

The

The fecond was of five hundred twenty-five thoufand florins, at five per cent. on the fame fund, by a deed executed the twenty-firft of March, one thoufand fix hundred ninety-one.　f. 525,000

The third was of five hundred fixty-feven thoufand florins, at five per cent. on the revenues of the upper quarter of Guelderland, by a deed of the fifteenth of January, one thoufand fix hundred ninety-two.　f. 567,000

The fourth and fifth loans, of five hundred thoufand, and two hundred thoufand florins, were made in purfuance of two deeds of the fourth and twenty-fecond of May, one thoufand fix hundred ninety-three, upon the duties in and out, collected at the Mary, at fix per cent.　f. 700,000

The fixth was of fix hundred fixty-five thoufand florins, on the fame fund, and at five per cent. borrowed by deed of the eleventh of April, one thoufand fix hundred ninety-five.　f. 665,000

The feventh was of a million four hundred and forty thoufand florins, on the fame fund, at five per cent. by deed of the twenty-fourth of November, one thoufand fix hundred ninety-five.　f. 1,440,000

The eighth, ninth, and tenth fums, of four hundred thoufand, one hundred thoufand, and three hundred thoufand florins, were borrowed by deeds of the tenth of December, one thoufand fix hundred ninety-five, the twelfth of Sep-　f. 800,000

tember,

tember, one thousand six hundred ninety-six, and the sixth of March, one thousand six hundred ninety-seven, at five
per cent. on the revenues collected at   f. 800,000
the Mary, and the demesnes of the
province of Namur, and supplement-
ally on the demesnes of the province of
Luxembourg, amounting together to

The eleventh sum, of five hundred
thousand florins, was borrowed by deed
of the thirtieth of April, one thousand   f. 500,000
six hundred ninety-six, at six per cent.
on the revenues of the provostship of
Mons.

The twelfth sum, of one million four
hundred thousand florins, at four per
cent. was borrowed upon the subsidies
of the provinces of the Netherlands, on
the remittances from Spain, and supple-
mentally on the revenues collected at
the Mary. Item, Two hundred and   f. 1,624,000
twenty-four thousand florins, for four
years interest of the principal, conformably to the tenor of the obligation of
the thirtieth of May, one thousand six
hundred ninety-eight; the total sum
amounting thus to   —   —

XXIII. In like manner his Imperial and Catholic
Majesty acknowledges, approves, and confirms, all
the contracts for money (the list of which is subjoined
at the end of this article) which were necessarily made
for the payment of several indispensable demands for
the preservation of the Spanish Netherlands, and for
maintaining the troops of his Imperial and Catholic
Majesty, during the provisional government of Great
Britain and the States General of the United Provinces,
and

and done by their High Mightineffes in concert with his Majefty of Great Britain. His Imperial and Catholic Majefty promifing to fatisfy the fame, and to caufe the faid contracts to be duly regiftered in the chambers of the Finances and of Accompts, and to caufe a certificate thereof in form to be delivered to their High Mightineffes, and the principal and intereft to be paid out of the funds and mortgages, both principal and additional, appropriated for that purpofe: nor fhall his Imperial and Catholic Majefty make, unlefs with the confent of the States General, any change in the direction or adminiftration of the mortgages upon which the contracts were entered into, but will leave them to their High Mightineffes, conformably to the tenor of the obligations; and if thofe funds fhould not be fufficient, the deficiencies fhall be made good by the States of the provinces of the faid Auftrian Netherlands.

An Account of the Sums negotiated during the provi-fional Government of his Britannic Majefty, and of their High Mightineffes, in the Netherlands.

IN one thoufand feven hundred and feven were borrowed three hundred thoufand florins, at five per cent. on the revenues of the poft-office, to be fent to the King at Barcelona; alfo four hundred thoufand florins, at five per cent. on the duties of importation and ex-portation in Flanders, for the neceffary fervices in the Netherlands: the intereft of the faid four hundred thoufand florins was affigned on the poft-office. } f. 700,000

In the month of February, one thou-fand feven hundred and nine, were bor-rowed two hundred and fifty thoufand florins, at five per cent. on the duties col-lected at the Mary, for maintaining the Imperial and Palatine troops. } f. 250,000

In

In the month of May, one thousand seven hundred and nine, was borrowed the sum of five hundred thousand florins, at five per cent, on the same conditions, on the same fund, and for the same use. } f. 500,000

In the month of August was farther borrowed a sum of ten hundred thousand florins, at five per cent. on the same terms, the same fund, and for the same use. } f. 1,000,000

In one thousand seven hundred and ten, was negotiated a sum of three hundred thousand florins, at six per cent. on the revenue of the post-office, for defraying the charge of the Imperial and Palatine troops in the service of his Imperial and Catholic Majesty. } f. 300,000

Item, on the duties in and out of Flanders, a sum of four hundred thousand florins, for supplying the expence of the Imperial troops, at six per cent. that is to say, five per cent. payable out of the duties in Flanders, and one per cent. out of the revenues at the Mary. } f. 400,000

Item, on the same fund, and at six per cent. namely, five per cent. on the duties in and out of Flanders, and one per cent. on the revenues at the Mary, the sum of three hundred thousand florins, for supporting the expence of the Imperial troops. } f. 300,000

Item, on the same fund, and at six per cent. viz. five per cent. on the duties in and out of Flanders, and one per cent. on the revenues at the Mary, the sum of three hundred and forty thousand six hundred and twenty-five florins, to supply the expence of the Imperial troops. } f. 340,625

Item,

Item, on the revenues of the Mary, at five per cent. the sum of three hundred thousand florins, for defraying the charge of the Imperial troops.	f. 300,000
In the month of March, one thousand seven hundred and eleven, was borrowed the sum of three hundred thousand florins, at six per cent. on the revenues of the post-office, for supplying the charge of the Imperial troops.	f. 300,000
In December, one thousand seven hundred and twelve, was negotiated on the revenues at the Mary, two hundred and twenty-eight thousand three hundred and thirty florins, at five per cent. for the necessary occasions, and for the fortifications of Mons, St. Ghilain, and Ath.	f. 228,330

All the said loans together making the sum of four millions six hundred and eighteen thousand nine hundred and fifty-five florins; the expenditure of which, as well as of the sum of five hundred and fifty thousand florins, which the receivers of the duties of importation and exportation in Flanders have paid in bills of exchange to the States General in the year one thousand seven hundred and ten, of an hundred thousand florins which they have received of the receiver of the Medianates, and of one hundred and five thousand florins (errors in the account excepted) which they have received of the third chamber of the council of Flanders, has been certified to the minister plenipotentiary of his Imperial and Catholic Majesty, in the manner the same is more particularly set forth by his declaration at the bottom of the account of the contracts and money lent, and of the expenditure of the said money, signed this day.

XXIV. An account shall be settled, as soon as the same can be done, of what has been paid of the intereſt and principal of the loans mentioned in the two preceding articles, in which account nothing ſhall be charged to their High Mightineſſes, but what ſhall appear to have been actually and really paid, by virtue of the ſaid obligations; nor, on the part of his Imperial and Catholic Majeſty, ſhall any difficulty be raiſed againſt the payment of the ſaid intereſt, or any pretence of abatement or diminution, on account of the non-poſſeſſion of mortgages, confiſcation in time of war, the ſinking of the value of the ſaid mortgages by reaſon of the diminution of the duties of importation and exportation, or any other cauſe or pretext whatever.

Nor while the ſaid account is ſettling, ſhall payment be diſcontinued on the part of his Imperial and Catholic Majeſty; but the intereſt and terms of reimburſement ſhall be continued, purſuant to the conditions expreſſed in the obligations, till it ſhall appear that all the loans and intereſt of them are entirely cleared and paid off, after which the mortgages ſhall be duly diſcharged and reſtored.

XXV. Moreover, by this preſent article are ratified and confirmed all the contracts for bread-waggons, and forage for the Imperial and Palatine troops, made by the miniſters of the two Powers at Bruſſels, or by the council of ſtate appointed for the government of the Netherlands, at the requiſition of the ſaid miniſters; and in like manner are confirmed and ratified all payments already made on thoſe contracts, by the council of the finances, and the orders delivered by the ſaid council for aſſigning what remains due for the ſaid bread, forage, and waggons, on the ſurpluſage of the duties ariſing by the four ſpecies, purſuant to the requiſitions of the council of ſtate; nor ſhall the ſaid ſurpluſage of thoſe duties be diverted to other uſes, under any pretext whatever, before the undertakers who furniſhed the ſaid bread, forage, and waggons, are entirely ſatisfied, according to the tenor of their contracts, purſuant to the requiſitions of the miniſters

of

of the two Potentates, and to the orders of the council of ſtate, and of that of the finances.

XXVI. As for what relates to commerce, it is agreed, that the ſhips, merchandizes, and goods, coming from Great Britain, and from the United Provinces, and entering into the Auſtrian Netherlands; as alſo the ſhips, merchandizes, and goods going out of the ſaid Netherlands for Great Britain and the United Provinces, ſhall pay the duties of importation and exportation upon the ſame foot on which they are collected at this time, and no other; and particularly in ſuch manner as they have been regulated before the ſigning of the preſent treaty, according to the requiſition made to the council of ſtate at Bruſſels by the miniſters of the two Potentates, dated the 6th of November; and ſo the whole ſhall remain, continue, and ſubſiſt in general on the ſaid foot, without any alteration, innovation, diminution, or augmentation, under any pretext whatever, till his Imperial and Catholic Majeſty, his Britannic Majeſty, and the Lords the States General ſhall agree otherwiſe by a treaty of commerce to be made as ſoon as may be; commerce, and every thing depending thereon, between the ſubjects of his Imperial and Catholic Majeſty in the Auſtrian Netherlands, and thoſe of the United Provinces, remaining in whole, and in part, on the eſtabliſhed foot, and in the manner ſpecified by the articles of the treaty made at Munſter the thirtieth of January, one thouſand ſix hundred forty-eight, between his Majeſty King Philip the Fourth, of glorious memory, and the ſaid Lords the States General, concerning commerce, which articles are now confirmed by this preſent article.

XXVII. That the fortifications, and all the works of the citadel of Liege, as alſo thoſe of the caſtle of Huy, with all the forts and works, ſhall be razed and demoliſhed, and never be rebuilt, or made up again: but it is underſtood that the ſaid demolition ſhall be

made

made at the expence of the States of the country of Liege, to whom the materials shall be left, to be sold, and to be removed elsewhere. The whole to be done by the orders and under the direction of the States General, who for that purpose shall send persons qualified for the direction of the said demolitions; the working upon which shall be begun immediately after the signing of the present treaty, and shall be finished within three months, or sooner, if possible; and in the mean time the garrisons of the States General shall not march out of the said places before the demolition is finished.

XXVIII. And for the greater security and fuller execution of the present treaty, his Britannic Majesty promises and engages to confirm it, and to guaranty it in all the points and articles thereof, as by this article he does confirm and guaranty the same.

XXIX. The present treaty shall be ratified and approved by his Imperial and Catholic Majesty, by his Britannic Majesty, and by the Lords the States General of the United Provinces, and the letters of ratification shall be delivered within the term of six weeks, or sooner, if possible, to be reckoned from the day of signing.

In witness whereof, we the Ministers Plenipotentiaries of his Imperial and Catholic Majesty, of his Britannic Majesty, and of the Lords the States General, by virtue of our respective powers, have in their said names signed these presents in our usual manner, and caused the seals of our arms to be put thereto. Done at Antwerp, this fifteenth of November, one thousand seven hundred and fifteen.

(L. S.) *J. L. C. de Kinigsegg.*　(L. S.) *Wm Cadogan.*
(L. S.) *B. V. Dussen.*　(L. S.) *Le Comte de Rechteren.*
　　　　　　　　　　(L. S.) *S. L. Gockinga.*
　　　　　　　　　　(L. S.) *Adr. Van Borssele.*
　　　　　　　　　　　　　Geldermalsen.

Form

Form of the Oath for the Governor of Dendermonde.

I *N. N.* appointed governor by his Imperial and Catholic Majefty at Dendermonde, promife and fwear, that I will never do any thing, nor fuffer any thing to be done in the faid town, that may be prejudicial to the fervice of their High Mightineffes the States General of the United Provinces, with refpect to the prefervation of the town and of the garrifon; and that I will give free paffage to their troops whenever and as often as they fhall defire it, provided requifition be previoufly made, and that the faid troops do not pafs but in a moderate number at a time; the whole conformably to the fifth article of the treaty of barrier, a copy of which has been communicated to me. So help me God.

Form of the Oath for the Governor of Places.

N. N. I fwear and promife to keep faithfully, in the fovereignty and propriety of his Imperial and Catholic Majefty .... which is intrufted to me, and never to deliver it up to any other Power; and that I will not meddle directly or indirectly, nor fuffer any one whatever under my government, to meddle in any affair concerning the civil government, religion, and matters ecclefiaftical, juftice, and finances, nor in any thing whatfoever againft the rights, privileges, and immunities of the inhabitants, as well clergy as laity, or in any other affair that has not immediate relation to the prefervation of the place which is intrufted to me, and to the maintaining of the garrifon committed to my care; but that I will leave all thofe things to his Imperial and Catholic Majefty, as the lawful Sovereign, and to the ftates and magiftrates, as well ecclefiaftical as civil, fo far as it belongs to either of them; promifing, on the contrary, to affift them by force and arms, whenever and as often as I fhall be required fo to do, for maintaining the civil order, and for the prefervation of tranquillity againft all who

would

would make oppofition thereto; but I am alfo to be allowed to execute the orders which the States General fhall give me, confonant to, and in execution of, the treaty between his Imperial and Catholic Majefty and their High Mightineffes. So help me God.

Here follows the Tenor of the Full Power of the Minifter Plenipotentiary of his Imperial and Catholic Majefty.

WE Charles the Sixth, by the Divine clemency elected Emperor of the Romans, always Auguft, King of Germany, Spain, Hungary, and Bohemia, &c. Archduke of Auftria, Duke of Burgundy, Brabant, Styria, Carinthia, Carniola, and Wirtemberg, Count of Flanders, Habfpurg, Tyrol, and Goritia, &c. &c. The negotiation of peace which in the month of March laft was begun at Raftad, between us and the moft Serene and Potent Prince and Lord Lewis XIV. the moft Chriftian King of France, being now, by the bleffing of God, in a fair way to a conclufion, and that affair being now in fuch forwardnefs, that the treaty for the fecurity of the States General of the United Netherlands, called the Limitary or Barrier Treaty, may forthwith be fet about, and amicably tranf-acted on both fides; we therefore, relying on the fide-lity, prudence, and experience of our and the Holy Roman Empire's beloved and faithful, the Illuftrious and Noble Jofeph Lothair Count Konigfegg, our Chamberlain, Counfellor of War, and Lieutenant Field-Marfhal-General, have by thefe prefents autho-rized him with full power for this purpofe, giving him all manner of licence, in our name to confer, treat, and tranfact with the Deputies of the forefaid States General, authorized with like orders, in fuch place as fhall be mutually chofen for this treaty, of and upon the faid limits; promifing, on our Imperial and Royal word, to confirm, ratify, and approve all and fingular the things he fhall fo treat, conclude, and tranfact, in the fame manner as if we ourfelves being

I   prefent

present had come and transacted them. In witness whereof we have signed thefe prefents with our own hand, and commanded our Imperial Royal feal to be put thereto. Given in our city of Vienna, the 16th day of Auguſt, in the year one thoufand feven hundred and fourteen, and in the third year of our Roman, the eleventh of our Spaniſh, and the fourth of our Hungarian and Bohemian reign.

. (Signed)   CHARLES.

And underneath, *Joan. Frid. C. à Seilern.*

Philip Lud. C. à Sinzendorff.

By his Sacred Imperial Majefty's exprefs command,
Signed,   *Joannes Georgius Buol.*

Here follows the Tenor of the Full Power of the Miniſter Plenipotentiary of his Britannic Majeſty.

GEORGE, by the grace of God, King of Great Britain, France, and Ireland, Defender of the Faith, &c. To all and fingular to whom thefe prefent letters ſhall come, greeting. Whereas by the treaty between our late deareſt fifter and coufin Anne, Queen of Great Britain, France, and Ireland, and the High and Mighty Lords the States General of the United Provinces of the Netherlands, made at Utrecht on the $\frac{\text{Nineteenth}}{\text{Thirtieth}}$ day of the month of January, in the year one thoufand feven hundred and $\frac{\text{Twelve}}{\text{Thirteen}}$, it was concluded and agreed, that the boundary commonly called the Barrier of the faid Lords the States General in the Spaniſh Netherlands ſhould be eſtabliſhed, and rules of commerce in the faid provinces fettled, when his Imperial and Catholic Majefty ſhould enter into the poffeffion of them; we have judged it for the intereſt of us and of our kingdoms, and very much for the advantage of our common friends, to nominate fome fit perfon, every way qualified for fuch a negotiation, to repair on our part to the congrefs which is to be held at Antwerp, and there carefully to fee

to

to the eftablifhing of the faid barrier and of commerce. Know ye, therefore, that we intirely relying
on the fidelity, prudence, and experience in negotiations, of our trufty and well-beloved William Cadogan, Efq; our Envoy Extraordinary to the High and
Mighty States General of the United Provinces of the
Netherlands, a Member of our Parliament of Great
Britain, Mafter of our Robes, Lieutenant General of
our forces, and Colonel of our fecond regiment of
guards, have named, conftituted, made, and ordained,
as by thefe prefents, figned with our Royal hand, we
do nominate, conftitute, make, and ordain him to be
our true, certain, and undoubted Commiffioner, Procurator, and Plenipotentiary, giving and granting to
him all and all manner of licence, power, and authority, together with general as well as fpecial order,
for us and in our name to meet, treat, confer, renew
and conclude, with the Minifters of his Imperial and
Catholic Majefty, and of the Lords the States General of the United Netherlands, and with the Minifters
of any other Princes and States whatfoever, authorized .
with like fufficient power, at Antwerp, or in any other
place, upon fuch alliances, conventions, and articles,
whether fecret or feparate, and all other things which
may moft conduce to the obtaining happily the forefaid end, and in our name to fign and mutually deliver and receive whatever fhall be by him fo renewed, concluded, and agreed, and to do and perform all
things elfe whatfoever which are neceffary to be done,
in as ample manner and form as we ourfelf, were
we prefent thereat, could do and perform ; engaging
and promifing, on our Royal word, to ratify, approve,
and accept in the beft manner, what fhall be renewed
and concluded by our faid Commiffioner, Procurator,
and Plenipotentiary, and never to fuffer the fame to
be violated or infringed in whole or in part by any
perfon whatfoever. In witnefs and confirmation
whereof we have caufed our great feal of Great Britain to be affixed to thefe prefents, figned with our
Royal

Royal hand. Given at our palace at St. James's, the eleventh day of October, in the year of our Lord one thousand seven hundred and fourteen, and of our reign the first.

(Signed) ·   GEORGE R.

- Here follows the Tenor of the Powers of the Ministers Plenipotentiaries of the Lords the States General.

THE States General of the United Provinces of the Netherlands, to all and singular whom it does or in any manner may concern, greeting. Whereas in the present state of affairs, nothing is more desired by us, than that a speedy agreement be made between his Sacred Imperial Majesty and us, upon every thing necessary for establishing the boundary commonly called the Barrier, in the provinces of the Spanish Netherlands, for our security; we therefore relying on the prudence, experience, and fidelity of M. Bruno Vander Duffen, formerly Burgomaster, now Senator, Counsellor, and Syndic of the town of Gouda, Assessor of the Council which has the administration of the territory of Schiland, and Dykegrave of the district of Crimp; Adolphus Henry Count Rechteren, Lord of Almeloe, chief Burgomaster of Zalland in Overyssel; Seato van Gockinga, Senator of the town of Groninguen; and Adrian van Borsselen, Lord of Gueldermalsen, Senator of the town of Flushing; the three former being Deputies in our Assembly from the provinces of Holland and Westfriseland, Overyssel and Groninguen, and the Ommelands, the fourth a Deputy from Zealand in the Council of State; have nominated, elected, and constituted, as we do hereby nominate, elect, and constitute them to be our true and undoubted Plenipotentiaries, for conferring, treating, and concluding, with him or them who on the part of his Sacred Imperial Majesty shall be appointed with like power, whatever they shall judge necessary and useful on both sides for establishing the said Barrier, with all things belonging thereto; giving and

granting for this purpose to all our said Plenipotentiaries jointly, or to some, and even to any one of
them separately, the rest being absent or otherwise hindered, full and all manner of power, together with
general as well as special order, to transact, conclude,
frame, sign, and subscribe the necessary instruments in
this affair, and finally to do every thing which we ourselves, were we present, might have power to do,
even though a more special order might seem requisite: promising *bona fide* to accept, ratify, and approve whatever all our above-named Plenipotentiaries
jointly, or some, or even one of them separately, the
rest being absent, or otherwise hindered, shall by virtue of these presents transact and conclude, and to
make out and deliver in due form the instruments of
ratification thereupon. In witness whereof we have
caused these presents to be sealed with our great seal,
and to be signed by the President of our Assembly,
and countersigned by our Greffier. Hague, the twen-
ty-eighth day of September, in the year one thousand
seven hundred and fourteen.

(Signed) .. *A. Vetters.*

By command of the forementioned States General,

(Countersigned) ' *F. Fagel.*

WE having seen and considered the treaty above-
written, have approved, ratified, and confirmed, as by
these presents, for us, our heirs and successors, we do
approve, ratify, and confirm the same, in all and every
the articles and clauses thereof; engaging and promising on our Royal word, sacredly and inviolably to perform and observe the foresaid treaty, and all and singular the contents thereof, and never to suffer (as far
as in us lies) any one to violate, or in any wise to
act contrary to the same. In witness and confirmation
whereof we have commanded our great seal of Great
Britain to be affixed to these presents, signed with
our Royal hand. Given at our palace at St. James's,
the

the thirteenth day of the month of November, in the year of our Lord 1715, and of our reign the second. GEORGE R.

GEORGE, by the Grace of God, King of Great Britain, France, and Ireland, Defender of the Faith, &c. To all and singular to whom these present letters shall come, greeting. Whereas a certain separate article, belonging to the treaty for establishing the boundary, commonly called the Barrier, concluded at Antwerp on the fifteenth day of this present month of November, was at the same place and on the same day signed by the same Ministers Plenipotentiaries empowered respectively with sufficient authority, in the form and words following.

Separate Article.

WHEREAS in the nineteenth article of Barrier for the States General of the United Provinces in the Austrian Netherlands, concluded this day, the fifteenth of November, one thousand seven hundred and fifteen, between his Imperial and Catholic Majesty, his Britannic Majesty, and the said Lords the States General, it is agreed to explain more particularly, by a separate article, what relates to the mortgages, and the methods of receiving the subsidy therein mentioned; his Imperial and Catholic Majesty, for the better securing and facilitating the payment of the said subsidy of five hundred thousand crowns, or twelve hundred and fifty thousand florins, Dutch money, yearly, agreed to and stipulated by the said article, does charge specially on the countries, towns, castellanies, and dependencies, yielded by France, the annual sum of six hundred and ten thousand florins, Dutch money, according to the following repartition; that is to say, on the town of Tournay fifty-five thousand florins, on the castellany of Tournay, called the Tournesis, twenty-five thousand florins, on the town and verge of Menin ninety thousand florins; and on the part of West Flanders,

Flanders, which was yielded by France, to be paid by a repartition among the towns, castellanies, and dependencies, according to the transport de Flandres, four hundred and forty thousand florins ; and for the rest, on the subsidies of the province of Brabant one third, being the sum of two hundred and thirteen thousand three hundred and thirty-three florins, and one-third of a florin ; and on those of the province of Flanders two-thirds, being the sum of four hundred twenty-six thousand six hundred sixty-six florins, and two-thirds of a florin, the said respective sums amounting together to the total sum five hundred thousand crowns, or twelve hundred and fifty thousand florins, Dutch money.

The share of the province of Brabant is charged on the contingent of the country of Waas, including Beveren, of the country of Oudenbourg, of the liberties of Bruges, of the country of Aloft, and of the town and country of Dendermonde, towards the subsidies of that province.

And for the better securing the regular payment of the said respective sums, his Imperial and Catholic Majesty promises and engages, that the payment shall be made every three months, to commence from the day of the signing this present treaty, to be paid on the day the same shall become due.

And in default of the said payment at the said end of three months, his Imperial and Catholic Majesty does now, and by this treaty order the States of the provinces and divisions, and the receivers of the subsidies, as well ordinary as extraordinary, and also those of his duties and demesnes, out of which the payment ought to be made conformably to the repartition above, that by virtue of this article, and at sight of a copy thereof, they take care to pay immediately at the end of each term, and without delay, to the receiver general of the said States General, or to his order, the sums above specified, and without waiting for any other order or assignment ; this present article being
to

to ftand for an order and affignment, now and for the time coming. And the faid payment fhall be allowed them on account, on the part of his Imperial and Catholic Majefty, as if it had been made to himfelf.

In default of which, or in cafe the faid States do not grant the fubfidies with requifite expedition, the States General fhall and may proceed to methods of compulfion and execution, and even by force of arms, against the receivers, ftates, and demefnes of the faid provinces and divifions, which his Imperial and Catholic Majefty fubjects thereto by virtue of this article; the whole without prejudice to the right of their High Mightineffes upon the other revenues of the fovereign over and above the fubfidy of the provinces, fuch as the duties of importation and exportation, the impofts, the tailles, tolls, and other demefnes.

Moreover it is agreed, that the payment of the faid fubfidy fhall not be delayed, much lefs refufed, under pretext of compenfation, clearing of accounts, or other pretenfions, of what name or nature foever they may be.

And this feparate article fhall have the fame force as the faid treaty of Barrier, and juft as if it were inferted therein word for word, and fhall be ratified at the fame time as that treaty.

In witnefs whereof we the Minifters Plenipotentiaries of his Imperial and Catholic Majefty, of his Britannic Majefty, and of the Lords the States General, have figned this prefent article, and caufed the feals of our arms to be put thereto. At Antwerp, this fifteenth of November, one thoufand feven hundred and fifteen.

(L. S.) *J. L. C. de Kinigfegg.*   (L. S.) *Wm Cadogan.*
(L. S.) *B. V. Duffen.*   (L. S.) *Le Comte de Rechteren.*
(L. S.) *S. L. Gockinga.*
(L. S.) *Adr. Van Borffele Geldermalfen.*

WE having feen and confidered the feparate article above-written, have approved, ratified, and confirmed, as by thefe prefents we do, for us, our heirs and fucceffors, approve, ratify, and confirm it in all and fingular the claufes thereof; engaging and promifing on our Royal word fincerely and faithfully to obferve and (as far as in us lies) to caufe to be obferved all and every the things contained in the forefaid feparate article. In witnefs and confirmation whereof we have commanded our great feal of Great Britain to be affixed to thefe prefents, figned with our Royal hand. Given at our palace at St. James's, the thirtieth day of the month of November, in the year of our Lord one thoufand feven hundred and fifteen, and of our reign the fecond.   GEORGE *R.*

Convention made at London *the 26th of* July, O. S. 1715.

HIS Britannic Majefty's Minifters having complained that the commerce of his faid Britannic Majefty with the Auftrian Netherlands is very much prejudiced by the high duties of importation laid upon the coarfe woollen cloths fent from Great Britain to the faid Auftrian Netherlands: the under-written Minifter and Plenipotentiary of his Imperial and Catholic Majefty for the treaty of Barrier at Antwerp, declares by thefe prefents, that his Imperial and Catholic Majefty will confent to the immediate reducing of the duties on the faid coarfe woollen cloths, according to the following fpecification: and that in all other refpects the commerce of the fubjects of his Britannic Majefty, with the Auftrian Netherlands, fhall remain, continue, and fubfift wholly on the fame foot as it does at prefent, without any alteration, innovation, diminution, or augmentation to be made under any pretext whatfoever, till all the parties interefted fhall agree upon a treaty of commerce.

Dyed Woollen Cloths.

Fl. Sols.

A piece of the value of above 60 florins, up to 90 — —	3	10
A piece of the value of above 40 florins, up to 60 — —	2	—
A piece of the value of 40 florins, and under — —	1	—

Mixed Woollen Cloths.

A piece of the value of above 60 florins, up to 90 — —	2	10
A piece of the value of above 40 florins, up to 60 — —	1	10
A piece of the value of 40 florins, and under — —	1	—

White Woollen Cloths.

A piece of the value of above 60 florins, up to 90 — —	2	10
A piece of the value of above 40 florins, up to 60 — —	2	—
A piece of the value of 40 florins, and under — —	1	—
Draps de Pie (cloth to lie upon floors) of all forts, the piece —	—	8

Done at London this 26th of July, O. S. 1715.

(L. S.) *J. L. de Kinigſegg.*

Requiſition made to the Council of State at Bruſſels, *the 6th of* November, 1715.

IT being abſolutely neceſſary, for the ſervice of his Imperial and Catholic Majeſty, to leſſen immediately the duties of importation on coarſe woollen cloths coming from Great Britain, and from the United Provinces, on the following foot.

Woollen Cloths Dyed.

A piece of the value of above 60 florins, up to 90 florins — —	3	10
From 40 to 60 — —	2	—
Of 40 and under — —	1	—

	Mixt.			Fl.	Sols.
A piece of the value of 60 florins, and so up to 90. — — —.				2	10
From 40 to 60 — —				1	10
Of 40 and under — —				1	—

White.

				Fl.	Sols.
A piece of the value of 60 florins, and so up to 90 — — —				2	10
From 40 to 60 — —				2	—
Of 40 and under — —				1	—
Draps de Pie (cloth to lie upon floors) of all sorts, the piece —				—	8

And to reduce the duties of importation on brandies distilled from corn coming from Great Britain, and from the United Provinces, to 3 florins the awm instead of 8 which is now paid. You are required, Gentlemen, to give forthwith the necessary directions in the finances, that the proper orders may be immediately issued for this purpose, and that the collectors of the duties of importation and exportation may conform themselves accordingly thereto. Done at the conference at Brussels, this 6th of November, 1715.

(Signed)   *Wm Cadogan,*
Johan Vander Bergh.

Attested to be a copy,
P. W. Francquen.

A Copy of the Resolution of the Council of State, minuted in the Margin of the Consultation of the Council of the Finances, the 7th of November, 1715.

HAVING made our representation to the Ministers of the conference, conformably to this consultation; and added also other reasons to enforce it, they have newly made this day another more pressing requisition to us, by which they insist absolutely that the former be put in execution; whereupon the council of the finances shall issue the orders therein specified;
but

but it is underftood that they fhall not have force nor effect, unlefs they be approved and ratified by his Imperial and Catholic Majefty in the treaty of Barrier: This laft claufe, however, which begins with the words *it is underftood*, and ends with the words *in the treaty of Barrier*, fhall not be inferted in the orders to be fent to the collectors.

(Signed)   *Voorfp.*

Attefted to be a copy,

P. W. Francquen.

Order of the Council of Finances to the Collectors of the Duties.

THE Counfellors and Commiffioners of the demefnes and finances of his Imperial and Catholic Majefty. Moft dear and fpecial friends, we herewith fend you, by exprefs order of the Council of State appointed for the general government of thefe countries, a copy of the requifition made to them by the Minifters of the conference, relating to the leffening of the duties of importation on the coarfe woollen cloths coming from Great Britain, and from the United Provinces; as alfo for reducing the faid duties on brandies diftilled from corn, commanding you, by exprefs order of the faid Council of State, to take care to regulate yourfelves purfuant thereto, in collecting the faid duties, and to give notice of it to your fubalterns. Moft dear and fpecial friends, God have you in his holy keeping. Bruffels, at the council of the faid finances, the 12th of November, 1715.

To the collectors of the duties of importation and
exportation at

Newport.	Fort St. Philip.
Oftend.	Borgerhout.
Bruges.	Mechlen.
Ghent.	Turnhout
Dendermonde.	Tirlemont.

This is a copy agreeing with the minutes kept in the
regiftry of the finances.

P. W. Francquen.

Extract

Extract from the Tariff settled the 14th of November, 1715.

N. B. A difficulty having risen about the intention of the requisition of the 6th of November, 1715, of which mention is made in the 26th article of the treaty of Barrier, it is agreed provisionally to cause the duties of importation on all the different sorts comprehended in the above tariff under the denomination of woollen cloths, to be collected according to the tenor of the said requisition of the 6th of November, till his Imperial and Catholic Majesty, and his Majesty the King of Great Britain, shall agree upon it otherwise; and in the mean while the King's collectors and officers shall permit the said manufactures to be imported, giving notice and taking security for the payment of the overplus duties of importation on the foot the same shall be settled.

A Letter from the Imperial Envoy Count Volkra, *to the Lord Viscount* Townshend, *principal Secretary of State.*

My Lord,

YOU have acquainted me that complaints are made here of contraventions to the twenty-sixth article of the treaty of Barrier, and I have had the honour to communicate to you what Count Kinigsegg has answered thereupon.

I can declare to you besides, that for the future there will be an exact performance of the said twenty-sixth article of the treaty of Barrier of the 15th of November, 1715, and of the convention at London of the 26th of July, 1715; as also of the declaration in the tariff of the 14th of November, 1715, that is to say, that the duties on the petite draperie (or woollen stuffs) of England will be collected on the foot of the coarse woollen cloths, according to the diminution expressed in the foresaid convention at London, without any alteration, till it be agreed otherwise between the Emperor

peror and the King, our masters; but in the mean time the merchants are to give security to pay the surplus, if the matter shall be so determined between the two respective courts.

London, ²⁰⁄₃₁ August,   I am, &c.
          1716.   *The Count Volkra.*

The Emperor's Ratification.

WE Charles the Sixth, by the Divine clemency elected Emperor of the Romans, always August, King of Germany, Spain, Hungary, Bohemia, Dalmatia, Croatia, and Sclavonia, Archduke of Austria, Duke of Burgundy, Brabant, Styria, Carinthia, Carniola, Limbourg, Luxembourg, Guelderland, Upper and Lower Silesia, and Wirtemberg, Prince of Swabia, Marquis of the Holy Roman Empire, of Burgaw, Moravia, Upper and Lower Lusatia, Count of Hapsburg, Flanders, Tyrol, Ferrete, Kyburg, Goritia, and Namur, Landgrave of Alsatia, Lord of the Marck of Sclavonia, Port Nao, and Salins, &c. &c. make known and attest to all and singular whom it concerns. Whereas peace being made with France last year at Baden in Switzerland, it was forthwith agreed between Us, the most Serene and most Potent King of Great Britain, and the States General of the United Netherlands, that what by the alliance made in the year one thousand seven hundred and one, on the seventh day of September, at the Hague, appeared yet remaining mutually to be performed, should without delay be adjusted in the Congress which was thought proper to be held at Antwerp by ministers respectively authorized with full power; and especially that those places, towns, and fortifications of our Netherlands, which for the future might serve for the security, defence, and safety, commonly called a Barrier, to the provinces and dominions of the foresaid States General, might be specified, and whatever else relates to that affair be settled; which by the favour of the Almighty,

2   and

and in especial manner by the friendly offices of the said most Serene King of Great Britain, was on the fifteenth day of November last determined and concluded by those Ministers Plenipotentiaries, whose names are hereunto subjoined, in the following words and articles:

It having pleased the Almighty to grant Peace for some Time past to Europe, &c.

That we have ratified and approved, as by virtue of these presents we do approve and ratify all and singular the things that by Ours, his Britannic Majesty's, and the States General's Ministers Plenipotentiaries, by virtue of an order empowering them, were, as is above recited, done, concluded, and transacted; promising on our Imperial, Royal, and Archiducal word, faithfully and religiously to perform and observe, and cause to be observed by our subjects, what relates to us, and not to suffer any thing to be done contrary thereto; assuredly trusting, that the Electors, Princes, and States of the Holy Roman Empire, duly considering the circumstances of affairs which in the present juncture obliged us to yield what by the twenty-seventh article above is stipulated, touching the razing of the fortifications and citadel of Liege, and of the castles and works of the town of Huy, will not scruple to concur therein with their consent. In witness whereof, we have signed these presents with our own hand, and caused our Imperial Royal seal to be put to it. Vienna, the twenty-first day of the month of December, in the year one thousand seven hundred and fifteen, the fifth of our Roman, the thirteenth of our Spanish, and the fifth of our Hungarian and Bohemian reign.

CHARLES (L. S.)

Philip Lud. C. à Sinzendorff.

By the express command of his Sacred Imperial and Catholic Majesty.

John George Buol.

The

The Emperor's Ratification of the separate Article.

WE Charles the Sixth, by the Divine clemency, elected Emperor of the Romans, always August, King of Germany, Spain, Hungary, Bohemia, Dalmatia, Croatia, and Sclavonia, Archduke of Austria, Duke of Burgundy, Brabant, Styria, Carinthia, Carniola, Limbourg, Luxembourg, Guelderland, Upper and Lower Silesia, and Wirtemberg, Prince of Swabia, Marquis of the Holy Roman Empire, of Burgaw, Moravia, Upper and Lower Lusatia, Count of Hapsburg, Flanders, Tyrol, Ferrete, Kyburg, Goritia, and Namur, Landgrave of Alsatia, Lord of the Marck of Sclavonia, Port Nao, and Salins, &c. &c. make known and attest to all and singular whom it concerns. Whereas for very weighty reasons it has been thought fit, by a separate article, to explain more particularly what by the nineteenth article of this treaty is stipulated in general words, touching the annual subsidy of five hundred thousand crowns to be allowed for the garrisons of the States General, and to assign the said subsidy by repartition on the several provinces of our Netherlands, and to secure the payment of the same in the following manner.

Separate Article.

Whereas in the Nineteenth Article of Barrier for the States General of the United Provinces in the Austrian Netherlands, concluded this Day, the Fifteenth of November, One thousand Seven hundred and Fifteen, &c.

That we have approved this separate article, and the contents thereof, in the like manner as the treaty itself, and by these presents we promise to observe it as faithfully and religiously, and to cause it to be observed by our subjects. In witness whereof we have signed these presents, and commanded our Imperial Royal seal to be set thereto. Given at Vienna, the 21st of the month of December, in the year one

thousand

thousand seven hundred and fifteen, the fifth of our Roman, the thirteenth of our Spanish, and the fifth of our Hungarian and Bohemian reign.

CHARLES (L.S.)
Philip Lud. à Sinzendorff.

By express command of his Sacred Imperial and Catholic Majesty, *John George Buol.*

The Ratification of the States General.

THE States General of the United Provinces of the Netherlands, to all who shall see these presents, greeting. Having seen and examined the treaty concluded and signed at Antwerp the fifteenth of the month of November, one thousand seven hundred and fifteen, by the Ministers Plenipotentiaries of his Imperial and Catholic Majesty, of his Majesty the King of Great Britain, and Ours, touching the manner in which the Austrian Netherlands are to serve henceforward for the barrier of Great Britain and of our State, as the said treaty here follows, inserted word for word.

It having pleased the Almighty to grant Peace for some Time past to Europe, &c.

We approving all that our Deputies and Ministers Plenipotentiaries have done, in concluding and signing this treaty, have consented to, approved, and ratified, consent to, approve, and ratify the same by these presents: promising sincerely and faithfully to keep, observe, and execute it in the whole, and in each of its articles, without acting contrary to it in any manner whatsoever, directly or indirectly. In witness whereof, we have caused our great seal to be affixed to these presents, and the same to be signed by the President of our Assembly, and countersigned by our Greffier. At the Hague, the fourteenth of January, one thousand seven hundred and sixteen. *W. Vander Does.*

By command of the above-mentioned Lords the States General, *F. Fagel.*

The

The States General's Ratification of the separate Article.

THE States General of the United Provinces of the Netherlands, to all who shall see these presents, greeting. Having seen and examined the separate article of the treaty concluded and signed at Antwerp the fifteenth of the month of November, one thousand seven hundred and fifteen, by the Ministers Plenipotentiaries of his Imperial and Catholic Majesty, of his Majesty the King of Great Britain, and Ours, touching the manner in which the Austrian Netherlands are to serve henceforward for the barrier of Great Britain, and of our State, the tenor of which separate article is as follows.

Separate Article.

Whereas in the Nineteenth Article of Barrier for the States General of the United Provinces in the Austrian Netherlands, concluded this Day, the Fifteenth of November, One thousand Seven hundred and Fifteen, &c.

We approving all that our Deputies and Ministers Plenipotentiaries have done, in concluding and signing this separate article, have consented to, approved, and ratified, consent to, approve, and ratify the same by these presents, promising sincerely and faithfully to keep, observe, and execute it, without acting contrary to it in any manner whatsoever, directly or indirectly. In witness whereof, we have caused our great seal to be affixed to these presents, and the same to be signed by the President of our Assembly, and countersigned by our Greffier. At the Hague, the fourteenth of January, one thousand seven hundred and sixteen.

W. Vander Does.

By command of the above-mentioned Lords the States General, *F. Fagel.*

[The

[The following is printed from the original.]

Count Volkra's *Declaration,* 1716, *about the Trade in the* Auſtrian Netherlands.

Milord,

VOUS m'avez témoigné qu'on ſe plaint ici des contraventions à l'article 26. du Traité de la Barrière; et j'ai eu l'honneur de vous communiquer ce que Monſieur le Comte de Kinigſegg a répondu là-deſſus.

Je puis vous déclarer outre cela, qu'on ſe tiendra à l'avenir exactement à l'obſervation du ſuſdit article 26. du Traité de la Barrière, du 15 Novembre, 1715, et à la convention de Londres, du 26 Juillet, 1715, comme encore à la déclaration du 14 Novembre, 1715; à ſavoir, qu'on louera les droits ſur la petite draperie d'Angleterre, ſur le pied des gros draps, ſuivant la diminution exprimée dans la ſuſdite convention de Londres, ſans aucune altération, juſques à ce qu'on en ſera convenu autrement entre l'Empereur et le Roi nos maîtres; mais que pourtant les marchands donneront caution de payer le ſurplus, ſi l'affaire ſera ainſi déterminée entre les deux reſpectives Cours.

J'eſpére, Milord, que vous ferez avancer, ſans plus de delai, l'emprunt de 200 piéces, ſelon la convention faite là-deſſus, en vous aſſurant que

Je ſuis, avec une très-parfaite eſtime,

Milord,

Votre très-humble et

très-obéiſſant ſerviteur,

Londres, ce $\frac{10}{11}$ Aout,   *Le Comte Volkra.*

1716.

[The

[The following is printed from the copy which was published by authority in 1718.]

The Treaty of Alliance for settling the Public Peace, signed at London, $\frac{22\ July}{2\ August}$, 1718.

GEORGE, by the grace of God, of Great Britain, France, and Ireland, King, Defender of the Faith, Duke of Brunswick and Lunenburg, Arch-Treasurer of the Holy Roman Empire, and Prince Elector, &c. To all and singular, to whom these presents shall come, greeting. Whereas a certain treaty, containing as well the conditions of peace to be made between the Emperor of the Romans and the King of Spain, and between the said Emperor and the King of Sicily, as the terms of a mutual alliance made between us and our good brother the said Emperor of the Romans, and our good brother the most Christian King, and our good friends the High and Mighty Lords the States General of the United Provinces of the Netherlands, by Plenipotentiaries on both sides sufficiently furnished with orders and authority for the same, in our city of London, the twenty-second day of July last past, O. S. has been concluded and signed in the form and words following:

In the Name of the most Holy and undivided Trinity.

Be it known to all whom it doth concern, or may any way concern.

Whereas the most Serene and most Potent Prince, George, of Great Britain, France, and Ireland, King, Duke of Brunswick and Lunenburgh, Elector of the Holy Roman Empire, &c. and the most Serene and most Potent Prince, Lewis the Fifteenth, the most Christian King, &c. as likewise the High and Mighty States General of the United Provinces of the Netherlands, being continually intent on preserving the blessing of peace, have duly considered, that however, by the triple alliance concluded by them on the 4th of January, 1717, their own kingdoms and provinces

were provided for, yet that the provifion was neither
fo general nor fo folid, as that the public tranquillity
could long flourifh and laft, unlefs at the fame time
the jealoufies which were ftill increafing between fome
of the Princes of Europe, as perpetual occafions of va-
riance, could be removed: and being convinced by
experience from the war kindled the laft year in Italy,
for the timely extinguifhing whereof, by a treaty made
in the year 1718, they agreed
amongft themfelves upon certain articles of pacification, according to which a peace might be brought
about and eftablifhed between his Sacred Imperial Majefty and the King of Spain; as likewife between his faid
Imperial Majefty and the King of Sicily; and farther
gave a friendly invitation to his Imperial Majefty, that,
out of his love for the public peace and quiet, he would
receive and approve the faid articles of convention in
his own name, and accordingly that he himfelf would
accede to the treaty made by them, the tenor of which
is as followeth.

*Conditions of Peace between his Imperial Majefty and his
Royal Catholic Majefty.*

I. For quieting the difturbances lately raifed contrary to the peace of Baden, concluded the 7th of September, 1714, as likewife to the neutrality eftablifhed
for Italy by the treaty of the 14th of March, 1713,
the moft Serene and moft Potent King of Spain obliges
himfelf to reftore to his Imperial Majefty, and accordingly fhall immediately, or at the fartheft after two
months, to be reckoned from the exchange of the ratifications of this prefent treaty, actually reftore to his
faid Imperial Majefty the ifland and kingdom of Sardinia, in the condition wherein he feized it, and fhall
renounce, in favour of his Imperial Majefty, all rights,
pretenfions, interefts, and claims upon the faid kingdom; fo that his Imperial Majefty fully and freely,
and in the manner which he judges beft, out of his
love to the public good, may difpofe of it as of his own
property.

II. Whereas

. II. Whereas the only method which could be·found out for fixing a durable balance in Europe was judged to be this, that it should be an eftablished rule that the kingdoms of France and Spain should never go together, or be united in one and the fame perfon, or in one and the fame line, and that thofe two monarchies should henceforward for ever remain feparate; and whereas for confirming this rule, fo neceffary for the public tranquillity, thofe Princes, to whom the prerogative of birth might have given a right of fucceeding in both kingdoms, have folemnly renounced one of thofe two kingdoms for themfelves and all their pofterity; fo that this feparation of the two monarchies has paffed into a fundamental law in the general affembly commonly called Las Cortes, which was received at Madrid the 9th of November, 1712, and confolidated by the treaties of Utrecht, the 11th of April, 1713; his Imperial Majefty, being willing to give the utmoft perfection to fo neceffary and wholefome a law, to take away all ground of fufpicion, and to promote the public tranquillity, doth accept and agree to thofe things which were done, ratified, and eftablished in the treaty of Utrecht, with regard to the right and order of fucceffion to the kingdoms of France and Spain, and doth renounce, as well for himfelf, as for his heirs, defcendants, and fucceffors, male and female, all rights, and all and every pretenfion whatfoever, not one in the leaft excepted, on any kingdoms whatfoever, dominions, and provinces of the Spanish monarchy, whereof the Catholic King was acknowledged to be the rightful poffeffor by the treaty of Utrecht, and will caufe to be made out in due form accordingly folemn acts of renunciation, which he will caufe to be published and regiftered in the proper courts, and promifes that he will exhibit the ufual inftruments thereupon to his Catholic Majefty, and to the contracting Powers.

III. By virtue of the faid renunciation, which his Imperial Majefty has made out of regard to the fecu

rity

rity of all Europe; and in confideration likewife that the
Duke of Orleans has for himfelf, and for his defcendants, renounced all his rights and claims upon the
kingdom of Spain, on condition that neither the Emperor, nor any of his defcendants, fhall ever fucceed
to the faid kingdom; his Imperial Majefty doth acknowledge Philip the Fifth to be lawful King of Spain
and of the Indies, and doth promife to give him the
titles and prerogatives belonging to his dignity and his
kingdoms : and moreover, he will allow him, his defcendants, heirs, and fucceffors, male and female, peaceably to enjoy all thofe dominions of the Spanifh monarchy in Europe, the Indies, and elfewhere, the poffeffion whereof was allowed to him by the treaties of
Utrecht, nor will he directly or indirectly difturb him
in the faid poffeffion at any time, nor will he claim to
himfelf any right to the faid kingdoms and provinces.

IV. In return for the renunciation and acknowledgment made by his Imperial Majefty in the two
foregoing articles, the Catholic King, as well in his
own, as in the name of his heirs, defcendants, and
fucceffors, male and female, doth renounce in favour
of his Imperial Majefty, his fucceffors, heirs, and defcendants, male and female, all rights and claims
whatfoever, none in the leaft being excepted, upon all
and every the kingdoms, provinces, and dominions,
which his Imperial Majefty doth poffefs in Italy or the
Netherlands, or may accrue to him by virtue of this
prefent treaty; and he doth wholly abdicate all rights,
kingdoms, and provinces in Italy, which heretofore
belonged to the Spanifh monarchy, amongft which the
marquifate of Final, yielded by his Imperial Majefty
to the republic of Genoa in the year 1713, is underftood to be exprefsly comprehended, and he will caufe
to be made out accordingly folemn acts of renunciation
in due form, which he will caufe to be publifhed and
regiftered in the proper courts, and promifes that he
will exhibit the ufual inftruments thereupon to his Imperial Majefty and the contracting Powers. His Catholic

tholic Majefty doth in like manner renounce the right
of reverfion of the kingdom of Sicily to the crown of
Spain, which he had referved to himfelf, and all other
claims and pretenfions under pretext whereof he might
difturb his Imperial Majefty, his heirs and fucceffors,
directly or indirectly, as well in the aforefaid kingdoms
and provinces, as in all other dominions, which he actually poffeffes in the Netherlands or elfewhere.

V. Whereas, in cafe the Grand Duke of Tufcany,
or the Duke of Parma and Placentia, or their fucceff-
fors, fhould die without male iffue, the pretenfions of
fucceffion to the dominions poffeffed by them might
kindle a new war in Italy, on account of the different
rights of fucceffion, whereby, after the deceafe of the
next heirs before her, the prefent Queen of Spain,
born Dutchefs of Parma, claims the faid dukedoms to
herfelf on the one part, and the Emperor and empire
on the other part. To the end that the great difputes,
and the evils arifing from them, may be timely obviated, it is agreed, that the ftates and dutchies at prefent
poffeffed by the Grand Duke of Tufcany, and Duke
of Parma and Placentia aforefaid, fhall in time to come
be held and acknowledged by all the contracting Powers
as undoubted male fiefs of the Holy Roman Empire.
His Imperial Majefty on his part doth confent, by himfelf as head of the empire, that whenever it fhall happen that the faid dutchies fhall lie open for want of heirs
male, the firft-born fon of the faid Queen of Spain, and
his defcendants, being males, born in lawful matrimony,
and in default of them, the fecond-born, or other the
younger fons of the faid Queen, if any fhall be born, together with their male defcendants, born in lawful marriage, fhall in like manner, fucceed to all the provinces
aforefaid. To which end, it being neceffary that the
confent of the empire be alfo given, his Imperial Majefty will ufe all his endeavours to obtain it; and having
obtained it, he will caufe the letters of expectative, containing the eventual inveftiture for the fon of the faid
Queen, or her fons, and their legitimate male de-

S 3   fcendants,

scendants, to be expedited in due form; and he will cause the said letters to be delivered to the Catholic King immediately, or at least after two months from the exchange of the ratifications; without any damage, nevertheless, or prejudice, to the Princes who now have possession of the said dutchies, which possession is to remain entirely safe to them.

It is farther agreed, between his Sacred Imperial Majesty, and the Catholic King, that the town of Leghorn may, and ought, perpetually to remain a free port, in the same manner as it now is.

By virtue of the renunciation made by the King of Spain, of all the dominions, kingdoms, and provinces in Italy, which heretofore belonged to the Kings of Spain, that King shall yield to the aforesaid Prince his son, the town of Porto Longone, together with that part of the island Elba, which he actually possesses therein; and shall deliver the same up to him, as soon as that Prince, on the extinction of the male posterity of the Grand Duke of Tuscany, shall be admitted into the actual possession of his territories.

It is moreover agreed to, and provided by solemn contract, that none of the aforesaid dutchies or dominions, at any time, or in any case, may or ought to be possessed by a Prince, who at the same time holds the kingdom of Spain; and that no King of Spain can ever take upon him the guardianship of that Prince, or may be allowed to exercise the same.

Lastly, it is agreed, and thereto all and singular the parties contracting have equally bound themselves, that it never shall be allowed, during the lives of the present possessors of the dutchies of Tuscany and Parma, or of their male successors, that any forces of any country whatsoever, whether their own or hired, shall either by the Emperor, the Kings of Spain and France, or even by the Prince appointed, as above, to the succession, be introduced into the provinces and lands of the said dutchies; nor shall any of them place any garrison in the cities, ports, towns, or fortresses therein situated.   But,

But, that the said son of the Queen of Spain, ap-. pointed by this treaty to the succeffion of the Great Duke of Tufcany and the Duke of Parma and Placentia, may be more fully fecured againft all events, and may more certainly depend on the execution of the fucceffion promifed him; and likewife that the fief, conftituted as above, may remain inviolable to the Emperor and empire; it is agreed on both fides, that garrifons, not exceeding however the number of fix thoufand men, fhall be put into the principal towns thereof, viz. Leghorn, Porto Ferraro, Parma, and Placentia, be taken from among the Swifs Cantons, which cantons are for this purpofe to be paid by the three contracting Powers, who have taken upon them the part of mediators. And the faid garrifons are therein to be continued till the cafe of the faid fucceffion fhall happen, when they fhall be obliged to deliver the towns to the faid Prince appointed to the fucceffion; neverthelefs, without any trouble or charge to the prefent poffeffors, and their fucceffors being males, to whom likewife the faid garrifons are to take an oath of fidelity, and are to affume to themfelves no other authority than only the guard of the cities committed to their charge.

But whereas this beneficial work may be longer delayed than is convenient, before an agreement can be made with the Swifs Cantons about the number, pay, and manner of eftablifhing fuch a force; his Sacred Royal Britannic Majefty, out of his fingular zeal for the faid work, and the public tranquillity, and for the earlier obtaining the end propofed, will not in the mean time refufe to lend his own forces for the ufe above-mentioned, if the reft of the contracting Powers think good, till the forces to be raifed in the Swifs Cantons can take upon them the guard and cuftody of the faid cities.

VI. His Catholic Majefty, to teftify his fincere inclination for the public tranquillity, doth confent to all things hereafter mentioned; with regard to what is fet-

tled

tled about the kingdom of Sicily for the advantage
of his Imperial Majefty, and doth renounce for himfelf, his heirs and fucceffors, male and female, the
right of reverfion of that kingdom to the crown of
Spain, which he exprefsly referved to himfelf by the
inftrument of ceffion dated the 10th of June, 1713.
Out of love to the public good he moreover departs
from the faid act of the 10th of June, 1713, as far as
is neceffary, as likewife from the fixth article of the
treaty of Utrecht, betwixt himfelf and his Royal
Highnefs the Duke of Savoy, as likewife in general
from every thing that may oppofe the retroceffion, difpofition, and permutation of the above-mentioned kingdom of Sicily, by this prefent treaty eftablifhed. On
condition, neverthelefs, that the right of reverfion of
the ifland and kingdom of Sardinia to the faid crown
may be yielded and allowed to him, as hereafter, in
the fecond article of the conventions between his Sacred Imperial Majefty and the King of Sicily, is farther explained.

VII. The Emperor and the Catholic King mutually promife and bind themfelves to a reciprocal defence and guaranty of all the kingdoms and provinces
which they actually poffefs, or the poffeffion whereof
ought to belong to them by virtue of the prefent
treaty.

VIII. His Imperial Majefty and his Royal Catholic Majefty fhall immediately after exchange of the
ratifications of thefe prefent conventions, put in execution all and every the conditions therein comprehended, and that within the fpace of two months at the
fartheft, and the inftruments of the ratifications of the
faid conventions fhall be exchanged at London within
the fpace of two months, to be computed from the
day of figning, or fooner if poffible. Which execution of the conditions being previoufly performed, their
Minifters and Plenipotentiaries, by them to be named,
fhall in the place of congrefs, which they fhall agree
upon,

upon, with all fpeed feverally fettle and determine the other points of their particular peace, under the mediation of the three contracting Powers.

It is farther agreed, that in the treaty of peace particularly to be made between the Emperor and the King of Spain, a general amnefty fhall be granted to all perfons, of any ftate, dignity, degree, or fex whatfoever, whether ecclefiaftical or military, political or civil, who followed the party of the one or the other Prince during the late war; in virtue whereof all and fingular the faid perfons fhall be permitted to receive, and they may receive full poffeffion and ufe of their goods, rights, privileges, honours, dignities, and immunities, and fhall ufe and enjoy the fame as freely as they did enjoy them at the beginning of the laft war, or at the time when they begun to join themfelves to the one or the other party, all confifcations, arrefts, and fentences, made, paffed, or pronounced, during the war, to the contrary notwithftanding, which fhall be held as null and of no effect. In virtue moreover of the aforefaid amnefty, it fhall be lawful and free for all and fingular the faid perfons, who followed one or the other party, to return to their country, and to enjoy their goods in the fame manner as if no war had happened; and a full licence is given them to take care of the faid effects, either by themfelves if they fhould be prefent, or by their attorneys, if they fhould choofe rather to abfent themfelves from their country, and they may either fell, or any other way, according to their pleafure, difpofe of them, entirely after the fame manner they might have done before the beginning of the war.

Conditions of the Treaty to be concluded between his Imperial Majefty *and the King of* Sicily.

I. WHEREAS the ceffion of Sicily, by the treaties of Utrecht, to the Houfe of Savoy, being folely made for rendering that peace folid, and not on the account of any right the King of Sicily had thereto, has

has been so far from bringing about the end proposed, that, as all Europe can witness, it has rather proved the great obstacle which hindered the Emperor from acceding to the said treaties, inasmuch as the separation of the kingdoms of Naples and Sicily, so long used to remain under the same dominion, and to be called by the name of both the Sicilies, has not only been found opposite to the common interests and mutual preservation of both kingdoms, but likewise to the repose of all Italy, being constantly productive of new commotions, while neither the ancient intercourse and mutual relation between the two nations can be destroyed, nor the interests of the different Princes can be easily reconciled : for this reason it is that the Princes, who first made the Utrecht treaties, have thought it lawful for them, even without the consent of the parties concerned, to abrogate that one article of those treaties which regards the kingdom of Sicily, and is not any principal part of the said treaty, founding themselves chiefly upon these reasons ; That the present treaty will receive its increase and completion from the Emperor's renunciation ; and that by the exchange of Sicily for Sardinia, the wars which threaten Italy may be prevented, inasmuch as the Emperor might rightfully attack Sicily, which he never yet renounced, and which, since the infraction of the neutrality of Italy by the seizure of Sardinia, he may rightfully recover by force of arms : besides that the King of Sicily may become possessed of a certain and durable dominion by the benefit of so solemn a treaty with his Imperial Majesty, and guarantied by the chief Princes of Europe. Being moved therefore by so great reasons, they have agreed that the King of Sicily shall restore to his Imperial Majesty the island and kingdom of Sicily, with all its dependencies and appendages, in the state wherein they now are, immediately, or in two months at the farthest from the exchange of the ratifications of the present treaty. And he shall in favour of the Emperor, his heirs

and

and fucceffors of both fexes, renounce all rights and pretenfions whatfoever to the faid kingdom, as well for himfelf as his heirs and fucceffors, male and female; the reverfion thereof to the crown of Spain being entirely taken away.

II. In return, his Imperial Majefty fhall yield to the King of Sicily the ifland and kingdom of Sardinia, in the fame condition wherein he fhall receive it from the Catholic King, and fhall renounce all rights and interefts in the faid kingdom, for himfelf, his heirs and fucceffors of both fexes, in favour of the King of Sicily, his heirs and fucceffors, that he may hereafter perpetually poffefs the fame, with the title of a kingdom, and all other honours annexed to the royal dignity, in the fame manner as he poffeffed the kingdom of Sicily; on condition, neverthelefs, that the reverfion of the faid kingdom of Sardinia fhall be referved to the crown of Spain, whenever it may happen that the King of Sicily fhall be without heirs male, and all the Houfe of Savoy fhall likewife be deftitute of heirs male. But in the fame manner altogether as the faid reverfion was fettled and ordained for the kingdom of Sicily by the treaties of Utrecht, and by the act of ceffion in purfuance thereof made by the King of Spain.

III. His Imperial Majefty fhall confirm to the King of Sicily all the ceffions made to him by the treaty figned at Turin the 8th of November, 1703, as well of that part of the dutchy of Montferrat, as of the provinces, cities, towns, caftles, lands, places, rights, and revenues of the ftate of Milan, which he now doth poffefs, in the manner wherein he actually doth poffefs them; and he will ftipulate for himfelf, his defcendants and fucceffors, that he never will difturb him, his heirs or fucceffors, in the poffeffion aforefaid: on condition, neverthelefs, that all other claims and pretenfions, which he may poffibly make in virtue of the faid treaty, fhall be and remain void.

IV. His

IV. His Imperial Majesty shall acknowledge the right of the King of Sicily, and his House, to succeed immediately to the kingdom of Spain and of the Indies, in case of the failure of King Philip V. and his posterity, in manner as is settled by the renunciations of the Catholic King, the Duke of Berry, and the Duke of Orleans, and by the treaties of Utrecht; and his Imperial Majesty shall promise, as well for himself as for his successors and descendants, that at no time he will directly or indirectly oppose, or any way act contrary to the same. It is declared, nevertheless, that no Prince of the House of Savoy, who shall succeed to the crown of Spain, may possess at the same time any province or dominion on the continent of Italy, and that in such case those provinces shall devolve to the collateral Princes of that House, who shall succeed therein one after another, according to the proximity of blood.

V. His Imperial Majesty and the King of Sicily shall give mutual guaranties for all the kingdoms and provinces which they actually possess in Italy, or which shall accrue to them by virtue of this present treaty.

VI. His Imperial Majesty and the King of Sicily, immediately after the exchange of the ratifications of these conventions, shall put in execution all and every the conditions therein contained, and that within the space of two months at the farthest: and the instruments of the ratifications of the said conventions shall be exchanged at London within two months from the day of signing, or sooner if possible. And immediately after the previous execution of the said conditions, their Ministers and Plenipotentiaries by them to be named shall, in the place of congress they shall agree upon, with all speed severally settle the other points of their particular peace, under the mediation of the three contracting Powers.

8

His

His above-named Imperial and Catholic Majesty, being extremely inclined to promote the peace proposed, and to avert the dreadful calamities of war, and out of his sincere desire to settle an universal pacification, hath accepted the afore-mentioned conventions, and all and singular the articles thereof, and hereby doth accept the same, and accordingly has entered into a particular treaty with the three Powers abovesaid, on the following conditions.

I. That there be and remain between his Sacred Imperial Catholic Majesty, his Sacred Royal Majesty of Great Britain, his Sacred Royal most Christian Majesty, and the High and Mighty Lords the States General of the United Netherlands, and their heirs and successors, a most strict alliance, in virtue whereof each of them are bound to preserve the dominions and subjects of the others, as likewise to maintain peace, to promote mutually the interests of the others as their own, and to prevent and repel all damages and injuries whatsoever.

II. The treaties made at Utrecht and Baden shall remain in their full strength and force, and shall be a part of this treaty, those articles excepted, from which it has been judged for the public good to depart; as likewise those articles of the Utrecht treaties excepted, which were abolished by the treaty of Baden. The treaty of alliance made at Westminster the 25th of May, 1716, between his Sacred Imperial and Catholic Majesty, and his Sacred Royal Majesty of Great Britain, as likewise the treaty made at the Hague the 4th of January, 1717, between the King of Great Britain and the most Christian King, and the States General of the United Provinces, shall nevertheless remain in full force in every particular.

III. His Sacred Britannic Majesty, as likewise his Sacred most Christian Majesty, and the Lords the States General of the United Netherlands, do covenant for themselves, their heirs and successors, that they never will, directly or indirectly, disturb his Sacred

cred

cred Imperial and Catholic Majefty, his heirs and fucceffors, in any of his kingdoms, dominions, and provinces, which he poffeffes by virtue of the treaties of
Utrecht and Baden, or which he fhall gain poffeffion
of by virtue of this prefent treaty. On the contrary,
they both will and ought to defend and guaranty the
provinces, kingdoms, and jurifdictions, which he now
poffeffes, or which fhall accrue to him in virtue of
this treaty, as well in Germany as in the Netherlands
and in Italy; and they promife that they will defend
the faid kingdoms and provinces of his Imperial and
Catholic Majefty, againft all and fingular who may
attempt to invade the fame in a hoftile manner; and
that they both will and ought, when the cafe happens, to furnifh him with fuch fuccours as he fhall
need, according to the conditions and repartition which
they have agreed upon as hereafter mentioned. In
like manner, their Royal Britannic and moft Chriftian Majefties, and the States General, exprefsly bind
themfelves, that they will not at any time give or grant
any protection or refuge, in any part of their dominions, to the fubjects of his Imperial and Catholic Majefty, who actually are, or hereafter fhall be by him
declared rebels, and in cafe any fuch fhall be found
in their kingdoms, provinces, or dominions, they fincerely promife that they will take effectual care to
expel them out of their territories, within eight days
after application made by his Imperial Majefty.

IV. On the other hand, his Sacred Imperial and
Catholic Majefty, his Sacred Royal Britannic Majefty, and the States General of the United Provinces, promife for themfelves, their heirs and fucceffors, that they never will, directly or indirectly, difturb his Sacred moft Chriftian Majefty in any of his
dominions to the crown of France now belonging. On
the contrary, they will and ought to guard and defend
the fame againft all and fingular who may attempt
to invade them in a hoftile manner, and in that cafe
they will and ought to furnifh fuch fuccours as his

moft

moft Chriftian Majefty fhall want, according as hereafter is agreed upon.

His Sacred Imperial and Catholic Majefty, his Sacred Royal Majefty of Great Britain, and the Lords the States General, do likewife promife and oblige themfelves, that they will and ought to maintain, guaranty, and defend the right of fucceffion in the kingdom of France, according to the tenor of the treaties made at Utrecht the 11th of April, 1713, obliging themfelves to ftand by the faid fucceffion, plainly according to the form of the renunciation made by the King of Spain the 5th of November, 1712, and by a folemn act accepted in the General Affembly of the States of Spain, the 9th day of the month and year aforefaid, which thereupon paffed into a law the 18th of March, 1713, and laftly was eftablifhed and fettled by the treaties of Utrecht: and this they fhall perform againft all perfons whatfoever who may prefume to difturb the order of the faid fucceffion, in contradiction to the previous acts, and treaties fubfequent thereupon; to which end they fhall furnifh the fuccours, according to the repartition agreed on below. Farther, when the matter may require it, they fhall defend the faid order of fucceffion with all their forces, by likewife declaring war againft him who may attempt to infringe or impugn the fame.

Moreover, his Imperial Royal Catholic Majefty, and his Royal Britannic Majefty, and the States General, do likewife promife, that they will not at any time give or grant any protection or refuge in their dominions to the fubjects of his Royal moft Chriftian Majefty, who actually are, or hereafter fhall be declared rebels; and in cafe any fuch fhall be found in their kingdoms, provinces, and dominions, they fhall command them to depart the fame within the fpace of eight days after application made by the faid King.

V. His Sacred Imperial and Royal Catholic Majefty, as alfo his Royal moft Chriftian Majefty, and the States General of the United Provinces, do bind

2   themfelves,

themselves, their heirs and successors, to maintain and guaranty the succession in the kingdom of Great Britain, as established by the laws of that kingdom, in the House of his Britannic Majesty now reigning, as likewise to defend all the dominions and provinces possessed by his Majesty. And they shall not give or grant any protection or refuge, in any part of their dominions, to the person, or his descendants, if he should have any, who, during the life of James the Second, took on him the title of Prince of Wales, and since the death of that King assumed the royal title of King of Great Britain; promising alike for themselves, their heirs and successors, that they will not give to the said person or his descendants, directly or indirectly, by sea or by land, any succour, counsel, or assistance whatsoever, either in money, arms, military stores, ships, soldiers, mariners, or any other manner whatsoever. The same they shall observe with regard to those who may be ordered or commissioned by the said person, or his descendants, to disturb the government of his Britannic Majesty, or the tranquillity of his kingdom, whether by open war or clandestine conspiracies, by raising seditions and rebellions, or by exercising piracy on his Britannic Majesty's subjects. In which last case his Imperial and Royal Catholic Majesty doth promise, that he will in no wise allow that there be any receptacle granted to such pirates in his ports in the Netherlands. The same do his Sacred most Christian Majesty, and the States General of the United Provinces, stipulate, with regard to the ports in their respective dominions: as, on the other hand, his Britannic Majesty doth promise, that he will refuse any refuge in the ports of his kingdoms to pirates infesting the subjects of his Sacred Imperial and Royal Catholic Majesty, of his Sacred Royal most Christian Majesty, or of the Lords the States General. Lastly, His Imperial and Royal Catholic Majesty, his Sacred Royal most Christian Majesty, and the Lords the States General, oblige themselves, that they never will

will give any refuge or protection, in any part of
their dominions, to such of his Britannic Majesty's
subjects as actually are, or hereafter shall be declared
rebels; and in case any such shall be found in any of
their kingdoms, provinces, and dominions, they shall
command them, within eight days after application
made by the said King, to depart out of their territories. And if it should happen that his Sacred Britannic Majesty should be invaded in any part in a
hostile manner, his Imperial and Royal Catholic Majesty, as likewise his Royal most Christian Majesty,
and the States General of the United Provinces, do
oblige themselves in that case to furnish the succours
hereafter specified. The same they are to do in favour
of his descendants, if ever it should happen that they
should be disturbed in the succession of the kingdom
of Great Britain.

VI. His Imperial and Royal Catholic Majesty, and
their Royal Britannic and most Christian Majesties,
do bind themselves, their heirs and successors, to protect and guaranty all the dominions, jurisdictions, and
provinces, which the Lords the States General of the
United Provinces actually possess, against all persons
whatsoever who may disturb or invade them, promising to furnish them in such case with the succours hereafter mentioned. His Imperial and Royal Catholic
Majesty, and their Royal Britannic and most Christian
Majesties, likewise oblige themselves, that they will
give no refuge or protection, in any of their kingdoms,
to the subjects of the States General, who are, or hereafter shall be declared rebels; and if any such shall
be found in any of their kingdoms, dominions, or
provinces, they will take care to send them out of their
dominions within the space of eight days after application made by the Republic.

VII. When it shall happen that any one of the four
contracting Powers shall be invaded by any other
Prince or State, or disturbed in the possession of their

Vol. I.   T   kingdoms

kingdoms or dominions, by the violent detention of their fubjects, fhips, goods, or merchandize, by fea or by land, then the three remaining Powers fhall, as foon as they are required thereto, ufe their good offices that the party fuffering may have fatisfaction for the damage and injury received, and that the aggreffor. may abftain from the profecution of his hoftility. But when thefe friendly offices for reconciliation, and procuring fatisfaction and reparation to the injured party; fhall have proved infufficient, in that cafe the high allies, within two months after application made, fhall furnifh the party invaded with the following fuccours, jointly or feparately; *viz.*

His Imperial and Royal Catholic Majefty, eight thoufand foot, and four thoufand horfe.

His Britannic Majefty, eight thoufand foot, and four thoufand horfe.

His moft Chriftian Majefty, eight thoufand foot, and four thoufand horfe.

And the Lords the States General, four thoufand foot, and two thoufand horfe.

But if the Prince or party injured, inftead of foldiers chufes rather fhips of war, or tranfports, or fubfidies in money, which is left to his difcretion, in that cafe, the fhips or money defired fhall be granted him in proportion to the charge of the foldiers to be furnifhed. And, that all ambiguity with regard to the calculation and charge of fuch fums may be taken away, it is agreed, that a thoufand foot by the month, fhall be reckoned at ten thoufand florins of Holland, and a thoufand horfe fhall be reckoned at thirty thoufand florins of Holland, by the month; the fame proportion being obferved with refpect to the fhips.

When the above-named fuccours fhall be found infufficient for the neceffity impending, the contracting Powers fhall, without delay, agree on contributing more ample fupplies. And farther, in cafe of exigency, they fhall affift their injured ally with all their forces, and declare war againft the aggreffor.

3 VIII. The

VIII. The Princes and States upon whom the contracting Powers fhall unanimoufly agree, may accede to this treaty; and the King of Portugal by name.

This treaty fhall be approved and ratified by their Imperial, Britannic, and moft Chriftian Majefties, and by the High and Mighty Lords the States General of the United Provinces, and the inftruments of ratification fhall be exchanged at London, and reciprocally delivered within the fpace of two months, or fooner, if poffible.

In witnefs whereof, we the underwritten (being furnifhed with full powers, which have been mutually communicated, and the copies whereof having been in due form by us collated and examined with the originals, are word for word inferted at the end of this inftrument) have fubfcribed this prefent treaty, and thereto put our feals. Done at London, the twenty fecond of July, O. S. fecond of Auguft, N. S. anno Domini one thoufand feven hundred and eighteen.

(L. S.) *Chrif. Penterridter ab Adelfhaufen.*

(L. S.) *Jo. Phil. Hoffman.*

(L. S.) *Dubois.*
(L. S.) *W. Cant.*
(L. S.) *Parker, C.*
(L. S.) *Sunderland, P.*
(L. S.) *Kingfton, C. P. S.*
(L. S.) *Kent.*
(L. S.) *Holles Newcaftle,*
(L. S.) *Bolton.*
(L. S.(*Roxburghe.*
(L. S.) *Barkeley.*
(L. S.) *J. Craggs.*

WE having feen and confidered the above-written treaty, have approved, ratified, and confirmed, as by thefe prefents, we do, for us, our heirs and fucceffors, approve, ratify, and confirm the fame in all and fingular its articles and claufes, engaging and promifing, upon our Royal word, fincerely and faithfully to perform

form all and fingular the contents of the faid treaty, and never to fuffer, as far as in us lies, any perfon to violate the fame, or in any manner to act contrary thereunto. In witnefs whereof, we have caufed our great feal of Great Britain to be affixed to thefe prefents, figned with our Royal hand. Given at our palace at Kenfington, the feventh day of Auguft, in the year of our Lord 1718, and of our reign the fifth.   GEORGE R.

GEORGE, by the grace of God, of Great Britain, France, and Ireland, King, Defender of the Faith, Duke of Brunfwick and Lunenburg, Arch-Treafurer of the Holy Roman Empire, and Prince Elector, &c. To all and fingular, to whom thefe prefents fhall come, greeting. Whereas, befides the treaty of pacification to be made between the Emperor of the Romans and the King of Spain, and between the faid Emperor and the King of Sicily, and the treaty made between us and our good brother the faid Emperor of the Romans, and our good brother the moft Chriftian King, and our good friends the High and Mighty Lords the States General of the United Netherlands, concluded by Plenipotentiaries fufficiently furnifhed on all fides with orders and authority, in our city of London, the twenty-fecond day of July laft paft, O. S. certain feparate and fecret articles, to the faid treaty belonging, were alfo concluded and figned by the faid Plenipotentiaries, in the fame place, and on the fame day, in the form and words following:

Separate and Secret Articles.

I. WHEREAS the moft Serene and moft Potent King of Great Britain, and the moft Serene and moft Potent the moft Chriftian King, as likewife the High and Mighty Lords the States General of the United Netherlands, by virtue of the treaty between them this day concluded and figned, have agreed on certain

tain conditions, whereby a peace may be made betwixt the moſt Serene and moſt Potent Emperor of the Romans, and the moſt Serene and moſt Potent King of Spain, as alſo between his Sacred Imperial Majeſty aforeſaid, and the King of Sicily (whom hereafter it is thought fit to call the King of Sardinia) which conditions they have communicated to the three Princes aforeſaid, as a baſis of the peace to be eſtabliſhed between them; his Sacred Imperial Majeſty, being moved by the moſt weighty reaſons which induced the King of Great Britain, the moſt Chriſtian King, and the States General aforeſaid, to take upon themſelves ſo great and ſo wholeſome a work, and, yielding to their circumſpect and urgent counſels and perſuaſions, declares that he doth accept the ſaid conditions or articles, none of them excepted, as fixed and immutable conditions, according to which he agrees to conclude a perpetual peace with the King of Spain and the King of Sardinia.

II. But becauſe the King of Spain and the King of Sardinia have not yet conſented to the ſaid conditions, his Imperial Majeſty, as likewiſe their Royal Britannic and moſt Chriſtian Majeſties, and the States General aforeſaid, have agreed to allow them, for conſenting thereto, the ſpace of three months, to be computed from the day of ſigning this preſent treaty, as judging this interval of time ſufficient for them duly to weigh the ſaid conditions, and finally determine and declare themſelves whether they are willing to accept them as fixed and immutable conditions of their pacification with his Imperial Majeſty, as from their piety and prudence it may be hoped they will do, and, following the example of his Imperial Majeſty, that they will be induced to moderate their paſſions, and, out of regard to humanity, that they will prefer the public tranquillity to their own private opinions; and at the ſame time not only ſpare the effuſion of their own people's blood, but avert the calamities of war from the other nations of Europe: to which end their Bri-

tannic

tannic and moft Chriftian Majefties, and the States General of the United Netherlands, will jointly and feparately contribute their moft effectual offices for inclining the faid Princes to fuch an acceptation. —

III. But if, contrary to all expectation of the parties above contracting, and the wifhes of all Europe, the King of Spain, and the King of Sardinia, after the term of three months elapfed, fhould decline to accept the faid conditions of pacification propofed betwixt them and his Imperial Majefty, fince it is not reafonable that the tranquillity of Europe fhould depend upon their refufal, or private defigns, their Britannic and moft Chriftian Majefties, and the States General, do promife that they will join their forces with thofe of his Imperial Majefty, in order to compel them to the acceptance and execution of the aforefaid conditions. To which end they will furnifh his Imperial Majefty, jointly and feparately, with the felffame fuccours with which they have agreed upon their reciprocal defence, by the feventh article of the treaty figned this day, unanimoufly confenting that the moft Chriftian King fhall, inftead of foldiers, contribute his quota in money. And if the fuccours fpecified in the faid feventh article fhall not be fufficient for compaffing the end propofed, then the four contracting parties fhall without delay agree of more ample fuccours to be furnifhed to his Imperial Majefty, and fhall continue the fame till his Imperial Majefty fhall have reduced the kingdom of Sicily, and till his kingdoms and provinces in Italy fhall enjoy full fecurity. It is farther agreed, and that in exprefs words, that if, by reafon of the fuccours which their Britannic and moft Chriftian Majefties, and the Lords the States General, fhall furnifh to his Imperial Majefty, by virtue and in execution of the prefent treaty, the Kings of Spain and Sardinia, or either of them, fhall declare or wage war againft any one of the faid contractors, either by attacking them in their dominions, or by violently detaining their fubjects or fhips, their goods and merchandizes,

chandizes, by fea or land, in that cafe the two other
of the contracting Powers fhall immediately declare
war againft the faid Kings of Spain and Sardinia, or
againft him of the two Kings who fhall have denounced or waged war againft any one of the faid
contracting Powers; nor fhall they lay down their
arms before the Emperor fhall be poffeffed of Sicily,
and made fecure with regard to his kingdoms and
provinces in Italy, and likewife juft fatisfaction fhall
be given to him of the three contracting Powers who
fhall have been invaded or fuffered damage by reafon
of the prefent treaty.

IV. When only one of the two Kings aforefaid,
who have not yet confented to the conditions of peace
to be made with his Imperial Majefty, fhall accept
them, he likewife fhall join himfelf with the four contracting Powers, to compel him that fhall refufe the
faid conditions, and fhall furnifh his quota of fuccours
according to the diftribution to be made thereupon.

V. If the Catholic King, out of regard to the public
good, and a perfuafion that an exchange of the kingdoms of Sicily and Sardinia is neceffary for the maintenance of the general peace, fhall agree thereto, and
embrace the conditions of peace to be made with the
Emperor as above, and on the other hand, if the King
of Sardinia fhall reject fuch an exchange, and perfift
in retaining Sicily; in that cafe the King of Spain fhall
reftore Sardinia to the Emperor, who (faving his fupreme dominion over it) fhail put the fame into the
cuftody of the moft Serene King of Great Britain,
and of the Lords the States General, for fo long time,
till Sicily being reduced, the King of Sardinia fhall
fign the above-mentioned conditions of a treaty with
the Emperor, and fhall agree to accept the kingdom
of Sardinia as an equivalent for the kingdom of
Sicily; which being done, he fhall be admitted into
the poffeffion thereof by the King of Great Britain
and the States General. But if his Imperial Majefty

fhould

fhould not be able to conquer Sicily, and reduce it under his power, in that cafe the King of Great Britain, and the States General, fhall reftore to him the kingdom of Sardinia; and in the mean time his Imperial Majefty fhall enjoy the revenues of the faid kingdom, which fhall exceed the charge of keeping it.

VI. But in cafe the King of Sardinia fhall confent to the faid exchange, and the King of Spain fhall refufe, in this cafe the Emperor, being aided by the fuccours of the reft of the contractors, fhall attack Sardinia; with which fuccours they on their part promife to furnifh him; as the Emperor promifes on his part, that he will not lay down his arms till he fhall have poffeffed himfelf of the whole kingdom of Sardinia, which immediately after fuch poffeffion he fhall give up to the King of Sardinia.

VII. But if both the Kings of Spain and Sardinia fhall oppofe the exchange of Sicily and Sardinia, the Emperor, together with the fuccours of the allies, fhall in the firft place attack Sicily, and having reduced it, he fhall turn his arms againft Sardinia, with fuch a number of forces, befides the fuccours of the allies, as he fhall judge neceffary for both expeditions: and, having likewife reduced Sardinia, his Imperial Majefty fhall commit the cuftody thereof to the King of Great Britain, and to the Lords the States General, till the King of Sardinia fhall have figned the conditions of peace to be made with the Emperor, and fhall confent to accept the kingdom of Sardinia as an equivalent for the kingdom of Sicily, which then is to be delivered up to him by his Britannic Majefty and the States General; and in the mean time his Imperial Majefty fhall enjoy the revenues of that kingdom, which fhall exceed the charge of keeping it.

VIII. In cafe the Catholic King and the King of Sardinia, or either of them, fhall refufe to accept and execute the abovefaid conditions of peace to them proposed,

propofed, and for that reafon the four contracting
Powers fhould be compelled to proceed againft them,
or either of them, by open force; it is exprefsly covenanted, that the Emperor (what progrefs foever his
arms may make againft the faid two Kings, or either
of them) fhall be content, and ought to acquiefce in
the advantages by mutual confent allotted to him in
the faid conditions, power neverthelefs being referved
to his Imperial Majefty of recovering the rights which
he pretends to have over that part of the dutchy of
Milan, which the King of Sardinia now poffeffes,
either by war, or by a treaty of peace fubfequent upon
fuch war; power being likewife referved to the other
three allies, in cafe fuch a war fhould be undertaken
againft the Kings of Spain and Sardinia, to agree with
his Imperial Majefty in appointing fome other Prince,
in whofe favour his Imperial Majefty may difpofe of
that part of the dutchy of Montferrat, now poffeffed
by the King of Sardinia, in exclufion of the faid King;
and to what other Prince or Princes he may, with the
confent of the empire, grant the letters of expectative,
containing the eventual inveftiture of the ftates now
poffeffed by the Grand Duke of Tufcany, and by the
Duke of Parma and Placentia, in exclufion of the
fons of the prefent Queen of Spain. This declaration being added, that in no time or cafe whatfoever,
either his Imperial Majefty, or any Prince of the
Houfe of Auftria, who fhall poffefs the kingdoms,
dominions, and provinces of Italy, may affert or gain
to himfelf the faid dutchies of Tufcany and Parma.

IX. But if his Imperial Majefty, after his efforts
by a fufficient number of forces, and the fuccours and
other means of the allies, and by ufing all convenient
diligence, fhould not be able by arms to fubdue, or to
eftablifh himfelf in the poffeffion of Sicily, the contracting Powers do agree and declare, that his Imperial
Majefty is, and fhall be in that cafe, altogether free
and difcharged from every obligation entered into by
this treaty, of agreeing to make a peace with the

Kings

Kings of Spain and Sardinia, on the conditions above-mentioned. All other the articles of this treaty nevertheless to remain good, which mutually regard his Imperial Majefty, their Britannic and most Chriftian Majefties, and the Lords the States General of the United Netherlands.

X. However, as the fecurity and tranquillity of Europe is the end and fcope of the renunciations to be made by his Imperial Majefty, and by his Catholic Majefty, for themfelves, their defcendants, and fucceffors, of all pretenfions to the kingdom of Spain, and the Indies, on the one part; and on the kingdoms, dominions, and provinces of Italy, and the Auftrian Netherlands, on the other part; the faid renunciations fhall be made, on the one and the other part, in manner and form as in the fecond and fourth articles of the conditions of a peace to be made between his Imperial Majefty, and his Royal Catholic Majefty, has been agreed. And though the Catholic King fhould refufe to accept the aforefaid conditions, the Emperor neverthelefs fhall caufe the inftruments of his renunciation to be difpatched, the publication whereof fhall however be deferred till the day of figning the peace with the Catholic King. And if the Catholic King fhould conftantly perfift in rejecting the faid peace, his Imperial Majefty neverthelefs, at the time when the ratifications of this treaty fhall be exchanged, fhall deliver to the King of Great Britain a folemn act of the faid renunciations, which his Britannic Majefty, purfuant to the common agreement of the contracting Powers, doth promife fhall not be exhibited to the moft Chriftian King before his Imperial Majefty fhall come into the poffeffion of Sicily. But that being obtained, then the exhibition, as well as publication of the faid act of his Imperial Majefty's renunciations, fhall be performed upon the firft demand of the moft Chriftian King. And thofe renunciations fhall take place, whether the Catholic King fhall fign the peace with the Emperor or no; by reafon that, in this laft

cafe,

cafe, the guaranty of the contracting parties fhall be to the Emperor in lieu of that fecurity which otherwife the renunciations of the Catholic King would have given to his Imperial Majefty for Sicily, the other States of Italy, and the provinces of the Netherlands.

XI. His Imperial Majefty doth promife that he will not attempt or enterprife any thing againft the Catholic King, or the King of Sardinia, or in general, againft the neutrality of Italy, in that fpace of three months allowed them for accepting the conditions of their peace with the Emperor. But if, within the faid fpace of three months, the Catholic King, inftead of accepting the faid conditions, fhall rather perfift in the profecuting of his hoftilities againft his Imperial Majefty; or if the King of Sardinia fhould with arms attack the provinces which the Emperor poffeffes in Italy; in that cafe their Britannic and moft Chriftian Majefties, and the Lords the States General, oblige themfelves inflantly to furnifh his Imperial Majefty, for his defence, with the fuccours which, in virtue of the treaty this day figned, they have mutually agreed to lend one another for their reciprocal defence; and that jointly or feparately, and without waiting the expiration of the two months otherwife prefixed in the faid treaty for the employing of friendly offices. And if the fuccours fpecified by the faid treaty fhould not be fufficient for the end propofed, the four contracting parties fhall immediately agree amongft themfelves to fend more powerful afliftance to his Imperial Majefty.

XII. The eleven foregoing articles are to be kept fecret by his Imperial Majefty, their Britannic and moft Chriftian Majefties, and the States General, for the fpace of three months, from the day of the figning, unlefs it fhall be unanimoufly agreed by them to fhorten or prolong the faid term: and though the faid eleven articles be feparate from the treaty of alliance this day figned by the four contracting parties aforefaid, they fhall neverthelefs have the fame power and
force

force as if they had been word for word inferted therein, fince they are deemed to be an effential part thereof.

The ratifications thereof fhall moreover be exchanged at the fame time as the other articles of the faid treaty.

In witnefs whereof, we the under-written, by virtue of the full powers this day mutually exhibited, have fubfcribed thefe feparate articles, and thereto have affixed our feals. Done at London, the $\frac{\text{22d of July, O. S.}}{\text{2d of Aug. N. S.}}$ anno Domini 1718.

(L.S.) *Chrif. Penterridter ab Adelfhaufen.*

(L.S.) *Jo. Phil. Hoffman.*

(L. S.) *Dubois.*
(L. S.) *W. Cant.*
(L. S.) *Parker, C.*
(L. S.) *Sunderland, P.*
(L. S.) *Kingfton, C. P. S.*
(L. S.) *Kent.*
(L. S.) *Holles Newcaftle.*
(L. S.) *Bolton.*
(L. S.) *Roxburghe.*
(L. S.) *Berkeley.*
(L. S.) *J. Craggs.*

WE having feen and confidered the feparate and fecret articles above-written, have approved, ratified, and confirmed, as by thefe prefents we do, for us, our heirs and fucceffors, approve, ratify, and confirm the fame, in all and fingular their claufes, engaging and promifing, upon our Royal word, fincerely and faithfully to perform and obferve all and fingular the contents of the faid feparate and fecret articles, and never to fuffer, as far as in us lies, any perfon to violate them, or in any manner to act contrary thereunto. In witnefs and confirmation whereof we have caufed our great feal of Great Britain to be affixed to thefe prefents, figned with our Royal hand. Given at our palace at Kenfington, the feventh day of Auguft, in the year of our Lord feventeen hundred and eighteen, and of our reign the fifth.   G E O R G E *R.*

G E O R G E,

GEORGE, by the grace of God, of Great Britain, France, and Ireland, King, Defender of the Faith, Duke of Brunfwick and Lunenburg, Arch-Treafurer of the Holy Roman Empire, and Prince Elector, &c. To all and fingular, to whom thefe prefents fhall come, greeting. Whereas, befides the treaty of pacification to be made between the Emperor of the Romans and the King of Spain, and between the faid Emperor and the King of Sicily, and the treaty made between us and our good brother the faid Emperor of the Romans, and our good brother the moft Chriftian King, and our good friends the High and Mighty Lords the States General of the United Netherlands, concluded by Plenipotentiaries fufficiently furnifhed on all fides with orders and authority, in our city of London, the twenty-fecond day of July laft paft, O. S. certain feparate articles, being four in number, to the faid treaty belonging, were alfo concluded and figned feverally by the faid Plenipotentiaries, in the fame place, and on the fame day, in the form and words following.

Separate Article.

WHEREAS the treaty, this day made and figned between his Imperial Majefty, his Britannic Majefty, and his moft Chriftian Majefty (containing as well fuch conditions as have been thought moft equitable and proper for eftablifhing a peace betwixt the Emperor and the Catholic King, and betwixt the faid Emperor and the King of Sicily, as the conditions of an alliance made for preferving the public peace between the faid contracting Powers) hath been communicated to the High and Mighty Lords the States General of the United Netherlands: and whereas the feparate and fecret articles likewife figned this day, and containing the meafures which it has been thought fit to take for putting the abovefaid treaty in execution, are likewife fhortly to be propofed to the States General aforefaid: the inclination which that Republic has fhewn for reftoring and eftablifhing the public tranquillity,

quillity, leaves no room of doubt but they will most readily accede thereto. The States General aforesaid are therefore by name inserted as contracting parties in the said treaty, in most certain hope that they will enter therein, as soon as the usual forms of their government will allow.

But if, contrary to the hopes and wishes of the contracting parties (which nevertheless is not in the least to be suspected) the said Lords the States General shall not take their resolution to accede to the said treaty, it is expresly agreed and covenanted between the said contracting parties, that the treaty above-mentioned, and this day signed, shall nevertheless have its effect among them, and shall in all its clauses and articles be put in execution in the same manner as therein is set forth, and the ratifications thereof shall be exhibited at the times above specified.

This separate article shall have the same force as if it had been word for word inserted in the treaty this day concluded and signed, and shall be ratified in the same manner, and the instruments of ratification shall be delivered within the same time, with the treaty itself.

In witness whereof we the under-written, by virtue of the full powers this day mutually exhibited, have signed this separate article, and thereto have affixed our seals. Done at London, the $\frac{21d\ of\ July,\ O.\ S.}{30\ of\ Aug.\ N.\ S.}$ anno Domini 1718.

(L. S.) *Chrif. Penterridter ab Adelfhaufen.*	(L. S.) *Dubois.*
	(L. S.) *W. Cant.*
	(L. S.) *Parker, C.*
(L. S.) *Jo. Phil. Hoffman.*	(L. S.) *Sunderland, P.*
	(L. S.) *Kingfton, C. P. S.*
	(L. S.) *Kent.*
	(L. S.) *Holles Newcaftle.*
	(L. S.) *Bolton.*
	(L. S.) *Roxburghe.*
	(L. S.) *Barkeley.*
	(L. S.) *J. Craggs.*

Separate

Separate Article.

BUT if the Lords the States General of the United Netherlands fhould happen to think it too hard for them to contribute their fhare of pay to the Swifs Cantons, for maintaining the garrifons of Leghorn, Porto-Ferraio, Parma, and Placentia, according to the tenor of the treaty of alliance this day concluded, it is exprefsly provided by this feparate article, and agreed between the four contracting Powers, that in fuch cafe the Catholic King may take upon him the faid fhare of the Lords the States General.

This feparate article fhall have the fame force as if it had been word for word inferted in the treaty this day concluded and figned, and fhall be ratified in the fame manner, and the inftruments of ratification fhall be delivered within the fame time, with the treaty itfelf.

In witnefs whereof we the under-written, by virtue of the full powers this day mutually exhibited, have figned this feparate article, and thereto have affixed our feals. Done at London, the $\frac{\text{22d of July, O. S.}}{\text{2d of Aug. N. S.}}$ anno Domini one thoufand feven hundred and eighteen.

(L. S.) *Chrif. Penterridter ab Adelfhaufen.*

(L. S.) *Jo. Phil. Hoffman.*

(L. S.) *Dubois.*
(L. S.) *W. Cant.*
(L. S.) *Parker, C.*
(L. S.) *Svnderland, P.*
(L. S.) *Kingfton, C. P. S.*
(L. S.) *Kent.*
(L. S.) *Holles Newcaflle.*
(L. S.) *Bolton.*
(L. S.) *Roxburghe.*
(L. S.) *Barkeley.*
(L. S.) *J. Craggs.*

Separate Article.

WHEREAS in the treaty of alliance this day to be figned with his Imperial and Catholic Majefty, as
likewife

likewife in the conditions of peace inferted therein, their Sacred Royal Britannic and moft Chriftian Majefties, and the Lords the States General of the United Netherlands, do ftyle the prefent poffeffor of Spain and the Indies Catholic King, and the Duke of Savoy King of Sicily, or alfo King of Sardinia: and whereas his Sacred Imperial and Catholic Majefty cannot acknowledge thefe two Princes as Kings, before they fhall have acceded to this treaty: his Sacred Imperial and Catholic Majefty, by this feparate article, which was figned before the treaty of alliance, doth therefore declare and proteft, that, by the titles there either given or omitted, he doth not mean in the leaft to prejudice himfelf, or to grant or allow the titles of King to the faid two Princes, only in that cafe when they fhall have acceded to the treaty this day to be figned, and fhall have agreed to the conditions of peace fpecified therein.

This feparate article fhall have the fame force as if it had been word for word inferted in the treaty this day concluded and figned, and fhall be ratified in the fame manner, and the inftruments of ratification fhall be delivered within the fame time, with the treaty itfelf.

In witnefs whereof, we the under-written, by virtue of the full powers this day mutually exhibited, have figned this feparate article, and thereto have affixed our feals. Done at London, the $\frac{\text{22d of July, O.S.}}{\text{2d of Aug. N.S.}}$ anno Domini 1718.

(L. S.) *Chrif. Penterridter ab Adelfhaufen.*

(L. S.) *Jo. Phil. Hoffman.*

(L. S.) *Dubois.*
(L. S.) *W. Cant.*
(L. S.) *Parker, C.*
(L. S.) *Sunderland, P.*
(L. S.) *Kingfton, C. P. S.*
(L. S.) *Kent.*
(L. S.) *Holles Newcaftle.*
(L. S.) *Bolton.*
(L. S.) *Roxburghe.*
(L. S.) *Barkeley.*
(L. S.) *J. Craggs.*

Separate

Separate Article.

WHEREAS some of the titles which his Sacred Imperial Majesty makes use of, either in his full powers, or in the treaty of alliance this day to be signed with him, cannot be acknowledged by his Sacred Royal most Christian Majesty; he doth declare and protest by this separate article, which was signed before the treaty of alliance, that by the said titles given in this treaty, he doth not mean to prejudice either himself or any other, or that he in the least gives any right thereby to his Imperial Majesty.

This separate article shall have the same force as if it had been word for word inserted in the treaty this day concluded and signed, and shall be ratified in the same manner, and the instruments of ratification shall be delivered within the same time, with the treaty itself.

In witness whereof we the under-written, by virtue of the full powers this day mutually exhibited, have signed this separate article, and thereto have affixed our seals. Done at London, the $\frac{\text{22d of July, O. S.}}{\text{2d of Aug. N. S.}}$, anno Domini one thousand seven hundred and eighteen.

(L. S.) *Chrif. Penterridter*   (L. S.) *Dubois.*
      ab Adelfhaufen.   (L. S.) *W. Cant.*
                         (L. S.) *Parker, C.*
(L. S.) *Jo. Phil. Hoffman.*   (L. S.) *Sunderland, P.*
                         (L. S.) *Kingfton, C. P. S.*
                         (L. S.) *Kent.*
                         (L. S.) *Holles Newtaftle.*
                         (L. S.) *Bolton.*
                         (L. S.) *Roxburghe.*
                         (L. S.) *Barkeley.*
                         (L. S.) *J. Craggs.*

WE having seen and considered the four separate articles above-written, have approved, ratified, and confirmed, as by these presents we do, for us, our heirs

and succeffors, approve, ratify, and confirm the fame,
in all and fingular their claufes, engaging and promifing,
upon our Royal word, fincerely and faithfully to perform and obferve all and fingular the contents of the
four feparate articles aforefaid, and never to fuffer, as
far as in us lies, any perfon to violate them, or in
any manner to act contrary thereunto. In witnefs and
confirmation whereof, we have caufed our great feal of
Great Britain to be affixed to thefe prefents, figned
with our Royal hand. Given at our palace at Kenfington, the feventh day of Auguft, in the year of our
Lord feventeen hundred and eighteen, and of our
reign the fifth.   GEORGE R.

The Act of Admiffion and Acceffion of the King of
Sardinia, &c.

WHEREAS a certain treaty, and feparate and
fecret articles, as likewife four other feparate articles
relating thereto, and all of them of the fame force with
the principal treaty, have been in due form concluded
and figned by the minifters plenipotentiaries of his Imperial and Catholic Majefty, of his Britannic Majefty,
and of his moft Chriftian Majefty, at London, the
22d day of July / 2d day of Aug. laft paft, between the contracting parties
above-mentioned, the tenor of all which, word for
word, here followeth.

Here were inferted,
The treaty.
Separate and fecret articles.
The four feparate articles.

And whereas farther the then King of Sicily, whom
it is now agreed to call by the name of King of Sardinia, according to the intention of the treaty and articles above inferted, has been invited to accede fully
and amply to all and fingular of them, and to join
himfelf in due form to the contracting parties, as if he
himfelf from the beginning had been one of the contractors: and whereas the faid King of Sardinia, having maturely weighed the conditions particularly ex-
pteffed

'preffed, in the treaty and articles above inferted, has not only declared himfelf willing to accept the fame, and to approve them by his acceffion, but has likewife granted fufficient full powers to his minifters appointed to perfect the faid work. That therefore an affair fo beneficial may have the defired fuccefs, we the under-written minifters plenipotentiaries of his Imperial and Catholic Majefty, of his Britannic Majefty, and of his moft Chriftian Majefty, in the name and by the authority of their faid Majefties, have admitted, joined, and affociated, and by thefe prefents do admit, join, and affociate, the aforefaid King of Sardinia into a full and total partnerfhip of the treaty above inferted, and of all and fingular the articles thereunto belonging; promifing by the fame authority, that their aforefaid Majefties, jointly and feparately, will entirely and exactly perform and fulfil to the faid King of Sardinia, all and fingular the conditions, ceffions, contracts, guaranties, and fecurities, contained and fet forth in the treaty and articles above-mentioned; it being farther provided, that all and fingular the things agreed upon by the fecret articles againft the faid King of Sardinia, fhall by this his prefent acceffion wholly ceafe, and be abolifhed. On the other hand alfo, we the under-written minifters plenipotentiaries of the King of Sardinia, by virtue of the full power in due form exhibited and allowed, a copy whereof is added at the end of this inftrument, do hereby teftify and promife in the name of the faid King, that our King and mafter aforefaid doth accede fully and amply to the treaty, and to all and fingular the articles therein above inferted: that by this folemn acceffion he doth join himfelf to the contracting parties abovefaid, as if he himfelf from the beginning had been a party contracting: and that, by virtue of this act, his faid Majefty the King of Sardinia doth mutually oblige and bind himfelf, both for himfelf, his heirs and fucceffors, to his Imperial and Catholic Majefty, to his Britannic Majefty, and to his moft Chriftian Majefty, and to

their

their heirs and fucceffors, jointly and feparately, that he will obferve, perform, and fulfil all and fingular the conditions, ceffions, contracts, guaranties, and fecurities, in the above-written treaties and articles expreffed and fet forth, towards all of them jointly, and each of them feparately, with the fame faith and confcience as if he had been a contracting party from the beginning, and had made, concluded, and figned, jointly or feparately, the fame conditions, ceffions, contracts, guaranties, and fecurities, with his Imperial and Catholic Majefty, his Britannic Majefty, and his moft Chriftian Majefty.

This inftrument of the admiffion and acceffion of the faid King of Sardinia fhall be ratified by all the contracting parties, and the ratifications, made out in due form, fhall be exchanged and mutually delivered at London, within the fpace of two months, or fooner, if poffible, to be reckoned from the day of the figning.

In witnefs whereof, we the plenipotentiaries of the parties contracting, being on every part furnifhed with fufficient powers, have figned thefe prefents with our hands, and thereto have put our feals; namely, the plenipotentiaries of his Imperial and Catholic Majefty, of his Britannic Majefty, of his Majefty the King of Sardinia, at London, the $\frac{23}{8}$ day of $\frac{October,}{November,}$ and the plenipotentiary of his moft Chriftian Majefty at Paris, the day of November, in the year of our Lord 1718.

(L. S.) *C. Provana.*
(L. S.) *C. de la Perroufe.*

(L. S.) *Chrif. Penterridter ab Adelfhaufen.*

(L. S.) *Jo. Phil. Hoffman.*

(L. S.) *Parker, C.*
(L. S.) *Sunderland, P.*
(L. S.) *Kent.*
(L. S.) *Holles Newcaftle.*
(L. S.) *Bolton.*
(L. S.) *Roxburghe.*
(L. S.) *Stanhope.*
(L. S.) *J. Craggs.*

His Imperial Majesty's Full Powers.

WE Charles the Sixth, by the Divine clemency elected Emperor of the Romans, always August, King of Germany, Spain, both Sicilies, Jerusalem, the Indies, Hungary, Bohemia, Dalmatia, Croatia, and Sclavonia, Archduke of Austria, Duke of Burgundy, Brabant, Styria, Carinthia, Carniola, and Wirtemberg, Count of Hapsburgh, Flanders, Tyrol, and Goritia, &c. &c. do make known and signify by these presents to whom it concerns. Whereas we have often been invited by the most friendly exhortations of the most Serene and most Potent Prince George, King of Great Britain, France, and Ireland, Elector of the holy Roman Empire, Duke of Brunswic, to enter with him into those measures whereby peace and quiet among all the Christian Princes throughout Europe might subsist, or be yet more certainly established against such accidents as seem to afford new occasions for wars hereafter, and even now to give them: into which measures we have been informed that the most Serene and most Potent Prince Lewis XV. the King of France, together with the States General of the United Netherlands, are likewise inclined to enter. Hence it is, that from our sincere disposition to the counsels of peace and quiet, we have thought fit to send the Honourable our Imperial and Aulic Counsellor, Assessor of the Belgic Austrian Council, Christopher Penterridter, of Adelshausen, ours and the holy Roman Empire's trusty and beloved, with full power to treat with the Ministers of the aforesaid Princes and with their confederates, of all things which may tend to bring about so beneficial a design, giving him full and entire power, together with our trusty and beloved the Honourable Philip Hoffman, our Resident at London, to whom for this purpose we give equal power, either together, or one of them being hindered, to treat and fully to conclude that affair with the said Ministers: promising, on our Imperial and Royal word, not only to ratify all and singular the things which they or either

U 3 of

of them fhall fo tranfaƈt, treat, and conclude in our
name, as if they had been done by ourfelves, but that
we will alfo deliver our inftrument of ratification within
the time agreed. In witnefs whereof, we have figned
thefe prefents with our own hand, and have caufed
them to be fealed with our Imperial Royal feal. Given
in our city of Vienna, the 27th of September, in the
year 1717, the fixth of our Roman, the fifteenth of
our Spanifh, and the feventh of our Hungarian and
Bohemian reign.   CHARLES.

(L. S.) *Philip Lud, C. of Sinzendorff.*

By the exprefs command of his Sacred Imperial
Catholic Royal Majefty.

John George Buol.

His Britannic *Majefty's Full Powers.*

GEORGE R.

GEORGE, by the grace of God, of Great Britain, France, and Ireland, King, Defender of the Faith,
Duke of Brunfwic and Lunenburg, Arch-Treafurer
of the Holy Roman Empire, and Prince Eleƈtor, &c.
to all and fingular to whom thefe prefent letters fhall
come, greeting. Whereas, after the conclufion of the
treaties of Utrecht and Baden, we perceived fo many
feeds of war to remain, that the calamities of Europe
feemed rather a little quieted and delayed, than wholly
extinguifhed; we inftantly applied all our care and
thoughts entirely to root out and cut off all occafions
of having recourfe to arms, by fettling on all fides
folid and durable conditions of peace. And whereas
the war which has arifen between the Emperor of the
Romans and the King of Spain rages more and more,
and begins to fpread more far and wide, we have thereupon redoubled our endeavours, without delay to reftore the public tranquillity, difturbed by thefe commotions. And whereas we underftand that the heads of
a pacification, which we, together with the moft Chrif-

tian

tian King, and the Lords the States General of the United Provinces, have thought may be juftly and equitably propofed to the parties, either now actually, or liable fhortly to be engaged in the war, have been agreeably received by the faid Emperor of the Romans, out of his zeal for the public good. And whereas we hope farther, that the reft of the Princes concerned, having duly weighed thefe conditions, will chearfully embrace the fame; we have thought fit to nominate perfons altogether qualified for that charge, to bring fo great and beneficial a work to its conclufion. Know ye, therefore, that we repofing great truft in the fidelity, prudence, integrity, and diligence of the moft Reverend Father in Chrift, our right trufty and right entirely beloved counfellor William Archbifhop of Canterbury, Primate and Metropolitan of all England; our right trufty and well-beloved counfellor Thomas Lord Parker, Baron of Macclesfield, our High Chancellor of Great Britain; our right trufty and right well-beloved coufin and counfellor Charles Earl of Sunderland, Prefident of our council; our right trufty and right entirely beloved coufins and counfellors, Evelyn Duke of Kingfton, Keeper of our Privy Seal; Henry Duke of Kent, Steward of our houfhold; Thomas Duke of Newcaftle, Chamberlain of our faid Houfhold; Charles Duke of Bolton, Lieutenant and Governor General of our kingdom of Ireland; John Duke of Marlborough, Captain General of our forces; and John Duke of Roxburghe, one of our principal Secretaries of State; our right trufty and right well-beloved coufins and counfellors James Earl of Berkeley, firft Commiffioner of our Admiralty; William Earl Cowper, Baron of Wingham; and James Earl Stanhope, one of our principal Secretaries of State; and our right trufty and well-beloved counfellor James Craggs, Efq; another of our principal Secretaries of State; have nominated, made, and conftituted, as by thefe prefents we do nominate, make,

and

and conftitute them our true, certain, and undoubted
Commiffioners, Procurators, and Plenipotentiaries,
giving and granting to them all, or any three or more
of them, all and all manner of leave, power, and
authority, and our general as well as fpecial command
(provided our general command do not derogate from
the fpecial, nor the contrary) to meet, treat, confer,
and conclude for us, and in our name, with the minifter or minifters, as well on the part of our good
brother the Emperor of the Romans, as on the part
of our good brother the moft Chriftian King, and alfo
on the part of the Lords the States General of the
United Provinces of the Netherlands, having fufficient
power thereto on each part, of and upon fuch conditions of peace, as may be moft conducive to quell the
commotions of war, and to reftore and fettle the common tranquillity of Europe, as alfo upon articles whether fecret or feparate, and laftly, upon all things
which fhall feem moft proper for promoting and perfecting the faid work: and in our name to fign and
mutually to deliver and receive what fhall be fo concluded and agreed, and to do and perform all other
things neceffary to be done, in as ample manner and
form as we ourfelves, were we prefent, would do and
perform; engaging and promifing, on our Royal word,
that whatever fhall be concluded by our faid Commiffioners, Procurators, and Plenipotentiaries, or any
three or more of them, we will ratify, approve, and
accept it all in the beft manner; and that we will never
fuffer any perfon to violate the fame in whole or in
part, or to act contrary thereto.   In witnefs and confirmation of all which, we have caufed our great feal
of Great Britain to be affixed to thefe prefents, figned
with our Royal hand.   Given at our palace at Kenfington, the 15th day of the month of July, in the year
of our Lord one thoufand feven hundred and eighteen,
and of our reign the fourth.

The

The most Christian King's Full Powers.

LEWIS, by the grace of God, King of France and Navarre, to all who shall see these present letters, greeting. Being willing to contribute, as much as in us lies, to maintain the public tranquillity restored by the treaties of Utrecht and Baden, and the establishment of the peace so necessary to all Europe: being besides desirous to answer the overtures which have been made to us on the part of our most dear and most beloved brother the King of Great Britain, with a design to prevent the consequences of the disturbance lately raised on occasion of the differences which subsist between our most dear and most beloved brother the Emperor of the Romans, and our most dear and most beloved brother and uncle the King of Spain: we having entire confidence in the capacity, experience, zeal, and fidelity for our service, of our beloved and faithful Abbot Dubois, counsellor in ordinary of our council of state, and in the council for foreign affairs, secretary of our cabinet. For these causes, and other good considerations us thereunto moving, by the advice of our most dear and most beloved uncle the Duke of Orleans, Regent, we have commissioned, ordered, and deputed, and by these presents, signed with our hand, do commission, order, and depute the said Abbot Dubois, and have given, and do give him full power, commission, and special order, in the quality of our Plenipotentiary, in our name, to agree with one or more ministers on the part of our said brother the Emperor of the Romans, on that of our said brother and uncle the King of Spain, on that of our said brother the King of Great Britain, and on that of their High Mightinesses our most dear and great friends the States General of the United Provinces of the Netherlands, alike authorized, by powers in due form, to settle, conclude, and sign, with the said ministers, together or separately, such treaties, articles, and conventions, as the said Abbot Dubois shall think good; ordering that he may act on this occasion with the same authority as

we

we fhould and might do if we were prefent thereat in
perfon, even though there fhould fomething arife requiring a more fpecial order than is contained in thefe
faid prefents. Promifing, on the faith and word of a
King, to approve, confirm, and keep for ever, to perform and execute punctually, all that the faid Abbot
Dubois fhall ftipulate, promife, and fign by virtue of
this prefent power, without ever infringing or fuffering
the fame to be infringed, for any caufe, or under any
pretext whatfoever: as alfo to difpatch our letters of
ratification thereof in due form, to be exchanged within
the time that fhall be agreed. For fuch is our pleafure.
In witnefs whereof, we have caufed our feal to be put
to thefe prefents. Given at Paris, May the 25th, in
the year of grace one thoufand feven hundred and eighteen, and of our reign the third.

LEWIS.

By the King,
The Duke of Orleans, Regent, prefent.

Phelypeaux.

The Full Power of his Majefty the King of Sardinia.

VICTOR Amedeo, by the grace of God, King
of Sicily, Jerufalem, and Cyprus, &c. Duke of
Savoy, Montferrat, &c. Prince of Piemont, &c. to all
thofe who fhall fee thefe prefents, greeting. The fincere
intention which we have always had to concur, as
much as in us lies, to the maintenance of the public
tranquillity, and to the fettlement of peace in Europe,
and to anfwer the defire of the three Powers on that
fubject, who have concluded the treaty of the quadruple alliance at London the fecond of Auguft laft paft,
N. S. and who have invited us to accede thereto, and
to accept the conditions of treaty therein contained
between his Imperial Majefty and us, determined us
thereto as foon as we were in a condition to do it. For
this purpofe, we trufting entirely in the capacity, experience, zeal, and fidelity for our fervice, of our dear, well-
beloved, and trufty the Count Provana, Knight, Great

Crofs,

Crofs, and Grand Confervator of the Military Order of St. Maurice and Lazarus, our Gentleman of the Chamber, and firft Secretary at War; and of the Count de la Peroufe, Counfellor of State, Knight of Honour to the Senate of Savoy, and our Envoy extraordinary to his Britannic Majefty; have chofen, nominated, and deputed, and by thefe prefents do chufe, nominate, and depute them to be our Plenipotentiaries; and have given, and do give them full power, commiffion, and fpecial order, in our name, and in the faid quality of our Plenipotentiaries, both of them jointly, or one of them alone, in cafe of ficknefs or other hinderance of the other, to accede to the abovefaid treaty of quadruple alliance of the faid fecond day of Auguft, to which we do accede from this prefent time; and to promife, as we do promife, to obferve the fame, and the conventions of treaty therein contained between his Imperial Majefty and us; and to that end to fign the act which fhall be made thereupon with the minifters, or the minifter, of the faid three Powers, jointly or feparately, as it fhall be agreed: as alfo to make, conclude, and fign the articles, treaties, and conventions, which they fhall think good. Ordering that they may act, on the occafions aforefaid, with the fame authority with which we fhould and might act if we were prefent in perfon, even though there fhould fomething arife requiring a more fpecial order than is contained in thefe prefents; promifing, on the faith and word of a King, to obferve, and caufe inviolably to be obferved, all which fhall be done, agreed, regulated, and figned, by the faid Counts Provana and de la Peroufe, our Plenipotentiaries, or by one of them, in cafe of ficknefs or hinderance of the other, without infringing, or fuffering the fame to be infringed, directly or indirectly, for any caufe, or under any pretext whatfoever: as alfo to caufe our letters of ratification to be difpatched in due form, to be exchanged within the time that fhall be agreed. In witnefs whereof, we have figned thefe prefents, caufed them to be counterfigned by the Marquis del Borgo,
Secretary

Secretary of our order, our Minister and principal
Secretary of State for foreign affairs, and have caused
our privy seal to be put thereunto. Given at our
castle of Rivoles, the 17th of October, in the year
of grace 1718, and of our reign the fifth.

V. AMEDEO.

(L. S.)   *Del Borgo.*

*His Imperial Majesty's Ratification of the Treaty for
settling the public Peace.*

WE Charles the Sixth, by the Divine clemency
elected Emperor of the Romans, always August, King
of Germany, Spain, Hungary, Bohemia, Dalmatia,
Croatia, and Sclavonia, Archduke of Austria, Duke
of Burgundy, Brabant, Milan, Mantua, Styria, Carinthia, Carniola, Limburg, Luxemburg, Gelderland,
the Upper and Lower Silesia, and Wurtemberg, Prince
of Suabia, Marquis of the Holy Roman Empire, of
Burgaw, Moravia, the Upper and Lower Lusatia,
Count of Habsburg, Flanders, Tirol, Ferret, Kyburg,
Goritia, and Namur, Landgrave of Alsatia, Lord of
the Marck of Sclavonia, of Port Naon, and of Salines, &c. do hereby make known and attest to all
whom it doth or in anywise may concern.

Whereas, by the Divine assistance, the following
treaties of peace and alliance between us and the most
Serene and most Potent Prince, George, King of
Great Britain and Ireland, Duke of Brunswic and
Lunenburg, Elector of the Holy Roman Empire, as
also the most Serene and most Potent Prince, Lewis
XV. King of France, and the High and Mighty
States General of the United Netherlands, were on
the 2d day of August, this present year 1718, concluded
and signed at London, by the underwritten Plenipotentiaries on all sides, furnished for that purpose with
sufficient orders, hereto annexed, to be ratified by all
of us respectively within the space of two months,
the tenor of which is as follows:

In

In the Name of the moft Holy and Undivided Trinity, &c.

We having read and fully examined the articles of
thofe treaties and conventions, have ratified and approved all and each of them entirely, as by virtue of
thefe prefents we do approve and ratify all and fingular
the fame, and generally all that was fo tranfacted, concluded, and figned; promifing, on our Imperial, Royal,
and Archducal word, firmly and religioufly to obferve
and perform them in every thing, and never to fuffer
them to be infringed by us or ours ever at any time.
In witnefs whereof, we have fubfcribed this prefent
inftrument of ratification with our own hand, and in
confirmation thereof caufed our ufual feal to be affixed thereto. Vienna, the 14th day of September,
in the year of our Lord one thoufand feven hundred
and eighteen, the feventh of our Roman, the fifteenth
of our Spanifh, and the eighth of our Hungarian and
Bohemian reigns.

CHARLES.

Philip Lud. Count Sinzendorff.

By the exprefs command of his Sacred Imperial
and Catholic Royal Majefty.

John George Buol.

*His Imperial Majefty's Ratification of the feparate and
fecret Articles.*

WE Charles the Sixth, by the Divine clemency
elected Emperor of the Romans, always Auguft, King
of Germany, Spain, Hungary, Bohemia, Dalmatia,
Croatia, and Sclavonia, Archduke of Auftria, Duke
of Burgundy, Brabant, Milan, Mantua, Styria, Carinthia, Carniola, Limburg, Luxemburg, Gelderland,
as alfo of the Upper and Lower Silefia, and of Wirtemberg, Prince of Swabia, Marquis of the Holy
Roman Empire, of Burgaw, Moravia, Upper and
Lower Lufatia, Count of Habfburg, Flanders, Tyrol,
Ferret,

Perret, Kyburg, Goritia, and Namur, Landgrave of
Alfatia, Lord of the Marck of Sclavonia, of Port
Naon, and of Salines, &c. make known to all and
every one whom it may concern. Whereas, for the
execution of the alliance this day concluded and figned
at London by our and their Plenipotentiaries, with the
moft Serene and moft Potent Kings of Great Britain
and France, and the High and Mighty States General
of the United Netherlands, certain feparate and fecret
articles likewife were agreed upon, the tenor whereof
is,

Separate and fecret Articles.

I. Whereas, &c.

We have entirely ratified and approved all and fingular the aforefaid articles fo concluded and figned by
the Plenipotentiaries in virtue of their order, in like
manner as the treaty of alliance itfelf, part of which
they are deemed to make, as by virtue of thefe prefents we do approve and ratify all and fingular the fame,
promifing, upon our Imperial, Royal, and Archducal
word, that we will facredly and religioufly perform and
obferve the faid articles, and each of them. In witnefs
whereof, we have figned this prefent inftrument of
ratification with our own hand, and thereto affixed our
feal. Vienna, the 14th day of September, in the year
of our Lord 1718, the feventh of our Roman, the
fifteenth of our Spanifh, and the eighth of our Hungarian and Bohemian reigns.

CHARLES.

Philip Lud. Count Sinzendorff.

By the exprefs command of his Sacred Imperial
and Catholic Royal Majefty.

John George Buol.

His

His Imperial Majesty's Ratification of the separate Article, N° 1.

WE Charles the Sixth, by the Divine clemency elected Emperor of the Romans, always August, King of Germany, Spain, Hungary, Bohemia, Dalmatia, Croatia, and Sclavonia, Archduke of Austria, Duke of Burgundy, Brabant, Milan, Mantua, Styria, Carinthia, Carniola, Limburg, Luxemburg, Gelderland, as also of the Upper and Lower Silesia, and of Wurtemberg, Prince of Swabia, Marquis of the Holy Roman Empire, of Burgaw, Moravia, Upper and Lower Lusatia, Count of Habsburg, Flanders, Tyrol, Ferret, Kyburg, Goritia, and Namur, Landgrave of Alsatia, Lord of the Marck of Sclavonia, of Port Naon, and of Salines, &c. make known to those whom it doth concern. Whereas, besides the treaty made this day at London, between us and the most Serene and most Potent Kings of Great Britain and France, and besides certain separate and secret articles concerning the execution of the said treaty, and making part thereof, the following separate article was likewise made, by virtue whereof those things which have been agreed, concluded, and signed between us, the three contractors in the said treaty of alliance and secret articles, are ratified and confirmed, even in case the High and Mighty States General of the United Netherlands, contrary to the hope and better confidence reposed in them, should not be willing to accede to the said treaties, the tenor of which is,

Separate Article.

Whereas the treaty, &c.

We have and do entirely ratify and approve the things which are contained, established, and provided in this separate article, in like manner as if they were inserted in the treaty itself; for the observation and execution whereof we do engage our Imperial, Royal, and Archducal word, by virtue of these presents, signed

with

with our name, and sealed with our seal. Vienna, the 14th day of the month of September, in the year of our Lord 1718, the seventh of our Roman, the fifteenth of our Spanish, and the eighth of our Hungarian and Bohemian reigns.

CHARLES.

Phil. Lud. Count Sinzendorf.

By the express command of his Sacred Imperial and Catholic Royal Majesty.

John George Buol.

His Imperial Majesty's Ratification of the separate Article, N° 2.

WE Charles the Sixth, by the Divine clemency elected Emperor of the Romans, always August, King of Germany, Spain, Hungary, Bohemia, Dalmatia, Croatia, and Sclavonia, Archduke of Austria, Duke of Burgundy, Brabant, Milan, Mantua, Styria, Carinthia, Carniola, Limburg, Luxemburg, Gelderland, as also of the Upper and Lower Silesia, and of Wurtemberg, Prince of Swabia, Marquis of the Holy Roman Empire, of Burgaw, Moravia, Upper and Lower Lusatia, Count of Habsburg, Flanders, Tyrol, Ferret, Kyburg, Goritia, and Namur, Landgrave of Alsatia, Lord of the Marck of Sclavonia, of Port Naon, and of Salines, &c. make known to all whom it doth concern. Whereas to the treaty made this day at London, between us and the most Serene and most Potent Kings of Great Britain and France, as also the High and Mighty the States General of the United Netherlands, amongst others also one separate article was added, which treats about the pay of the Swiss garrisons to be put in the places therein expressed, the tenor of which follows:

Separate Article.

But if, &c.

We do entirely approve and ratify this article, as making

making a part of the principal treaty. In witness and confirmation whereof, we have set our name and seal to these presents. Vienna, the 14th day of the month of September, in the year of our Lord 1718, the seventh of our Roman, the fifteenth of our Spanish, and the eighth of our Hungarian and Bohemian reigns.

CHARLES.

Philip Lud. Count Sinzendorf.

By the express command of his Sacred Imperial and Catholic Royal Majesty.

John George Buol.

His Imperial Majesty's Ratification of the separate Article, Nº 3.

W.E. Charles the Sixth, by the Divine clemency elected Emperor of the Romans, always August, King of Germany, Spain, Hungary, Bohemia, Dalmatia, Croatia, and Sclavonia, Archduke of Austria, Duke of Burgundy, Brabant, Styria, Carinthia, Carniola, Milan, Mantua, Limburg, Luxemburg, Gelderland, as also of the Upper and Lower Silesia, and of Wurtemberg, Prince of Swabia, Marquis of the Holy Roman Empire, of Burgaw, Moravia, Upper and Lower Lusatia, Count of Habsburg, Flanders, Tyrol, Ferret, Kyburg, Goritia, and Namur, Landgrave of Alsatia, Lord of the Marck of Sclavonia, of Port Naon, and of Salines, &c. make known and testify by these presents. Whereas before the signing the treaty of alliance made the 2d day of the month of August, with the most Serene and most Potent Kings of Great Britain and France, as also with the High and Mighty States General of the United Netherlands, the following article was proposed to us.

Separate Article.

Whereas in the treaty of alliance, &c.

That we have ratified and approved, as we do hereby

ratify and approve the fame. In witnefs whereof, we have caufed thefe prefents, figned by our own hand, to be fealed with our feal. Vienna, the 14th day of the month of September, in the year of our Lord 1718, the feventh of our Roman, the fifteenth of our Spanifh, and the eighth of our Hungarian and Bohemian reigns.

CHARLES.

Philip Lud. Count Sinzendorf.

By the exprefs command of his Sacred Imperial and Catholic Royal Majefty.

John George Buol.

His Imperial Majefty's Ratification of the feparate Article, N° 4.

WE Charles the Sixth, by the Divine clemency elected Emperor of the Romans, always Auguft, King of Germany, Spain, Hungary, Bohemia, Dalmatia, Croatia, and Sclavonia, Archduke of Auftria, Duke of Burgundy, Brabant, Milan, Mantua, Styria, Carinthia, Carniola, Limburg, Luxemburg, Gelderland, as alfo of the Upper and Lower Silefia, and of Wurtemberg, Prince of Swabia, Marquis of the Holy Roman Empire, of Burgaw, Moravia, Upper and Lower Lufatia, Count of Habfburg, Flanders, Tyrol, Ferret, Kyburg, Goritia, and Namur, Landgrave of Alfatia, Lord of the Marck of Sclavonia, of Port Naon, and of Salines, &c. make known and teftify by thefe prefents. Whereas before the figning the treaty of alliance made the 2d day of the month of Auguft, with the moft Serene and moft Potent Kings of Great Britain and France, as alfo with the High and Mighty States General of the United Netherlands, the following article was propofed to us:

Separate Article.

Whereas fome of the titles, &c.

That we have ratified and approved, as we do hereby

3

by ratify and approve the fame. In witneſs whereof, we have caufed thefe prefents, figned by our own hand, to be fealed with our feal. Vienna, the 14th day of the month of September, in the year of our Lord 1718, the feventh of our Roman, the fifteenth of our Spaniſh, and the eighth of our Hungarian and Bohe-mian reigns.   CHARLES.

Philip Lud. Count Sinzendorf.

By the exprefs command of his Sacred Imperial and Catholic Royal Majefty.

John George Buol.

The moſt Chriſtian King's Ratification of the Treaty, and of Three of the ſeparate Articles, N° 2, 3, 4.

LEWIS, by the grace of God, King of France and Navarre, to all who fhall fee thefe prefents, greet-ing. Whereas our beloved and faithful the Abbot du Bois, counfellor in ordinary of our Council of State, and of the Council for foreign affairs, Secretary of our Cabinet, and our Plenipotentiary, has, by virtue of full powers which we gave him for that purpofe, con-cluded, agreed, and figned at London, the 2d of this prefent month of Auguft, with M. Chriftopher Pen-terridter, of Adelfhaufen, Imperial Aulic Counfellor, and Affeffor of the Council of the Auftrian Nether-lands, and John Philip Hoffman, Refident of our moft dear and moft beloved brother the Emperor of the Romans at London, his Plenipotentiaries, furnifhed in like manner with his full powers; and with Wil-liam Archbifhop of Canterbury, Primate and Metro-politan of all England; Thomas Lord Parker, Baron of Macclesfield, Lord High Chancellor of our moft dear and moft beloved brother the King of Great Britain; Charles Earl of Sunderland, Prefident of the Council of our faid brother; Evelyn Duke of King-fton, Lord Privy Seal; Henry Duke of Kent, Lord High Steward of the Houfhold of our faid brother; Thomas Duke of Newcaftle, Lord Chamberlain of

the

the Houfhold of our faid brother; Charles Duke of
Bolton, Lord Lieutenant and Governor General of
the Kingdom of Ireland; John Duke of Roxburghe,
one of the principal Secretaries of State of Great Britain; James Earl of Berkeley, firft Commiffioner of
the Admiralty; and James Craggs, likewife one of
the principal Secretaries of State of Great Britain, furnifhed in like manner with his full powers, the treaty
of alliance, and the feparate articles, the tenor whereof
follows.

In the name, &c.

We approving the above-mentioned treaties of alliance and feparate articles in all and every the points
therein contained, have by the advice of our moft dear
and moft beloved uncle the Duke of Orleans, Regent
of our kingdom, as well for us, as for our heirs, fucceffors, kingdoms, countries, territories, lordfhips, and
fubjects, accepted, approved, ratified, and confirmed,
and by thefe prefents, figned with our hand, do accept,
approve, ratify, and confirm the fame; and promife,
on the word and faith of a King, to keep and obferve
the whole inviolably, without ever acting one way or
other to the contrary, directly or indirectly, in any kind
or manner whatever. In witnefs whereof, we have
caufed our feal to be affixed to thefe prefents. Given
at Paris, the 30th of Auguft, in the year of grace one
thoufand feven hundred and eighteen, and of our reign
the third.

                                    LEWIS.

        By the King.
The Duke of Orleans, Regent, prefent.

                              Phelypeaux.

*The moft Chriftian King's Ratification of the feparate
and fecret Articles, and of one of the feparate Articles, N° 1.*

LEWIS, by the grace of God, King of France
and Navarre, to all who fhall fee thefe prefents, greet-
                                    ing.

·ing. Whereas our beloved and faithful the Abbot du Bois, counfellor in ordinary of our Council of State, and of the Council for foreign affairs, Secretary of our Cabinet, and our Plenipotentiary, has, by virtue of full powers which we gave him for that purpofe, concluded, agreed, and figned at London, the 2d of this prefent month of Auguft, with M. Chriftopher Penterridter, of Adelfhaufen, Imperial Aulic Counfellor, and Affeffor of the Council of the Auftrian Netherlands, and John Philip Hoffman, Refident of our moft dear and moft beloved brother the Emperor of the Romans at London, his Plenipotentiaries, furnifhed in like manner with his full powers; and with William Archbifhop of Canterbury, Primate and Metropolitan of all England; Thomas Lord Parker, Baron of Macclesfield, Lord High Chancellor of our moft dear and moft beloved brother the King of Great Britain; Charles Earl of Sunderland, Prefident of the Council of our faid brother; Evelyn Duke of Kingfton, Lord Privy Seal; Henry Duke of Kent, Lord High Steward of the Houfhold of our faid brother; Thomas Duke of Newcaftle, Lord Chamberlain of the Houfhold of our faid brother; Charles Duke of Bolton, Lord Lieutenant and Governor General of the Kingdom of Ireland; John Duke of Roxburghe, one of the principal Secretaries of State of Great Britain; James Earl of Berkeley, firft Commiffioner of the Admiralty; and James Craggs, likewife one of the principal Secretaries of State of Great Britain, Plenipotentiaries of our faid brother the King of Great Britain, furnifhed in like manner with his full powers, feparate and fecret articles, the tenor whereof follows.

Separate Articles, &c.

We approving the above-mentioned feparate and fecret articles, in all and every the points therein contained, have by the advice of our moft dear and moft beloved uncle the Duke of Orleans, Regent of our kingdom, as well for us as for our heirs, fucceffors,

kingdoms,

kingdoms, countries, territories, lordfhips and fubjects, accepted, approved, ratified, and confirmed, and
by thefe prefents, figned with our hand, do accept, approve, ratify, and confirm the fame, and promife, on
the word and faith of a King, to keep and obferve
the whole inviolably, without ever acting one way or
other to the contrary, directly or indirectly, in any
kind or manner whatfoever. In witnefs whereof, we
have caufed our feal to be affixed to thefe prefents,
Given at Paris, the 30th of Auguft, in the year of grace
one thoufand feven hundred and eighteen, and of our
reign the third.   LEWIS.

By the King.
The Duke of Orleans, Regent, prefent.

Phelypeaux.

---

*The Treaty of Peace and Alliance between the Emperor
Charles VI. and George II. King of Great Britain, in which the States of the United Provinces
of the Netherlands are included. Made at Vienna, the 16th of March, 1731.*

In the name of the moft Holy and Undivided Trinity.
Amen.

TO all to whom it does or may any way appertain. Be it known, that the moft Serene and moft
Potent Prince and Lord, Charles VI. Emperor of the
Romans, King of Spain, of both the Sicilies, Hungary, and Bohemia, Archduke of Auftria, &c. &c. and
the moft Serene and moft Potent Prince and Lord,
George II. King of Great Britain, France, and Ireland, together with the High and Mighty Lords the
States General of the United Provinces of the Netherlands, having taken into confideration the prefent un-
                                                    fettled

fettled and perplexed ftate of affairs in Europe, feri-
oufly bethought themfelves of finding proper methods,
not only to prevent thofe evils which muft naturally
arife from the cavils and divifions that were daily increafing, but alfo to eftablifh the public tranquillity
upon a fure and lafting foundation, and in as eafy and
fpeedy a manner as it was poffible : for this end their
faid Majefties, and the faid States General, being fully
animated with a fincere defire to promote fo wholefome a work, and to bring it to perfection, judged it
expedient to agree among themfelves upon certain
general conditions, which might ferve as the bafis for
reconciling the animofities and fettling the differences
of the chief Princes of Europe, which, as they are
heightened among themfelves, do greatly endanger the
public tranquillity.

For which purpofe, the moft High Prince and
Lord, Eugene, Prince of Savoy and Piedmont, actual
Privy Counfellor to his Sacred Imperial and Catholic
Majefty, Prefident of the Council of the Auftrian Netherlands at Vienna, and his Lieutenant General, Major General of the holy Roman Empire, and Vicar
General of the kingdoms and ftates of the faid Empire
in Italy, Colonel of a regiment of dragoons, Knight
of the Golden Fleece ; and alfo the moft Illuftrious
and moft Excellent Lord, Philip Lewis, Hereditary
Treafurer of the holy Roman Empire, Count of Zinzendorf, Free Baron of Ernftbrunn, Lord of the Dy-
nafties of Gfoll, Upper Selowitz, Porlitz, Sabor, Mul-
fig, Loof-zan, and Drefkau, Burgrave of Rheineck,
Hereditary Mafter of the Horfe in Upper and Lower
Auftria, Knight of the Golden Fleece, Chamberlain
to his Sacred Imperial Majefty, actual Privy Counfellor, and firft Chancellor of the Court, &c. and alfo
the moft Illuftrious and moft Excellent Lord, Gundacker Thomas, Count of the holy Roman Empire,
by the titles of Staremberg, Schatomburg, and Wax-
emburg, Lord of the domains of Efchelberg, Liech-
tenhagen, Roteneg, Freyftadt, Haus, Oberwalfe, Sef-
fenberg,

X 4

fenberg, Bodendorf, Hatwan, Knight of the Golden
Fleece, actual Privy Counsellor to his Sacred Imperial and Catholic Majesty, Hereditary Marshal of the
Archdutchy of Upper and Lower Austria, on the part
of his Sacred Imperial and Catholic Majesty; and
Thomas Robinson, Esq; Member of the Parliament
of Great Britain, and Minister of his Majesty of Great
Britain to his said Imperial and Catholic Majesty, on
the part of his Sacred Royal Majesty of Great Britain: and   on the part of the
High and Mighty States of the United Provinces of
the Netherlands; being all furnished with full powers,
after they had held conferences together, and exchanged
their credential letters and full powers, agreed upon
the following articles and conditions.

I. That there shall be from this time forward, between his Sacred Imperial Catholic Majesty, his Sacred Royal Majesty of Great Britain, the heirs and
successors of both, and the High and Mighty Lords
the States General of the United Provinces of the Netherlands, a firm, sincere, and inviolable friendship,
for the mutual advantage of the provinces and subjects
belonging to each of the contracting Powers; and that
this peace be so established, that each of the contractors shall be obliged to defend the territories and
subjects of the others; to maintain the peace, and promote the advantages of the other contractors as much
as their own; and to prevent and avert all damages
and injuries of every kind whatsoever, which might be
done to them. For this end, all the former treaties
or conventions of peace, friendship, and alliance, shall
have their full effect, and shall preserve in all and
every part their full force and virtue, and shall even
be looked upon as renewed and confirmed by virtue
of the present treaty, except only such articles, clauses,
and conditions, from which it has been thought fit to
derogate by the present treaty. And moreover, the
said contracting parties have expressly obliged themselves, by virtue of this present article, to a mutual
defence,

defence, or, as it is called, guaranty of all the kingdoms, states, and territories, which each of them possesses, and even of the rights and immunities each of them enjoys, or ought to enjoy, in such manner, that they have mutually declared and promised to one another, that they will with all their forces oppose the enterprizes of all and every one who shall (perhaps contrary to expectation) undertake to disturb any of the contractors, or their heirs and successors, in the peaceable possession of their kingdoms, states, provinces, lands, rights, and immunities, which each of the contracting parties doth or ought to enjoy, at the time of the conclusion of the present treaty.

II. Moreover, as it has been frequently remonstrated on the part of his Imperial and Catholic Majesty, that the public tranquillity could not reign and last long, and that no other sure way could be found out for maintaining the balance of Europe, than a general defence, engagement, and eviction, or, as they call it, a guaranty for the order of his succession, as it is settled by the Imperial declaration of 1713, and received in the most Serene House of Austria; his Sacred Royal Majesty of Great Britain, and the High and Mighty Lords the States of the United Provinces of the Netherlands, moved thereto by their ardent desire to secure the public tranquillity, and to preserve the balance of Europe, as also by a view of the terms agreed upon in the following articles, which are exceedingly well adapted to answer both purposes, do, by virtue of the present article, take upon them the general guaranty of the said order of succession, and oblige themselves to maintain it as often as there shall be occasion, against all persons whatsoever; and consequently they promise, in the most authentic and strongest manner that can be, to defend, maintain, and (as it is called) to guaranty, with all their forces, that order of succession which his Imperial Majesty has declared and established by a solemn act of the 19th of April, 1713; in manner of a perpetual,

tual, indivisible, and inseparable feoffment of trust, in favour of primogeniture, for all his Majesty's heirs of both sexes; of which act there is a copy annexed at the end of this treaty: which said act was readily and unanimously received by the orders and estates of all the kingdoms, archdutchies, principalities, provinces, and domains, belonging by right of inheritance to the most Serene House of Austria; all which have humbly and thankfully acknowledged it, and transcribed it into their public registers, as having the force of a law and pragmatic sanction, which is to subsist for ever in full force. And whereas, according to this rule and order of succession, if it should please God of his mercy to give his Imperial and Catholic Majesty issue male, then the eldest of his sons, or, he being dead before, the eldest son's eldest son; and in case there be no male issue, on his Imperial and Catholic Majesty's demise, the eldest of his daughters, the most Serene Archdutchesses of Austria, by the order and right of seniority, which has always been indivisibly preserved, is to succeed his Imperial Majesty in all his kingdoms, provinces, and domains, in the same manner as he now possesses them: nor shall they at any time, upon any account, or for any reason whatever, be divided or separated in favour of him, or her, or them who may be of the second, the third, or more distant branch. And this same order and indivisible right of seniority is to be preserved in all events, and to be observed in all ages, as well in his Imperial Majesty's male issue, if God grants him any, as in his Imperial Majesty's female issue, after the extinction of the male heirs; or, in short, in all cases wherein the succession of the kingdoms, provinces, and hereditary dominions of the most Serene House of Austria shall be called in question. For this purpose, his Majesty of Great Britain, and the High and Mighty Lords the States General of the United Provinces of the Netherlands, promise and engage to maintain him, or her, who ought to succeed according to the rule and

order

order above set forth, in the kingdoms, provinces, or domains of which his Imperial Majesty is now actually in possession; and they engage to defend the same for ever against all such as shall perhaps presume to disturb that possession in any manner whatsoever.

III. And forasmuch as it hath been often represented to his Imperial and Catholic Majesty, in terms full of friendship, on the part of his Sacred Royal Majesty of Great Britain, and the High and Mighty Lords the States General of the United Provinces, that there was no surer nor more speedy method for establishing the public tranquillity so long desired, than by rendering the succession of the dutchies of Tuscany, Parma, and Placentia, designed for the most Serene the Infante Don Carlos, yet more secure by the immediate introduction of 6000 Spanish soldiers into the strong places of those dutchies; his said Sacred Imperial and Catholic Majesty, desiring to promote the pacific views and intentions of his Britannic Majesty, and the High and Mighty States General of the United Netherlands, will by no means oppose the peaceable introduction of the said 6000 Spaniards into the strong places of the dutchies of Tuscany, Parma, and Placentia, in pursuance of the abovementioned engagements entered into by his said Britannic Majesty, and by the States General. And whereas, to this end, his Imperial and Catholic Majesty judges the consent of the Empire necessary, he promises, at the same time, that he will use his utmost endeavours to obtain the said consent within the space of two months, or sooner, if possible. And to obviate as readily as may be the evils which threaten the public peace, his Imperial and Catholic Majesty moreover promises, that, immediately after the mutual exchange of the ratifications, he will notify the consent which he, as head of the Empire, has given to the said peaceable introduction, to the Minister of the Great Duke of Tuscany, and to the Minister of Parma residing at his court, or wherever else it shall be thought proper.

proper. His said Imperial and Catholic Majesty likewise promises and affirms, that he is so far from any
thought of raising, or causing any hinderance, directly
or indirectly, to the Spanish garrisons being admitted
into the places aforesaid, that on the contrary he will
interpose his good offices and authority for removing
any unexpected obstruction or difficulty that may oppose the said introduction, and consequently that the
6000 Spanish soldiers may be introduced quietly, and
without any delay, in the manner aforesaid, into the
strong places as well of the great dutchy of Tuscany, as of the dutchies of Parma and Placentia.

IV. That therefore all the articles thus agreed to,
with the irrevocable consent of the contracting parties, be so firmly and reciprocally established, and so
entirely decided, that it shall not be lawful for the
contracting parties to deviate from them in any wise;
meaning as well those which are to be put in execution without delay, and immediately after the exchange
of the ratifications, as those which ought to remain
for ever inviolable.

V. Whereas, for attaining to the end which the contracting parties in this treaty propose to themselves,
it has been found necessary to pluck up every root of
division and dissension, and therefore that the antient
friendship which united the said contracting parties,
may not only be renewed, but knit closer and closer
every day, his Imperial Catholic Majesty promises,
and, by virtue of the present article, binds himself to
cause all commerce and navigation to the East Indies
to cease immediately and for ever in the Austrian
Netherlands, and in all the other countries which in
the time of Charles II. Catholic King of Spain, were
under the dominion of Spain; and that he will *bonâ
fide* act in such manner, that neither the Ostend company, nor any other, either in the Austrian Netherlands, or in the countries which, as is abovesaid,
were under the dominion of Spain in the time of the
late

late Catholic King Charles II. shall at. any time, directly or indirectly, contravene this rule established. for ever. Excepting that the Ostend company may send, for once only, two ships, which shall sail from the said port to the East Indies, and from thence return to Ostend, where the said company may, when they think fit, expose the merchandizes so brought from the Indies to sale. And his Sacred Royal Majesty of Great Britain, and the High and Mighty States General of the United Provinces, do likewise promise on their part, and oblige themselves, to make a new treaty with his Imperial Majesty without delay, concerning commerce and the rule of imposts, commonly called a Tariff, as far as relates to the Austrian Netherlands, and agreeable to the intention of the 26th article of the treaty, commonly called (by reason of the limits therein settled) the Barrier. And for this purpose the contracting parties shall immediately name commissioners, who shall meet at Antwerp within the space of two months, to be computed from the day of signing the present treaty, to agree together upon every thing that regards the entire execution of the said barrier treaty, which was concluded at Antwerp the $\frac{6}{17}$th day of November, anno 1715, and of the convention since signed at the Hague the $\frac{11}{22}$ day of December, 1718; and particularly to conclude a new treaty there, as has been said, concerning commerce, and the rate of imposts, as far as relates to the Austrian Netherlands, and according to the intention of the aforesaid 26th article. It is moreover agreed, and solemnly-stipulated, that every thing which it hath been thought fit to leave to the commissioners who are to meet at Antwerp, shall be brought to a final issue, with all the justice and integrity, as soon as possible, and in such manner that the last hand may be put to that work, at least within the space of two years.

VI. As the examination and discussion of the other points which remain to. be discussed, either between the contracting parties; or any of their confederates, require

require much more time than can be spared in this critical situation of affairs, therefore, to avoid all delays, which might be too prejudicial to the common welfare, it is covenanted and agreed to declare mutually, that all the treaties and conventions which any of the said contracting Powers have made with other Princes and States, shall subsist as they now are, excepting only so far as they may be contrary to any of the points regulated by the present treaty; and moreover, that all the disputes which are actually between the said contracting parties, or any of their allies, shall be amicably adjusted as soon as possible; and in the mean time the contracting parties shall mutually endeavour to prevent any of those who have differences, from having recourse to arms to support their pretensions.

VII. To take away all manner of doubt from the subjects of the King of Great Britain, and the Lords the States General, touching their commerce in the kingdom of Sicily, his Imperial and Catholic Majesty has been pleased to declare, that from this time forward they shall be treated in the same manner, and upon the same foot as they were or ought to have been treated in the time of Charles II. King of Spain, of glorious memory, and as any nation in the strictest friendship has been usually treated.

VIII. There shall be included in this treaty of peace, all those who, within the space of six months after its ratifications are exchanged, shall be proposed by either party, and by common consent.

IX. This present treaty shall be approved and ratified by his Imperial and Catholic Majesty, by his Sacred Royal Majesty of Great Britain, and by the High and Mighty Lords the States General of the United Netherlands, and the ratifications shall be given and exchanged at Vienna, within six weeks, to be computed from the day of signing.

In witness and confirmation whereof, as well the
Imperial

Imperial Commiſſioners, in quality of Ambaſſadors Extraordinary and Plenipotentiaries, as the
Miniſter of the King of Great Britain, equally
furniſhed with full powers, have ſigned this treaty
with their own hands, and ſealed it with their
ſeals. Done at Vienna in Auſtria, the 16th day
of March, in the year of our Lord 1731.

.(L. S.) *Eugene of Savoy.*
(L. S.) *Philip Lewis of Zinzendorf.*
(L. S.) *Gundacker Thomas of Staremberg.*
(L. S.) *Thomas Robinſon.*

' *Separate Article.*

THOUGH by the firſt article of the treaty concluded this day between his Imperial and Catholic
Majeſty, his Sacred Royal Majeſty of Great Britain,
and the Lords the States General of the United Provinces of the Netherlands, the contracting parties did
mutually promiſe, among other things, that they would
with all their forces oppoſe the enterprizes of any perſon or perſons who ſhould (perhaps contrary to expectation) offer to give diſturbance to any of the contracting parties, their heirs or ſucceſſors, in the peaceable poſſeſſion of their kingdoms, dominions, provinces, countries, rights or immunities, which each of
the contractors doth or ought to enjoy at the time of
the concluſion of the preſent treaty; the ſaid contracting parties have nevertheleſs agreed among themſelves, by virtue of the preſent ſeparate article, that
if it ſhould happen, perhaps, in proceſs of time, that
the Turks ſhould offer to diſturb his Sacred Imperial
and Catholic Majeſty, his heirs and ſucceſſors, in the
quiet poſſeſſion of the kingdoms, dominions, provinces, countries, rights, or immunities, which his Imperial Majeſty actually doth, or ought to enjoy, the
guaranties ſtipulated in the ſaid firſt article are not to
be extended to this caſe now mentioned. '

This ſeparate article ſhall have the ſame force, &c.

Declaration

Declaration concerning the Spanish *Garrisons, which are to be introduced into the strong Places of* Tuscany, Parma, *and* Placentia.

FORASMUCH as his Sacred Imperial Catholic Majesty was desirous to have all manner of security, before he would consent on his part to the 3d article of the treaty concluded this day, which regulates the immediate introduction of the Spanish garrisons into the strong places of Tuscany, Parma, and Placentia, agreeably to the real views and intentions contained in the promises made and signed in the treaty of Seville, partly on the 9th, and partly on the 21st day of November, anno 1729; his Sacred Royal Majesty of Great Britain, and the High and Mighty Lords the States General of the United Netherlands, have not only exhibited those promises *bona fide*, as they are here subjoined, to his Sacred Imperial and Catholic Majesty, but moreover they have not hesitated to affirm, in the strongest manner, that when they agreed to introduce the Spanish garrisons into the strong places of Tuscany, Parma, and Placentia, they had no intention to depart in the least from those things which had been settled by the 5th article of the Quadruple Alliance, concluded at London $\frac{\text{July 22}}{\text{August 2}}$, 1718, either with regard to the rights of his Imperial Majesty, and the Empire, or to the security of the kingdoms and states which his Imperial Majesty actually possesseth in Italy, or lastly, to the preservation of the quiet and dignity of those who were then the lawful possessors of those dutchies. For this purpose, his Royal Majesty of Great Britain, and the High and Mighty Lords the States General of the United Netherlands, have declared, and do declare, that they are entirely disposed and ready to give his Imperial and Catholic Majesty, as they do by these presents, all the strong and solemn promises, evictions, or, as they are called, guaranties, that can be desired, as well in relation to the points above-mentioned, as in relation to all the

other

other points ftill contained in the faid 5th article of the treaty called Quadruple.

This prefent declaration fhall have the fame force, &c.

Declaration concerning the Succeffion of Parma.

IT being apprehended that the unexpected death of the late moft Serene Prince, Anthony Farnefe, in his life-time Duke of Parma and Placentia, might in fome fort retard or obftruct the conclufion of this treaty, it having happened at the very time when it was upon the point of being concluded; his Imperial and Catholic Majefty doth, by virtue of this prefent act, declare and engage, that in cafe the hopes of the pregnancy of the moft Serene Dutchefs Dowager, wife of the faid moft Serene Duke Anthony whilft he lived, do not prove abortive, and the faid Dutchefs Dowager fhould bring a man-child into the world, all that has been regulated, as well by the 3d article of the treaty concluded this day, as by the act of declaration above recited, fhall take place, as much as if the unforefeen death of the Duke had not happened: but that if the hopes conceived of the pregnancy of the faid Dutchefs Dowager fhould vanifh, or fhe fhould bring a pofthumous daughter into the world, then his faid Imperial Majefty declares, and binds himfelf, that inftead of introducing the Spanifh foldiers into the ftrong places of Parma and Placentia, the moft Serene Infante of Spain, Don Carlos, fhall be put into the poffeffion of the faid dutchies, in the fame manner as was agreed upon with the court of Spain, by confent of the Empire, and purfuant to the letters of eventual inveftiture, the tenor of which fhall be looked upon as repeated and confirmed in all its articles, claufes, and conditions; in fuch manner notwithftanding, that the faid Infante of Spain, as alfo the court of Spain, fhall firft of all fulfil the former treaties, wherein the Emperor is a contracting party with the confent of the Empire. And whereas upon the deceafe of the faid Duke Anthony Farnefe, the

Vol. I. Y Imperial

Imperial troops were not put into the ftrong places of Parma and Placentia, with a yiew to hinder the eventual fucceffion, as it was fecured to the moft Serene Infante Don Carlos by the treaty of London, commonly called the Quadruple Alliance, but only to prevent any enterprize which might have difturbed the tranquillity of Italy; his Sacred Imperial and Catholic Majefty perceiving, that by the treaty concluded this day, the public tranquillity is reftored and confirmed as far as poffible, he doth again declare, that in putting his troops into the ftrong places of Parma and Placentia, he had no other intention than to fupport, as far as lay in his power, the fucceffion of the moft Serene Infante Don Carlos, as it is fecured to the faid Infante by the faid treaty of London : and that, very far from oppofing the faid fucceffion, in cafe the male branch of the Houfe of Farnefe fhould be utterly extinct; or from oppofing the introduction of the Spanifh garrifons, if the Dutchefs Dowager fhould happen to bring a pofthumous fon into the world; his Imperial Majefty doth on the contrary declare and promife, that the faid forces fhall by his exprefs orders be withdrawn, either that the faid Infante Don Carlos may be put into poffeffion of the faid dutchies, according to the tenor of the letters of eventual inveftiture, or that the Spanifh garrifons may be introduced peaceably, and without any refiftance whatever ; which faid garrifons are to ferve for no other ufe than to fecure the execution of the promife made to him, in cafe the male branch of the Houfe of Farnefe fhould be utterly extinct.

The prefent declaration fhall have the fame force, &c.

Declaration figned by the Minifters of the King of Great Britain, and the Lords the States General, by virtue of their Full Powers.

WHEREAS among feveral articles agreed upon in the treaty of Seville, on the 9th and 21ft day of November,

November, 1729, in favour of the Great Duke of Tufcany, as well as of the dutchies of Parma and Placentia, it was likewife provided, that as foon as the moft Serene Infante of Spain, Don Carlos, or the , Prince to whom his rights may devolve, fhould be in peaceable poffeffion of the fucceffion defigned for him, and fecure from any infults of enemies, and againft any juft caufe of fear, then his Royal Catholic Majefty fhould prefently give orders for withdrawing his own troops out of the faid dutchies, but not thofe belonging to the Infante Don Carlos, or to the Prince upon whom, as above-mentioned, his rights may devolve.

The under-written Minifters of the King of Great Britain, and the Lords the States General, do, by virtue of this prefent inftrument, declare, that as his faid Royal Majefty of Great Britain, and the High and Mighty Lords the States General of the United Netherlands, are always accuftomed to fulfil what they have promifed, fo it is ftill their meaning and intention, that in the cafes aforefaid, the Spanifh troops fhall be immediately withdrawn from the dutchies of Tufcany, Parma, and Placentia.

This declaration is to be kept fecret, but is, neverthelefs, to be of the fame force, &c.

Separate Article.

WHEREAS the treaty concluded this day between his Imperial Catholic Majefty, his Britannic Majefty, and the High and Mighty Lords the States General of the United Provinces of the Netherlands, could not be fubfcribed or figned by the Minifter of the faid States General refiding at the Imperial court, becaufe, according to the cuftom of the Republic, and the form of its government, the full powers could not be difpatched to the faid Minifter fo foon as was neceffary; it is agreed between his Imperial Majefty, and his Royal Majefty of Great-Britain, that the faid States

General

General (there being feveral conditions in the faid treaty, wherein they are particularly concerned) fhall be held and reputed as a principal contracting party, according as they are alfo named in the faid treaty, in firm hope and confidence that they would accede to it, as foon as the ufual form of their government would admit of it. And becaufe the zeal which that Republic manifefts for eftablifhing and fecuring the public tranquillity, leaves their faid Majefties no room to doubt, that the faid Republic is defirous of becoming, as foon as may be, a principal contracting party in the faid treaty, to the end fhe may partake of the advantages therein ftipulated for her; both their Majefties will therefore unite their endeavours, that this treaty may be figned at the Hague, on the part of the faid States General, within the fpace of three months, to be computed from the day of the figning of the prefent treaty, or fooner if poffible; for it appeared neceffary both to his Imperial and to his Royal Britannic Majefty, in order to obtain the end propofed by the prefent treaty, and for completing the public tranquillity, that the faid States General fhould enter into a part and partnerfhip of the faid conventions.

This feparate article fhall have the fame force, &c.

A Declaration concerning Eaft Friefland.

THE States General of the United Provinces of the Netherlands having, upon feveral occafions, affured his Imperial and Catholic Majefty, that how much foever they are interefted in the re-eftablifhment and prefervation of the peace in their neighbourhood, and by confequence that of the province of Eaft Friefland, it was never their intention to prejudice in the leaft the dependence of the faid province of Eaft Friefland upon the Emperor and the Empire; his faid Imperial and Catholic Majefty, to give the States a frefh proof of his defire to oblige them, as far as is confiftent with juftice, has been pleafed to explain

plain to them his true fentiments on that affair; and by that means to recover them from the fears they feem to have received. In order to this, no hefitation has been made to declare to them on his part, by the prefent act, that his intention always was and ftill is,

I. That an amnefty, which he has moft gracioufly granted to thofe of Embden and their adherents, fhall have its entire effect; and therefore that the feveral pains and penalties pronounced againft thofe of Embden and their adherents, upon the fcore of their renitency (refiftance) fhall not be put in execution. And as for thofe of them which have actually been executed fince the moft gracious acceptance of the fubmiffion made by the people of Embden and their adherents, the whole fhall be reftored upon the foot it ftood before the faid fubmiffion was accepted, that is to fay, before the 3d of May, 1729, faving what is hereafter mentioned, of an agreement to indemnify thofe for their loffes, who were plundered during the late troubles.

II. His Imperial and Catholic Majefty having, by his refolution of the 12th of September, 1729, moft gracioufly permitted thofe of the town of Embden, and their adherents, to draw up a frefh account of their grievances, or matters wherein they thought themfelves aggrieved by the decrees of 1721, and the years following, concerning the ground of the affairs upon which they differed with the Prince; and the faid grievances having been afterwards exhibited to the Imperial Aulic Council, with all fubmiffion, the of November the fame year; his faid Majefty has already ordained, by his moft gracious refolution of the 31ft of Auguft, that thofe grievances fhould be examined as foon as poffible. And, as it has been often declared, it has been and ftill is his conftant defire, that they fhould be determined and decided with all the juftice and difpatch that is poffible, according to the agreements, conventions, and decifions, which

Y 3 make

make the particular law of the province of Eaft
Friefland, and which are referred to in the Prince's
reverfal letters, paffed and fworn to at his acceffion
to the regency: provided, neverthelefs, that under
the denomination of thofe agreements, conventions,
and decifions, none be comprehended which were abrogated and annulled by his Imperial Majefty's auguft
predeceffors in the Empire, or which ftrike at the fupreme rights of the Emperor and the Empire over
the province of Eaft Friefland. And his Imperial
and Catholic Majefty, as a farther proof of his moft
gracious intention to cut as fhort as juftice will admit
him, the examination of the grievances of the people
of Embden, and their adherents, has already ordained,
by his refolution of the 31ft of Auguft laft year, that,
as foon as the account thereof is delivered to thofe
who are properly to take cognizance of the fame, according to the tenor of the refolution above-mentioned, they fhall anfwer it very foon, and once for all;
after which his Imperial Majefty, with the advice
of his Imperial Aulic Council, will redrefs every complaint, article by article, which fhall appear to be
grounded on the agreements above-mentioned.

III. It having been already ordained, purfuant to
his Imperial and Catholic Majefty's laft refolution of
the 31ft of Auguft, 1730, that the people of the town
of Embden, and their adherents, ought to be admitted into the Affembly of the States, which is to be
called together to deliberate freely upon the affairs
that lie before them; his Imperial and Catholic Majefty will take care that this refolution fhall have its
intire effect, and that none of thofe who have a right
to affift therein be excluded, contrary to the tenor
of it.

IV. As to the indemnification, his Imperial Majefty thinks it proper, that an account be taken of the
damages, which, according to the tenor of the amnefty
publifhed the   in the year 1728, and of the
refolution

resolution of the 12th of September, 1729, ought to be made good by the renitents ; and that the said account be communicated to them, that they may make their objections : after which, his Imperial and Catholic Majesty will cause the difference to be amicably adjusted, or, on failure of an accommodation, will, with the utmost equity, fix the sum which shall be required to make good the damages sustained.

V. His Imperial and Catholic Majesty persists in the intention he always had to take particular care of the payment of the interest of the sums which the States of East Friesland, and of the town of Embden, have borrowed of the subjects of the United Provinces, as also of the reimbursement of the capital, according to the engagements entered into on that account.

F R A N C E.

1259.
to
1632.

THE more ancient treaties, between England and France, which are frequent and numerous, may be seen in

Rym. Fœd. vol. i. part ii. p. 50.
vol. iii. part ii. p. 3.
vol. iv. part iii. p. 171.
vol. vi. part ii. p. 88.
vol. xii. p. 690.
vol. xv. p. 211—640.
vol. xvi. p. 645.
vol. xix. p. 66.
Corps Dip. tom. vi. part. i. p. 31-33.
Pap. Off. B. 11.
Treat. 1732, vol. ii. p. 41—310.

1648.   The treaty of Weſtphalia, which is recited by the treaty of Verſailles, in 1783, as
one of its foundations.

> *Mably, Dr. Pub.* vol. i. ch. 1.
> *Treat.* 1732, vol. i. p. 1.—vol. ii. p.
>   335.
> *Treat.* 1785, vol. i. p. 1—44.

1655
to
1659.   The treaties between the Cromwells and
France.

> *Pap. Off.* B. 12—13—14.
> *Treat.* 1732, vol. iii. p. 149—199.
> *Treat.* 1785, vol. i. p. 81—86—93
>   —4—100—101.

1667.
$\frac{2}{1}$ July.   The treaty between Great Britain and
France, concluded at Bredah.

> *Pap. Off.* B. 17.
> *Treat.* 1732, vol. i. p. 127.
> *Treat.* 1785, vol. i. p. 186.

167$\frac{4}{5}$.
24 Feb.   The marine and commercial treaty between Great Britain and France.

> *Treat.* 1685, p. 243.
> *Treat.* 1732, vol. i. p. 170.
> *Treat.* 1785, vol. i. p. 209.

1678.
1679.   The treaties of Nimeguen, between France
and the States General, in 1678, and between France and Spain, in 1679, are recited by the treaty of Verſailles, in 1783, as
two of its foundations.

> *Treat.* 1732, vol. i. p. 193—245.
> *Corps Dip.* vol. vii. p. 350—365.

1686.
16 Nov.   The treaty of peace and neutrality in
America, between Great Britain and France,

> *Pap. Off.* B. 25.
> *Treat.* 1732, vol. i. p. 246.
> *Treat.* 1785, vol. i. p. 261.

1697.   .. The treaty of peace between Great Bri-
⁴⁰⁄₁₈.Sept.   tain and France, concluded at Ryſwick;
which ſee at p. 332.
> *Pap. Off.* B. 26.
> *Treat.* 1732, vol. i. p. 302.
> *Treat.* 1785, vol. i. p. 299.

1698.   The treaty, uſually called the *Firſt Parti-*
19 Aug. *tion Treaty,* between Great Britain, France,
,and the States General. '
> *Treat.* 1732, vol. i. p. 386.
> *Treat.* 1785, vol. i. p. 305.

1700.   The treaty, uſually called the *Second Par-*
21 Feb. *tition Treaty,* between Great Britain, France,
and the States General, with the ſeparate
and ſecret articles.
> *Pap. Off.* B. 28.
> *Treat.* 1732, vol. i. p. 407.
> *Treat.* 1785, vol. i. p. 319.

1713.   The treaty of peace and friendſhip be-
31 Mar. tween Great Britain and France, concluded
11 Apr. at Utrecht.
> *Pap. Off.* B. 31—32. ·
> *Treat.* 1732, vol. iii. p. 398.
> *Treat.* 1785, vol. ii. p. 5.

1713.   The treaty of navigation and commerce,
31 Mar. between Great Britain and France, concluded
11 Apr. at Utrecht.
> *Pap. Off.* B. 34.
> *Treat.* 1732, vol. iii. p. 440.
> *Treat.* 1785, vol. ii. p. 40.

1714. .   The treaty of BADEN, between the Em-
7 Sept.   peror and France, is recited by the treaty of
Verſailles, in 1783, as one of its foundations.
> *Treat.* 1732, vol. iv. p. 358.
> *Rouſſet, Recueil,* vol. i. p. 1.

1717. The treaty of defensive alliance, between
4 Jan. Great Britain, France, and the States General, which was concluded at the Hague,
and which is usually called The Triple Alliance. *Pap. Off.* B. 37.
>*Treat.* 1732, vol. iv. p. 39.
>*Treat.* 1785, vol. ii. p. 185.
>*Rousset, Recueil Historique,* tom. i. p. 89.

1718. The Quadruple Alliance, between
22 July Great Britain, the Emperor, France, and the
—— States General, with the separate and secret
2 Aug. articles, which is printed before, page 257,
under the head of The Austrian Netherlands.
>*Pap. Off.* B. 44.
>*Treat.* 1732, vol. iv. p. 53.
>*Treat.* 1785, vol. ii. p. 199.
>*Rousset, Recueil Historique,* tom. i. p. 180.

1721. The treaty of defensive alliance, between
13 June. Great Britain, France, and Spain, with the
separate articles, concluded at Madrid.
>*Pap. Off.* B. 50.
>*Treat.* 1732, vol. iv. p. 123.
>*Treat.* 1785, vol. ii. p. 268.

1721. The triple defensive alliance, between
13 June. Great Britain, France, and Spain, with the
separate article, concluded at Madrid.
>*Pap. Off.* B. 53.

1725. The treaty between Great Britain, France,
3 Sept. and Prussia, concluded at Hanover.
>*Pap. Off.* B. 58.
>*Rousset, Recueil Historique,* tom. ii. p. 189.
>*Treat.* 1732, vol. iv. p. 146.
>*Treat.* 1785, vol. ii. p. 274.

1727.

1727.   ·The defenſive treaty, between Great Bri-
16 Apr. tain, France, and Denmark, concluded at
         Copenhagen.

> *Pap. Off.* B. 62.
> *Rouſſet, Recueil Hiſtorique,* tom. iv. p. 244.
> *Treat.* 1732, vol. iv. p. 167.
> *Treat.* 1785, vol. ii. p. 295.

1729.   The treaty of peace, union, and mutual
9 Nov.   defence, with the ſeparate and ſecret articles,
         between Great Britain, France, and Spain,
         concluded at Seville.

> *Pap. Off.* B. 64.
> *Rouſſet, Recueil Hiſtorique,* tom. v.
>   part. ii. p. 1.
> *Treat.* 1732, vol. iv. p. 201.
> *Treat.* 1785, vol. ii. p. 306.

1738.   The treaty of VIENNA, between the Em-
         peror and other Powers, is recited by the
         treaty of Verſailles, in 1783, as one of its
         foundations.

> *Mably, Dr. Pub.* vol. iii. p. 57.

1748.   The treaty of peace, with the ſeparate and
7/7 Oct. ſecret articles, between Great Britain, France,
         and the States General, concluded at Aix-la-
         Chapelle.

> *Pap. Off.* B. 76.
> *Treat.* 1785, vol. ii. p. 370.

1763.   The definitive treaty of peace, between
10 Feb. Great Britain, France, and Spain, concluded
         at Paris.

> *Treat.* 1785, vol. iii. p. 177.

1783. · The treaty of peace, between Great Bri-
3 Sept. tain and France, concluded at Verfailles.. :
Treat. 1785, vol. iii. p. 354.

1786. The treaty of navigation and commerce,
26 Sept. between Great Britain and France, concluded at Verfailles..

1787. The convention between Great Britain
15 Jan. and France, concluded at Verfailles.

1787. The convention between Great Britain
31 Aug. and France, concluded at Verfailles.

[The TREATY OF RYSWICK, is printed from the copy
which was publifhed by authority in 1697.]

*The Articles of Peace between the moft Serene and
Mighty Prince* William *the Third, King of* Great
Britain, *and the moft Serene and Mighty Prince*
Lewis *the Fourteenth, the moft Chriftian King, con-
cluded in the Royal Palace at* Ryfwick, *the* $\frac{10}{20}$ *Day
of* September, 1697.

I. THAT there be an univerfal perpetual peace,
and a true and fincere friendfhip, between the moft
Serene and Mighty Prince William the Third, King
of Great Britain, and the moft Serene and Mighty
Prince Lewis the Fourteenth, the moft Chriftian King,
their heirs and fucceffors, and between the kingdoms,
ftates, and fubjects of both ; and that the fame be fo
fincerely and inviolably obferved and kept, that the
one fhall promote the intereft, honour, and advantage
of the other, and that on both fides a faithful neighbourhood, and true obfervation of peace and friendfhip, may daily flourifh and increafe.

II. That all enmities, hoftilities, difcords, and wars,
between the faid King of Great Britain and the moft
Chriftian King, and their fubjects, ceafe and be abolifhed, fo that on both fides they forbear and abftain
hereafter

hereafter from all plundering, depredation, harm-do-ing, injuries, and infeſtation whatſoever, as well by land as by ſea, and on freſh waters, every where; and eſpecially throughout all the kingdoms, territories, do-minions, and places, belonging to each other, of what condition ſoever they be.

III. That all offences, injuries, damages, which the ſaid King of Great Britain and his ſubjects, or the ſaid moſt Chriſtian King and his ſubjects, have ſuf-fered from each other during this war, ſhall be forgot-ten, ſo that neither on account of them, or for any other cauſe or pretence, neither party, or the ſubjects of either, ſhall hereafter do, cauſe, or ſuffer to be done, any hoſtility, enmity, moleſtation, or hinderance to the other, by himſelf or others, ſecretly or openly, directly or indirectly, by colour of right or way of fact.

IV. And ſince the moſt Chriſtian King was never more deſirous of any thing, than that the peace be firm and inviolable, the ſaid King promiſes and agrees, for himſelf and his ſucceſſors, that he will on no account whatſoever diſturb the ſaid King of Great Britain in the free poſſeſſion of the kingdoms, countries, lands, or dominions which he now enjoys; and therefore engages his honour, upon the faith and word of a King, that he will not give or afford any aſſiſtance, directly or indirectly, to any enemy or enemies of the ſaid King of Great Britain; and that he will in no manner whatſoever favour the conſpiracies or plots which any rebels, or ill-diſpoſed perſons, may in any place excite or contrive againſt the ſaid King; and for that end promiſes and engages, that he will not aſſiſt with arms, ammunition, ſhips, proviſions, or mo-ney, or in any other way, by ſea or land, any perſon or perſons, who ſhall hereafter, under any pretence whatſoever, diſturb or moleſt the ſaid King of Great Britain in the free and full poſſeſſion of his king-doms, countries, lands, and dominions. The King of Great Britain likewiſe promiſes and engages, for

himſelf

himself and fucceffors, Kings of Great Britain, that he will inviolably do and perform the fame towards the faid moft Chriftian King, his kingdoms, countries, lands, and dominions.

V. That there be a free ufe of navigation and commerce between the fubjects of both the faid Kings, as was formerly in the time of peace, and before the declaration of the late war, fo that every one of them may freely come into the kingdoms, marts, ports, and rivers of either of the faid Kings with their merchandizes, and may there continue and trade without any moleftation, and fhall ufe and enjoy all liberties, immunities, and privileges, granted by folemn treaties and ancient cuftom.

VI. That the ordinary adminiftration of juftice fhall be reftored and fet open, throughout the kingdoms and dominions of both Kings, fo that it fhall be free for all the fubjects of either, to claim and obtain their rights, pretenfions, and actions, according to the laws, conftitutions, and ftatutes of each kingdom.

VII. The moft Chriftian King fhall reftore to the faid King of Great Britain, all countries, iflands, forts, and colonies, wherefoever fituated, which the Englifh did poffefs before the declaration of this prefent war. And in like manner the King of Great Britain fhall reftore to the moft Chriftian King all countries, iflands, forts, and colonies, wherefoever fituated, which the French did poffefs before the faid declaration of war; and this reftitution fhall be made, on both fides, within the fpace of fix months, or fooner if it can be done. And to that end, immediately after the ratification of this treaty, each of the faid Kings fhall deliver, or caufe to be delivered, to the other, or to commiffioners authorized in his name for that purpofe, all acts of conceffion, inftruments, and neceffary orders, duly made and in proper form, fo that they may have their effect.

VIII. Com-

VIII. Commiſſioners ſhall be appointed on both ſides, to examine and determine the rights and pretenſions which either of the ſaid Kings hath to the places ſituated in Hudſon's Bay; but the poſſeſſion of thoſe places which were taken by the French, during the peace that preceded this preſent war, and were retaken by the Engliſh during this war, ſhall be left to the French, by virtue of the foregoing article.   The capitulation made by the Engliſh on the fifth of September, 1696, ſhall be obſerved, according to its form and tenor; the merchandizes therein mentioned ſhall be reſtored; the governor of the fort taken there ſhall be ſet at liberty, if it be not already done; the differences ariſen concerning the execution of the ſaid capitulation, and the value of the goods there loſt, ſhall be adjudged and determined by the ſaid commiſſioners; who, immediately after the ratification of the preſent treaty, ſhall be inveſted with ſufficient authority for ſettling the limits and confines of the lands to be reſtored on either ſide, by virtue of the foregoing article, and likewiſe for exchanging of lands, as may conduce to the mutual intereſt and advantage of both Kings.

And to this end the commiſſioners ſo appointed ſhall, within the ſpace of three months from the time of the ratification of the preſent treaty, meet in the city of London, and within ſix months, to be reckoned from their firſt meeting, ſhall determine all differences and diſputes which may ariſe concerning this matter; after which, the articles the ſaid commiſſioners ſhall agree to, ſhall be ratified by both Kings, and ſhall have the ſame force and vigour as if they were inſerted word for word in the preſent treaty.

IX. All letters, as well of repriſal as of marque and counter-marque, which hitherto have for any cauſe been granted on either ſide, ſhall be and remain null and void; nor ſhall any the like letters be hereafter granted by either of the ſaid Kings againſt the ſubjects of the other, unleſs it be firſt made manifeſt feft that right hath been denied; and it fhall not be taken for a denial of right, unlefs the petition of the perfon, who defires letters of reprifal to be granted to him, be firft fhewn to the minifter refiding there on the part of the King againft whofe fubjects thofe letters are defired; that within the fpace of four months, or fooner, he may inquire into the contrary, or procure that fatisfaction be made with all fpeed from the party offending to the complainant. But if the King againft whofe fubjects reprifals are demanded, have no minifter refiding there, letters of reprifal fhall not be granted, till after the fpace of four months, to be reckoned from the day on which his petition was made and prefented to the King againft whofe fubjects reprifals are defired, or to his privy council.

X. For cutting off all matter of difpute and contention, which may arife concerning the reftitution of fhips, merchandizes, and other moveable goods, which either party may complain to be taken and detained from the other, in countries and on coafts far diftant, after the peace is concluded, and before it be notified there; all fhips, merchandizes, and other moveable goods, which fhall be taken by either fide, after the figning and publication of the prefent treaty, within the fpace of twelve days in the Britifh and North feas, as far as the Cape St. Vincent; within the fpace of ten weeks beyond the faid Cape, and on this fide of the Equinoctial Line or Equator, as well in the ocean and Mediterranean fea as elfewhere; laftly, within the fpace of fix months beyond the faid Line, throughout the whole world, fhall belong and remain unto the poffeffors, without any exception or further diftinction of time or place, or any confideration to be had of reftitution or compenfation.

XI. But if it happens, through inadvertency or imprudence, or any other caufe whatever, that any fubject of either of the faid two Kings fhall do or commit any thing, by land or fea, or on frefh water, any

I   where,

where, contrary to the prefent treaty, or that any particular article thereof is not fulfilled; this peace and
good correfpondence between the faid two Kings fhall
not on that account be interrupted or infringed, but
fhall remain in its former force, ftrength, and vigour,
and the faid fubject only fhall anfwer for his own fact,
and undergo the punifhment to be inflicted, according
to the cuftom and law of nations.

XII. But if (which God forbid) the differences now
compofed between the faid Kings fhould at any time
be renewed, and break out into open war, the fhips,
merchandizes, and all kind of moveable goods of either party, which fhall be found to be and remain
in the ports and dominions of the adverfe party, fhall
not be confifcated or brought under any inconveniency, but the whole fpace of fix months fhall be allowed to the fubjects of both of the faid Kings, that
they may carry away and tranfport the forefaid goods,
and any thing elfe that is theirs, whither they fhall
think fit, without any moleftation.

XIII. For what concerns the principality of Orange,
and other lands and dominions belonging to the faid
King of Great Britain, the feparate article of the
treaty of Nimeguen, concluded between the moft
Chriftian King and the States General of the United
Provinces, the 10th day of Auguft, 1678, fhall, according to its form and tenor, have full effect, and all
things that have been innovated and altered fhall be
reftored as they were before. All decrees, edicts, and
other acts, of what kind foever they be, without exception, which are in any manner contrary to the faid
treaty, or were made after the conclufion thereof, fhall
be held to be null and void, without any revival or
confequence for the future: and all things fhall be
reftored to the faid King in the fame ftate, and in the
fame manner, as he held and enjoyed them before he
was difpoffeffed thereof in the time of the war which
was ended by the faid treaty of Nimeguen, or which

he ought to have held and enjoyed, according to the said treaty. And, that an end may be put to all trouble, differences, processes, and questions, which may arise concerning the same, both the said Kings will name commissioners, who, with full and summary power, may compose and settle all these matters. And forasmuch as, by the authority of the most Christian King, the King of Great Britain was hindered from enjoying the revenues, rights, and profits, as well of his principality of Orange, as of other his dominions, which, after the conclusion of the treaty of Nimeguen, until the declaration of the present war, were under the power of the said most Christian King; the said most Christian King will restore, and cause to be restored in reality, with effect, and with the interest due, all those revenues, rights, and profits, according to the declarations and verifications that shall be made before the said commissioners.

XIV. The treaty of peace concluded between the most Christian King, and the late Elector of Brandenburgh, at St. Germains in Laye, the 29th of June, 1679, shall be restored in all its articles, and remain in its former vigour between his Sacred most Christian Majesty, and his Electoral Highness of Brandenburgh.

XV. Whereas it will greatly conduce to the public tranquillity, that the treaty be observed, which was concluded between his Sacred most Christian Majesty, and his Royal Highness of Savoy, on the 9th of August, 1696, it is agreed that the said treaty shall be confirmed by this article.

XVI. Under this present treaty of peace shall be comprehended those who shall be named by either party, with common consent, before the exchange of ratifications, or within six months after. But in the mean time, the most Serene and Mighty Prince William, King of Great Britain, and the most Serene and Mighty Prince Lewis, the most Christian King,

gratefully

gratefully acknowledging the sincere offices and indefatigable endeavours, which have been employed by
the most Serene and Mighty Prince Charles King of
Sweden, by the interposition of his mediation, in bringing this happy work of the peace, with the Divine af-
sistance, to the desired conclusion; and to shew the
like affection to him, it is by consent of all parties
stipulated and agreed, that his said Sacred Royal Majesty of Sweden shall, with all his kingdoms, countries, provinces, and rights, be included in this treaty,
and comprehended, in the best manner, in the present
pacification.

XVII. Lastly, The solemn ratifications of this present agreement and alliance, made in due form, shall
be delivered on both sides, and mutually and duly exchanged at the royal palace of Ryswick, in the province of Holland, within the space of three weeks, to
be reckoned from the day of the subscription, or sooner
if it may be.

In testimony of all and every the things before mentioned, and for their greater force, and to give
them all the vigour and full authority they ought
to have, the under-written Ambassadors Extraordinary and Plenipotentiaries, together with the
Illustrious and most Excellent the Extraordinary
Ambassador Mediator, have signed and sealed the
present instrument of peace. Done, &c.

Signed by the English and French Ambassadors, and
by the Mediator.

Separate Article.

BESIDES all that is concluded and stipulated by the
treaty of peace signed this present day, the 20th of
September, it is moreover agreed by the present separate article, which shall have the same force and
effect as if it was inserted word for word in the said
treaty, that the most Christian King shall covenant.

and

and agree, and by the prefent article he does covenant and agree, that it fhall be free for the Emperor
and the Empire, until the firft day of November
next, to accept the conditions of peace lately propofed by the moft Chriftian King, according to the declaration made on the firft day of this prefent month,
unlefs in the mean time it fhall be otherwife agreed
between his Imperial Majefty and the Empire, and
his moft Chriftian Majefty. And in cafe his Imperial Majefty does not, within the time prefixed, accept
thofe conditions, or that it be not otherwife agreed
between his Imperial Majefty and the Empire, and
his moft Chriftian Majefty, the faid treaty fhall have
its full effect, and be duly put in execution according to its form and tenor: and it fhall not be lawful for the King of Great Britain, directly or indirectly, on any account or caufe whatfoever, to act
contrary to the faid treaty.

[The TREATY OF UTRECHT, is printed from the copy
which was publifhed by authority in 1713.]

*The Treaty of Peace and Friendfhip between the moft
Serene and moft Potent Princefs* Anne, *by the grace
of God, Queen of* Great Britain, France, *and* Ireland, *and the moft Serene and moft Potent Prince*
Lewis *the* XIVth, *the moft Chriftian King, concluded
at* Utrecht, *the* $\frac{11}{1}$ *day of* $\frac{March}{April}$, 1713.

WHEREAS it has pleafed Almighty God, for
the glory of his name, and for the univerfal welfare, fo
to direct the minds of Kings for the healing, now in his
own time, the miferies of the wafted world, that they
are difpofed towards one another with a mutual defire
of making peace: be it therefore known to all and fingular whom it may concern, that under this Divine
guidance, the moft Serene and moft Potent Princefs
and Lady Anne, by the grace of God, Queen of
Great

Great Britain, France, and Ireland, and the moft
Serene and moft Potent Prince and Lord Lewis the
XIVth, by the grace of God, the moft Chriftian
King, confulting as well the advantage of their fubjects, as providing (as far as mortals are able to do)
for the perpetual tranquillity of the whole Chriftian
world, have refolved at laft to put an end to the war,
which was unhappily kindled, and has been obftinately
carried on above thefe ten years, being both cruel and
deftructive, by reafon of the frequency of battles, and
the effufion of Chriftian blood. And for promoting
this their royal purpofe, of their own proper motion,
and from that paternal care which they delight to ufe
towards their own fubjects, and the public weal of
Chriftendom, have nominated and appointed the moft
noble, illuftrious, and excellent Lords, their Royal
Majefties refpective Ambaffadors Extraordinary and
Plenipotentiaries, *viz.* her Sacred Royal Majefty of
Great Britain, the Right Reverend John, by Divine
permiffion, Bifhop of Briftol, Keeper of the Privy
Seal of England, one of her Majefty's Privy Council,
Dean of Windfor, and Regifter of the moft Noble
Order of the Garter; as alfo the moft Noble, Illuf-
trious, and Excellent Lord, Thomas Earl of Strafford,
Vifcount Wentworth of Wentworth Woodhoufe, and
Stainborough, Baron of Raby, one of her Majefty's Privy
Council, her Ambaffador Extraordinary and Plenipo-
tentiary to the High and Mighty Lords the States
General of the United Netherlands, Colonel of the
Royal regiment of Dragoons, Lieutenant General of
her Majefty's forces, firft Lord Commiffioner of the
Admiralty of Great Britain and Ireland, and Knight
of the moft Noble Order of the Garter; and his Sa-
cred Royal moft Chriftian Majefty, the moft Noble,
Illuftrious, and Excellent Lords, Nicolas, Marquis
of Huxelles, Marfhal of France; Knight of the King's
Orders, and Lieutenant General of the dukedom of
Burgundy; and Nicolas Mefnager, Knight of the King's
Order of St. Michael: and have furnifhed the faid

Ambaf-

Ambaſſadors Extraordinary with full and ample power to treat, agree of, and conclude a firm and laſting peace between their Royal Majeſties. Wherefore the aforeſaid Ambaſſadors, after divers and important conſultations had in the congreſs held at Utrecht for that purpoſe, having at length overcome, without the intervention of any mediator, all the obſtacles which hindered the end of ſo wholeſome a deſign, and having invoked the Divine aſſiſtance, that God would be pleaſed to preſerve this their work intire and unviolated, and to prolong it to the lateſt poſterity, after having mutually communicated and duly exchanged their full powers (copies whereof are inſerted word for word at the end of this inſtrument) they have agreed on the reciprocal conditions of peace and friendſhip between their above-mentioned Majeſties, and their people and ſubjects, as follows:.

I. That there be an univerſal perpetual peace, and a true and ſincere friendſhip, between the moſt Serene and moſt Potent Princeſs Anne, Queen of Great Britain, and the moſt Serene and moſt Potent Prince Lewis the XIVth, the moſt Chriſtian King, and their heirs and ſucceſſors, as alſo the kingdoms, ſtates, and ſubjects of both, as well without as within Europe; and that the ſame be ſo ſincerely and inviolably preſerved and cultivated, that the one do promote the intereſt, honour, and advantage of the other, and that a faithful neighbourhood on all ſides, and a ſecure cultivating of peace and friendſhip, do daily flouriſh again and increaſe.

II. That all enmities, hoſtilities, diſcords, and wars, between the ſaid Queen of Great Britain and the ſaid moſt Chriſtian King, and their ſubjects, do ceaſe and be aboliſhed, ſo that on both ſides they do wholly refrain and deſiſt from all plundering, depredation, harm-doing, injuries, and annoyance whatſoever, as well by land, as by ſea and freſh waters, in all parts of the world, and chiefly through all tracts, dominions, and

and places of what kind foever, of the kingdoms, countries, and territories of either fide.

III. All offences, injuries, harms, and damages, which the aforefaid Queen of Great Britain, and her fubjects, or the aforefaid moft Chriftian King, and his fubjects, have fuffered the one from the other, during this war, fhall be buried in oblivion, fo that neither on account, or under pretence thereof, or of any other thing, fhall either hereafter, or the fubjects of either, do or give, caufe or fuffer to be done or given, to the other, any hoftility, enmity, moleftation, or hinderance, by themfelves or by others, fecretly or openly, directly or indirectly, under colour of right, or by way of fact.

IV. Furthermore, for adding a greater ftrength to the peace which is reftored, and to the faithful friendfhip which is never to be violated, and for cutting off all occafions of diftruft, which might at any time arife from the eftablifhed right and order of the hereditary fucceffion to the crown of Great Britain, and the limitation thereof by the laws of Great Britain (made and enacted in the reigns of the late King William the Third, of glorious memory, and of the prefent Queen) to the iffue of the abovefaid Queen, and in default thereof, to the moft Serene Princefs Sophia, Dowager of Brunfwic-Hanover, and her heirs in the Proteftant line of Hanover. That therefore the faid fucceffion may remain fafe and fecure, the moft Chriftian King fincerely and folemnly acknowledges the abovefaid limitation of the fucceffion to the kingdom of Great Britain, and on the faith and word of a King, on the pledge of his own and his fucceffors honour, he does declare and engage, that he accepts and approves the fame, and that his heirs and fucceffors do and fhall accept and approve the fame for ever. And under the fame obligation of the word and honour of a King, the moft Chriftian King promifes, that no one befides the Queen herfelf, and her fucceffors, according to the feries of the faid limitation, fhall ever by him, or by his heirs or fucceffors, be acknowledged or reputed to be King or

Queen

Queen of Great Britain. And for adding more ample credit to the said acknowledgment and promises, the most Christian King does engage, that whereas the person who, in the life-time of the late King James the Second, did take upon him the title of Prince of Wales, and since his decease, that of King of Great Britain, is lately gone, of his own accord, out of the kingdom of France, to reside in some other place, he the aforesaid most Christian King, his heirs and successors, will take all possible care that he shall not at any time hereafter, or under any pretence whatsoever, return into the kingdom of France, or any the dominions thereof.

V. Moreover, the most Christian King promises, as well in his own name, as in that of his heirs and successors, that they will at no time whatever disturb or give any molestation to the Queen of Great Britain, her heirs and successors, descended from the aforesaid Protestant line, who possess the crown of Great Britain, and the dominions belonging thereunto. Neither will the aforesaid most Christian King, or any one of his heirs, give at any time any aid, succour, favour, or counsel, directly or indirectly, by land or by sea, in money, arms, ammunition, warlike provision, ships, soldiers, seamen, or any other way, to any person or persons, whosoever they be, who for any cause, or under any pretext whatsoever, should hereafter endeavour to oppose the said succession, either by open war, or by fomenting seditions and forming conspiracies against such Prince or Princes who are in possession of the throne of Great Britain, by virtue of the acts of parliament afore-mentioned, or against that Prince or Princess to whom the succession to the crown of Great Britain shall be open, according to the said acts of parliament.

VI. Whereas the most destructive flame of war, which is to be extinguished by this peace, arose chiefly from thence, that the security and liberties of Europe could by no means bear the union of the kingdoms of

France

France and Spain under one and the same King; and
whereas it has at length been brought to pass, by the
assistance of the Divine Power, upon the most earnest
instances of her Sacred Royal Majesty of Great Britain, and with the consent both of the most Christian
and of the Catholic King, that this evil should in all
times to come be obviated, by means of renunciations
drawn in the most effectual form, and executed in the
most solemn manner, the tenor whereof is as follows:

Letters Patents by the KING,

*Which admit the Renunciation of the King of Spain
to the Crown of France, and those of M. the Duke
of Berry, and of M. the Duke of Orleans, to the
Crown of Spain.*

LEWIS, by the grace of God, King of France
and Navarre: to all people present and to come, greeting. During the various revolutions of a war, wherein
we have fought only to maintain the justice of the rights
of the King, our most dear, and most beloved grandson, to the monarchy of Spain, we have never ceased
to desire peace. The greatest successes did not at all
dazzle us, and the contrary events, which the hand of
God made use of to try us, rather than to destroy us,
did not give birth to that desire in us, but found it
there. But the time marked out by Divine Providence,
for the repose of Europe, was not yet come; the diftant fear of seeing one day our crown, and that of Spain,
upon the head of one and the same Prince, did always
make an equal impression on the Powers which were
united against us; and this fear, which had been the
principal cause of the war, seemed also to lay an infu-
perable obstacle in the way to peace. At last, after
many fruitless negotiations, God being moved with
the sufferings and groans of so many people, was
pleased to open a surer way to come at so difficult a
peace. But the same alarms still subsisting, the first
and principal condition, which was proposed to us by

our

our moſt dear and moſt beloved ſiſter the Queen of
Great Britain, as the eſſential and neceſſary foundation
of treating, was, that the King of Spain, our ſaid brother and grandſon, keeping the monarchy of Spain and
of the Indies, ſhould renounce for himſelf and his
deſcendants for ever, the rights which his birth might
at any time give him and them to our crown; that on
the other hand, our moſt dear and moſt beloved grandſon the Duke of Berry, and our moſt dear and moſt
beloved nephew the Duke of Orleans, ſhould likewiſe
renounce, for themſelves, and for their deſcendants,
male and female for ever, their rights to the monarchy
of Spain and the Indies. Our ſaid ſiſter cauſed it to
be repreſented to us, that without a formal and po-
ſitive aſſurance upon this point, which alone could be
the bond of peace, Europe would never be at reſt; all
the Powers which ſhare the ſame being equally per-
ſuaded, that it was for their general intereſt, and for
their common ſecurity, to continue a war, whereof
no one could foreſee the end, rather than to be expoſed
to behold the ſame Prince become one day maſter of
two monarchies ſo powerful as thoſe of France and
Spain. But as this Princeſs (whoſe indefatigable zeal
for re-eſtabliſhing the general tranquillity we cannot
ſufficiently praiſe) was ſenſible of all the reluctancy we
had to conſent that one of our children, ſo worthy to inherit the ſucceſſion of our forefathers, ſhould neceſſarily
be excluded from it, if the misfortunes, wherewith it has
pleaſed God to afflict us in our family, ſhould moreover take from us, in the perſon of the Dauphin, our
moſt dear and moſt beloved great grandſon, the only re-
mainder of thoſe Princes which our kingdom has ſo
juſtly lamented with us; ſhe entered into our pain, and
after having jointly ſought out gentler means of ſecuring the peace, we agreed with our ſaid ſiſter to propoſe
to the King of Spain other dominions, inferior, indeed,
to thoſe which he poſſeſſes, yet the value thereof would
ſo much the more increaſe under his reign, inaſmuch
as in that caſe he would preſerve his rights, and annex

to

to our crown a part of the said dominions, if he came one time or other to succeed us. We employed therefore the strongest reasons to persuade him to accept this alternative. We gave him to understand, that the duty of his birth was the first which he ought to consult; that he owed himself to his house, and to his country, before he was obliged to Spain; that if he were wanting to his first engagements, he would perhaps one day in vain regret his having abandoned those rights which he would be no more able to maintain. We added to these reasons, the personal motives of friendship and of tender love, which we thought likely to move him; the pleasure we should have in seeing him from time to time near us, and in passing some part of our days with him, which we might promise ourselves from the neighbourhood of the dominions that were offered him, the satisfaction of instructing him ourselves concerning the state of our affairs, and of relying upon him for the future; so that, if God should preserve to us the Dauphin, we could give our kingdom, in the person of the King our brother and grandson, a regent instructed in the art of government; and that if this child, so precious to us and to our subjects, were also taken from us, we should at least have the consolation of leaving to our people a virtuous King, fit to govern them, and who would likewise annex to our crown very considerable dominions. Our instances, reiterated with all the force, and with all the tender affection necessary to persuade a son, who so justly deserves those efforts which we made for preserving him to France, produced nothing but reiterated refusals on his part, ever to abandon such brave and faithful subjects, whose zeal for him had been distinguished in those conjunctures when his throne seemed to be the most shaken. So that, persisting with an invincible firmness in his first resolution, asserting likewise, that it was more glorious and more advantageous for our house, and for our kingdom, than that which we pressed him to take, he declared in the meet-

ing

ing of the States of the kingdom of Spain, affembled at Madrid for that purpofe, that for obtaining a ge-. neral peace, and fecuring the tranquillity of Europe by a balance of power, he of his own proper motion, of his own free will, and without any conftraint, renounced for himfelf, for his heirs and fucceffors for ever and ever, all pretenfions, rights, and titles, which he or or any of his defcendants have at prefent, or may have at any time to come whatfoever, to the fuc- ceffion of our crown; that he held for excluded there- from, himfelf, his children, heirs, and defcendants for ever; that he confented for himfelf and for them, that now, as well as then, his right, and that of his defcendants, fhould pafs over and be transferred to him among the Princes whom the law of fucceffion and the order of birth calls or fhall call to inherit our crown, in default of our faid brother and grandfon the King of Spain, and of his defcendants, as it is more amply fpecified in the act of renunciation ap- proved by the States of his kingdom; and confequently he declared, that he defifted particularly from the right which hath been added to that of his birth by our letters patents of the month of December, 1700, whereby we declared, that it was our will that the King of Spain, and his defcendants, fhould always preferve the rights of their birth and original, in the fame manner as if they refided actually in our kingdom; and from the regiftry which was made of our faid letters patents, both in our court of parliament, and in our chamber of accounts at. Paris. We are fen- fible, as King, and as Father, how much it were to be defired that the general peace could have been con- cluded without a renunciation, which makes fo great a change in our Royal Houfe, and in the ancient order of fucceeding to our crown; but we are yet more fenfible how much it is our duty to fecure fpeedily to our fubjects a peace, which is fo neceffary for them. We fhall never forget the efforts which they made for us during the long continuance of a war which we

could

could not have fupported if their zeal had not been much more extenfive than their power. The welfare of a people fo faithful, is to us a fupreme law, which ought to be preferred to any other confideration. It is to this law that we this day facrifice the right of a grandfon who is fo dear to us, and by the price which the general peace will coft our tender love, we fhall at leaft have the comfort of fhewing our fubjects, that, even at the expence of our blood, they will always keep the firft place in our heart.

For thefe caufes, and other important confiderations us thereunto moving, after having feen in our council the faid act of renunciation of the King of Spain, our faid brother and grandfon, of the fifth of November laft, as alfo the acts of renunciation which our faid grandfon the Duke of Berry, and our faid nephew the Duke of Orleans, made reciprocally of their rights to the crown of Spain, as well for themfelves as for their defcendants, male and female, in confequence of the renunciation of our faid brother and grandfon the King of Spain, the whole hereunto annexed, with a copy collated of the faid letters patents of the month of December, 1700, under the counter-feal of our chancery, of our fpecial grace, full power, and Royal authority, we have declared, decreed, and ordained, and by thefe prefents, figned with our hand, we do declare, decree, and ordain, we will, and it is our pleafure, that the faid act of renunciation of our faid brother and grandfon the King of Spain, and thofe of our faid grandfon the Duke of Berry, and of our faid nephew the Duke of Orleans, which we have admitted, and do admit, be regiftered in all our courts of par- liament, and chambers of our accounts in our king- dom, and other places where it fhall be neceffary, in order to their being executed according to their form and tenor. And confequently, we will and intend, that our faid letters patents of the month of December, 1700, be and remain null, and as if they had never been made, that they be brought back to us, and that

in

in the margin of the registers of our said court of parliament; and of our said chamber of accounts, where the enrolment of the said letters patents is, the extract of these presents be placed and inserted, the better to signify our intention as to the revocation and nullity of the said letters. We will, that in conformity to the said act of renunciation of our said brother and grandson the King of Spain, he be from henceforth looked upon and considered as excluded from our succession, that his heirs, successors, and descendants be likewise excluded for ever, and looked upon as incapable of enjoying the same. We understand that in failure of them, all rights to our said crown, and succession to our dominions, which might at any time whatsoever belong and appertain to them, be and remain transferred to our most dear and most beloved grandson the Duke of Berry, and to his children and descendants, being males born in lawful marriage; and successively, in failure of them, to those of the Princes of our Royal House, and their descendants, who in right of their birth, or by the order established since the foundation of our monarchy, ought to succeed to our crown. And so we command our beloved and trusty counsellors, the members of our court of parliament at Paris, that they do cause these presents, together with the acts of renunciation made by our said brother and grandson the King of Spain, by our said grandson the Duke of Berry, and by our said nephew the Duke of Orleans, to be read, published, and registered, and the contents thereof to be kept, observed, and executed, according to their form and tenor, fully, peaceably, and perpetually, ceasing, and causing to cease, all molestations and hinderances, notwithstanding any laws, statutes, usages, customs, decrees, regulations, and other matters contrary thereunto; whereto, and to the derogations of the derogations therein contained, we have derogated, and do derogate by these presents, for this purpose only, and without being brought into precedent. For such is our pleasure.

And

And to the end that this may be a matter firm and
lasting for ever, we have caused our seal to be affixed
to these presents. Given at Versailles, in the month
of March, in the year of our Lord 1713, and of our
reign the seventieth. Signed, L E W I S; and underneath, By the King, *Phelypeaux*. *Visa Phelypeaux*.
And sealed with the great seal on green wax, with
strings of red and green silk.

Read and published, the court being assembled, and
registered among the rolls of the court, the King's
attorney-general being heard, and moving for the
same, to the end that they may be executed according to their form and tenor, in pursuance of,
and in conformity to the acts of this day. At
Paris, in parliament, the 15th of March, 1713.

(Signed)   *Dongois.*

The KING.

WHEREAS, on the 5th of November, in this
present year 1712, before Don Manuel of Vadillo
and Velasco, my secretary of state, and chief notary
of the kingdoms of Castille and Leon, and witnesses,
I delivered, swore to, and signed a public instrument
of the tenor following, which is word for word as here
ensues:

D. Philip, by the grace of God, King of Castille,
Leon, Arragon, the Two Sicilies, Jerusalem, Navarre,
Granada, Toledo, Valentia, Galicia, Majorca, Se-
ville, Sardinia, Corduba, Corsica, Murcia, Jaen, the
Algarves, Algezira, Gibraltar, the Canary Islands, the
East and West Indies, the Islands and Terra Firma of
the ocean, Archduke of Austria, Duke of Burgundy,
Brabant, and Milan, Count of Habspurg, Flanders,
Tirol, and Barcelona, Lord of Biscay, and Molina,
&c. By the account and information of this instru-
ment and writing, of renunciation and relinquishment,
and that it may remain for a perpetual remembrance,
I do

I do make known and declare to Kings, Princes, Potentates, Commonwealths, Communities, and particular persons, which now are, and shall be in future ages; That it being one of the principal positions of the treaties of peace depending between the crowns of Spain and of France, with that of England, for the rendering it firm and lasting, and proceeding to a general one, on the maxim of securing for ever the universal good and quiet of Europe, by an equal weight of power, so that many being united in one, the balance of the equality desired might not turn to the advantage of one, and the danger and hazard of the rest; it was proposed and insisted on by England, and it was agreed to on my part, and on that of the King my grandfather, that for avoiding at any time whatever the union of this monarchy with that of France, and the possibility that it might happen in any case, reciprocal renunciations should be made by me, and for all my descendants, to the possibily of succeeding to the monarchy of France, and on the part of those Princes, and of all their race, present and to come, to that of succeeding to this monarchy; by forming a proper project of abdication of all rights which might be claimed by the two Royal houses of this and of that monarchy, as to their succeeding mutually to each other; by separating, by the legal means of my renunciation, my branch from the Royal stem of France, and all the branches of France from the stem of the blood-royal of Spain; by taking care at the same time, in pursuance of the fundamental and perpetual maxim of the balance of power in Europe, which persuades and justifies the avoiding, in all cases imaginable, the union of the monarchy of France with that of Spain, that the inconvenience should likewise be provided against, lest, in default of my issue, the case should happen that this monarchy should devolve again to the House of Austria, whose dominions and dependencies, even without the union of the Empire, would make it formidable; a motive which at other times made it justifiable to se-

parate

parate the hereditary dominions of the Houfe of Auftria from the body of the Spanifh monarchy; it being
agreed and fettled to this end by England with me, and
with the King my grandfather, that in failure of me,
and of my iffue, the Duke of Savoy, and his fons and
defcendants, being males, born in conftant lawful
marriage, are to enter upon the fucceffion of this monarchy; and in default of his male line, the Prince
Amadeo of Carignan, and his fons and defcendants,
being males, born in conftant lawful marriage; and in
default of his line, Prince Thomas, brother of the
Prince of Carignan, his fons and defcendants, being
males, born in conftant lawful marriage, who, as defcendants of the Infanta Donna Catharina, daughter
of Philip the Second, and being exprefsly called, have
a clear and known right, fuppofing the friendfhip and
perpetual alliance which the Duke of Savoy, and his
defcendants, are to folicit and obtain from this crown;
it being to be believed, that by this perpetual and
never-ceafing hope, the needle of the balance may
remain invariable, and all the Powers, wearied with
the toil and uncertainty of battles, may be amicably
kept in an equal poife; it not remaining in the difpofal
of any of the parties to alter this federal equilibrium
by way of any contract of renunciation, or retroceffion, fince the fame reafon which induced its being
admitted, demonftrates its permanency, a fundamental
conftitution being formed, which may fettle by an unalterable law the fucceffion of what is to come.   In
confequence of what is above faid, and for the love I
bear to the Spaniards; and from the knowledge I have
of what I owe to them, and the repeated experience
of their fidelity, and for making a return to Divine
· Providence, by this refignation to its deftiny, for the
great benefit of having placed and maintained me on
the throne, among fuch illuftrious and well-deferving
vaffals, I have determined to abdicate, for. myfelf, and
all my defcendants, the right of fucceeding to the
· crown of France, defiring not to depart from living

-and dying with my beloved and faithful Spaniards;
leaving to all my defcendants the infeparable bond of
their fidelity and love.   And to the end that this refolution may have its due effect, and that the matter
may ceafe which has been looked upon as one of the
principal motives of the war which has hitherto afflicted Europe, of my own motion, free, fpontaneous,
and unconftrained will, I Don Philip, by the grace
of God, King of Caftille, Leon, Arragon, the Two
Sicilies, Jerufalem, Navarre, Granada, Toledo, Valencia, Galicia, Majorca, Seville, Sardinia, Corduba, Corfica,
Murcia, Jaen, the Algarves, Algezira, Gibraltar, the
Canary Iflands, the Eaft and Weft Indies, the Iflands
and Terra Firma of the ocean, Archduke of Auftria,
Duke of Burgundy, Brabant, and Milan, Count of
Habfpurg, Flanders, Tirol, and Barcelona, Lord of
Bifcay and Molina, &c. do by this prefent inftrument,
for myfelf, for my heirs and fucceffors, renounce, quit,
and relinquifh, for ever and ever, all pretenfions, rights,
and titles, which I have, or any defcendant of mine
hath at prefent, or may have at any time to come, to
the fucceffion of the crown of France; and I declare,
and hold myfelf for excluded and feparated, me and
my fons, heirs, and defcendants for ever, for excluded
and difabled abfolutely, and without limitation, difference, and diftinction of perfons, degrees, fexes, and
times, from the act and right of fucceeding to the
crown of France.   And I will and confent, for myfelf
and my faid defcendants, that now, as well as then, it
may be taken to be paffed over and transferred to him,
who by mine and their being excluded, difabled, and incapacitated, fhall be found next and immediate in degree to the King by whofe death it fhall become vacant:
and the fucceffion to the faid crown of France is at
any time, and in any cafe, to be fettled on and given to
him, to have and to hold the fame as true and lawful
fucceffor, in the fame manner as if I and my defcendants had not been born, or been in the world; fince
for fuch are we to be held and efteemed, becaufe in
my perfon, and in that of my defcendants, there is no
                                        confideration

confideration to be had, or foundation to be made of
active or paffive reprefentation, beginning, or continuation of lineage effective, or contentive of fubftance,
blood, or quality, nor can the defcent or computation
of degrees of thofe perfons be derived from the moft
Chriftian King, my lord and grandfather, nor from
the Dauphin, my father, nor from the glorious Kings
their progenitors; nor by any other means can they
come into the fucceffion, nor take poffeffion of the
degree of proximity, and exclude from it the perfon
who, as is abovefaid, fhall be found next in degree.
I will and confent for myfelf, and for my defcendants,
that from this time, as well as then, this right be looked
upon and confidered as paffed over and transferred to
the Duke of Berry, my brother, and to his fons and
defcendants, being males, born in conftant lawful
marriage; and in default of his male iffue, to the Duke
of Orleans, my uncle, and to his fons and defcendants, being males, born in conftant lawful marriage;
and in default of his iffue, to the Duke of Bourbon,
my coufin, and to his fons and defcendants, being males,
born in conftant lawful marriage; and in like manner
fucceffively to all the Princes of the blood of France,
their fons and defcendants, being males, for ever and
ever, according to the place and order in which they
fhall be called to the crown by right of their birth;
and confequently to that perfon among the faid Princes,
who (I and all my faid defcendants being, as is abovefaid, excluded, difabled, and incapacitated) fhall be found
the neareft in immediate degree after that King by
whofe death the vacancy of the crown of France fhall
happen, and to whom the fucceffion ought to belong
at any time, and in any cafe whatfoever, that he may
poffefs the fame as true and lawful fucceffor, in the
fame manner as if I and my defcendants had not been
born.   And for the greater ftrength of this act of abdication of all the rights and titles which appertained
to me, and to all my fons and defcendants, of fucceeding to the aforefaid crown of France, I depart

from and relinquifh efpecially that which might moreover accrue to the rights of birth from the letters patents, or inftrument, whereby the King my grandfather preferved and referved to me, and enabled me
to enjoy the right of fucceffion to the crown of France;
which inftrument was difpatched at Verfailles in the
month of December, in the year 1700, and paffed,
and approved, and regiftered by the Parliament. I
will that it cannot ferve me for a foundation to the
purpofes therein provided for, and I reject and renounce
it, and hold it for null, void, and of no force, and for
cancelled, and as if no fuch inftrument had ever been
executed. I promife and oblige myfelf, on the faith
of a King's word, that as much as fhall relate to my
part, and that of my fons and defcendants, which are
and fhall be, I will take care of the obfervation and
accomplifhment of this writing, without permitting or
confenting that any thing be done contrary thereunto,
directly or indirectly, in the whole, or in part; and I
relinquifh and depart from all and all manner of remedies, known or unknown, ordinary or extraordinary,
and which by common right, or fpecial privilege,
might belong to us, to me, and to my fons and defcendants, to reclaim, mention, or alledge againft what
is abovefaid; and I renounce them all, and efpecially
that of evident prejudice, enormous, and moft enormous, which may be reckoned to have happened in
this relinquifhment and renunciation of the right of
being able at any time to fucceed to the crown afore-
mentioned. I will that none of the faid remedies,
nor others, of whatfoever name, ufe, importance, and
quality they may be, do avail us, or can avail us.
And if in fact, or under any colour, we fhould endeavour to feize the faid kingdom by force of arms, by
making or moving war, offenfive or defenfive, from
this time for ever, that is to be held, judged, and declared, for an unlawful, unjuft, and wrongfully undertaken war, and for violence, invafion, and ufurp-
ation, done againft reafon and confcience; and on the

3   contrary,

contrary, that is to be judged and efteemed a juft, lawful, and allowed war, which fhall be made or moved in behalf of him who, by the exclufion of me, and of my faid fons and defcendants, ought to fucceed to the faid crown of France, to whom the fubjects and natives thereof are to apply themfelves, and to obey him, to take and perform the oath and homage of fealty, and to ferve him as their lawful king and lord. And the relinquifhment and renunciation, for me, and my faid fons and defcendants, is to be firm, ftable, valid, and irrevocable perpetually, for ever and ever. And I declare and promife, that I have not made, neither will I make, any proteftation or reclaiming, in public or in fecret, to the contrary, which may hinder or diminifh the force of what is contained in this writing; and that if I fhould make it, although it be fworn to, it is not to be valid, neither can it have any force; and for the greater ftrength and fecurity of what is contained in this renunciation, and of what is faid and promifed on my part therein, I give again the pledge of my faith and Royal word, and I fwear folemnly by the Gofpels contained in this Miffal, upon which I lay my right hand, that I will obferve, maintain, and accomplifh this act and inftrument of renunciation, as well for myfelf as for all my fucceffors, heirs, and defcendants, in all the claufes therein contained, according to the moft natural, literal, and plain fenfe and conftruction; and that I have not fought, neither will I feek, any difpenfation from this oath; and if it fhall be fought for by any particular perfon, or fhall be granted *motu proprio*, I will not ufe it, nor take any advantage of it. Nay, in fuch cafe as that it fhould be granted me, I make another the like oath, that there may always be and remain one oath above and beyond all difpenfations which may be granted me. And I deliver this writing before the prefent fecretary, notary of this my kingdom, and I have figned it, and commanded it to be fealed with my Royal feal; there being provided and called as witneffes, the Car-

dinal

dinal Don Francisco de Judice, Inquisitor General,
and Archbishop of Montreal, one of my Council of
State; Don Joseph Fernandez, of Velasco and Tobar,
Constable of Castille, Duke of Frias, Gentleman of
my Chamber, my High Steward of my Houshold,
great Cup-bearer, and great Huntsman; Don Juan
Claros Alfonso Perez de Gusman el Bueno, Duke of
Medina Sidonia, Knight of the Order of the Holy
Ghost, my great Master of the Horse, Gentleman of
my Chamber, and one of my Council of State; Don
Francisco Andres de Benavides, Count of Santistevan,
one of my Council of State, and High Steward to the
Queen; Don Carlos Homodei Laco de la Vega,
Marquis of Almonacir, and Count of Casa Palma,
Gentleman of my Chamber, one of my Council of
State, and Great Master of the Horse to the Queen;
Don Restayno Cantelmo, Duke of Popoli, Knight of
the Order of the Holy Ghost, Gentleman of my
Chamber, and Captain of my Italian Life Guards;
Don Fernando of Arragon and Moncada, Duke of
Montalto, Marquis of los Velez, Commander of Silla
and Benaful in the Order of Montessa, Gentleman of
my Chamber, and one of my Council of State; Don
Antonio Sebastian de Toledo, Marquis of Mansera,
Gentleman of my Chamber, one of my Council of
State, and President of that of Italy; Don Juan Do-
mingo, of Haro and Guzman, great Commander in
the Order of St. James, one of my Council of State;
Don Joachim Ponce de Leon, Duke of Arcos, Gentleman of my Chamber, great Commander in the
Order of Calatrava, one of my Council of State; Don
Domingo de Giudice, Duke of Giovenazzo, one of
my Council of State; Don Manuel Coloma, Marquis
of Canales, Gentleman of my Chamber, one of my
Council of State, and Captain General of the Artillery of Spain; Don Joseph de Solis, Duke of Mon-
tellano, one of my Council of State; Don Rodrigo
Manuel Manrique de Lara, Count of Frigiliana, Gentleman of my Chamber, one of my Council of State;
and

and President of that of the Indies; Don Isidro de la-
Cueva, Marquis of Bedmar, Knight of the Order of
the Holy Ghost, Gentleman of my Chamber, one of
my Council of State, President of that of the Orders,
and first Minister of War; Don Francisco Ronquillo
Briceño, Count of Gramedo, Governor of my Council of Castille; Don Lorenzo Armangual, Bishop of
Gironda, one of my Council and Chamber of Castille, and Governor of that of the Revenues; Don
Carlos de Borja and Centellas, Patriarch of the Indies, one of my Council of the Orders, my Chaplain
and Great Almoner, and Vicar General of my Armies;
Don Martin de Guzman, Marquis of Montealegre,
Gentleman of my Chamber, and Captain of my Guard
of Halberdiers; Don Pedro de Toledo Sarmiento,
Count of Gondomar, one of my Council and Chamber of Castille; Don Francisco Rodrigues de Menda-
rosqueta, Commissary General of the Cruzada; and
Don Melchior de Avellaneda, Marquis of Valdecañas,
one of my Council of War, and Director General of
the Infantry of Spain.

I the K I N G.

I Don Manuel of Vadillo and Velasco, Knight of
the Order of Saint James, and Commander of Bo-
fuelo in that of Calatrava, Secretary of State to his
Majesty, Public Notary, and Writer, in his kingdoms
and dominions, who was present at the delivery, and
at all the rest herein above contained, do testify the
same: and in witness of the truth I have signed it, and
put my name thereto, in Madrid, the fifth of November, 1712.   *Manuel Vadillo y Velasco.*

Now in regard to the federal conventions, whereof
mention is made in the said instrument here inserted,
and to the end it may appear authentically to all the
parties where it appertains, and who may pretend to
make use of the contents thereof; and for all the effects
which may take place in right, and which may be de-

A a 4   rived

rived from the delivery hereof, under the claufes, conditions, and fuppofitions therein contained, I have
commanded thefe prefents to be made out, figned with
my hand, and fealed with the feal of my Royal arms,
and counterfigned by my underwritten Secretary of
State, and Chief Notary of thefe my kingdoms, at
Buen Retiro, the feventh of November, 1712.

(L. S.)   *I the* **K I N G.**

Manuel de Vadillo y Velafco.

Read and publifhed, the court being affembled, and
   regiftered in the rolls of the court, the King's
   advocate general being heard, and moving for the
   fame, to the end that it may be executed according to the form and tenor thereof, in purfuance
   of, and in conformity to the acts of this day.
   At Paris, in parliament, the 15th of March,
   1713.

(Signed)   *Dongois.*

I Don Francifco Antonio le Quincoces, Knight of
the Order of St. James, one of his Majefty's Council,
and Secretary of that of the Chamber, and of State
of Caftille, Public Notary and Writer in his kingdoms
and dominions,

   Do certify, that in purfuance of the propofition
which the King our Lord (whom God preferve) made
to the kingdom affembled in Cortes, reprefented by
all the knights deputies from the cities and towns
which have a vote therein, the fifth day of this prefent
month and year, in his Royal palace of Buen Retiro,
and upon fight of the inftrument of renunciation, delivered by his Majefty the fame day, month, and year,
before Don Manuel of Vadillo and Velafco, his Secretary of State, and Public Notary and Writer in all his
kingdoms and dominions, which his Majefty ordered
him to prefent, and which was read and publifhed in
the meeting of the Cortes, which the kingdom held
for

for this alone, the ninth of this month, the following refolution was agreed upon:

That the moſt humble repreſentation be made by the kingdom, laying ourſelves at the Royal feet of his Majeſty, giving him immortal thanks for the immenſe benefits, and exceeding great favours, wherewith he has been pleaſed to honour and exalt the Spaniſh nation, by taking care of the greateſt good and advantage of his moſt loving vaſſals, by procuring to this monarchy the eaſe of this deſired peace and tranquillity. And that the kingdom, deſiring on their part to contribute to the attaining the Royal intention of his Majeſty, aſſents to, and if it were neceſſary for the greater authority, validity, and ſtrength, approves and confirms the renunciation which his Majeſty is pleaſed to make for himſelf, and in the name of all his Royal deſcendants, to the ſucceſſion which poſſibly may happen of the monarchy of France, with this circumſtance, that the like renunciation to this crown is to be executed by the Princes of that Royal family, and their deſcendants: and likewiſe the perpetual excluſion of the Houſe of Auſtria from the dominions of this monarchy; and in like manner, in caſe of failure (which God forbid) of the Royal iſſue of his Majeſty, the calling of the Houſe of the Duke of Savoy, and of all his ſons, and male deſcendants, born in conſtant lawful matrimony; and in default of all theſe lines, of the Prince Amadeus of Carignan, his ſons, and male deſcendants, born in conſtant lawful matrimony; and in failure thereof, of the Prince Thomas, brother of the ſaid Prince of Carignan, his ſons, and male deſcendants, born in conſtant lawful matrimony, who as deſcendants of the Infanta Donna Catharina, daughter of Philip the Second, and being expreſsly called, have a clear and known right, ſuppoſing the friendſhip and perpetual alliance with this crown, which ought to be ſought and obtained by the Duke of Savoy, and his deſcendants. And that the kingdom approves, agrees to, and ratifies all theſe three things, and each of
them,

them, with the fame qualities, conditions, and fuppofitions, as are expreffed, inferred, and concluded in.
the faid inftrument of renunciation executed by his
Majefty, which has been mentioned and referred to.
And laftly, that for fecuring and eftablifhing the
ftrength of thefe treaties, thefe kingdoms oblige them-:
felves, with all their power and force, to caufe to be,
maintained the Royal refolutions of his Majefty, fa-:
crificing in his Royal fervice, even to the laft drop of·
their blood, offering to his Majefty their lives and for-
tunes in token of their love. And that for the eternal
remembrance and obfervance of the Royal deliberation
of his Majefty, and agreement of the kingdom, it be
defired in their name (as in effect they have defired and
petitioned by their reprefentation and confultation made
the fame ninth day of this month) that his Majefty
would be pleafed to order, that by annulling all that
fhall be found to the contrary, it be eftablifhed as a
fundamental law, as well the aforefaid renunciations,
as the perpetual exclufion of the Houfe of Auftria
from the dominions of this crown, and the calling of.
that of Savoy to the fucceffion of thefe kingdoms, in
default (which God forbid) of defcendants from his
Majefty; which the kingdom, with the approbation
of his Majefty, does even now agree to, as the foundation whereon depends the greateft good and advantage of this monarchy, fo much purfued, favoured,
and exalted by the Royal benevolence of his Majefty.
And the King our lord, having agreed to this unanimous and uniform refolution and reprefentation of
all the knights deputies in the Cortes of the kingdom, he has been pleafed, by his Royal decree of the
feventeenth of this month, to command it to be re-
mitted to his fupreme council, jointly with the writing
of renunciation, ordaining that the tenor of the law
be forthwith formed, extended, and difpofed, with all
the circumftances of clearnefs and ftrength, for its
more inviolable and perpetual obfervation.

As

As all that is abovefaid does more largely appear from the aforementioned inftruments, the refolution, and fupplication of the kingdom, which are cited, and to which I refer.   And this certificate, figned with my hand, fealed with the feal of the Royal arms of his Majefty, I give by virtue of his Royal order, in the paper of the Marquis of Mejorada and of Breña, one of his Council, Gentleman of his Chamber, his Secretary of State, and of the univerfal difpatch.   At Madrid, the ninth of November, 1712.

(L. S.) *Don Francifco de Quincoces.*

CHARLES, fon ·of France, Duke of Berry, Alenfon, and Angoulefme, Vifcount of Vernon, Andely, and Gifors, Lord of the Chatellenies of Coignac and Merpins; to all Kings, Princes, Commonwealths, Communities, and to all other bodies, and private perfons, prefent and to come, be it known.   All the Powers of Europe finding themfelves almoft ruined on account of the prefent wars, which have carried defolation to the frontiers, and into many other parts of the richeft monarchies, and other dominions, it has been agreed, in the conferences and treaties of peace which are negotiating with Great Britain, to eftablifh an equilibrium, and political boundaries between the kingdoms, whereof the interefts have been, and are ftill, the fad occafion of a bloody difpute; and to hold it for a fundamental maxim, in order to preferve this peace, that provifion ought to be made that the forces of thefe kingdoms may not become formidable, nor be able to caufe any jealoufy, which, it has been thought, cannot be fettled more folidly, than by hindering them from extending themfelves, and by keeping a certain proportion, to the end that the weaker being united together may defend themfelves againft the more powerful, and fupport themfelves refpectively againft their equals.

For this purpofe the King, our moft honoured lord and grandfather, and the King of Spain, our moft dear brother, have agreed and concluded with the Queen of
Great

Great Britain, that reciprocal renunciations fhall be made by all the Princes, both prefent and to come, of the crown of France, and of that of Spain, of all rights which may appertain to each of them, to the fucceffion of the one or of the other kingdom, by eftablifhing an habitual right to the fucceffion to the crown of Spain, in that line which fhall be made capable thereof, and declared immediate after that of King Philip the Fifth our brother, by the Eftates of Spain, who were to affemble for this purpofe; by making an immoveable balance to maintain the equilibrium, which is intended to be placed in Europe, and by going on to particularife all the cafes of union which are forefeen, to ferve as a example for all fuch as may happen. It has likewife been agreed and concluded between the King our moft honoured lord and grandfather, King Philip the Fifth, our brother, and the Queen of Great Britain, that the faid King Philip fhall renounce for himfelf, and for all his defcendants, the hopes of fucceeding to the crown of France; that on our fide we fhall renounce in like manner, for us, and for our defcendants, the crown of Spain; that the Duke of Orleans, our moft dear uncle, fhall do the fame thing: fo that all the lines of France and of Spain, refpectively and relatively, fhall be excluded for ever, and by all kind of ways, from all the right which the lines of France might have to the crown of Spain, and the lines of Spain to the crown of France: and laftly, that care fhall be taken, that under pretence of the faid renunciations, or under any other pretence whatfoever, the Houfe of Auftria may not make ufe of the pretenfions which it might have to the fucceffion of the monarchy of Spain; forafmuch as by uniting this monarchy to the hereditary countries and dominions of that Houfe, it would become formidable, even without the union of the Empire, to the other Powers, which are between both, and which would find themfelves as it were furrounded; which would deftroy the equality that is eftablifhing at prefent, to fecure

and

and ftrengthen more perfectly the peace of Chriftendom, and to take away all manner of jealoufy from
the Powers of the North and of the Weft, which is the
end that is propofed by this political equilibrium; by
removing and excluding all thefe branches, and calling
to the crown of Spain, in default of the lines of King
Philip the Fifth, our brother, and of all his children
and defcendants, the Houfe of the Duke of Savoy,
which defcends from the Infanta Catharina, daughter
of Philip the Second; it having been confidered, that
in making the faid Houfe of Savoy fucceed immediately in this manner, this equality and balance between
the three Powers may be fixed as it were in its centre,
without which it would be impoffible to extinguifh the
flame of war which has been kindled, and is capable or
deftroying every thing.

Being willing therefore to concur by our relinquifhment, and by the abdication of all our rights, for us, our
fucceffors and defcendants, to the eftablifhing of the
univerfal repofe, and the fecuring the peace of Europe,
becaufe we believe that this method is the fureft and
moft effectual in the terrible circumftances of this con-
juncture, we have refolved to renounce the hopes of
fucceeding to the crown of Spain, and all the rights
thereunto, which belong to us, and may belong to us,
under any title, and by any means whatfoever. And
to the end that this refolution may have its full effect,
and alfo by reafon that King Philip the Fifth, our
brother, did on his part, the fifth of this prefent month
of November, make his renunciation of the crown of
France, we of our mere, free, and frank will, and
without being moved thereunto by any refpectful awe,
or by any other regard, except thofe above-mentioned,
do declare, and hold ourfelves from this prefent, we,
our children, and defcendants, excluded and difabled
abfolutely for ever, without limitation or diftinction
of perfons, degrees, or fexes, from every act, and from
all right of fucceeding to the crown of Spain. We
will and confent, for us, our faid children, and defcendants,

fcendants, that from this time, and for ever, we and they, in confequence of thefe prefents, be held to be excluded and difabled, in like manner as all the other defcendants of the Houfe of Auftria, who, as it has been faid and fuppofed, ought alfo to be excluded, in whatever degree we may be, both the one and the other; and if the fucceffion falls to us, our line, that of all our defcendants, and all the others of the Houfe of Auftria, as it has been faid, ought to be feparated and excluded therefrom. That for this reafon the kingdom of Spain be accounted as devolved and transferred to him, to whom in fuch cafe the fucceffion ought to devolve and be transferred at any time whatfoever, fo that we do take and hold him for true and lawful fucceffor, becaufe for the fame reafons and motives, and in confequence of thefe prefents, neither we, nor our defcendants, ought any more to be confidered as having any foundation of reprefentation, active or paffive, or making any continuation of line effective, or contentive of fubftance, blood or quality, or likewife to derive any right from our defcent, or to reckon our degrees from the perfons of the Queen Maria Therefa of Auftria, our moft honoured lady and grandmother, of the Queen Anne of Auftria, our molt honoured lady and great-grandmother, or of the glorious Kings their anceftors; on the contrary, we ratify the claufes of their wills, and the renunciations made by the faid ladies, our grandmother and great-grandmother; we renounce likewife the right which may belong to us, and to our children and defcendants, by virtue of the will of King Charles the Second, which, notwithftanding what is above-mentioned, calls us to the fucceffion of the crown of Spain, in cafe of failure of the line of Philip the Fifth. We therefore relinquifh this right, and renounce the fame, for us, our children, and defcendants; we promife and engage, for us, our faid children and defcendants, to employ ourfelves with all our might in caufing this prefent act to be fulfilled, without allowing or fuffering that the fame be violated,

directly

directly or indirectly, in the whole or in part; and we relinquish all means, ordinary or extraordinary, which by common right, or by any special privilege, might belong to us, our children, and descendants; which means we likewise renounce absolutely and particularly, that of evident, enormous, and most enormous prejudice, which may be found in the said renunciation of the succession to the crown of Spain. And we will, that none of the said means may or can have any effect, and that if, under this pretext, or any other colour, we would possess ourselves of the said kingdom by force of arms, the war which we should make, or stir up, be deemed unjust, unlawful, and unduly undertaken. And on the contrary, that the war which he should make upon us, who by virtue of this renunciation should have right to succeed to the crown of Spain, be deemed just and allowable. And that all the subjects and people of Spain do acknowledge him, obey him, defend him, do him homage, and swear fealty to him, as to their King and lawful lord.

And for the greater security of all that we say and promise for ourselves, and in the name of our children and descendants, we swear solemnly on the Gospels contained in this Missal, upon which we lay our right hand, that we will keep, maintain, and fulfil the same in all and every part thereof; that we will never ask to be relieved from the same, and if any one do ask it for us, or if it be granted us *motu proprio*, we will not make use or take advantage of it. But rather, in case it should be granted us, we over and above make this other oath, and this shall subsist and remain for ever, whatever dispensations may be granted us. We swear and promise likewise, that we have not made, neither will we make, in public or in secret, any protestation or reclamation to the contrary, which may hinder what is contained in these presents, or lessen the force thereof; and if we should make any, whatever oaths they may be accompanied with, they shall not have any force or virtue, or produce any effect.

In

In witness whereof, and to render these presents authentic, they have been passed before masters Alexander le Fevre, and Anthony le Moyne, counsellors to the King, notaries, minute-keepers to his Majesty, and seal-keepers in the Chatelet of Paris, here-under written, who have wholly delivered this present act; and for causing these presents to be published and registered, wherever it shall be necessary, my Lord the Duke of Berry has constituted the bearers of these dispatches, by duplicates thereof, his general and special attornies, to whom my said Lord has, by these said presents, given special power and authority in that behalf. At Marly, the twenty-fourth day of November, 1712, before noon, and has signed the present duplicate and another, and the minute thereof remaining in the hands of the said le Moyne, notary.

(Signed)   CHARLES.

Le Fevre, Le Moyne.

WE Jerome d'Argouges, Knight, Lord of Fleury, counsellor to the King in his councils, honorary master of the requests of his household, civil lieutenant of the city, provostship, and vicounty of Paris, do certify to all to whom it may appertain, that masters Alexander le Fevre, and Anthony le Moyne, who have signed the act on the other side, are counsellors to the King, notaries, minute-keepers to his Majesty, and seal-keepers at the Chatelet of Paris, and that faith is to be given, as well in court as out of it, to the acts received by them. In witness whereof, we have signed these presents, caused the same to be countersigned by our secretary, and the seal of our arms to be affixed. At Paris, the twenty-fourth of November, 1712.

(Signed)   *D'Argouges.*

By my said Lord, *Barbey.*

Read and published, the court sitting, and registered in the rolls of the court, the King's attorney general being heard, and moving for the same, in order

order to its being executed according to its form
and tenor, in purfuance of and in conformity to
the acts of this day. At Paris, in parliament,
the fifteenth of March, 1713.

(Signed)   *Dongcis.*

PHILIP, grandfon of France, Duke of Orleans,
Valois, Chartres, and Nemours: to all Kings, Princes,
Commonwealths, Potentates, Communities, and to all
perfons, as well prefent as to come, we make known
by thefe prefents; that the fear of the union of the
crowns of France and Spain, having been the principal motive of the prefent war, and the other Powers
of Europe having always apprehended left thefe two
crowns fhould come upon one head, it has been laid
down as the foundation of the peace, which is treated
of at prefent, and which it is hoped may be cemented
more and more, for the repofe of fuch a number of
countries which have facrificed themfelves, as fo many
victims, to oppofe the dangers wherewith they thought
themfelves threatened, that it was neceffary to eftablifh
a kind of equality and equilibrium between the Princes
who were in difpute, and to feparate for ever, in an
irrevocable manner, the rights which they pretend to
have, and which they defended, fword in hand, with a
reciprocal flaughter on each fide.

That with intent to eftablifh this equality, the
Queen of Great Britain propofed, and upon her in-
ftances it has been agreed by the King, our moft
honoured lord and uncle, and by the Catholic King,
our moft dear nephew, that for avoiding at any time
whatfoever the union of the crowns of France and
Spain, reciprocal renunciations fhould be made, that
is to fay, by the Catholic King Philip the Fifth our
nephew, for himfelf, and for all his defcendants, of the
fucceffion to the crown of France, as alfo by the
Duke of Berry, our moft dear nephew, and by us,
for ourfelves, and for all our defcendants, of the crown
of Spain; on condition likewife, that neither the

House of Austria, nor any of the descendants thereof, shall be able to succeed to the crown of Spain, because this House itself, without the union of the Empire, would become formidable, if it should add a new power to its ancient dominions; and consequently this equilibrium, which is designed to be established for the good of the Princes and States of Europe, would cease. Now it is certain, that without this equilibrium, either the states suffer from the weight of their own greatness, or envy engages their neighbours to make alliances to attack them, and to reduce them to such a point, that these great Powers may inspire less fear, and may not aspire to an universal monarchy.

For attaining the end, which is proposed, and by reason that his Catholic Majesty has on his part made his renunciation the fifth of this present month, we consent that, in failure of Philip the Fifth, our nephew, and of his descendants, the crown of Spain do pass over to the House of the Duke of Savoy, whose rights are clear and known, inasmuch as he descends from the Infanta Catharina, daughter of Philip the Second, and as he is called by the other Kings his successors; so that his right to the succession of Spain is indisputable.

And we desiring on our side to concur towards the glorious end, which is proposed for re-establishing the public tranquillity, and for preventing the fears which the rights of our birth, or all others which might appertain unto us, might occasion, have resolved to make this relinquishment, this abdication, and this renunciation of all our rights, for ourselves, and in the name of all our successors and descendants; and for the accomplishing of this resolution, which we have taken of our mere, free, and frank will, we declare and hold ourselves from this present, us, our children, and descendants, for excluded and disabled, absolutely, and for ever, and without limitation or distinction of persons, of degrees, and of sexes, from every act, and

from

from all right of fucceeding to the crown of Spain. We will and confent, for us and our defcendants, that from this time, and for ever, we be held, we and ours, for excluded, difabled, and incapacitated, in whatever degree we may happen to be, and in what manner foever the fucceffion may fall to our line, and to all others, whether of the Houfe of France or of that of Auftria, and of all the defcendants both of the one and the other Houfe, which, as it is faid and fuppofed, ought likewife to hold themfelves for cut off and excluded; and that for this reafon, the fucceffion to the faid crown of Spain be deemed to be devolved and transferred to him to whom the fucceffion of Spain ought to be transferred, in fuch cafe, and at any time whatfoever; fo that we do take and hold him for true and lawful fucceffor, becaufe neither we, nor our defcendants, ought any more to be confidered as having any foundation of reprefentation, active or paffive, or making a continuation of a line effective, or contenuve of fubftance, blood, or quality, nor ought we to derive any right from our defcent, or reckon the degrees from Queen Anne of Auftria, our moft honoured lady and grandmother, nor from the glorious Kings her anceftors. On the contrary, we ratify the renunciation which the faid lady Queen Anne made, and all the claufes which the kings Philip the Third and Philip the Fourth inferted in their wills. We renounce in like manner all the right which may appertain to us, and to our children and defcendants, by virtue of the declaration made at Madrid, the twenty-ninth of October, 1703, by Philip the Fifth King of Spain, our nephew; and any right which might appertain to us, for us, and our defcendants, we relinquifh the fame, and renounce it for us and for them; we promife and engage, for us, our faid children and defcendants, prefent and to come, to employ ourfelves, with all our might, in caufing thefe prefents to be obferved and fulfilled, without allowing or fuffering that directly or indirectly the fame be violated, whether in the whole or in part. And we relinquifh all means, ordinary or extraordinary, which by common right, or any fpecial privilege, might appertain to us, our children, and defcendants; which means we renounce abfolutely, and in particular that of evident, enormous, and moft enormous prejudice, which may be found in the renunciation of the fucceffion to the faid crown of Spain; and we will that any of the faid means neither may nor can ferve or avail us. And if under this pretext, or any other colour whatever, we would poffefs ourfelves of the faid kingdom of Spain by force of arms, that the war which we fhould make, or flir up, be held for unjuft, unlawful, and unduly undertaken; and that on the contrary, that which he fhould make upon us, who by virtue of this renunciation fhould have right to fucceed to the crown of Spain, be held for juft and allowable; and that all the fubjects and people of Spain do acknowledge him, obey him, defend him, do homage to him, and take the oath of fealty to him, as to their King and lawful lord.

And for the greater affurance and fecurity of all that we fay and promife, for us, and in the name of our fucceffors and defcendants, we fwear folemnly on the holy Gofpels contained in this Miffal, whereon we lay our right hand, that we will keep, maintain, and fulfil the fame, wholly and entirely; and that we will at no time afk to have ourfelves relieved therefrom; and if any perfon afks it, or if it is granted us *motu proprio*, we will not make ufe or avail ourfelves thereof; but rather, in cafe it fhould be granted us, we make another oath, that this fhall fubfift and remain for ever, what difpenfation foever may be granted us. We further fwear and promife, that we have not made, neither will we make, either in public or in fecret, any proteftation or reclamation to the contrary, which may hinder that which is contained in thefe prefents, or leffen the force thereof, and if we fhould make any, what oath foever they may be attended with, they
                                                                        fhall

ſhall not have either force or virtue, or produce any effect.

And for greater ſecurity, we have paſſed and do paſs the preſent act of renunciation, abdication, and relinquiſhment, before maſters Anthony le Moyne and Alexander le Fevre, counſellors to the King, notaries, minute-keepers, and ſeal-keepers at the Chatelet of Paris, here-under written, in our palace royal at Paris, 1712, the nineteenth of November, before noon; and for cauſing theſe preſents to be inſinuated and regiſtered in every place where it ſhall appertain, we have conſtituted the bearer to be our attorney, and we have ſigned theſe preſents, and the minute thereof remaining in the poſſeſſion of the ſaid le Fevre, notary.

Philip of Orleans.

Le Moyne, Le Fevre.

WE Jerome d'Argouges, Knight, Lord of Fleury, counſellor to the King in his councils, honorary maſter of the requeſts of his houſehold, civil lieutenant of the city, provoſtſhip, and vicounty of Paris, do certify to all to whom it ſhall appertain, that maſter Anthony le Moyne, and Alexander le Fevre, who have ſigned the act of renunciation on the other ſide, are counſellors to the King, notaries at the Chatelet of Paris, and that faith ought to be given, as well in judgment as out of the ſame, to the acts by them received. In witneſs whereof we have ſigned theſe preſents, cauſed the ſame to be counter-ſigned by our ſecretary, and the ſeal of our arms to be affixed. At Paris, the twenty-firſt of November, 1712.

(Signed) *D'Argouges.*

By my ſaid Lord, *Barbey.*

Read and publiſhed, the court being aſſembled, and regiſtered in the rolls of the court, the King's attorney general being heard, and requiring the

fame, that it may be executed according to its
form and tenor, in purfuance of, and in conformity to the acts of this day. At Paris, in Parliament, the fifteenth of March, 1713.

(Signed)   *Dongois.*

The King's Letters Patents of the Month of December,
1700.

LEWIS, by the grace of God, King of France
and Navarre, to all prefent and to come, greeting.
The profperities which it has pleafed God to heap upon
us during the courfe of our reign, are fo many motives to us, to apply ourfelves, not only for the time
prefent, but alfo for the future, to the happinefs and
tranquillity of the people whereof Divine Providence
has entrufted to us the government.   His impenetra-
ble judgments let us only fee, that we ought not to
place our confidence, neither in our forces, nor in the
extent of our dominions, nor in a numerous pofterity;
and that thefe advantages, which we receive from his
goodnefs alone, have no other folidity than what it
pleafes him to give them.   But as it is, however, his
will, that the Kings, whom he chufes to lead his people, fhould forefee afar off the events able to produce
diforders, and the moft bloody wars; that they fhould
make ufe of the lights, which his divine wifdom pours
upon them; we fulfil his defigns, when, in the midft
of the univerfal rejoicings of our kingdom, we look
upon, as a poffible thing, a fad futurity, which we pray
God to avert for ever.   At the fame time that we
accept the will of the late King of Spain; that our
moft dear and moft beloved fon the Dauphin renounces his lawful right to that crown, in favour of his fecond fon the Duke of Anjou, our moft dear and moft
beloved grandfon, inftituted by the late King of Spain,
his univerfal heir; that this Prince, known at prefent by
the name of Philip the Fifth, King of Spain, is ready to
enter his kingdom, and to anfwer the earneft wifhes of
                                                    his

his new subjects; this great event does not hinder us from carrying our views beyond the time present, and when our succession appears the best established, we judge it to be equally the duty of a King, and of a Father, to declare, for the future, our will conformably to the sentiments which these two qualities inspire in us. Wherefore, being persuaded that the King of Spain, our grandson, will always preserve for us, for our house, for the kingdom wherein he is born, the same tenderness, and the same sentiments, whereof he has given us so many proofs, that his example, uniting his new subjects to ours, is going to form a perpetual amity, and the most perfect correspondence between them; we should think likewise that we do him an injustice, whereof we are incapable, and occasion an irreparable prejudice to our kingdom, if we should hereafter look upon as a stranger, a Prince, whom we grant to the unanimous requests of the Spanish nation.

For these causes, and other great considerations us hereunto moving, of our special grace, full power, and royal authority, we have resolved, declared, and ordained, and by these presents, signed with our hand, we do resolve, declare, and ordain, we will, and it is our pleasure, that our most dear and most beloved grandson the King of Spain do preserve for ever the rights of his birth, in the same manner as if he made his actual residence in our kingdom; wherefore our most dear and most beloved only son the Dauphin, being the true and lawful successor and heir of our crown, and of our dominions, and after him our most dear and most beloved grandson the Duke of Burgundy, if it should happen (which God forbid) that our said grandson the Duke of Burgundy should come to die without male children, or that those which he should have in good and lawful marriage should die before him, or if the said male children should not leave any male children after them, born in lawful marriage, in such case our said grandson the

King

King of Spain, making use of the rights of his birth, is to be the true and lawful successor to our crown, and to our dominions, notwithstanding he should be at that time absent, and residing out of our said kingdom; and immediately after his decease, his heirs male begot in lawful marriage, shall come into the said succession, notwithstanding that they may be born, or that they may dwell out of our kingdom; we will that, for the abovesaid causes, neither our said grandson the King of Spain, nor his children, being males, be deemed and reputed less able and capable to enter upon the said succession, or upon others which may fall to them within our said kingdom. On the contrary, we intend, that all rights, and generally other things whatever, which may at present, or for the future, belong and appertain to them, be and remain preserved whole and intire, as if they did reside and dwell constantly within our kingdom to the time of their decease, and as if their heirs had been natives and inhabitants of the kingdom; having for this purpose, as far as there is or shall be need, enabled and dispensed with them, as we do enable and dispense with them by these presents. And so we give it in command to our beloved and trusty counsellors, the members of our Court of Parliament, and Chamber of our Accounts at Paris, Presidents and Treasurers General of France in the office of our Exchequer established in the same place, and to all others our officers and justices to whom it shall appertain, that they cause these presents to be registered, and our said grandson the King of Spain, his children and descendants, being male, born in lawful marriage, to enjoy and use the contents thereof, fully and peaceably, any thing to the contrary notwithstanding; to which, by our grace and authority, as abovesaid, we have derogated, and do derogate, for this is our pleasure. And that this may be a matter firm and lasting for ever, we have caused our seal to be put to these presents. Given at Versailles, in the month of December,

ber, in the year of our Lord 1700, and of our reign the 58th. Signed LEWIS; and on the fold, By the King, *Phelipeaux*; and fealed with the great feal on green wax, with ftrings of red and green filk.

' Regiftered, the King's attorney general being heard, and requiring the fame, in order to their being executed according to their form and tenor, purfuant to the act of this day. At Paris, in Parliament, the firft of February, 1701.

(Signed) *Dongois.*

NOW whereas it is provided and fettled by the preceding renunciation (which is always to have the force of a pragmatic, fundamental, and inviolable law) that at no time whatever either the Catholic King himfelf, or any one of his lineage, fhall feek to obtain the crown of France, or afcend the throne thereof; and by reciprocal renunciations on the part of France, and by fettlements of the hereditary fucceffion there, tending to the fame purpofe, the crowns of France and Spain are fo divided and feparated from each other, that the aforefaid renunciations, and the other tranfactions relating thereto, remaining in force, and being truly and faithfully obferved, they can never be joined in one. Wherefore the moft Serene Queen of Great Britain, and the moft Serene the moft Chriftian King, engage to each other folemnly, and on their Royal words, that nothing ever fhall be done by them, or their heirs and fucceffors, or allowed to be done by others, whereby the aforefaid renunciations, and the other tranfactions aforementioned, may not have their full effect : but rather, on the contrary, their Royal Majefties, with joint counfels and forces, will always fincerely take that care, and ufe thofe endeavours, that the faid foundations of the public fafety may remain unfhaken, and be preferved untouched for ever.

Moreover, the moft Chriftian King confents and engages, that he will not, for the intereft of his fubjects,

jects, hereafter endeavour to obtain, or accept of any other usage of navigation and trade to Spain, and the Spanish Indies, than what was practised there in the reign of the late King Charles the Second of Spain, or than what shall likewise be fully given and granted, at the same time, to other nations and people concerned in trade.

VII. That there be a free use of navigation and commerce between the subjects of both their Royal Majesties, as it was formerly in time of peace, and before the declaration of this last war, and also as it is agreed and concluded by the treaty of commerce this day made between the two nations.

VIII. That the ordinary distribution of justice be revived, and open again, through the kingdoms and dominions of each of their Royal Majesties, so that it may be free for all the subjects on both sides to sue for and obtain their rights, pretensions, and actions, according to the laws, constitutions, and statutes of each kingdom.

IX. The most Christian King shall take care that all the fortifications of the city of Dunkirk be razed, that the harbour be filled up, and that the sluices or moles which serve to cleanse the harbour be levelled, and that at the said King's own expence, within the space of five months after the conditions of peace are concluded and signed; that is to say, the fortifications towards the sea, within the space of two months, and those towards the land, together with the said banks, within three months; on this express condition also, that the said fortifications, harbour, moles, or sluices, be never repaired again. All which shall not, however, be begun to be ruined, till after that every thing is put into his Christian Majesty's hands, which is to be given him, instead thereof, or as an equivalent.

X. The said most Christian King shall restore to the kingdom and Queen of Great Britain, to be possessed

feffed in full right for ever, the bay and ftreights of
Hudfon, together with all lands, feas, fea-coafts, ·ri-
vers, and places fituate in the faid bay and ftreights,
and which belong thereunto, no tracts of land or of
fea being excepted, which are at prefent poffeffed by
the fubjects of France. All which, as well as any
buildings there made, in the condition they now are,
and likewife all fortreffes there erected, either befoie
or fince the French feized the fame, fhall, within fix
months from the ratification of the prefent treaty, or
fooner, if poffible, be well and truly delivered to the
Britifh fubjects, having commiffion from the Queen
of Great Britain to demand and receive the fame,
entire and undemolifhed, together with all the cannon
and cannon-ball which are therein, as alfo with a quantity of powder, if it be there found, in proportion to
the cannon-ball, and with the other provifion of war
ufually belonging to cannon. It is, however, provided, that it may be entirely free for the company of
Quebec, and all other the fubjects of the moft Chriftian King whatfoever, to go by land, or by fea, whitherfoever they pleafe, out of the lands of the faid bay,
together with all their goods, merchandizes, arms,
and effects, of what nature or condition foever, except fuch things as are above referved in this article.
But it is agreed on both fides, to determine within a
year, by commiffaries to be forthwith named by each
party, the limits which are to be fixed between the
faid Bay of Hudfon and the places appertaining to
the French; which limits both the Britifh and French
fubjects fhall be wholly forbid to pafs over, or thereby
to go to each other by fea or by land. The fame
commiffaries fhall alfo have orders to defcribe and fettle, in like manner, the boundaries between the other
Britifh and French colonies in thofe parts.

XI. The abovementioned moft Chriftian King fhall
take care that fatisfaction be given, according to the
rule of juftice and equity, to the Englifh company
trading to the Bay of Hudfon, for all damages and
spoil

spoil done to their colonies, ships, persons, and goods, by the hostile incursions and depredations of the French, in time of peace, an estimate being made thereof by commissaries to be named at the requisition of each party. The same commissaries shall moreover inquire as well into the complaints of the British subjects concerning ships taken by the French in time of peace, as also concerning the damages sustained last year in the island called Montserat, and others, as into those things of which the French subjects complain, relating to the capitulation in the island of Nevis, and castle of Gambia, also to French ships, if perchance any such have been taken by British subjects in time of peace; and in like manner into all disputes of this kind, which shall be found to have arisen between both nations, and which are not yet ended; and due justice shall be done on both sides without delay.

XII. The most Christian King shall take care to have delivered to the Queen of Great Britain, on the same day that the ratifications of this treaty shall be exchanged, solemn and authentic letters, or instruments, by virtue whereof it shall appear, that the island of St. Christopher's is to be possessed alone hereafter by British subjects, likewise all Nova Scotia or Acadie, with its ancient boundaries, as also the city of Port Royal, now called Annapolis Royal, and all other things in those parts, which depend on the said lands and islands, together with the dominion, propriety, and possession of the said islands, lands, and places, and all right whatsoever, by treaties, or by any other way obtained, which the most Christian King, the crown of France, or any the subjects thereof, have hitherto had to the said islands, lands, and places, and the inhabitants of the same, are yielded and made over to the Queen of Great Britain, and to her crown, for ever, as the most Christian King doth at present yield and make over all the particulars abovesaid; and that in such ample manner and form, that the

subjects

subjects of the most Christian King shall hereafter be excluded from all kind of fishing in the said seas, bays, and other places, on the coasts of Nova Scotia, that is to say, on those which lie towards the east, within 30 leagues, beginning from the island commonly called Sable, inclusively, and thence stretching along towards the south-west.

XIII. The island called Newfoundland, with the adjacent islands, shall from this time forward belong of right wholly to Britain; and to that end the town and fortress of Placentia, and whatever other places in the said island are in the possession of the French, shall be yielded and given up, within seven months from the exchange of the ratifications of this treaty, or sooner, if possible, by the most Christian King, to those who have a commission from the Queen of Great Britain for that purpose. Nor shall the most Christian King, his heirs and successors, or any of their subjects, at any time hereafter, lay claim to any right to the said island and islands, or to any part of it, or them. Moreover, it shall not be lawful for the subjects of France to fortify any place in the said island of Newfoundland, or to erect any buildings there, besides stages made of boards, and huts necessary and usual for drying of fish; or to resort to the said island, beyond the time necessary for fishing, and drying of fish. But it shall be allowed to the subjects of France to catch fish, and to dry them on land, in that part only, and in no other besides that, of the said island of Newfoundland, which stretches from the place called Cape Bonavista to the northern point of the said island, and from thence running down by the western side, reaches as far as the place called Point Riche. But the island called Cape Breton, as also all others, both in the mouth of the river of St. Lawrence, and in the gulph of the same name, shall hereafter belong of right to the French, and the most Christian King shall have all manner of liberty to fortify any place or places there.

XIV. It

XIV. It is exprefsly provided, that in all the said places and colonies to be yielded and reftored by the moft Chriftian King, in purfuance of this treaty, the fubjeƈts of the faid King may have liberty to remove themfelves, within a year, to any other place, as they fhall think fit, together with all their moveable effeƈts. But thofe who are willing to remain there, and to be fubjeƈt to the kingdom of Great Britain, are to enjoy the free exercife of their religion, according to the ufage of the church of Rome, as far as the laws of Great Britain do allow the fame.

XV. The fubjeƈts of France inhabiting Canada, and others, fhall hereafter give no hinderance or moleftation to the five nations or cantons of Indians, fubjeƈt to the dominion of Great Britain, nor to the other natives of America, who are friends to the fame. In like manner, the fubjeƈts of Great Britain fhall behave themfelves peaceably towards the Americans who are fubjeƈts or friends to France; and on both fides they fhall enjoy full liberty of going and coming on account of trade. As alfo the natives of thofe countries fhall, with the fame liberty, refort, as they pleafe, to the Britifh and French colonies, for promoting trade on one fide and the other, without any moleftation or hinderance, either on the part of the Britifh fubjeƈts or of the French. But it is to be exaƈtly and diftinƈtly fettled by commiffaries, who are, and who ought to be accounted the fubjeƈts and friends of Britain or of France.

XVI. That all letters, as well of reprifal as of mark and counter-mark, which have hitherto on any account been granted on either fide, be and remain null, void, and of no effeƈt; and that no letters of this kind be hereafter granted by either of their faid Royal Majefties, againft the fubjeƈts of the other, unlefs there fhall have been plain proof beforehand of a denial or wrongful delay of juftice; and unlefs the petition of him, who defires the grant of letters of re-

prifal,

prifal, be exhibited and fhewn to the minifter, who refides there in the name of that Prince, againft whofe fubjects thofe letters are demanded, that he within the fpace of four months, or fooner, may make enquiry to the contrary, or procure that fatisfaction be forthwith given to the plaintiff by the party accufed. But in cafe no minifter be refiding there from that Prince, againft whofe fubjects reprifals are demanded, that letters of reprifal be not granted till after the fpace of four months, to be computed from the day whereon the petition was exhibited and prefented to the Prince, againft whofe fubjects reprifals are defired, or to his privy council.

XVII. Whereas it is exprefsly ftipulated, among the conditions of the fufpenfion of arms, made between the abovementioned contracting parties the $\frac{11}{22}$ day of Auguft laft paft, and afterwards prolonged for four months more, in what cafes fhips, merchandizes, and other moveable effects, taken on either fide, fhould either become prize to the captor, or be reftored to the former proprietor; it is therefore agreed, that in thofe cafes the conditions of the aforefaid fufpenfion of arms fhall remain in full force, and that all things relating to fuch captures, made either in the Britifh and Northern feas, or in any other place, fhall be well and truly executed according to the tenor of the fame.

XVIII. But in cafe it happen through inadvertency, or imprudence, or any other caufe whatfoever, that any fubject of their aforefaid Royal Majefties do or commit any thing, by land, by fea, or on frefh waters, in any part of the world, whereby this prefent treaty be not obferved, or whereby any particular article of the fame hath not its effect, this peace and good correfpondence, between the Queen of Great Britain and the moft Chriftian King, fhall not be therefore interrupted or broken, but fhall remain in its former ftrength, force, and vigour. But that fub-

§   ject

ject alone shall be answerable for his own fact, and shall suffer the punishment which is inflicted by the rules and directions of the law of nations.

XIX. However, in case (which God Almighty forbid) the dissensions which have been laid asleep should at any time be renewed, between their said Royal Majesties, or their successors, and break out into open war, the ships, merchandizes, and all the effects, both moveable and immoveable, on both sides, which shall be found to be and remain in the ports, and in the dominions of the adverse party, shall not be confiscated, or any wise endamaged; but the entire space of six months, to be reckoned from the day of the rupture, shall be allowed to the said subjects of each of their Royal Majesties, in which they may sell the aforesaid things, or any part else of their effects, or carry and remove them from thence whither they please, without any molestation, and retire from thence themselves.

XX. Just and reasonable satisfaction shall be given to all and singular the allies of the Queen of Great Britain, in those matters which they have a right to demand from France.

XXI. The most Christian King will, in consideration of the friendship of the Queen of Great Britain, grant, that in making the treaty with the Empire, all things concerning the state of religion, in the aforesaid Empire, shall be settled conformable to the tenor of the treaties of Westphalia, so that it shall plainly appear, that the most Christian King neither will have, nor would have had any alteration made in the said treaties.

XXII. Moreover, the most Christian King engages, that he will forthwith, after the peace is made, cause justice to be done to the family of Hamilton, concerning the dukedom of Chatelraut; to the Duke of Richmond, concerning such requests as he has to
make

make in France; as alfo to Charles Douglas, concerning certain lands to be reclaimed by him, and to others.

XXIII. By the mutual confent of the Queen of Great Britain, and of the moft Chriftian King, the fubjects of each party, who were taken prifoners during the war, fhall be fet at liberty, without any diftinction or ranfom, paying fuch debts as they fhall have contracted in the time of their being prifoners.

XXIV. It is mutually agreed, that all and fingular the conditions of the peace, made this day between his Sacred Royal moft Chriftian Majefty, and his Sacred Royal Majefty of Portugal, be confirmed by this treaty; and her Sacred Royal Majefty of Great Britain takes upon herfelf the guaranty of the fame, to the end that it may be more firmly and inviolably obferved.

XXV. The treaty of peace made this day between his Sacred Royal moft Chriftian Majefty, and his Royal Highnefs the Duke of Savoy, is particularly included in this treaty, as an effential part of it, and is confirmed by it, in the fame manner as if it were word for word inferted therein; her Royal Majefty of Great Britain declaring exprefsly, that fhe will be bound by the ftipulations of fecurity and guaranty promifed therein, as well as by thofe which fhe has formerly taken upon herfelf.

XXVI. The moft Serene King of Sweden, with his kingdoms, dominions, provinces, and rights, as alfo the Great Duke of Tufcany, the Republic of Genoa, and the Duke of Parma, are in the beft manner included in this treaty.

XXVII. Their Majefties have alfo been pleafed to comprehend in this treaty the Hans-Towns, namely, Lubec, Bremen, and Hamburg, and the city of Dantzic, with this effect, that as foon as the general peace shall be concluded, the Hans-Towns and the city of Dantzic may, for the future, as common friends, enjoy the ancient advantages which they have heretofore had in the business of trade, either by treaties or by old custom.

XXVIII. Those shall be comprehended in this present treaty of peace, who shall be named by common consent, on the one part and on the other, before the exchange of the ratifications, or within six months after.

XXIX. Lastly, Solemn ratifications of this present treaty, and made in due form, shall be exhibited on both sides at Utrecht, and mutually and duly exchanged within the space of four weeks, to be computed from the day of the signing, or sooner if possible.

XXX. In witness whereof, we the under-written Ambassadors Extraordinary and Plenipotentiaries of the Queen of Great Britain, and of the most Christian King, have put our seals to these present instruments, subscribed with our own hands, at Utrecht, the $\frac{3}{4}\frac{1}{4}$ day of $\frac{March}{April}$, in the year 1713.

(L. S.) *Joh. Bristol, C. P. S.*　(L. S.) *Huxelles.*
(L. S.) *Strafford.*　　　　　(L. S.) *Mesnager.*

ANNE *R.*

ANNE, by the grace of God, Queen of Great Britain, France, and Ireland, Defender of the faith, &c.; to all and singular to whom these presents shall come, greeting. Whereas the Congress that was held at Utrecht in the beginning of the last year, for making a general peace, has been drawn out into length above these fourteen months by various obstacles, which have been thrown in the way, contrary to our hopes and wishes; but now, by the favour and goodness of Almighty God (who has been pleased to inspire the love of concord more strongly into the breasts of the

parties

parties engaged in war) it feems happily to tend to-wards the end fo long defired, and fo neceffary for the tranquillity and welfare of Europe; we, having at laft adjufted with our good brother the moft Chriftian King our matters on both fides, relating both to peace and to commerce, to the end that our minifters, who have hitherto, under the title of Plenipotentiaries, ap-plied themfelves, with our higheft approbation, to the difcharge of this employment, may, with greater fplen-dor, put an end to this moft wholefome work, have thought fit to give them the moft honourable character of our Ambaffadors Extraordinary. Now know ye, that we repofing efpecial confidence in the loyalty, induftry, experience, and fagacity in managing matters of great importance, of the Right Reverend Father in God our right trufty and well-beloved Coun-fellor John Bifhop of Briftol, Keeper of our Privy Seal, Dean of Windfor, and Regifter of our moft Noble Order of the Garter; and of our right trufty and right well-beloved Coufin and Counfellor Thomas Earl of Strafford, Vifcount Wentworth of Wentworth Wood-houfe and Stainborough, Baron of Raby, Lieutenant General of our forces, Firft Commiffioner of our Ad-miralty, Knight of our moft Noble Order of the Gar-ter, and our Ambaffador Extraordinary and Plenipo-tentiary to the High and Mighty Lords the States Ge-neral of the United Netherlands; have named, made, and conftituted them, as by thefe prefents we do name, make, and conftitute them, our true, certain, and un-doubted Ambaffadors Extraordinary, Commiffaries, Procurators, and Plenipotentiaries, giving and grant-ing to them, jointly and feparately, all and all manner of power, faculty, and authority, as alfo both general and fpecial order (but fo as the general do not dero-gate from the fpecial, nor on the contrary) to meet and confer in the city of Utrecht, or in any other place, with the Ambaffadors Extraordinary and Ple-nipotentiaries, which the faid moft Chriftian King fhall have deputed on his part, being furnifhed with fuffi-

C c 2   cient

cient authority, and to treat, agree, and conclude concerning fafe, lafting, and honourable conditions of peace
and friendfhip between us and the faid moft Chriftian
King; and to fign for us, and in our name, all fuch
things as fhall be fo agreed and concluded; and to
make out fuch and fo many inftruments of what is concluded, as fhall be neceffary, and to exchange and
mutually receive the fame; and generally to do and
perform all fuch things as they fhall judge neceffary,
or any way conducible towards making and fettling
the conditions of peace and friendfhip, as is abovefaid,
in as ample manner and form, and with the like force
and effect, as we ourfelves might do and perform, if
we were prefent; engaging and promifing on our Royal
word, that we will accept, approve, and ratify, in the
fame manner and form as they have been agreed, all
and every thing that by virtue of thefe prefents fhall
happen to be tranfacted, concluded, and figned by our
faid Ambaffadors Extraordinary, Commiffaries, Procurators, and Plenipotentiaries, jointly or feparately.
In witnefs and confirmation whereof we have commanded our great feal of Great Britain to be affixed
to thefe prefents, figned with our Royal hand. Given
at our palace of St. James's, the 24th day of the month
of March, in the year of our Lord 17$\frac{1}{3}$, and of our
reign the twelfth.

LEWIS, by the grace of God, King of France
and Navarre, to all who fhall fee thefe prefents, greeting. Whereas we have omitted nothing for contributing with all our might towards the re-eftablifhment
of a fincere and folid peace; and as our moft dear
and moft beloved fifter the Queen of Great Britain
has fhewn the fame defire, and as there is room to
hope, that the conferences which are held at Utrecht,
for attaining to fo defirable a good, will in a little time
have a happy iffue; and being willing likewife to apply all our care for promoting the effect thereof, and
repofing entire confidence in the capacity, experience,

ence, zeal, and fidelity for our fervice, of our moft
dear and well-beloved coufin, the Marquis d'Huxelles, Marfhal of France, Knight of our Orders, and
our Lieutenant General of the government of Burgundy, and of our dear and well-beloved the Sieur
Mefnager, Knight of our Order of St. Michael.   For
thefe caufes, and other good confiderations us hereunto moving, we have commiffioned, ordained, and
deputed, as by thefe prefents, figned with our h and,
we do commiffion, ordain, and depute the faid Sieurs
Marfhal d'Huxelles and Mefnager, and have given,
and do give to them full power, commiffion, and fpecial command, in quality of our Ambaffadors Extraordinary, and our Plenipotentiaries, to confer, negotiate, and treat with the Ambaffadors Extraordinary,
Plenipotentiaries of our faid fifter, provided with her
powers in due form, to agree, conclude, and fign fuch
treaties of peace, articles, and conventi ns, as they
fhall fee good.   We will that in cafe of abfence of one
of them by ficknefs, or through any other lawful
caufe, the other have the fame power to c nfer, negotiate, treat, agree, conclude, and fign fuch treaties
of peace, articles, and conventions, as fhall be agreeable to the good of the peace which we propofe to
ourfelves, and to the reciprocal advantage of our fubjects, fo that our faid Ambaffadors Extraordinary and
Plenipotentiaries may act, in all which fhall belong to
the negotiation with our faid fifter, with the fame authority as we fhould and might do, if we were prefent
in perfon, although there fhould be fomething which
might require a more. fpecial order than is contained
in thefe prefents.   We promife, on the faith and word
of a King, to approve, and to keep firm and lafting
for ever, to fulfil and execute punctually, all that the
faid Sieurs Marfhal d'Huxelles and Mefnager, or one
of them, in the faid cafes of abfence, or of ficknefs,
fhall ftipulate, promife, and fign, by virtue of this prefent power, without ever acting contrary thereto, or
permitting that any thing be done to the contrary, on

C c 3   any

any cauſe, or under any pretence whatſoever; as likewiſe to cauſe our letters ratifying the 'ſame to be diſ-
patched, in good form, and to cauſe them to be delivered, in order to be ,exchanged, within the time
which ſhall be agreed on by the treaties to be made.
For this is our pleaſure. In witneſs whereof we have
cauſed our ſeal to be affixed to theſe preſents. Given
at Verſailles, the fourth day of March, in 'the year of
our Lord 1713, and of our reign the ſeventieth. Signed LEWIS; and on the fold, By the King, *Colbert.*

[The following is printed from the copy, which was
publiſhed by authority in 1713.

*The Treaty of Navigation and Commerce between the
most Serene and most Potent Princeſs Anne, by the
Grace of God, Queen of Great Britain, France,
and Ireland, and the most Serene and most Potent
Prince Lewis the XIVth, the most Chriſtian King,
concluded at Utrecht the $\frac{11}{11}$ Day of $\frac{March}{April}$ 1713.*

WHEREAS the most Serene and most Potent
Princeſs and Lady Anne, by the grace of God,
Queen of Great Britain, France, and Ireland, and the
most Serene and most Potent Prince and Lord Lewis
the Fourteenth, by the grace of God, the most Chriſtian King, ſince they applied their minds, by the diſpoſal of the Almighty, to the ſtudy of peace, have
both been moved with an earneſt deſire to increaſe the
advantages of their ſubjects, which are to ariſe therefrom, by a reciprocal liberty of navigation and commerce, which ought to be as well the principal fruit
as eſtabliſhment of peace: and to that end they have
most graciouſly given inſtructions to their Ambaſſadors Extraordinary and Plenipotentiaries, going to the
congreſs at Utrecht, that they ſhould employ their
utmoſt diligence and care both to re-eſtabliſh peace,
and to renew the former treaties of commerce between
the two nations, and to adapt them to the preſent
ſtate

ftate of affairs; that is to fay, her Sacred Royal Majefty of Great Britain, to the Right Reverend John, by Divine permiffion, Bifhop of Briftol, Keeper of the Privy Seal of England, one of her Majefty's Privy Council, Dean of Windfor, and Regifter of the moft Noble Order of the Garter: as alfo to the moft Noble, Illuftrious, and Excellent Lord Thomas Earl of Strafford, Vifcount Wentworth of Wentworth-Woodhoufe, and Stainborough, Baron of Raby, one of her Majefty's Privy Council, her Ambaffador Extraordinary and Plenipotentiary to the High and Mighty Lords the States General of the United Netherlands, Colonel of her Majefty's regiment of dragoons, Lieutenant General of her Majefty's forces, Firft Lord Commiffioner of the Admiralty of Great Britain and Ireland, and Knight of the moft Noble Order of the Garter: and his Sacred Royal moft Chriftian Majefty, to the moft Noble, Illuftrious, and Excellent Lords Nicolas Marquis of Huxelles, Marfhál of France, Knight of the King's Orders, and Lieutenant General of the dukedom of Burgundy; and Nicolas Mefnager, Knight of the King's Order of St. Michael. Whereupon the faid Ambaffadors, to the end that the defign of their Royal Majefties, which is fo pious and wholefome, might attain the defired effect, having had feveral conferences upon that affair, and having adjufted the principal matters on both fides, as far as they could in fo fhort a time, after having communicated to each other, and duly exchanged, the full powers wherewith they were provided for this purpofe, copies whereof are inferted word for word at the end of this inftrument, have agreed upon articles of navigation and commerce, in manner and form as follows.

I. IT is agreed and concluded between the moft Serene and moft Potent Queen of Great Britain, and the moft Serene and moft Potent the moft Chriftian King, that there fhall be a reciprocal and entirely perfect liberty of navigation and commerce between the

fubjects on each part, through all and every the kingdoms, ftates, dominions, and provinces of their Royal
Majefties in Europe, concerning all and fingular kinds
of goods, in thofe places, and on thofe conditions, and
in fuch manner and form, as is fettled and adjufted in
the following articles.

II. But that the commerce and friendfhip between
the fubjects of the abovefaid parties may be hereafter
fecure, and free from all trouble and moleftation, it is
agreed and concluded, that if at any time any ill underftanding and breach of friendfhip, or rupture, fhould
happen between the crowns of their Royal Majefties
(which God forbid) in fuch cafe the term of fix months
fhall be allowed, after the faid rupture, to the fubjects
and inhabitants on each part, refiding in the dominions
of the other, in which they themfelves may retire, together with their families, goods, merchandizes, and
effects, and carry them whitherfoever they fhall pleafe;
as likewife at the fame time the felling and difpofing of
their goods, both moveable and immoveable, fhall be
allowed them freely, and without any difturbance; and
in the mean time their goods, effects, wares, and merchandizes, and particularly their perfons, fhall not be
detained or troubled by arreft or feizure: but rather, in
the mean while, the fubjects on each fide fhall have
and enjoy good and fpeedy juftice, fo that, during the
faid fpace of fix months, they may be able to recover
their goods and effects, entrufted as well to the public
as to private perfons.

III. It is likewife agreed and concluded, that the
fubjects and inhabitants of the kingdoms, provinces,
and dominions of each of their Royal Majefties, fhall
exercife no acts of hoftility and violence againft each
other, neither by fea nor by land, nor in rivers, ftreams,
ports, or havens, under any colour or pretence whatfoever; fo that the fubjects of either party fhall receive
no patent, commiffion, or inftruction, for arming and
acting at fea as privateers, nor letters of reprifal, as
they

they are called, from any princes or ftates, which are
enemies to one fide or the other; nor, by virtue or
under colour of fuch patents, commiffions, or reprifals,
fhall they difturb, or infeft, or any way prejudice or damage the aforefaid fubjects and inhabitants of the
Queen of Great Britain, or of the moft Chriftian King;
neither fhall they arm fhips in fuch manner as is abovefaid, or go out to fea therewith.   To which end, as
often as it is required by either fide, ftrict and exprefs
prohibitions fhall be renewed and publifhed in all the
regions, dominions, and territories of each party wherefoever, that no one fhall in any wife ufe fuch commiffions or letters of reprifal, under the fevereft punifhment
that can be inflicted on the tranfgreffors, befides reftitution and full fatisfaction to be given to thofe to
whom they have done any damage; neither fhall any
letters of reprifal be hereafter granted on either fide,
by the faid confederates, to the detriment or difadvantage of the fubjects of the other, except in fuch cafe
only as juftice is denied or delayed, to which denial or
delay credit fhall not be given, unlefs the petition of
the perfon who defires the faid letters of reprifal be
communicated to the Minifter refiding there on the
part of the Prince againft whofe fubjects they are to
be granted, that within the fpace of four months, or
fooner, if it be poffible, he may evince the contrary, or
procure the performance of what is due to juftice.

IV. The fubjects and inhabitants of each of the
aforefaid confederates fhall have liberty, freely and
fecurely, without licence or paffport, general or fpecial,
by land or by fea, or any other way, to go into the
kingdoms, countries, provinces, lands, iflands, cities,
villages, towns, walled or unwalled, fortified or unfortified, ports, dominions, or territories whatfoever, of
the other confederate, in Europe, there to enter, and
to return from thence, to abide there, or to pafs
through the fame, and in the mean time to buy and
purchafe, as they pleafe, all things neceffary for their
fubfiftence and ufe; and they fhall be treated with all
                                                    mutual

mutual kindnefs and favour. Provided, however, that in all thefe matters they behave and comport themfelves conformably to the laws and ftatutes, and live and converfe with each other friendly and peaceably, and keep up reciprocal concord by all manner of good underftanding.

V. The fubjects of each of their Royal Majefties may have leave and licence to come with their fhips, as alfo with the merchandizes and goods on board the fame (the trade and importation whereof are not prohibited by the laws of either kingdom) to the lands, countries, cities, ports, places, and rivers of either fide, in Europe, to enter into the fame, to refort thereto, to remain and refide there, without any limitation of time; alfo to hire houfes, or to lodge with other people, and to buy all lawful kinds of merchandizes, where they think fit, from the firft workman or feller, or in any other manner, whether in the public market for the fale of things, in mart towns, fairs, or wherefoever thofe goods are manufactured or fold; they may likewife lay up and keep in their magazines and warehoufes, and from thence expofe to fale, merchandizes brought from other parts; neither fhall they be in any wife obliged, unlefs willingly and of their own accord, to bring their faid merchandizes to the marts and fairs, on this condition, however, that they fhall not fell the fame by retail in fhops, or any where elfe. But they are not to be loaded with any impofitions or taxes on account of the faid freedom of trade, or for any other caufe whatfoever, except what are to be paid for their fhips and goods according to the laws and cuftoms received in each kingdom. And moreover they fhall have free leave, without any moleftation, to remove themfelves, alfo, if they fhall happen to be married, their wives, children, and fervants, together with their merchandizes, wares, goods, and effects, either bought or imported, whenfoever and whitherfoever they fhall think fit, out of the bounds of each kingdom, by land and by fea, on the rivers and frefh waters, difcharging

8   the

the ufual duties, notwithftanding any law, privilege, grant, immunity, or cuftom, in any wife importing the contrary. But in the bufinefs of religion, there fhall be an entire liberty allowed to the fubjects of each of the confederates, as alfo, if they are married, to their wives and children; neither fhall they be compelled to go to the churches, or to be prefent at the religious worfhip in any other place. On the contrary, they may, without any kind of moleftation, perform their religious exercifes after their own way, although it be forbid by the laws of the kingdom, privately and within their own walls, and without the admittance of any other perfons whatfoever. Moreover, liberty fhall not be refufed to bury the fubjects of either party, who die in the territories of the other, in convenient and decent places, to be appointed for that purpofe, as occafion fhall require; neither fhall the dead bodies of thofe that are buried be any ways molefted. The laws and ftatutes of each kingdom fhall remain in full force, and fhall be duly put in execution, whether they relate to commerce and navigation, or to any other right, thofe cafes only being excepted, concerning which it is otherwife determined in the articles of this prefent treaty.

VI. The fubjects of each party fhall pay the tolls, cuftoms, and duties of import and export through all the dominions and provinces of either party, as are due and accuftomed. And, that it may be certainly known to every one what are all the faid tolls, cuftoms, and duties of import and export, it is likewife agreed, that tables fhewing the cuftoms, port-duties, and impofts, fhall be kept in public places, both at London, and in other towns within the dominions of the Queen of Great Britain, and at Roan, and other towns of France, where trading is ufed; whereunto recourfe may be had, as often as any queftion or difpute arifes concerning fuch port-duties, cuftoms, and impofts; which are to be demanded in fuch manner, and no otherwife, as fhall be

agreeable

agreeable to the plain words and genuine fenfe of the
abovefaid tables. And if any officer, or other perfon
in his name, fhall, under any pretence, publicly or
privately, directly or indirectly, afk or take of a merchant, or of any other perfon, any fum of money, or
any thing elfe, on account of right, dues, ftipend, exhibition, or compenfation, although it be under the
name of a free gift, or in any other manner, or under
any other pretence, more, or otherwife, than what is
prefcribed above, in fuch cafe the faid officer, or his
deputy, if he be found guilty, and convicted of the
fame before a competent judge, in the country where
the crime was committed, fhall give full fatisfaction
to the party that is wronged, and fhall likewife be punifhed according to the direction of the laws.

VII. Merchants, mafters of fhips, owners, mariners,
men of all kinds, fhips, and all merchandizes in general, and effects of one of the confederates, and of
his fubjects and inhabitants, fhall on no public or private account, by virtue of any general or fpecial edict,
be feized in any the lands, ports, havens, fhores, or
dominions whatfoever of the other confederate, for the
public ufe, for warlike expeditions, or for any other
caufe; much lefs, for the private ufe of any one, fhall
they be detained by arrefts, compelled by violence, or
under any colour thereof, or in any wife molefted or
injured. Moreover, it fhall be unlawful for the fubjects of both parties to take any thing, or to extort it
by force, except the perfon to whom it belongs confent,
and it be paid for with ready money. Which, however, is not to be underftood of that detention and
feizure which fhall be made by the command and authority of juftice, and by the ordinary methods, on
account of debt, or crimes; in refpect whereof the
proceeding muft be by way of law, according to the
form of juftice.

VIII. Furthermore, it is agreed and concluded, as a
general rule, that all and fingular the fubjects of the moft

Serene Queen of Great Britain, and of the moft Serene,
the moft Chriftian King, in all countries and places fubject to their power on each fide, as to all duties, impofitions, or cuftoms whatfoever, concerning perfons, goods,
and merchandizes, fhips, freights, feamen, navigation,
and commerce, fhall ufe and enjoy the fame privileges,
liberties, and immunities at leaft, and have the like
favour in all things, as well in the courts of juftice, as
in all fuch things as relate either to commerce, or to
any other rights whatever, which any foreign nation, the
moft favoured, has, ufes, and enjoys, or may hereafter
have, ufe, and enjoy.

IX. It is further agreed, that within the fpace of
two months after a law fhall be made in Great Britain,
whereby it fhall be fufficiently provided, that no more
cuftoms or duties be paid for goods and merchandizes
brought from France to Great Britain, than what are
payable for goods and merchandizes of the like nature
imported into Great Britain from any other country in
Europe; and that all laws made in Great Britain fince
the year 1664, for prohibiting the importation of any
goods and merchandizes coming from France, which
were not prohibited before that time, be repealed; the
general tariff made in France the 18th day of September
in the year 1664, fhall take place there again, and the
duties payable in France by the fubjects of Great Britain, for goods imported and exported, fhall be paid
according to the tenor of the tariff above-mentioned,
and fhall not exceed the rule therein fettled, in the
provinces whereof mention is there made, and in the
other provinces the duty fhall not be payable otherwife than according to the rule at that time prefcribed:
and all prohibitions, tariffs, edicts, declarations, or decrees, made in France fince the faid tariff of the year
1664, and contrary thereunto, in refpect to the goods
and merchandizes of Great Britain, fhall be repealed.
But whereas it is urged on the part of France, that
certain merchandizes, that is to fay, manufactures of
wool, fugar, falted fifh, and the product of whales, be

3   excepted

excepted out of the rule of the above-mentioned tariff, and likewife other heads of matters belonging to this treaty remain, which having been propofed on the part of Great Britain, have not yet been mutually adjufted, a fpecification of all which is contained in a feparate inftrument fubfcribed by the Ambaffadors Extra-ordinary and Plenipotentiaries on both fides; it is hereby provided and agreed, that within two months from the exchange of the ratifications of this treaty, commiffaries on both fides fhall meet at London, to confider of and remove the difficulties concerning the merchandizes to be excepted out of the tariff of the year 1664, and concerning the other heads, which, as is abovefaid, are not yet wholly adjufted. And at the fame time the faid commiffaries fhall likewife endea-vour (which feems to be very much for the intereft of both nations) to have the methods of commerce on one part, and of the other, more thoroughly examined, and to find out and eftablifh juft and beneficial means on both fides for removing the difficulties in this mat-ter, and for regulating the duties mutually. But it is always underftood and provided, that all and fingular the articles of this treaty do in the mean while remain in their full force, and efpecially that nothing be deemed, under any pretence whatfoever, to hinder the benefit of the general tariff of the year 1664 from being granted to the fubjects of her Royal Majefty of Great Britain, and the faid Britifh fubjects from hav-ing and enjoying the fame, without any delay or ter-giverfation, within the fpace of two months after a law is made in Great Britain as abovefaid, in as ample manner and form as the fubjects of any nation, the moft favoured, might have and enjoy the benefit of the aforefaid tariff, any thing to be done or difcuffed by the faid commiffaries to the contrary in any wife not-withftanding.

X. The duties on tobacco imported into France, either in the leaf, or prepared, fhall be reduced here-after to the fame moderate rate as the faid tobacco

of

of the growth of any country in Europe or America, being brought into France, does or shall pay. The subjects on both sides shall also pay the same duties in France for the said tobacco; there shall be likewise an equal liberty of selling it; and the British subjects shall have the same laws as the merchants of France themselves have and enjoy.

XI. It is likewise concluded, that the imposition or tax of 50 *sols Tournois*, laid on British ships in France for every ton, shall wholly cease, and be from henceforward annulled. In like manner the tax of five shillings sterling laid on French ships in Great Britain for every ton, shall cease; neither shall the same, or any the like impositions, be laid hereafter on the ships of the subjects on either side.

XII. It is further agreed and concluded, that it shall be wholly free for all merchants, commanders of ships, and other the subjects of the Queen of Great Britain, in all places of France, to manage their own business themselves, or to commit them to the management of whomsoever they please, nor shall they be obliged to make use of any interpreter, or broker, nor to pay them any salary, unless they chuse to make use of them. Moreover, masters of ships shall not be obliged, in loading or unloading their ships, to make use of those workmen, either at Bourdeaux, or in any other places, as may be appointed by public authority for that purpose; but it shall be entirely free for them to load or unload their ships by themselves, or to make use of such persons in loading or unloading the same as they shall think fit, without the payment of any salary to any other whomsoever; neither shall they be forced to unload any sort of merchandizes, either into other ships, or to receive them into their own, or to wait for their being loaded longer than they please. And all and every the subjects of the most Christian King shall reciprocally have and enjoy the same pri-

vileges

vileges and liberty, in all places in Europe subject to the dominion of Great Britain.

XIII. It shall be wholly lawful and free for merchants and others, being subjects either to the Queen of Great Britain or to the most Christian King, by will, and any other disposition made, either during the time of sickness, or at any other time before, or at the point of death, to devise or give away their merchandizes, effects, money, debts belonging to them, and all moveable goods which they have or ought to have at the time of their death, within the dominions and any other places belonging to the Queen of Great Britain, and to the most Christian King. Moreover, whether they die, having made their will, or intestate, their lawful heirs and executors, or administrators, residing in either of the kingdoms, or coming from any other part, although they be not naturalized, shall freely and quietly receive and take possession of all the said goods and effects whatsoever, according to the laws of Great Britain and France respectively; in such manner, however, that the wills, and right of entering upon the inheritances of persons intestate, must be proved according to law, as well by the subjects of the Queen of Great Britain, as by the subjects of the most Christian King, in those places where each person died, whether that may happen in Great Britain or in France, any law, statute, edict, custom, or *droit d'aubeine* whatsoever to the contrary notwithstanding.

XIV. A dispute arising between any commander of the ships on both sides and his seamen, in any port of the other party, concerning wages due to the said seamen, or other civil causes, the magistrate of the place shall require no more from the person accused, than that he give to the accuser a declaration in writing, witnessed by the magistrate, whereby he shall be bound to answer that matter before a competent judge in his own country; which being done, it shall not be lawful
either

either for the feamen to defert their fhip, or to hinder
the commander from profecuting his voyage. It fhall
moreover be lawful for the merchants on both fides, in
the places of their abode, or elfewhere, to keep books
of their accounts and affairs, as they fhall think fit,
and to have an intercourfe of letters, in fuch language
or idiom as they fhall pleafe, without any moleftation
or fearch whatfoever. But if it fhould happen to be
neceffary for them to produce their books of accounts,
for deciding any difpute and controverfy, in fuch cafe
they fhall be obliged to bring into court the entire
books or writings, but fo as that the judge may not
have liberty to infpect any other articles in the faid
books than fuch as fhall relate to the teftimony or authority in queftion, or fuch as fhall be neceffary to give
credit to the faid books; neither fhall it be lawful, under any pretence, to take the faid books or writings
forcibly out of the hands of the owners, or to retain
them; the cafe of bankruptcy only excepted: neither
fhall the faid fubjects of the Queen of Great Britain
be obliged to write their accounts, copies of letters,
acts or inftruments relating to trade, on ftamped paper,
in French, *papier timbrè*, except their day-book, which,
that it may be produced as evidence in any law-fuit,
ought, according to the laws, which all perfons trading
in France are to obferve, to be fubfcribed *gratis* by the
judge, and marked or flourifhed with his own hand.

XV. It fhall not be lawful for any foreign privateers, not being fubjects of one or of the other of the
confederates, who have commiffions from any other
Prince or State in enmity with either nation, to fit their
fhips in the ports of one or the other of the aforefaid
parties, to fell what they have taken, or in any other
manner whatever to exchange either fhips, merchandizes, or any other ladings; neither fhall they be allowed even to purchafe victuals, except fuch as fhall be
neceffary for their going to the next port of that
Prince fiom whom they have commiffions.

XVI. The ſhips of both parties being laden, ſailing along the coaſts or ſhores of the other, and being forced by ſtorm into the havens or ports, or coming to land in any other manner, ſhall not be obliged there to unlade their goods, or any part thereof, or to pay any duty, unleſs they do of their own accord unlade their goods there, or diſpoſe of any part of their lading: but it may be lawful to take out of the ſhip, and to ſell (leave being firſt obtained from thoſe who have the inſpection of ſea affairs) a ſmall part of their lading, for this end only, that neceſſaries either for the refreſhment or victualling of the ſhip may be purchaſed; and in that caſe the whole lading of the ſhip ſhall not be ſubject to pay the duties, but that ſmall part only which has been taken out and ſold.

XVII. It ſhall be lawful for all and ſingular the ſubjects of the Queen of Great Britain, and of the moſt Chriſtian King, to ſail with their ſhips with all manner of liberty and ſecurity, no diſtinction being made who are the proprietors of the merchandizes laden thereon, from any port, to the places of thoſe who are now, or ſhall be hereafter, at enmity with the Queen of Great Britain, or the moſt Chriſtian King; it ſhall likewiſe be lawful for the ſubjects and inhabitants aforeſaid to ſail with the ſhips and merchandizes aforementioned, and to trade with the ſame liberty and ſecurity from the places, ports, and havens of thoſe who are enemies of both, or of either party, without any oppoſition or diſturbance whatſoever, not only directly from the places of the enemy aforementioned to neutral places, but alſo from one place belonging to an enemy to another place belonging to an enemy, whether they be under the juriſdiction of the ſame Prince, or under ſeveral. And as it is now ſtipulated concerning ſhips and goods, that free ſhips ſhall alſo give a freedom to goods, and that every thing ſhall be deemed to be free and exempt which ſhall be found on board the ſhips belonging to the ſubjects of either of the confederates, although the whole
lading,

lading, or any part thereof, fhould appertain to the
enemies of either of their Majefties, contraband goods
being always excepted, on the difcovery whereof, matters fhall be managed according to the fenfe of the
fubfequent articles; it is alfo agreed, in like manner,
that the fame liberty be extended to perfons who are
on board a free fhip, with this effect, that although they
be enemies to both, or to either party, they are not to be
taken out of that free fhip, unlefs they are foldiers, and
in actual fervice of the enemies.

XVIII. This liberty of navigation and commerce
fhall extend to all kinds of merchandizes, excepting
thofe only which follow in the next article, and which
are fignified by the name of Contraband.

XIX. Under this name of contraband or prohibited
goods, fhall be comprehended arms, great guns, bombs,
with their fufees and other things belonging to them;
fire-balls, gunpowder, match, cannon-ball, pikes,
fwords, lances, fpears, halberds, mortars, petards, granadoes, falt-petre, mufkets, mufket-ball, helmets, head-
pieces, breaft-plates, coats of mail, and the like kinds
of arms proper for arming foldiers, mufket-refts, belts,
horfes with their furniture, and all other warlike inftruments whatever.

XX. Thefe merchandizes which follow fhall not be
reckoned among prohibited goods, that is to fay, all
forts of cloths, and all other manufactures woven of
any wool, flax, filk, cotton, or any other materials
whatever; all kinds of cloaths and wearing-apparel,
together with the fpecies whereof they are ufed to be
made; gold and filver, as well coined as uncoined,
tin, iron, lead, copper, brafs, coals; as alfo wheat and
barley, and any other kind of corn and pulfe; tobacco,
and likewife all manner of fpices, falted and fmoked
flefh, falted fifh, cheefe and butter, beer, oils, wines,
fugars, and all forts of falt, and, in general, all provifions which ferve for the nourifhment of mankind
and the fuftenance of life. Furthermore, all kinds of

cotton,

cotton, hemp, flax, tar, pitch, ropes, cables, sails, sail-cloths, anchors, and any parts of anchors; also ship-masts, planks, boards, and beams, of what trees foever; and all other things proper either for building or repairing ships; and all other goods whatever, which have not been worked into the form of any inftrument or thing prepared for war, by land or by fea, shall not be reputed contraband, much lefs fuch as have been already wrought and made up for any other ufe; all which shall wholly be reckoned among free goods, as likewife all other merchandizes and things which are not comprehended and particularly mentioned in the preceding article, fo that they may be tranfported and carried, in the freeft manner, by the fubjects of both confederates, even to places belonging to an enemy, fuch towns or places being only excepted as are at that time befieged, blocked up round about, or invefted.

XXI. To the end that all manner of diffenfions and quarrels may be avoided and prevented on one fide and the other, it is agreed, that in cafe either of their Royal Majefties, who are allied, fhould be engaged in war, the ships and veffels belonging to the fubjects of the other ally muft be furnifhed with fea-letters or paffports, expreffing the name, property, and bulk of the ship, as alfo the name and place of habitation of the mafter or commander of the faid ship, that it may appear thereby that the ship really and truly belongs to the fubjects of one of the Princes; which paffports shall be made out and granted according to the form annexed to this treaty; they shall likewife be recalled every year, that is, if the ship happens to return home within the fpace of a year. It is likewife agreed, that fuch ships being laden, are to be provided, not only with paffports, as above-mentioned, but alfo with certificates containing the feveral particulars of the cargo, the place whence the ship failed, and whither she is bound, that fo it may be known whether any forbidden

bidden or contraband goods, as are enumerated in the nineteenth article of this treaty, be on board the same; which certificates shall be made out by the officers of the place whence the ship set sail, in the accustomed form. And if any one shall think it fit or advisable to express in the said certificates the person to whom they belong, he may freely do so.

XXII. The ships of the subjects and inhabitants of both their most Serene Royal Majesties, coming to any of the sea-coasts within the dominions of either of the confederates, but not willing to enter into port, or being entered, yet not being willing to shew or to sell the cargoes of their ships, shall not be obliged to give an account of their lading, unless they are suspected, upon sure evidence, of carrying to the enemies of the other confederate prohibited goods, called contraband.

XXIII. And in case of the said manifest suspicion, the said subjects and inhabitants of the dominions of both their most Serene Royal Majesties shall be obliged to exhibit in the ports their passports and certificates, in the manner before specified.

XXIV. But in case the ships of the subjects and inhabitants of both their most Serene Royal Majesties, either on the sea-coast, or on the high seas, shall meet with the men of war of the other, or with privateers, the said men of war and privateers, for preventing any inconveniences, are to remain out of cannon-shot, and to send a boat to the merchant-ship which has been met with, and shall enter her with two or three men only, to whom the master or commander of such ship or vessel shall shew his passport, concerning the property thereof, made out according to the form annexed to this present treaty; and the ship which shall exhibit one, shall have free passage, and it shall be wholly unlawful any way to molest her, search, or compel her to quit her intended course.

XXV. But

XXV. But that merchant-ship of the other party, which intends to go to a port at enmity with the other confederate, or concerning whose voyage, and the fort of goods on board, there may be juft fufpicion, fhall be obliged to exhibit, either on the high feas, or in the ports and havens, not. only her paffports, but her certificates, expreffing that they are not of the kind of goods prohibited, which are fpecified in the nineteenth article.

XXVI. But if one party, in the exhibiting the abovefaid certificates, mentioning the particulars of the things on board, fhould difcover any goods of that kind which are declared contraband or prohibited, by the nineteenth article of this treaty, defigned for a port fubject to the enemy of the other, it fhall be unlawful to break up the hatches of that fhip wherein the fame fhall happen to be found, whether fhe belong to the fubjects of Great Eritain or of France, to open the chefts, packs, or cafks therein, or to remove even the fmallest parcel of the goods, unlefs the lading be brought on fhore in the prefence of the officers of the court of admiralty, and an inventory thereof made; but there fhall be no allowance to fell, exchange, or alienate the fame in any manner, unlefs after that due and lawful procefs fhall have been had againft fuch prohibited goods, and the judges of the admiralty refpectively fhall, by a fentence pronounced, have confifcated the fame; faving always, as well the fhip itfelf, as the other goods found therein, which by this treaty are to be efteemed free; neither may they be detained on pretence of their being, as it were, infected by the prohibited goods, much lefs fhall they be confifcated as lawful prize: but if not the whole cargo, but only part thereof fhall confift of prohibited or contraband goods, and the commander of the fhip fhall be ready and willing to deliver them to the captor who has difcovered them, in fuch cafe the captor, having received thofe goods, fhall forthwith difcharge the fhip, and not

hinder

hinder her by any means freely to profecute the voyage on which fhe was bound.

XXVII. On the contrary, it is agreed, that whatever fhall be found to be laden by the fubjects and inhabitants of either party, on any fhip belonging to the enemy of the other, and his fubjects, the whole, although it be not of the fort of prohibited goods, may be confifcated, in the fame manner as if it belonged to the enemy himfelf, except thofe goods and merchandizes as were put on board fuch fhip before the declaration of war, or even after fuch declaration, if fo be it were done within the time and limits following; that is to fay, if they were put on board fuch fhip, in any port and place within the fpace of fix weeks after fuch declaration, within the bounds called the Naze in Norway, and the Soundings; of two months, from the Soundings to the city of Gibraltar; of ten weeks, in the Mediterranean fea; and of eight months, in any other country or place in the world: fo that the goods of the fubjects of either Prince, whether they be of the nature of fuch as are prohibited, or otherwife, which, as is aforefaid, were put on board any fhip belonging to an enemy before the war, or after the declaration of the fame, within the time and limits abovefaid, fhall no ways be liable to confifcation, but fhall well and truly be reftored without delay to the proprietors demanding the fame; but fo as that if the faid merchandizes be contraband, it fhall not be any ways lawful to carry them afterwards to the ports belonging to the enemy.

XXVIII. And, that more abundant care may be taken for the fecurity of the fubjects of both their moft Serene Royal Majefties, that they fuffer no injury by the men of war or privateers of the other party, all the commanders of the fhips of the Queen of Great Britain, and of the moft Chriftian King, and all their fubjects, fhall be forbid doing any injury or damage to the other fide; and if they act to the con-

trary,

trary, they fhall be punifhed, and fhall moreover be bound to make fatisfaction for all caufe of damage, and the intereft thereof, by reparation, under the bond and obligation of their perfon and goods.

· XXIX. For this caufe, all commanders of privateers, before they receive their patents or fpecial commiffions, fhall hereafter be obliged to give, before a competent judge, fufficient fecurity by good bail, who are men able to pay, and have no intereft in the faid fhip, and are each bound in the whole for the fum of 1,500*l.* fterling, or 16,500 *livres Tournois*; or, if fuch fhip be provided with above one hundred and fifty feamen or foldiers, for the fum of 3,000 *l.* fterling, or 33,000 *livres Tournois*, that they will make entire fatisfaction for any damages and injuries whatfoever, which they, or their officers, or others in their fervice, commit during their courfe at fea, contrary to this prefent treaty, or the edicts of either of their moft Serene Royal Majefties publifhed by virtue thereof; under penalty likewife of having their fpecial commiffions and patents revoked and annulled.

XXX. Both their above-named Royal Majefties being willing to fhew a mutual and equal favour, in all their dominions refpectively, to the fubjects of each other, in the fame manner as if they were their own fubjects, will give fuch orders as fhall be neceffary and effectual, that juftice be adminiftered concerning prizes in the court of admiralty, according to the rule of equity and right, and the articles of this treaty, by judges who are above all fufpicion, and who have no manner of intereft in the caufe in difpute.

· XXXI. Whenfoever the ambaffadors of each of their Royal Majefties above-named, and other their minifters, having a public character, and refiding in the court of the other Prince, fhall complain of the unjuftnefs of the fentences which have been given, their Majefties on each fide fhall take care that the fame be revifed and re-examined in their refpective

councils,

councils, that it may appear whether the directions and provisions prescribed in this treaty have been observed, and have had their due effect: they shall likewise take care that this matter be effectually provided for, and that right be done to every complainant within the space of three months. However, before or after judgment given, the revision thereof still depending, for the avoiding of all damage, it shall not be lawful to sell the goods in dispute, or to unlade them, unless with the consent of the persons concerned.

XXXII. A suit being commenced between the captors of prizes on one part, and the reclaimers of the same on the other, and a sentence or decree being given in favour of the reclaimer, that same sentence or decree, security being given, shall be put in execution, the appeal of the captor to a superior judge in any wise notwithstanding; which, however, is not to be observed when judgment has been given against the reclaimers.

XXXIII. In case that either ships of war, or merchantmen, forced by storm, or other misfortune, be driven on rocks or shelves on the coasts of one or the other party, and are there broken to pieces and shipwrecked, whatever part of the ships or tackling thereof, as also of the goods and merchandizes, shall be saved, or the produce thereof, shall be faithfully restored to the proprietors, reclaimers, or their factors, paying only the expences of preserving the same, in such manner as it may be settled on both sides concerning the rate of salvage; saving, at the same time, the rights and customs of each nation: and both their most Serene Royal Majesties will interpose their authority, that such of their subjects may be severely punished, who in the like accident shall be found guilty of inhumanity.

XXXIV. It shall be free for the subjects of each party to employ such advocates, attornies, notaries, solicitors, and factors, as they shall think fit; to which end

end the said advocates, and others abovementioned, may be appointed by the ordinary judges, if it be needful, and the judges be required thereunto.

XXXV. And, that commerce and navigation may be more securely and freely followed, it is further agreed, that neither the Queen of Great Britain, nor the most Christian King, shall receive any pirates and robbers into any of their ports, havens, cities, or towns, neither shall they permit them to be received into their ports, to be protected or assisted by any manner of harbouring or support, by any the subjects or inhabitants of either of them; but they shall rather cause all such pirates and sea-robbers, or whoever shall receive, conceal, or assist them, to be apprehended and punished as they deserve, for a terror and example to others. And all the ships, goods, or merchandizes, being piratically taken by them, and brought into the ports of the kingdom of either, as much as can be found, although they have by sale been conveyed to others, shall be restored to the lawful owners, or their deputies, having instruments of delegation, and an authority of procuration for reclaiming the same; and indemnisation shall be made, proper evidence being first given in the court of admiralty for proving the property. And all ships and merchandizes, of what nature soever, which can be rescued out of their hands on the high seas, shall be brought into some port of either kingdom, and shall be delivered to the custody of the officers of that port, with this intention, that they be delivered entire to the true proprietor, as soon as due and sufficient proof shall have been made concerning the property thereof.

XXXVI. It shall be lawful, as well for the ships of war of both their most Serene Royal Majesties, as for privateers, to carry whithersoever they please the ships and goods taken from their enemies, neither shall they be obliged to pay any thing to the officers of the admiralty, or to any other judges; nor shall the aforementioned prizes, when they come to and enter the ports

ports of either of their moſt Serene Royal Majeſties, be detained by arreſt, neither ſhall ſearchers, or other officers of thoſe places, make examination concerning them, or the validity thereof; but rather they ſhall have liberty to hoiſt ſail at any time, to depart, and to carry their prizes to that place which is mentioned in their commiſſion or patent, which the commanders of ſuch ſhips of war ſhall be obliged to ſhew: on the contrary, no ſhelter or refuge ſhall be given in their ports to ſuch as have made a prize upon the ſubjects of either of their Royal Majeſties. And if perchance ſuch ſhips ſhall come in, being forced by ſtreſs of weather, or the danger of the ſea, particular care ſhall be taken (as far as it is not repugnant to former treaties made with other Kings and States) that they go from thence, and retire elſewhere, as ſoon as poſſible.

XXXVII. Neither of their moſt Serene Royal Majeſties ſhall permit that the ſhips or goods of the other be taken upon the coaſts, or in the ports or rivers of their dominions, by ſhips of war, or others having commiſſion from any Prince, Commonwealth, or town whatſoever, and in caſe ſuch a thing ſhould happen, both parties ſhall uſe their authority and united force that the damage done be made good.

XXXVIII. If hereafter it ſhall happen, through inadvertency, or otherwiſe, that any contraventions or inconveniences, on either ſide, ariſe concerning the obſervation of this treaty, the friendſhip and good intelligence ſhall not immediately thereupon be broke off; but this treaty ſhall ſubſiſt in all its force, and a proper remedy for removing the inconveniences ſhall be procured, as likewiſe reparation of the contraventions; and if the ſubjects of the one or the other be found in fault, they only ſhall be ſeverely puniſhed and chaſtiſed.

XXXIX. But if it ſhall appear that a captor made uſe of any kind of torture upon the maſter of the ſhip, the ſhip's crew, or others who ſhall be on board any

ſhip

ship belonging to the subjects of the other party; in such case, not only the ship itself, together with the persons, merchandizes, and goods whatsoever, shall be forthwith released without any further delay, and set entirely free, but also such as shall be found guilty of so great a crime, as also the accessaries thereunto, shall suffer the most severe punishment, suitable to their crime: this the Queen of Great Britain, and the most Christian King, do mutually engage shall be done, without any respect of persons.

Form of the Passports to be desired of, and given by, the Lord High Admiral of Great Britain, *&c. or by the Lords Commissioners for executing the Office of High Admiral of* Great Britain, *&c. according to the Direction of the twenty-first Article of this Treaty.*

TO all to whom these presents shall come, greeting. We ' high admiral of Great Britain, &c. (or) We commissioners for executing the office of high admiral of Great Britain, &c: do make known and testify by these presents, That *A. B.* of *C.* the usual place of his dwelling, master or commander of the ship called *D.* appeared before us, and declared by solemn oath, (or) produced a certificate under the seal of the magistrate, or of the officers of the customs of the town and port of *E.* Dated the day of the month of in the year of our Lord 17 of and concerning the oath made before them, that the said ship and vessel *D.* burthen tons, whereof he himself is at this time master or commander, doth really and truly belong to the subjects of her most Serene Majesty our most gracious Sovereign. And whereas it would be most acceptable to us, that the said master or commander should be assisted in the affairs wherein he is justly and honestly employed, we desire you, and all and every of you, that wheresoever the said master or commander shall bring his ship, and the goods on board thereof, you would cause

him

him to be kindly received, to be civilly treated, and in paying the lawful and accuſtomed duties, and other things, to be admitted to enter, to remain in, to depart out of, your ports, rivers, and dominions, and to enjoy all manner of right, and all kind of navigation, traffic, and commerce, in all places where he ſhall think it proper and convenient. For which we ſhall always be moſt willing and ready to make returns to you in a grateful manner. In witneſs and confirmation whereof, we have ſigned theſe preſents, and cauſed our ſeal to be put thereunto. Given at the   day of the month of in the year 17

> *Form of the Certificates to be required of, and to be given by, the Magiſtrate, or Officers of the Cuſtoms, of the Town and Port, in their reſpective Towns and Ports, to the Ships and Veſſels which ſail from thence, according to the Direction of the twenty-firſt Article of this preſent Treaty.*

WE *A. B.*   magiſtrate (or) officers of the cuſtoms of the town and port of *C.* do certify and atteſt, That on the   day of the month of   in the year of our Lord 17   *D. E.* of *F.*   perſonally appeared before us, and declared by a ſolemn oath, that the ſhip or veſſel called *G.*   of about tons, whereof *H. I.* of *K.* his uſual place of habitation, is maſter or commander, does rightfully and properly belong to him and others, ſubjects of her moſt Serene Majeſty our moſt gracious Sovereign, and to them alone; that ſhe is now bound from the port of *L.*   to the port of *M.*   laden with the goods and merchandizes hereunder particularly deſcribed and enumerated, that is to ſay, as follows:

In witneſs whereof, we have ſigned this certificate, and ſealed it with the ſeal of our office. Given the   day of the month of in the year of our Lord 17

Form

*Form of the Paſsports and Letters which are to be
given, in the Admiralty of France, to the Ships and
Barks which ſhall go from thence, according to the
twenty-firſt Article of this preſent Treaty.*

LEWIS, Count of Thoulouſe, Admiral of France,
to all who ſhall ſee theſe preſents, greeting. We make
known, that we have given leave and permiſſion to
                         maſter and commander of the ſhip
called   of the town of   burthen
           tons, or thereabouts, lying at preſent in the
port and haven of   and bound for
and laden with   after that his ſhip has
been viſited, and before ſailing, he ſhall make oath
before the officers who have the juriſdiction of maritime affairs, that the ſaid ſhip belongs to one or more
of the ſubjects of his Majeſty, the act whereof ſhall be
put at the end of theſe preſents; as likewiſe that he
will keep, and cauſe to be kept by his crew on board,
the marine ordinances and regulations, and enter in the
proper office a liſt ſigned and witneſſed, containing the
names and ſurnames, the places of birth and abode
of the crew of his ſhip, and of all who ſhall embark
on board her, whom he ſhall not take on board without the knowledge and permiſſion of the officers of
the marine; and in every port or haven where he ſhall
enter with his ſhip, he ſhall ſhew this preſent leave to
the officers and judges of the marine, and ſhall give a
faithful account to them of what paſſed and was done
during his voyage. And he ſhall carry the colours,
arms, and enſigns of the King, and of us, during his
voyage. In witneſs whereof, we have ſigned theſe
preſents, and put the ſeal of our arms thereunto, and
cauſed the ſame to be counterſigned by our ſecretary
of the marine, at   the   day of
           17   Signed LEWIS, Count of Thou-
louſe; and underneath, by

Form

Form of the Act containing the Oath.

· WE   of the admiralty of
do certify, That   mafter of the fhip named
in the above paffport, has taken the oath mentioned
therein. Done at   the   day of
    17

XL. The prefent treaty fhall be ratified by the Queen of Great Britain, and by the moft Chriftian King, and the ratifications thereof fhall be duly exchanged at Utrecht within four weeks, or fooner if offible.

XLI. In witnefs whereof, we the underwritten Ambaffadors Extraordinary and Plenipotentiaries of the Queen of Great Britain, and of the moft Chriftian King, have fet our hands and feals to this prefent treaty, at Utrecht, the $\frac{11}{12}$ day of $\frac{March}{April}$, in the year of of our Lord 1713.

(L. S.) *Joh. Briftol*, C. P. S.   (L. S.) *Huxelles.*
(L. S.) *Strafford.*   (L. S.) *Mefnager.*

ANNE *R.*

ANNE, by the grace of God, Queen of Great Britain, France, and Ireland, Defender of the Faith, &c.; to all and fingular to whom thefe prefents fhall come, greeting. Whereas the congrefs that was held at Utrecht in the beginning of the laft year, for making a general peace, has been drawn out into length above thefe fourteen months, by various obftacles which have been thrown in the way, contrary to our hopes and wifhes; but now, by the favour and goodnefs of Almighty God (who has been pleafed to infpire the love of concord more ftrongly into the breafts of the parties engaged in war) it feems happily to tend towards the end fo long defired, and fo neceffary for the tranquillity and welfare of Europe; we having at
2   . laft

laft adjufted, with our good brother the moft Chriftian
King, our matters on both fides, relating both to peace
and to commerce, to the end that our Minifters, who
have hitherto, under the title of Plenipotentiaries, ap-
plied themfelves, with our higheft approbation, to the
difcharge of this employment, may with greater fplen-
dor put an end to this moft wholefome work, have
thought fit to give them the moft honourable character
of our Ambaffadors Extraordinary. Now know ye,
that we repofing efpecial confidence in the loyalty, induftry, experience, and fagacity in managing matters
of great importance, of the Right Reverend Father in
God our right trufty and well-beloved counfellor John
Bifhop of Briftol, Keeper of our Privy Seal, Dean of
Windfor, and Regifter of our moft Noble Order of
the Garter; and of our right trufty and right well beloved coufin and counfellor Thomas Earl of Strafford, Vifcount Wentworth of Wentworth Woodhoufe
and Stainborough, Baron of Raby, Lieutenant General of our forces, Firft Commiffioner of our Admiralty,
Knight of our moft Noble Order of the Garter, and
our Ambaffador Extraordinary and Plenipotentiary to
the High and Mighty Lords the States General of
the United Netherlands, have named, made, and
conftituted them, as by thefe prefents we do name,
make, and conftitute them, our true, certain, and
undoubted Ambaffadors Extraordinary, Commiffaries,
Procurators, and Plenipotentiaries, giving and granting
to them, jointly and feparately, all and all manner of
power, faculty, and authority, as alfo both general
and fpecial order (but fo as the general do not derogate from the fpecial, nor on the contrary) to meet
and confer in the city of Utrecht, or in any other
place, with the Ambaffadors Extraordinary and Plenipotentiaries which the faid moft Chriftian King fhall
have deputed on his part, being furnifhed with fufficient authority, and to treat, agree, and conclude concerning the adjufting, in the moft friendly manner,
the conditions of navigation and commerce between

§   our

our fubjects and thofe of the faid moft Chriftian King; and to fign for us, and in our name, all fuch things as fhall be fo agreed and concluded; and to make out fuch and fo many inftruments of what is concluded, as fhall be neceffary, and to exchange and mutually receive the fame; and generally to do and perform all fuch things as they fhall judge neceffary, or any way conducible towards making and fettling the conditions of navigation and commerce, as is abovefaid, in as ample manner and form, and with the like force and effect, as we ourfelves might do and perform, if we were prefent; engaging and promifing, on our Royal word, that we will accept, approve, and ratify, in the fame manner and form as they have been agreed, all and every thing that by virtue of thefe prefents fhall happen to be tranfacted, concluded, and figned by our faid Ambaffadors Extraordinary, Commiffaries, Procurators, and Plenipotentiaries, jointly or feparately. In witnefs and confirmation whereof, we have commanded our great feal of Great Britain to be affixed to thefe prefents, figned with our Royal hand. Given at our palace of St. James's, the 24th day of the month of March, in the year of our Lord 17$\frac{11}{12}$, and of our reign the twelfth.

LEWIS, by the grace of God, King of France and Navarre, to all who fhall fee thefe prefents, greeting. Whereas we have omitted nothing for contributing with all our might towards the re-eftablifhment of a fincere and folid peace; and as our moft dear and moft beloved fifter the Queen of Great Britain has fhewn the fame defire; and as there is room to hope, that the conferences which are held at Utrecht, for attaining to fo defirable a good, will in a little time have a happy iffue; and being willing likewife to apply all our care for promoting the effect thereof, and repofing entire confidence in the capacity, experience, zeal, and fidelity for our fervice, of our moft dear and well-beloved coufin the Marquis

d'Huxelles, Marſhal of France, Knight of our Orders, and our Lieutenant General of the government of
Burgundy, and of our dear and well-beloved the Sieur
Meſnager, Knight of our Order of St. Michael. For
theſe cauſes, and other good conſiderations us hereunto
moving, we have commiſſioned, ordained, and deputed, as by theſe preſents, ſigned with our hand, we do
commiſſion, ordain, and depute the ſaid Sieurs Marſhal d'Huxelles and Meſnager, and have given, and
do give to them full power, commiſſion, and ſpecial
command, in quality of our Ambaſſadors Extraordinary, and our Plenipotentiaries, to confer, negotiate,
and treat with the Ambaſſadors Extraordinary, Plenipotentiaries of our ſaid ſiſter, provided with her
powers in due form, to agree, conclude, and ſign ſuch
treaties of commerce, articles, and conventions, as
they ſhall ſee good. We will that in caſe of abſence
of one of them by ſickneſs, or through any other lawful
cauſe, the other have the ſame power to confer, negotiate, treat, agree, conclude, and ſign ſuch treaties
of commerce, articles, and conventions, as ſhall be
agreeable to the good which we propoſe to ourſelves,
and to the reciprocal advantage of our ſubjects, ſo that
our ſaid Ambaſſadors Extraordinary and Plenipotentiaries may act, in all which ſhall belong to the negotiation with our ſaid ſiſter, with the ſame authority
as we ſhould and might do, if we were preſent in perſon, although there ſhould be ſomething which might
require a more ſpecial order than is contained in theſe
preſents. We promiſe, on the faith and word of a
King, to approve, and to keep firm and laſting for
ever, to fulfil and execute punctually, all that the ſaid
Sieurs Marſhal d'Huxelles and Meſnager, or one of
them, in the ſaid caſes of abſence, or of ſickneſs, ſhall
ſtipulate, promiſe, and ſign, by virtue of this preſent
power, without ever acting contrary thereto, or permitting that any thing be done to the contrary, on
any cauſe, or under any pretence whatſoever; as likewiſe to cauſe our letters ratifying the ſame to be diſ-
patched,

patched, in good form, and to caufe them to be delivered, in order to be exchanged, within the time
which fhall be agreed on by the treaties to be made.
For this is our pleafure. In witnefs whereof, we have
caufed our feal to be affixed to thefe prefents. Given
at Verfailles, the fourth day of March, in the year of
our Lord 1713, and of our reign the feventieth. Signed
LEWIS; and on the fold, By the King. *Colbert.*

BE it known unto all men, that whereas in the
9th article of the treaty of commerce, concluded this
day between the moft Serene Queen of Great Britain and the moft Serene the moft Chriftian King, by
their Majefties Ambaffadors Extraordinary and Plenipotentiaries, mention is made of fome heads of matters; which being propofed on the part of Great Britain, have not as yet been mutually adjufted; and
therefore it was thought fit to refer them to be difcuffed and determined by commiffioners: we therefore, the under-written Ambaffadors, that it may certainly appear what are thofe heads of matters which
are to be referred to commiffioners, have refolved to
give a particular defcription of them in this writing;
declaring that they are the fame, and no other than
what follow:

I. No manufactures of either kingdom, and the
dominions belonging thereunto, fhall hereafter be fubject to be infpected and confifcated, under any pretence of fraud or defect in making or working them,
or becaufe of any other imperfection therein; but abfolute freedom fhall be allowed to the buyer and feller, to bargain and agree for the fame as they fhall
fee good; any law, ftatute, edict, arreft, privilege,
grant, or cuftom, to the contrary notwithftanding.

II. And forafmuch as a certain ufage, not confirmed by any law, has obtained in feveral towns of
Great Britain and of France; that is to fay, that every
one, for coming in, and going out, fhall pay a kind

of tax, called in Englifh, Head-Money, and in French, Du Chef; it is concluded, that neither the fame, nor any other duty on that account, fhall any more be exacted.

III. And the Britifh merchants fhall not hereafter be forbidden to fell the faid tobacco to any buyer whom they pleafe; for which purpofe, the letting out the duties on the faid tobacco to farmers, which has been hitherto practifed, fhall ceafe, neither fhall fuch farming be ufed again hereafter.

IV. The following cafe only being excepted, that is to fay, where Britifh fhips fhall take up merchandizes in one port, and carry them to another port of France, in which cafe, and in no other, the Britifh fubjects fhall be obliged to pay the duties abrogated and abolifhed by this article, only in proportion to the goods which they take in, and not according to the bulk of the fhip.

V. Whereas feveral kinds of goods, contained in cafks, chefts, or other cafes, for which the duties are paid by weight, will be exported from, and imported into, France by Britifh fubjects, it is therefore agreed, that in fuch cafe the aforefaid duties fhall be payable only according to the weight of the goods themfelves; but the weight of the cafks, chefts, and other cafes whatever, fhall be deducted in fuch manner, and in fuch proportion, as has been hitherto in ufe in England, and is ftill practifed.

VI. It is further agreed, that if any miftake or error fhall on either fide be committed by any mafter of a fhip, his interpreter, or factor, or by others employed by him, in making the entry or declaration of the goods on board his fhip, for fuch defect, if fo be fome fraud does not evidently appear, neither the fhip nor the lading thereof fhall be fubject to be confifcated, but it fhall be free for the proprietors to take back again fuch goods as were omitted in the entry or declaration

claration of the master of the ship, paying only the accustomed duties according to the rates settled in the books; neither shall the merchants, or the master of the ship, lose the said goods, or suffer any other punishment, if so be that the said goods, so omitted, were not brought on shore before the declaration made, and the customs paid for the same.

VII. And whereas the quality of the ship, master, and goods, will sufficiently appear from such passports and certificates, it shall not be lawful for the commanders of men of war to exact any other verification, under any title whatsoever. But if any merchant ship shall want such passports or certificates, then it may be examined by a proper judge, but in such manner as, if it shall be found, from other proofs and documents, that it does truly belong to the subjects of either of the confederates, and does not contain any prohibited goods, designed to be carried to the enemy of the other, it shall not be liable to confiscation, but shall be released, together with its cargo, in order to proceed on its voyage, since it may often happen that such papers could not come to the ship when she was setting sail from any port, or that they have been lost by some chance or other, or that they have been taken away from the ship. And if, besides the passports and certificates made according to the form of their treaty, other passports and certificates happen to be found in the ship, in another form, and perhaps according to the prescription of treaties made with others, no pretence shall be taken from thence of detaining, or in any wise molesting, either the ship, or men, or goods. If the master of the ship named in the passports be removed by death, or any other cause, and another be put in his place, the passports shall nevertheless retain their force, and the ships, and goods laden thereon, shall be secure.

VIII. It is further provided on both sides, and shall be taken for a general rule, that a ship and goods, although they have remained in the enemy's power for four

four and twenty hours, shall not therefore be esteemed as capture, and be immediately made prize; but if, on other accounts, they ought to be restored, they may be reclaimed, and shall be given again to the proprietors.

IX. It shall be free for both their Royal Majesties, for the advantage of their subjects trading to the kingdoms and dominions of the other, to constitute national consuls of their own subjects, who shall enjoy that right and liberty which belongs to them by reason of the exercise of their function; but as to the places where such consuls are to be appointed, both sides shall afterwards agree between themselves.

In witness whereof, we the Ambassadors Extraordinary and Plenipotentiaries of her Sacred Royal Majesty of Great Britain, and of his Sacred Royal most Christian Majesty, have subscribed this present instrument with our hands, and set our seals thereunto. At Utrecht, the $\frac{11}{1}$ day of the month of $\frac{March}{April}$, in the year 1713.

(L. S.) *Joh. Bristol, C. P. S.*   (L. S. *Huxelles.*
(L. S.) *Strafford.*   (L. S.) *Mesnager.*

BE it known unto all men, that whereas, in the 9th article of the treaty of navigation and commerce, concluded the $\frac{11}{1}$ day of $\frac{March}{April}$, 1713, between the most Serene Queen of Great Britain, and the most Serene the most Christian King, by the Ambassadors Extraordinary and Plenipotentiaries of their Majesties, certain merchandizes, namely, woollen manufactures, sugar, salt-fish, and what is produced from whales, are excepted in general words from the rule of the tariff made the 18th day of the month of September, in the year 1664, in order to be afterwards referred to the discussion of commissaries; to prevent therefore all mistakes and ambiguity, which might
perhaps

perhaps arife from fuch general terms; and to make it more evidently appear what particular forts of goods are to come under the confideration of the aforefaid commiffaries, we the under-written Ambaffadors Extraordinary and Plenipotentiaries have declared by thefe prefents, and do declare, that the exception of the above-mentioned merchandizes is to be underftood in the manner following.

I. Whalebone cut and prepared, fins and oils of whales, fhall pay, at all places of importation in the kingdom, the duties appointed by the tariff of the 7th of December, 1699.

II. Cloths, ratines, and ferges, fhall be likewife fubject to the fame duties of the tariff of the 7th of December, 1699; and in order to facilitate the trade thereof, it fhall be allowed to import them by St. Valery upon the Somme, by Rouen, and by Bourdeaux, where thefe goods fhall be fubject to vifitation in the fame manner as thofe which are made in the kingdom.

III. Salt-fifh in barrels only is to be imported into the kingdom; and at all places of entrance in the kingdom, countries, and territories under the dominion of the King, even at all free ports, the duties of landing and of confumption fhall be paid which were appointed before the tariff of 1664; and befides 40 livres per laft, confifting of 12 barrels, weighing each 300 *lb.* for the duty of entry; which entry fhall not be permitted but by St. Valery upon the Somme, Rouen, Nants, Libourn, and Bourdeaux, and fhall remain prohibited at all other harbours or ports, as well in the ocean as in the Mediterranean.

IV. Refined fugar in loaf or in powder, white and brown fugar-candy, fhall pay the duties appointed by the tariff of 1699.

In confirmation of which, we the under-written Ambaffadors Extraordinary and Plenipotentiaries of her Majesty the Queen of Great Britain, and the most Christian King, have signed and sealed these presents, at Utrecht, the $\frac{2\cdot 8}{3}$ day of $\frac{April}{May}$, in the year 1713.

(L. S.) *Joh. Bristol, C. P. S.*   (L. S.) *Huxelles.*
(L. S.) *Strafford.*   (L. S.) *Mesnager.*

[The treaty of AIX-LA-CHAPELLE, 1748, is printed from the copy which was published by authority in 1749.]

The Definitive Treaty of Peace and Friendship between his Britannic *Majesty, the most* Christian *King, and the* States General *of the* United Provinces ; *concluded at* Aix-la-Chapelle, *the* 18*th Day of* October, *N.S.* 1748 ; *to which the Empress Queen of* Hungary, *the Kings of* Spain *and* Sardinia, *the Duke of* Modena, *and the Republic of* Genoa, *have acceded.*

In the name of the most holy and undivided Trinity, the Father, Son, and Holy Ghost.

BE it known to all those whom it shall or may concern, in any manner whatsoever. Europe sees the day, which the Divine Providence had pointed out for the re-establishment of its repose. A general peace succeeds to the long and bloody war, which had arose between the most Serene and most Potent Prince George II. by the grace of God, King of Great Britain, France, and Ireland, Duke of Brunswick and Lunenbourg, Arch-Treasurer and Elector of the Holy Roman Empire, &c. and the most Serene and most Potent Princess Mary Theresia, by the grace of God, Queen of Hungary and Bohemia, &c. Empress of the Romans, on the one part; and the most Serene and most Potent Prince Lewis XV. by the grace of God, the most Christian King, on the other; as also between the King of Great Britain, the
Empress

Emprefs Queen of Hungary and Bohemia, and the moft Serene and moft Potent Prince Charles Emanuel III. by the grace of God, King of Sardinia, on the one part, and the moft Serene and moft Potent Prince Philip V. by the grace of God, King of Spain and the Indies (of glorious memory) and after his deceafe, the moft Serene and moft Potent Prince Ferdinand VI. by the grace of God, King of Spain and the Indies, on the other: in which war the High and Mighty Lords the States General of the United Provinces of the Low Countries had taken part, as auxiliaries to the King of Great Britain and the Emprefs Queen of Hungary and Bohemia; and the moft Serene Duke of Modena, and the moft Serene Republic of Genoa, as auxiliaries to the King of Spain. God, in his mercy, made known to all thefe Powers, at the fame time, the way which he had decreed for their reconciliation, and for the reftoration of tranquillity to the people, whom he had fubjected to their government. They fent their Minifters to Aix-la-Chapelle, where thofe of the King of Great Britain, his moft Chriftian Majefty, and of the States General of the United Provinces, having agreed upon preliminary conditions for a general pacification; and thofe of the Emprefs Queen of Hungary and Bohemia, of his Catholic Majefty, of the King of Sardinia, of the Duke of Modena, and of the Republic of Genoa, having acceded thereunto, a general ceffation of hoftilities, by fea and land, happily enfued. In order to complete, at Aix-la-Chapelle, the great work of a peace, equally ftable and convenient for all parties, the high contracting Powers have nominated, appointed, and provided with their full powers, the moft illuftrious and moft excellent Lords their Ambaffadors Extraordinary and Minifters Plenipotentiary, viz. his Sacred Majefty the King of Great Britain, John Earl of Sandwich, Vifcount Hinchinbrook, Baron Montagu of St. Neots, Peer of England, Firft Lord Commiffioner of the Admiralty, one of the

Lords

Lords Regents of the kingdom, his Minister Plenipotentiary to the States General of the United Provinces, and Sir Thomas Robinson, Knight of the
most honourable Order of the Bath, and his Minister
Plenipotentiary to his Majesty the Emperor of the
Romans, and her Majesty the Empress Queen of
Hungary and Bohemia.

His Sacred most Christian Majesty, Alphonso Maria Lewis Count de St. Severin of Arragon, Knight
of his Orders, and John Gabriel de la Porte du
Theil, Knight of the Order of our Lady of Mount
Carmel, and of St. Lazarus of Jerusalem, Counsellor
of the King in his Councils, Secretary of the Chamber, and of the Cabinet of his Majesty, of the Orders
of the Dauphin, and of Mesdames of France.

Her Sacred Majesty the Empress Queen of Hungary and Bohemia, Wenceslaus Anthony Count of
Kaunitz Rittberg, Lord of Essens, Stedesdorff, Wittmund, Austerlitz, Hungrischbrod, Wite, &c. actual
intimate Counsellor of State to their Imperial Majesties.

His Sacred Catholic Majesty, the Lord Don James
Maffone de Lima and Sotto Major, Gentleman of the
Bed-chamber to his Catholic Majesty, and Major Ge-
neral of his forces.

His Sacred Majesty the King of Sardinia, Don
Joseph Ossorio, Knight, Grand Croix and Grand Con-
servator of the Military Order of the Saints Maurice
and Lazarus, and Envoy Extraordinary of his Majesty the King of Sardinia to his Majesty the King of
Great Britain; and Joseph Borré Count Chavanne,
his Counsellor of State, and his Minister to the Lords
the States General of the United Provinces.

The High and Mighty Lords the States General of
the United Provinces, William Count Bentinck, Lord
of Rhoon and Pendrecht, one of the Nobles of the
province of Holland and West Friesland, Curator of
the University of Leyden, &c. &c. &c. Frederick
Henry Baron of Wassenaer, Lord of Catwyck and
Zand,

Zand, one of the Nobles of the province of Holland and Weſt Frieſland, Hoog-Heemrade of Rhynland, &c. Gerard Arnout Haſſelaer, Burgo-maſter and Counſellor of the city of Amſterdam, Director of the Eaſt India Company; John Baron of Borſele, Firſt Noble and Repreſentative of the Nobility in the States, in the Council and Admiralty of Zeland, Director of the Eaſt India Company; Onno Zwier Van Haren, Grietman of Weſt Sterlingwerf, Deputy Counſellor of the province of Frieſland, and Commiſſary General of all the Swiſs and Griſon troops in the ſervice of the aforeſaid States General, and reſpective Deputies in the Aſſembly of the States General, and in the Council of State, on the part of the provinces of Holland and Weſt Frieſland, Zealand, and Frieſland.

· The moſt Serene Duke of Modena, the Sieur Count de Monzone, his Counſellor of State, and Colonel in his ſervice, and his Miniſter Plenipotentiary to his moſt Chriſtian Majeſty.

The moſt Serene Republic of Genoa, the Sieur Francis Marquis Doria.

Who, after having communicated their full poweis to each other in due form, copies whereof are annexed at the end of this preſent treaty, and having conferred on the ſeveral objects, which their Sovereigns have judged proper to be inſerted in this inſtrument of general pacification, have agreed to the ſeveral articles, which are as follow.

I. There ſhall be à chriſtian, univerſal, and perpetual peace, as well by ſea as land, and a ſincere and laſting friendſhip, between the eight Powers abovementioned, and between their heirs and ſucceſſors, kingdoms, ſtates, provinces, countries, ſubjects, and vaſſals, of what rank, and condition ſoever they may be, without exception of places or perſons. So that the high contracting Powers may have the greateſt attention to maintain, between them and their ſaid ſtates and ſubjects, this reciprocal friendſhip and correſpondence,

not

not permitting any fort of hoſtilities to be committed, on one ſide or the other, on any cauſe, or under any pretence whatſoever; and avoiding every thing that may, for the future, diſturb the union happily re-eſtabliſhed between them; and, on the contrary, endeavouring to procure, on all occaſions, whatever may contribute to their mutual glory, intereſts, and advantage, without giving any aſſiſtance or protection, directly or indirectly, to thoſe who would injure or prejudice any of the ſaid high contracting parties.

II. There ſhall be a general oblivion of whatever may have been done or committed during the war now ended. And all perſons, upon the day of the exchange of the ratifications of all the parties, ſhall be maintained or re-eſtabliſhed in the poſſeſſion of all the effects, dignities, eccleſiaſtical benefices, honours, revenues, which they enjoyed, or ought to have enjoyed, at the commencement of the war, notwithſtanding all diſpoſſeſſions, ſeizures, or confiſcations, occaſioned by the ſaid war.

III. The treaties of Weſtphalia of 1648; thoſe of Madrid, between the crowns of England and Spain, of 1667 and 1670; the treaties of peace of Nimeguen of 1678 and 1679; of Ryſwick of 1697; of Utrecht of 1713; of Baden of 1714; the treaty of the triple alliance of the Hague of 1717; that of the quadruple alliance of London of 1718; and the treaty of peace of Vienna of 1738, ſerve as a baſis and foundation to the general peace, and to the preſent treaty; and, for this purpoſe, they are renewed and confirmed in the beſt form, and as if they were herein inſerted word for word; ſo that they ſhall be punctually obſerved for the future in all their tenor, and religiouſly executed on the one ſide and the other; ſuch points, however, as have been derogated from in the preſent treaty excepted.

IV. All the priſoners made on the one ſide and the other, as well by ſea as by land, and the hoſtages required

quired or given during the war, and to this day, fhall
be reftored, without ranfom, in fix weeks at lateft, to
be reckoned from the exchange of the ratification of
the prefent treaty; and it fhall be immediately proceeded upon after that exchange: and all the fhips of
war, as well as merchant veffels, that fhall have been
taken fince the expiration of the terms agreed upon
for the ceffation of hoftilities at fea, fhall be, in like
manner, faithfully reftored, with all their equipages
and cargoes; and fureties fhall be given on all fides
for payment of the debts, which the prifoners or hoftages may have contracted, in the ftates where they
had been detained, until their full difcharge.

V. All the conquefts, that have been made fince
the commencement of the war, or which, fince the
conclufion of the preliminary articles, figned the 30th
of April laft, may have been or fhall be made, either
in Europe, or the Eaft or Weft Indies, or in any
other part of the world whatfoever, being to be reftored without exception, in conformity to what was ftipulated by the faid preliminary articles, and by the
declarations fince figned; the high contracting parties
engage to give orders immediately for proceeding to
that reftitution, as well as to the putting the moft Serene Infant Don Philip in poffeffion of the ftates,
which are to be yielded to him by virtue of the faid
preliminaries, the faid parties folemnly renouncing, as
well for themfelves as for their heirs and fucceffors,
all rights and claims, by what title or pretence foever, to all the ftates, countries, and places, that they
refpectively engage to reftore or yield; faving, however, the reverfion ftipulated of the ftates yielded to
the moft Serene Infant Don Philip.

VI. It is fettled and agreed, that all the refpective
reftitutions and ceffions in Europe fhall be entirely
made and executed on all fides in the fpace of fix
weeks, or fooner if poffible, to be reckoned from the
day of the exchange of the ratifications of the prefent
treaty

treaty of all the eight parties above-mentioned; so that, within the same term of six weeks, the most Christian King shall restore, as well to the Empress Queen of Hungary and Bohemia, as to the States General of the United Provinces, all the conquests which he has made upon them during this war.

The Empress Queen of Hungary and Bohemia shall be put, in consequence hereof, in full and peaceable possession of all that she possessed before the present war in the Low Countries, and elsewhere, except what is otherwise regulated by the present treaty.

In the same time the Lords the States General of the United Provinces shall be put in full and peaceable possession, and such as they had before the present war, of the places of Bergen-op-Zoom and Maestricht, and of all they possessed before the said present war in Dutch Flanders, Dutch Brabant, and elsewhere:

And the towns and places in the Low Countries, the sovereignty of which belongs to the Empress Queen of Hungary and Bohemia, in which their High Mightinesses have the right of garrison, shall be evacuated to the troops of the Republic, within the same space of time.

The King of Sardinia shall be in like manner, and within the same time, entirely re-established and maintained in the dutchy of Savoy, and in the county of Nice, as well as in all the states, countries, places, and forts conquered and taken from him on occasion of the present war.

The most Serene Duke of Modena, and the most Serene Republic of Genoa, shall be also, within the same time, entirely re-established and maintained in the states, countries, places, and forts conquered and taken from them during the present war, conformably to the tenor of the 13th and 14th articles of this treaty, which relate to them.

All the restitutions and cessions of the said towns, forts, and places, shall be made, with all the artillery
and

and warlike ftores that were found there on the day of their furrender, during the courfe of the war, by the Powers who are to make the faid ceffions and reftitutions, and this according to the inventories which have been made of them, or which fhall be delivered *bonâ -fide*, on each fide. Provided that, as to the pieces of artillery, that have been removed elfewhere to be new caft, or for other ufes, they fhall be replaced by the fame number of the fame bore, or weight in metal. Provided alfo, that the places of Charleroy, Mons, Athe, Oudenarde, and Menin, the outworks of which have been demolifhed, fhall be reftored without artillery. Nothing fhall be demanded for the charges and expences employed in the fortifications of all the other places; nor for other public or private works, which have been done in the countries that are to be reftored.

VII. In confideration of the reftitutions that his moft Chriftian Majefty, and his Catholic Majefty, make, by the prefent treaty, either to her Majefty the Queen of Hungary and Bohemia, or to his Majefty the King of Sardinia, the dutchies of Parma, Placentia, and Guaftella fhall, for the future, belong to the moft Serene Infant Don Philip, to be poffeffed by him and his male defcendants, born in lawful marriage, in the fame manner, and in the fame extent, as they have been, or ought to be, poffeffed by the prefent poffeffors; and the faid moft Serene Infant, or his male defcendants, fhall enjoy the faid three dutchies, conformably and under the conditions expreffed in the acts of ceffion of the Emprefs Queen of Hungary and Bohemia, and of the King of Sardinia.

Thefe acts of ceffion of the Emprefs Queen of Hungary and Bohemia, and of the King of Sardinia, fhall be delivered, together with their ratifications of the prefent treaty, to the Ambaffador Extraordinary and Plenipotentiary of the Catholic King; in like manner as the Ambaffadors Extraordinary and Plenipotentiaries of the moft Chriftian King, and Catholic King,

King, shall deliver, with the ratifications of their Majesties, to the Ambassador Extraordinary and Plenipotentiary of the King of Sardinia, the orders to the Generals of the French and Spanish troops to restore Savoy and the county of Nice to the persons appointed by that Prince to receive them; so that the restitution of the said states, and the taking possession of the dutchies of Parma, Placentia, and Guastalla, by or in the name of the most Serene Infant Don Philip, may be effected within the same time, conformably to the acts of cession, the tenor whereof follows.

WE Mary Theresia, &c. make known by these presents: Whereas, in order to put an end to the fatal war, certain preliminary articles were agreed upon, the 30th of April of this year, between the Ministers Plenipotentiaries of the most Serene and most Potent Prince George II. King of Great Britain, and the most Serene and most Potent Prince Lewis XV. the most Christian King, and their High Mightinesses the States General of the United Provinces, which have been since ratified by all the Powers concerned: the tenor of the 4th article whereof is conceived in the following manner.

The dutchies of Parma, Placentia, and Guastalla, shall be yielded to the most Serene Infant Don Philip, to serve him as an establishment, with the right of reversion to the present possessors; after that his Majesty the King of the Two Sicilies shall have succeeded to the crown of Spain: as also in case the said most Serene Infant Don Philip should happen to die without children.

And whereas a definitive treaty of peace having since been concluded, the several points relating to this affair have been, by virtue of the articles thereof, explained, by the common consent of the parties concerned, in the following manner.

In consideration of the restitutions that his most Christian Majesty and his Catholic Majesty make, by the present treaty, either to her Majesty the Queen of
                                          Hungary

Hungary and Bohemia, or to his Majesty the King of Sardinia, the dutchies of Parma, Placentia, and Guastalla shall, for the future, belong to the most Serene Infant Don Philip, to be possessed by him, and his male descendants born in lawful marriage, in the same manner, and in the same extent, as they have been or ought to be possessed by the present possessors; and the said most Serene Infant, or his male descendants, shall enjoy the said three dutchies, conformably and under the conditions expressed in the acts of cession of the Empress Queen of Hungary and Bohemia, and of the King of Sardinia.

These acts of cession of the Empress Queen of Hungary and Bohemia, and of the King of Sardinia, shall be delivered, together with their ratifications of the present treaty, to the Ambassador Extraordinary and Plenipotentiary of the Catholic King, in like manner, as the Ambassadors Extraordinary and Plenipotentiaries of the most Christian King and Catholic King shall deliver, with the ratifications of their Majesties, to the Ambassadors Extraordinary and Plenipotentiaries of the King of Sardinia, the orders to the generals of the French and Spanish troops to restore Savoy and the county of Nice to the persons appointed by that Prince to receive them; so that the restitution of the said States, and the taking possession of the dutchies of Parma, Placentia, and Guastalla, by or in the name of the most Serene Infant Don Philip, may be effected in the same time, conformably to the said acts of cession.

Wherefore, in order to fulfil those things, to which we have bound ourselves by the articles before inserted, and in the firm hope that the most Christian and Catholic Kings, and the future possessor of the aforesaid three dutchies, and his male descendants, will, on their part, *bonâ fide*, and punctually, fulfil the tenor of the articles above-mentioned, and will likewise restore to us, within the same time, the states and places which are to be restored to us in consequence of the second

and

and eighteenth articles of the same preliminaries,
we do yield and renounce, for us and our successors,
under the conditions expressed in the above-mentioned articles, all rights, claims, and pretensions to
us, under any title or cause whatsoever belonging,
upon the aforesaid three dutchies of Parma, Placentia,
and Guastalla, formerly possessed by us; and transfer
the same rights, claims, and pretensions, in the best
and most solemn manner possible, to the most Serene
Don Philip Infant of Spain, and his male descendants
to be born in lawful marriage, absolving all the inhabitants of the said dutchies from the allegiance and
oath which they have taken to us, who shall be obliged for the future to pay the same allegiance to those
to whom we have yielded our rights; all which however is to be understood only for that space of time
that either the said most Serene Infant Don Philip, or
one of his descendants, shall not have ascended either
the throne of the Two Sicilies, or of Spain; for at
that time, and in case the aforesaid Infant should die
without male descendants, we expresly reserve to ourselves, our heirs and successors, all rights, claims, and
pretensions, which have heretofore belonged to us,
and consequently the right of reversion to the said
dutchies.

In witness whereof, &c.

CHARLES Emanuel, &c. The desire we have
to contribute, on our part, to the most speedy re-
establishment of the public tranquillity, which lately
induced us to accede to the preliminary articles, signed
the 30th of April last, between the Ministers of his
Britannic Majesty, his most Christian Majesty, and the
Lords the States General of the United Provinces,
which we did on the 31st of May last, by our Plenipotentiary accordingly accede to, inducing us now to
accomplish as much as is to be performed on our part
in pursuance of them; and particularly for the execution of what is contained in the fourth article of the
said preliminaries, by virtue whereof the dutchies of
Parma,

Parma, Placentia, and Guaftalla, are to be yielded to the moft Serene Prince Don Philip, Infant of Spain, to hold, as an eftablifhment, with the right of reverfion to the prefent poffeffors; as foon as his Majefty the King of the Two Sicilies fhall have fucceeded to the crown of Spain, or that the faid Infant fhould happen to die without iffue male, we, in conformity thereto, do, by the prefent act, renounce, yield, and transfer, for ourfelves and our fucceffors, to the aforefaid moft Serene Infant Don Philip, and to his male iffue, and their defcendants born in lawful marriage, the town of Placentia, and the Plaifantine (whereof we were poffeffed) to be held and poffeffed by him as Duke of Placentia; renouncing to this end all rights, claims, and pretenfions, which we have upon them; referving, however, exprefsly, to us and our fucceffors, the right of reverfion in the cafes above-mentioned.

In witnefs whereof, &c.

VIII. In order to fecure and effectuate the faid reftitutions and ceffions, it is agreed, that they fhall be entirely executed and accomplifhed on all fides, in Europe, within the term of fix weeks, or fooner if poffible, to be reckoned from the day of the exchange of the ratifications of all the eight Powers; it being provided, that in fifteen days after the figning of the prefent treaty, the generals, or other perfons, whom the high contracting parties fhall think proper to appoint for that purpofe, fhall meet at Bruffels and at Nice, to concert and agree on the method of proceeding to the reftitutions, and of putting the parties in poffeffion, in a manner equally convenient for the good of the troops, the inhabitants, and the refpective countries; but fo that all and each of the high contracting Powers may be, agreeable to their intentions, and to the engagements contracted by the prefent treaty, in full and peaceable poffeffion, without any exception, of all that is to be acquired to them, either by reftitution or ceffion, within the faid term of fix weeks, or fooner if poffible, after the exchange of the ratifications of the prefent treaty by all the faid eight Powers.

IX. In confideration that, notwithftanding the reciprocal engagement taken by the eighteenth article of the preliminaries, importing that all the reftitutions and ceffions fhould be carried on equally, and fhould be executed at the fame time, his moft Chriftian Majefty engages, by the fixth article of the prefent treaty, to reftore within the fpace of fix weeks, or fooner if poffible, to be reckoned from the day of the exchange of the ratifications of the prefent treaty, all the conquefts which he has made in the Low Countries; whereas it is not poffible, confidering the diftance of the countries, that what relates to America fhould be effected within the fame time, or even to fix the time of its entire execution; his Britannic Majefty likewife engages on his part to fend to his moft Chriftian Majefty, immediately after the exchange of the ratifications of the prefent treaty, two perfons of rank and confideration, who fhall remain there as hoftages, till there fhall be received a certain and authentic account of the reftitution of Ifle Royal, called Cape Breton, and of all the conquefts which the arms or fubjects of his Britannic Majefty may have made, before or after the figning of the preliminaries, in the Eaft and Weft Indies.

Their Britannic and moft Chriftian Majefties oblige themfelves likewife to caufe to be delivered, upon the exchange of the ratifications of the prefent treaty, the duplicates of the orders addreffed to the commiffaries appointed to reftore and receive, refpectively, whatever may have been conquered on either fide in the faid Eaft and Weft Indies, agreeably to the fecond article of the preliminaries, and to the declarations of the 21ft and 31ft of May, and the 8th of July laft, in regard to what concerns the faid conquefts in the Eaft and Weft Indies. Provided neverthelefs, that Ifle Royal, called Cape Breton, fhall be reftored, with all the

the artillery and warlike ftores which fhall have been found therein on the day of its furrender, conformably to the inventories which have been made thereof, and in the condition that the faid place was in on the faid day of its furrender.   As to the other reftitutions, they fhall take place conformably to the meaning of the fecond article of the preliminaries, and of the declarations and convention of the 21ft and 31ft of May, and the 8th of July laft, in the condition in which things were on the 11th of June, N. S. in the Weft Indies, and on the 31ft of October alfo, N. S. in the Eaft Indies. And every thing befides fhall be re-eftablifhed on the foot that they were or ought to be before the prefent war.

The faid refpective commiffaries, as well thofe for the Weft, as thofe for the Eaft Indies, fhall be ready to fet out on the firft advice that their Britannic and moft Chriftian Majefties fhall receive of the exchange of the ratifications, furnifhed with all the neceffary inftructions, commiffions, powers, and orders, for the moft expeditious accomplifhment of their faid Majefties intentions, and of the engagements taken by the prefent treaty.

X. The ordinary revenues of the countries that are to be refpectively reftored or yielded, and the impofitions laid upon thofe countries for the entertainment and winter quarters of the troops, fhall belong to the Powers that are in poffeffion of them, till the day of the exchange of the ratifications of the prefent treaty, without, however, its being permitted to proceed to any kind of execution, provided fufficient fecurity has been given for the payment; it being always to be underftood, that the forage and utenfils for the troops fhall be furnifhed till the evacuations; in confequence of which, all the Powers promife and engage not to demand or exact impofitions and contributions which they may have laid upon the countries, towns, and places that they have poffeffed during the courfe of the war, and which had not been paid at the time that the

events

events of the faid war had obliged them to abandon the faid countries, towns, and places; all pretenfions of this nature being made void by the prefent treaty.

XI. All the papers, letters, documents, and archives, which were in the countries, eftates, towns, and places which are reftored, and thofe belonging to the countries yielded, fhall be refpectively, and *bonâ fide*, delivered or given up at the fame time, if poffible, as poffeffion fhall be taken, or at fartheft two months after the exchange of the ratifications of the prefent treaty of all the eight parties, in whatever places the faid papers or documents may be, namely, thofe which may have been removed from the archive of the great council of Mechlin.

XII. His Majefty the King of Sardinia fhall remain in poffeffion of all that he antiently and newly enjoyed, and particularly of the acquifition which he made in the year 1743 of the Vigevanafque, a part of the Pavefan, and the county of Anghiera, in the manner as this Prince now poffeffes them, by virtue of the ceffions that have been made of them to him.

XIII. The moft Serene Duke of Modena, by virtue as well of the prefent treaty, as of his rights, prerogatives, and dignities, fhall take poffeffion fix weeks, or fooner if poffible, after the exchange of the ratifications of the faid treaty, of all his ftates, places, forts, countries, effects, and revenues, and, in general, of all that he enjoyed before the war.

At the fame time fhall be likewife reftored to him his archives, documents, writings, and moveables, of what nature foever they may be, as alfo the artillery and warlike ftores which fhall have been found in his countries at the time of their being feized. As to what fhall be wanting, or fhall have been converted into another form, the juft value of the things fo taken away, and which are to be reftored, fhall be paid in ready money; which money, as well as the equivalent for the fiefs which the moft Serene Duke of Modena

poffeffed

poffeffed in Hungary, if they are not reftored to him,
fhall.be fettled and adjufted by the refpective.generals
or commiffaries, who, according to the eighth article
of the prefent treaty, are to affemble at Nice in fifteen
·days after the fignature, in order to agree upon the
means for executing the reciprocal reftitutions and putting in poffeffion, fo that at the fame time, and on the
fame day as the moft Serene Duke of Modena fhall
take poffeffion of all his ftates, he may likewife enter
into the enjoyment, either of his fiefs in Hungary, or
of the faid equivalent, and receive the value of fuch
things as cannot be reftored to him.   Juftice fhall alfo
be done him, within the fame time of fix weeks after
the exchange of the ratifications, with refpect to the
allodial effects of the Houfe of Guaftalla.

XIV. The moft Serene Republic of Genoa, as
well by virtue of the prefent treaty, as of its rights,
prerogatives, and dignities, fhall re-enter into the poffeffion, fix weeks, or fooner if possible, after the exchange of the ratifications of the faid treaty, of all the
ftates, forts, places, countries, effects, of what nature
foever they may be, rents and revenues, that it enjoyed
before the war; particularly, all and every one of the
members and fubjects of the faid republic fhall, within
the aforefaid term after the exchange of the ratifications of the prefent treaty, re-enter into the poffeffion,
enjoyment, and liberty of difpofing of all the funds
which they had in the bank of Vienna, in Auftria,
in Bohemia, or in any other part whatfoever of the
ftates of the Emprefs Queen of Hungary and Bohemia, and of thofe of the King of Sardinia; and the
intereft fhall be exactly and regularly paid them, to be
reckoned from the faid day of the exchange of the
ratifications of the prefent treaty.

XV: It has been fettled and agreed upon between
the eight high contracting parties, that, for the advantage and maintenance of the peace in general, and for

the

the tranquillity of Italy in particular, all things fhall remain there in the condition they were in before the war; faving, and after, the execution of the difpofitions made by the prefent treaty.

XVI. The treaty of the Affiento for the trade of negroes, figned at Madrid on the 26th of March, 1713, and the article of the annual fhip, making part of the faid treaty, are particularly confirmed by the prefent treaty, for the four years during which the enjoyment thereof has been interrupted, fince the commencement of the prefent war, and fhall be executed on the fame footing, and under the fame conditions, as they have or ought to have been executed before the faid war.

XVII. Dunkirk fhall remain fortified on the fide of the land, in the fame condition as it is at prefent; and as to the fide of the fea, it fhall remain on the footing of former treaties.

XVIII. The demands of money that his Britannic Majefty has, as Eletor of Hanover, upon the crown of Spain; the differences relating to the abbey of St. Hubert; the enclaves of Hainault, and the bureaux newly eftablifhed in the Low Countries; the pretenfions of the Eletor Palatine; and the other articles, which could not be regulated fo as to enter into the prefent treaty, fhall be amicably adjufted immediately by the commiffaries appointed for that purpofe on both fides, or otherwife, as fhall be agreed on by the Powers concerned.

XIX. The fifth article of the treaty of the quadruple alliance, concluded at London the 2d of Auguft, 1718, containing the guaranty of the fucceffion to the kingdom of Great Britain in the Houfe of his Britannic Majefty now reigning, and by which every thing has been provided for that can relate to the perfon who has taken the title of King of Great Britain, and to his defcendants of both fexes, is exprefsly confirmed

. firmed and renewed by the prefent article, as if it was here inferted in its full extent.'

XX. His Britannic Majefty, as Elector of Brunf-wic Lunenburg, as well for himfelf, as for his heirs and fucceffors, and all the ftates and poffeffions of his faid Majefty in Germany, are included and guarantied· by the prefent treaty of peace.

XXI. All the Powers interefted in the prefent treaty, who have guarantied the pragmatic fanction of the 19th of April, 1713, for the whole inheritance of the late Emperor Charles the Sixth, in favour of his daughter the Emprefs Queen of Hungary and Bohe-mia, now reigning, and of her defcendants for ever, according to the order eftablifhed by the faid pragmatic fanction, renew it in the beft manner poffible; except however the ceffions already made, either by the faid Emperor, or the faid Princefs, and thofe ftipulated by the prefent treaty.

XXII. The dutchy of Silefia, and the county of Glatz, as his Pruffian Majefty now poffeffes them, are guarantied to that Prince by all the Powers, parties, and contractors of the prefent treaty.

XXIII. All the Powers contracting and interefted in the prefent treaty, reciprocally and refpectively gua-ranty the execution thereof.

XXIV. The folemn ratifications of the prefent treaty, expedited in good and due form, fhall be ex-changed in this city of Aix-la-Chapelle, between all the eight parties, within the fpace of one month, or fooner if poffible, to be reckoned from the day of its fignature.

In witnefs whereof, we the under-written their Am-baffadors Extraordinary and Minifters Plenipo-tentiaries have figned with our hands, in their name, and by virtue of our full powers, the pre-fent

...fent treaty of peace, and have caused the feals of
our arms to be put thereto.

Done at Aix-la-Chapelle, the 18th of October,
1748.

(Signed)

(L. S.) *Sandwich.*   (L. S.) *W. Bentinck.*
(L. S.) *T. Robinfon.*   (L. S.) *G. A. Haffelaer.*
(L. S.) *St. Severin d'Aragon.* (L. S.) *J. V. Bouffele.*
(L. S.) *La Porte du Theil.*   (L. S.) *O. Z. Van Haren.*

Separate Articles.

I. SOME of the titles made ufe of by the contracting Powers, either in the full powers, and other
acts during the courfe of the negotiation, or in the
preamble of the prefent treaty, not being generally
acknowledged, it has been agreed, that no prejudice
fhall at any time refult therefrom to any of the faid
contracting parties; and that the titles taken or omitted
on either fide, on account of the faid negotiation, and
of the prefent treaty, fhall not be cited, or any confequence drawn therefrom.

II. It has been agreed and determined, that the
French language, made ufe of in all the copies of the
prefent treaty, and which may be ufed in the acts of
acceffion, fhall not be made a precedent that may be
alledged, or drawn into confequence, or in any manner
prejudice any of the contracting Powers; and that
they conform themfelves for the future to what has
been and ought to be obferved with regard to, and on
the part of Powers, who are ufed and have a right to
give and receive copies of like treaties and acts in another language than the French.

The prefent treaty, and the acceffions which fhall
intervene, having ftill the fame force and effect as if
the aforefaid practice had been therein obferved; and
the prefent feparate articles fhall have likewife the fame
force as if they were inferted in the treaty.

In

, In witnefs whereof, we the under-written Ambaffadors Extraordinary and Minifters Plenipotentiaries of his Britannic Majefty, of his moft Chriftian Majefty, and of the Lords the States General of the United Provinces, have figned the
prefent feparate articles, and caufed the feals of
our arms to be put thereto.

Done at Aix-la-Chapelle, the 18th of October,
1748.

(Signed)

(L. S.) *Sandwich.*   (L. S.) *W. Bentinck.*
(L. S.) *T. Robinfon.*   (L. S.) *G. A. Haffelaer.*
  (L. S.) *St. Severin d'Aragon.* (L. S.) *J. V. Borffele.*
  (L. S.) *La Porte du Theil.*   (L. S.) *O. Z. Van Haren.*

His Britannic *Majefty's Full Power.*

GEORGE *R.*

GEORGE the Second, by the grace of God, of
Great Britain, France, and Ireland, King, Defender
of the Faith, Duke of Brunfwic and Lunenburg,
Arch-treafurer of the Holy Roman Empire, and
Prince Elector, &c.; to all to whom thefe prefents
fhall come, greeting. Whereas, in order to perfect the
work of a general peace, fo happily begun, and to
bring it as foon as poffible to the defired conclufion,
we have thought proper to inveft two fit perfons with
the title and character of our Ambaffadors Extraordinary and Plenipotentiaries at the prefent congrefs:
Know ye therefore, that we having entire confidence
in the zeal, judgment, fkill, and abilities in managing
great affairs, of our right trufty and well-beloved coufin John Earl of Sandwich, as alfo our trufty and well-
beloved Thomas Robinfon, Knight of the moft honourable Order of the Bath, and our Minifter Plenipotentiary to our good fifter the Emprefs of Germany,
Queen of Hungary and Bohemia, have named, made,
conftituted, and appointed, as we by thefe prefents
name, make, conftitute, and appoint them our true
and

and undoubted Ambassadors Extraordinary, Ministers, Commissioners, Deputies, Procurators, and Plenipotentiaries, giving unto them, or each of them, jointly or separately, all and all manner of power and authority, as well as our general and special command (yet so that the general do not derogate from the special, or otherwise) to repair to Aix-la-Chapelle, or to any other place where the treaty and negotiations for the above-mentioned peace and tranquillity may be to be carried on; and there, for us, and in our name, together with the Ambassadors, Commissioners, Deputies, and Plenipotentiaries of the Princes and States whom it may concern, properly vested with the same power and authority to meet in congress and conference, either singly and separately, or jointly and in a body; and with them to agree upon, treat, consult, and conclude what may be necessary for making a firm and stable peace, and re-establishing a sincere friendship and good harmony; and to sign for us, and in our name, every thing so agreed upon and concluded; and to make a treaty or treaties upon what shall have been so agreed and concluded, and to do and transact all other matters which may appertain to the finishing the abovesaid work, in as ample manner and form, and with equal force and efficacy, as we ourselves could do, if personally present; engaging, and on our Royal word promising, that whatever things shall be transacted and concluded by our said Ambassadors Extraordinary and Plenipotentiaries, or by either of them, shall be agreed to, acknowledged, and accepted by us, in the fullest manner; and that we will never suffer, either in the whole or in part, any person whatsoever to infringe or act contrary to the same. In witness whereof, we have signed these presents with our Royal hand, and have caused to be affixed thereto our great seal of Great Britain. Given at our palace at Herrnhausen, the $\frac{\text{Thirtieth}}{\text{Tenth}}$ day of $\frac{\text{July}}{\text{August,}}$ in the year of our Lord 1748, and in the twenty-second year of our reign.

The

The moſt Chriſtian King's Full Power:

LEWIS, by the grace of God, King of France, and Navarre; to all thoſe to whom theſe preſents ſhall come, greeting. Whereas we are deſirous of omitting nothing in our power in order to accelerate the concluſion of the great and ſalutary work of peace, and the re-eſtabliſhment of the public tranquillity, truſting entirely to the capacity and experience, zeal and fidelity for our ſervice, of our dear and well-beloved the Count de St. Severin d'Aragon, Knight of our Orders, and the Sieur de la Porte du Theil, Counſellor in our councils, Secretary of our chamber and cabinet, and of the commands of our moſt dear and moſt beloved ſon the Dauphin. For theſe cauſes, and other good conſiderations us thereto moving, we have commiſſioned and ordained them, and by theſe preſents, ſigned with our hand, do commiſſion and ordain, and have given them, and do give to the one and to the other jointly, as well as to either of them ſeparately, in caſe of abſence or indiſpoſition of the other, full power, commiſſion, and ſpecial order, in our name, and in the quality of our Ambaſſadors Extraordinary and Plenipotentiaries, to agree with the Ambaſſadors and Miniſters actually aſſembled at Aix-la-Chapelle for the concluſion of a peace, provided with full powers in good form on the part of their maſters, to ſettle, conclude, and ſign ſuch treaties, articles, and conventions, as the one and the other together, or either of them, in the aforeſaid caſe of abſence or indiſpoſition of the other, ſhall think good, and chiefly the definitive treaty, which ſhall re-eſtabliſh a ſolid peace and perfect union between us and the Princes and States formerly at war, or auxiliaries of the Powers at war; promiſing, on the faith and word of a King, to accept, keep firm and ſtable for ever, accompliſh and execute punctually, all that the ſaid Count de St. Severin d'Aragon, and the ſaid Sieur de la Porte du Theil, or either of them, in the ſaid caſes

of

of abfence or indifpofition of the other, fhall have ftipulated, promifed, and figned by virtue of this prefent power, without ever contravening the fame, or fuffering it to be contravened, for what caufe or under what pretext foever; as alfo to caufe our letters of ratification thereof to be difpatched in good form, and exchanged in the time that fhall be agreed upon: for fuch is our pleafure. In witnefs whereof, we have caufed our feal to be put to thefe prefents. Given at Fontainebleau, the 7th day of October, in the year of grace 1748, and of our reign the thirty-fourth.

(Signed)　　LEWIS.

(And lower)
　　By the King,
　　　　(Signed)　　　*Brulart.*

And fealed with the great feal in yellow wax.

The States General's Full Power.

THE States General of the United Provinces of the Netherlands; to all thofe who fhall fee thefe prefents, greeting. Whereas we defire nothing more ardently than to fee the war, with which Chriftendom is at prefent afflicted, terminated by a good peace; and the city of Aix-la-Chapelle has been agreed upon for the place of the conferences; we, by the fame defire of putting a ftop, as far as fhall be in us, to the defolation of fo many provinces, and to the effufion of fo much Chriftian blood, have been willing to contribute thereto all that depends upon us; and, to this end, to depute to the faid affembly fome perfons out of our own body, who have given feveral proofs of the knowledge and experience which they have of public affairs; as well as of the affection which they have for the good of our State.

And whereas the Sieurs William Count Bentinck, Lord of Rhoon and Pendrecht, of the body of Nobles of the province of Holland and Weft Frizeland,

Curator

Curator. of: the Univerfity. of Leyden, &c.; Frederic
Henry Baron Waffenaer, Lord of Catwyck and Zand;
of the body of Nobles of. the province, of Holland
and Weft Frizeland, Hoog-Heemrade of Rhynland,
&c.; Gerard Arnold Haffelaer, Schepen and Senator
of. the city of Amfterdam, and Director of the Eaft
India Company; and Onno Zwier van Haren, Grietman of Weft Stellingwerf; deputed counfellor of the
province of Frizeland; and Commiffary General of all
the Swifs and Grifon troops in our fervice; refpective
deputies in our Affembly, and in the Council of State,
on the part of the provinces of Holland and Weft
Frizeland, and Frizeland, have diftinguifhed themfelves
in feveral employments of importance for our fervice,
in which they have given marks of their fidelity, application, and addrefs in the management of affairs : for
thefe caufes, and other good confiderations us thereunto moving, we have commiffioned, ordained, and
deputed the faid Sieurs Bentinck, Waffenaer, Haffelaer,
and van Haren, do commiffion, ordain, and depute
them by thefe prefents, and have given and do give
unto them full power, commiffion, and fpecial order,
to go to Aix-la-Chapelle, in quality of our Ambaffadors Extraordinary and Plenipotentiaries for the peace,
and there to confer with the Ambaffadors Extraordinary
and Plenipotentiaries of his moft Chriftian Majefty,
and his allies, provided with fufficient powers, and
there to treat of the means of terminating and pacifying the differences which at prefent occafion the war;
and our faid Ambaffadors Extraordinary and Plenipotentiaries all together, or any of them, or any one
among them, in cafe of abfence of the others, by
ficknefs or other impediment, fhall have power to
agree about the fame, and thereupon to conclude and
fign a good and fure peace, and in general to tranfact,
negotiate, promife, and grant whatever they fhall think
neceffary to the faid effect of the peace, and generally
to do every thing that we could do if we were there
prefent, even though a more fpecial power and order;

8

not

not contained in these presents, should be necessary for that purpose; promising sincerely and *bonâ fide* to accept and keep firm and stable what by our said Ambassadors Extraordinary and Plenipotentiaries, or by any, or any one of them, in case of sickness, absence, or other impediment of the others, shall have been stipulated, promised, and granted, and thereof to cause our letters of ratification to be dispatched in the time that they shall have promised in our name to furnish them.   Given at the Hague, in our assembly, under our great seal, the paraphe of the president of our assembly, and the signature of our first greffier, the eighth day of March, 1748.

(Signed)   H. van Isselmuden, V.

(Lower)
By order of the said Lords the States General,
(Signed)   H. Fagel.

The States General's Full Power.

THE States General of the United Provinces of the Netherlands ; to all those who shall see these presents, greeting.   Whereas we desire nothing more ardently than to see the war, with which Christendom is at present afflicted, terminated by a good peace; and the city of Aix-la-Chapelle has been agreed upon for the place of the conferences: we, by the same desire of putting a stop, as far as shall be in us, to the desolation of so many provinces, and to the effusion of so much Christian blood, have been willing to contribute thereto all that depends upon us; and, to this end, have already deputed some persons heretofore to the said assembly out of our own body, who have given several proofs of the knowledge and experience which they have of public affairs, as well as of the affection which they have for the good of our State; to wit, the Sieurs William Bentinck, Lord of Rhoon and Pendrecht, of the body of Nobles of the province of Holland and West Frizeland, Curator of the university

fity

fity of Leyden, &c.; Frederic Henry Baron Wassenaer,
Lord of Catwyck and Zand, of the body of Nobles
of the province of Holland and West-Friesland, Hoog-
Heemrade of Rhynland, &c.; Gerard Arnold Hasselaer, Schepen and Senator of the city of Amsterdam,
and Director of the East India Company; and Onno
Zwier van Haren, Grietman of West-Stellingwerff, Deputed Counsellor of the province of Friesland, and Commissary General of all the Swiss and Grison troops in
our service; respective Deputies in our Assembly, and
in the Council of State, on the part of the provinces
of Holland and West-Friesland, and Friesland. And
whereas we have at present thought proper to join a
fifth person to the four above-mentioned, for this same
purpose; and the Sieur John Baron Van Borssele, first
Noble, and representing the nobility, in the States,
in the Council, and in the Admiralty of Zeeland, Director of the East India Company, and Deputy in
our Assembly on the part of the said province of Zeeland, has distinguished himself in several employments
of importance for our service, in which he has given
marks of his fidelity, application, and address in the
management of affairs: for these causes, and other good
considerations us thereunto moving, we have commissioned, ordained, and deputed the said Sieur van Borssele, do commission, ordain, and depute him, by these
presents, and have given and do give unto him full
power, commission, and special order, to go to Aix-
la-Chapelle, in quality of our Ambassador Extraordinary and Plenipotentiary for the peace, and there to
confer with the Ambassadors Extraordinary and Plenipotentiaries of his most Christian Majesty and his allies, provided with sufficient full powers, and there to
treat of the means of terminating and pacifying the
differences which at present occasion the war; and our
said Ambassador Extraordinary and Plenipotentiary,
together with the said Sieurs Bentinck, Wassenaer,
Hasselaer, and Van Haren, our other four Ambassadors Extraordinary and Plenipotentiaries; or with any

or any one of them, or even alone, in cafe of abfence
of the others by ficknefs or other impediment, fhall
have power to agree about the fame, and thereupon to
conclude and fign a good and fure peace, and in general to tranfact, negotiate, promife, and grant whatever he fhall think neceffary for the faid effect of the
peace, and generally do every thing that we could do
if we were there prefent, even though a more fpecial
power and order, not contained in thefe prefents, fhould
be neceffary for that purpofe; promifing fincerely, and
bonâ fide, to accept and keep firm and ftable whatever
by the faid Sieur van Borffele, together with our
other four Ambaffadors Extraordinary and Plenipotentiaries, or any or any one of them, or by him alone,
in cafe of ficknefs, abfence, or other impediment of
the others, fhall have been ftipulated, promifed, and
granted, and thereof to caufe our letters of ratification to be difpatched in the time that they fhall have
promifed in our name to furnifh them.   Given at the
Hague, in our Affembly, under our great feal, the paraphe of the Prefident of our Affembly, and the fignature of our firft Greffier, the 25th day of April,
1748.

(Signed)   *H. V. Hamerfter, V*.

(Lower)

By order of the faid Lords the States General,
(Signed)   *H. Fagel.*

The Acceffion of the Emprefs Queen of Hungary.

In the Name of the moft Holy and Undivided Trinity, Father, Son, and Holy Ghoft.

BE it known to all whom it fhall or may concern.
The Ambaffadors Extraordinary and Plenipotentiaries
of his Britannic Majefty, of his moft Chriftian Majefty, and of the High and Mighty Lords the States
General of the United Provinces, having concluded
and figned, in this city of Aix-la-Chapelle, on the 18th
day of this prefent month of October, upon the bafis
of

óf the preliminaries which were agreed upon arid concluded between them the 30th day of April of the
prefent year, a general and definitive treaty of peace,
and two feparate articles, the tenor of which treaty and
feparate articles follows.

[Fiat Infertio.]

And the faid Ambaffadors Extraordinary and Plenipotentiaries having, in a friendly manner, invited the
Ambaffador Extraordinary and Plenipotentiary of her
Majefty the Emprefs Queen of Hungary and Bohemia, to accede thereto, in the name of her faid Majefty;

The Ambaffadors underwritten, that is to fay, on
the part of the moft Serene and moft Potent Prince,
George the Second, by the grace of God, King of
Great Britain, John Earl of Sandwich, Vifcount
Hinchinbrooke, Baron Montagu of St. Neots, Peer
of England, Firft Lord Commiffioner of the Admiralty, one of the Lords of the Regency of the kingdom, his Minifter Plenipotentiary to the Lords the
States General of the United Provinces; and Sir Thomas Robinfon, Knight of the moft honourable Order
of the Bath, and his Minifter Plenipotentiary to his
Majefty the Emperor of the Romans, and to her Majefty the Emprefs Queen of Hungary and Bohemia:
and on the part of the moft Serene and moft Potent
Princefs Maria Therefia, by the grace of God, Queen
of Hungary and Bohemia, Emprefs, the Lord Wen-
ceflas Anthony Count de Kaunitz Rittberg, Lord of
Effens, Steteſdorff, Wittmund, Aufterlitz, Hungrifch-
brod, Wiefe, &c. actual Privy Counfellor to their
Imperial Majefties, by virtue of their full powers,
which they have communicated to each other, and
copies whereof are annexed to the end of this prefent
act, have agreed on what follows.

That her Majefty the Emprefs Queen of Hungary
and Bohemia, being defirous of contributing to re-
eftablifh and confirm, as foon as poffible, the repofe of

Europe, accedes, by virtue of the present act, to the said treaty and two separate articles, without any reserve or exception, in the firm confidence that every thing, which is therein promised to her said Majesty, will be *bonâ fide* fulfilled; declaring, at the same time, and promising, that she will, in like manner, most faithfully perform all the articles, clauses, and conditions which relate to her.

His Britannic Majesty likewise accepts the present accession of the Empress Queen of Hungary and Bohemia, and promises, in like manner, to perform, without any reserve or exception, all the articles, clauses, and conditions, contained in the said treaty, and the two separate articles before inserted.

The ratifications of the present act shall be exchanged, in this city of Aix-la-Chapelle, within the space of three weeks, to be computed from this day.

In witness whereof, we the Ambassadors Extraordinary and Plenipotentiaries of his Britannic Majesty, and her Majesty the Empress Queen of Hungary and Bohemia, have signed the present act, and have thereunto affixed the seal of our arms.

Done at Aix-la-Chapelle, the 23d day of October, 1748.

(L. S.) *Le Comte V. A. de Kaunitz Rittberg.*

The Empress Queen of Hungary's *Full Power.*

WE Maria Theresia, by the grace of God, Empress of the Romans, and of Germany, of Hungary, Bohemia, Dalmatia, Croatia, Sclavonia, &c. Queen; Arch-Dutchess of Austria, Dutchess of Burgundy, Brabant, Milan, Styria, Carinthia, Carniolia, Mantua, Parma and Placentia, Limburgh, Luxemburgh, Gueldre, Wurtemberg, of the Upper and Lower Silesia; Princess of Suabia and Transylvania; Marchioness of the Holy Roman Empire, Burgovia, Moravia, and the Upper and Lower Lusatia; Countess of Habspurg,

purg, Flanders, Tirol, Ferrete, Kybourg, Goritia, Gra-
difca, and Artois; Countefs of Namur; Lady of the
marches of Slavonia, the Port of Naon, Saline, and
Mechlin, &c.; Dutchefs of Lorraine and Barr, Great
Dutchefs of Tufcany, &c. do make known and certify,
by virtue of thefe prefents. Whereas we are informed
that the Congrefs, which had been opened at Breda, is
diffolved; and that conferences are to be held at Aix-la-
Chapelle, between the Minifters of the feveral Princes
engaged in the prefent war, authorized to agree upon
the means of terminating the differences that have
arifen between them, and reftoring peace, and, as we
have nothing more at heart, than to do every thing, that
depends upon us, towards obtaining, as foon as poffible,
fo defirable an end, in the moft fecure and effectual
manner, we lofe no time in doing our part towards
the promoting fo falutary a work, by fending thither
our Minifters Plenipotentiaries, whom we have, moreover, invefted with the character of our Ambaffadors.
Confiding therefore entirely in the often tried fidelity,
experience in bufinefs, and great prudence of our
actual Privy Counfellor, Wenceflaus Anthony de Kaunitz and Rittberg, Count of the Holy Roman Empire,
as alfo of Thaddæus, Free Baron of Reifchach, our
Lord of the Bed-chamber, Counfellor for the government of Anterior Auftria, and our Minifter to the High
and Mighty the States General of the United Provinces; both of whom, and each of them, we have
invefted with the character of our Ambaffador, as well
as with full powers, as we do accordingly, by thefe prefents, inveft them both, and each of them, in cafe of
the abfence or hinderance of the other, in the moft ample manner poffible; to the end that both or either of
them, in cafe of the abfence or hinderance of the other,
may join their endeavours with our allies and their Minifters, hold friendly conferences with thofe of other
Princes, engaged in the prefent war againft us or our allies, and with any one or more of them, furnifhed with
the like full powers, and agree upon any matters and

G g 3   things

things relating thereto, and whatever shall have been so agreed upon, whether jointly or separately, to sign and seal; and, in a word, to do all those things, in our name, which we ourselves could do if personally present: promising, on our Imperial, Royal, and Archiducal word, that we will agree to, accept of, and faithfully fulfil, all and singular such acts as our aforesaid Ministers Plenipotentiaries, invested over and above with the characters of our Ambassadors, shall have so done, concluded, and signed. In witness whereof, and for its greater force, we have signed the present full powers with our own hand, and ordered our Imperial, Royal, and Archiducal seal to be affixed thereto. Given in our city of Vienna, the 19th day of December, in the year 1747, the eighth year of our reign.

(Signed)   MARIA THERESIA.
             C. Count Ulfeld.

By command of her Sacred Imperial Royal Majesty,   *John Christoph, Bartenstein.*

His Catholic Majesty's Accession.

In the Name of the most Holy and Undivided Trinity, Father, Son, and Holy Ghost.

BE it known to all those to whom it shall belong or can belong. The Ambassadors and Plenipotentiaries of his Britannic Majesty, of his most Christian Majesty, and of the High and Mighty Lords the States General of the United Provinces, having concluded and signed at Aix-la-Chapelle, the 18th of October of this year, a definitive treaty of peace, and two separate articles; the tenor of which treaty and separate articles is as follows.

[*Fiat Insertio.*]

And the said Ambassadors and Plenipotentiaries having amicably invited the Ambassador Extraordinary and Plenipotentiary of his Catholic Majesty to accede thereto, in the name of his said Majesty; the under-written Ambassadors, to wit, on the part of the most

†   Serene

Serene and moſt Potent Prince, George the Second, by
the grace of God, King of Great Britain, France,
and Ireland, Duke of Brunſwic and Lunenburg, Arch-
treaſurer and Elector of the Holy Roman Empire, &c.
the Lords John Earl of Sandwich, Viſcount of Hinchinbrooke, Baron Montagu of St. Neots, Peer of
England, firſt Lord Commiſſioner of the Admiralty,
one of the Lords Regents of the kingdom, his Miniſter Plenipotentiary to the Lords the States General
of the United Provinces; and Thomas Robinſon,
Knight of the moſt honourable Order of the Bath, and
his Miniſter Plenipotentiary to his Majeſty the Emperor of the Romans, and her Majeſty the Empreſs
Queen of Hungary and Bohemia: and on the part
of the moſt Serene and moſt Potent Prince, Ferdinand
the Sixth, by the grace of God, King of Spain and of
the Indies, the Lord Don James Maſſone de Lima y
Soto Mayor, Lord of the Bed-chamber of his ſaid
Catholic Majeſty, and Major General of his armies.
By virtue of their full powers, which they have communicated, and copies whereof are added at the end
of the preſent act, have agreed upon what follows.

That his Catholic Majeſty, deſiring to contribute and
concur to re-eſtabliſh and ſettle, as ſoon as poſſible,
the peace of Europe, accedes, by virtue of the preſent act, to the ſaid treaty, and two ſeparate articles,
without any reſerve or exception, in a firm confidence,
that whatſoever is promiſed therein to his ſaid Majeſty,
ſhall be faithfully fulfilled; declaring, at the ſame time,
and promiſing, that he will alſo perform moſt faithfully all the articles, clauſes, and conditions which
concern him.

In like manner his Britannic Majeſty accepts the
preſent acceſſion of his Catholic Majeſty; and likewiſe promiſes to perform, without any reſerve or exception, all the articles, clauſes, and conditions contained in the ſaid treaty, and two ſeparate articles, inſerted above.

The

The ratifications of the prefent act fhall be exchanged in this city of Aix-la-Chapelle in the fpace of a month, to be computed from this day.

In teftimony whereof, we the Ambaffadors Extraordinary and Plenipotentiaries of his Britannic Majefty, and of his Catholic Majefty, have figned the prefent act, and have caufed the feal of our arms to be fet thereto.

Done at Aix-la-Chapelle, the 20th of October, 1748.

(L. S.) *Sandwich.*   (L. S.) *Don Jayme Mafones de*
(L. S.) *T. Robinfon.*   *Lima y Soto Mayor.*

His Catholic Majefty's Full Power.

FERDINAND, by the grace of God, King of Caftille, of Leon, of Aragon, of the Two Sicilies, of Jerufalem, of Navarre, of Granada, of Toledo, of Valencia, of Galicia, of Majorca, of Seville, of Sardinia, of Cordova, of Corfica, of Murcia, of Jaen, of the Algarves, of Algezira, of Gibraltar, of the Canary Iflands, of the Eaft and Weft Indies, the Iflands and Terra Firma of the Ocean Sea, Archduke of Auftria, Duke of Burgundy, of Brabant and Milan, Count of Hapfburg, of Flanders, Tirol, and Barcelona, Lord of Bifcay and of Molina, &c. Whereas it has been my moft earneft defire, ever fince Divine Providence has trufted me with the government of the vaft dominions annexed to my crown, to put an honourable end to the troubles in which I found my arms involved, and to concur in giving peace to Europe, by all the juft means that fhould appear moft conducive to that end: and whereas I knowing that feveral Minifters, and particularly thofe of the Powers now at war, are meeting at Aix-la-Chapelle with the fame view to a general pacification; and it being therefore neceffary that I fhould appoint one to affift on my part, endowed with that fidelity, zeal, and underftanding, requifite for fuch a purpofe, and finding in you, Don
Jaime

Jaime-Mafone de Lima, Lord of my Bed-chamber, and Major General of my armies, thefe fpecial and diftinguifhed qualifications; I do chufe and nominate you, to the end that, invefted with the charaƐter of my Ambaffador Extraordinary and Plenipotentiary, you do repair, in my name, to Aix-la-Chapelle, and, reprefenting at that place my own perfon, you do treat and confer with the Minifter or Minifters of the Powers now at war, who do already, or fhall hereafter, refide there, or in any other place where it fhall be thought convenient to treat; and to the end that you may, in the fame manner, conclude and fign with the faid Minifters, the treaty or treaties which fhall tend to the fole view of producing a folid and honourable peace; and whatever you may thus treat of, conclude, and fign, I do from this time acknowledge as accepted and ratified, and promife, upon my Royal word, to obferve and fulfil, and to caufe the fame to be obferved and fulfilled, in the fame manner as if I myfelf had treated and conferred upon, concluded and figned the fame. To which end, I do hereby give you all my authority and full power, in the moft ample manner as by law required. In witnefs whereof, I have caufed the prefents to be difpatched, figned with my hand, fealed with my fecret feal, and counterfigned by my under-written counfellor, and fecretary of ftate, and of the general difpatch of war, the revenues, Indies, and marine. Given at Aranjués, the 12th of May, 1748. *I the* KING.

Cenon de Somo de Villa.

His Sardinian Majefty's Acceffion.

In the Name of the moft Holy and Undivided Trinity, Father, Son, and Holy Ghoft.

BE it known to all thofe to whom it fhall or may belong.

The Ambaffadors Extraordinary and Plenipotentiaries of his Britannic Majefty, of his moft Chriftian Majefty,

Majefty, and of the High and Mighty Lords the States General of the United Provinces, having concluded and figned in this city of Aix-la-Chapelle, the 18th of the month of October laft, upon the foundation of the preliminaries at firft agreed to and fettled amongft them the thirtieth of April of this year, a general and definitive treaty of peace, and two feparate articles, the tenor of which treaty and feparate articles is as fol-lows.

[*Fiat Infertio.*]

And the faid Ambaffadors Extraordinary and Pleni-potentiaries having amicably invited the Ambaffadors Extraordinary and Plenipotentiaries of his Majefty the King of Sardinia to accede thereto, in the name of his faid Majefty;

The under-written Ambaffadors, to wit, on the part of the moft Serene and moft Powerful Prince, George the Second, by the grace of God, King of Great Bri-tain, France, and Ireland, the Lords John Earl of Sandwich, Vifcount of Hinchinbrooke, Baron Mon-tagu of Saint Neots, Peer of England, Firft Lord Commiffioner of the Admiralty, one of the Lords Re-gents of the kingdom, his Minifter Plenipotentiary to the Lords the States General of the United Provinces; and Thomas Robinfon, Knight of the moft honourable Order of the Bath, and his Minifter Plenipotentiary to his Majefty the Emperor of the Romans, and her Ma-jefty the Emprefs Queen of Hungary and Bohemia: and on the part of the moft Serene and moft Potent Prince, Charles Emanuel the Third, by the grace of God, King of Sardinia, the Lords Don Jofeph Offo-rio, Chevalier Grand Croix, and Grand Confervator of the Military Order of the Saints Maurice and Lazarus, and Envoy Extraordinary of his Majefty the King of Sardinia to his Majefty the King of Great Britain; and Jofeph Borré, Count de la Chavanne, his Counfellor of State, and his Minifter to the Lords the States Ge-neral of the United Provinces, by virtue of their full powers, which they have communicated to each other,

and

and copies whereof are added at the end of the present act, have agreed upon what follows.

That his Majefty the King of Sardinia, defiring to contribute and concur to re-eftablifh and fettle, as foon as poffible, the peace of Europe, accedes, by virtue of the prefent act, to the faid treaty, and two feparate articles, in a firm confidence, that whatfoever is promifed therein to his faid Majefty, fhall be faithfully fulfilled; declaring at the fame time, and promifing, that he will alfo perform, moft faithfully, all the articles, claufes, and conditions, which regard him.

In like manner his Britannic Majefty accepts the prefent acceflion of his Majefty the King of Sardinia; and likewife promifes to perform, without any referve or exception, all the articles, claufes, and conditions, contained in the faid treaty, and the two feparate articles, inferted above.

The ratifications of the prefent act fhall be exchanged in this city of Aix-la-Chapelle, in the fpace of twenty-five days, to be computed from this day.

In teftimony whereof, we the Ambaffadors Extraordinary and Plenipotentiaries of his Britannic Majefty, and of his Majefty the King of Sardinia, have figned the prefent act, and have caufed the feal of our arms to be fet thereto.

Done at Aix-la-Chapelle, the feventh of November, one thoufand feven hundred forty-eight.

(L. S.) *T. Robinfon.*   (L. S.) *Offorio.*
(L. S.) *De la Chavanne.*

The King of Sardinia's *Full Power.*

CHARLES EMANUEL, by the grace of God, King of Sardinia, of Cyprus, and of Jerufalem; Duke of Savoy, of Montferrat, of Aofte, of Chablais, of Genevois, and of Plaifance; Prince of Piedmont and of Oneille; Marquis of Italy, of Saluces, of Sufa, of Ivrée, of Ceve, of Maro, of Oriftan, and of Sefane; Count of Maurienne, of Geneva, of Nice, of Tende,

of

of Romont, of Aft, of Alexandria, of Gocean, of No-
vara, of Tortona, of Vigevano, and of Bobbio; Baron of Vaud and of Faucigny; Lord of Verceil, of
Pignerol, of Tarantaise, of the Lumelline, and of the
Valley of Sesia; Prince and Perpetual Vicar of the
Holy Empire in Italy, &c.; to all who shall see these
presents, greeting. Whereas, after having acceded to
the preliminary articles of peace, signed the 30th of
April last at Aix-la-Chapelle, we are sincerely desirous
of concurring in the perfect re-establishment of the
general peace in Europe, to which all the Powers,
that have signed and acceded, as we have done, to the
aforesaid preliminary articles, are disposed to give their
assistance, by reducing those same preliminary articles,
and other acts depending thereon, into one definitive treaty of general peace. For these reasons, and
other considerations us thereunto moving, we, trusting
in the capacity, experience, zeal and fidelity for our
service, of our dear, well-beloved, and trusty, the Chevalier Ossorio, Knight, Grand Croix and Grand Con-
servator of our Military Order of the Saints Maurice
and Lazarus, and our Envoy Extraordinary to the
King of Great Britain; and the Count Borré de la
Chavanne, our Counsellor of State, our Minister to
the Lords the States General of the United Provinces, and our Minister Plenipotentiary to the conferences of Aix-la-Chapelle, have named and deputed
them, as by these presents we do name and depute
them, our Ambassadors Extraordinary and Plenipotentiaries; and have given them, and do give them, power, commission, and special order, in our name, and in
the said quality of our Ambassadors Extraordinary and
Plenipotentiaries, to make, conclude, and sign, both
jointly, or one of them alone, in case of absence, sickness, or other hinderance of the other, with the respective Ambassadors Extraordinary and Plenipotentiaries
of the above-mentioned Powers, jointly or separately,
provided with powers for that purpose, such definitive
treaty of peace, articles, conventions, or acts, as they
shall

fhall think fit, for re-eftablifhing, in a folid manner, the general peace in Europe, or to accede to thofe which fhall have been already concluded and figned for the fame end; willing, that they fhould, upon thofe occafions, act with the fame authority as we would do, if we were prefent in perfon, and even if any thing fhould occur, which might require a more fpecial order, not contained in thefe prefents: promifing, upon the faith and word of a King, to obferve and caufe to be obferved inviolably all that fhall be done, agreed, regulated, and figned by the above-mentioned Chevalier Offorio and Count de la Chavanne, our Ambaffadors Extraordinary and Plenipotentiaries, without contravening, or fuffering any contravention thereto, directly or indirectly, for what caufe or under what pretext foever it fhall or may be; as alfo to caufe to be difpatched our letters of ratification thereof in due form, to be exchanged within the term which fhall be agreed on. In witnefs whereof, we have figned thefe prefents with our hand, and caufed them to be counterfigned by the Marquis D. Leopold de Carret de Gorzegne, our Firft Secretary of State for foreign affairs, and caufed the fecret feal of our arms to be affixed thereto. Given at Turin, the twenty-fourth of the month of Auguft, in the year of our Lord one thoufand feven hundred and forty-eight, and of our reign the nineteenth.

(L S.) C. EMANUEL.

(Lower)   *Carret de Gorzegne.*

The Acceffion of the Duke of Modena.

In the Name of the moft Holy and Undivided Trinity, Father, Son, and Holy Ghoft.

BE it known to all thofe to whom it fhall or may belong. The Ambaffadors Extraordinary and Plenipotentiaries of his Britannic Majefty, of his moft Chriftian Majefty, and of the High and Mighty Lords the States General of the United Provinces, having

concluded

concluded and figned, in this city of Aix-la-Chapelle, the 18th of the prefent month of October, upon the foundation of the preliminaries, at firft agreed upon and concluded amongft them the 30th day of April of this year, a general and definitive treaty of peace, and two feparate articles, the tenor of which treaty and feparate articles follows.

[*Fiat Infertio.*]

And the faid Ambaffadors Extraordinary and Plenipotentiaries having amicably invited the Minifter Plenipotentiary of his moft Serene Highnefs, Francis the Third, by the grace of God, Duke of Modena, Reggio, Mirandola, &c. to accede thereto, in the name of his moft Serene Highnefs;

The under-written Ambaffadors and Minifter Plenipotentiary, to wit, on the part of the moft Serene and moft Potent Prince George the Second, by the grace of God King of Great Britain, France, and Ireland, the Lords, John Earl of Sandwich, Vifcount of Hinchinbrooke, Baron Montagu of St. Neots, Peer of England, Firft Lord Commiffioner of the Admiralty, one of the Lords Regents of the kingdom, his Minifter Plenipotentiary to the Lords the States General of the United Provinces; and Thomas Robinfon, Knight of the moft honourable Order of the Bath, and his Minifter Plenipotentiary to his Majefty the Emperor of the Romans, and her Majefty the Emprefs Queen of Hungary and Bohemia: and on the part of his moft Serene Highnefs the Duke of Modena, the Sieur Count de Monzone, his Counfellor of State, and Colonel in his fervice, and his Minifter Plenipotentiary to his moft Chriftian Majefty; by virtue of their full powers, which they have communicated to each other, and of which copies are added at the end of the prefent act, have agreed on what follows.

That his moft Serene Highnefs the Duke of Modena, defiring to contribute and concur to re-eftablifh and fettle, as foon as poffible, the peace of Europe, accedes,

accedes, by virtue of the prefent act, to the faid treaty
and two feparate articles, without any referve or exception, in a firm confidence, that what is promifed
to his faid moft Serene Highnefs therein, fhall be
faithfully fulfilled; declaring and promifing, at the
fame time, that he will alfo perform, moft faithfully,
all the articles, claufes, and conditions, which concern
him.

In like manner his Britannic Majefty accepts the
prefent acceffion of his moft Serene Highnefs the Duke
of Modena, and promifes likewife to fulfil, without
any referve or exception, all the articles, claufes, and
conditions, contained in the faid treaty and the two feparate articles, inferted above.

The ratifications of the prefent act fhall be exchanged, in this city of Aix-la-Chapelle, in the fpace
of three weeks, to be computed from this day.

. In teftimony whereof, we the Ambaffadors Extraor-
- dinary and Minifter Plenipotentiary of his Britannic Majefty, and of his moft Serene Highnefs the Duke of Modena, have figned the prefent act, and have caufed the feal of our arms to
be fet thereto.

Done at Aix-la-Chapelle, the 25th of October,
1748.

(L. S.) T. Robinfon.   (L. S.) Le Comte de Monzone.

The Duke of Modena's *Full Power*.

Francis Duke of Modena, Reggio, Mirandola.

WHEREAS, in the conferences to be held at
Aix-la-Chapelle, for a general pacification between
the Powers concerned in the prefent war, affairs are to
be treated of which regard us; for which it is neceffary to have a Minifter there, on whofe ability, fidelity,
and prudence we may fafely rely, we have not thought
that we could employ any perfon with greater confidence, on this occafion, than the Count de Monzone,
                                                    our

out Counfellor of State, Minifter Plenipotentiary at the
court of his moft Chriftian Majefty, and Colonel in
our fervice; for which reafon, we do chufe and depute him for our Minifter Plenipotentiary at the faid
Congrefs, by giving and granting to him faculty, authority, and full power, with general and fpecial order,
to treat there, in our name, of all matters which concern us, and to promife, agree to, conclude, ftipulate,
and fign, on our part, whatever he fhall judge moft
convenient for our fervice; defiring, for this end, tho
Minifters Plenipotentiary of all the Courts concerned,·
which fhall be prefent at the faid Congrefs, to accept of
and acknowledge him as our Minifter Plenipotentiary;
promifing, on the faith and word of a Prince, to hold
as confirmed and ratified, and to approve and obferve
all that fhall be concluded, accepted of, and ftipulated,
by the fame Minifter Plenipotentiary.

In witnefs whereof, we have figned thefe prefents,
which fhall be counterfigned by one of our Minifters, and have our feal affixed thereto. Given
at Marfeilles, this 30th of November, 1748.

(Signed)   FRANCESCO.

(And underneath counterfigned)

De Bondigli.

The Republic of Genoa's *Acceffion.*

In the Name of the moft Holy and Undivided Trinity, Father, Son, and Holy Ghoft.

BE it known to all thofe to whom it fhall or may
belong.

The Ambaffadors Extraordinary and Plenipotentiaries of his Britannic Majefty, of his moft Chriftian
Majefty, and of the High and Mighty Lords the
States General of the United Provinces, having concluded and figned, in this city of Aix-la-Chapelle, the
18th of the prefent month of October, upon the
foundation

foundation, of the preliminaries, at firft agreed upon and fettled amongft them the 30th of April of this year, a general and definitive treaty of peace, and two fepa-rate articles; of which treaty and feparate articles the tenor is as follows.

[Fiat Infertio.]

And the faid Ambaffadors Extraordinary and Ple-nipotentiaries having amicably invited the Minifter Plenipotentiary of the moft Serene Republic of Ge-noa to accede thereto, in the name of the faid moft Serene Republic;

The under-written Ambaffadors and Minifter Ple-nipotentiary; to wit, on the part of the moft Serene and moft Potent Prince, George the Second, by the grace of God, King of Great Britain, France, and Ireland, the Lords, John Earl of Sandwich, Vifcount of Hinchinbrooke, Baron Montagu of St. Neots, Peer of England, Firft Lord Commiffioner of the Ad-miralty, one of the Lords Regents of the kingdom, his Minifter Plenipotentiary to the Lords the States General of the United Provinces; and Thomas Ro-binfon, Knight of the moft honourable Order of the Bath, and his Minifter Plenipotentiary to his Majefty the Emperor of the Romans, and her Majefty the Emprefs Queen of Hungary and Bohemia: and on the part of the moft Serene Republic of Genoa, the Sieur Francis Marquis Doria, by virtue of their full powers, which they have communicated to each other, and copies whereof are added at the end of the pre-fent act, have agreed upon what follows.

That the moft Serene Republic of Genoa, defiring to contribute and concur to re-eftablifh and fettle the quiet of Europe, accedes, by virtue of the prefent act, to the faid treaty and two feparate articles, without any referve or exception, in a firm confidence, that whatfoever is promifed therein to the faid moft Serene Republic, fhall be faithfully fulfilled; declaring at the fame time, and promifing, that fhe will alfo perform, moſt faithfully, all the articles, clauſes, and conditions, which regard her.

In like manner his Britannic Majeſty accepts the preſent acceſſion of the moſt Serene Republic of Genoa; and likewiſe promiſes to perform, without any reſerve or exception, all the articles, clauſes, and conditions contained in the ſaid treaty, and the two ſeparate articles, inſerted above.

The ratifications of the preſent act ſhall be exchanged in this city of Aix-la-Chapelle, in the ſpace of twenty-five days, to be computed from this day.

In teſtimony whereof, we the Ambaſſadors Extraordinary and Miniſter Plenipotentiary of his Britannic Majeſty, and of the moſt Serene Republic of Genoa, have ſigned the preſent act, and have cauſed the ſeal of our arms to be affixed thereto.

Done at Aix-la-Chapelle, the 28th of October 1748.

(L. S.) *T. Robinſon.*

(L. S.) *Fr.ᶜᵒⁱˢ M.ⁱᵉ Marquis D'Oria.*

The Republic of Genoa's *Full Power.*

The Doge, Governors, and Procurators of the Republic of Genoa.

CONSCIOUS of the experience, fidelity, and zeal of our Patrician Franceſco Maria D'Oria, we have choſen and deputed him as our Miniſter Plenipotentiary at the conferences of peace at Aquiſgrano, otherwiſe Aix-la-Chapelle, or any other place where the ſaid conferences of peace may hereafter be held, or transferred to, and we have given and conferred upon him, as we do give and confer upon him, ample faculty and full power, with general and ſpecial order, to treat there in our name, upon the affairs which regard us, and to agree to, conclude, ſtipulate, and ſign, on our part, whatever he ſhall apprehend to be moſt ſuitable to our intereſts, and that in the ſame manner as we ourſelves, were we preſent, could do, although a more full

§   and

and special order than the prefent might be requifite, defiring, for this end, the Minifters Plenipotentiaries of all the courts concerned, which fhall be prefent at the faid conferences, to accept of and acknowledge him as our Minifter Plenipotentiary; promifing, on the faith and word of a Prince, to hold as confirmed and ratified, and to obferve all that fhall be concluded, accepted, ftipulated, and figned by the fame, in virtue of the prefent full power; as alfo to difpatch our ratifications in due form, to be exchanged within the time which fhall be agreed upon.

In witnefs whereof, thefe prefents fhall be figned by our under-written Secretary of State, with our ufual feal affixed thereto.

Given at our royal palace, this 1ft of March 1748.

(L. S.) *C. Giufeppe Maria Sertorio,*
Secretary of State.

[The treaty of PARIS, 1763 is printed from the copy, which was publifhed by authority in 1763.]

The Definitive Treaty of Peace and Friendfhip, between his Britannic *Majefty, the moft Chriftian King, and the King of* Spain; *concluded at* Paris, *the 10th Day of* February, 1763. *To which the King of* Portugal *acceded on the fame Day.*

In the Name of the moft Holy and Undivided Trinity, Father, Son, and Holy Ghoft.   So be it.

BE it known to all thofe to whom it fhall or may in any manner belong.

It has pleafed the Moft High to diffufe the fpirit of union and concord among the Princes, whofe divifions had fpread the troubles in the four parts of the world, and to infpire them with the inclination to caufe the comforts of peace to fucceed to the misfortunes of a long and bloody war, which, having arifen between

England

England and France, during the reign of the most
Serene and most Potent Prince George the Second,
by the grace of God, King of Great Britain, of glorious memory, continued under the reign of the most
Serene and most Potent Prince George the Third,
his succeffor, and, in its progrefs, communicated itfelf to Spain and Portugal: confequently, the most
Serene and most Potent Prince, George the Third,
by the grace of God, King of Great Britain, France,
and Ireland, Duke of Brunfwic and Lunenbourg,
Arch-Treafurer and Elector of the Holy Roman Empire; the most Serene and most Potent Prince,
Lewis the Fifteenth, by the grace of God, most Chriftian King; and the most Serene and Most Potent
Prince, Charles the Third, by the grace of God,
King of Spain and of the Indies, after having laid the
foundations of peace in the preliminaries, figned at
Fontainebleau the 3d of November laft; and the
most Serene and most Potent Prince, Don Jofeph the
Firft, by the grace of God, King of Portugal and of
the Algarves, after having acceded thereto, determined
to compleat, without delay, this great and important
work. For this purpofe, the high contracting parties
have named and appointed their refpective Ambaffadors Extraordinary and Minifters Plenipotentiary, viz.
His facred Majefty the King of Great Britain, the
most Illuftrious and most Excellent Lord, John Duke
and Earl of Bedford, Marquis of Taviftock, &c.
his Minifter of State, Lieutenant General of his armies, Keeper of his privy feal, Knight of the most noble Order of the Garter, and his Ambaffador Extraordinary and Minifter Plenipotentiary to his most
Chriftian Majefty; his Sacred Majefty the most Chriftian King, the most Illuftrious and most Excellent
Lord Cæfar Gabriel de Choifeul, Duke of Praflin,
Peer of France, Knight of his Orders, Lieutenant
General of his Armies, and of the province of Bri-
tanny, Counfellor in all his Councils, and Minifter and
Secretary of State, and of his commands and finances;

I.   *   his

his facred Majefty the Catholic King, the moft Illuftrious and moft Excellent Lord, Dom Jerome Grimaldi, Marquis de Grimaldi, Knight of the moft Chriftian King's Orders, Gentleman of his Catholic Majefty's
Bed-chamber in employment, and his Ambaffador Extraordinary to his moft Chriftian Majefty; his Sacred
Majefty the moft Faithful King, the moft Illuftrious and
moft Excellent Lord, Martin de Mello and Caftro,
Knight profeffed of the Order of Chrift, of his moft Faithful Majefty's Council, and his Ambaffador and Minifter Plenipotentiary to his moft Chriftian Majefty.

Who, after having duly communicated to each other
their full powers, in good form, copies whereof are
tranfcribed at the end of the prefent treaty of peace,
have agreed upon the articles, the tenor of which is as
follows.

I. There fhall be a Chriftian, univerfal, and perpetual peace, as well by fea as by land, and a fincere and
conftant friendfhip fhall be re-eftablifhed between their
Britannic, moft Chriftian, Catholic, and moft Faithful
Majefties, and between their heirs and fucceffors, kingdoms, dominions, provinces, countries, fubjects, and
vaffals, of what quality or condition foever they be,
without exception of places or of perfons: fo that the
high contracting parties fhall give the greateft attention
to maintain between themfelves and their faid dominions and fubjects, this reciprocal friendfhip and correfpondence, without permitting, on either fide, any kind
of hoftilities, by fea or by land, to be committed, from
henceforth, for any caufe, or under any pretence whatfoever, and every thing fhall be carefully avoided,
which might, hereafter, prejudice the union happily
re-eftablifhed, applying themfelves, on the contrary,
on every occafion, to procure for each other whatever
may contribute to their mutual glory, interefts, and
advantages, without giving any affiftance or protection,
directly or indirectly, to thofe who would caufe any
prejudice to either of the high contracting parties:
there fhall be a general oblivion of every thing that

H h 3   may

may have been done or committed before, or since, the commencement of the war, which is juft ended.

II. The treaties of Weftphalia of 1648; thofe of Madrid, between the crowns of Great Britain and Spain, of 1667 and 1670; the treaties of peace of Nimeguen of 1678 and 1679; of Ryfwyck of 1697; thofe of peace and of commerce of Utretcht of 1713; that of Baden of 1714; the treaty of the triple alliance of the Hague of 1717; that of the quadruple alliance of London of 1718; the treaty of peace of Vienna of 1738; the definitive treaty of Aix-la-Chapelle of 1748; and that of Madrid, between the crowns of Great Britain and Spain, of 1750; as well as the treaties between the crowns of Spain and Portugal, of the 13th of February 1668; of the 6th of February 1715; and of the 12th of February 1761; and that of the 11th of April 1713, between France and Portugal, with the guaranties of Great Britain; ferve as a bafis and foundation to the peace, and to the prefent treaty: and for this purpofe, they are all renewed and confirmed in the beft form, as well as all the treaties in general, which fubfifted between the high contracting parties before the war, as if they were inferted here word for word, fo that they are to be exactly obferved, for the future, in their whole tenor, and religioufly executed on all fides, in all their points which fhall not be derogated from by the prefent treaty, notwithftanding all that may have been ftipulated to the contrary by any of the high contracting parties: and all the faid parties declare, that they will not fuffer any privilege, favour, or indulgence, to fubfift, contrary to the treaties above confirmed, except what fhall have been agreed and ftipulated by the prefent treaty.

III. All the prifoners made, on all fides, as well by land as by fea, and the hoftages carried away, or given during the war, and to this day, fhall be reftored, without ranfom, fix weeks, at lateft, to be computed from the day of the exchange of the ratification of the prefent

fent treaty, each crown respectively paying the advances, which shall have been made for the subsistence and maintenance of their prisoners, by the Sovereign of the country where they shall have been detained, according to the attested receipts and estimates, and other authentic vouchers, which shall be furnished on one side and the other: and securities shall be reciprocally given for the payment of the debts which the prisoners shall have contracted, in the countries where they have been detained, until their entire liberty. And all the ships of war and merchant vessels, which shall have been taken, since the expiration of the terms agreed upon for the cessation of hostilities by sea, shall be likewise restored *bonâ fide*, with all their crews and cargoes: and the execution of this article shall be proceeded upon immediately after the exchange of the ratifications of this treaty.

IV. His most Christian Majesty renounces all pretensions, which he has heretofore formed, or might form, to Nova Scotia or Acadia, in all its parts, and guaranties the whole of it, and with all its dependencies, to the King of Great Britain: moreover, his most Christian Majesty cedes and guaranties to his said Britannic Majesty, in full right, Canada, with all its dependencies, as well as the Island of Cape Breton, and all the other islands and coasts in the gulph and river St. Laurence, and, in general, every thing that depends on the said countries, lands, islands, and coasts, with the sovereignty, property, possession, and all rights, acquired by treaty or otherwise, which the most Christian King, and the crown of France, have had till now over the said countries, islands, lands, places, coasts, and their inhabitants, so that the most Christian King cedes and makes over the whole to the said King, and to the crown of Great Britain, and that in the most ample manner and form, without restriction, and without any liberty to depart from the said cession and guaranty, under any pretence, or to disturb Great Britain in the possessions above-mentioned. His Britan-

nic

nic Majesty, on his side, agrees to grant the liberty of
the Catholic religion to the inhabitants of Canada: he
will consequently give the most precise and most effectual orders, that his new Roman Catholic subjects
may profess the worship of their religion, according to
the rites of the Romish church, as far as the laws of
Great Britain permit. His Britannic Majesty further
agrees, that the French inhabitants, or others who had
been subjects of the most Christian King in Canada,
may retire, with all safety and freedom, wherever they
shall think proper, and may sell their estates, provided
it be to subjects of his Britannic Majesty, and bring
away their effects, as well as their persons, without being restrained in their emigration, under any pretence
whatsoever, except that of debts, or of criminal prosecutions: the term limited for this emigration shall be
fixed to the space of eighteen months, to be computed from the day of the exchange of the ratifications of the present treaty.

V. The subjects of France shall have the liberty of
fishing and drying, on a part of the coasts of the Island
of Newfoundland, such as it is specified in the XIIIth
article of the treaty of Utrecht; which article is renewed and confirmed by the present treaty (except
what relates to the island of Cape Breton, as well as
to the other islands and coasts in the mouth and in
the gulph of St. Laurence:) and his Britannic Majesty consents to leave to the subjects of the most
Christian King the liberty of fishing in the gulph St.
Laurence, on condition that the subjects of France do
not exercise the said fishery but at the distance of three
leagues from all the coasts belonging to Great Britain,
as well those of the continent, as those of the islands
situated in the said gulph St. Laurence. And as to
what relates to the fishery on the coasts of the island
of Cape Breton out of the said gulph, the subjects of
the most Christian King shall not be permitted to exercise the said fishery but at the distance of fifteen
leagues from the coasts of the island of Cape Breton;
and

and the fishery on the coasts of Nova Scotia or Acadia, and every where else out of the said gulph, shall remain on the foot of former treaties.

VI. The King of Great Britain cedes the islands of St. Pierre and Miquelon, in full right, to his most Christian Majesty, to serve as a shelter to the French fishermen: and his said most Christian Majesty engages not to fortify the said islands; to erect no buildings upon them, but merely for the convenience of the fishery; and to keep upon them a guard of fifty men only for the police.

VII. In order to re-establish peace on solid and durable foundations, and to remove for ever all subject of dispute with regard to the limits of the British and French territories on the continent of America; it is agreed, that, for the future, the confines between the dominions of his Britannic Majesty, and those of his most Christian Majesty, in that part of the world, shall be fixed irrevocably by a line drawn along the middle of the river Mississippi, from its source to the river Iberville, and from thence, by a line drawn along the middle of this river, and the lakes Maurepas and Pontchartrain, to the sea; and for this purpose, the most Christian King cedes in full right, and guaranties to his Britannic Majesty, the river and port of the Mobile, and every thing which he possesses, or ought to possess, on the left side of the river Mississippi, except the town of New Orleans, and the island in which it is situated, which shall remain to France; provided that the navigation of the river Mississippi shall be equally free, as well to the subjects of Great Britain as to those of France, in its whole breadth and length, from its source to the sea, and expresly that part which is between the said island of New Orleans and the right bank of that river, as well as the passage both in and out of its mouth. It is further stipulated, that the vessels belonging to the subjects of either nation shall not be stopped, visited, or subjected to the payment of

any

any duty whatsoever. The stipulations, inserted in the IVth article, in favour of the inhabitants of Canada, shall also take place with regard to the inhabitants of the countries ceded by this article.

VIII. The King of Great Britain shall restore to France the islands of Guadeloupe, of Marie Galante, of Desirade, of Martinico, and of Belleisle; and the fortresses of these islands shall be restored in the same condition they were in when they were conquered by the British arms; provided that his Britannic Majesty's subjects, who shall have settled in the said islands, or those who shall have any commercial affairs to settle there, or in the other places restored to France by the present treaty, shall have liberty to sell their lands and their estates, to settle their affairs, to recover their debts, and to bring away their effects, as well as their persons, on board vessels, which they shall be permitted to send to the said islands, and other places restored as above, and which shall serve for this use only, without being restrained on account of their religion, or under any other pretence whatsoever, except that of debts or of criminal prosecutions: and for this purpose, the term of eighteeen months is allowed to his Britannic Majesty's subjects, to be computed from the day of the exchange of the ratifications of the present treaty; but, as the liberty, granted to his Britannic Majesty's subjects, to bring away their persons and their effects, in vessels of their nation, may be liable to abuses, if precautions were not taken to prevent them; it has been expresly agreed between his Britannic Majesty and his most Christian Majesty, that the number of English vessels, which shall have leave to go to the said islands and places restored to France, shall be limited, as well as the number of tons of each one; that they shall go in ballast; shall set sail at a fixed time; and shall make one voyage only, all the effects, belonging to the English, being to be embarked at the same time. It has been further agreed, that his most Christian Majesty shall cause the neeessary passports to be given to
the

the faid veffels; that, for the greater fecurity, it fhall
be allowed to place two French clerks, or.guards, in
each of the faid veffels, which fhall be vifited in the
landing places and ports of the faid iflands, and places,
reftored to France, and that the merchandife, which
fhall be found therein, fhall be confifcated.

IX. The moft Chriftian King cedes and guaranties
to his Britannic Majefty, in full right, the iflands of
Grenada, and of the Grenadines, with the fame ftipulations in favour of the inhabitants of this colony, inferted in the IVth article for thofe of Canada : and the
partition of the iflands, called Neutral, is agreed and
fixed, fo that thofe of St. Vincent, Dominica, and Tobago, fhall remain in full right to Great Britain, and
that of St. Lucia fhall be delivered to France, to enjoy the fame likewife in full right; and the high contracting parties guaranty the partition fo ftipulated.

X. His Britannic Majefty fhall reftore to France the
ifland of Gorée, in the condition it was in when conquered : and his moft Chriftian Majefty cedes, in full
right, and guaranties to the King of Great Britain, the
river Senegal, with the forts and factories of St. Lewis,
Podor, and Galam ; and with all the rights and dependencies of the faid river Senegal.

XI. In the Eaft Indies, Great Britain fhall reftore
to France, in the condition they are now in, the different factories, which that crown poffeffed, as well on
the coaft of Coromandel and Orixa, as on that of Malabar, as alfo in Bengal, at the beginning of the year
1749. And his moft Chriftian Majefty renounces all
pretenfion to the acquifitions which he had made on
the coaft of Coromandel and Orixa, fince the faid beginning of the year 1749. His moft Chriftian Majefty fhall reftore, on his fide, all that he may have
conquered from Great Britain, in the Eaft Indies, during the prefent war ; and will exprefly caufe Nattal and
Tapanoully, in the ifland of Sumatra, to be reftored ;
he engages further, not to erect fortifications, or to
keep

keep troops in any part of the dominions of the fubah; of Bengal. And in order to preferve future peace on the coaft of Coromandel and Orixa, the Englifh and French fhall acknowledge Mahomet Ally Khan for lawful nabob of the Carnatic, and Salabat Jing for lawful fubah of the Decan; and both parties fhall re-nounce all demands and pretenfions of fatisfaction, with which they might charge each other, or their In-dian allies, for the depredations or pillage committed, on the one fide or on the other, during the war.

XII. The ifland of Minorca fhall be reftored to his Britannic Majefty, as well as Fort St. Philip, in the fame condition they were in when conquered by the arms of the moft Chriftian King; and with the artil-lery which was there when the faid ifland and the faid fort were taken.

XIII. The town and port of Dunkirk fhall be put into the ftate fixed by the laft treaty of Aix-la-Cha-pelle, and by former treaties. The Cunette fhall be deftroyed immediately after the exchange of the rati-fications of the prefent treaty, as well as the forts and batteries which defend the entrance on the fide of the fea; and provifion fhall be made, at the fame time, for the wholefomenefs of the air, and for the health of the inhabitants, by fome other means, to the fatisfac-tion of the King of Great Britain.

XIV. France fhall reftore all the countries belong-ing to the electorate of Hanover, to the Landgrave of Heffe, to the Duke of Brunfwic, and to the Count of La Lippe Buckebourg, which are or fhall be occu-pied by his moft Chriftian Majefty's arms: the for-treffes of thefe different countries fhall be reftored in the fame condition they were in, when conquered by the French arms; and the pieces of artillery, which fhall have been carried elfewhere, fhall be replaced by the fame number, of the fame bore, weight, and metal.

XV. In

L' XV. In cafe the ftipulations, contained in the XIIIth
article of the preliminaries, fhould not be compleated
at the time of the fignature of the prefent treaty, as
well with regard to the evacuations to be made by the
armies of France of the fortreffes of Cleves, Wefel,
Guelders, and of all the countries belonging to the
King of Pruffia, as with regard to the evacuations to
be made by the Britifh and French armies of the countries which they occupy in Weftphalia, Lower Saxony,
on the Lower Rhine, the Upper Rhine, and in all the
empire, and to the retreat of the troops into the dominions of their refpective fovereigns; their Britannic
and moft Chriftian Majefties promife to proceed, *bonâ
fide*, with all the difpatch the cafe will permit of, to the
faid evacuations, the entire completion whereof they
ftipulate before the 15th of March next, or fooner if it
can be done; and their Britannic and moft Chriftian
Majefties further engage, and promife to each other,
not to furnifh any fuccours, of any kind, to their refpective allies, who fhall continue engaged in the war
in Germany.

XVI. The decifion of the prizes made, in time of
peace, by the fubjects of Great Britain, on the Spaniards, fhall be referred to the courts of juftice of the
admiralty of Great Britain, conformably to the rules
eftablifhed among all nations, fo that the validity of
the faid prizes, between the Britifh and Spanifh nations, fhall be decided and judged, according to the
law of nations, and according to treaties, in the courts
of juftice of the nation who fhall have made the
capture.

XVII. His Britannic Majefty fhall caufe to be demolifhed all the fortifications which his fubjects fhall have
erected in the Bay of Honduras, and other places of
the territory of Spain in that part of the world, four
months after the ratification of the prefent treaty:
and his Catholic Majefty fhall not permit his Britannic
Majefty's fubjects, or their workmen, to be difturbed

or

or molested, under any pretence whatsoever, in the said places, in their occupation of cutting, loading, and carrying away logwood: and for this purpose, they may build without hinderance, and occupy without interruption, the houses and magazines which are necessary for them, for their families, and for their effects: and his Catholic Majesty assures to them, by this article, the full enjoyment of those advantages, and powers, on the Spanish coasts and territories, as above stipulated, immediately after the ratification of the present treaty.

XVIII. His Catholic Majesty desists, as well for himself, as for his successors, from all pretension, which he may have formed, in favour of the Guipuscoans, and other his subjects, to the right of fishing in the neighbourhood of the island of Newfoundland.

XIX. The King of Great Britain shall restore to Spain all the territory which he has conquered in the island of Cuba, with the fortress of the Havana, and this fortress, as well as all the other fortresses of the said island, shall be restored in the same condition they were in when conquered by his Britannic Majesty's arms; provided, that his Britannic Majesty's subjects, who shall have settled in the said island, restored to Spain by the present treaty, or those who shall have any commercial affairs to settle there, shall have liberty to sell their lands, and their estates, to settle their affairs, to recover their debts, and to bring away their effects, as well as their persons, on board vessels which they shall be permitted to send to the said island restored as above, and which shall serve for that use only, without being restrained on account of their religion, or under any other pretence whatsoever, except that of debts, or of criminal prosecutions: and for this purpose, the term of eighteen months is allowed to his Britannic Majesty's subjects, to be computed from the day of the exchange of the ratifications of the present treaty: but as the liberty, granted to his Britannic Majesty's subjects, to bring away their persons, and their effects, in

vessels

veffels of their nation, may be liable to abufes, if precautions were not taken to prevent them; it has been
expreſly agreed, between his Britannic Majefty and his
Catholic Majefty, that the number of Englifh veffels,
which fhall have leave to go to the faid ifland reftored
to Spain, fhall be limited, as well as the number of
tons of each one; that they fhall go in ballaft; fhall
fet fail at a fixed time; and fhall make one voyage
only; all the effects belonging to the Englifh being to
be embarked at the fame time: it has been further
agreed, that his Catholic Majefty fhall caufe the neceffary paffports to be given to the faid veffels; that, for
the greater fecurity, it fhall be allowed to place two
Spanifh clerks, or guards, in each of the faid veffels,
which fhall be vifited in the landing-places and ports
of the faid ifland reftored to Spain, and that the merchandize, which fhall be found therein, fhall be confifcated.

XX. In confequence of the reftitution ftipulated in
the preceding article, his Catholic Majefty cedes and
guaranties, in full right, to his Britannic Majefty, Flo-
rida, with Fort St. Auguftin, and the Bay of Penfacola,
as well as all that Spain poffeffes on the continent of
North America, to the eaft, or to the fouth-eaft, of the
river Miffiffipi; and, in general, every thing that depends on the faid countries, and lands, with the fovereignty, property, poffeffion, and all rights, acquired by
treaties or otherwife, which the Catholic King, and the
crown of Spain, have had, till now, over the faid
countries, lands, places, and their inhabitants; fo that
the Catholic King cedes and makes over the whole to
the faid King, and to the crown of Great Britain, and
that in the moſt ample manner and form. His Bri-
tanic Majefty agrees, on his fide, to grant to the inhabitants of the countries, above ceded, the liberty of
the Catholic religion: he will confequently give the
moft exprefs and the moft effectual orders, that his new
Roman Catholic fubjects may profefs the worfhip of
their religion, according to the rites of the Romifh
church,

church, as far as the laws of Great Britain permit:
his Britannic Majesty further agrees, that the Spanish
inhabitants, or others, who had been subjects of the
Catholic King in the said countries, may retire, with
all safety and freedom, wherever they think proper;
and may sell their estates, provided it be to his Britannic Majesty's subjects, and bring away their effects, as
well as their persons, without being restrained in their
emigration, under any pretence whatsoever, except that
of debts, or of criminal prosecutions: the term limited
for this emigration being fixed to the space of eighteen
months, to be computed from the day of the exchange
of the ratifications of the present treaty. It is moreover stipulated, that his Catholic Majesty shall have
power to cause all the effects, that may belong to
him, to be brought away, whether it be artillery or
other things.

XXI. The French and Spanish troops shall eva-
cuate all the territories, lands, towns, places, and castles, of his most Faithful Majesty, in Europe, without
any reserve, which shall have been conquered by the
armies of France and Spain, and shall restore them in
the same condition they were in when conquered, with
the same artillery and ammunition which were found
there: and, with regard to the Portuguese colonies in
America, Africa, or in the East Indies, if any change
shall have happened there, all things shall be restored
on the same footing they were in, and conformably to
the preceding treaties which subsisted between the
courts of France, Spain, and Portugal, before the
present war.

XXII. All the papers, letters, documents, and archives, which were found in the countries, territories,
towns, and places, that are restored, and those belonging to the countries ceded, shall be respectively and
bonâ fide delivered, or furnished, at the same time, if
possible, that possession is taken, or, at latest, four
months after the exchange of the ratifications of the
present

present treaty, in whatever places the said papers or documents may be found.

XXIII. All the countries and territories, which may have been conquered, in whatsoever part of the world, by the arms of their Britannic and most Faithful Majesties, as well as by those of their most Christian and Catholic Majesties, which are not included in the present treaty, either under the title of Cessions, or under the title of Restitutions, shall be restored without difficulty, and without requiring any compensation.

XXIV. As it is necessary to assign a fixed epoch for the restitutions, and the evacuations, to be made by each of the high contracting parties; it is agreed, that the British and French troops shall compleat, before the 15th of March next, all that shall remain to be executed of the XIIth and XIIIth articles of the preliminaries, signed the 3d day of November last, with regard to the evacuation to be made in the empire, or elsewhere. The island of Belleisle shall be evacuated six weeks after the exchange of the ratifications of the present treaty, or sooner if it can be done; Guadeloupe, Desirade, Marie Galante, Martinico, and St. Lucia, three months after the exchange of the ratifications of the present treaty, or sooner if it can be done. Great Britain shall likewise, at the end of three months after the exchange of the ratifications of the present treaty, or sooner if it can be done, enter into possession of the river and port of the Mobile, and of all that is to form the limits of the territory of Great Britain, on the side of the river Mississippi, as they are specified in the VIIth article. The island of Gorée shall be evacuated by Great Britain, three months after the exchange of the ratifications of the present treaty; and the island of Minorca, by France, at the same epoch, or sooner if it can be done: and according to the conditions of the VIth article, France shall likewise enter into possession of the islands of St. Peter, and of Miquelon, at the end of three months after the exchange of the ratifications of the prefent treaty. The factories in the Eaft Indies fhall be reftored fix months after the exchange of the ratifications of the prefent treaty, or fooner if it can be done. The fortrefs of the Havana, with all that has been conquered in the ifland of Cuba, fhall be reftored three months after the exchange of the ratifications of the prefent treaty, or fooner if it can be done: and, at the fame time, Great Britain fhall enter into poffeffion of the country ceded by Spain, according to the XXth article. All the places and countries of his moft Faithful Majefty, in Europe, fhall be reftored immediately after the exchange of the ratifications of the prefent treaty; and the Portuguefe colonies, which may have been conquered, fhall be reftored in the fpace of three months in the Weft Indies, and of fix months in the Eaft Indies, after the exchange of the ratifications of the prefent treaty, or fooner if it can be done. All the fortreffes, the reftitution whereof is ftipulated above, fhall be reftored with the artillery and ammunition which were found there at the time of the conqueft. In confequence whereof, the neceffary orders fhall be fent by each of the high contracting parties, with reciprocal paffports for the fhips that fhall carry them, immediately after the exchange of the ratifications of the prefent treaty.

XXV. His Britannic Majefty, as Elector of Brunfwick Lunenburg, as well for himfelf, as for his heirs and fucceffors, and all the dominions and poffeffions of his faid Majefty in Germany, are included and guarantied by the prefent treaty of peace.

XXVI. Their Sacred Britannic, moft Chriftian, Catholic, and moft Faithful Majefties, promife to obferve, fincerely and *bonâ fide*, all the articles contained and fettled in the prefent treaty; and they will not fuffer the fame to be infringed, directly or indirectly, by their refpective fubjects; and the faid high contracting parties, generally and reciprocally, guaranty

ranty to each other all the stipulations of the present treaty.

XXVII. The solemn ratifications of the present treaty, expedited in good and due form, shall be exchanged in this city of Paris, between the high contracting parties, in the space of a month, or sooner if possible, to be computed from the day of the signature of the present treaty.

In witness whereof, we the underwritten, their Ambassadors Extraordinary, and Ministers Plenipotentiary, have signed with our hand, in their name, and in virtue of our full powers, the present definitive treaty, and have caused the seal of our arms to be put thereto.

Done at Paris, the 10th of February, 1763.

Bedford, C.P.S.	*Choiseul, Duc*	*El Marq' de*
(L. S.)	*de Praslin.*	*Grimaldi.*
	(L. S.)	(L. S.)

Separate Articles.

I. SOME of the titles made use of by the contracting Powers, either in the full powers, and other acts, during the course of the negotiation, or in the preamble of the present treaty, not being generally acknowledged; it has been agreed, that no prejudice shall ever result therefrom to any of the said contracting parties, and that the titles, taken or omitted, on either side, on occasion of the said negotiation, and of the present treaty, shall not be cited, or quoted as a precedent.

II. It has been agreed and determined, that the French language, made use of in all the copies of the present treaty, shall not become an example, which may be alledged or made a precedent of, or prejudice, in any manner, any of the contracting Powers; and that they shall conform themselves, for the future, to what has been observed, and ought to be

observed,

observed, with regard to and on the part of Powers, who are used, and have a right, to give and to receive copies of like treaties in another language than French; the present treaty having still the same force and effect as if the aforesaid custom had been therein observed.

III. Though the King of Portugal has not signed the present definitive treaty, their Britannic, most Christian, and Catholic Majesties, acknowledge, nevertheless, that his most Faithful Majesty is formally included therein as a contracting party, and as if he had expresßly signed the said treaty: consequently, their Britannic, most Christian, and Catholic Majesties, respectively and conjointly, promise to his most Faithful Majesty, in the most express and most binding manner, the execution of all and every the clauses contained in the said treaty, on his act of accession.

The present separate articles shall have the same force as if they were inserted in the treaty.

In witness whereof, we the under-written Ambassadors Extraordinary and Ministers Plenipotentiary of their Britannic, most Christian, and Catholic Majesties, have signed the present separate articles, and have caused the seal of our arms to be put thereto.

Done at Paris, the 10th of February, 1763.

Bedford, C. P. S.	Choiseul, Duc	El Marq¹ de
(L. S.)	de Praslin.	Grimaldi.
	(L. S.)	(L. S.)

His Britannic Majesty's Full Power.

GEORGE R.

GEORGE the Third, by the grace of God, King of Great Britain, France, and Ireland, Defender of the Faith, Duke of Brunswic and Lunenburg, Arch-treasurer and Prince Elector of the Holy Roman Empire, &c.; to all and singular to whom these pre-
                                                      sents

ſents ſhall come, greeting. Whereas, in order to perfect the peaee between us and our good brother the moſt Faithful King, on the one part, and our good brothers the moſt Chriſtian and Catholic Kings, on the other, which has been happily begun by the pre-liminary articles already ſigned at Fontainebleau the 3d of this month, and to bring the ſame to the de-ſired end, we have thought proper to inveſt ſome fit perſon with full authority, on our part; Know ye, that we, having moſt entire confidence in the fidelity, judgment, ſkill, and ability, in managing affairs of the greateſt conſequence, of our right truſty and right entirely beloved couſin and counſellor, John Duke and Earl of Bedford, Marquis of Taviſtock, Baron Ruſſel of Cheneys, Baron Ruſſel of Thornhaugh, and Baron Howland of Streatham, Lieutenant General of our forces, Keeper of our Privy Seal, Lieutenant and Cuſtos Rotulorum of the counties of Bedford and Devon, Knight of our moſt noble Order of the Gar-ter, and our Ambaſſador Extraordinary and Plenipo-tentiary to our good brother the moſt Chriſtian King, have nominated, made, conſtituted, and appointed, as by theſe preſents we do nominate, make, conſtitute, and appoint him our true, certain, and undoubted Miniſter, Commiſſary, Deputy, Procurator, and Ple-nipotentiary, giving to him all and all manner of pow-er, faculty, and authority, as well as our general and ſpecial command (yet ſo as that the general do not derogate from the ſpecial, or on the contrary) for us and in our name to meet and confer, as well ſingly and ſeparately, as jointly and in a body, with the Am-baſſadors, Commiſſaries, Deputies, and Plenipoten-tiaries of the Princes whom it may concern, veſted with ſufficient power and authority for that purpoſe, and with them to agree upon, treat, conſult, and con-clude concerning the re-eſtabliſhing, as ſoon as may be, a firm and laſting peace, and ſincere friendſhip and concord; and whatever ſhall be ſo agreed and concluded, for us and in our name to ſign, and to

I i 3 make

make a treaty or treaties on what fhall have been fo
agreed and concluded, and to tranfact every thing elfe
that may belong to the happy completion of the aforefaid work, in as ample a manner and form, and with
the fame force and effect, as we ourfelves, if we were
prefent, could do and perform; engaging and promifing, on our Royal word, that we will approve, ratify,
and accept, in the beft manner, whatever fhall happen to be tranfacted and concluded by our faid Plenipotentiary, and that we will never fuffer any perfon
to infringe or act contrary to the fame, either in the
whole or in part. In witnefs and confirmation whereof, we have caufed our great feal of Great Britain to
be affixed to thefe prefents, figned with our Royal
hand. Given at our palace at St. James's, the 12th
day of November, 1762, in the third year of our
reign.

His moft Chriftian Majefty's Full Power.

LEWIS, by the grace of God, King of France
and Navarre, to all who fhall fee thefe prefents, greeting. Whereas the preliminaries, figned at Fontainebleau the 3d of November of the laft year, laid the
foundation of the peace re-eftablifhed between us and
our moft dear and moft beloved good brother and
coufin the King of Spain, on the one part, and our
moft dear and moft beloved good brother the King of
Great Britain, and our moft dear and moft beloved
good brother and coufin the King of Portugal, on the
other, we have had nothing more at heart, fince that
happy epoch, than to confolidate and ftrengthen, in
the moft lafting manner, fo falutary and fo important
a work, by a folemn and definitive treaty between us
and the faid Powers. For thefe caufes, and other
good confiderations us thereunto moving, we trufting
entirely in the capacity and experience, zeal and fidelity for our fervice, of our moft dear and well-beloved
coufin, Cæfar Gabriel de Choifeul, Duke of Praflin,
Peer of France, Knight of our Orders, Lieutenant
General

General of our forces, and of the province of Britany, Counsellor in all our Councils, Minister and Secretary of State, and of our Commands and Finances, we have named, appointed, and deputed him, and by these presents, signed with our hand, do name, appoint, and depute him, our Minister Plenipotentiary, giving him full and absolute power to act in that quality, and to confer, negotiate, treat, and agree, jointly with the Minister Plenipotentiary of our most dear and most beloved good brother the King of Great Britain, the Minister Plenipotentiary of our most dear and most beloved good brother and cousin the King of Spain, and the Minister Plenipotentiary of our most dear and most beloved good brother and cousin the King of Portugal, vested with full powers, in good form, to agree, conclude, and sign, such articles, conditions, conventions, declarations, definitive treaty, accessions, and other acts whatsoever, that he shall judge proper for securing and strengthening the great work of peace, the whole with the same latitude and authority that we ourselves might do, if we were there in person, even though there should be something which might require a more special order than what is contained in these presents; promising, on the faith and word of a King, to approve, keep firm and stable for ever, to fulfil and execute punctually, all that our said cousin, the Duke of Praslin, shall have stipulated, promised, and signed, in virtue of the present full power, without ever acting contrary thereto, or permitting any thing contrary thereto, for any cause, or under any pretence whatsoever; as also to cause our letters of ratification to be expedited in good form, and to cause them to be delivered, in order to be exchanged within the time that shall be agreed upon. For such is our pleasure. In witness whereof, we have caused our seal to be put to these presents. Given at Versailles, the 7th day of the month of February, in the year of grace 1763, and of our reign the forty-eighth. Signed LEWIS; and on the fold, By the King, The

Duke

Duke of *Choifeul*. Sealed with the great feal of yellow wax.

His Catholic Majefty's Full Power.

DON CARLOS, by the grace of God, King
of Caftille, of Leon, of Arragon, of the Two Sicilies, of Jerufalem, of Navarre, of Granada, of Toledo, of Valencia, of Galicia, of Majorca, of Seville,
of Sardinia, of Cordova, of Corfica, of Murcia, of
Jaen, of the Algarves, of Algecira, of Gibraltar, of the
Canary Iflands, of the Eaft and Weft Indies, iflands
and continent, of the Ocean; Archduke of Auftria;
Duke of Burgundy, of Brabant, and Milan; Count of
Hapfburg, of Flanders, of Tirol and Barcelona; Lord
of Bifcay, and of Molino, &c. Whereas preliminaries of a folid and lafting peace, between this crown
and that of France on the one part, and that of England and Portugal on the other, were concluded and
figned in the Royal refidence of Fontainebleau, the
3d of November of the prefent year, and the refpective ratifications thereof exchanged on the 22d of the
fame month, by Minifters authorized for that purpofe, wherein it is promifed, that a definitive treaty
fhould be forthwith entered upon, having eftablifhed
and regulated the chief points upon which it is to
turn : and whereas in the fame manner as I granted to
you, Don Jerome Grimaldi, Marquis de Grimaldi,
Knight of the Order of the Holy Ghoft, Gentleman of
my Bed-chamber with employment, and my Ambaffador Extraordinary to the moft Chriftian King, my
full power to treat, adjuft, and fign the before-men-
tioned preliminaries, it is neceffary to grant the fame
to you, or to fome other, to treat, adjuft, and fign
the promifed definitive treaty of peace as aforefaid :
therefore, as you the faid Don Jerome Grimaldi,
Marquis de Grimaldi, are at the convenient place, and
as I have every day frefh motives, from your approved fidelity and zeal, capacity and prudence, to
entruft to you this and other like concerns of my

crown,

crown, I have appointed you my Minister Plenipotentiary, and granted to you my full power, to the
end that, in my name, and reprefenting my perfon,
you may treat, regulate, fettle, and fign the faid definitive treaty of peace, between my crown and that of
France on the one part, that of England and that of
Portugal on the other, with the Minifters who fhall
be equally and fpecially authorized by their refpective
Sovereigns for the fame purpofe; acknowledging, as I
do from this time acknowledge, as accepted and ratified, whatever you fhall fo treat, conclude, and fign;
promifing, on my Royal word, that I will obferve and
fulfil the fame, will caufe it to be obferved and fulfilled, as if it had been treated, concluded, and figned
by myfelf. In witnefs whereof, I have caufed thefe
prefents to be difpatched, figned by my hand, fealed
with my privy feal, and counterfigned by my under-
written Counfellor of State, and Firft Secretary for
the department of State and of War.　Buen Retiro,
the tenth of December, 1762.

　　　　(Signed)　　-　　*I the* KING.
　　　　(And lower)　　　*Richard Wall.*

*Declaration of his moft Chriftian Majefty's Plenipo-
tentiary, with regard to the Debts due to the Canadians.*

THE King of Great Britain having defired, that
the payment of the letters of exchange and bills, which
had been delivered to the Canadians for the neceffaries
furnifhed to the French troops, fhould be fecured, his
moft Chriftian Majefty, entirely difpofed to render to
every one that juftice which is legally due to them,
has declared, and does declare, that the faid bills, and
letters of exchange, fhall be punctually paid, agreeably to a liquidation made in a convenient time, according to the diftance of the places, and to what
fhall be poffible, taking care, however, that the bills
and letters of exchange, which the French fubjects
　　　　　　　　　　　　　　　　　　　may

may have at the time of this declaration, be not confounded with the bills and letters of exchange which are in the poffeffion of the new fubjects of the King of Great Britain.

In witnefs whereof, we the under-written Minifter of his moft Chriftian Majefty, duly authorized for this purpofe, have figned the prefent declaration, and caufed the feal of our arms to be put thereto.

Done at Paris, the 10th of February, 1763.

Choifeul, Duc de Praflin. (L. S.)

Declaration of his Britannic Majefty's Ambaffador Extraordinary and Plenipotentiary, with regard to the Limits of Bengal, *in the* Eaft Indies.

WE the under-written Ambaffador Extraordinary and Plenipotentiary of the King of Great Britain, in order to prevent all fubject of difpute on account of the limits of the dominions of the Subah of Bengal, as well as of the coaft of Coromandel and Orixa, declare, in the name and by order of his faid Britannic Majefty, that the faid dominions of the Subah of Bengal fhall be reputed not to extend farther than Yanaon exclufively, and that Yanaon fhall be confidered as included in the north part of the coaft of Coromandel or Orixa.

In witnefs whereof, we the under-written Minifter Plenipotentiary of his Majefty the King of Great Britain, have figned the prefent declaration, and have caufed the feal of our arms to be put thereto.

Done at Paris, the 10th of February, 1763.

Bedford, C. P. S. (L. S.)

Acceffion of his moft Faithful Majefty.

In the Name of the moft Holy and Undivided Trinity, Father, Son, and Holy Ghoft. So be it.

BE it known to all thofe to whom it fhall or may belong; the Ambaffadors and Plenipotentiaries of his
Britannic

Britannic Majesty, of his most Christian Majesty, and
of his Catholic Majesty, having concluded and signed
at Paris, the 10th of February of this year, a definitive treaty of peace, and separate articles, the tenor
of which is as follows.

[*Fiat Insertio.*]

And the said Ambassadors and Plenipotentiaries
having, in a friendly manner, invited the Ambassador
and Minister Plenipotentiary of his most Faithful Majesty to accede thereto, in the name of his said Majesty; the under-written Ministers Plenipotentiary,
viz. on the part of the most Serene and most Potent
Prince George the Third, by the grace of God, King
of Great Britain, France, and Ireland, Duke of
Brunswic and Lunenburg, Arch-treasurer and Elector of the Holy Roman Empire, the most Illustrious and most Excellent Lord, John Duke and Earl
of Bedford, Marquis of Tavistock, &c. Minister of
State of the King of Great Britain, Lieutenant General of his forces, Keeper of his Privy Seal, Knight of
the most Noble Order of the Garter, and his Ambassador Extraordinary and Plenipotentiary to his most
Christian Majesty; and on the part of the most Serene and most Potent Prince Don Joseph the First, by
the grace of God, King of Portugal and of the Algarves, the most Illustrious and most Excellent Lord,
Martin de Mello and Castro, Knight professed of the
Order of Christ, of his most Faithful Majesty's Council, and his Ambassador and Minister Plenipotentiary
to his most Christian Majesty, in virtue of their full
powers, which they have communicated to each other,
and of which copies shall be added at the end of the
present act, have agreed upon what follows, viz. His
most Faithful Majesty desiring most sincerely to concur in the speedy re-establishment of peace, accedes,
in virtue of the present act, to the said definitive treaty
and separate articles, as they are above transcribed,
without any reserve or exception, in the firm confidence

dence that every thing that is promised to his said
Majesty, will be *bonâ fide* fulfilled; declaring at the
same time, and promising to fulfil, with equal fidelity,
all the articles, clauses, and conditions, which concern him. On his side, his Britannic Majesty accepts
the present accession of his most Faithful Majesty, and
promises likewise to fulfil, without any reserve or exception, all the articles, clauses, and conditions, contained in the said definitive treaty and separate articles above inserted. The ratifications of the present
treaty shall be exchanged in the space of one month,
to be computed from this day, or sooner if it can be
done.

> In witness whereof, we, Ambassadors and Ministers
> Plenipotentiary of his Britannic Majesty, and
> of his most Faithful Majesty, have signed the
> present act, and have caused the seal of our arms
> to be put thereto.

Done at Paris, the 10th of February, 1763.

Bedford, C.P.S. (L.S.)   *De Mello et Castro.* (L.S.)

His most Faithful Majesty's Full Power.

DON JOSEPH, by the grace of God, King of
Portugal, and of the Algarves, on this side the sea,
and on that side in Africa, Lord of Guinea, and of the
conquest, navigation, commerce of Ethiopia, Ara-
bia, Persia, and India, &c. I make known to those
who shall see these my letters patent, that, desiring
nothing more than to see the flame of war, which has
raged so many years in all Europe, extinguished, and
to co-operate (as far as depends upon me) towards
its being succeeded by a just peace, established upon
solid principles: and being informed, that great part
of the belligerent Powers entertain the same pacific
dispositions, I am to nominate a person, to assist, in
my name, at the assemblies and conferences to be held
upon this important business, who, by his nobility,
prudence,

prudence, and dexterity, is worthy of my confidence: whereas thefe feveral qualities concur in Martin de Mello de Caftro; of my Council, and my Envoy Extraordinary and Plenipotentiary to the court of London; and as from the experience I have, that he has always ferved me to my fatisfaction, in every thing I have charged him with, relying, that I fhall, from henceforward, have frefh caufe for the confidence I have placed in him, I nominate and conftitute him my Ambaffador and Plenipotentiary, in order that he may, as fuch, affift, in my name, at any congreffes, affemblies, or conferences, as well public as private, in which the bufinefs of pacification may be treated: negotiating and agreeing with the Ambaffadors and Plenipotentiaries of the faid belligerent Powers, whatever may relate to the faid peace, and concluding what he fhall negotiate between me and any belligerent Kings and Princes, under the conditions he fhall ftipulate in my Royal name: therefore, for the above purpofes, I grant him all the full powers and authority, general and fpecial, which may be neceffary; and I promife, upon the faith and word of a King, that I will acknowledge to be firm and valid, and will ratify within the time agreed upon, whatever fhall be contracted and ftipulated by my faid Ambaffador and Plenipotentiary, with the aforefaid Ambaffadors and Minifters of the belligerent Kings and Princes, who fhall be furnifhed by them with equal powers. In witnefs whereof, I have ordered thefe prefents to be made out, figned by myfelf, fealed with the feal of my arms thereunto affixed, and counterfigned by my Secretary and Minifter of State for foreign Affairs and War. Given at the palace of our Lady of Ajuda, the eighteenth day of September, of the year from the birth of our Lord Jefus Chrift 1762.

Locus	The KING.
Sigilli	Don Lewis da Cunha.
pendentis.	

Letters patent whereby your Majesty is pleased to nominate Martin de Mello de Castro to be your Ambassador and Plenipotentiary for the negotiation and conclusion of peace, in the form above set forth.

For your Majesty's inspection.

Declaration of his most Faithful Majesty's Ambassador and Minister Plenipotentiary, with regard to Alternating with Great Britain *and* France.

WHEREAS, on the conclusion of the negotiation of the definitive treaty, signed at Paris this 10th day of February, a difficulty arose as to the order of signing, which might have retarded the conclusion of the said treaty, we the under-written, Ambassador and Minister Plenipotentiary of his most Faithful Majesty, declare, that the alternative observed, on the part of the King of Great Britain, and the most Christian King, with the most Faithful King, in the act of accession of the court of Portugal, was granted, by their Britannic and most Christian Majesties, solely with a view to accelerate the conclusion of the definitive treaty, and by that means the more speedily to consolidate so important and so salutary a work ; and that this complaisance of their Britannic and most Christian Majesties shall not be made any precedent of for the future ; the court of Portugal shall not alledge it as an example in their favour; shall derive therefrom no right, title, or pretension, for any cause, or under any pretence whatsoever.

In witness whereof, we, Ambassador and Minister Plenipotentiary of his most Faithful Majesty, duly authorized for this purpose, have signed the present declaration, and have caused the seal of our arms to be put thereto.

Done at Paris, the 10th of February, 1763.

Martin de Mello et Castro. (L. S.)

[The

[The treaty of VERSAILLES, 1783, is printed from the copy which was publifhed by authority, in 1783.]

The Definitive Treaty of Peace and Friendfhip, between his Britannic Majefty, and the moft Chriftian King; figned at Verfailles, the 3d of September, 1783.

In the name of the moft Holy and Undivided Trinity, Father, Son, and Holy Ghoft.   So be it.

BE it known to all thofe whom it fhall or may in any manner concern.   The moft Serene and moft Potent Prince, George the Third, by the grace of God, King of Great Britain, France, and Ireland, Duke of Brunfwic and Lunenburg, Arch-trefurer and Elector of the Holy Roman Empire, &c. and the moft Serene and moft Potent Prince, Lewis the Sixteenth, by the grace of God, moft Chriftian King, being equally defirous to put an end to the war which for feveral years paft afflicted their refpective dominions, accepted the offer which their Majefties the Emperor of the Romans, and the Emprefs of all the Ruffias, made to them of their interpofition, and of their mediation: but their Britannic and moft Chriftian Majefties, animated with a mutual defire of accelerating the re-eftablifhment of peace, communicated to each other their laudable intention; which Heaven fo far bleffed, that they proceeded to lay the foundations of peace, by figning preliminary articles at Verfailles, the 20th of January, in the prefent year.   Their faid Majefties the King of Great Britain, and the moft Chriftian King, thinking it incumbent upon them to give their Imperial Majefties a fignal proof of their gratitude for the generous offer of their mediation, invited them, in concert, to concur in the completion of the great and falutary work of peace, by taking part, as mediators, in the definitive treaty to be concluded between their Britannic and moft Chriftian Majefties.   Their faid Imperial Majefties having readily accepted that invitation, they have named as their reprefentatives, viz.

*

His

His Majefty the Emperor of the Romans, the moft illuftrious and moft excellent Lord Florimond, Count Mercy-Argenteau, Vifcount of Loo, Baron of Crichegnée, Knight of the Golden Fleece, Chamberlain, actual Privy Counfellor of State to his Imperial and Royal Apoftolic Majefty, and his Ambaffador to his moft Chriftian Majefty; and her Majefty the Emprefs of all the Ruffias, the moft illuftrious and moft excellent Lord, Prince Iwan Bariatinfkoy, Lieutenant General of the forces of her Imperial Majefty of all the Ruffias, Knight of the Orders of St. Anne, and of the Swedifh Sword, and her Minifter Plenipotentiary to his moft Chriftian Majefty, and the Lord Arcadi de Marcoff, Counfellor of State to her Imperial Majefty of all the Ruffias, and her Minifter Plenipotentiary to his moft Chriftian Majefty. In confequence, their faid Majefties the King of Great Britain, and the moft Chriftian King, have named and conftituted for their Plenipotentiaries, charged with the concluding and figning of the definitive treaty of peace, *viz.* the King of Great Britain, the moft illuftrious and moft excellent Lord, George Duke and Earl of Manchefter, Vifcount Mandeville, Baron of Kimbolton, Lord Lieutenant and Cuftos Rotulorum of the county of Huntingdon, actual Privy Counfellor to his Britannic Majefty, and his Ambaffador Extraordinary and Plenipotentiary to his moft Chriftian Majefty; and the moft Chriftian King, the moft illuftrious and moft excellent Lord, Charles Gravier, Count de Vergennes, Baron of Welferding, &c. the King's Counfellor in all his Councils, Commander in his Orders, Prefident of the Royal Council of Finances, Counfellor of State Military, Minifter and Secretary of State, and of his Commands and Finances: who, after having exchanged their refpective full powers, have agreed upon the following articles:

I. There fhall be a Chriftian, univerfal, and perpetual peace, as well by fea as by land, and a fincere and conftant friendfhip fhall be re-eftablifhed between
their

their Britannic and moſt Chriſtian Majeſties, and be-·
tween their heirs and ſucceſſors, kingdoms, dominions,
provinces, countries, ſubjects, and vaſſals, of what
quality or condition ſoever they be, without exception
either of places or perſons; ſo that the high contracting parties ſhall give the greateſt attention to the maintaining between themſelves, and their ſaid dominions
and ſubjects, this reciprocal friendſhip and intercourſe,
without permitting hereafter, on either part, any kind
of hoſtilities to be committed, either by ſea or by land,
for any cauſe, or under any pretence whatſoever; and
they ſhall carefully avoid, for the future, every thing
which might prejudice the union happily re-eſtabliſhed,
endeavouring, on the contrary, to procure reciprocally for each other, on every occaſion, whatever may
contribute to their mutual glory, intereſts, and advantage, without giving any aſſiſtance or protection, directly or indirectly, to thoſe who would do any injury
to either of the high contracting parties. There ſhall
be a general oblivion and amneſty of every thing which
may have been done or committed before or ſince the
commencement of the war which is juſt ended.

II. The treaties of Weſtphalia of 1648; the treaties of peace of Nimeguen of 1678 and 1679; of
Ryſwick of 1697; thoſe of peace and of commerce
of Utrecht of 1713; that of Baden of 1714; that of
the triple alliance of the Hague of 1717; that of the
quadruple alliance of London of 1718; the treaty
of peace of Vienna of 1738; the definitive treaty of
Aix-la-Chapelle of 1748; and that of Paris of 1763,
ſerve as a baſis and foundation to the peace, and to
the preſent treaty; and, for this purpoſe, they are all
renewed and confirmed in the beſt form, as well as
all the treaties in general which ſubſiſted between the
high contracting parties before the war, as if they were
herein inſerted word for word; ſo that they are to be
exactly obſerved for the future in their full tenor, and
religiouſly executed by both parties, in all the points

VOL. I. K k which

which shall not be derogated from by the present treaty of peace.

III. All the prisoners taken on either side, as well by land as by sea, and the hostages carried away or given during the war, and to this day, shall be restored, without ransom, in six weeks at latest, to be computed from the day of the exchange of the ratifications of the present treaty; each crown respectively discharging the advances which shall have been made for the subsistence and maintenance of their prisoners by the Sovereign of the country where they shall have been detained, according to the receipts and attested accounts, and other authentic vouchers, which shall be furnished on each side: and sureties shall be reciprocally given for the payment of the debts which the prisoners may have contracted in the countries where they may have been detained, until their entire release. And all ships, as well men of war as merchant-ships, which may have been taken since the expiration of the terms agreed upon for the cessation of hostilities by sea, shall likewise be restored, *bonâ fide*, with all their crews and cargoes. And the execution of this article shall be proceeded upon immediately after the exchange of the ratifications of this treaty.

IV. His Majesty the King of Great Britain is maintained in his right to the island of Newfoundland, and to the adjacent islands, as the whole were assured to him by the thirteenth article of the treaty of Utrecht; excepting the islands of St. Pierre and Miquelon, which are ceded in full right, by the present treaty, to his most Christian Majesty.

V. His Majesty the most Christian King, in order to prevent the quarrels which have hitherto arisen between the two nations of England and France, consents to renounce the right of fishing, which belongs to him in virtue of the aforesaid article of the treaty of Utrecht, from Cape Bonavista to Cape St. John, situated on the eastern coast of Newfoundland, in fifty

degrees

degrees north latitude; and his Majesty the King of Great Britain consents on his part, that the fishery assigned to the subjects of his most Christian Majesty, beginning at the said Cape St. John, passing to the north, and descending by the western coast of the island of Newfoundland, shall extend to the place called Cape Raye, situated in forty-seven degrees fifty minutes latitude. The French fishermen shall enjoy the fishery which is assigned to them by the present article, as they had the right to enjoy that which was assigned to them by the treaty of Utrecht.

VI. With regard to the fishery in the gulph of St. Laurence, the French shall continue to exercise it conformably to the fifth article of the treaty of Paris.

VII. The King of Great Britain restores to France the island of St. Lucia, in the condition it was in when it was conquered by the British arms: and his Britannic Majesty cedes and guaranties to his most Christian Majesty the island of Tobago. The Protestant inhabitants of the said island, as well as those of the same religion who shall have settled at St. Lucia, whilst that island was occupied by the British arms, shall not be molested in the exercise of their worship: and the British inhabitants, or others who may have been subjects of the King of Great Britain in the aforesaid islands, shall retain their possessions upon the same titles and conditions by which they have acquired them; or else they may retire in full security and liberty, where they shall think fit, and shall have the power of selling their estates, provided it be to subjects of his most Christian Majesty, and of removing their effects, as well as their persons, without being restrained in their emigration under any pretence whatsoever, except on account of debts, or of criminal prosecutions. The term limited for this emigration is fixed to the space of eighteen months, to be computed from the day of the exchange of the ratifications of the present treaty. And for the better securing the possessions of the inhabi-

tants

tants of the aforefaid ifland of Tobago, the moft
Chriftian King fhall iffue letters patent, containing an
abolition of the *droit d'aubaine* in the faid ifland.

VIII. The moft Chriftian King reftores to Great
Britain the iflands of Grenada, and the Grenadines, St.
Vincent's, Dominica, St. Chriftopher's, Nevis, and
Montferrat; and the fortreffes of thefe iflands fhall be
delivered up in the condition they were in when the
conqueft of them was made. The fame ftipulations
inferted in the preceding article fhall take place in favour of the French fubjects, with refpect to the iflands
enumerated in the prefent article.

IX. The King of Great Britain cedes, in full
right, and guaranties to his moft Chriftian Majefty,
the river Senegal, and its dependencies, with the forts
of St. Louis, Podor, Galam, Arguin, and Portendic;
and his Britannic Majefty reftores to France the ifland
of Gorée, which fhall be delivered up in the condition
it was in when the conqueft of it was made.

X. The moft Chriftian King, on his part, guaranties
to the King of Great Britain the poffeffion of fort
James, and of the river Gambia.

XI. For preventing all difcuffion in that part of the
world, the two high contracting parties fhall, within
three months after the exchange of the ratifications of
the prefent treaty, name commiffaries, who fhall be
charged with the fettling and fixing of the boundaries
of the refpective poffeffions. As to the gum trade,
the Englifh fhall have the liberty of carrying it on,
from the mouth of the river St. John, to the bay and
fort of Portendic inclufively. Provided that they
fhall not form any permanent fettlement, of what nature foever, in the faid river St. John, upon the coaft,
or in the bay of Portendic.

XII. As to the refidue of the coaft of Africa, the
Englifh and French fubjects fhall continue to refort
thereto,

thereto, according to the ufage which has hitherto prevailed.

XIII. The King of Great Britain reftores to his moft Chriftian Majefty all the fettlements which belonged to him at the beginning of the prefent war, upon the coaft of Orixa, and in Bengal, with liberty to furround Chandernagore with a ditch for carrying off the waters: and his Britannic Majefty engages to take fuch meafures as fhall be in his power for fecuring to the fubjects of France in that part of India, as well as on the coafts of Orixa, Coromandel, and Malabar, a fafe, free, and independent trade, fuch as was carried on by the French Eaft India Company, whether they exercife it individually, or united in a company.

XIV. Pondicherry fhall be in like manner delivered up and guarantied to France, as alfo Karikal; and his Britannic Majefty fhall procure, for an additional dependency to Pondicherry, the two diftricts of Valanour and Bahour; and to Karikal, the four Magans bordering thereupon.

XV. France fhall re-enter into the poffeffion of Mahé, as well as of its factory at Surat; and the French fhall carry on their trade in this part of India conformably to the principles eftablifhed in the thirteenth article of this treaty.

XVI. Orders having been fent to India by the high contracting parties, in purfuance of the fixteenth article of the preliminaries, it is further agreed, that if, within the term of four months, the refpective allies of their Britannic and moft Chriftian Majefties fhall not have acceded to the prefent pacification, or concluded a feparate accommodation, their faid Majefties fhall not give them any affiftance, directly or indirectly, againft the Britifh or French poffeffions, or againft the ancient poffeffions of their refpective allies, fuch as they were in the year 1776.

XVII. The King of Great Britain, being defirous

to give to his most Christian Majesty a sincere proof of reconciliation and friendship, and to contribute to render solid the peace re-established between their said Majesties, consents to the abrogation and suppression of all the articles relative to Dunkirk, from the treaty of peace concluded at Utrecht in 1713, inclusive, to this day.

XVIII. Immediately after the exchange of the ratifications, the two high contracting parties shall name commissaries to treat concerning new arrangements of commerce between the two nations, on the basis of reciprocity and mutual convenience; which arrangements shall be settled and concluded within the space of two years, to be computed from the first of January, in the year 1784.

XIX. All the countries and territories which may have been, or which may be conquered, in any part of the world whatsoever, by the arms of his Britannic Majesty, as well as by those of his most Christian Majesty, which are not included in the present treaty, neither under the head of Cessions, nor under the head of Restitutions, shall be restored without difficulty, and without requiring any compensation.

XX. As it is necessary to appoint a certain period for the restitutions and evacuations to be made by each of the high contracting parties, it is agreed that the King of Great Britain shall cause to be evacuated the islands of St. Pierre and Miquelon, three months after the ratification of the present treaty, or sooner, if it can be done; St. Lucia (one of the Charibee islands) and Gorée in Africa, three months after the ratification of the present treaty, or sooner, if it can be done. The King of Great Britain shall, in like manner, at the end of three months after the ratification of the present treaty, or sooner, if it can be done, enter again into the possession of the islands of Grenada, the Grenadines, St. Vincent's, Dominica, St. Christopher's, Nevis, and Montserrat. France shall be put in posseffion of the towns and factories which are restored to her in the East Indies, and of the territories which are procured for her, to serve as additional dependencies to Pondicherry, and to Karikal, six months after the ratification of the present treaty, or sooner, if it can be done. France shall deliver up, at the end of the like term of six months, the towns and territories which her arms may have taken from the English, or their allies, in the East Indies. In consequence whereof, the necessary orders shall be sent by each of the high contracting parties, with reciprocal passports for the ships which shall carry them, immediately after the ratification of the present treaty.

XXI. The decision of the prizes and seizures made prior to the hostilities shall be referred to the respective courts of justice; so that the legality of the said prizes and seizures shall be decided according to the law of nations, and to treaties, in the courts of justice of the nation-which shall have made the capture, or ordered the seizures.

XXII. For preventing the revival of the law-suits which have been ended in the islands conquered by either of the high contracting parties, it is agreed, that the judgments pronounced in the last resort, and which have acquired the force of matters determined, shall be confirmed and executed according to their form and tenor.

XXIII. Their Britannic and most Christian Majesties promise to observe sincerely, and *bonâ fide*, all the articles contained and established in the present treaty; and they will not suffer the same to be infringed, directly or indirectly, by their respective subjects: and the said high contracting parties guaranty to each other, generally and reciprocally, all the stipulations of the present treaty.

XXIV. The solemn ratifications of the present treaty, prepared in good and due form, shall be ex-

K k 4 changed

changed in this city of Verſailles, between the high contracting parties, in the ſpace of a month, or ſooner if poſſible, to be computed from the day of the ſignature of the preſent treaty.

In witneſs whereof, we the under-written Ambaſſador Extraordinary and Miniſters Plenipotentiary have ſigned with our hands, in their names, and in virtue of our reſpective full powers, the preſent definitive treaty, and have cauſed the ſeals of our arms to be affixed thereto.

Done at Verſailles, the third day of September, one thouſand ſeven hundred and eighty-three.

Mancheſter. (L. S.)   *Gravier de Vergennes.* (L. S.)

Separate Articles.

I. SOME of the titles made uſe of by the contracting parties, whether in the full powers, and other inſtruments, during the courſe of the negotiation, or in the preamble of the preſent treaty, not being generally acknowledged, it has been agreed, that no prejudice ſhould ever reſult therefrom to either of the ſaid contracting parties; and that the titles taken or omitted on either ſide, upon occaſion of the ſaid negotiation, and of the preſent treaty, ſhall not be cited, or quoted as a precedent.

II. It has been agreed and determined, that the French language, made uſe of in all the copies of the preſent treaty, ſhall not form an example which may be alledged or quoted as a precedent, or in any manner prejudice either of the contracting Powers; and that they ſhall conform for the future to what has been obſerved, and ought to be obſerved, with regard to, and on the part of Powers, who are in the practice and poſſeſſion of giving and receiving copies of like treaties in a different language from the French; the preſent treaty having, neverthelefs, the ſame force and virtue as if the aforeſaid practice had been therein obſerved.

In

In witnefs whereof, we the under-written Ambaffador Extraordinary and Minifters Plenipotentiary of their Britannic and moft Chriftian Majefties, have figned the prefent feparate articles,
and have caufed the feals of our arms to be
affixed thereto.

Done at Verfailles, the third of September, one
thoufand feven hundred and eighty-three.

Manchefter. (L. S.) *Gravier de Vergennes.* (L. S.)

Declaration.

T H E King having entirely agreed with his moft
Chriftian Majefty upon the articles of the definitive
treaty, will feek every means which fhall not only infure the execution thereof, with his accuftomed good
faith and punctuality, but will befides give, on his
part, all poffible efficacy to the principles which fhall
prevent even the leaft foundation of difpute for the
future.

To this end, and in order that the fifhermen of the
two nations may not give caufe for daily quarrels, his
Britannic Majefty will take the moft pofitive meafures for preventing his fubjects from interrupting, in
any manner, by their competition, the fifhery of the
French, during the temporary exercife of it which is
granted to them upon the coafts of the ifland of Newfoundland; and he will, for this purpofe, caufe the fixed
fettlements, which fhall be formed there, to be removed.
His Britannic Majefty will give orders that the French
fifhermen be not incommoded, in cutting the wood neceffary for the repair of their fcaffolds, huts, and fifhing-veffels.

The thirteenth article of the treaty of Utrecht, and
the method of carrying on the fifhery, which has at all
times been acknowledged, fhall be the plan upon
which the fifhery fhall be carried on there; it fhall
not be deviated from by either party; the French fifhermen building only their fcaffolds, confining themselves

felves to the repair of their fifhing-veffels, and not wintering there; the fubjects of his Britannic Majefty, on their part, not molefting in any manner the French fifhermen during their fifhing, nor injuring their fcaffolds during their abfence.

The King of Great Britain, in ceding the iflands of St. Pierre and Miquelon to France, regards them as ceded for the purpofe of ferving as a real fhelter to the French fifhermen, and in full confidence that thefe poffeffions will not become an object of jealoufy between the two nations; and that the fifhery between the faid iflands and that of Newfoundland fhall be limited to the middle of the channel.

With regard to India, Great Britain having granted to France every thing that can afcertain and confirm the trade which the latter requires to carry on there, his Majefty relies with confidence on the repeated affurances of the court of Verfailles, that the power of furrounding Chandernagore with a ditch for carrying off the waters, fhall not be exercifed in fuch a manner as to make it become an object of umbrage.

The new ftate in which commerce may perhaps be found in all parts of the world, will demand revifions and explanations of the fubfifting treaties; but an entire abrogation of thofe treaties, in whatever period it might be, would throw commerce into fuch confufion as would be of infinite prejudice to it.

In fome of the treaties of this fort, there are not only articles which relate merely to commerce, but many others which infure reciprocally to the refpective fubjects, privileges, facilities for conducting their affairs, perfonal protections, and other advantages, which are not, and which ought not to be of a changeable nature, fuch as the regulations relating merely to the value of goods and merchandize, variable from circumftances of every kind.

When therefore the ftate of the trade between the two nations fhall be treated upon, it is requifite to be underftood, that the alterations which may be made in

§   the

the fubfifting treaties are to extend only to arrangements merely commercial; and that the privileges and
advantages, mutual and particular, be not only preferved on each fide, but even augmented, if it can be
done.

In this view, his Majefty has confented to the ap-
pointment of commiffaries on each fide, who fhall
treat folely upon this objeft.

> In witnefs whereof, we his Britannic Majefty's Am-
> baffador Extraordinary and Minifter Plenipoten-
> tiary, being thereto duly authorized, have figned
> the prefent declaration, and caufed the feal of
> our arms to be fet thereto.
> Given at Verfailles, the third of September, one
> thoufand feven hundred and eighty-three.

(L. S.) Manchefter.

Counter-Declaration.

THE principles which have guided the King in
the whole courfe of the negotiations which preceded
the re-eftablifhment of peace, muft have convinced
the King of Great Britain, that his Majefty has had
no other defign than to render it folid and lafting, by
preventing, as much as poffible, in the four quarters
of the world, every fubjeft of difcuffion and quarrel.
The King of Great Britain undoubtedly places too
much confidence in the uprightnefs of his Majefty's
intentions, not to rely upon his conftant attention to
prevent the iflands of St. Pierre and Miquelon from
becoming an objeft of jealoufy between the two nations.

As to the fifhery on the coafts of Newfoundland,
which has been the objeft of the new arrangements fettled by the two Sovereigns upon this matter, it is fufficiently afcertained by the fifth article of the treaty of
peace figned this day, and by the declaration likewife
delivered to-day, by his Britannic Majefty's Ambaffador
Extraordinary

Extraordinary and Plenipotentiary; and his Majesty declares that he is fully satisfied on this head.

In regard to the fishery between the island of New-foundland, and those of St. Pierre and Miquelon, it is not to be carried on, by either party, but to the middle of the channel; and his Majesty will give the most positive orders, that the French fishermen shall not go beyond this line. His Majesty is firmly persuaded that the King of Great Britain will give like orders to the English fishermen.

The King's desire to maintain the peace comprehends India as well as the other parts of the world; his Britannic Majesty may therefore be assured, that his Majesty will never permit that an object so inoffensive and so harmless as the ditch with which Chandernagore is to be surrounded, should give any umbrage to the court of London.

The King, in proposing new arrangements of commerce, had no other design than to remedy, by the rules of reciprocity and mutual convenience, whatever may be defective in the treaty of commerce signed at Utrecht, in one thousand seven hundred and thirteen. The King of Great Britain may judge from thence, that his Majesty's intention is not in any wise to cancel all the stipulations in the above-mentioned treaty; he declares, on the contrary, from henceforth, that he is disposed to maintain all the privileges, facilities, and advantages expressed in that treaty, as far as they shall be reciprocal, or compensated by equivalent advantages. It is to attain this end, desired on each side, that commissaries are to be appointed to treat upon the state of the trade between the two nations, and that a considerable space of time is to be allowed for compleating their work. His Majesty hopes that this object will be pursued with the same good faith, and the same spirit of conciliation, which presided over the discussion of all the other points comprized in the definitive treaty; and his said Majesty is firmly persuaded
that

that the refpective commiffaries will employ the utmoft diligence for the completion of this important work.

> In witnefs whereof, we the under-written Minifter Plenipotentiary of his moft Chriftian Majefty, being thereto duly authorized, have figned the prefent counter-declaration, and have caufed the feal of our arms to be affixed thereto.

> Given at Verfailles, the third of September, one thoufand feven hundred and eighty-three.

(L. S.) *Gravier de Vergennes.*

WE, Ambaffador Plenipotentiary of his Imperial and Royal Apoftolic Majefty, having acted as mediator in the work of pacification, declare that the treaty of peace figned this day at Verfailles, between his Britannic Majefty and his moft Chriftian Majefty, with the two feparate articles thereto annexed, and of which they form a part, as alfo with all the claufes, conditions, and ftipulations which are therein contained, was concluded by the mediation of his Imperial and Royal Apoftolic Majefty. In witnefs whereof, we have figned thefe prefents with our hand, and have caufed the feal of our arms to be affixed thereto. Done at Verfailles, the third of September, one thoufand feven hundred and eighty-three.

(L. S.) *Le Comte de Mercy Argenteau.*

WE, Minifters Plenipotentiary of her Imperial Majefty of all the Ruffias, having acted as mediators in the work of pacification, declare that the treaty of peace, figned this day at Verfailles, between his Britannic Majefty, and his moft Chriftian Majefty, with the two feparate articles thereto annexed, and of which they form a part, as alfo with all the claufes, conditions, and ftipulations which are therein contained, was concluded by the mediation of her Imperial Majefty of all the Ruffias. In witnefs whereof, we have figned thefe prefents with our hands, and have caufed the

feals

feals of our arms to be affixed thereto. Done at Verfailles, the third of September, one thoufand feven
hundred and eighty-three.

(L. S.) *Prince Iwan Bariatinſkoy.*
(L. S.) *A. Marcoff.*

His Britannic *Majeſty's Full Power.*

GEORGE *R.*

GEORGE the Third, by the grace of God, King
of Great Britain, France, and Ireland, Defender
of the Faith, Duke of Brunſwic and Lunenburg,
Arch-treafurer, and Prince Elector of the Holy Roman Empire, &c.; to all and fingular to whom thefe
prefents fhall come, greeting. Whereas, for perfecting
the peace between us and our good brother the moſt
Chriſtian King, which has been happily begun by the
preliminary articles already figned at Verfailles, on the
twentieth day of January laſt, and for bringing the
fame to the defired conclufion, we have thought proper to inveſt fome fit perfon with full authority on our
part; and whereas our right trufty and right entirely
beloved coufin and counfellor George Duke and Earl
of Mancheſter, Vifcount Mandeville, Baron of Kimbolton, Lord Lieutenant and Cuſtos Rotulorum of the
county of Huntingdon, has merited our favour by his
illuſtrious defcent, eminent qualities of mind, fingular
experience in affairs, and approved fidelity, on whom
therefore we have conferred the character of our Ambaſſador Extraordinary and Plenipotentiary to our faid
good brother the moſt Chriſtian King, being perfuaded
that he will highly dignify the office which we have
refolved to entruſt to him; Know ye therefore, that we
have made, conſtituted, and appointed, and, by thefe
prefents, do make, conſtitute, and appoint, him the faid
George Duke of Mancheſter, our true, certain, and undoubted Plenipotentiary, Commiſſioner, and Procurator, giving and granting to him full and all manner
of power and authority, as alfo our general and fpecial

cial command, for us, and in our name, to meet and
confer with the said most Christian King, and his Ministers, Commissioners, or Procurators, furnished with
sufficient authority, as also with the Ambassadors, Commissioners, Deputies, and Plenipotentiaries of the other
Princes and States whom it may concern, being likewise furnished with sufficient authority, whether singly
and separately, or collectively and jointly, and with
them to agree, treat, consult, and conclude upon the
re-establishing, as soon as may be, of a firm and lasting peace, and sincere friendship and concord; and for
us, and in our name, to sign whatever may be so agreed
upon and concluded; and also to make, and mutually
deliver and receive, a treaty or treaties, or such other
and so many instruments as shall be requisite, upon the
business concluded, and to transact all other matters
which may relate to the happily accomplishing of the
aforesaid work, in as ample manner and form, and
with equal force and effect, as we, if we were present,
could do and perform: engaging and promising, on our
Royal word, that we will approve, ratify, and accept,
in every more perfect form, whatever may happen to
be transacted and concluded by our said Plenipotentiary,
and that we will never suffer the same to be violated or
infringed by any one, either in the whole or in part.
In witness, and for the greater validity of all which,
we have caused our great seal of Great Britain to be
affixed to these presents, signed with our Royal hand.
Given at our court at St. James's, the twentieth day
of April, in the year of our Lord one thousand seven
hundred and eighty-three, and in the twenty-third
year of our reign.

His most Christian Majesty's Full Power.

LEWIS, by the grace of God, King of France
and Navarre; to all those who shall see these presents,
greeting. The preliminaries signed at Versailles the
twentieth of January, in the present year, laid the foundation of the peace re-established between us and our
most

moſt dear and moſt beloved good brother the King
of Great Britain. We have nothing more at heart
than to confolidate that ſalutary and important work,
by a ſolemn and definitive treaty: for theſe cauſes,
and other good conſiderations us thereunto moving,
we confiding entirely in the capacity and experience,
zeal and fidelity in our ſervice, of our moſt dear
and well-beloved the Sieur Count de Vergennes,
our Counſellor in all our Councils, Commander in
our Orders, Preſident of our Royal Council of Finances, Counſellor of State Military, Miniſter and
Secretary of State, and of our Commands and Finances, having the department of foreign affairs, we
have named, appointed, and deputed him, and by
theſe preſents, ſigned with our hand, do name, appoint, and depute him our Miniſter Plenipotentiary,
giving him full and abſolute power to act in that
quality, and to confer, negotiate, treat, and agree,
jointly with the Miniſter Plenipotentiary of our moſt
dear and moſt beloved good brother the King of
Great Britain, inveſted with full powers in good form,
to agree upon, conclude, and ſign ſuch articles, conditions, conventions, declarations, definitive treaty, ac-
ceſſions, and other acts whatſoever, that he ſhall judge
proper for ſecuring and confirming the great work of
peace, the whole with the ſame latitude and authority
as we ourſelf might do, if we were there preſent in
perſon, even though there ſhould be ſomething which
might require a more ſpecial order than what is contained in theſe preſents; promiſing, on the faith and
word of a King, to approve, keep firm and ſtable for
ever, fulfil and execute punctually, every thing that the
ſaid Sieur Count de Vergennes ſhall have ſtipulated
and ſigned, in virtue of the preſent full power, without
ever infringing, or permitting the ſame to be infringed, for any cauſe or under any pretence whatſoever; as alſo to cauſe our letters of ratification thereof
to be expedited in good form, and to cauſe them to be
delivered, in order to their being exchanged, in the time
which

which shall be agreed upon: for such is our pleasure: In witness whereof, we have caused our seal to be put to these presents. Given at Versailles, the fourth day of the month of February, in the year of grace one thousand seven hundred and eighty-three, and in the ninth year of our reign. Signed, LOUIS; and on the fold, By the King, *La Croix*, Marshal *de Castries*; and sealed with the great seal of yellow wax.

The Emperor's Full Power.

WE Joseph the Second, by the Divine favour, Emperor elect of the Romans, always August, King of Germany, Jerusalem, Hungary, Bohemia, Dalmatia, Croatia, Slavonia, and Lodomeria; Archduke of Austria; Duke of Burgundy, Lorrain, Stiria, Carinthia, and Carniolia; Great Duke of Tuscany; Great Prince of Transilvania; Marquis of Moravia; Duke of Brabant, Limburg, Luxemburg and Gueldres, Wirtemberg, Upper and Lower Silesia, Milan, Mantua, Parma, Placentia and Guastalla, Osvecinia and Zatoria, Calabria, Barri, Montferat and Teschin; Prince of Suevia and Carolopolis; Count of Hapsburg, Flanders, Tyrol, Hainault, Kiburg, Goritia, and Gradisca; Marquis of the Holy Roman Empire, of Burgovia, Upper and Lower Lusatia, Mussopont, and Nomeny; Count of Namur, Provence, Vaudemont, Albimont, Zutphen, Sarwar, Salm, and Falkenstein; Lord of Marchpurg, Slavonia, and Mechlin;—

By the tenor of these presents make known and testify to all and singular whom it doth or may in any manner concern. During the time that the late extensive war overspread almost the whole world, we, and her Majesty the Empress and sole Monarch of all the Russias, animated with an equal desire of putting an end as soon as possible to the calamities of the war, did not omit frequently to manifest our earnest inclination that by the interposition of our respective and mutual friendly offices, a reconciliation of the belligerent parties might be promoted, and the former peace and sincere concord between them be restored. It was

very agreeable to us to underſtand that our common endeavours had not failed of the deſired effect; for a more
pacific diſpoſition afterwards prevailing in the minds of
the Princes engaged in the war, and the buſineſs being
already ſo far happily advanced, that previous conditions of peace, or preliminary articles, were agreed
upon between them, on which the general work of
pacification might be founded, the aforeſaid moſt
Serene and moſt Potent Princes deſired, in a friendly
manner, that, in concert with her Imperial Majeſty of
all the Ruſſias, we would apply our joint attention to
this ſalutary buſineſs, and interpoſe our friendly offices
for eſtabliſhing the peace, of which the foundations
were happily laid by the above-mentioned previous
conditions, in order that by the united efforts of the
mediators, the great work of peace might on every
ſide be the more certainly accompliſhed. We, ever
intent upon that object, perceived with the greater
ſatisfaction the ſentiments of the above-mentioned
Princes, and, having previouſly concerted meaſures
with her Majeſty the Empreſs of all the Ruſſias, did
not heſitate to confirm the expectations they had conceived on our part, by accepting, with a willing and
chearful mind, the truſt committed to us. For which
end we have made choice of the illuſtrious and noble,
our faithful and beloved Florimond Count de Mercy-
Argenteau, Knight of the Golden Fleece, our actual
Privy Counſellor, and our Ambaſſador reſiding at the
court of the moſt Serene and moſt Potent King of
France and Navarre, a perſon of ſingular fidelity, integrity, and experience in the proper conduct of affairs,
and have appointed, and hereby given him full power
to take upon him, in our name, the office of mediator,
conjointly with ſuch perſon or perſons who ſhall be appointed and furniſhed with equal full power, as well
on the part of her Majeſty the Empreſs of all the
Ruſſias, as co-mediatrix, as on the part of the other
Princes who may be intereſted therein, and to contribute his counſel and aſſiſtance for concluding, by the
inter-

interpofition of friendly offices and united efforts, fuch treaties, conventions, or regulations whatfoever, as may appear to be neceffary for completing the work of peace; all which he fhall fubfcribe and fign, and fhall alfo deliver fuch inftrument or inftruments, on his part, as may be proper and required of him for perfecting the bufinefs: promifing, on our Imperial, Royal, and Archducal word, that we will ratify, accept, and faithfully fulfil all fuch things as our faid Ambaffador fhall have concluded, promifed, and figned, by virtue of thefe prefents, and that we will order letters of ratification to be expedited at the time agreed upon. In witnefs, and for the greater validity whereof, we have figned this inftrument of full power with our hand, and have ordered it to be confirmed with our Imperial, Royal, and Archducal feal affixed thereto. Given in our city of Vienna, the fixteenth day of April, in the year of our Lord one thoufand feven hundred and eighty-three, in the twentieth of our Roman-Germanic reign, and the third of our hereditary reign.

JOSEPHUS.

W. Kaunitz Rietberg.

By his Sacred Imperial and Royal Apoftolic Majefty's fpecial command.

Ant. Spielmann.

The Emprefs of Ruffia's Full Power.

BY the grace of God, we Catherine the Second, Emprefs and fole Monarch of all the Ruffias, of Mufcovy, Kiovia, Vlodomiria, Novogorod, Czarina of Cafan, Czarina of Aftracan, Czarina of Siberia, Lady of Plefcau, and Great Dutchefs of Smolenfko; Dutchefs of Eftonia, of Livonia, Carelia, Twer, Ingoria, Germia, Viatkia, Bulgaria, and other countries; Lady and Great Dutchefs of Lower Novogorod, of Czernigovia, Refan, Roftow, Jaroflow, Belo-Oforia, Udoria, Obdoria, Condihia; Ruler of all the fide of the North; Lady of Iveria; and Hereditary Princefs and Sovereign of the Czars of Cartalinia and Georgia, as alfo of Cabardinia, of the Princes of Circaffia, of Gorfki, &c. Being intent, during all the courfe of the late war, which had extended over every part of the earth, to teftify how much we had it at heart to fee the calamities thereof terminated, we were inclined, in conjunction with his Majefty the Emperor of the Romans, King of Hungary and Bohemia, to employ our good offices, in order to find means of conciliation proper for re-eftablifhing peace and good underftanding between the belligerent Powers. We have had the fatisfaction to obferve that our common endeavours were not fruit-lefs; and the pacific fentiments with which the faid Powers were happily animated, having ripened and ftrengthened fo far that they proceeded to conclude preliminary articles, ferving as a bafis to the definitive treaties, they invited us, conjointly with his Majefty the Emperor of the Romans, King of Hungary and Bohemia, to carry our united mediation into full exe-cution, and to interpofe our good offices in this falutary work, by concurring to confolidate and fully eftablifh the peace, the foundations of which were laid by the aforefaid preliminary articles, and thus to accomplifh the bufinefs of pacification fo happily begun. We, equally induced by the fentiments above expreffed, as by a juft acknowledgment of thofe which were mani-fefted to us on the part of the faid Powers, did not hefitate, in concert with his Majefty the Emperor of the Romans, to confirm their expectation, and to charge ourfelf with the important employment which was tendered to us. For this end, we have made choice of, named, and deputed, and by thefe prefents do make choice of, name, and depute, our Minifters Plenipoten-tiary to his moft Chriftian Majefty, our beloved and trufty Prince, Iwan Bariatinfkoy, Lieutenant General of our forces, Knight of the Order cf St. Anne, and the Sieur Arcadius de Marcoff, our Counfellor of Chan-cery, giving them full power, in cur name, and on our behalf,

2

behalf, in quality of mediators, jointly with him or them who shall be named for this purpose, and likewise furnished with full powers, on the part of his Majesty the Emperor of the Romans, King of Hungary and Bohemia, co-mediator, as well as on the part of the other Powers interested therein, to act or interpose, and assist with our mediation and good offices in the arrangement and completion of all such treaties, conventions, or other instruments, as shall be judged necessary for the consolidation and entire confirmation of the work begun; and also to sign and deliver, on their part, such act or acts as may be required and deemed conducive to the attainment of that end: promising, on our faith and Imperial word, to approve and faithfully perform every thing which shall have been done, concluded, promised, and signed, in virtue of the present full power, by the said Prince Bariatinskoy and Sieur Marcoff, as also to cause our ratifications thereof to be expedited in the time agreed upon.   In witness whereof, we have signed these presents with our own hand, and have caused the great seal of the empire to be fixed thereto.   Given at our residence of St. Petersburgh, the twelfth of March, in the year of grace one thousand seven hundred and eighty-three, and in the twenty-first year of our reign.

CATHERINE.

Count John d'Ostermann.

[The COMMERCIAL TREATY, 1786, is printed from the copy, which was published by authority, in 1786.]

The Treaty of Navigation and Commerce between his Britannic Majesty and the most Christian King; Signed at Versailles, the 26th of September, 1786.

HIS Britannic Majesty, and his most Christian Majesty, being equally animated with the desire

not

not only of confolidating the good harmony which actually fubfifts between them, but alfo of extending the happy effects thereof to their refpective fubjects, have thought that the moft efficacious means for attaining thofe objects, conformably to the eighteenth article of the treaty of peace figned the 6th of September, 1783, would be to adopt a fyftem of commerce on the bafis of reciprocity and mutual convenience, which, by difcontinuing the prohibitions and prohibitory duties which have exifted for almoft a century between the two nations, might procure the moft folid advantages on both fides to the national productions and induftry, and put an end to contraband trade, no lefs injurious to the public revenue than to that lawful commerce which is alone entitled to protection. For this end, their faid Majefties have named for their Commiffaries and Plenipotentiaries, to wit, the King of Great Britain, William Eden, Efq; Privy Counfellor in Great Britain and Ireland, Member of the Britifh Parliament, and his Envoy Extraordinary and Minifter Plenipotentiary to his moft Chriftian Majefty; and the moft Chriftian King, the Sieur Jofeph Mathias Gerard de Rayneval, Knight, Counfellor of State, Knight of the Royal Order of Charles III; who, after having exchanged their refpective full powers, have agreed upon the following articles.

I. It is agreed and concluded between the moft Serene and moft Potent King of Great Britain, and the moft Serene and moft Potent the moft Chriftian King, that there fhall be a reciprocal and entirely perfect liberty of navigation and commerce between the fubjects of each party, in all and every the kingdoms, ftates, provinces, and territories, fubject to their Majefties, in Europe, for all and fingular kinds of goods, in thofe places, upon the conditions, and in fuch manner and form as is fettled and adjufted in the following articles.

II. For

II. For the future fecurity of commerce and friendfhip between the fubjects of their faid Majefties, and
to the end that this good correfpondence may be preferved from all interruption and difturbance, it is concluded and agreed, that if at any time there fhould
arife any mifunderftanding, breach of friendfhip, or
rupture, between the crowns of their Majefties, which
God forbid! (which rupture fhall not be deemed to ex-
ift until the recalling or fending home of the refpective
Ambaffadors and Minifters) the fubjects of each of the
two parties, refiding in the dominions of the other, fhall
have the privilege of remaining and continuing their
trade therein, without any manner of difturbance, fo
long as they behave peaceably, and commit no offence againft the laws and ordinances: and in cafe their
conduct fhould render them fufpected, and the refpective governments fhould be obliged to order them to
remove, the term of twelve months fhall be allowed
them for that purpofe, in order that they may remove,
with their effects and property, whether entrufted to
individuals or to the State. At the fame time it is to
be underftood, that this favour is not to be extended
to thofe who fhall act contrary to the eftablifhed
laws.

III. It is likewife agreed and concluded, that the
fubjects and inhabitants of the kingdoms, provinces,
and dominions of their Majefties, fhall exercife no acts
of hoftility or violence againft each other, either by
fea or by land, or in rivers, ftreams, ports, or havens,
under any colour or pretence whatfoever; fo that the
fubjects of either party, fhall receive no patent, commiffion, or inftruction for arming and acting at fea as
privateers, nor letters of reprifal, as they are called,
from any Princes or States, enemies to the other party;
nor by viriue or under colour of fuch patents, commiffions, or reprifals, fhall they difturb, infeft, or any
way prejudice or damage the aforefaid fubjects and inhabitants of the King of Great Britain, or of the
moft Chriftian King; neither fhall they arm fhips in

fuch

such manner as is abovesaid, or go out to sea there-with. To which end, as often as it is required by either party, strict and express prohibitions shall be renewed and published in all the territories, countries, and dominions of each party wheresoever, that no one shall in any wise use such commissions or letters of re-prisal, under the severest punishment that can be in-flicted on the transgressors, besides being liable to make full restitution and satisfaction to those to whom they have done any damage: neither shall any letters of reprisal be hereafter granted by either of the said high contracting parties, to the prejudice or detriment of the subjects of the other, except only in such case wherein justice is denied or delayed; which denial or delay of justice shall not be regarded as verified, un-less the petition of the person who desires the said let-ters of reprisal be communicated to the Minister re-siding there on the part of the Prince against whose subjects they are to be granted, that within the space of four months, or sooner, if it be possible, he may ma-nifest the contrary, or procure the satisfaction which may be justly due.

IV. The subjects and inhabitants of the respective dominions of the two Sovereigns shall have liberty, freely and securely, without licence or passport, general or special, by land or by sea, or any other way, to enter into the kingdoms, dominions, provinces, coun-tries, islands, cities, villages, towns, walled or unwalled, fortified or unfortified, ports, or territories whatsoever, of either Sovereign, situated in Europe, and to return from thence, to remain there, or to pass through the same, and therein to buy and purchase, as they please, all things necessary for their subsistence and use, and they shall mutually be treated with all kindness and favour. Provided, however, that in all these matters they behave and conduct themselves conformably to the laws and statutes, and live with each other in a friendly and peaceable manner, and promote reciprocal concord by maintaining a mutual good understanding.

V. The

ᴸ V. The subjects of each of their said Majesties may
have leave and licence to come with their ships, as
also with the merchandizes and goods on board the
same, the trade and importation whereof are not prohibited by the laws of either kingdom, and to enter
into the countries, dominions, cities, ports, places, and
rivers of either party, situated in Europe, to resort
thereto, and to remain and reside there, without any
limitation of time; also to hire houses, or to lodge
with other persons, and to buy all lawful kinds of merchandizes where they think fit, either from the first
maker or the seller, or in any other manner, whether
in the public market for the sale of merchandizes, or
in fairs, or wherever such merchandizes are manufactured or sold. They may likewise deposit and keep
in their magazines and warehouses the merchandizes
brought from other parts, and afterwards expose the
same to sale, without being in any wise obliged, unless
willingly and of their own accord, to bring the said
merchandizes to the marts and fairs. Neither are they
to be burthened with any impositions or duties on account of the said freedom of trade, or for any other
cause whatsoever, except those which are to be paid
for their ships and merchandizes conformably to the
regulations of the present treaty, or those to which the
subjects of the two contracting parties shall themselves
be liable. And they shall have free leave to remove
themselves, as also their wives, children, and servants,
together with their merchandizes, property, goods, or
effects, whether bought or imported, wherever they
shall think fit, out of either kingdom, by land and by
sea, on the rivers and fresh waters, after discharging
the usual duties, any law, privilege, grant, immunities,
or customs to the contrary thereof in any wise notwithstanding. In matters of religion, the subjects of
the two crowns shall enjoy perfect liberty: they shall
not be compelled to attend Divine service, whether
in the churches or elsewhere; but, on the contrary,
they shall be permitted, without any molestation, to
perform

.perform. the . exercifes, of their religion privately in
their own houfes,· and in, their own way. Liberty
fhall not be refufed to bury the fubjects of either kingdom, who die in the territories of the other, in convenient places to be appointed for that purpofe; nor fhall
the funerals or fepulchres of the deceafed be in any
wife difturbed. The laws and· ftatutes of each kingdom fhall remain in. force and vigour, and fhall be
duly put in execution, whether. they relate to commerce and navigation, or to any other right, thofe cafes
only excepted, concerning which it is otherwife determined in the articles of this prefent treaty. . .

VI. The two high contracting parties have thought
proper to fettle the duties on certain goods and merchandizes, in order to fix invariably the footing on
which the trade therein fhall be eftablifhed between
the two nations. In confequence of which they have
agreed upon the following tariff, *viz.*

1ft. The wines of France, imported directly from
France· into Great Britain, fhall in no cafe pay any
higher duties than thofe which the wines of Portugal
now pay.

The wines of France, imported directly from France
into Ireland, fhall pay no higher duties than thofe
which they now pay.

2d. The vinegars of France, inftead of fixty-feven
pounds, five fhillings and three pence, and twelve twentieths of a penny fterling, per ton, which they now
pay, fhall not for the future pay in Great Britain any
higher duties than thirty-two pounds eighteen fhillings
and ten pence, and fixteen twentieths of a penny fterling, per ton.

3d. The brandies of France, inftead of nine fhillings and fix pence, and twelve twentieths of a penny
fterling, fhall for the future pay in Great Britain only
feven fhillings fterling per gallon, making four quarts,
Englifh meafure.

4th. Oil of olives, coming directly from France,
fhall

shall for the future pay no higher duties than are now paid for the same from the moft favoured nations.

5th. Beer shall pay reciprocally a duty of thirty per cent. ad valorem.

6th. The duties on hardware, cutlery, cabinet ware, and turnery, and also all works, both heavy and light, of iron, steel, copper, and brass, shall be classed; and the highest duty shall not exceed ten per cent. ad valorem.

7th. All sorts of cottons manufactured in the dominions of the two Sovereigns in Europe, and also woollens, whether knit or wove, including hosiery, shall pay, in both countries, an import duty of twelve per cent. ad valorem; all manufactures of cotton or wool, mixed with silk, excepted, which shall remain prohibited on both sides.

8th. Cambrics and lawns shall pay, in both countries, an import duty of five shillings, or six *livres Tournois*, per demi piece of seven yards and three quarters, English measure; and linens, made of flax or hemp, manufactured in the dominions of the two Sovereigns in Europe, shall pay no higher duties, either in Great Britain or France, than linens manufactured in Holland or Flanders, imported into Great Britain, now pay.

And linens made of flax or hemp, manufactured in Ireland or France, shall reciprocally pay no higher duties than linens manufactured in Holland, imported into Ireland, now pay.

9th. Sadlery shall reciprocally pay an import duty of fifteen per cent. ad valorem.

10th. Gauzes of all sorts shall reciprocally pay ten per cent. ad valorem.

11th. Millinery made up of muslin, lawn, cambric, or gauze of every kind, or of any other article admitted under the present tariff, shall pay reciprocally a duty of twelve per cent. ad valorem: and if any articles shall be used therein which are not specified in the tariff, they shall pay no higher duties than those

paid

paid for the same articles by the most favoured nations.

12th. Porcelain, earthen-ware, and pottery, shall pay reciprocally twelve per cent. ad valorem.

13th. Plate-glass, and glass-ware in general, shall be admitted on each side, paying a duty of twelve per cent. ad valorem.

His Britannic Majesty reserves the right of countervailing, by additional duties on the under-mentioned merchandizes, the internal duties actually imposed upon the manufactures, or the import duties which are charged on the raw materials; namely, on all linens or cottons, stained or printed, on beer, glass-ware, plate-glass, and iron.

And his most Christian Majesty also reserves the right of doing the same, with regard to the following merchandizes; namely, cottons, iron, and beer.

And for the better securing the due collection of the duties payable, ad valorem, which are specified in the above tariff, the said contracting parties will concert with each other as well the form of the declarations to be made, as also the proper means of preventing fraud with respect to the real value of the said goods and merchandizes.

But if it shall hereafter appear that any mistakes have inadvertently been made in the above tariff, contrary to the principles on which it is founded, the two Sovereigns will concert with good faith upon the means of rectifying them.

VII. The duties above specified are not to be altered but by mutual consent; and the merchandizes not above specified shall pay, in the dominions of the two Sovereigns, the import and export duties payable in each of the said dominions by the most favoured European nations, at the time the present treaty bears date; and the ships belonging to the subjects of the said dominions shall also respectively enjoy therein all the privileges and advantages which are granted to those of the most favoured European nations.

And

And it being the intention of the two high contracting parties, that their respective subjects should be, in
the dominions of each other, upon a footing as advantageous as those of other European nations, they agree
that, in case they shall hereafter grant any additional advantages in navigation or trade to any other European
nation, they will reciprocally allow their said subjects to
participate therein, without prejudice however to the
advantages which they reserve, *viz.* France, in favour
of Spain, in consequence of the twenty-fourth article
of the family compact, signed the 10th of May, 1761,
and England according to what she has practised in
conformity to, and in consequence of the convention
of 1703, between England and Portugal.

And, to the end that every person may know with
certainty the state of the aforesaid imposts, customs,
import and export duties, whatever they may be, it is
agreed that tariffs, indicating the imposts, customs,
and established duties, shall be affixed in public places,
as well in Rouën and the other trading cities of France,
as in London and the other trading cities under the
dominion of the King of Great Britain, that recourse
may be had to them whenever any difference shall
arise concerning such imposts, customs, and duties;
which shall not be levied otherwise than in conformity
to what is clearly expressed in the said tariffs, and according to their natural construction. And if any
officer, or other person in his name, shall, under any
pretence, publicly or privately, directly or indirectly,
demand or take of a merchant, or of any other person,
any sum of money, or any thing else, on account of
duties, impost, search, or compensation, although it
be under the name of a free gift, or under any other
pretence, more or otherwise than what is above prescribed; in such case, the said officer, or his deputy, if
he be accused and convicted of the same before a competent judge, in the place where the crime was committed, shall give full satisfaction to the injured party,
and shall likewise suffer the penalty prescribed by the
laws.

VIII. No

VIII. No merchandize exported from the countries
respectively under the dominion of their Majesties,
shall hereafter be subject to be inspected or confiscated,
under any pretence of fraud or defect in making or
working them, or of any other imperfection whatsoever; but absolute freedom shall be allowed to the
buyer and seller to bargain and fix the price for the
same, as they shall see good; any law, statute, edict,
proclamation, privilege, grant, or custom to the contrary notwithstanding.

IX. Whereas several kinds of merchandizes, which
are usually contained in casks, chests, or other cases,
and for which the duties are paid by weight, will be
exported from and imported into France by British
subjects; it is agreed, that, in such case, the aforesaid
duties shall be demanded only according to the real
weight of the merchandizes; and the weight of the
casks, chests, and other cases whatever, shall be deducted, in the same manner as has been and is now
practised in England.

X. It is further agreed, that if any mistake or error
shall be committed by any master of a ship, his interpreter or factor, or by others employed by him, in
making the entry or declaration of her cargo, neither
the ship nor the cargo, for such defect, shall be subject
to confiscation; but it shall be lawful for the proprietors to take back again such goods as were omitted
in the entry or declaration of the master of the ship,
paying only the accustomed duties according to the
pancart; provided always, that there be no manifest
appearance of fraud. Neither shall the merchants, or
the masters of ships, or the merchadize, be subject to
any penalties by reason of such omission, in case the
goods omitted in the declaration shall not have been
landed before the declaration has been made.

XI. In case either of the two high contracting parties shall think proper to establish prohibitions, or to
augment the import duties upon any goods or merchandize

x

chandize of the growth or manufacture of the other, which are not fpecified in the tariff, fuch prohibitions or augmentations fhall be general, and fhall comprehend the like goods and merchandizes of the other moft favoured European nations, as well as thofe of either ftate: and in cafe either of the two contracting parties fhall revoke the prohibitions, or diminifh the duties, in favour of any other European nation, upon any goods or merchandize of its growth or manufacture, whether on importation or exportation, fuch revocations or diminutions fhall be extended to the fubjects of the other party, on condition that the latter fhall grant to the fubjects of the former the importation and exportation of the like goods and merchandizes under the fame duties; the cafes referved in the feventh article of the prefent treaty always excepted.

XII. And forafmuch as a certain ufage, not authorized by any law, has formerly obtained in divers parts of Great Britain and France, by which French fubjects have paid in England a kind of capitation tax, called in the language of that country Head-money; and Englifh fubjects a like duty in France, called *Argent du chef*; it is agreed, that the faid impoft fhall not be demanded for the future, on either fide, neither under the ancient name, nor under any other name whatfoever.

XIII. If either of the high contracting parties has granted or fhall grant any bounties for encouraging the exportation of any articles being of the growth, produce, or manufacture of his dominions, the other party fhall be allowed to add to the duties already impofed, by virtue of the prefent treaty, on the faid goods and merchandizes imported into his dominions, fuch an import duty as fhall be equivalent to the faid bounty. But this ftipulation is not to extend to the cafes of reftitutions of duties and impofts (called drawbacks) which are allowed upon exportation.

XIV. The

XIV. The advantages granted by the prefent treaty, to the fubjects of his Britannic Majefty, fhall take effect, as far as relates to the kingdom of Great Britain, as foon as laws fhall be paffed there for fecuring to the fubjects of his moft Chriftian Majefty the reciprocal enjoyment of the advantages which are granted to them by the prefent treaty.

And the advantages granted by all thefe articles, except the tariff, fhall take effect, with regard to the kingdom of Ireland, as foon as laws fhall be paffed there for fecuring to the fubjects of his moft Chriftian Majefty the reciprocal enjoyment of the advantages which are granted to them by this treaty; and, in like manner, the advantages granted by the tariff fhall take effect in what relates to the faid kingdom, as foon as laws fhall be paffed there for giving effect to the faid tariff.

XV. It is agreed, that fhips belonging to his Britannic Majefty's fubjects, arriving in the dominions of his moft Chriftian Majefty from the ports of Great Britain or Ireland, or from any other foreign port, fhall not pay freight duty, or any other like duty. In the fame manner, French fhips fhall be exempted, in the dominions of his Britannic Majefty, from the duty of five fhillings, and from every other fimilar duty or charge.

XVI. It fhall not be lawful for any foreign privateers, not being fubjects of either crown, who have commiffions from any other Prince or State, in enmity with either nation, to arm their fhips in the ports of either of the faid two kingdoms, to fell what they have taken, or in any other manner whatever to exchange the fame; neither fhall they be allowed even to purchafe victuals, except fuch as fhall be neceffary for their going to the neareft port of that Prince from whom they have obtained commiffions.

XVII. When any difpute fhall arife between any commander of a fhip and his feamen, in the ports of either kingdom, concerning wages due to the faid feamen,

men, or other civil caufes whatever, the magiftrate of the place fhall require no more from the perfon accufed than that he give to the accufer a declaration in writing, witneffed by the magiftrate, whereby he fhall be bound to anfwer that matter before a competent judge in his own country; which being done, it fhall not be lawful either for the feamen to defert their fhip, or to hinder the commander from profecuting his voyage. It fhall moreover be lawful for the merchants, in the places of their abode, or elfewhere, to keep books of their accounts and affairs, as they fhall think fit, and to have an intercourfe of letters in fuch language or idiom as they fhall chufe, without any moleftation or fearch whatfoever. But if it fhould happen to be neceffary for them to produce their books of accounts for deciding any difpute or controverfy, in fuch cafe, they fhall be obliged to bring into court the entire books or writings, but fo as the judge may not have liberty to take cognizance of any other articles in the faid books than fuch as fhall relate to the affair in queftion, or fuch as fhall be neceffary to give credit to the faid books; neither fhall it be lawful, under any pretence, to take the faid books or writings forcibly out of the hands of the owners, or to retain them, the cafe of bankruptcy only excepted. Nor fhall the fubjects of the King of Great Britain be obliged to write their accounts, letters, or other inftruments relating to trade, on ftamped paper, except their day-book, which, that it may be produced as evidence in any law-fuit, ought, according to the laws which all perfons trading in France are to obferve, to be indorfed and attefted *gratis* by the judge, under his own hand.

XVIII. It is further agreed and concluded, that all merchants, commanders of fhips, and others, the fubjects of the King of Great Britain, in all the dominions of his moft Chriftian Majefty in Europe, fhall have full liberty to manage their own affairs themfelves, or to commit them to the management of whomfoever they pleafe; nor fhall they be obliged to employ any interpreter or broker, nor to pay them any falary, unlefs they fhall chufe to employ them. Moreover, mafters of fhips fhall not be obliged, in loading or unloading their fhips, to make ufe of thofe perfons who may be appointed by public authority for that purpofe, either at Bourdeaux or elfewhere; but it fhall be entirely free for them to load or unload their fhips by themfelves, or to make ufe of fuch perfons in loading or unloading the fame as they fhall think fit, without the payment of any reward to any other whom-foever; neither fhall they be forced to unload into other fhips, or to receive into their own any merchan-dize whatever, or to wait for their lading any longer than they pleafe. And all the fubjects of the moft Chriftian King fhall reciprocally have and enjoy the fame privileges and liberties, in all the dominions of his Britannic Majefty in Europe.

XIX. The fhips of either party being laden, failing along the coafts of the other, and being forced by ftorm into the havens or ports, or making land there in any other manner whatever, fhall not be obliged to unlade their goods, or any part thereof, or to pay any duty, unlefs they of their own accord unlade their goods there, and fell fome part thereof. But it fhall be lawful, permiffion having been firft obtained from thofe who have the direction of maritime affairs, to unlade and fell a fmall part of their cargo, merely for the end of purchafing neceffaries, either for victual-ling or refitting the fhip; and in that cafe the whole lading fhall not be fubject to pay the duties, but that fmall part only which fhall have been taken out and fold.

XX. It fhall be lawful for all the fubjects of the King of Great Britain, and of the moft Chriftian King, to fail with their fhips, with perfect fecurity and liberty, no diftinction being made who are the proprietors of the merchandizes laden thereon, from any port what-ever, to the countries which are now or fhall be here-after

after at war with the King of Great Britain, or the moſt Chriſtian King. It ſhall likewiſe be lawful for, the aforeſaid ſubjects to ſail and traffic with their ſhips and merchandizes, with the ſame liberty and ſecurity, from the countries, ports, and places of thoſe who are enemies of both, or of either party, without any oppoſition or diſturbance whatſoever, and to paſs directly not only from the places of the enemy afore-mentioned to neutral places, but alſo from one place belonging to an enemy to another place belonging to an enemy, whether they be under the juriſdiction of the ſame or of ſeveral Princes. And as it has been ſtipulated concerning ſhips and goods, that every thing ſhall be deemed to be free which ſhall be found on board the ſhips belonging to the ſubjects of the reſpective kingdoms, although the whole lading, or part thereof, ſhould belong to the enemies of their Majeſties, contraband goods being always excepted, on the ſtopping of which, ſuch proceedings ſhall be had as are conformable to the ſpirit of the following articles; it is likewiſe agreed, that the ſame liberty be extended to perſons who are on board a free ſhip, to the end that, although they be enemies to both or to either party, they may not be taken out of ſuch free ſhip, unleſs they are ſoldiers actually in the ſervice of the enemies, and on their voyage for the purpoſe of being employed in a military capacity in their fleets or armies.

XXI. This liberty of navigation and commerce ſhall extend to all kinds of merchandizes, excepting thoſe only which are ſpecified in the following article, and which are deſcribed under the name of Contraband.

XXII. Under this name of Contraband, or prohibited goods, ſhall be comprehended arms, cannon, harquebuſſes, mortars, petards, bombs, grenades, ſauciſſes, carcaſſes, carriages for cannon, muſket-reſts, bandoleers, gunpowder, match, ſalt-petre, ball, pikes, ſwords, head-pieces, helmets, cuiraſſes, halberds, javelins, holſters, belts, horſes and harneſs, and all other

M m 2 like

like kinds of arms and warlike implements fit for the use of troops.

XXIII. Thefe merchandizes which follow fhall not be reckoned among contraband goods, that is to fay, all forts of cloth, and all other manufactures of wool, flax, filk, cotton, or any other materials; all kinds of wearing apparel, together with the articles of which they are ufually made; gold, filver, coined or uncoined, tin, iron, lead, copper, brafs, coals; as alfo wheat and barley, and any other kind of corn and pulfe, tobacco, and all kinds of fpices, falted and fmoked flefh, falted fifh, cheefe and butter, beer, oil, wines, fugar, all forts of falt, and of provifions which ferve for fuftenance and food to mankind; alfo all kinds of cotton, cordage, cables, fails, failcloth, hemp, tallow, pitch, tar and rofin, anchors, and any parts of anchors, fhip-mafts, planks, timber of all kinds of trees, and all other things proper either for building or repairing fhips. Nor fhall any other goods whatever, which have not been worked into the form of any inftrument or furniture for warlike ufe, by land or by fea, be reputed contraband, much lefs fuch as have been already wrought and made up for any other purpofe. All which things fhall be deemed goods not contraband, as likewife all others which are not comprehended and particularly defcribed in the preceding article; fo that they may be freely carried, by the fubjects of both kingdoms, even to places belonging to an enemy, excepting only fuch places as are befieged, blocked up, or invefted.

XXIV. To the end that all manner of diffenfions and quarrels may be avoided and prevented on both fides, it is agreed, that in cafe either of their Majefties fhould be engaged in war, the fhips and veffels belonging to the fubjects of the other fhall be furnifhed with fea-letters or paffports, expreffing the name, property, and bulk of the fhip, as alfo the name and place of abode of the mafter or commander of the

said

said ship, that it may appear thereby, that the ship really and truly belongs to the subjects of one of the Princes; which passports shall be made out and grant-ed, according to the form annexed to the present treaty: they shall likewise be renewed every year, if the ship happens to return home within the space of a year. It is also agreed, that such ships when laden are to be provided not only with passports as above-mentioned, but also with certificates containing the several particulars of the cargo, the place from whence the ship sailed, and whither she is bound, so that it may be known whether she carries any of the prohibited or contraband goods specified in the 22d article of this treaty; which certificates shall be prepared by the officers of the place from whence the ship set sail, in the accustomed form. And if any one shall think fit to express in the said certificates the person to whom the goods belong, he may freely do so.

XXV. The ships belonging to the subjects and inhabitants of the respective kingdoms, coming to any of the coasts of either of them, but without being willing to enter into port, or, being entered, yet not willing to land their cargoes or break bulk, shall not be obliged to give an account of their lading, unless they are suspected, upon sure evidence, of carrying prohibited goods, called contraband, to the enemies of either of the two high contracting parties.

XXVI. In case the ships belonging to the said subjects and inhabitants of the respective dominions of their most Serene Majesties, either on the coast, or on the high seas, shall meet with any men of war belonging to their most Serene Majesties, or with privateers, the said men of war and privateers, for preventing any inconveniencies, are to remain out of cannon-shot, and to send their boats to the merchant ship which may be met with, and shall enter her to the number of two or three men only, to whom the master or commander of such ship or vessel shall shew his pass-

port,

port, containing the proof of the property of the ſhip, made out according to the form annexed to this preſent treaty; and the ſhip which ſhall have exhibited the ſame, ſhall have liberty to continue her voyage, and it ſhall be wholly unlawful any way to moleſt or ſearch her, or to chaſe or compel her to alter her courſe,

XXVII. The merchant ſhips belonging to the ſubjeſts of either of the two high contracting parties, which intend to go to a port at enmity with the other Sovereign, concerning whoſe voyage, and the ſort of goods on board, there may be juſt cauſe of ſuſpicion, ſhall be obliged to exhibit, as well on the high ſeas as in the ports and havens, not only her paſſports, but alſo her certificates, expreſſing that the goods are not of the kind which are contraband, as ſpecified in the 22d article of this treaty.

XXVIII. If, on exhibiting the above-mentioned certificates, containing a liſt of the cargo, the other party ſhould diſcover any goods of that kind which are declared contraband, or prohibited, by the 22d article of this treaty, and which are deſigned for a port ſubject to his enemies, it ſhall be unlawful to break up or open the hatches, cheſts, caſks, bales, or other veſſels found on board ſuch ſhip, or to remove even the ſmalleſt parcel of the goods, whether the ſaid ſhip belongs to the ſubjects of the King of Great Britain, or of the moſt Chriſtian King, unleſs the lading be brought on ſhore, in the preſence of the officers of the court of admiralty, and an inventory made by them of the ſaid goods: nor ſhall it be lawful to ſell, exchange, or alienate the ſame in any manner, unleſs after due and lawful proceſs ſhall have been had againſt ſuch prohibited goods, and the judges of the Admiralty reſpectively ſhall, by ſentence pronounced, have confiſcated the ſame, ſaving always as well the ſhip itſelf, as the other goods found therein, which by this treaty are to be accounted free; neither may they be

detained

detained on pretence of their being mixed with prohibited goods, much lefs fhall they be confifcated as lawful prize : and if when only part of the cargo fhall confift of contraband goods, the mafter of the fhip fhall agree, confent, and offer to deliver them to the captor who has difcovered them, in fuch cafe, the captor, having received thofe goods as lawful prize, fhall forthwith releafe the fhip, and not hinder her, by any means, from profecuting her voyage to the place of her deftination.

XXIX. On the contrary, it is agreed, that whatever fhall be found to be laden by the fubjects and inhabitants of either party, on any fhip belonging to the enemies of the other, although it be not contraband goods, fhall be confifcated in the fame manner as if it belonged to the enemy himfelf; except thofe goods and merchandizes which were put on board fuch fhip before the declaration of war, or the general order for reprifals, or even after fuch declaration, if it were done within the times following; that is to fay, if they were put on board fuch fhip in any port or place, within the fpace of two months after fuch declaration, or order for reprifals, between Archangel, St. Peterfburgh, and the Scilly iflands, and between the faid iflands and the city of Gibraltar; of ten weeks in the Mediterranean fea; and of eight months in any other country or place in the world : fo that the goods of the fubjects of either Prince, whether they be contraband, or otherwife, which, as aforefaid, were put on board any fhip belonging to an enemy before the war, or after the declaration of the fame, within the time and limits above-mentioned, fhall no ways be liable to confifcation, but fhall well and truly be reftored, without delay, to the proprietors demanding the fame; provided neverthelefs that, if the faid merchandizes be contraband, it fhall not be any ways lawful to carry them afterwards to the ports belonging to the enemy.

M m 4   XXX. And,

XXX. And, that more abundant care may be taken for the fecurity of the refpective fubjects of their moft Serene Majefties, to prevent their fuffering any injury by the men of war or privateers of either party, all the commanders of the fhips of the King of Great Britain, and of the moft Chriftian King, and all their fubjects, fhall be forbid doing any damage to thofe of the other party, or committing any outrage againft them; and if they act to the contrary they fhall be punifhed, and fhall moreover be bound, in their perfons and eftates, to make fatisfaction and reparation for all damages, and the intereft thereof, of what nature foever.

XXXI. For this caufe, all commanders of privateers, before they receive their patents or fpecial commiffions, fhall hereafter be obliged to give, before a competent judge, fufficient fecurity by good bail, who are refponfible men, and have no intereft in the faid fhip, each of whom fhall be bound in the whole for the fum of thirty-fix thoufand *livres Tournois*, or fifteen hundred pounds fterling; or, if fuch fhip be provided with above one hundred and fifty feamen or foldiers, for the fum of feventy-two thoufand *livres Tournois*, or three thoufand pounds fterling, that they will make entire fatisfaction for all damages and injuries whatfoever, which they, or their officers, or others in their fervice, may commit during their cruize, contrary to the tenor of this prefent treaty, or the edicts made in confequence thereof by their moft Serene Majefties, under penalty likewife of having their patents and fpecial commiffions revoked and annulled.

XXXII. Their faid Majefties being willing mutually to treat in their dominions the fubjects of each other as favourably as if they were their own fubjects, will give fuch orders as fhall be neceffary and effectual, that the judgments and decrees, concerning prizes in the court of admiralty, be given conformably to

the

the rules of juſtice and equity, and to the ſtipulations of this treaty, by judges who are above all ſuſpicion, and who have no manner of intereſt in the cauſe in diſpute.

XXXIII. And when the quality of the ſhip, goods, and maſter, ſhall ſufficiently appear, from ſuch paſſports and certificates, it ſhall not be lawful for the commanders of men of war to exact any further proof, under any pretext whatſoever. But if any merchant ſhip ſhall not be provided with ſuch paſſports or certificates, then it may be examined by a proper judge, but in ſuch manner as, if it ſhall be found, fiom other proofs and documents, that it truly belongs to the ſubjects of one of the Sovereigns, and does not contain any contraband goods, deſigned to be carried to the enemy of the other, it ſhall not be liable to confiſcation, but ſhall be releaſed, together with its cargo, in order to proceed on its voyage.

If the maſter of the ſhip named in the paſſports ſhould happen to die, or be removed by any other cauſe, and another put in his place, the ſhips and goods laden thereon ſhall nevertheleſs be equally ſecure, and the paſſports ſhall remain in full force.

XXXIV. It is further provided and agreed, that the ſhips of either of the two nations, retaken by the privateers of the other, ſhall be reſtored to the former owner, if they have not been in the power of the enemy for the ſpace of four and twenty hours, ſubject to the payment, by the ſaid owner, of one third of the value of the ſhip retaken, and of its cargo, guns, and apparel; which third part ſhall be amicably adjuſted by the parties concerned; but if not, and in caſe they ſhould diſagree, they ſhall make application to the officers of the admiralty of the place where the privateer which retook the captured-veſſel ſhall have carried her.

If the ſhip retaken has been in the power of the enemy above four and twenty hours, ſhe ſhall wholly belong to the privateer which retook her.

In

In cafe of a fhip being retaken by any man of war belonging to his Britannic Majefty, or to his moft Chriftian Majefty, it fhall be reftored to the former owner, on payment of the thirtieth part of the value of fuch fhip, and of its cargo, guns, and apparel, if it was retaken within the four and twenty hours; and the tenth part, if it was retaken after the four and twenty hours; which fums fhall be diftributed, as a reward, amongft the crews of the fhips which fhall have retaken fuch prize. The valuation of the thirtieth and tenth parts above-mentioned fhall be fettled conformably to the regulations in the beginning of this article.

XXXV. Whenfoever the Ambaffadors of either of their faid Majefties, or other their Minifters having a public character, and refiding at the court of the other Prince, fhall complain of the injuftice of the fentences which have been given, their Majefties fhall refpectively caufe the fame to be revifed and re-examined in their councils, unlefs their councils fhould already have decided thereupon, that it may appear, with certainty, whether the directions and provifions prefcribed in this treaty have been followed and obferved. Their Majefties fhall likewife take care that this matter be effectually provided for, and that juftice be done to every complainant within the fpace of three months. However, before or after judgment given, and pending the revifion thereof, it fhall not be lawful to fell the goods in difpute, or to unlade them, unlefs with the confent of the perfons concerned, for preventing any kind of lofs; and laws fhall be enacted on both fides for the execution of the prefent article.

XXXVI. If any differences fhall arife refpecting the legality of prizes, fo that a judicial decifion fhould become neceffary, the judge fhall direct the effects to be unladen, an inventory and appraifement to be made thereof, and fecurity to be required refpectively from the captor for paying the cofts, in cafe the fhip fhould

not

not be declared lawful prize; and from the claimant for paying the value of the prize, in cafe it fhould be declared lawful; which fecurities being given by both parties, the prize fhall be delivered up to the claimant. But if the claimant fhould refufe to give fufficient fecurity, the judge fhall direct the prize to be delivered to the captor, after having received from him good and fufficient fecurity for paying the full value of the faid prize, in cafe it fhould be adjudged illegal. Nor fhall the execution of the fentence of the judge be fufpended by reafon of any appeal, when the party againft whom fuch appeal fhall be brought, whether claimant or captor, fhall have given fufficient fecurity for reftoring the fhip or effects, or the value of fuch fhip or effects, to the appellant, in cafe judgment fhould be given in his favour.

XXXVII. In cafe any fhips of war or merchantmen, forced by ftorms or other accidents, be driven on rocks or fhelves, on the coafts of either of the high contracting parties, and fhould there be dafhed to' pieces and fhipwrecked; all fuch parts of the faid fhips, or of the furniture or apparel thereof, as alfo of the goods and merchandizes, as fhall be faved, or the produce thereof, fhall be faithfully reftored, upon the fame being claimed by the proprietors, or their factors, duly authorized, paying only the expences incurred in the prefervation thereof, according to the rate of falvage fettled on both fides; faving at the fame time the rights and cuftoms of each nation, the abolition or modification of which fhall however be treated upon, in the cafes where they fhall be contrary to the ftipulations of the prefent article; and their Majefties will mutually interpofe their authority, that fuch of their fubjects, as fhall be fo inhuman as to take advantage of any fuch misfortune, may be feverely punifhed.

XXXVIII. It fhall be free for the fubjects of each party to employ fuch advocates, attornies, notaries, folicitors,

x

solicitors, and factors, as they shall think fit; to which end, the said advocates, and others above-mentioned, shall be appointed by the ordinary judges, if it be needful, and the judges be thereunto required.

XXXIX. And, for the greater security and liberty of commerce and navigation, it is further agreed, that both the King of Great Britain, and the moſt Chriſtian King, shall not only refuſe to receive any pirates or sea-rovers whatſoever into any of their havens, ports, cities, or towns, or permit any of their subjects, citizens, or inhabitants, on either part, to receive or protect them in their ports, to harbour them in their houſes, or to aſſiſt them in any manner whatſoever; but further, they shall cauſe all ſuch pirates and sea-rovers, and all perſons who shall receive, conceal, or aſſiſt them, to be brought to condign puniſhment, for a terror and example to others. And all their ſhips, with the goods or merchandizes taken by them, and brought into the ports of either kingdom, shall be ſeized, as far as they can be diſcovered, and shall be reſtored to the owners, or their factors duly authorized or deputed by them in writing, proper evidence being firſt given in the court of admiralty, for proving the property, even in caſe ſuch effects should have paſſed into other hands by ſale, if it be proved that the buyers knew, or might have known, that they had been piratically taken. And generally all ſhips and merchandizes, of what nature ſoever, which may be taken on the high ſeas, shall be brought into ſome port of either kingdom, and delivered into the cuſtody of the officers of that port, that they may be reſtored entire to the true proprietor, as ſoon as due and ſufficient proof shall have been made concerning the property thereof.

XL. It shall be lawful, as well for the ſhips of war of their Majeſties, as for privateers belonging to their subjects, to carry whitherſoever they pleaſe the ſhips and goods taken from their enemies, without being
obliged

obliged to pay any fee to the officers of the admiralty, or to any judges whatever; nor shall the said prizes, when they arrive at and enter the ports of their said Majesties, be detained or seized; neither shall the searchers, or other officers of those places, visit or take cognizance of the validity of such prizes; but, they shall be at liberty to hoist sail at any time, to depart, and to carry their prizes to the place mentioned in the commissions or patents, which the commanders of such ships of war shall be obliged to shew: on the contrary, no shelter or refuge shall be given in their ports to such as have made a prize upon the subjects of either of their Majesties; but if forced by stress of weather, or the dangers of the sea, to enter therein, particular care shall be taken to hasten their departure, and to cause them to retire from thence as soon as possible, as far as it is not repugnant to former treaties made in this respect with other Sovereigns or States.

XLI. Neither of their said Majesties shall permit the ships or goods belonging to the subjects of the other to be taken within cannon-shot of the coast, or in the ports or rivers of their dominions, by ships of war, or others having commission from any prince, republic or city whatsoever: but in case it should so happen, both parties shall employ their united force to obtain reparation of the damage thereby occasioned.

XLII. But if it shall appear that the captor made use of any kind of torture upon the master of the ship, the crew, or others who shall be on board any ship belonging to the subjects of the other party, in such case, not only the ship itself, together with the persons, merchandizes, and goods whatsoever, shall be forthwith released, without ony delay, and set entirely free, but also such as shall be convicted of so enormous a crime, together with their accomplices, shall suffer the most severe punishment suitable to their offences.

fences: this the King of Great Britain and the moft Chriftian King mutually engage fhall be obferved, without any refpect of perfons whatfoever.

XLIII. Their Majefties fhall refpectively be at liberty, for the advantage of their fubjects trading to the kingdoms and dominions of either of them, to appoint therein national confuls, who fhall enjoy the right, immunity, and liberty belonging to them, by reafon of their duties and their functions; and places fhall hereafter be agreed upon where the faid confuls fhall be eftablifhed, as well as the nature and extent of their functions. The convention relative to this point fhall be concluded immediately after the fignature of the prefent treaty, of which it fhall be deemed to conftitute a part.

XLIV. It is alfo agreed, that in whatever relates to the lading and unlading of fhips, the fafety of merchandize, goods, and effects, the fucceffion to perfonal eftates, as well as the protection of individuals, and their perfonal liberty, as alfo the adminiftration of juftice, the fubjects of the two high contracting parties fhall enjoy, in their refpective dominions, the fame privileges, liberties, and rights, as the moft favoured nation.

XLV. If hereafter it fhall happen, through inadvertency or otherwife, that any infractions or contraventions of the prefent treaty fhould be committed on either fide, the friendfhip and good underftanding fhall not immediately thereupon be interrupted; but this treaty fhall fubfift in all its force, and proper remedies fhall be procured for removing the inconveniencies, as likewife for the reparation of the contraventions: and if the fubjects of either kingdom fhall be found guilty thereof, they only fhall be punifhed and feverely chaftifed.

XLVI. His Britannic Majefty and his moft Chriftian Majefty have referved the right of revifing and
re-examining

re-examining the feveral ftipulations of this treaty, after the term of twelve years, to be computed from the day of paffing laws for its execution in Great Britain and Ireland refpectively, to propofe and make fuch alterations as the times and circumftances may have rendered proper or neceffary for the commer-cial interefts of their refpective fubjects; and this re-vifion is to be compleated in the fpace of twelve months; after which term the prefent treaty fhall be of no effect, but in that event, the good harmony and friendly correfpondence between the two nations fhall not fuffer the leaft diminution.

XLVII. The prefent treaty fhall be ratified and confirmed by his Britannic Majefty, and by his moft Chriftian Majefty, in two months, or fooner, if it can be done, after the exchange of fignatures between the Plenipotentiaries.

In witnefs whereof, we the underfigned Commif-faries and Plenipotentiaries of the King of Great Britain and the moft Chriftian King, have figned the prefent treaty with our hands, and have fet thereto the feals of our arms.

Done at Verfailles, the twenty-fixth of September, one thoufand feven hundred and eighty-fix.

Wm. Eden. (L. S.)   *Gerard de Rayneval.* (L. S.)

Form of the Paffports and Sea-Letters which are to be granted by the refpective Admiralties of the Domini-ons of the two high contracting Parties, to the Ships and Veffels failing from thence, purfuant to the 24th Article of the prefent Treaty.

N. N. TO all who fhall fee thefe prefents, greet-ing. Be it known, that we have granted licence and permiffion to N. of the city (or place) of N. mafter or commander of the fhip N. belonging to N. of the port of N. burthen   tons or there-abouts, now lying in the port or haven of N. to fail

to *N.* laden with *N.* the said ship having been examined before her departure, in the usual manner, by the
officers of the place appointed for that purpose. And
the said *N.* or such other person as shall happen to
succeed him, shall produce this licence in every port
or haven which he may enter with his ship, to the
officers of the place, and shall give a true account to
them of what shall have passed or happened during
his voyage; and he shall carry the colours, arms, and
ensigns of *N.* during his voyage.

  In witness whereof, we have signed these presents,
   and set the seal of our arms thereto, and caused
   the same to be countersigned by *N.* at
   day of   in the year, &c. &c.

[The following CONVENTION of January 1787 is
 printed from the copy which was published by
authority in 1787.]

 The Convention between his Britannic *Majesty and
  the Most* Christian *King.* Signed at Versailles, *the*
  15*th of* January, 1787.

THE King of Great Britain, and the most Christian King, being willing, in conformity to the 6th
and 43d articles of the treaty of navigation and commerce, signed at Versailles the 26th of September,
1786, to explain and settle certain points which had
been reserved, their Britannic and most Christian
Majesties, always disposed more particularly to confirm the good understanding in which they are happily united, have named, for that purpose, their respective Plenipotentiaries, to wit, on the part of his
Britannic Majesty, William Eden, Esq; Privy Counsellor in Great Britain and Ireland, Member of the
British Parliament, and his Envoy Extraordinary and
Minister Plenipotentiary to his most Christian Majesty; and on the part of his most Christian Majesty,
the Count de Vergennes, Minister and Secretary of
             State

State for the department of Foreign Affairs, and Chief of the Royal Council of Finances; who, after having communicated to each other their respective full powers, have agreed upon the following articles.

I. Their Majesties having stipulated, in the 6th article of the said treaty, " That the duties on hard-" ware, cutlery, cabinet ware, and turnery, and on all, " works, both heavy and light, of iron, steel, copper, " and brass, shall be classed; and that the highest " duty shall not exceed ten per cent. ad valorem," it is agreed, that cabinet ware and turnery, and every thing that is included under those denominations, as also musical instruments, shall pay ten per cent. ad valorem.

All articles made of iron or steel, pure or mixed, or worked or mounted with other substances, not exceeding in value sixty *livres Tournois*, or fifty shillings per quintal, shall pay only five per cent. ad valorem; and all other wares, as buttons, buckles, knives, scissars, and all the different articles included under the description of hardware and cutlery, as also all other works of iron, steel, copper, and brass, pure or mixed, or worked or mounted with other substances, shall pay ten per cent. ad valorem.

If either of the two Sovereigns should think proper to admit the said articles, or only some of them, from any other nation, by reason of their utility, at a lower duty, the subjects of the other Sovereign shall be allowed to participate in such diminution, in order that no foreign nation may enjoy in this respect any preference to their disadvantage.

The works of iron, steel, copper, and brass abovementioned, are not to be understood to extend to bar iron or pig iron, or in general to any kind of iron, steel, copper, or brass, in the state of the raw material.

II. Their Majesties having also stipulated in the 6th article, " That, for the better securing the due

" collection of the duties payable ad valorem, which
" are fpecified in the tariff, they will concert with
" each other the form of the declarations to be made,
" and the proper means of preventing fraud with re-
" fpect to the real value of the goods and merchan-
" dizes," it is agreed that each declaration fhall be
given in writing, figned by the merchant, owner, or
factor, who anfwers for the merchandizes at their entry; which declaration fhall contain an exact lift of
the faid merchandizes, and of their packages, of the
marks, numbers, and cyphers, and of the contents
of each bale or cafe, and fhall certify that they are
of the growth, produce, or manufacture of the kingdom from whence they are imported, and fhall alfo
exprefs the true and real value of the faid merchandizes, in order that the duties may be paid in confequence thereof. That the officers of the cuftom-houfe
where the declaration may be made, fhall be at liberty to make fuch examination as they fhall think
proper of the faid merchandizes, upon their being
landed, not only for the purpofe of verifying the facts
alledged in the faid declaration, that the merchandizes
are of the produce of the country therein mentioned,
and that the ftatement of their value and quantity is
exact, but alfo for that of preventing the clandeftine
introduction of other merchandizes in the fame bales
or cafes: Provided, neverthelefs, that fuch examinations fhall be made with every poffible attention to the
convenience of the traders, and to the prefervation of
the faid merchandizes.

In cafe the officers of the cuftoms fhould not be fatisfied with the valuation made of the merchandizes
in the faid declaration, they fhall be at liberty, with
the confent of the principal officer of the cuftoms at
the port, or of fuch other officer as fhall be appointed
for that purpofe, to take the faid merchandizes according to the valuation made by the declaration, allowing to the merchant or owner an overplus of ten
per cent. and refunding to him the duties he may
                                                    have

have paid for the said merchandizes. In which case, the whole amount shall be paid without delay, by the custom-house of the port, if the value of the effects in question shall not exceed four hundred and eighty *livres Tournois*, or twenty pounds sterling; and within fifteen days, at latest, if their value shall exceed that sum.

And if doubts should happen to arise, either respecting the value of the said merchandizes, or the country of which they are the produce, the officers of the customs at the port shall come to a determination thereupon, with all possible dispatch, and no greater space of time shall be employed for that purpose, in any case, than eight days, in the ports where the officers who have the principal direction of the customs reside, and fifteen days in any other port whatsoever.

It is supposed and understood, that the merchandizes admitted by the present treaty shall be respectively of the growth, produce, or manufacture of the dominions of the two Sovereigns in Europe.

To oblige the traders to be accurate in the declarations required by the present article, as also to prevent any doubt that might arise on that part of the tenth article of the said treaty, which provides, that if any of the effects are omitted in the declaration delivered by the master of the ship, they shall not be liable to confiscation, unless there be a manifest appearance of fraud; it is understood that, in such case, the said effects shall be confiscated, unless satisfactory proof be given to the officers of the customs that there was not any intention of fraud.

III. In order to prevent the introduction of callicoes, manufactured in the East Indies, or in other countries, as if they had been manufactured in the respective dominions of the two Sovereigns in Europe, it is agreed, that the callicoes manufactured in the said dominions for exportation from one country to the other respectively, shall have at the two ends of each piece a particular mark, woven in the piece, to

be fettled in concert by the two governments, of which
mark the refpective governments fhall give nine
months previous notice to the manufacturers; and the
faid mark fhall be altered from time to time, as the
cafe may require. It is further agreed, that until the
faid precaution can be put in execution, the faid callicoes mutually exported, fhall be accompanied by a
certificate of the officers of the cuftoms, or of fuch
other officer as fhall be appointed for that purpofe,
declaring that they were fabricated in the country from
whence they were exported, and alfo that they are
furnifhed with the marks already prefcribed in the refpective countries, to diftinguifh fuch callicoes from
thofe which come from other countries.

IV. In fettling the duties upon cambricks and
lawns, it is underftood that the breadth fhould not exceed, for the cambricks, feven-eighths of a yard, Englifh meafure (about three quarters of an ell of France)
and for the lawns, one yard and a quarter, Englifh
meafure (one ell of France) and if any fhall hereafter
be made of a greater breadth than what is above-
mentioned, they fhall pay a duty of ten per cent. ad
valorem.

V. It is alfo agreed, that the ftipulations in the
18th article of the treaty fhall not be conftrued to derogate from the privileges, regulations, and ufages already eftablifhed in the cities or ports of the refpective dominions of the two Sovereigns : and further,
that the 25th article of the faid treaty fhall be conftrued to relate only to fhips fufpected of carrying, in
time of war, to the enemies of either of the high contracting parties, any prohibited articles, denominated
contraband ; and the faid article is not to hinder the
examinations of the officers of the cuftoms, for the
purpofe of preventing illicit trade in the refpective dominions.

VI. Their Majefties having ftipulated, by the 43d
article of the faid treaty, that the nature and extent of

I   the

the functions of the confuls fhould be determined,
" and that a convention relative to this point fhould
" be concluded immediately after the fignature of the
" prefent treaty, of which it fhould be deemed to
" conftitute a part," it is agreed that the faid ulterior
convention fhall be fettled within the fpace of two
months, and that, in the mean time, the confuls general, confuls, and vice confuls, fhall conform to the
ufages which are now obferved, relative to the conful-
fhip, in the refpective dominions of the two Sovereigns; and that they fhall enjoy all the privileges,
rights, and immunities belonging to their office, and
which are allowed to the confuls general, confuls,
and vice confuls of the moft favoured nation.

VII. It fhall be lawful for the fubjects of his Britannic Majefty to profecute their debtors in France,
for the recovery of debts contracted in the dominions
of his faid Majefty, or elfewhere, in Europe, and
there to bring actions againft them, in conformity to
the practice of law in ufe in the kingdom: provided
that there fhall be the like ufage, in favour of French
fubjects, in the European dominions of his Britannic
Majefty.

VIII. The articles of the prefent convention fhall
be ratified and confirmed by his Britannic Majefty,
and by his moft Chriftian Majefty, in one month, or
fooner, if it can be done, after the exchange of fignatures between the Plenipotentiaries.

In witnefs whereof, we the Minifters Plenipotentiary
    have figned the prefent convention, and have
    caufed the feals of our arms to be fet thereto.
Done at Verfailles, the fifteenth of January, one
    thoufand feven hundred and eighty-feven.

Wm. Eden. (L. S.)   *Gravier de Vergennes.* (L. S.)

[The

[The following CONVENTION, of Auguſt 1787, is printed from the copy, which was publiſhed by au-thority, in 1787.]

The Convention between his Britannic *Majeſty and the Moſt* Chriſtian *King. Signed at* Verſailles, *the* 31ſt *of* Auguſt, 1787.

DIFFICULTIES having ariſen in the Eaſt In-dies, relative to the meaning and extent of the thir-teenth article of the treaty of peace, ſigned at Ver-ſailles the third of September, one thouſand ſeven hundred and eighty-three, his Britannic Majeſty and his moſt Chriſtian Majeſty, with a view to remove every cauſe of diſpute between their reſpective ſub-jects in that part of the world, have thought proper to make a particular convention, which may ſerve as an explanation of the thirteenth article above-mentioned: in this view, their ſaid Majeſties have named for their reſpective Plenipotentiaries, to wit, on the part of his Britannic Majeſty, William Eden, Eſq; Privy Coun-ſellor in Great Britain and Ireland, Member of the Britiſh Parliament, and his Envoy Extraordinary and Miniſter Plenipotentiary to his moſt Chriſtian Ma-jeſty; and on the part of his moſt Chriſtian Majeſty, the Sieur Armand Mark, Count de Montmorin de St. Herem, Marſhal of his Camps and Forces, Counſel-lor in all his Councils, Knight of his Orders, and of the Golden Fleece, Miniſter and Secretary of State, and of his Commands and Finances, having the de-partment of foreign affairs; who, after having com-municated to each other their reſpective full powers, have agreed upon the following articles.

I. His Britannic Majeſty again engages "to take "ſuch meaſures as ſhall be in his power for ſecuring "to the ſubjects of France a ſafe, free, and independ-"ant trade, ſuch as was carried on by the French Eaſt "India Company," and as is explained in the follow-ing articles, "whether they exerciſe it individually, or "as a company," as well in the Nabobſhip of Arcot, and the countries of Madura and Tanjore, as in the provinces

provinces of Bengal, Bahar, and Orixa, the Northern Circars, and in general in all the British poffeffions on the coafts of Orixa, Coromandel, and Malabar.

II. In order to prevent all abufes and difputes relative to the importation of falt, it is agreed that the French fhall not import annually into Bengal more than two hundred thoufand maunds of falt: the faid falt fhall be delivered at a place of depofit appointed for that purpofe by the government of Bengal, and to officers of the faid government, at the fixed price of one hundred and twenty rupees for every hundred maunds.

III. There fhall be delivered annually for the French commerce, upon the demand of the French agent in Bengal, eighteen thoufand maunds of faltpetre, and three hundred chefts of opium, at the price eftablifhed before the late war.

IV. The fix antient factories, namely, Chandernagore, Coffimbuzar, Dacca, Jugdea, Balafore, and Patna, with the territories belonging to the faid factories, fhall be under the protection of the French flag, and fubject to the French jurifdiction.

V. France fhall alfo have poffeffion of the ancient houfes of Soopore, Keerpoy, Cannicole, Mohunpore, Serampore, and Chittagong, as well as the dependencies on Soopore, viz. Gautjurat, Allende, Chintzabad, Patorcha, Monepore, and Dolobody, and fhall further have the faculty of eftablifhing new houfes of commerce; but none of the faid houfes fhall have any jurifdiction, or any exemption from the ordinary juftice of the country exercifed over British fubjects.

VI. His Britannic Majefty engages to take meafures to fecure to French fubjects without the limits of the ancient factories above-mentioned, an exact and impartial adminiftration of juftice, in all matters concerning their perfons or properties, or the carrying on their trade, in the fame manner and as effectually as to his own fubjects.

N n 4   VII. All

VII. All Europeans, as well as natives, againſt whom judicial proceedings ſhall be inſtituted, within the limits of the ancient factories above-mentioned, for offences committed, or debts contracted, within the ſaid limits, and who ſhall take refuge out of the ſame, ſhall be delivered up to the chiefs of the ſaid factories: and all Europeans, or others whoſoever, againſt whom judicial proceedings ſhall be inſtituted, without the ſaid limits, and who ſhall take refuge within the ſame, ſhall be delivered up by the chiefs of the ſaid factories, upon demand being made of them by the government of the country.

VIII. All the ſubjects of either nation reſpectively, who ſhall take refuge within the factories of the other, ſhall be delivered up on each ſide, upon demand being made of them.

IX. The factory of Yanam, with its dependencies, having, in purſuance of the ſaid treaty of peace, been delivered up by Mr. William Hamilton, on the part of his Britannic Majeſty, to Mr. Peter Paul Martin, on the part of his moſt Chriſtian Majeſty, the reſtitution thereof is confirmed by the preſent convention, in the terms of the inſtrument bearing date the ſeventh of March, one thouſand ſeven hundred and eighty-five, and ſigned by Meſſrs. Hamilton and Martin.

X. The preſent convention ſhall be ratified and confirmed in the ſpace of three months, or ſooner, if it can be done, after the exchange of ſignatures between the Plenipotentiaries.

In witneſs whereof, we, Miniſters Plenipotentiary, have ſigned the preſent convention, and have cauſed the ſeals of our arms to be affixed thereto.

Done at Verſailles, the thirty-firſt of Auguſt, one thouſand ſeven hundred and eighty-ſeven.

Wm. Eden. (L. S.)   *Le Cᵗᵉ de Montmorin.* (L. S.)

The

The SUPPLEMENT to the Treaties with FRANCE.

[The following is the FAMILY COMPACT, which is referred to in the Commercial Treaty 1786, between Great Britain and France.]

The Family Compact of the House of Bourbon; *signed at* Paris, Auguſt 15*th*, 1761.

IN the name of the moſt holy and indiviſible Trinity, Father, Son, and Holy Ghoſt. Amen. The ties of blood, which unite the two monarchs now reigning in France and Spain, and the particular ſentiments which have animated each other, of which they have given ſo many proofs, have engaged their moſt Chriſtian and Catholic Majeſties to form, and conclude between them, a treaty of friendſhip and union, under the title of The Family Compact; the principal objeckt of which is to render permanent and indiviſible, as well for their ſaid Majeſties, as for their deſcendants and ſucceſſors, thoſe duties which are the natural conſequences of conſanguinity and friendſhip. The intention of their moſt Chriſtian and Catholic Majeſties, in contracting the engagements formed by this treaty, is to perpetuate in their poſterity the ſentiments of Lewis XIV. of glorious memory, their common and auguſt great grandfather; and to preſerve for ever a ſolemn monument of their reciprocal intereſt, which ought to be the foundation of the views of their courts, and of the proſperity of their royal families.

With this view, and to attain ſo agreeable and ſalutary an end, their moſt Chriſtian and Catholic Majeſties have given their full powers, *i. e.* his moſt Chriſtian Majeſty, to the Duke de Choiſeul, a Peer of France, Knight of his Orders, and Lieutenant General of his Majeſty's armies, Governor of Touraine, High Steward and Superintendant General, and Se-

cretary

cretary of State in the department of War and Foreign Affairs; and his Catholic Majesty, to the Marquis of Grimaldi, Gentleman of his Bed-chamber, and his Ambassador Extraordinary to his most Christian Majesty; who, being informed of the dispositions of their respective Sovereigns, and after having communicated their credentials to each other, have agreed to the following articles:

I. Their most Christian and Catholic Majesties declare, that in consequence of their intimate ties of consanguinity and friendship, and the union they contract by the present treaty, the two Crowns will hereafter consider every Power as their common enemy who shall become such to either of them.

II. The two contracting Kings reciprocally guaranty, in the most absolute and authentic manner, all the estates, lands, islands, and places which they possess in any part of the world whatever, without any reserve or exception; and the possessions, the object of their guaranty, shall be fixed according to the actual state in which they shall be found, as soon as either of the two Crowns shall be at peace with all other Powers.

III. Their most Christian and Catholic Majesties grant the same absolute and authentic guaranty to the King of the Two Sicilies, and to the Infant Don Philip, Duke of Parma, for all the estates, territories, and places which they possess; provided that his Sicilian Majesty, and the said Infant Duke of Parma, also guaranty, on their part, all the estates and possessions of their most Christian and Catholic Majesties.

IV. Though the inviolable and mutual guaranty, to which their most Christian and Catholic Majesties bind themselves, ought to be supported with all their power, and though their Majesties thus understand it, according to the fundamental principles of this treaty, that *whoever attacks one crown, attacks the other*, yet the two contracting parties have thought it proper to
ascertain

afcertain the firft fuccours, which the Power requefted fhall be obliged to, furnifh to the Power requefting.

V. The two Kings have-agreed, that the crown requefted to furnifh fuccours fhall, within three months after fuch requifition, have twelve fhips of the line, and fix armed frigates, in one or more of its ports, at the entire difpofition of the requefting court.

VI. The Power requefted fhall have ready, within the fpace of three months, at the difpofition of the Power requefting, 18,000 foot, and 6,000 horfe, if France fhall be the Power requefted; and if Spain be the Power requefted, 10,000 foot, and 2,000 horfe. In this difference of number, attention muft be paid to the greater number of forces actually kept on foot in France than in Spain; but if it fhould at any time fo happen, that the number of forces kept on foot by them fhall be equal, then the obligation fhall alfo be equal to furnifh reciprocally the fame number. The Power requefted engages to affemble the ftipulated fuccours, and to place them in fuch fituations (without immediate marching them out of the kingdom) as the party requefting fhall appoint, in order that they may be the more readily employed in the fervices for which the faid troops were demanded; and when, to gain fuch place of deftination, a paffage by fea, or marches by land, may be neceffary, the expences thereof fhall be borne by the Power requefted, to whom the faid fuccours properly belong.

VII. As to what regards the difference in the faid number of troops to be furnifhed, his Catholic Majefty excepts the cafe wherein they may be found neceffary to defend the poffeffions of the King of the Two Sicilies, his fon, or thofe of the Infant Duke of Parma, his brother; fo that freely acknowledging the preference, which the ties of blood and kindred impofe on him, then the Catholic King, in thofe two circumftances, promifes to furnifh the fuccours of 18,000 foot and 6,000 horfe, and even to employ all his forces, without claiming of his moft Chriftian Majefty any

more

more than the number of troops above specified, and such other efforts as his tender friendship for the Princes of his own blood may induce him to exert in their favour.

VIII. His most Christian Majesty excepts also, on his part, the wars he may engage in, either as principal or auxiliary, in consequence of the engagements he has contracted by the treaty of Westphalia, and other alliances with the German and other Northern Powers; and, considering that the said wars can in no manner interfere with the crown of Spain, his most Christian Majesty promises not to demand any assistance from his Catholic Majesty, unless some maritime Powers should take part in the said wars, or that the event should be so unfavourable to France, that she should be attacked by land in her own territories; then, in this last case, his Catholic Majesty promises to furnish his most Christian Majesty, without any exception, not only with the said 10,000 foot and 2,000 horse, but even, in case of necessity, with 18,000 foot and 6,000 horse, being the number stipulated to be furnished for the use of the Catholic King, by his most Christian Majesty; his Catholic Majesty engaging, in such case, to pay no regard to the disproportion between the land forces of France and those of Spain.

IX. The requesting Power shall be permitted to send one or more commissaries, chosen from among their own subjects, in order to assure themselves, that the Power requested has collected, within the three months from the time of requisition, in one or more of their ports, twelve ships of the line and six armed frigates, as well as the stipulated number of land forces, ready to march.

X. The said ships, frigates, and troops, shall act agreeably to the will of the Power that shall have occasion for and demand them; and the Power requested shall be allowed to make no more than one representation reprefentation concerning the motives or objects to which the faid land and fea forces are deftined.

XI. What is above agreed upon fhall immediately take place, as often as the requefting Power fhall demand fuccours for any offenfive or defenfive enterprize, either by land or fea, and it muft be underftood in fuch cafe, that the fhips and frigates of the requefted Power fhall be collected in fome port of its dominions, fince it fhall then be fufficient that the land and fea forces are in readinefs in thofe ports of their kingdoms which fhall be appointed by the requefting Power, as moft convenient to its intentions.

XII. The demand which one of the two Sovereigns fhall make of the other, for the fuccours ftipulated by the prefent treaty, fhall be fufficient to conftitute the neceffity of one party, and the obligation of the other to furnifh the faid fuccours, without being obliged to enter into any explication whatever, nor, under any pretence, to elude the moft fpeedy and perfect execution of this engagement.

XIII. In confequence of the preceding article, no difcuffion of the offenfive or defenfive cafe fhall take place, with refpect to furnifhing the twelve fhips, the fix frigates, and the land troops, fince thofe forces are to be confidered, in all points, *three months after the requifition*, as properly belonging to the Power that fhall requeft them.

XIV. The Power that fhall furnifh thefe fuccours, whether in fhips and frigates, or in troops, fhall pay them, wherever its ally fhall call them to act, as if thofe forces were directly employed in their own fervice; and the requefting Power fhall be obliged, whether the faid fhips, frigates, or troops remain a fhort or long time in their ports, to fupply them with every thing neceffary, at the fame price as if they properly belonged to them, and to allow them the fame prerogatives and privileges as their own troops enjoy. It is agreed, that in no cafe the faid fhips or troops fhall

be

be at the expence of the Power to whom they are sent, and that they shall be at their difposition during the war in which they shall be employed.

XV. Their moft Chriftian and Catholic Majefties oblige themfelves to keep compleat and well armed the fhips, frigates, and troops which their Majefties fhall reciprocally furnifh, fo that, as foon as the Power requefted fhall furnifh the fuccours ftipulated by the fifth and fixth articles of the prefent treaty, fuch Power fhall arm in its ports a number of fhips, fufficient immediately to replace fuch as may be loft by the events of war or the dangers of the fea; the fame Power fhall be equally prepared to recruit and make the neceffary reparations in the land troops it fhall furnifh.

XVI. The fuccours ftipulated in the preceding articles, according to the time and manner fpecified, fhould be confidered as an obligation of the ties of blood and friendfhip, and as an intimate union, which the two contracting Monarchs defire to perpetuate among their defcendants; and thefe ftipulated fuccours fhall be the leaft which the Power requefted fhall give to the other in cafe of neceffity: but, as the intention of the two Kings is, that a war, beginning by or againft one of the two Crowns, ought to intereft the other, it is agreed, that when the two Kings fhall find themfelves engaged in a war againft the fame enemy or enemies, the obligation of the faid ftipulated fuccours fhall ceafe, and inftead thereof the two Crowns oblige themfelves to make war conjointly, and to employ all their forces therein; and for this purpofe, the two high contracting parties will then enter into particular agreements, relative to the circumftances of the war in which they fhall find themfelves engaged; they will reciprocally join in their efforts and refpective advantages, as alfo in their plans and military and political operations; and, thefe agreements being made, the two Kings will conjointly execute them with one common and perfect accord.

XVII. Their

XVII. Their moft Chriftian and Catholic Majefties engage and promife, in cafe they fhall find themfelves engaged in a war, neither to liften to nor make any propofitions of peace, neither to treat nor conclude any thing with their enemy or enemies, but by mutual and common confent and agreement, and reciprocally to communicate every thing that fhall come to their knowledge, interefting to the two Crowns, and in particular on the terms of peace; fo that in war as in peace, each of the two Crowns fhall regard as his own intereft that of his ally.

XVIII. In conformity to this principle, and the engagement contracted in confequence thereof, their moft Chriftian and Catholic Majefties have agreed, that when they fhall terminate by peace the war they fhall have fupported in common, they will balance the advantages which one of the two Powers may have received, againft the loffes of the other; fo that, on the conditions of peace, as in the operations of war, the two Monarchs of France and Spain, throughout the extent of their Empire, fhall be confidered, and will act, as if they formed but one and the fame Power.

XIX. The King of the Two Sicilies, having the fame ties of blood and friendfhip, and the fame interefts, which intimately unite their moft Chriftian and Catholic Majefties, his Catholic Majefty ftipulates for the King of the Two Sicilies, his fon, and obliges himfelf to make him ratify, as well for himfelf, as his defcendants for ever, all the articles of the prefent treaty; and, as to what regards the proportion of fuccours to be furnifhed by his Sicilian Majefty, they fhall be fettled in his act of acceffion to the faid treaty, according to the extent of his power.

XX. Their moft Chriftian, Catholic, and Sicilian Majefties engage, not only to concur in the maintenance and fplendor of their kingdoms, in their prefent ftate, but alfo to fupport, on every occafion whatever, the dignity and rights of their Houfes; fo that each Prince, who fhall have the honour to defcend from the same blood, may be affured at all times of the protection and affiftance of three Crowns.

XXI. The prefent treaty being to be confidered, as hath been already announced in the preamble, as a *Family Compact* between all the branches of the auguft Houfe of Bourbon, no other Power, but thofe of that Houfe, can be invited or admitted to accede thereto.

XXII. The ftrict friendfhip which unites the contracting Monarchs, and the engagements they take by this treaty, determine them alfo to ftipulate, that their dominions and refpective fubjects fhall partake of the advantages, and of the union eftablifhed between thofe Sovereigns; and their Majefties promife not to fuffer, in any cafe, nor under any pretence whatever, their faid fubjects to do or undertake any thing contrary to that perfect correfpondence which ought inviolably to fubfift between the three Crowns.

XXIII. The more effectually to preferve this harmony, and thefe reciprocal advantages between the fubjects of the two Crowns, it is agreed, that the Spaniards fhall no longer be confidered as *foreigners* in France; and confequently his moft Chriftian Majefty engages to abolifh, in their favour, the right of efcheatage, fo that they may difpofe by will, donations, or otherwife, of all their effects, without exception, of what nature foever, which they poffefs in his kingdom, and which their heirs, fubjects of his Catholic Majefty, refident in France or elfewhere, fhall have power to receive as their inheritance, even where no will is made, either by themfelves, their attornies, or particular order (though they may not have obtained letters of naturalization) and convey them out of his moft Chriftian Majefty's dominions, notwithftanding all the laws, edicts, ftatutes, cuftoms, or rights to the contrary, which his moft Chriftian Majefty hereby annuls, as far as is neceffary. His Catholic Majefty engages, on his part, to grant the fame privileges, and in the fame

manner,

manner, in every part of his dominions in Europe, to all the French subjects of his most Christian Majesty, with respect to the free disposal of the effects they shall possess in any part of the Spanish monarchy; so that the subjects of the two crowns shall be generally treated (in what regards this article) in both dominions, as the proper and natural subjects of the Power in whose territories they reside.　Every thing abovesaid, respecting the abolition of the right of escheatage, and the advantages which the French are to enjoy in the Spanish dominions in Europe, and the Spaniards in France, is granted to the subjects of the King of the Two Sicilies, who shall be comprised under the same condition in this article; and the subjects of their most Christian and Catholic Majesties shall reciprocally enjoy the same exemption and advantages in the dominions of his Sicilian Majesty.

XXIV. The subjects of the high contracting parties shall be treated, with respect to commerce and duties, in each of the two kingdoms in Europe, as the proper subjects of the country in which they live or resort to; so that the Spanish flag shall enjoy in France the same rights and prerogatives as the French flag; and, in like manner, the French flag shall be treated in Spain with the same favour as the Spanish flag. The subjects of the two monarchies, in declaring their merchandizes, shall pay the same duties as shall be paid by the natives.　The importation and exportation shall be equally free to them as to the natural subjects; neither shall they pay any other duty than what shall be received from the natural subjects of the Sovereign, nor any goods be liable to confiscation, but such as are prohibited to the natives themselves; and as to what concerns these objects, all interior treaties, conventions, or engagements between the two monarchies, are hereby abolished.　And farther, that no other foreign Power shall enjoy in Spain, any more than in France, any privileges more advantageous than those of the two nations; the same rules shall be observed

in both France and Spain, with regard to the flag
and subjects of the King of the Two Sicilies; and his
Sicilian Majesty shall reciprocally cause to be observed
the same, with respect to the flag and subjects of the
Crowns of France and Spain.

XXV. If the high contracting parties shall hereafter conclude a treaty of commerce with other Powers,
and grant them, or have already granted them, in their
ports or dominions, the treatment granted to the most
favoured nation, notice shall be given to the said
Powers, that the treatment of Spaniards in France, and
in the Two Sicilies, of Frenchmen in Spain, and in
like manner in the Two Sicilies, and of Neapolitans
and Sicilians in France and Spain, upon the same footing, is excepted in that respect, and ought not to be
quoted, or serve as an example, their most Christian, Catholic, and Sicilian Majesties being unwilling
that any other nation should partake of those privileges
which they judged convenient for the reciprocal enjoyment of their respective subjects.

XXVI. The high contracting parties will rea-
cally confide in all the alliances which they shall hereafter form, and the negotiations they shall engage in,
especially such as shall have any influence on their
common interests; and, consequently, their most Christian, Catholic, and Sicilian Majesties will order all
their respective ministers, that they endeavour, in the
other courts of Europe, to maintain among themselves the most perfect harmony and entire confidence,
that every step taken in the name of either of the three
Crowns, may tend to their glory and common advantages, and be a constant pledge of the intimacy which
their said Majesties would for ever establish among
them.

XXVII. The delicate object of precedence in public acts, employments, and ceremonies, is often an
obstacle to good harmony and the intimate confidence
which ought to be supported between the respective

9　　　　　　　　Ministers

Minifters of France and Spain, becaufe fuch contentions, whatever method may be taken to ftop them,
indifpofe the mind. Thefe naturally arofe when the
two Crowns belonged to Princes; of two different
Houfes; but now (and at all times hereafter) and as
long as Providence has determined to maintain on the
two thrones Sovereigns of the fame Houfe, it is not
agreeable that there fhould fubfift between them a
continual occafion for altercation and difcontent; their
moft Chriftian and Catholic Majefties have therefore
agreed entirely to remove that occafion, in determining, as an invariable rule to their Minifters, invefted
with the fame character in foreign courts, as well as
in thofe of the family (for fuch now certainly are thofe
of Naples and Parma) that the Minifters of the chief
Monarch of the Houfe fhall always have the precedence in every act, employment, or ceremony whatever, which precedence fhall be regarded as the confequence of the advantage of birth; and that, in all
other courts, the Minifter (whether of France or
Spain) who fhall laft arrive, or whofe refidence fhall
be more recent, fhall give place to the Minifter of the
other Crown, and of the fame character, who fhall
have arrived firft, or whofe refidence fhall have been
prior, fo that henceforth, in that refpect, there will be
a certain and brotherly alternative, to which no other
Power can be fubject, nor fhall be admitted, feeing
that this arrangement, which is equally a confequence
of the prefent *Family Compact*, would ceafe, if the
Princes of the fame Houfe no longer filled the thrones
of the two monarchies, and that then each Crown
would refume its rights or pretenfions to precedence.
It is agreed alfo, that if, by accident, the Minifters of
the two Crowns fhould arrive precifely at the fame
time in any other court than that of the family, the
Minifter of the Sovereign chief of the Houfe fhall
take place of the Minifter of the Sovereign who is a
junior of the fame Houfe.

XXVIII. The

XXVIII. The prefent treaty, or family compact, fhall be ratified, and the ratification exchanged within the fpace of one month, or fooner if may be, to be reckoned from the day of the figning of the faid treaty.

In witnefs whereof, we, the underfigned Minifters Plenipotentiary for their moft Chriftian and Catholic Majefties, by virtue of full powers, have hereunto fixed our hands and feals.

Given at Paris, Auguft 15, 1761.

      (Signed)   *The Duke de Choifeul.*

THE END OF THE FIRST VOLUME.

www.ingramcontent.com/pod-product-compliance
Lightning Source LLC
La Vergne TN
LVHW012208040326
832903LV00003B/192